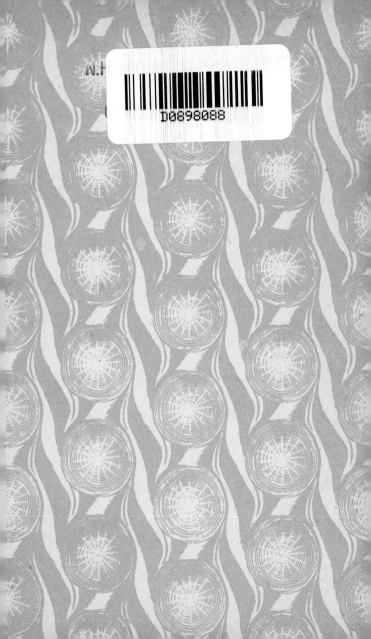

Everyman, I will go with thee, and be thy guide,
In thy most need to go by thy side.

EVERYMAN'S LIBRARY

No. 436

HISTORY

THE DECLINE AND FALL
OF THE ROMAN EMPIRE
BY EDWARD GIBBON · EDITED
BY OLIPHANT SMEATON, M.A.
IN 6 VOLS.   VOL. 3

EDWARD GIBBON, born in 1737 at Putney. Educated at Westminster School, Oxford and privately at Lausanne. Toured Italy, 1764–5, and conceived the plan of his 'History.' Settled in London in 1772, and sat in Parliament from 1774–83. Lived in Lausanne, 1787–93, and died in London in 1794.

THE DECLINE AND FALL OF
THE ROMAN EMPIRE
VOLUME THREE

EDWARD GIBBON

LONDON: J. M. DENT & SONS LTD.
NEW YORK: E. P. DUTTON & CO. INC.

CONTENTS

THE
HISTORY OF THE DECLINE AND FALL
OF THE
ROMAN EMPIRE

CHAPTER XXVI

Manners of the Pastoral Nations—Progress of the Huns from China to Europe—Flight of the Goths—They pass the Danube—Gothic War—Defeat and Death of Valens—Gratian invests Theodosius with the Eastern Empire—His Character and Success—Peace and Settlement of the Goths

In the second year of the reign of Valentinian and Valens, on the morning of the twenty-first day of July, the greatest part of the Roman world was shaken by a violent and destructive earthquake. The impression was communicated to the waters; the shores of the Mediterranean were left dry by the sudden retreat of the sea; great quantities of fish were caught with the hand; large vessels were stranded on the mud; and a curious spectator [1] amused his eye, or rather his fancy, by contemplating the various appearance of valleys and mountains which had never, since the formation of the globe, been exposed to the sun. But the tide soon returned with the weight of an immense and irresistible deluge, which was severely felt on the coasts of Sicily, of Dalmatia, of Greece, and of Egypt; large boats were transported and lodged on the roofs of houses, or at the distance of two miles from the shore; the people, with their habitations, were swept away by the waters; and the city of Alexandria annually commemorated the fatal day on which fifty thousand persons had lost their lives in the inundation. This calamity, the report of which was magnified from one province to another, astonished and terrified the subjects of Rome, and their affrighted imagination enlarged the real extent of a momentary evil. They

---

[1] Such is the bad taste of Ammianus (xxvi. 10), that it is not easy to distinguish his facts from his metaphors. Yet he positively affirms that he saw the rotten carcase of a ship, ad *secundum lapidem*, at Methone, or Modon, in Peloponnesus.

recollected the preceding earthquakes, which had subverted the
cities of Palestine and Bithynia; they considered these alarming
strokes as the prelude only of still more dreadful calamities;
and their fearful vanity was disposed to confound the symptoms
of a declining empire and a sinking world.[1]   It was the fashion
of the times to attribute every remarkable event to the particular
will of the Deity; the alterations of nature were connected, by
an invisible chain, with the moral and metaphysical opinions of
the human mind; and the most sagacious divines could distinguish, according to the colour of their respective prejudices,
that the establishment of heresy tended to produce an earthquake, or that a deluge was the inevitable consequence of the
progress of sin and error.   Without presuming to discuss the
truth or propriety of these lofty speculations, the historian may
content himself with an observation, which seems to be justified
by experience, that man has much more to fear from the passions
of his fellow-creatures than from the convulsions of the elements.[2]
The mischievous effects of an earthquake or deluge, a hurricane
or the eruption of a volcano, bear a very inconsiderable proportion to the ordinary calamities of war, as they are now moderated
by the prudence or humanity of the princes of Europe, who
amuse their own leisure and exercise the courage of their subjects
in the practice of the military art.   But the laws and manners of
modern nations protect the safety and freedom of the vanquished
soldier; and the peaceful citizen has seldom reason to complain
that his life or even his fortune is exposed to the rage of war.
In the disastrous period of the fall of the Roman empire, which
may justly be dated from the reign of Valens, the happiness
and security of each individual were personally attacked, and
the arts and labours of ages were rudely defaced by the barbarians of Scythia and Germany.   The invasion of the Huns
precipitated on the provinces of the West the Gothic nation,
which advanced, in less than forty years, from the Danube to
the Atlantic, and opened a way, by the success of their arms,

[1] The earthquakes and inundations are variously described by Libanius
(Orat. de ulciscendâ Juliani nece, c. x. in Fabricius, Bibl. Græc. tom. vii.
p. 158, with a learned note of Olearius), Zosimus (l. iv. [c. 18] p. 221), Sozomen (l. vi. c. 2), Cedrenus (p. 310, 314 [tom. i. p. 543, 550, ed. Bonn]), and
Jerom (in Chron. p. 186 [tom. viii. p. 809, ed. Vallars.], and tom. i. p. 250,
in Vit. Hilarion [tom. ii. p. 36, ed. Vallars.]).   Epidaurus must have been
overwhelmed, had not the prudent citizens placed St. Hilarion, an Egyptian monk, on the beach.   He made the sign of the cross; the mountain-
wave stopped, bowed, and returned.
[2] Dicæarchus the Peripatetic composed a formal treatise to prove this
obvious truth, which is not the most honourable to the human species
(Cicero, de Officiis, ii. 5).

to the inroads of so many hostile tribes more savage than themselves. The original principle of motion was concealed in the remote countries of the North, and the curious observation of the pastoral life of the Scythians [1] or Tartars [2] will illustrate the latent cause of these destructive emigrations.

The different characters that mark the civilised nations of the globe may be ascribed to the use and the abuse of reason, which so variously shapes and so artificially composes the manners and opinions of an European or a Chinese. But the operation of instinct is more sure and simple than that of reason; it is much easier to ascertain the appetites of a quadruped than the speculations of a philosopher; and the savage tribes of mankind, as they approach nearer to the condition of animals, preserve a stronger resemblance to themselves and to each other. The uniform stability of their manners is the natural consequence of the imperfection of their faculties. Reduced to a similar situation, their wants, their desires, their enjoyments still continue the same; and the influence of food or climate, which, in a more improved state of society, is suspended or subdued by so many moral causes, most powerfully contributes to form and to maintain the national character of barbarians. In every age the immense plains of Scythia or Tartary have been inhabited by vagrant tribes of hunters and shepherds, whose indolence refuses to cultivate the earth, and whose restless spirit disdains the confinement of a sedentary life. In every age the Scythians

---

[1] The original Scythians of Herodotus (l. iv. c. 47-57, 99-101) were confined by the Danube and the Palus Mæotis within a square of 4000 stadia (400 Roman miles). See D'Anville (Mém. de l'Académie, tom. xxxv. p. 573-591). Diodorus Siculus (tom. i. l. ii. [c. 43] p. 155, edit. Wesseling) has marked the gradual progress of the *name* and nation.

[2] The *Tatars* or Tartars were a primitive tribe, the rivals, and at length the subjects, of the Moguls. In the victorious armies of Zingis Khan and his successors, the Tartars formed the vanguard; and the name which first reached the ears of foreigners was applied to the whole nation (Fréret, in the Hist. de l'Académie, tom. xviii. p. 60). In speaking of all or any of the northern shepherds of Europe or Asia, I indifferently use the appellations of *Scythians* or *Tartars*.

[The Tartars were a tribe nearly allied to the Mongols in race, who dwelt near Lake Bouyir to the eastward of Mongolia. They were among the first of the Mongol conquests, and they afterwards took so conspicuous a place in the army of Gengkes Khan that their name became synonymous with that of the Mongols. Their proper name was Tatars. It is said to have been changed into "Tartar" in consequence of an expression of St. Louis who, when he heard of the devastation of Gengkes Khan (which excited so much horror in Europe) said, "Erigat nos, mater, cœleste solatium, quia si proveniant ipsi, vel nos ipsos quos vocamus Tartaros ad suas Tartareas sedes, unde exierunt, retrudemus, vel hand ipsi nos omnes ad cœlum advehant." Prichard, Physical History of Mankind, vol. iv. p. 278-332; also Harmsworth's History of the World, vol. v.—O. S.]

and Tartars have been renowned for their invincible courage and rapid conquests. The thrones of Asia have been repeatedly overturned by the shepherds of the North, and their arms have spread terror and devastation over the most fertile and warlike countries of Europe.[1] On this occasion, as well as on so many others, the sober historian is forcibly awakened from a pleasing vision, and is compelled, with some reluctance, to confess that the pastoral manners, which have been adorned with the fairest attributes of peace and innocence, are much better adapted to the fierce and cruel habits of a military life. To illustrate this observation, I shall now proceed to consider a nation of shepherds and of warriors in the three important articles of, I. Their diet; II. Their habitation; and III. Their exercises. The narratives of antiquity are justified by the experience of modern times;[2] and the banks of the Borysthenes, of the Volga, or of the Selinga will indifferently present the same uniform spectacle of similar and native manners.[3]

I. The corn, or even the rice, which constitutes the ordinary and wholesome food of a civilised people, can be obtained only by the patient toil of the husbandman. Some of the happy savages who dwell between the tropics are plentifully nourished by the liberality of nature, but in the climates of the North a nation of shepherds is reduced to their flocks and herds. The skilful practitioners of the medical art will determine (if they are able to determine) how far the temper of the human mind may be affected by the use of animal or of vegetable food; and whether the common association of carnivorous and cruel deserves to be considered in any other light than that of an innocent, perhaps a

---

[1] Imperium Asiæ *ter* quæsivere: ipsi perpetuo ab alieno imperio, aut intacti, aut invicti, mansere. Since the time of Justin (ii. 3) they have multiplied this account. Voltaire, in a few words (tom. x. p. 64, Hist. Générale, c. 156), has abridged the Tartar conquests.

Oft o'er the trembling nations from afar
        Has Scythia breath'd the living cloud of war.

[2] The fourth book of Herodotus affords a curious though imperfect portrait of the Scythians. Among the moderns, who describe the uniform scene, the Khan of Khowaresm, Abulghazi Bahadur, expresses his native feelings; and his Genealogical History of the *Tatars* has been copiously illustrated by the French and English editors. Carpin, Ascelin, and Rubruquis (in the Hist. des Voyages, tom. vii.), represent the Moguls of the fourteenth century. To these guides I have added Gerbillon and the other Jesuits (Description de la Chine, par Du Halde, tom. iv.), who accurately surveyed the Chinese Tartary, and that honest and intelligent traveller, Bell of Antermony (two volumes in 4to, Glasgow, 1763).

[3] The Uzbeks are the most altered from their primitive manners; 1, by the profession of the Mahometan religion; and 2, by the possession of the cities and harvests of the Great Bucharia.

salutary, prejudice of humanity.[1] Yet, if it be true that the
sentiment of compassion is imperceptibly weakened by the sight
and practice of domestic cruelty, we may observe that the horrid
objects which are disguised by the arts of European refinement
are exhibited in their naked and most disgusting simplicity in
the tent of a Tartarian shepherd. The ox or the sheep are
slaughtered by the same hand from which they were accustomed
to receive their daily food; and the bleeding limbs are served,
with very little preparation, on the table of their unfeeling
murderer. In the military profession, and especially in the
conduct of a numerous army, the exclusive use of animal food
appears to be productive of the most solid advantages. Corn
is a bulky and perishable commodity, and the large magazines,
which are indispensably necessary for the subsistence of our
troops, must be slowly transported by the labour of men or
horses. But the flock and herds which accompany the march
of the Tartars afford a sure and increasing supply of flesh and
milk; in the far greater part of the uncultivated waste the
vegetation of the grass is quick and luxuriant; and there are
few places so extremely barren that the hardy cattle of the
North cannot find some tolerable pasture. The supply is
multiplied and prolonged by the undistinguishing appetite and
patient abstinence of the Tartars. They indifferently feed on
the flesh of those animals that have been killed for the table
or have died of disease. Horseflesh, which in every age and
country has been proscribed by the civilised nations of Europe
and Asia, they devour with peculiar greediness, and this singular
taste facilitates the success of their military operations. The
active cavalry of Scythia is always followed, in their most distant
and rapid incursions, by an adequate number of spare horses,
who may be occasionally used either to redouble the speed or
to satisfy the hunger of the barbarians. Many are the resources
of courage and poverty. When the forage round a camp of
Tartars is almost consumed, they slaughter the greatest part
of their cattle, and preserve the flesh, either smoked or dried in
the sun. On the sudden emergency of a hasty march, they
provide themselves with a sufficient quantity of little balls of

---

[1] Il est certain que les grands mangeurs de viande sont en général cruels
et féroces plus que les autres hommes. Cette observation est de tous les
lieux, et de tous les tems: la barbarie Angloise est connue, etc. Emile de
Rousseau, tom. i. p. 274. Whatever we may think of the general observation, *we* shall not easily allow the truth of his example. The good-natured
complaints of Plutarch, and the pathetic lamentations of Ovid, seduce our
reason by exciting our sensibility.

cheese, or rather of hard curd, which they occasionally dissolve in water, and this unsubstantial diet will support, for many days, the life, and even the spirits, of the patient warrior. But this extraordinary abstinence, which the Stoic would approve and the hermit might envy, is commonly succeeded by the most voracious indulgence of appetite. The wines of a happier climate are the most grateful present or the most valuable commodity that can be offered to the Tartars; and the only example of their industry seems to consist in the art of extracting from mare's milk a fermented liquor which possesses a very strong power of intoxication. Like the animals of prey, the savages, both of the old and new world, experience the alternate vicissitudes of famine and plenty, and their stomach is inured to sustain, without much inconvenience, the opposite extremes of hunger and of intemperance.

II. In the ages of rustic and martial simplicity, a people of soldiers and husbandmen are dispersed over the face of an extensive and cultivated country; and some time must elapse before the warlike youth of Greece or Italy could be assembled under the same standard, either to defend their own confines, or to invade the territories of the adjacent tribes. The progress of manufactures and commerce insensibly collects a large multitude within the walls of a city; but these citizens are no longer soldiers, and the arts which adorn and improve the state of civil society corrupts the habits of the military life. The pastoral manners of the Scythians seem to unite the different advantages of simplicity and refinement. The individuals of the same tribe are constantly assembled, but they are assembled in a camp, and the native spirit of these dauntless shepherds is animated by mutual support and emulation. The houses of the Tartars are no more than small tents, of an oval form, which afford a cold and dirty habitation for the promiscuous youth of both sexes. The palaces of the rich consist of wooden huts, of such a size that they may be conveniently fixed on large waggons, and drawn by a team perhaps of twenty or thirty oxen. The flocks and herds, after grazing all day in the adjacent pastures, retire, on the approach of night, within the protection of the camp. The necessity of preventing the most mischievous confusion in such a perpetual concourse of men and animals must gradually introduce, in the distribution, the order, and the guard of the encampment, the rudiments of the military art. As soon as the forage of a certain district is consumed, the tribe, or rather army, of shepherds makes a regular march to some fresh pastures, and thus acquires, in the ordinary occupations of the pastoral life, the practical knowledge of one of the most important and difficult operations of war. The choice of stations is regulated by the difference of the seasons; in the summer the Tartars advance towards the North, and pitch their tents on the banks of a river, or, at least, in the neighbourhood of a running stream. But in the winter they return to the South, and shelter their camp, behind some convenient eminence, against the winds, which are chilled in their passage over the bleak and icy regions of Siberia. These manners are admirably adapted to diffuse among the wandering tribes the spirit of emigration and conquest. The connection between the people and their territory is of so frail a texture that it may be broken by the slightest accident. The camp, and not the soil, is the native country of the genuine Tartar. Within the precincts of that camp his family, his companions, his property, are always included, and in the most distant marches he is still surrounded by the objects which are dear or valuable or familiar in his eyes. The thirst of rapine, the fear or the resentment of injury, the impatience of servitude, have, in every age, been sufficient causes to urge the tribes of Scythia boldly to advance into some unknown countries, where they might hope to find a more plentiful subsistence or a less formidable enemy. The revolutions of the North have frequently determined the fate of the South; and in the conflict of hostile nations the victor and the vanquished have alternately drove, and been driven, from the confines of China to those of Germany.[1] These great emigrations, which have been sometimes executed with almost incredible diligence, were rendered more easy by the peculiar nature of the climate. It is well known that the cold of Tartary is much more severe than in the midst of the temperate zone might reasonably be expected; this uncommon rigour is attributed to the height of the plains, which rise, especially towards the east, more than half a mile above the level of the sea, and to the quantity of saltpetre with which the soil is deeply impregnated.[2] In the

---

[1] These Tartar emigrations have been discovered by M. de Guignes (Histoire des Huns, tom. i. ii.), a skilful and laborious interpreter of the Chinese language, who has thus laid open new and important scenes in the history of mankind.

[2] A plain in the Chinese Tartary, only eighty leagues from the great wall, was found by the missionaries to be three thousand geometrical paces above the level of the sea. Montesquieu, who has used and abused the relations of travellers, deduces the revolutions of Asia from this important circumstance, that heat and cold, weakness and strength, touch each other without any temperate zone (Esprit des Loix, l. xvii. c. 3).

winter season, the broad and rapid rivers that discharge their waters into the Euxine, the Caspian, or the Icy Sea, are strongly frozen, the fields are covered with a bed of snow, and the fugitive or victorious tribes may securely traverse, with their families, their waggons, and their cattle, the smooth and hard surface of an immense plain.

III. The pastoral life, compared with the labours of agriculture and manufactures, is undoubtedly a life of idleness; and as the most honourable shepherds of the Tartar race devolve on their captives the domestic management of the cattle, their own leisure is seldom disturbed by any servile and assiduous cares. But this leisure, instead of being devoted to the soft enjoyments of love and harmony, is usefully spent in the violent and sanguinary exercise of the chase. The plains of Tartary are filled with a strong and serviceable breed of horses, which are easily trained for the purposes of war and hunting. The Scythians of every age have been celebrated as bold and skilful riders, and constant practice had seated them so firmly on horseback that they were supposed by strangers to perform the ordinary duties of civil life, to eat, to drink, and even to sleep, without dismounting from their steeds. They excel in the dexterous management of the lance; the long Tartar bow is drawn with a nervous arm, and the weighty arrow is directed to its object with unerring aim and irresistible force. These arrows are often pointed against the harmless animals of the desert, which increase and multiply in the absence of their most formidable enemy—the hare, the goat, the roebuck, the fallow-deer, the stag, the elk, and the antelope. The vigour and patience both of the men and horses are continually exercised by the fatigues of the chase, and the plentiful supply of game contributes to the subsistence and even luxury of a Tartar camp. But the exploits of the hunters of Scythia are not confined to the destruction of timid or innoxious beasts: they boldly encounter the angry wild boar when he turns against his pursuers, excite the sluggish courage of the bear, and provoke the fury of the tiger as he slumbers in the thicket. Where there is danger, there may be glory; and the mode of hunting which opens the fairest field to the exertions of valour may justly be considered as the image and as the school of war. The general hunting matches, the pride and delight of the Tartar princes, compose an instructive exercise for their numerous cavalry. A circle is drawn, of many miles in circumference, to encompass the game of an extensive district; and the troops that form the circle regularly advance towards a common centre, where the captive animals, surrounded on every side, are abandoned to the darts of the hunters. In this march, which frequently continues many days, the cavalry are obliged to climb the hills, to swim the rivers, and to wind through the valleys, without interrupting the prescribed order of their gradual progress. They acquire the habit of directing their eye and their steps to a remote object, of preserving their intervals, of suspending or accelerating their pace according to the motions of the troops on their right and left, and of watching and repeating the signals of their leaders. Their leaders study in this practical school the most important lesson of the military art, the prompt and accurate judgment of ground, of distance, and of time. To employ against a human enemy the same patience and valour, the same skill and discipline, is the only alteration which is required in real war, and the amusements of the chase serve as a prelude to the conquest of an empire.[1]

The political society of the ancient Germans has the appearance of a voluntary alliance of independent warriors. The tribes of Scythia, distinguished by the modern appellation of *Hords*, assume the form of a numerous and increasing family, which, in the course of successive generations, has been propagated from the same original stock. The meanest and most ignorant of the Tartars preserve with conscious pride the inestimable treasure of their genealogy, and, whatever distinctions of rank may have been introduced by the unequal distribution of pastoral wealth, they mutually respect themselves and each other as the descendants of the first founder of the tribe. The custom, which still prevails, of adopting the bravest and most faithful of the captives, may countenance the very probable suspicion that this extensive consanguinity is, in a great measure, legal and fictitious. But the useful prejudice which has obtained the sanction of time and opinion produces the effects of truth; the haughty barbarians yield a cheerful and voluntary obedience to the head of their blood, and their chief, or *mursa*, as the representative of their great father, exercises the authority of a judge in peace and of a leader in war. In the original state of the pastoral world, each of the *mursas* (if we may continue to use a

---

[1] Petit de la Croix (Vie de Gengiscan, l. iii. c. 7) represents the full glory and extent of the Mogul chace. The Jesuits Gerbillon and Verbiest followed the emperor Kamhi when he hunted in Tartary (Du Halde, Description de la Chine, tom. iv. p. 81, 290, etc., folio edit.). His grandson, Kienlong, who unites the Tartar discipline with the laws and learning of China, describes (Eloge de Moukden, p. 273-285), as a poet, the pleasures which he had often enjoyed as a sportsman.

modern appellation) acted as the independent chief of a large
and separate family, and the limits of their peculiar territories
were gradually fixed by superior force or mutual consent. But
the constant operation of various and permanent causes contributed to unite the vagrant Hords into national communities,
under the command of a supreme head. The weak were desirous
of support, and the strong were ambitious of dominion; the
power which is the result of union oppressed and collected the
divided forces of the adjacent tribes; and, as the vanquished
were freely admitted to share the advantages of victory, the
most valiant chiefs hastened to range themselves and their
followers under the formidable standard of a confederate nation.
The most successful of the Tartar princes assumed the military
command, to which he was entitled by the superiority either of
merit or of power. He was raised to the throne by the acclamations of his equals, and the title of *Khan* expresses in the language
of the North of Asia the full extent of the regal dignity. The
right of hereditary succession was long confined to the blood of
the founder of the monarchy; and at this moment all the Khans
who reign from Crimea to the wall of China are the lineal
descendants of the renowned Zingis.[1] But, as it is the indispensable duty of a Tartar sovereign to lead his warlike subjects
into the field, the claims of an infant are often disregarded, and
some royal kinsman, distinguished by his age and valour, is
intrusted with the sword and sceptre of his predecessor. Two
distinct and regular taxes are levied on the tribes to support the
dignity of their national monarch and of their peculiar chief, and
each of those contributions amounts to the tithe both of their
property and of their spoil. A Tartar sovereign enjoys the
tenth part of the wealth of his people; and as his own domestic
riches of flocks and herds increase in a much larger proportion,
he is able plentifully to maintain the rustic splendour of his court,
to reward the most deserving or the most favoured of his
followers, and to obtain from the gentle influence of corruption
the obedience which might be sometimes refused to the stern
mandates of authority. The manners of his subjects, accustomed, like himself, to blood and rapine, might excuse in their
eyes such partial acts of tyranny as would excite the horror of a

---

[1] See the second volume of the Genealogical History of the Tartars, and
the lists of the Khans at the end of the life of Gengis, or Zingis. Under the
reign of Timur, or Tamerlane, one of his subjects, a descendant of Zingis,
still bore the regal appellation of Khan; and the conqueror of Asia contented himself with the title of Emir or Sultan. Abulghazi, part v. c. 4.
D'Herbelot, Bibliothèque Orientale, p. 878.

civilised people, but the power of a despot has never been acknowledged in the deserts of Scythia. The immediate jurisdiction of the khan is confined within the limits of his own tribe, and the exercise of his royal prerogative has been moderated by the ancient institution of a national council. The Coroultai,[1] or Diet, of the Tartars was regularly held in the spring and autumn in the midst of a plain, where the princes of the reigning family and the mursas of the respective tribes may conveniently assemble on horseback with their martial and numerous trains, and the ambitious monarch who reviewed the strength, must consult the inclination, of an armed people. The rudiments of a feudal government may be discovered in the constitution of the Scythian or Tartar nations, but the perpetual conflict of those hostile nations has sometimes terminated in the establishment of a powerful and despotic empire. The victor, enriched by the tribute and fortified by the arms of dependent kings, has spread his conquests over Europe or Asia; the successful shepherds of the North have submitted to the confinement of arts, of laws, and of cities; and the introduction of luxury, after destroying the freedom of the people, has undermined the foundations of the throne.[2]

[1] See the Diets of the ancient Huns (De Guignes, tom. ii. p. 26), and a curious description of those of Zingis (Vie de Gengiscan, l. i. c. 6, l. iv. c. 11). Such assemblies are frequently mentioned in the Persian history of Timur, though they served only to countenance the resolutions of their master.

[2] Montesquieu labours to explain a difference, which has not existed, between the liberty of the Arabs and the *perpetual* slavery of the Tartars (Esprit des Loix, l. xvii. c. 5, l. xviii. c. 19, etc.).

[Since the time of Gibbon (as Dr. Smith says) our knowledge of the languages of the nomadic tribes of Asia has been enlarged, and we are now able to classify them with greater accuracy than was possible at an earlier period. The nomadic tribes of Asia inhabit the vast area reaching from the Uralian Mountains to the Chinese Sea and Japan, and from the northern limits of Persia and India to the frozen zone of Siberia, although a portion of the latter country is also occupied by other races. These various tribes were originally one race, as the evidence of their languages reveals, though, like the members of the Indo-European race, they are now divided into different families, speaking languages which, though in some cases mutually unintelligible, yet bear a strong resemblance to each other. They are divided into four great branches, called respectively the Mongolian, Tungusian, Turkish, and Ugrian.

I. THE MONGOLIAN RACE.—The Mongolians are the least numerous of the four, and were confined to a comparatively small territory till the time of their national hero, Gengkis Khan, when they first occur in history. Even in his armies and those of his successors, most of the soldiers were Turks, while the officers were Mongolians. With the exception of a few scattered hordes, the Mongolians are still confined to the country north of the great Wall of China, and westward of the Manchu country.

II. THE TUNGUSIAN RACE.—Extends on the east from the Yenesei River to the Sea of Okhotsk, and on the north from the coast of the " Icy Sea," between the Yenesei and the Lena to the Yellow Sea on the south-

The memory of past events cannot long be preserved in the frequent and remote emigrations of illiterate barbarians. The modern Tartars are ignorant of the conquests of their ancestors;[1] and our knowledge of the history of the Scythians is derived from their intercourse with the learned and civilised nations of the South—the Greeks, the Persians, and the Chinese. The Greeks, who navigated the Euxine, and planted their colonies along the sea-coast, made the gradual and imperfect discovery of Scythia, from the Danube and the confines of Thrace, as far as the frozen Mæotis, the seat of eternal winter, and Mount Caucasus, which, in the language of poetry, was described as the utmost boundary of the earth. They celebrated, with simple credulity, the virtues of the pastoral life:[2] they entertained a more rational apprehension of the strength and numbers of the warlike barbarians,[3] who contemptuously baffled the immense armament of Darius, the son of Hystaspes.[4] The Persian

east. Among the numerous tribes of the Tungusian race, some of which are very barbarous, the only one which has exercised an influence on the history of the world is that of the Manchus, the present rulers of China.

III. THE TURKISH RACE.—This is the most widely extended of the four, and is also one of the most considerable of the families of the world, occupying as it does the vast extent of country from Lake Baikal, 110° E. long. to the eastern boundaries of the Greek and Slavonic countries of Europe. One isolated tribe, the Yakuts, dwell in the remote east, on the River Lena and the coasts of the Icy Sea. The chief divisions of the Turks are, (1) the *Ouigours*, on the west of the Mongol frontier, the most anciently civilised division of the Turkish race. (2) Turks of the Sandy Desert, conterminous with Mongolia and Tibet. (3) Turks of *Khoten, Kashgar,* and *Yarkend,* conterminous with Tibet. (4) The *Kirghis* in Independent Tartary. (5) The *Uzbeks,* the Turks of Bokhara. (6) The *Turkomans,* inhabiting the Persian frontier of Independent Tartary from Balk to the Caspian. (7) The *Osmanli,* or *Ottoman Turks,* those of the Turkish Empire. (8) The *Nogays,* dwelling north of the Caucasus, between the lower Don and lower Volga. (9) The Turks of the Russian Empire.

IV. THE UGRIAN RACE.—Also called the Finnish or Tschudish. This people left the great eastern plateau and settled in the north-west of Asia and the north of Europe at a period long antecedent to all historical documents. They extend as a continuous population from the Yenesei on the east to Norway on the west. The eastern branches of this race are the Voguls and the Ostiaks, between the Ural mountains and the Yenesei, inhabiting the country formerly called Ugrien, Jugrien, or Jugoria, the most important of the western branches being the Finns and Lapps. The Magyars of Hungary are also members of the Ugrian race. Cf. Latham, *The National History of the Varieties of Man.*—O. S.]

[1] Abulghazi Khan, in the two first parts of his Genealogical History, relates the miserable fables and traditions of the Uzbek Tartars concerning the times which preceded the reign of Zingis.

[2] In the thirteenth book of the Iliad, Jupiter turns away his eyes from the bloody fields of Troy to the plains of Thrace and Scythia. We would not, by changing the prospect, behold a more peaceful or innocent scene.

[3] Thucydides, l. ii. c. 97.

[4] See the fourth book of Herodotus. When Darius advanced into the Moldavian desert, between the Danube and the Dniester, the king of the

monarchs had extended their western conquests to the banks of the Danube and the limits of European Scythia. The eastern provinces of their empire were exposed to the Scythians of Asia, the wild inhabitants of the plains beyond the Oxus and the Jaxartes, two mighty rivers, which direct their course towards the Caspian Sea. The long and memorable quarrel of Iran and Touran is still the theme of history or romance: the famous, perhaps the fabulous, valour of the Persian heroes, Rustan and Asfendiar, was signalised, in the defence of their country, against the Afrasiabs of the North; [1] and the invincible spirit of the same barbarians resisted, on the same ground, the victorious arms of Cyrus and Alexander. [2] In the eyes of the Greeks and Persians, the real geography of Scythia was bounded, on the east, by the mountains of Imaus or Caf; and their distant prospect of the extreme and inaccessible parts of Asia was clouded by ignorance, or perplexed by fiction. But those inaccessible regions are the ancient residence of a powerful and civilised nation, [3] which ascends, by a probable tradition, above forty centuries; [4] and which is able to verify a series of near two thousand years by the

Scythians sent him a mouse, a frog, a bird, and five arrows; a tremendous allegory!

[1] These wars and heroes may be found under their respective *titles*, in the Bibliothèque Orientale of D'Herbelot. They have been celebrated in an epic poem of sixty thousand rhymed couplets, by Ferdusi, the Homer of Persia. See the history of Nadir Shah, p. 145, 165. The public must lament that Mr. Jones has suspended the pursuit of Oriental learning.

[Ferdusi, the Persian poet, *circa* 940-1020, was the poetical title of Abu Kasim Mansur, author of the *Shahnamah*, or Book of Kings, which contains the legendary annals of the ancient monarchs of Persia, down to the Arab invasion of 641 A.D. Ferdusi, who was a native of Tus, laboured on the *Shahnamah* for thirty-five years, and then presented the poem to Mahmud. Displeased by the reward given by the latter, he fled to the caliph of Bagdad, for whom he wrote the poem, *Yusaf and Zuleikha*, describing the loves of Joseph and Potiphar's wife.—O. S.]

[2] The Caspian Sea, with its rivers and adjacent tribes, are laboriously illustrated in the Examen Critique des Historiens d'Alexandre, which compares the true geography and the errors produced by the vanity or ignorance of the Greeks.

[3] The original seat of the nation appears to have been in the north-west of China, in the provinces of Chensi and Chansi. Under the two first dynasties the principal town was still a movable camp; the villages were thinly scattered; more land was employed in pasture than in tillage; the exercise of hunting was ordained to clear the country from wild beasts; Petcheli (where Pekin stands) was a desert; and the southern provinces were peopled with Indian savages. The dynasty of the *Han* (before Christ 206) gave the empire its actual form and extent.

[4] The era of the Chinese monarchy has been variously fixed from 2952 to 2132 years before Christ; and the year 2637 has been chosen for the lawful epoch by the authority of the present emperor. The difference arises from the uncertain duration of the two first dynasties; and the vacant space that lies beyond them, as far as the real, or fabulous, times of Fohi or Hoangti. Sematsien dates his authentic chronology from the year 841;

perpetual testimony of accurate and contemporary historians.[1]
The annals of China [2] illustrate the state and revolutions of the
pastoral tribes, which may still be distinguished by the vague
appellation of Scythians or Tartars—the vassals, the enemies,
and sometimes the conquerors of a great empire, whose policy
has uniformly opposed the blind and impetuous valour of the
barbarians of the North. From the mouth of the Danube to the
sea of Japan, the whole longitude of Scythia is about one hundred
and ten degrees, which, in that parallel, are equal to more than
five thousand miles. The latitude of these extensive deserts
cannot be so easily or so accurately measured; but, from the
fortieth degree, which touches the wall of China, we may securely
advance above a thousand miles to the northward, till our progress is stopped by the excessive cold of Siberia. In that dreary
climate, instead of the animated picture of a Tartar camp, the
smoke which issues from the earth, or rather from the snow,

the thirty-six eclipses of Confucius (thirty-one of which have been verified)
were observed between the years 722 and 480 before Christ. The *historical
period* of China does not ascend above the Greek Olympiads.
[The ablest Chinese scholars in Europe accept the statements of Chinese
authors respecting the antiquity of their monarchy. Remusat says that
the history of China goes back with certainty to the twenty-second century
before our era, and that traditions, entitled to respect, enable us to date
its commencement four centuries earlier, in the year 2637 B.C., in the sixty-
first year of the reign of Hoang-ti. But the laws of historical criticism
oblige us to reject this ancient date. The earliest extant history of China
is by Ssema-Thsian (called by Gibbon Sematsien), who was born B.C. 145,
and published his work about the beginning of the first century before our
era. Even if Ssema-Thsian recovered most of the ancient annals, we do
not know anything of their value, whether they were written by contemporaries of the deeds they record, or whether, like the Greek genealogies
of the heroic ages, they were the invention of a later period. At all events
we cannot, with certainty, place the commencement of the historical period
in China earlier than B.C. 206, the beginning of the Han dynasty.—O. S.]

[1] After several ages of anarchy and despotism, the dynasty of the Han
(before Christ 206) was the era of the revival of learning. The fragments
of ancient literature were restored; the characters were improved and
fixed; and the future preservation of books was secured by the useful in-
ventions of ink, paper, and the art of printing. Ninety-seven years before
Christ, Sematsien published the first history of China. His labours were
illustrated and continued by a series of one hundred and eighty historians.
The substance of their works is still extant; and the most considerable of
them are now deposited in the king of France's library.

[2] China has been illustrated by the labours of the French; of the missionaries at Pekin, and Messrs. Fréret and De Guignes at Paris. The substance of the three preceding notes is extracted from the *Chou-king*, with
the preface and notes of M. de Guignes, Paris, 1770; The *Tong-Kien-Kang-
Mou*, translated by the P. de Mailla, under the name of Hist. Générale de
la Chine, tom. i. p. xlix.-cc.; the Mémoires sur la Chine, Paris, 1776, etc.,
tom. i. p. 1-323, tom. ii. p. 5-364; the Histoire des Huns, tom. i. p. 1-131,
tom. v. p. 345-362; and the Mémoires de l'Académie des Inscriptions, tom.
x. p. 377-402, tom. xv. p. 495-564, tom. xviii. p. 178-295, tom. xxxvi.
p. 164-238.

betrays the subterraneous dwellings of the Tongouses and the Samoiedes: the want of horses and of oxen is imperfectly supplied by the use of reindeer and of large dogs; and the conquerors of the earth insensibly degenerate into a race of deformed and diminutive savages, who tremble at the sound of arms.[1]

The Huns, who under the reign of Valens threatened the empire of Rome, had been formidable, in a much earlier period, to the empire of China.[2] Their ancient, perhaps their original, seat was an extensive, though dry and barren, tract of country immediately on the north side of the great wall. Their place is at present occupied by the forty-nine Hords or Banners of the Mongous, a pastoral nation, which consists of about two hundred thousand families.[3] But the valour of the Huns had extended the narrow limits of their dominions; and their rustic chiefs, who assumed the appellation of *Tanjou*, gradually became the conquerors and the sovereigns of a formidable empire. Towards the east their victorious arms were stopped only by the ocean; and the tribes, which are thinly scattered between the Amoor and the extreme peninsula of Corea, adhered with reluctance to the standard of the Huns. On the west, near the head of the Irtish, and in the valleys of Imaus, they found a more ample space, and more numerous enemies. One of the lieutenants of the Tanjou subdued, in a single expedition, twenty-six nations; the Igours,[4]

---

[1] See the Histoire Générale des Voyages, tom. xviii.; and the Genealogical History, vol. ii. p. 620-664.

[2] M. de Guignes (tom. ii. p. 1-124) has given the original history of the ancient Hiong-nou, or Huns. The Chinese geography of their country (tom. i. part ii. p. lv.-lxiii.) seems to comprise a part of their conquests. [Much controversy has been waged with regard to the origin of the Huns. But three theories may be said to represent all that has been said. (1) Niebuhr's theory that they were Mongols. (2) That they were Ugrians, which is maintained by Humboldt and the chief writers on the subject. (3) That they were Turks, which is upheld by Zeuss, Prichard, and Latham. The last is the one now generally accepted. De Guignes identifies the Hiongnou or Hiong-nú with the Huns, the word signifying "revolted slaves."—O. S.]

[3] See in Du Halde (tom. iv. p. 18-65) a circumstantial description, with a correct map, of the country of the Mongous.

[4] The Igours, or Vigours, were divided into three branches—hunters, shepherds, and husbandmen; and the last class was despised by the two former. See Abulghazi, part ii. c. 7. [The history of the Igours or Ouigours has been collected from Chinese sources by Visdelon, Remusat, and Klaproth. Their language represents the old Turkish language before it became corrupted by the infusion of Persian and Arabic words. It was reduced to writing many centuries before letters were known among the other nations in Central Asia. The alphabet of the Ouigours is derived from the Syrian Estranghelo, being introduced among them by the missionaries of the Nestorian Christians. In turn the Syrian alphabet was diffused among the Mongolian and Tungusian nations by the Ouigours.—O. S.]

distinguished above the Tartar race by the use of letters, were in the number of his vassals; and, by the strange connection of human events, the flight of one of those vagrant tribes recalled the victorious Parthians from the invasion of Syria.[1] On the side of the north, the ocean was assigned as the limit of the power of the Huns. Without enemies to resist their progress, or witnesses to contradict their vanity, they might securely achieve a real, or imaginary, conquest of the frozen regions of Siberia. The *Northern Sea* was fixed as the remote boundary of their empire. But the name of that sea, on whose shores the patriot Sovou embraced the life of a shepherd and an exile,[2] may be transferred, with much more probability, to the Baikal, a capacious basin, above three hundred miles in length, which disdains the modest appellation of a lake,[3] and which actually communicates with the seas of the North, by the long course of the Angara, the Tonguska, and the Yenesei. The submission of so many distant nations might flatter the pride of the Tanjou; but the valour of the Huns could be rewarded only by the enjoyment of the wealth and luxury of the empire of the South. In the third century before the Christian era, a wall of fifteen hundred miles in length was constructed, to defend the frontiers of China against the inroads of the Huns;[4] but this stupendous work, which holds a conspicuous place in the map of the world, has never contributed to the safety of an unwarlike people. The cavalry of the Tanjou frequently consisted of two or three hundred thousand men, formidable by the matchless dexterity with which they managed their bows and their horses; by their hardy patience in supporting the inclemency of the weather; and by

[1] Mémoires de l'Académie des Inscriptions, tom. xxv. p. 17-33. The comprehensive view of M. de Guignes has compared these distant events.

[2] The fame of Sovou, or So-ou, his merit, and his singular adventures, are still celebrated in China. See the Eloge de Moukden, p. 20, and notes, p. 241-247; and Mémoires sur la Chine, tom. iii. p. 317-360.

[3] See Isbrand Ives in Harris's Collection, vol. ii. p. 931; Bell's Travels, vol. i. p. 247-254; and Gmelin, in the Hist. Générale des Voyages, tom. xviii. p. 283-329. They all remark the vulgar opinion, that the *holy sea* grows angry and tempestuous if any one presumes to call it a *lake*. This grammatical nicety often excites a dispute between the absurd superstition of the mariners and the absurd obstinacy of travellers.

[Lake Baikal figured greatly in the recent (1905) Russo-Japanese War, in which the Russians laid a line over the frozen surface of the lake, by which troops could be hurried to the front, a saving of distance amounting to over 100 miles.—O. S.]

[4] The construction of the wall of China is mentioned by Du Halde (tom. ii. p. 45) and De Guignes (tom. ii. p. 59).

[The "Great Wall of China" was finished by Chi-hoangti of the dynasty of Thsin, B.C. 244. According to Chinese authorities, its length is 10,000 *li* (about 1350 miles), and its height averages from 20 to 25 feet.—O. S.]

the incredible speed of their march, which was seldom checked by torrents or precipices, by the deepest rivers, or by the most lofty mountains.

They spread themselves at once over the face of the country; and their rapid impetuosity surprised, astonished, and disconcerted the grave and elaborate tactics of a Chinese army. The emperor Kaoti,[1] a soldier of fortune, whose personal merit had raised him to the throne, marched against the Huns with those veteran troops which had been trained in the civil wars of China. But he was soon surrounded by the barbarians; and, after a siege of seven days, the monarch, hopeless of relief, was reduced to purchase his deliverance by an ignominious capitulation. The successors of Kaoti, whose lives were dedicated to the arts of peace, or the luxury of the palace, submitted to a more permanent disgrace. They too hastily confessed the insufficiency of arms and fortifications. They were too easily convinced that, while the blazing signals announced on every side the approach of the Huns, the Chinese troops, who slept with the helmet on their head, and the cuirass on their back, were destroyed by the incessant labour of ineffectual marches.[2] A regular payment of money and silk was stipulated as the condition of a temporary and precarious peace; and the wretched expedient of disguising a real tribute under the names of a gift or subsidy was practised by the emperors of China as well as by those of Rome. But there still remained a more disgraceful article of tribute, which violated the sacred feelings of humanity and nature. The hardships of the savage life, which destroy in their infancy the children who are born with a less healthy and robust constitution, introduce a remarkable disproportion between the numbers of the two sexes. The Tartars are an ugly and even deformed race; and while they consider their own women as the instruments of domestic labour, their desires, or rather their appetites, are directed to the enjoyment of more elegant beauty. A select band of the fairest maidens of China

[1] See the life of Lieoupang, or Kaoti, in the Hist. de la Chine, published at Paris, 1777, etc., tom. i. p. 442-522. This voluminous work is the translation (by the P. de Mailla) of the *Tong-Kien-Kang-Mou*, the celebrated abridgment of the great History of Semakouang (A.D. 1084) and his continuators.

[2] See a free and ample memorial, presented by a Mandarin to the emperor Venti (before Christ 180-157), in Du Halde (tom. ii. p. 412-426), from a collection of State papers, marked with the red pencil by Kamhi himself (p. 384-612). Another memorial from the minister of war (Kang-Mou, tom. ii. p. 555) supplies some curious circumstances of the manners of the Huns.

was annually devoted to the rude embraces of the Huns; [1] and
the alliance of the haughty Tanjous was secured by their
marriage with the genuine, or adopted, daughters of the Imperial
family, which vainly attempted to escape the sacrilegious pollu-
tion.   The situation of these unhappy victims is described in the
verses of a Chinese princess, who laments that she had been condemned by her parents to a distant exile, under a barbarian
husband; who complains that sour milk was her only drink,
raw flesh her only food, a tent her only palace; and who expresses,
in a strain of pathetic simplicity, the natural wish that she were
transformed into a bird, to fly back to her dear country, the object
of her tender and perpetual regret. [2]

The conquest of China has been twice achieved by the pastoral
tribes of the North: the forces of the Huns were not inferior to
those of the Moguls, or of the Mantcheoux; and their ambition
might entertain the most sanguine hopes of success.   But their
pride was humbled, and their progress was checked, by the arms
and policy of Vouti, [3] the fifth emperor of the powerful dynasty of
the Han.   In his long reign of fifty-four years, the barbarians of
the southern provinces submitted to the laws and manners of
China; and the ancient limits of the monarchy were enlarged
from the great river of Kiang to the port of Canton.   Instead of
confining himself to the timid operations of a defensive war, his
lieutenants penetrated many hundred miles into the country of
the Huns.   In those boundless deserts, where it is impossible to
form magazines, and difficult to transport a sufficient supply of
provisions, the armies of Vouti were repeatedly exposed to
intolerable hardships: and, of one hundred and forty thousand
soldiers who marched against the barbarians, thirty thousand
only returned in safety to the feet of their master.   These losses,
however, were compensated by splendid and decisive success.
The Chinese generals improved the superiority which they
derived from the temper of their arms, their chariots of war, and
the service of their Tartar auxiliaries.   The camp of the Tanjou
was surprised in the midst of sleep and intemperance; and,
though the monarch of the Huns bravely cut his way through
the ranks of the enemy, he left above fifteen thousand of his subjects on the field of battle.   Yet this signal victory, which was

---

[1] A supply of women is mentioned as a customary article of treaty and
tribute (Hist. de la Conquête de la Chine par les Tartares Mantcheoux,
tom. i. p. 186, 187, with the note of the editor).

[2] De Guignes, Hist. des Huns, tom. ii. p. 62.

[3] See the reign of the emperor Vouti, in the Kang-Mou, tom. iii. p. 1-98.
His various and inconsistent character seems to be impartially drawn.

preceded and followed by many bloody engagements, contributed much less to the destruction of the power of the Huns, than the effectual policy which was employed to detach the tributary nations from their obedience. Intimidated by the arms, or allured by the promises, of Vouti and his successors, the most considerable tribes, both of the East and of the West, disclaimed the authority of the Tanjou. While some acknowledged themselves the allies or vassals of the empire, they all became the implacable enemies of the Huns: and the numbers of that haughty people, as soon as they were reduced to their native strength, might perhaps have been contained within the walls of one of the great and populous cities of China.[1] The desertion of his subjects, and the perplexity of a civil war, at length compelled the Tanjou himself to renounce the dignity of an independent sovereign, and the freedom of a warlike and high-spirited nation. He was received at Sigan, the capital of the monarchy, by the troops, the mandarins, and the emperor himself, with all the honours that could adorn and disguise the triumph of Chinese vanity.[2] A magnificent palace was prepared for his reception; his place was assigned above all the princes of the royal family; and the patience of the barbarian king was exhausted by the ceremonies of a banquet, which consisted of eight courses of meat, and of nine solemn pieces of music. But he performed, on his knees, the duty of a respectful homage to the emperor of China; pronounced, in his own name, and in the name of his successors, a perpetual oath of fidelity; and gratefully accepted a seal, which was bestowed as the emblem of his regal dependence. After this humiliating submission, the Tanjous sometimes departed from their allegiance, and seized the favourable moments of war and rapine; but the monarchy of the Huns gradually declined, till it was broken, by civil dissension, into two hostile and separate kingdoms. One of the princes of the nation was urged by fear and ambition to retire towards the south with eight hordes, which composed between forty and fifty thousand families. He obtained, with the title of Tanjou, a convenient territory on the verge of the Chinese provinces; and his constant attachment to the service of the empire was

[1] This expression is used in the memorial to the emperor Venti (Du Halde, tom. ii. p. 417). Without adopting the exaggerations of Marco Polo and Isaac Vossius, we may rationally allow for Pekin two millions of inhabitants. The cities of the south, which contain the manufactures of China, are still more populous.

[2] See the Kang-Mou, tom. iii. p. 150, and the subsequent events under the proper years. This memorable festival is celebrated in the Eloge de Moukden, and explained in a note by the P. Gaubil, p. 89, 90.

secured by weakness and the desire of revenge. From the time of this fatal schism, the Huns of the north continued to languish about fifty years, till they were oppressed on every side by their foreign and domestic enemies. The proud inscription [1] of a column, erected on a lofty mountain, announced to posterity that a Chinese army had marched seven hundred miles into the heart of their country. The Sienpi,[2] a tribe of Oriental Tartars, retaliated the injuries which they had formerly sustained; and the power of the Tanjous, after a reign of thirteen hundred years, was utterly destroyed before the end of the first century of the Christian era.[3]

The fate of the vanquished Huns was diversified by the various influence of character and situation.[4] Above one hundred thousand persons, the poorest, indeed, and the most pusillanimous of the people, were contented to remain in their native country, to renounce their peculiar name and origin, and to mingle with the victorious nation of the Sienpi. Fifty-eight hordes, about two hundred thousand men, ambitious of a more honourable servitude, retired towards the south, implored the protection of the emperors of China, and were permitted to inhabit and to guard the extreme frontiers of the province of Chansi and the territory of Ortous. But the most warlike and powerful tribes of the Huns maintained in their adverse fortune the undaunted spirit of their ancestors. The Western world was open to their valour, and they resolved, under the conduct of their hereditary chieftains, to discover and subdue some remote country which was still inaccessible to the arms of the Sienpi and to the laws of China.[5] The course of their emigration soon carried them beyond the mountains of Imaus and the limits of the Chinese geography; but *we* are able to distinguish the two great divisions of these formidable exiles, which directed their march towards the Oxus and towards the Volga. The first of these colonies established their dominion in the fruitful and extensive plains

---

[1] This inscription was composed on the spot by Pankou, President of the Tribunal of History (Kang-Mou, tom. iii. p. 392). Similar monuments have been discovered in many parts of Tartary (Histoire des Huns, tom. ii. p. 122).

[2] M. de Guignes (tom. i. p. 189) has inserted a short account of the Sienpi.

[3] The era of the Huns is placed by the Chinese 1210 years before Christ. But the series of their kings does not commence till the year 230. (Hist. des Huns, tom. ii. p. 21, 123).

[4] The various accidents of the downfall and flight of the Huns are related in the Kang-Mou, tom. iii. p. 88, 91, 95, 139, etc. The small numbers of each horde may be ascribed to their losses and divisions.

[5] M. de Guignes has skilfully traced the footsteps of the Huns through the vast deserts of Tartary (tom. ii. p. 123, 277, etc. 325, etc.).

of the Sogdiana, on the eastern side of the Caspian, where they preserved the name of Huns, with the epithet of Euthalites or Nephalites. Their manners were softened, and even their features were insensibly improved, by the mildness of the climate and their long residence in a flourishing province,[1] which might still retain a faint impression of the arts of Greece.[2] The *white* Huns, a name which they derived from the change of their complexions, soon abandoned the pastoral life of Scythia. Gorgo, which, under the appellation of Carizme, has since enjoyed a temporary splendour, was the residence of the king, who exercised a legal authority over an obedient people. Their luxury was maintained by the labour of the Sogdians; and the only vestige of their ancient barbarism was the custom which obliged all the companions, perhaps to the number of twenty, who had shared the liberality of a wealthy lord, to be buried alive in the same grave.[3] The vicinity of the Huns to the provinces of Persia involved them in frequent and bloody contests with the power of that monarchy. But they respected, in peace, the faith of treaties; in war, the dictates of humanity; and their memorable victory over Peroses, or Firuz, displayed the moderation as well as the valour of the barbarians. The *second* division of their countrymen, the Huns who gradually advanced towards the north-west, were exercised by the hardships of a colder climate and a more laborious march. Necessity compelled them to exchange the silks of China for the furs of Siberia; the imperfect rudiments of civilised life were obliterated;

---

[1] Mohammed, sultan of Carizme, reigned in Sogdiana when it was invaded (A.D. 1218) by Zingis and his Moguls. The Oriental historians (see D'Herbelot, Petit de la Croix, etc.) celebrate the populous cities which he ruined, and the fruitful country which he desolated. In the next century the same provinces of Chorasmia and Mawaralnahr were described by Abulfeda (Hudson, Geograph. Minor. tom. iii.). Their actual misery may be seen in the Genealogical History of the Tartars, p. 423-469.

[Euthalites seems to be a misprint for Ephthalites, which is the name that appears in Procopius (Bell. Persic. i. c. 3). The Armenian writers who frequently mention the wars carried on by this people against the Persians call them Hephthal. The Ephthalites, according to Parker, were not part of the Hiung-nu, but seem to have been the Yueh-chih, who possessed part of the long, straggling province now known as Kan Suh. They were conquered by Meghder, and being forced westward by his successor about 162 B.C., divided Bactria with the Parthians.—O. S.]

[2] Justin (xli. 6) has left a short abridgment of the Greek kings of Bactriana. To their industry I should ascribe the new and extraordinary trade which transported the merchandises of India into Europe by the Oxus, the Caspian, the Cyrus, the Phasis, and the Euxine. The other ways, both of the land and sea, were possessed by the Seleucides and the Ptolemies. (See l'Esprit des Loix, l. xxi.)

[3] Procopius de Bell. Persico, l. i. c. 3, p. 9 [tom. i. p. 16, ed. Bonn.].

and the native fierceness of the Huns was exasperated by their intercourse with the savage tribes, who were compared, with some propriety, to the wild beasts of the desert. Their independent spirit soon rejected the hereditary succession of the Tanjous; and while each horde was governed by its peculiar mursa, their tumultuary council directed the public measures of the whole nation. As late as the thirteenth century their transient residence on the eastern banks of the Volga was attested by the name of Great Hungary.[1] In the winter they descended with their flocks and herds towards the mouth of that mighty river; and their summer excursions reached as high as the latitude of Saratoff, or perhaps the conflux of the Kama. Such at least were the recent limits of the black Calmucks,[2] who remained about a century under the protection of Russia, and who have since returned to their native seats on the frontiers of the Chinese empire. The march and the return of those wondering Tartars, whose united camp consists of fifty thousand tents or families, illustrate the distant emigrations of the ancient Huns.[3]

It is impossible to fill the dark interval of time which elapsed after the Huns of the Volga were lost in the eyes of the Chinese, and before they showed themselves to those of the Romans. There is some reason, however, to apprehend that the same force which had driven them from their native seats still continued to impel their march towards the frontiers of Europe. The power of the Sienpi, their implacable enemies, which extended above three thousand miles from east to west,[4] must have gradually oppressed them by the weight and terror of a

[1] In the thirteenth century, the monk Rubruquis (who traversed the immense plain of Kipzak in his journey to the court of the Great Khan) observed the remarkable name of *Hungary*, with the traces of a common language and origin (Hist. des Voyages, tom. vii. p. 269.)

[2] Bell (vol. i. p. 29-34) and the editors of the Genealogical History (p. 539) have described the Calmucks of the Volga in the beginning of the present century.

[3] This great transmigration of 300,000 **Calmucks**, or Torgouts, happened in the year 1771. The original narrative of Kien-long, the reigning emperor of China, which was intended for the inscription of a column, has been translated by the missionaries of Pekin (Mémoires sur la Chine, tom. i. p. 401-418). The emperor affects the smooth and specious language of the Son of Heaven, and the Father of his People.

[4] The Kang-Mou (tom. iii. p. 447) ascribes to their conquests a space of 14,000 *lis*. According to the present standard, 200 *lis* (or more accurately 193) are equal to one degree of latitude; and one English mile consequently exceeds three miles of China. But there are strong reasons to believe that the ancient *li* scarcely equalled one-half of the modern. See the elaborate researches of M. d'Anville, a geographer who is not a stranger in any age or climate of the globe. (Mémoires de l'Acad. tom. ii. p. 125-502. Mesures Itinéraires, p. 154-167.)

formidable neighbourhood; and the flight of the tribes of Scythia
would inevitably tend to increase the strength or to contract
the territories of the Huns. The harsh and obscure appellations
of those tribes would offend the ear, without informing the understanding, of the reader; but I cannot suppress the very natural
suspicion *that* the Huns of the North derived a considerable reinforcement from the ruin of the dynasty of the South, which, in
the course of the third century, submitted to the dominion of
China; *that* the bravest warriors marched away in search of their
free and adventurous countrymen; *and* that, as they had been
divided by prosperity, they were easily reunited by the common
hardships of their adverse fortune.[1] The Huns, with their flocks
and herds, their wives and children, their dependents and allies,
were transported to the West of the Volga, and they boldly
advanced to invade the country of the Alani, a pastoral people,
who occupied, or wasted, an extensive tract of the deserts of
Scythia. The plains between the Volga and the Tanais were
covered with the tents of the Alani, but their name and manners
were diffused over the wide extent of their conquests; and the
painted tribes of the Agathyrsi and Geloni were confounded
among their vassals. Towards the north they penetrated into
the frozen regions of Siberia, among the savages who were
accustomed, in their rage or hunger, to the taste of human
flesh; and their southern inroads were pushed as far as the
confines of Persia and India. The mixture of Sarmatic and
German blood had contributed to improve the features of the
Alani, to whiten their swarthy complexions, and to tinge their
hair with a yellowish cast, which is seldom found in the Tartar
race. They were less deformed in their persons, less brutish in
their manners, than the Huns; but they did not yield to those
formidable barbarians in their martial and independent spirit;
in the love of freedom, which rejected even the use of domestic
slaves; and in the love of arms, which considered war and rapine
as the pleasure and the glory of mankind. A naked scimetar,
fixed in the ground, was the only object of their religious worship;
the scalps of their enemies formed the costly trappings of their
horses; and they viewed with pity and contempt the pusillanimous warriors who patiently expected the infirmities of age
and the tortures of lingering disease.[2] On the banks of the

---

[1] See the Histoire des Huns, tom. ii. p. 125-144. The subsequent history
(p. 145-277) of three or four Hunnic dynasties evidently proves that their
martial spirit was not impaired by a long residence in China.

[2] Utque hominibus quietis et placidis otium est voluptabile, ita illos
pericula juvant et bella. Judicatur ibi beatus qui in prœlio profuderit

Tanais the military power of the Huns and the Alani encountered
each other with equal valour, but with unequal success. The
Huns prevailed in the bloody contest; the king of the Alani
was slain; and the remains of the vanquished nation were
dispersed by the ordinary alternative of flight or submission.[1]
A colony of exiles found a secure refuge in the mountains of
Caucasus, between the Euxine and the Caspian, where they still
preserve their name and their independence. Another colony
advanced, with more intrepid courage, towards the shores of the
Baltic; associated themselves with the northern tribes of Germany; and shared the spoil of the Roman provinces of Gaul and
Spain. But the greatest part of the nation of the Alani embraced
the offers of an honourable and advantageous union; and the
Huns, who esteemed the valour of their less fortunate enemies,
proceeded, with an increase of numbers and confidence, to invade
the limits of the Gothic empire.

The great Hermanric, whose dominions extended from the
Baltic to the Euxine, enjoyed, in the full maturity of age and
reputation, the fruit of his victories, when he was alarmed by
the formidable approach of an host of unknown enemies,[2] on

animam: senescentes etiam et fortuitis mortibus mundo digressos, ut
degeneres et ignavos, conviciis atrocibus insectantur. [Ammian. xxxi. 2.]
We must think highly of the conquerors of *such* men.

[1] On the subject of the Alani, see Ammianus (xxxi. 2), Jornandes (de
Rebus Geticis, c. 24), M. de Guignes (Hist. des Huns, tom. ii. p. 279), and
the Genealogical History of the Tartars (tom. ii. p. 617).
[With regard to the Alani there has been much dispute regarding their
ethnological affinities. Milman maintains that the remains of them still
exist in the Ossetæ, a people of Mount Caucasus, who are said by ancient
travellers also to have borne the name of Alans. But these Ossetæ appear
to be an Indo-European people; while all the descriptions of the Alani by
ancient writers seem to prove that they belonged to the Tartar or nomadic
races of Asia. Lucian says that their language and dress were the same
as those of the Scythians, and Ammianus describes them as resembling
the Huns, but less savage in form and manners. This would seem to point
to a Turkish origin, which is conformed by the fact that their area, the
country north of the Caucasus, between the lower Don and the lower
Volga, is now occupied by the Nogay Turks, who are of ancient introduction into the country. If Persian tradition as represented by the poems
of Ferdusi is to be relied upon, the Alani dwelt in the most ancient
times on the northern side of the country of the Paropamisus, near the
land Gkur or Ghordseh. Klaproth says the Alani are mentioned in
Chinese annals under the names Yanthsai, Alanna, Alan, and subsequently
Suthle and Suth. Legge also affirms the same, and Latham. Cf. Klaproth, *Tableaux Historiques de l'Asie*, p. 174-190; Latham, *The Germania*
of Tacitus, *Epilegomena*.—O. S.]
[2] As we are possessed of the authentic history of the Huns, it would be
impertinent to repeat or to refute the fables which misrepresent their
origin and progress, their passage of the mud or water of the Mæotis in
pursuit of an ox or stag, les Indes qu'ils avoient découvertes, etc. (Zosimus
l. iv. [c. 20] p. 224. Sozomen, l. vi. c. 37. Procopius, Hist. Miscell. c. 5.
Jornandes, c. 24. Grandeur et Décadence, etc., des Romains, c. 17.)

whom his barbarous subjects might, without injustice, bestow the epithet of barbarians. The numbers, the strength, the rapid motions, and the implacable cruelty of the Huns were felt, and dreaded, and magnified by the astonished Goths, who beheld their fields and villages consumed with flames and deluged with indiscriminate slaughter. To these real terrors they added the surprise and abhorrence which were excited by the shrill voice, the uncouth gestures, and the strange deformity of the Huns. These savages of Scythia were compared (and the picture had some resemblance) to the animals who walk very awkwardly on two legs, and to the misshapen figures, the *Termini*, which were often placed on the bridges of antiquity. They were distinguished from the rest of the human species by their broad shoulders, flat noses, and small black eyes, deeply buried in the head; and as they were almost destitute of beards, they never enjoyed either the manly graces of youth or the venerable aspect of age.[1] A fabulous origin was assigned worthy of their form and manners—that the witches of Scythia, who, for their foul and deadly practices, had been driven from society, had copulated in the desert with infernal spirits, and that the Huns were the offspring of this execrable conjunction.[2] The tale, so full of horror and absurdity, was greedily embraced by the credulous hatred of the Goths; but while it gratified their hatred it increased their fear, since the posterity of dæmons and witches might be supposed to inherit some share of the preternatural powers as well as of the malignant temper of their parents. Against these enemies, Hermanric prepared to exert the united forces of the Gothic state; but he soon discovered that his vassal tribes, provoked by oppression, were much more inclined to second than to repel the invasion of the Huns. One of the chiefs of

[1] Prodigiosæ formæ, et pandi; ut bipedes existimes bestias; vel quales in commarginandis pontibus, effigiati stipites dolantur incompti. Ammian. xxxi. 2. Jornandes (c. 24) draws a strong caricature of a Calmuck face. Species pavendâ nigredine . . . quædam deformis offa, non facies; habensque magis puncta quam lumina. See Buffon, Hist. Naturelle, tom. iii. p. 380.

[With regard to the appearance of the Huns, art added to their native ugliness, but (as Milman says) it is difficult to ascribe the proper share in the features of this hideous picture to nature, to the barbarous skill with which they were self-disfigured, or to the terror and hatred of the Romans. Their noses were flattened by their nurses, their cheeks were gashed by an iron instrument that the scars might look more fearful and prevent the growth of the beard.—O. S.]

[2] This execrable origin, which Jornandes (c. 24) describes with the rancour of a Goth, might be originally derived from a more pleasing fable of the Greeks (Herodot. l. iv. c. 9, etc.).

the Roxolani [1] had formerly deserted the standard of Hermanric, and the cruel tyrant had condemned the innocent wife of the traitor to be torn asunder by wild horses. The brothers of that unfortunate woman seized the favourable moment of revenge. The aged king of the Goths languished some time after the dangerous wound which he received from their daggers; but the conduct of the war was retarded by his infirmities; and the public councils of the nation were distracted by a spirit of jealousy and discord. His death, which has been imputed to his own despair, left the reins of government in the hands of Withimer, who, with the doubtful aid of some Scythian mercenaries, maintained the unequal contest against the arms of the Huns and the Alani till he was defeated and slain in a decisive battle. The Ostrogoths submitted to their fate: and the royal race of the Amali will hereafter be found among the subjects of the haughty Attila. But the person of Witheric, the infant king, was saved by the diligence of Alatheus and Saphrax; two warriors of approved valour and fidelity, who, by cautious marches, conducted the independent remains of the nation of the Ostrogoths towards the Danastus, or Dniester, a considerable river, which now separates the Turkish dominions from the empire of Russia. On the banks of the Dniester the prudent Athanaric, more attentive to his own than to the general safety, had fixed the camp of the Visigoths; with the firm resolution of opposing the victorious barbarians, whom he thought it less advisable to provoke. The ordinary speed of the Huns was checked by the weight of baggage and the encumbrance of captives; but their military skill deceived and almost destroyed the army of Athanaric. While the Judge of the Visigoths defended the banks of the Dniester he was encompassed and attacked by a numerous detachment of cavalry, who, by the light of the moon, had passed the river in a fordable place; and it was not without the utmost efforts of courage and conduct that he was able to effect his retreat towards the hilly country. The undaunted general had already formed a new and judicious plan of defensive war; and the strong lines which he was preparing to construct between the mountains, the Pruth, and the Danube, would have secured the extensive and fertile territory that bears the modern name of Wallachia from the destructive inroads of the Huns.[2]

---

[1] The Roxolani may be the fathers of the Ῥῶς, the *Russians* (D'Anville, Empire de Russie, p. 1-10), whose residence (A.D. 862) about Novogrod Veliki cannot be very remote from that which the Geographer of Ravenna (i. 12, iv. 4, 46, v. 28, 30) assigns to the Roxolani (A.D. 886).

[2] The text of Ammianus seems to be imperfect or corrupt; but the nature

But the hopes and measures of the Judge of the Visigoths were soon disappointed by the trembling impatience of his dismayed countrymen, who were persuaded by their fears that the interposition of the Danube was the only barrier that could save them from the rapid pursuit and invincible valour of the barbarians of Scythia. Under the command of Fritigern and Alavivus,[1] the body of the nation hastily advanced to the banks of the great river, and implored the protection of the Roman emperor of the East. Athanaric himself, still anxious to avoid the guilt of perjury, retired, with a band of faithful followers, into the mountainous country of Caucaland, which appears to have been guarded and almost concealed by the impenetrable forests of Transylvania.[2]

After Valens had terminated the Gothic war with some appearance of glory and success, he made a progress through his dominions of Asia, and at length fixed his residence in the capital of Syria. The five years [3] which he spent at Antioch were employed to watch, from a secure distance, the hostile designs of the Persian monarch; to check the depredations of the Saracens and Isaurians; [4] to enforce, by arguments more prevalent than those of reason and eloquence, the belief of the Arian theology; and to satisfy his anxious suspicions by the promiscuous execution of the innocent and the guilty. But the attention of the emperor was most seriously engaged by the important intelligence which he received from the civil and military officers who were intrusted with the defence of the Danube. He was informed that the North was agitated by a furious tempest; that the irruption of the Huns, an unknown and monstrous race of savages, had subverted the power of the Goths; and that the suppliant multitudes of that warlike nation, whose pride was now humbled in the dust, covered a space of many miles along the banks of the river. With outstretched arms and pathetic

of the ground explains, and almost defines, the Gothic rampart. Mémoires de l'Académie, etc. tom. xxviii. p. 444-462.

[1] M. de Buat (Hist. des Peuples de l'Europe, tom. vi. p. 407) has conceived a strange idea, that Alavivus was the same person as Ulphilas the Gothic bishop; and that Ulphilas, the grandson of a Cappadocian captive, became a temporal prince of the Goths.

[2] Ammianus (xxxi. 3) and Jornandes (de Rebus Geticis, c. 24) describe the subversion of the Gothic empire by the Huns.

[3] The chronology of Ammianus is obscure and imperfect. Tillemont has laboured to clear and settle the annals of Valens.

[4] Zosimus, l. iv. [c. 20] p. 223. Sozomen, l. vi. c. 38. The Isaurians, each winter, infested the roads of Asia Minor, as far as the neighbourhood of Constantinople. Basil, Epist. ccl. apud Tillemont, Hist. des Empereurs, tom. v. p. 106.

lamentations they loudly deplored their past misfortunes and their present danger; acknowledged that their only hope of safety was in the clemency of the Roman government; and most solemnly protested that, if the gracious liberality of the emperor would permit them to cultivate the waste lands of Thrace, they should ever hold themselves bound, by the strongest obligations of duty and gratitude, to obey the laws and to guard the limits of the republic. These assurances were confirmed by the ambassadors of the Goths, who impatiently expected from the mouth of Valens an answer that must finally determine the fate of their unhappy countrymen. The emperor of the East was no longer guided by the wisdom and authority of his elder brother, whose death happened towards the end of the preceding year; and as the distressful situation of the Goths required an instant and peremptory decision, he was deprived of the favourite resource of feeble and timid minds, who consider the use of dilatory and ambiguous measures as the most admirable efforts of consummate prudence. As long as the same passions and interests subsist among mankind, the questions of war and peace, of justice and policy, which were debated in the councils of antiquity, will frequently present themselves as the subject of modern deliberation. But the most experienced statesman of Europe has never been summoned to consider the propriety or the danger of admitting or rejecting an innumerable multitude of barbarians, who are driven by despair and hunger to solicit a settlement on the territories of a civilised nation. When that important proposition, so essentially connected with the public safety, was referred to the ministers of Valens, they were perplexed and divided; but they soon acquiesced in the flattering sentiment which seemed the most favourable to the pride, the indolence, and the avarice of their sovereign. The slaves, who were decorated with the titles of præfects and generals, dissembled or disregarded the terrors of this national emigration— so extremely different from the partial and accidental colonies which had been received on the extreme limits of the empire. But they applauded the liberality of fortune which had conducted, from the most distant countries of the globe, a numerous and invincible army of strangers to defend the throne of Valens, who might now add to the royal treasures the immense sums of gold supplied by the provincials to compensate their annual proportion of recruits. The prayers of the Goths were granted, and their service was accepted by the Imperial court; and orders were immediately despatched to the civil and military governors of the Thracian diocese to make the necessary preparations for the passage and subsistence of a great people, till a proper and sufficient territory could be allotted for their future residence. The liberality of the emperor was accompanied, however, with two harsh and rigorous conditions, which prudence might justify on the side of the Romans, but which distress alone could extort from the indignant Goths. Before they passed the Danube they were required to deliver their arms, and it was insisted that their children should be taken from them and dispersed through the provinces of Asia, where they might be civilised by the arts of education, and serve as hostages to secure the fidelity of their parents.

During this suspense of a doubtful and distant negotiation, the impatient Goths made some rash attempts to pass the Danube without the permission of the government whose protection they had implored. Their motions were strictly observed by the vigilance of the troops which were stationed along the river, and their foremost detachments were defeated with considerable slaughter; yet such were the timid councils of the reign of Valens, that the brave officers who had served their country in the execution of their duty were punished by the loss of their employments, and narrowly escaped the loss of their heads. The Imperial mandate was at length received for transporting over the Danube the whole body of the Gothic nation; [1] but the execution of this order was a task of labour and difficulty. The stream of the Danube, which in those parts is above a mile broad,[2] had been swelled by incessant rains, and in this tumultuous passage many were swept away and drowned by the rapid violence of the current. A large fleet of vessels, of boats, and of canoes, was provided; many days and nights they passed and repassed with indefatigable toil; and the most strenuous diligence was exerted by the officers of Valens that not a single barbarian, of those who were reserved to subvert the foundations of Rome, should be left on the opposite shore. It was thought expedient that an accurate account should be taken of their numbers; but the

---

[1] The passage of the Danube is exposed by Ammianus (xxxi. 3, 4), Zosimus (l. iv. [c. 20] p. 223, 224), Eunapius in Excerpt. Legat. (p. 19, 20 [p. 49, 50, ed. Bonn]), and Jornandes (c. 25, 26). Ammianus declares (c. 5) that he means only ipsas rerum digerere *summitates*. But he often takes a false measure of their importance, and his superfluous prolixity is disagreeably balanced by his unseasonable brevity.

[2] Chishull, a curious traveller, has remarked the breadth of the Danube, which he passed to the south of Bucharest, near the conflux of the Argish (p. 77). He admires the beauty and spontaneous plenty of Mæsia, or Bulgaria.

persons who were employed soon desisted, with amazement and dismay, from the prosecution of the endless and impracticable task;[1] and the principal historian of the age most seriously affirms that the prodigious armies of Darius and Xerxes, which had so long been considered as the fables of vain and credulous antiquity, were now justified, in the eyes of mankind, by the evidence of fact and experience. A probable testimony has fixed the number of the Gothic warriors at two hundred thousand men; and if we can venture to add the just proportion of women, of children, and of slaves, the whole mass of people which composed this formidable emigration must have amounted to near a million of persons, of both sexes and of all ages. The children of the Goths, those at least of a distinguished rank, were separated from the multitude. They were conducted without delay to the distant seats assigned for their residence and education; and as the numerous train of hostages or captives passed through the cities, their gay and splendid apparel, their robust and martial figure, excited the surprise and envy of the provincials. But the stipulation, the most offensive to the Goths and the most important to the Romans, was shamefully eluded. The barbarians, who considered their arms as the ensigns of honour and the pledges of safety, were disposed to offer a price which the lust or avarice of the Imperial officers was easily tempted to accept. To preserve their arms, the haughty warriors consented, with some reluctance, to prostitute their wives or their daughters; the charms of a beauteous maid, or a comely boy, secured the connivance of the inspectors, who sometimes cast an eye of covetousness on the fringed carpets and linen garments of their new allies,[2] or who sacrificed their duty to the mean consideration of filling their farms with cattle and their houses with slaves. The Goths, with arms in their hands, were permitted to enter the boats; and, when their strength was collected on the other side of the river, the immense camp which was spread over the plains and the hills of the Lower Mæsia assumed a threatening and even hostile aspect. The leaders of the Ostrogoths, Alatheus and Saphrax, the guardians of their infant king, appeared soon

[1] Quem qui scire velit, Libyci velit æquoris idem
Discere quam multæ Zephyro turbentur arenæ.
Ammianus has inserted in his prose these lines of Virgil (Georgic. l. ii. 105), originally designed by the poet to express the impossibility of numbering the different sorts of vines. See Plin. Hist. Natur. l. xiv.

[2] Eunapis and Zosimus curiously specify these articles of Gothic wealth and luxury. Yet it must be presumed that they were the manufactures of the provinces, which the barbarians had acquired as the spoils of war, or as the gifts or merchandise of peace.

afterwards on the northern banks of the Danube, and immediately despatched their ambassadors to the court of Antioch to solicit, with the same professions of allegiance and gratitude, the same favour which had been granted to the suppliant Visigoths. The absolute refusal of Valens suspended their progress, and discovered the repentance, the suspicions, and the fears of the Imperial council.

An undisciplined and unsettled nation of barbarians required the firmest temper and the most dexterous management. The daily subsistence of near a million of extraordinary subjects could be supplied only by constant and skilful diligence, and might continually be interrupted by mistake or accident. The insolence or the indignation of the Goths, if they conceived themselves to be the objects either of fear or of contempt, might urge them to the most desperate extremities, and the fortune of the state seemed to depend on the prudence, as well as the integrity, of the generals of Valens. At this important crisis the military government of Thrace was exercised by Lupicinus and Maximus, in whose venal minds the slightest hope of private emolument outweighed every consideration of public advantage, and whose guilt was only alleviated by their incapacity of discerning the pernicious effects of their rash and criminal administration. Instead of obeying the orders of their sovereign, and satisfying, with decent liberality, the demands of the Goths, they levied an ungenerous and oppressive tax on the wants of the hungry barbarians. The vilest food was sold at an extravagant price, and, in the room of wholesome and substantial provisions, the markets were filled with the flesh of dogs and of unclean animals who had died of disease. To obtain the valuable acquisition of a pound of bread, the Goths resigned the possession of an expensive though serviceable slave, and a small quantity of meat was greedily purchased with ten pounds of a precious but useless metal.[1] When their property was exhausted, they continued this necessary traffic by the sale of their sons and daughters; and notwithstanding the love of freedom which animated every Gothic breast, they submitted to the humiliating maxim that it was better for their children to be maintained in a servile con-

---

[1] *Decem libras ;* the word *silver* must be understood. Jornandes betrays the passions and prejudices of a Goth. The servile Greeks, Eunapius and Zosimus, disguise the Roman oppression, and execrate the perfidy of the barbarians. Ammianus, a patriot historian, slightly and reluctantly touches on the odious subject. Jerom, who wrote almost on the spot, is fair, though concise. Per avaritiam Maximi ducis, ad rebellionem fame *coacti* sunt (in Chron. [tom. viii. p. 817, ed. Vallars.]).

dition than to perish in a state of wretched and helpless independence. The most lively resentment is excited by the tyranny of pretended benefactors, who sternly exact the debt of gratitude which they have cancelled by subsequent injuries; a spirit of discontent insensibly arose in the camp of the barbarians, who pleaded, without success, the merit of their patient and dutiful behaviour, and loudly complained of the inhospitable treatment which they had received from their new allies. They beheld around them the wealth and plenty of a fertile province, in the midst of which they suffered the intolerable hardships of artificial famine. But the means of relief, and even of revenge, were in their hands, since the rapaciousness of their tyrants had left to an injured people the possession and the use of arms. The clamours of a multitude, untaught to disguise their sentiments, announced the first symptoms of resistance, and alarmed the timid and guilty minds of Lupicinus and Maximus. Those crafty ministers, who substituted the cunning of temporary expedients to the wise and salutary counsels of general policy, attempted to remove the Goths from their dangerous station on the frontiers of the empire, and to disperse them, in separate quarters of cantonment, through the interior provinces. As they were conscious how ill they had deserved the respect or confidence of the barbarians, they diligently collected from every side a military force that might urge the tardy and reluctant march of a people who had not yet renounced the title or the duties of Roman subjects. But the generals of Valens, while their attention was solely directed to the discontented Visigoths, imprudently disarmed the ships and the fortifications which constituted the defence of the Danube. The fatal oversight was observed and improved by Alatheus and Saphrax, who anxiously watched the favourable moment of escaping from the pursuit of the Huns. By the help of such rafts and vessels as could be hastily procured, the leaders of the Ostrogoths transported, without opposition, their king and their army, and boldly fixed an hostile and independent camp on the territories of the empire.[1]

Under the name of Judges, Alavivus and Fritigern were the leaders of the Visigoths in peace and war; and the authority which they derived from their birth was ratified by the free consent of the nation. In a season of tranquillity their power might have been equal as well as their rank; but, as soon as their countrymen were exasperated by hunger and oppression, the superior abilities of Fritigern assumed the military command,

[1] Ammianus, xxxi. 4, 5.

which he was qualified to exercise for the public welfare. He restrained the impatient spirit of the Visigoths till the injuries and the insults of their tyrants should justify their resistance in the opinion of mankind: but he was not disposed to sacrifice any solid advantages for the empty praise of justice and moderation. Sensible of the benefits which would result from the union of the Gothic powers under the same standard, he secretly culti-vated the friendship of the Ostrogoths; and while he professed an implicit obedience to the orders of the Roman generals, he proceeded by slow marches towards Marcianopolis, the capital of the Lower Mæsia, about seventy miles from the banks of the Danube. On that fatal spot the flames of discord and mutual hatred burst forth into a dreadful conflagration. Lupicinus had invited the Gothic chiefs to a splendid entertainment; and their martial train remained under arms at the entrance of the palace. But the gates of the city were strictly guarded, and the barbarians were sternly excluded from the use of a plentiful market, to which they asserted their equal claim of subjects and allies. Their humble prayers were rejected with insolence and derision; and as their patience was now exhausted, the towns-men, the soldiers, and the Goths were soon involved in a conflict of passionate altercation and angry reproaches. A blow was imprudently given; a sword was hastily drawn; and the first blood that was spilt in this accidental quarrel became the signal of a long and destructive war. In the midst of noise and brutal intemperance Lupicinus was informed by a secret messenger that many of his soldiers were slain and despoiled of their arms; and as he was already inflamed by wine and oppressed by sleep, he issued a rash command, that their death should be revenged by the massacre of the guards of Fritigern and Alavivus. The clamorous shouts and dying groans apprised Fritigern of his extreme danger; and, as he possessed the calm and intrepid spirit of a hero, he saw that he was lost if he allowed a moment of deliberation to the man who had so deeply injured him. " A trifling dispute," said the Gothic leader, with a firm but gentle tone of voice, " appears to have arisen between the two nations; but it may be productive of the most dangerous consequences, unless the tumult is immediately pacified by the assurance of our safety and the authority of our presence." At these words Fritigern and his companions drew their swords, opened their passage through the unresisting crowd, which filled the palace, the streets, and the gates of Marcianopolis, and, mounting their horses, hastily vanished from the eyes of the astonished Romans.

The generals of the Goths were saluted by the fierce and joyful acclamations of the camp; war was instantly resolved, and the resolution was executed without delay: the banners of the nation were displayed according to the custom of their ancestors; and the air resounded with the harsh and mournful music of the barbarian trumpet.[1] The weak and guilty Lupicinus, who had dared to provoke, who had neglected to destroy, and who still presumed to despise his formidable enemy, marched against the Goths, at the head of such a military force as could be collected on this sudden emergency. The barbarians expected his approach about nine miles from Marcianopolis; and on this occasion the talents of the general were found to be of more prevailing efficacy than the weapons and discipline of the troops. The valour of the Goths was so ably directed by the genius of Fritigern, that they broke, by a close and vigorous attack, the ranks of the Roman legions. Lupicinus left his arms and standards, his tribunes and his bravest soldiers, on the field of battle; and their useless courage served only to protect the ignominious flight of their leader. "That successful day put an end to the distress of the barbarians and the security of the Romans: from that day the Goths, renouncing the precarious condition of strangers and exiles, assumed the character of citizens and masters, claimed an absolute dominion over the possessors of land, and held, in their own right, the northern provinces of the empire, which are bounded by the Danube." Such are the words of the Gothic historian,[2] who celebrates, with rude eloquence, the glory of his countrymen. But the dominion of the barbarians was exercised only for the purposes of rapine and destruction. As they had been deprived by the ministers of the emperor of the common benefits of nature and the fair intercourse of social life, they retaliated the injustice on the subjects of the empire; and the crimes of Lupicinus were expiated by the

---

[1] Vexillis de *more* sublatis, auditisque *triste sonantibus classicis*. Ammian. xxxi. 5. These are the *rauca cornua* of Claudian (in Rufin. ii. 57), the large horns of the *Uri*, or wild bull—such as have been more recently used by the Swiss cantons of Uri and Unterwald (Simler de Republicâ Helvet. l. ii. p. 201, edit. Fuselin. Tigur. 1734). Their military horn is finely, though perhaps casually, introduced in an original narrative of the battle of Nancy (A.D. 1477). " Attendant le combat le dit cor fut corné par trois fois, tant que le vent du souffleur pouvoit durer: ce qui esbahit fort Monsieur de Bourgoigne; *car déja à Morat l'avoit ouy*." (See the Pièces Justificatives in the 4to edition of Philippe de Comines, tom. iii. p. 493.)

[2] Jornandes de Rebus Geticis, c. 26, p. 648, edit. Grot. These *splendidi anni* (they are comparatively such) are undoubtedly transcribed from the larger histories of Priscus, Ablavius, or Cassiodorus.

ruin of the peaceful husbandmen of Thrace, the conflagration of their villages, and the massacre or captivity of their innocent families. The report of the Gothic victory was soon diffused over the adjacent country; and while it filled the minds of the Romans with terror and dismay, their own hasty imprudence contributed to increase the forces of Fritigern and the calamities of the province. Some time before the great emigration a numerous body of Goths, under the command of Suerid and Colias, had been received into the protection and service of the empire.[1] They were encamped under the walls of Hadrianople: but the ministers of Valens were anxious to remove them beyond the Hellespont, at a distance from the dangerous temptation which might so easily be communicated by the neighbourhood and the success of their countrymen. The respectful submission with which they yielded to the order of their march might be considered as a proof of their fidelity; and their moderate request of a sufficient allowance of provisions and of a delay of only two days was expressed in the most dutiful terms. But the first magistrate of Hadrianople, incensed by some disorders which had been committed at his country-house, refused this indulgence; and arming against them the inhabitants and manufacturers of a populous city, he urged, with hostile threats, their instant departure. The barbarians stood silent and amazed, till they were exasperated by the insulting clamours and missile weapons of the populace: but when patience or contempt was fatigued, they crushed the undisciplined multitude, inflicted many a shameful wound on the backs of their flying enemies, and despoiled them of the splendid armour [2] which they were unworthy to bear. The resemblance of their sufferings and their actions soon united this victorious detachment to the nation of the Visigoths; the troops of Colias and Suerid expected the approach of the great Fritigern, ranged themselves under his standard, and signalised their ardour in the siege of Hadrianople. But the resistance of the garrison informed the barbarians that in the attack of regular fortifications the efforts of unskilful courage are seldom effectual. Their general acknowledged his error, raised the siege, declared that " he was at peace with stone walls," [3] and revenged his disappointment on the adjacent

---

[1] Cum populis suis longe ante suscepti. We are ignorant of the precise date and circumstances of their transmigration.

[2] An imperial manufacture of shields, etc., was established at Hadrianople; and the populace were headed by the *Fabricenses*, or workmen (Vales. ad Ammian. xxxi. 6).

[3] Pacem sibi esse cum parietibus memorans. Ammian. xxxi. 6.

country. He accepted with pleasure the useful reinforcement of hardy workmen who laboured in the gold-mines of Thrace [1] for the emolument and under the lash of an unfeeling master: [2] and these new associates conducted the barbarians through the secret paths to the most sequestered places, which had been chosen to secure the inhabitants, the cattle, and the magazines of corn. With the assistance of such guides nothing could remain impervious or inaccessible: resistance was fatal; flight was impracticable; and the patient submission of helpless innocence seldom found mercy from the barbarian conqueror. In the course of these depredations a great number of the children of the Goths, who had been sold into captivity, were restored to the embraces of their afflicted parents; but these tender interviews, which might have revived and cherished in their minds some sentiments of humanity, tended only to stimulate their native fierceness by the desire of revenge. They listened with eager attention to the complaints of their captive children, who had suffered the most cruel indignities from the lustful or angry passions of their masters, and the same cruelties, the same indignities, were severely retaliated on the sons and daughters of the Romans. [3]

The imprudence of Valens and his ministers had introduced into the heart of the empire a nation of enemies; but the Visigoths might even yet have been reconciled by the manly confession of past errors and the sincere performance of former engagements. These healing and temperate measures seemed to concur with the timorous disposition of the sovereign of the East: but on this occasion alone Valens was brave; and his unseasonable bravery was fatal to himself and to his subjects. He declared his intention of marching from Antioch to Constantinople, to subdue this dangerous rebellion; and, as he was not ignorant of

[1] These mines were in the country of the Bessi, in the ridge of mountains, the Rhodope, that runs between Philippi and Philippopolis, two Macedonian cities, which derived their name and origin from the father of Alexander. From the mines of Thrace he annually received the value, not the weight, of a thousand talents (£200,000)—a revenue which paid the phalanx and corrupted the orators of Greece. See Diodor. Siculus, tom. ii. l. xvi. [c. 8] p. 88, edit. Wesseling. Godefroy's Commentary on the Theodosian Code, tom. iii. p. 496. Cellarius, Geograph. Antiq. tom. i. p. 676, 857. D'Anville, Géographie Ancienne, tom. i. p. 336.

[2] As those unhappy workmen often ran away, Valens had enacted severe aws to drag them from their hiding-places. Cod. Theodosian. l. x. tit. xix. leg. 5, 7.

[3] See Ammianus xxxi. 5, 6. The historian of the Gothic war loses time and space by an unseasonable recapitulation of the ancient inroads of the barbarians.

the difficulties of the enterprise, he solicited the assistance of his nephew, the emperor Gratian, who commanded all the forces of the West. The veteran troops were hastily recalled from the defence of Armenia; that important frontier was abandoned to the discretion of Sapor; and the immediate conduct of the Gothic war was intrusted, during the absence of Valens, to his lieutenants, Trajan and Profuturus, two generals who indulged themselves in a very false and favourable opinion of their own abilities. On their arrival in Thrace they were joined by Richomer, count of the domestics; and the auxiliaries of the West that marched under his banner were composed of the Gallic legions, reduced indeed by a spirit of desertion to the vain appearances of strength and numbers. In a council of war, which was influenced by pride rather than by reason, it was resolved to seek and to encounter the barbarians, who lay encamped in the spacious and fertile meadows near the most southern of the six mouths of the Danube.[1] Their camp was surrounded by the usual fortification of waggons;[2] and the barbarians, secure within the vast circle of the enclosure, enjoyed the fruits of their valour and the spoils of the province. In the midst of riotous intemperance, the watchful Fritigern observed the motions and penetrated the designs of the Romans. He perceived that the numbers of the enemy were continually increasing; and, as he understood their intention of attacking his rear as soon as the scarcity of forage should oblige him to remove his camp, he recalled to their standard his predatory detachments, which covered the adjacent country. As soon as they descried the flaming beacons[3] they obeyed with incredible speed the signal of their leader; the camp was filled with the martial crowd of barbarians; their impatient clamours demanded the battle, and their tumultuous zeal was approved and animated by the spirit of their chiefs. The evening was already far advanced; and the two armies prepared themselves for the approaching

---

[1] The Itinerary of Antoninus (p. 226, 227, edit. Wesseling) marks the situation of this place about sixty miles north of Tomi, Ovid's exile; and the name of *Salices* (the willows) expresses the nature of the soil.

[2] This circle of waggons, the *Carrago*, was the usual fortification of the barbarians (Vegetius de Re Militari, l. iii. c. 10. Valesius ad Ammian. xxxi. 7). The practice and the name were preserved by their descendants as late as the fifteenth century. The *Charroy*, which surrounded the *Ost*, is a word familiar to the readers of Froissart, or Comines.

[3] Statim ut accensi malleoli [Amm. xxxi. 7]. I have used the literal sense of real torches or beacons; but I almost suspect that it is only one of those turgid metaphors, those false ornaments, that perpetually disfigure the style of Ammianus.

combat, which was deferred only till the dawn of day. While the trumpets sounded to arms, the undaunted courage of the Goths was confirmed by the mutual obligation of a solemn oath; and, as they advanced to meet the enemy, the rude songs which celebrated the glory of their forefathers were mingled with their fierce and dissonant outcries, and opposed to the artificial harmony of the Roman shout. Some military skill was displayed by Fritigern to gain the advantage of a commanding eminence; but the bloody conflict, which began and ended with the light, was maintained on either side by the personal and obstinate efforts of strength, valour, and agility. The legions of Armenia supported their fame in arms, but they were oppressed by the irresistible weight of the hostile multitude: the left wing of the Romans was thrown into disorder, and the field was strewed with their mangled carcasses. This partial defeat was balanced, however, by partial success; and when the two armies, at a late hour of the evening, retreated to their respective camps, neither of them could claim the honours or the effects of a decisive victory. The real loss was more severely felt by the Romans, in proportion to the smallness of their numbers; but the Goths were so deeply confounded and dismayed by this vigorous, and perhaps unexpected, resistance, that they remained seven days within the circle of their fortifications. Such funeral rites as the circumstances of time and place would admit were piously discharged to some officers of distinguished rank; but the indiscriminate vulgar was left unburied on the plain. Their flesh was greedily devoured by the birds of prey, who in that age enjoyed very frequent and delicious feasts; and, several years afterwards, the white and naked bones which covered the wide extent of the fields presented to the eyes of Ammianus a dreadful monument of the battle of Salices.[1]

The progress of the Goths had been checked by the doubtful event of that bloody day; and the Imperial generals, whose army would have been consumed by the repetition of such a contest, embraced the more rational plan of destroying the barbarians by the wants and pressure of their own multitudes. They prepared to confine the Visigoths in the narrow angle of land between the Danube, the desert of Scythia, and the moun-

---

[1] Indicant nunc usque albentes ossibus campi. Ammian. xxxi. 7. The historian might have viewed these plains, either as a soldier or as a traveller. But his modesty has suppressed the adventures of his own life subsequent to the Persian wars of Constantius and Julian. We are ignorant of the time when he quitted the service and retired to Rome, where he appears to have composed his History of his Own Times.

tains of Hæmus, till their strength and spirit should be insensibly wasted by the inevitable operation of famine. The design was prosecuted with some conduct and success; the barbarians had almost exhausted their own magazines and the harvests of the country; and the diligence of Saturninus, the master-general of the cavalry, was employed to improve the strength and to contract the extent of the Roman fortifications. His labours were interrupted by the alarming intelligence that new swarms of barbarians had passed the unguarded Danube, either to support the cause or to imitate the example of Fritigern. The just apprehension that he himself might be surrounded and overwhelmed by the arms of hostile and unknown nations, compelled Saturninus to relinquish the siege of the Gothic camp; and the indignant Visigoths, breaking from their confinement, satiated their hunger and revenge by the repeated devastation of the fruitful country which extends above three hundred miles from the banks of the Danube to the straits of the Hellespont.[1] The sagacious Fritigern had successfully appealed to the passions as well as to the interest of his barbarian allies; and the love of rapine and the hatred of Rome seconded, or even prevented, the eloquence of his ambassadors. He cemented a strict and useful alliance with the great body of his countrymen who obeyed Alatheus and Saphrax as the guardians of their infant king: the long animosity of rival tribes was suspended by the sense of their common interest; the independent part of the nation was associated under one standard; and the chiefs of the Ostrogoths appear to have yielded to the superior genius of the general of the Visigoths. He obtained the formidable aid of the Taifalæ, whose military renown was disgraced and polluted by the public infamy of their domestic manners. Every youth, on his entrance into the world, was united by the ties of honourable friendship and brutal love to some warrior of the tribe; nor could he hope to be released from this unnatural connection till he had approved his manhood by slaying in single combat a huge bear or a wild boar of the forest.[2] But the most powerful auxiliaries of the Goths were drawn from the camp of those enemies who had expelled them from their native seats. The

[1] Ammian. xxxi. 8.

[2] Hanc Taifalorum gentem turpem, et obscenæ vitæ flagitiis ita accipimus mersam, ut apud eos nefandi concubitûs fœdere copulentur maribus puberes, ætatis viriditatem in eorum pollutis usibus consumpturi. Porro, si qui jam adultus aprum exceperit solus, vel interemerit ursum immanem, colluvione liberatur incesti. Ammian. xxxi. 9. Among the Greeks likewise, more especially among the Cretans, the holy bands of friendship were confirmed and sullied by unnatural love.

loose subordination and extensive possessions of the Huns and the Alani delayed the conquests and distracted the councils of that victorious people. Several of the hordes were allured by the liberal promises of Fritigern; and the rapid cavalry of Scythia added weight and energy to the steady and strenuous efforts of the Gothic infantry. The Sarmatians, who could never forgive the successor of Valentinian, enjoyed and increased the general confusion; and a seasonable irruption of the Alemanni into the provinces of Gaul engaged the attention and diverted the forces of the emperor of the West.[1]

One of the most dangerous inconveniences of the introduction of the barbarians into the army and the palace was sensibly felt in their correspondence with their hostile countrymen, to whom they imprudently or maliciously revealed the weakness of the Roman empire. A soldier of the life-guards of Gratian was of the nation of the Alemanni, and of the tribe of the Lentienses, who dwelt beyond the lake of Constance. Some domestic business obliged him to request a leave of absence. In a short visit to his family and friends he was exposed to their curious inquiries, and the vanity of the loquacious soldier tempted him to display his intimate acquaintance with the secrets of the state and the designs of his master. The intelligence that Gratian was preparing to lead the military force of Gaul and of the West to the assistance of his uncle Valens, pointed out to the restless spirit of the Alemanni the moment and the mode of a successful invasion. The enterprise of some light detachments, who in the month of February passed the Rhine upon the ice, was the prelude of a more important war. The boldest hopes of rapine, perhaps of conquest, outweighed the considerations of timid prudence or national faith. Every forest and every village poured forth a band of hardy adventurers; and the great army of the Alemanni, which on their approach was estimated at forty thousand men by the fears of the people, was afterwards magnified to the number of seventy thousand by the vain and credulous flattery of the Imperial court. The legions which had been ordered to march into Pannonia were immediately recalled or detained for the defence of Gaul; the military command was divided between Nanienus and Mellobaudes; and the youthful emperor, though he respected the long experience and sober wisdom of the former, was much more inclined to admire and

---

[1] Ammian. xxxi. 8, 9. Jerom (tom. i. p. 26 [tom. i. p. 342, ed. Vallars.]) enumerates the nations, and marks a calamitous period of twenty years. This epistle to Heliodorus was composed in the year 397 (Tillemont, Mém. Ecclés. tom. xii. p. 645).

to follow the martial ardour of his colleague, who was allowed to unite the incompatible characters of count of the domestics and of king of the Franks. His rival Priarius, king of the Alemanni, was guided, or rather impelled, by the same headstrong valour; and as their troops were animated by the spirit of their leaders, they met, they saw, they encountered each other near the town of Argentaria, or Colmar,[1] in the plains of Alsace. The glory of the day was justly ascribed to the missile weapons and well-practised evolutions of the Roman soldiers: the Alemanni, who long maintained their ground, were slaughtered with unrelenting fury: five thousand only of the barbarians escaped to the woods and mountains; and the glorious death of their king on the field of battle saved him from the reproaches of the people, who are always disposed to accuse the justice or policy of an unsuccessful war. After this signal victory, which secured the peace of Gaul and asserted the honour of the Roman arms, the emperor Gratian appeared to proceed without delay on his Eastern expedition; but, as he approached the confines of the Alemanni, he suddenly inclined to the left, surprised them by his unexpected passage of the Rhine, and boldly advanced into the heart of their country. The barbarians opposed to his progress the obstacles of nature and of courage; and still continued to retreat from one hill to another till they were satisfied, by repeated trials, of the power and perseverance of their enemies. Their submission was accepted as a proof, not indeed of their sincere repentance, but of their actual distress; and a select number of their brave and robust youth was exacted from the faithless nation, as the most substantial pledge of their future moderation. The subjects of the empire, who had so often experienced that the Alemanni could neither be subdued by arms nor restrained by treaties, might not promise themselves any solid or lasting tranquillity; but they discovered, in the virtues of their young sovereign, the prospect of a long and auspicious reign. When the legions climbed the mountains and scaled the fortifications of the barbarians, the valour of Gratian was distinguished in the foremost ranks: and the gilt and variegated armour of his guards was pierced and shattered by the blows which they had received in their constant attachment to the person of their sovereign. At the age of nineteen the son of Valentinian seemed to possess the talents of peace and war;

[1] The field of battle, *Argentaria* or *Argentovaria*, is accurately fixed by M. d'Anville (Notice de l'Ancienne Gaule, p. 96-99) at twenty-three Gallic leagues, or thirty-four and a half Roman miles, to the south of Strasburg. From its ruins the adjacent town of *Colmar* has arisen.

and his personal success against the Alemanni was interpreted as a sure presage of his Gothic triumphs.[1]

While Gratian deserved and enjoyed the applause of his subjects, the emperor Valens, who at length had removed his court and army from Antioch, was received by the people of Constantinople as the author of the public calamity. Before he had reposed himself ten days in the capital he was urged by the licentious clamours of the Hippodrome to march against the barbarians whom he had invited into his dominions: and the citizens, who are always brave at a distance from any real danger, declared, with confidence, that if they were supplied with arms, *they* alone would undertake to deliver the province from the ravages of an insulting foe.[2] The vain reproaches of an ignorant multitude hastened the downfall of the Roman empire: they provoked the desperate rashness of Valens, who did not find, either in his reputation or in his mind, any motives to support with firmness the public contempt. He was soon persuaded by the successful achievements of his lieutenants to despise the power of the Goths, who, by the diligence of Fritigern, were now collected in the neighbourhood of Hadrianople. The march of the Taifalæ had been intercepted by the valiant Frigerid; the king of those licentious barbarians was slain in battle; and the suppliant captives were sent into distant exile to cultivate the lands of Italy, which were assigned for their settlement in the vacant territories of Modena and Parma.[3] The exploits of Sebastian,[4] who was recently engaged in the service of Valens, and promoted to the rank of master-general of the infantry, were still more honourable to himself, and useful to the republic. He obtained the permission of selecting three hundred soldiers from each of the legions, and this separate

---

[1] The full and impartial narrative of Ammianus (xxxi. 10) may derive some additional light from the Epitome of Victor, the Chronicle of Jerom, and the History of Orosius (l. vii. c. 33, p. 552, edit. Havercamp).

[2] Moratus paucissimos dies, seditione popularium levium pulsus. Ammian. xxxi. 11. Socrates (l. iv. c. 38) supplies the dates and some circumstances.

[3] Vivosque omnes circa Mutinam, Regiumque, et Parmam, Italica oppida, rura culturos exterminavit. Ammianus, xxxi. 9. Those cities and districts, about ten years after the colony of the Taifalæ, appear in a very desolate state. See Muratori, Dissertazioni sopra le Antichità Italiane, tom. i. Dissertat. xxi. p. 354.

[4] Ammian. xxxi. 11. Zosimus, l. iv. [c. 23] p. 228-230. The latter expatiates on the desultory exploits of Sebastian, and despatches in a few lines the important battle of Hadrianople. According to the ecclesiastical critics, who hate Sebastian, the praise of Zosimus is disgrace (Tillemont, Hist. des Empereurs, tom. v. p. 121). His prejudice and ignorance undoubtedly render him a very questionable judge of merit.

detachment soon acquired the spirit of discipline and the exercise of arms, which were almost forgotten under the reign of Valens. By the vigour and conduct of Sebastian, a large body of the Goths was surprised in their camp; and the immense spoil which was recovered from their hands filled the city of Hadrianople and the adjacent plain. The splendid narratives which the general transmitted of his own exploits alarmed the Imperial court by the appearance of superior merit; and though he cautiously insisted on the difficulties of the Gothic war, his valour was praised, his advice was rejected; and Valens, who listened with pride and pleasure to the flattering suggestions of the eunuchs of the palace, was impatient to seize the glory of an easy and assured conquest. His army was strengthened by a numerous reinforcement of veterans; and his march from Constantinople to Hadrianople was conducted with so much military skill that he prevented the activity of the barbarians, who designed to occupy the intermediate defiles, and to intercept either the troops themselves or their convoys of provisions. The camp of Valens, which he pitched under the walls of Hadrianople, was fortified, according to the practice of the Romans, with a ditch and rampart; and a most important council was summoned to decide the fate of the emperor and of the empire. The party of reason and of delay was strenuously maintained by Victor, who had corrected, by the lessons of experience, the native fierceness of the Sarmatian character; while Sebastian, with the flexible and obsequious eloquence of a courtier, represented every precaution and every measure that implied a doubt of immediate victory as unworthy of the courage and majesty of their invincible monarch. The ruin of Valens was precipitated by the deceitful arts of Fritigern and the prudent admonitions of the emperor of the West. The advantages of negotiating in the midst of war were perfectly understood by the general of the barbarians; and a Christian ecclesiastic was despatched, as the holy minister of peace, to penetrate and to perplex the councils of the enemy. The misfortunes, as well as the provocations, of the Gothic nation were forcibly and truly described by their ambassador, who protested, in the name of Fritigern, that he was still disposed to lay down his arms, or to employ them only in the defence of the empire, if he could secure for his wandering countrymen a tranquil settlement on the waste lands of Thrace, and a sufficient allowance of corn and cattle. But he added, in a whisper of confidential friendship, that the exasperated barbarians were averse to these reasonable conditions; and that

Fritigern was doubtful whether he could accomplish the conclusion of the treaty unless he found himself supported by the
presence and terrors of an Imperial army. About the same
time, Count Richomer returned from the West to announce the
defeat and submission of the Alemanni; to inform Valens that
his nephew advanced by rapid marches at the head of the veteran
and victorious legions of Gaul; and to request, in the name of
Gratian and of the republic, that every dangerous and decisive
measure might be suspended till the junction of the two emperors
should ensure the success of the Gothic war. But the feeble
sovereign of the East was actuated only by the fatal illusions of
pride and jealousy. He disdained the importunate advice; he
rejected the humiliating aid; he secretly compared the ignominious, at least the inglorious, period of his own reign with the
fame of a beardless youth; and Valens rushed into the field to
erect his imaginary trophy before the diligence of his colleague
could usurp any share of the triumphs of the day.

On the 9th of August, a day which has deserved to be marked
among the most inauspicious of the Roman calendar,[1] the
emperor Valens, leaving, under a strong guard, his baggage and
military treasure, marched from Hadrianople to attack the Goths,
who were encamped about twelve miles from the city.[2] By
some mistake of the orders, or some ignorance of the ground, the
right wing or column of cavalry arrived in sight of the enemy
whilst the left was still at a considerable distance; the soldiers
were compelled, in the sultry heat of summer, to precipitate their
pace; and the line of battle was formed with tedious confusion
and irregular delay. The Gothic cavalry had been detached to
forage in the adjacent country; and Fritigern still continued to
practise his customary arts. He despatched messengers of peace,
made proposals, required hostages, and wasted the hours, till
the Romans, exposed without shelter to the burning rays of the
sun, were exhausted by thirst, hunger, and intolerable fatigue.
The emperor was persuaded to send an ambassador to the Gothic
camp; the zeal of Richomer, who alone had courage to accept
the dangerous commission, was applauded; and the count of
the domestics, adorned with the splendid ensigns of his dignity,

---

[1] Ammianus (xxxi. 12, 13) almost alone describes the councils and actions
which were terminated by the fatal battle of Hadrianople. We might
censure the vices of his style, the disorder and perplexity of his narrative;
but we must now take leave of this impartial historian; and reproach is
silenced by our regret for such an irreparable loss.

[2] The difference of the eight miles of Ammianus, and the twelve of Idatius,
can only embarrass those critics (Valesius ad loc.) who suppose a great
army to be a mathematical point, without space or dimensions.

had proceeded some way in the space between the two armies when he was suddenly recalled by the alarm of battle. The hasty and imprudent attack was made by Bacurius the Iberian, who commanded a body of archers and targeteers: and, as they advanced with rashness, they retreated with loss and disgrace. In the same moment the flying squadrons of Alatheus and Saphrax, whose return was anxiously expected by the general of the Goths, descended like a whirlwind from the hills, swept across the plain, and added new terrors to the tumultuous but irresistible charge of the barbarian host. The event of the battle of Hadrianople, so fatal to Valens and to the empire, may be described in a few words: the Roman cavalry fled; the infantry was abandoned, surrounded, and cut in pieces. The most skilful evolutions, the firmest courage, are scarcely sufficient to extricate a body of foot encompassed on an open plain by superior numbers of horse; but the troops of Valens, oppressed by the weight of the enemy and their own fears, were crowded into a narrow space, where it was impossible for them to extend their ranks, or even to use, with effect, their swords and javelins. In the midst of tumult, of slaughter, and of dismay, the emperor, deserted by his guards, and wounded, as it was supposed, with an arrow, sought protection among the Lancearii and the Mattiarii, who still maintained their ground with some appearance of order and firmness. His faithful generals, Trajan and Victor, who perceived his danger, loudly exclaimed that all was lost unless the person of the emperor could be saved. Some troops, animated by their exhortation, advanced to his relief: they found only a bloody spot, covered with a heap of broken arms and mangled bodies, without being able to discover their unfortunate prince either among the living or the dead. Their search could not indeed be successful, if there is any truth in the circumstances with which some historians have related the death of the emperor. By the care of his attendants, Valens was removed from the field of battle to a neighbouring cottage, where they attempted to dress his wound and to provide for his future safety. But this humble retreat was instantly surrounded by the enemy; they tried to force the door; they were provoked by a discharge of arrows from the roof; till at length, impatient of delay, they set fire to a pile of dry faggots, and consumed the cottage with the Roman emperor and his train. Valens perished in the flames; and a youth, who dropped from the window, alone escaped, to attest the melancholy tale and to inform the Goths of the inestimable prize which they had lost by their own rashness. A great number of brave and distinguished officers perished in the battle of Hadrianople, which equalled in the actual loss, and far surpassed in the fatal consequences, the misfortune which Rome had formerly sustained in the fields of Cannæ.[1] Two master-generals of the cavalry and infantry, two great officers of the palace, and thirty-five tribunes, were found among the slain; and the death of Sebastian might satisfy the world that he was the victim as well as the author of the public calamity. Above two-thirds of the Roman army were destroyed: and the darkness of the night was esteemed a very favourable circumstance, as it served to conceal the flight of the multitude, and to protect the more orderly retreat of Victor and Richomer, who alone, amidst the general consternation, maintained the advantage of calm courage and regular discipline.[2]

While the impressions of grief and terror were still recent in the minds of men, the most celebrated rhetorician of the age composed the funeral oration of a vanquished army and of an unpopular prince, whose throne was already occupied by a stranger. "There are not wanting," says the candid Libanius, "those who arraign the prudence of the emperor, or who impute the public misfortune to the want of courage and discipline in the troops. For my own part, I reverence the memory of their former exploits; I reverence the glorious death which they bravely received, standing and fighting in their ranks; I reverence the field of battle, stained with *their* blood and the blood of the barbarians. Those honourable marks have been already washed away by the rains; but the lofty monuments of their bones, the bones of generals, of centurions, and of valiant warriors, claim a longer period of duration. The king himself fought and fell in the foremost ranks of the battle. His attendants presented him with the fleetest horses of the Imperial stable, that would soon have carried him beyond the pursuit of the enemy. They

---

[1] Nec ulla, annalibus, præter Cannensem pugnam, ita ad internecionem res legitur gesta. Ammian. xxxi. 13. According to the grave Polybius, no more than 370 horse and 3000 foot escaped from the field of Cannæ; 10,000 were made prisoners; and the number of the slain amounted to 5630 horse and 70,000 foot (Polyb. l. iii. [c. 117] p. 371, edit. Casaubon, in 8vo.). Livy (xxii. 49) is somewhat less bloody; he slaughters only 2700 horse and 40,000 foot. The Roman army was supposed to consist of 87,200 effective men (xxii. 36).

[2] We have gained some faint light from Jerom (tom. i. p. 26 [tom. i. p. 342, ed. Vallars.], and in Chron. p. 188 [tom. viii. p. 817, ed. Vallars.]), Victor (in Epitome), Orosius (l. vii. c. 33, p. 554), Jornandes (c. 27), Zosimus (l. iv. [c. 24] p. 230), Socrates (l. iv. c. 38), Sozomen (l. vi. c. 40), Idatius (in Chron.). But their united evidence, if weighed against Ammianus alone, is light and unsubstantial.

vainly pressed him to reserve his important life for the future service of the republic. He still declared that he was unworthy to survive so many of the bravest and most faithful of his subjects; and the monarch was nobly buried under a mountain of the slain. Let none, therefore, presume to ascribe the victory of the barbarians to the fear, the weakness, or the imprudence of the Roman troops. The chiefs and the soldiers were animated by the virtue of their ancestors, whom they equalled in discipline and the arts of war. Their generous emulation was supported by the love of glory, which prompted them to contend at the same time with heat and thirst, with fire and the sword, and cheerfully to embrace an honourable death as their refuge against flight and infamy. The indignation of the gods has been the only cause of the success of our enemies." The truth of history may disclaim some parts of this panegyric, which cannot strictly be reconciled with the character of Valens or the circumstances of the battle; but the fairest commendation is due to the eloquence, and still more to the generosity, of the sophist of Antioch.[1]

The pride of the Goths was elated by this memorable victory; but their avarice was disappointed by the mortifying discovery that the richest part of the Imperial spoil had been within the walls of Hadrianople. They hastened to possess the reward of their valour; but they were encountered by the remains of a vanquished army with an intrepid resolution, which was the effect of their despair and the only hope of their safety. The walls of the city and the ramparts of the adjacent camp were lined with military engines that threw stones of an enormous weight, and astonished the ignorant barbarians by the noise and velocity, still more than by the real effects, of the discharge. The soldiers, the citizens, the provincials, the domestics of the palace, were united in the danger and in the defence; the furious assault of the Goths was repulsed; their secret arts of treachery and treason were discovered; and after an obstinate conflict of many hours they retired to their tents, convinced by experience that it would be far more advisable to observe the treaty which their sagacious leader had tacitly stipulated with the fortifications of great and populous cities. After the hasty and impolitic massacre of three hundred deserters, an act of justice extremely useful to the discipline of the Roman armies, the Goths indignantly raised the siege of Hadrianople. The scene of war and tumult was instantly converted into a silent solitude; the

---

[1] Libanius de ulciscend. Julian. Nece, c. 3, in Fabricius, Bibliot. Græc. tom. vii. p. 146-148.

multitude suddenly disappeared; the secret paths of the woods and mountains were marked with the footsteps of the trembling fugitives, who sought a refuge in the distant cities of Illyricum and Macedonia; and the faithful officers of the household and the treasury cautiously proceeded in search of the emperor, of whose death they were still ignorant. The tide of the Gothic inundation rolled from the walls of Hadrianople to the suburbs of Constantinople. The barbarians were surprised with the splendid appearance of the capital of the East, the height and extent of the walls, the myriads of wealthy and affrighted citizens who crowded the ramparts, and the various prospect of the sea and land. While they gazed with hopeless desire on the inaccessible beauties of Constantinople, a sally was made from one of the gates by a party of Saracens,[1] who had been fortunately engaged in the service of Valens. The cavalry of Scythia was forced to yield to the admirable swiftness and spirit of the Arabian horses; their riders were skilled in the evolutions of irregular war; and the Northern barbarians were astonished and dismayed by the inhuman ferocity of the barbarians of the South. A Gothic soldier was slain by the dagger of an Arab, and the hairy, naked savage, applying his lips to the wound, expressed a horrid delight while he sucked the blood of his vanquished enemy.[2] The army of the Goths, laden with the spoils of the wealthy suburbs and the adjacent territory, slowly moved from the Bosphorus to the mountains which form the western boundary of Thrace. The important pass of Succi was betrayed by the fear or the misconduct of Maurus; and the barbarians, who no longer had any resistance to apprehend from the scattered and vanquished troops of the East, spread themselves over the face of a fertile and cultivated country, as far as the confines of Italy and the Hadriatic Sea.[3]

[1] Valens had gained, or rather purchased, the friendship of the Saracens, whose vexatious inroads were felt on the borders of Phœnicia, Palestine, and Egypt. The Christian faith had been lately introduced among a people reserved in a future age to propagate another religion (Tillemont, Hist. des Empereurs, tom. v. p. 104, 106, 141; Mém. Ecclés. tom. vii. p. 593).

[2] Crinitus quidam, nudus omnia præter pubem, subraucum et lugubre strepens. Ammian. xxxi. 16, and Vales. ad loc. The Arabs often fought naked—a custom which may be ascribed to their sultry climate and ostentatious bravery. The description of this unknown savage is the lively portrait of Derar, a name so dreadful to the Christians of Syria. See Ockley's Hist. of the Saracens, vol. i. p. 72, 84, 87.

[3] The series of events may still be traced in the last pages of Ammianus (xxxi. 15, 16). Zosimus (l. iv. [c. 22] p. 227, 231), whom we are now reduced to cherish, misplaces the sally of the Arabs before the death of Valens. Eunapius (in Excerpt. Legat. p. 20 [p. 51, ed. Bonn]) praises the fertility of Thrace, Macedonia, etc.

The Romans, who so coolly and so concisely mention the acts of *justice* which were exercised by the legions,[1] reserve their compassion and their eloquence for their own sufferings when the provinces were invaded and desolated by the arms of the successful barbarians. The simple circumstantial narrative (did such a narrative exist) of the ruin of a single town, of the misfortunes of a single family,[2] might exhibit an interesting and instructive picture of human manners; but the tedious repetition of vague and declamatory complaints would fatigue the attention of the most patient reader. The same censure may be applied, though not perhaps in an equal degree, to the profane and the ecclesiastical writers of this unhappy period; that their minds were inflamed by popular and religious animosity, and that the true size and colour of every object is falsified by the exaggerations of their corrupt eloquence. The vehement Jerom [3] might justly deplore the calamities inflicted by the Goths and their barbarous allies on his native country of Pannonia, and the wide extent of the provinces from the walls of Constantinople, to the foot of the Julian Alps; the rapes, the massacres, the conflagrations, and, above all, the profanation of the churches that were turned into stables, and the contemptuous treatment of the relics of holy martyrs. But the saint is surely transported beyond the limits of nature and history when he affirms, "that in those desert countries nothing was left except the sky and the earth; that, after the destruction of the cities and the extirpation of the human race, the land was overgrown with thick forests and inextricable brambles; and that the universal desolation, announced by the prophet Zephaniah, was accomplished in the scarcity of the beasts, the birds, and even of the fish." These complaints were pronounced about twenty years after the death of Valens; and the Illyrian provinces, which were constantly

---

[1] Observe with how much indifference Cæsar relates, in the Commentaries of the Gallic war, *that* he put to death the whole senate of the Veneti, who had yielded to his mercy (iii. 16); *that* he laboured to extirpate the whole nation of the Eburones (vi. 43); *that* forty thousand persons were massacred at Bourges by the just revenge of his soldiers, who spared neither age nor sex (vii. 27), etc.

[2] Such are the accounts of the sack of Magdeburg, by the ecclesiastic and the fisherman, which Mr. Harte has transcribed (Hist. of Gustavus Adolphus, vol. i. p. 313-320), with some apprehension of violating the *dignity* of history.

[3] Et vastatis urbibus, hominibusque interfectis, solitudinem et *raritatem bestiar\,m* quoque fieri, *et volatilium, pisciumque :* testis Illyricum est, testis Thracia, testis in quo ortus sum solum (Pannonia); ubi præter cœlum et terram, et crescentes vepres, et condensa silvarum *cuncta perierunt.* Tom. vii. p. 250, ad 1. Cap. Sophonias; and tom. i. p. 26 [tom. i. p. 342, ed. Vallars.].

exposed to the invasion and passage of the barbarians, still continued, after a calamitous period of ten centuries, to supply new materials for rapine and destruction. Could it even be supposed that a large tract of country had been left without cultivation and without inhabitants, the consequences might not have been so fatal to the inferior productions of animated nature. The useful and feeble animals, which are nourished by the hand of man, might suffer and perish if they were deprived of his protection; but the beasts of the forest, his enemies or his victims, would multiply in the free and undisturbed possession of their solitary domain. The various tribes that people the air or the waters are still less connected with the fate of the human species; and it is highly probable that the fish of the Danube would have felt more terror and distress from the approach of a voracious pike than from the hostile inroad of a Gothic army.

Whatever may have been the just measure of the calamities of Europe, there was reason to fear that the same calamities would soon extend to the peaceful countries of Asia. The sons of the Goths had been judiciously distributed through the cities of the East, and the arts of education were employed to polish and subdue the native fierceness of their temper. In the space of about twelve years their numbers had continually increased; and the children who in the first emigration were sent over the Hellespont had attained with rapid growth the strength and spirit of perfect manhood.[1] It was impossible to conceal from their knowledge the events of the Gothic war; and, as those daring youths had not studied the language of dissimulation, they betrayed their wish, their desire, perhaps their intention, to emulate the glorious example of their fathers. The danger of the times seemed to justify the jealous suspicions of the provincials; and these suspicions were admitted as unquestionable evidence that the Goths of Asia had formed a secret and dangerous conspiracy against the public safety. The death of Valens had left the East without a sovereign; and Julius, who filled the important station of master-general of the troops, with a high reputation of diligence and ability, thought it his duty to consult the senate of Constantinople, which he considered, during the vacancy of the throne, as the representative council of the nation. As soon as he had obtained the discretionary

---

[1] Eunapius (in Excerpt. Legat. p. 20 [p. 50, ed. Bonn]) foolishly supposes a preternatural growth of the young Goths, that he may introduce Cadmus's armed men, who sprung from the dragon's teeth, etc. Such was the Greek eloquence of the times.

power of acting as he should judge most expedient for the good of the republic, he assembled the principal officers and privately concerted effectual measures for the execution of his bloody design. An order was immediately promulgated that, on a stated day, the Gothic youth should assemble in the capital cities of their respective provinces; and, as a report was industriously circulated that they were summoned to receive a liberal gift of lands and money, the pleasing hope allayed the fury of their resentment, and perhaps suspended the motions of the conspiracy. On the appointed day the unarmed crowd of the Gothic youth was carefully collected in the square or forum; the streets and avenues were occupied by the Roman troops, and the roofs of the houses were covered with archers and slingers. At the same hour, in all the cities of the East, the signal was given of indiscriminate slaughter; and the provinces of Asia were delivered, by the cruel prudence of Julius, from a domestic enemy, who in a few months might have carried fire and sword from the Hellespont to the Euphrates.[1] The urgent consideration of the public safety may undoubtedly authorise the violation of every positive law. How far that or any other consideration may operate to dissolve the natural obligations of humanity and justice, is a doctrine of which I still desire to remain ignorant.

The emperor Gratian was far advanced on his march towards the plains of Hadrianople when he was informed, at first by the confused voice of fame, and afterwards by the more accurate reports of Victor and Richomer, that his impatient colleague had been slain in battle, and that two-thirds of the Roman army were exterminated by the sword of the victorious Goths. Whatever resentment the rash and jealous vanity of his uncle might deserve, the resentment of a generous mind is easily subdued by the softer emotions of grief and compassion; and even the sense of pity was soon lost in the serious and alarming consideration of the state of the republic. Gratian was too late to assist, he was too weak to revenge, his unfortunate colleague; and the valiant and modest youth felt himself unequal to the support of a sinking world. A formidable tempest of the barbarians of Germany seemed ready to burst over the provinces of Gaul, and the mind of Gratian was oppressed and distracted

[1] Ammianus evidently approves this execution, efficacia velox et salutaris, which concludes his work (xxxi. 16). Zosimus, who is curious and copious (l. iv. [c. 26] p. 233-236), mistakes the date, and labours to find the reason why Julius did not consult the emperor Theodosius, who had not yet ascended the throne of the East.

by the administration of the Western empire. In this important crisis the government of the East and the conduct of the Gothic war required the undivided attention of a hero and a statesman. A subject invested with such ample command would not long have preserved his fidelity to a distant benefactor; and the Imperial council embraced the wise and manly resolution of conferring an obligation rather than of yielding to an insult. It was the wish of Gratian to bestow the purple as the reward of virtue; but at the age of nineteen it is not easy for a prince, educated in the supreme rank, to understand the true characters of his ministers and generals. He attempted to weigh, with an impartial hand, their various merits and defects; and whilst he checked the rash confidence of ambition, he distrusted the cautious wisdom which despaired of the republic. As each moment of delay diminished something of the power and resources of the future sovereign of the East, the situation of the times would not allow a tedious debate. The choice of Gratian was soon declared in favour of an exile, whose father, only three years before, had suffered, under the sanction of *his* authority, an unjust and ignominious death. The great Theodosius, a name celebrated in history and dear to the catholic church,[1] was summoned to the Imperial court, which had gradually retreated from the confines of Thrace to the more secure station of Sirmium. Five months after the death of Valens the emperor Gratian produced before the assembled troops *his* colleague and *their* master, who, after a modest, perhaps a sincere resistance, was compelled to accept, amidst the general acclamations, the diadem, the purple, and the equal title of Augustus.[2] The provinces of Thrace, Asia, and Egypt, over which Valens had reigned, were resigned to the administration of the new emperor; but as he was specially intrusted with the conduct of the Gothic war, the Illyrian præfecture was dis-

---

[1] A Life of Theodosius the Great was composed in the last century (Paris, 1679, in 4to; 1680, in 12mo), to inflame the mind of the young dauphin with Catholic zeal. The author, Fléchier, afterwards bishop of Nismes, was a celebrated preacher; and his history is adorned or tainted with pulpit eloquence; but he takes his learning from Baronius, and his principles from St. Ambrose and St. Augustin.

[2] The birth, character, and elevation of Theodosius, are marked in Pacatus (in Panegyr. Vet. xii. 10, 11, 12), Themistius (Orat. xiv. p. 182), Zosimus (l. iv. [c. 24] p. 231), Augustin (de Civitat. Dei, v. 25), Orosius (l. vii. c. 34), Sozomen (l. vii. c. 2), Socrates (l. v. c. 2), Theodoret (l. v. c. 5), Philostorgius (l. ix. c. 17, with Godefroy, p. 393), the Epitome of Victor, and the Chronicles of Prosper, Idatius, and Marcellinus, in the Thesaurus Temporum of Scaliger.

membered, and the two great dioceses of Dacia and Macedonia were added to the dominions of the Eastern empire.[1]

The same province, and perhaps the same city,[2] which had given to the throne the virtues of Trajan and the talents of Hadrian, was the original seat of another family of Spaniards, who, in a less fortunate age, possessed, near fourscore years, the declining empire of Rome.[3] They emerged from the obscurity of municipal honours by the active spirit of the elder Theodosius, a general whose exploits in Britain and Africa have formed one of the most splendid parts of the annals of Valentinian. The son of that general, who likewise bore the name of Theodosius, was educated, by skilful preceptors, in the liberal studies of youth; but he was instructed in the art of war by the tender care and severe discipline of his father.[4] Under the standard of such a leader, young Theodosius sought glory and knowledge in the most distant scenes of military action; inured his constitution to the difference of seasons and climates; distinguished his valour by sea and land; and observed the various warfare of the Scots, the Saxons, and the Moors. His own merit, and the recommendation of the conqueror of Africa, soon raised him to a separate command; and, in the station of duke of Mæsia, he vanquished an army of Sarmatians; saved the province; deserved the love of the soldiers; and provoked the envy of the court.[5] His rising fortunes were soon blasted by the disgrace and execution of his illustrious father; and Theodosius obtained, as a favour, the permission of retiring to a private life in his native province of Spain. He displayed a firm and temperate character in the ease with which he adapted himself to this new situation. His time was almost equally

---

[1] Tillemont, Hist. des Empereurs, tom. v. p. 716, etc.

[2] *Italica*, founded by Scipio Africanus for his wounded veterans of *Italy*. The ruins still appear, about a league above Seville, but on the opposite bank of the river. See the Hispania Illustrata of Nonius—a short though valuable treatise—c. xvii. p. 64-67.

[3] I agree with Tillemont (Hist. des Empereurs, tom. v. p. 726), in suspecting the royal pedigree, which remained a secret till the promotion of Theodosius. Even after that event, the silence of Pacatus outweighs the venal evidence of Themistius, Victor, and Claudian, who connect the family of Theodosius with the blood of Trajan and Hadrian.

[4] Pacatus compares, and consequently prefers, the youth of Theodosius, to the military education of Alexander, Hannibal, and the second Africanus, who, like him, had served under their fathers (xii. 8).

[5] Ammianus (xxix. 6) mentions this victory of Theodosius Junior Dux Mæsiæ, primâ etiam tum lanugine juvenis, princeps postea perspectissimus. The same fact is attested by Themistius and Zosimus; but Theodoret (l. v. c. 5), who adds some curious circumstances, strangely applies it to the time of the interregnum.

The following is the genealogical table of the family of Theodosius:—

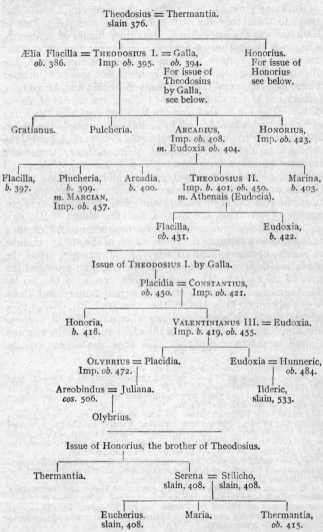

Theodosius = Thermantia.
slain 376.

Ælia Flacilla = THEODOSIUS I. = Galla,   Honorius.
ob. 386.   Imp. *ob.* 395.   *ob.* 394.   For issue of
                             For issue of   Honorius
                             Theodosius   see below.
                             by Galla,
                             see below.

Gratianus.   Pulcheria.   ARCADIUS,   HONORIUS,
                            Imp. *ob.* 408.   Imp. *ob.* 423.
                       m. Eudoxia *ob.* 404.

Flacilla,   Plucheria,   Arcadia,   THEODOSIUS II.   Marina,
b. 397.   *b.* 399.   *b.* 400.   Imp. *b.* 401, *ob.* 450.   *b.* 403.
      m. MARCIAN,   *m.* Athenais (Eudocia).
      Imp. *ob.* 457.

Flacilla,   Eudoxia,
ob. 431.   *b.* 422.

Issue of THEODOSIUS I. by Galla.

Placidia = CONSTANTIUS,
ob. 450. | Imp. *ob.* 421.

Honoria,   VALENTINIANUS III. = Eudoxia.
b. 418.   Imp. *b.* 419, *ob.* 455.

OLYBRIUS = Placidia.   Eudoxia = Hunneric,
Imp. *ob.* 472.   *ob.* 484.

Areobindus = Juliana.   Ilderic,
cos. 506.   slain, 533.

Olybrius.

Issue of Honorius, the brother of Theodosius.

Thermantia.   Serena = Stilicho,
              slain, 408. | slain, 408.

Eucherius,   Maria.   Thermantia,
slain, 408.   *ob.* 415.

divided between the town and country; the spirit which had animated his public conduct was shown in the active and affectionate performance of every social duty; and the diligence of the soldier was profitably converted to the improvement of his ample patrimony,[1] which lay between Valladolid and Segovia, in the midst of a fruitful district, still famous for a most exquisite breed of sheep.[2] From the innocent, but humble, labours of his farm, Theodosius was transported, in less than four months, to the throne of the Eastern empire: and the whole period of the history of the world will not perhaps afford a similar example of an elevation at the same time so pure and so honourable. The princes who peaceably inherit the sceptre of their fathers claim and enjoy a legal right, the more secure as it is absolutely distinct from the merits of their personal characters. The subjects who, in a monarchy of a popular state, acquire the possession of supreme power, may have raised themselves, by the superiority either of genius or virtue, above the heads of their equals: but their virtue is seldom exempt from ambition; and the cause of the successful candidate is frequently stained by the guilt of conspiracy or civil war. Even in those governments which allow the reigning monarch to declare a colleague or a successor, his partial choice, which may be influenced by the blindest passions, is often directed to an unworthy object. But the most suspicious malignity cannot ascribe to Theodosius, in his obscure solitude of Caucha, the arts, the desires, or even the hopes of an ambitious statesman; and the name of the Exile would long since have been forgotten, if his genuine and distinguished virtues had not left a deep impression in the Imperial court. During the season of prosperity he had been neglected; but, in the public distress, his superior merit was universally felt and acknowledged. What confidence must have been reposed in his integrity, since Gratian could trust that a pious son would forgive, for the sake of the republic, the murder of his father! What expectations must have been formed of his abilities, to encourage the hope that a single man could save, and restore, the empire of the East! Theodosius was invested with the purple in the thirty-third year of his age. The vulgar gazed with admiration on the manly beauty of his face and the graceful majesty of his person, which they were pleased to

---

[1] Pacatus (in Panegyr. Vet. xii. 9) prefers the rustic life of Theodosius to that of Cincinnatus; the one was the effect of choice, the other of poverty.

[2] M. d'Anville (Géographie Ancienne, tom. i. p. 25) has fixed the situation of Caucha, or Coca, in the old province of Gallicia, where Zosimus and Idatius have placed the birth or patrimony of Theodosius.

compare with the pictures and medals of the emperor Trajan; whilst intelligent observers discovered, in the qualities of his heart and understanding, a more important resemblance to the best and greatest of the Roman princes.

It is not without the most sincere regret that I must now take leave of an accurate and faithful guide, who has composed the history of his own times without indulging the prejudices and passions which usually affect the mind of a contemporary. Ammianus Marcellinus, who terminates his useful work with the defeat and death of Valens, recommends the more glorious subject of the ensuing reign to the youthful vigour and eloquence of the rising generation.[1] The rising generation was not disposed to accept his advice, or to imitate his example; [2] and, in the study of the reign of Theodosius, we are reduced to illustrate the partial narrative of Zosimus by the obscure hints of fragments and chronicles, by the figurative style of poetry or panegyric, and by the precarious assistance of the ecclesiastical writers, who, in the heat of religious faction, are apt to despise the profane virtues of sincerity and moderation. Conscious of these disadvantages, which will continue to involve a considerable portion of the decline and fall of the Roman empire, I shall proceed with doubtful and timorous steps. Yet I may boldly pronounce that the battle of Hadrianople was never revenged by any signal or decisive victory of Theodosius over the barbarians; and the expressive silence of his venal orators may be confirmed by the observation of the condition and circumstances of the times. The fabric of a mighty state, which has been reared by the labours of successive ages, could not be overturned by the misfortune of a single day, if the fatal power of the imagination did not exaggerate the real measure of the calamity. The loss of forty thousand Romans, who fell in the plains of Hadrianople, might have been soon recruited in the

---

[1] Let us hear Ammianus himself. Hæc, ut miles quondam et Græcus, a principatu Cæsaris Nervæ exorsus, adusque Valentis interitum, pro virium explicavi mensurâ: opus veritatem professum nunquam, ut arbitror, sciens, silentio ausus corrumpere vel mendacio. Scribant reliqua potiores ætate, doctrinisque florentes. Quos id, si libuerit, aggressuros, procudere linguas ad majores moneo stilos. Ammian. xxxi. 16. The first thirteen books, a superficial epitome of two hundred and fifty-seven years, are now lost; the last eighteen, which contain no more than twenty-five years, still preserve the copious and authentic history of his own times.

[2] Ammianus was the last subject of Rome who composed a profane history in the Latin language. The East, in the next century, produced some rhetorical historians, Zosimus, Olympiodorus, Malchus, Candidus, etc. See Vossius de Historicis Græcis, l. ii. c. 18; de Historicis Latinis, l. ii. c. 10, etc.

populous provinces of the East, which contained so many millions of inhabitants. The courage of a soldier is found to be the cheapest and most common quality of human nature; and sufficient skill to encounter an undisciplined foe might have been speedily taught by the care of the surviving centurions. If the barbarians were mounted on the horses, and equipped with the armour, of their vanquished enemies, the numerous studs of Cappadocia and Spain would have supplied new squadrons of cavalry; the thirty-four arsenals of the empire were plentifully stored with magazines of offensive and defensive arms; and the wealth of Asia might still have yielded an ample fund for the expenses of the war. But the effects which were produced by the battle of Hadrianople on the minds of the barbarians and of the Romans, extended the victory of the former, and the defeat of the latter, far beyond the limits of a single day. A Gothic chief was heard to declare, with insolent moderation, that, for his own part, he was fatigued with slaughter; but that he was astonished how a people who fled before him like a flock of sheep could still presume to dispute the possession of their treasures and provinces.[1] The same terrors which the name of the Huns had spread among the Gothic tribes were inspired, by the formidable name of the Goths, among the subjects and soldiers of the Roman empire.[2] If Theodosius, hastily collecting his scattered forces, had led them into the field to encounter a victorious enemy, his army would have been vanquished by their own fears; and his rashness could not have been excused by the chance of success. But the *great* Theodosius, an epithet which he honourably deserved on this momentous occasion, conducted himself as the firm and faithful guardian of the republic. He fixed his headquarters at Thessalonica, the capital of the Macedonian diocese;[3] from whence he could watch the irregular motions of the barbarians, and direct the operations of his lieutenants, from the gates of Constantinople to the shores of the Hadriatic. The fortifications and garrisons of the cities were strengthened; and the troops, among whom a sense of order and discipline was revived, were insensibly emboldened by the confidence of their own safety.

---

[1] Chrysostom, tom. i. p. 344, edit. Montfaucon. I have verified and examined this passage; but I should never, without the aid of Tillemont (Hist. des Emp. tom. v. p. 152), have detected an historical anecdote in a strange medley of moral and mystic exhortations, addressed, by the preacher of Antioch, to a young widow.

[2] Eunapius, in Excerpt. Legation. p. 21 [p. 52, ed. Bonn].

[3] See Godefroy's Chronology of the Laws. Codex Theodos. tom. i. Prolegomen. p. xcix.-civ.

From these secure stations they were encouraged to make frequent sallies on the barbarians, who infested the adjacent
country; and, as they were seldom allowed to engage, without
some decisive superiority, either of ground or of numbers, their
enterprises were, for the most part, successful; and they were
soon convinced, by their own experience, of the possibility of
vanquishing their *invincible* enemies. The detachments of these
separate garrisons were gradually united into small armies; the
same cautious measures were pursued, according to an extensive
and well-concerted plan of operations; the events of each day
added strength and spirit to the Roman arms; and the artful
diligence of the emperor, who circulated the most favourable
reports of the success of the war, contributed to subdue the
pride of the barbarians, and to animate the hopes and courage
of his subjects. If, instead of this faint and imperfect outline,
we could accurately represent the counsels and actions of Theodosius in four successive campaigns, there is reason to believe
that his consummate skill would deserve the applause of every
military reader. The republic had formerly been saved by the
delays of Fabius; and, while the splendid trophies of Scipio, in
the field of Zama, attract the eyes of posterity, the camps and
marches of the dictator among the hills of Campania may claim
a juster proportion of the solid and independent fame which the
general is not compelled to share either with fortune or with his
troops. Such was likewise the merit of Theodosius; and the
infirmities of his body, which most unseasonably languished
under a long and dangerous disease, could not oppress the vigour
of his mind, or divert his attention from the public service.[1]

The deliverance and peace of the Roman provinces [2] was the
work of prudence, rather than of valour: the prudence of Theodosius was seconded by fortune; and the emperor never failed
to seize, and to improve, every favourable circumstance. As
long as the superior genius of Fritigern preserved the union and
directed the motions of the barbarians, their power was not
inadequate to the conquest of a great empire. The death of
that hero, the predecessor and master of the renowned Alaric,
relieved an impatient multitude from the intolerable yoke of

---

[1] Most writers insist on the illness and long repose of Theodosius at Thessalonica: Zosimus, to diminish his glory; Jornandes, to favour the Goths;
and the ecclesiastical writers, to introduce his baptism.

[2] Compare Themistius (Orat. xiv. p. 181) with Zosimus (l. iv. [c. 25]
p. 232), Jornandes (c. xxvii. p. 649), and the prolix Commentary of M.
de Buat (Hist. des Peuples, etc., tom. vi. p. 477-552). The Chronicles
of Idatius and Marcellinus allude, in general terms, to magna certamina,
magna multaque prælia. The two epithets are not easily reconciled.

discipline and discretion. The barbarians, who had been restrained by his authority, abandoned themselves to the dictates of their passions; and their passions were seldom uniform or consistent. An army of conquerors was broken into many disorderly bands of savage robbers; and their blind and irregular fury was not less pernicious to themselves than to their enemies. Their mischievous disposition was shown in the destruction of every object which they wanted strength to remove, or taste to enjoy; and they often consumed, with improvident rage, the harvests, or the granaries, which soon afterwards became necessary for their own subsistence. A spirit of discord arose among the independent tribes and nations, which had been united only by the bands of a loose and voluntary alliance. The troops of the Huns and the Alani would naturally upbraid the flight of the Goths, who were not disposed to use with moderation the advantages of their fortune: the ancient jealousy of the Ostrogoths and the Visigoths could not long be suspended; and the haughty chiefs still remembered the insults and injuries which they had reciprocally offered or sustained while the nation was seated in the countries beyond the Danube. The progress of domestic faction abated the more diffusive sentiment of national animosity; and the officers of Theodosius were instructed to purchase, with liberal gifts and promises, the retreat or service of the discontented party. The acquisition of Modar, a prince of the royal blood of the Amali, gave a bold and faithful champion to the cause of Rome. The illustrious deserter soon obtained the rank of master-general, with an important command; surprised an army of his countrymen, who were immersed in wine and sleep; and, after a cruel slaughter of the astonished Goths, returned with an immense spoil, and four thousand waggons, to the Imperial camp.[1] In the hands of a skilful politician the most different means may be successfully applied to the same ends; and the peace of the empire, which had been forwarded by the divisions, was accomplished by the re-union of the Gothic nation. Athanaric, who had been a patient spectator of these extraordinary events, was at length driven, by the chance of arms, from the dark recesses of the woods of Caucaland. He no longer hesitated to pass the Danube; and a very considerable part of the subjects of Fritigern, who already felt the inconveniences of anarchy, were easily persuaded to acknowledge for their king a Gothic Judge, whose birth they respected, and whose

---

[1] Zosimus (l. iv. [c. 25] p. 232) styles him a Scythian, a name which the more recent Greeks seem to have appropriated to the Goths.

abilities they had frequently experienced. But age had chilled
the daring spirit of Athanaric; and instead of leading his people
to the field of battle and victory, he wisely listened to the fair
proposal of an honourable and advantageous treaty. Theodosius,
who was acquainted with the merit and power of his new ally,
condescended to meet him at the distance of several miles from
Constantinople; and entertained him in the Imperial city, with
the confidence of a friend, and the magnificence of a monarch.
" The barbarian prince observed, with curious attention, the
variety of objects which attracted his notice, and at last broke
out into a sincere and passionate exclamation of wonder. I now
behold (said he) what I never could believe, the glories of this
stupendous capital! And as he cast his eyes around, he viewed
and he admired the commanding situation of the city, the strength
and beauty of the walls and public edifices, the capacious harbour
crowded with innumerable vessels, the perpetual concourse of
distant nations, and the arms and discipline of the troops.
Indeed (continued Athanaric), the emperor of the Romans is a
god upon earth; and the presumptuous man who dares to lift
his hand against him is guilty of his own blood." [1] The Gothic
king did not long enjoy this splendid and honourable reception;
and, as temperance was not the virtue of his nation, it may justly
be suspected that his mortal disease was contracted amidst the
pleasures of the Imperial banquets. But the policy of Theodosius derived more solid benefit from the death than he could
have expected from the most faithful services of his ally. The
funeral of Athanaric was performed with solemn rites in the
capital of the East; a stately monument was erected to his
memory; and his whole army, won by the liberal courtesy and
decent grief of Theodosius, enlisted under the standard of the
Roman empire. [2] The submission of so great a body of the
Visigoths was productive of the most salutary consequences;
and the mixed influence of force, of reason, and of corruption,

---

[1] The reader will not be displeased to see the original words of Jornandes, or the author whom he transcribed. Regiam urbem ingressus est,
miransque, En, inquit, cerno quod sæpe incredulus audiebam, famam
videlicet tantæ urbis. Et huc illuc oculos volvens, nunc situm urbis,
commeatumque navium, nunc mœnia clara prospectans, miratur; popu-
losque diversarum gentium, quasi fonte in uno e diversis partibus scatu-
riente undâ, sic quoque militem ordinatum aspiciens; Deus, inquit, sine
dubio est terrenus Imperator, et quisquis adversus eum manum moverit,
ipse sui sanguinis reus existit. Jornandes (c. xxviii. p. 650) proceeds to
mention his death and funeral.

[2] Jornandes, c. xxviii. p. 650. Even Zosimus (l. iv. [c. 34] p. 246) is
compelled to approve the generosity of Theodosius, so honourable to himself and so beneficial to the public.

became every day more powerful and more extensive. Each independent chieftain hastened to obtain a separate treaty, from the apprehension that an obstinate delay might expose *him*, alone and unprotected, to the revenge or justice of the conqueror. The general, or rather the final, capitulation of the Goths, may be dated four years, one month, and twenty-five days, after the defeat and death of the emperor Valens.[1]

The provinces of the Danube had been already relieved from the oppressive weight of the Gruthungi, or Ostrogoths, by the voluntary retreat of Alatheus and Saphrax, whose restless spirit had prompted them to seek new scenes of rapine and glory. Their destructive course was pointed towards the West; but we must be satisfied with a very obscure and imperfect knowledge of their various adventures. The Ostrogoths impelled several of the German tribes on the provinces of Gaul; concluded, and soon violated, a treaty with the emperor Gratian; advanced into the unknown countries of the North; and, after an interval of more than four years, returned with accumulated force to the banks of the Lower Danube. Their troops were recruited with the fiercest warriors of Germany and Scythia; and the soldiers, or at least the historians, of the empire no longer recognised the name and countenances of their former enemies.[2] The general who commanded the military and naval powers of the Thracian frontier soon perceived that his superiority would be disadvantageous to the public service; and that the barbarians, awed by the presence of his fleet and legions, would probably defer the passage of the river till the approaching winter. The dexterity of the spies whom he sent into the Gothic camp allured the barbarians into a fatal snare. They were persuaded that, by a bold attempt, they might surprise, in the silence and darkness of the night, the sleeping army of the Romans; and the whole multitude was hastily embarked in a fleet of three thousand canoes.[3] The bravest of the Ostrogoths led the van; the main body consisted of the remainder of their subjects and

---

[1] The short, but authentic, hints in the *Fasti* of Idatius (Chron. Scaliger. p. 52) are stained with contemporary passion. The fourteenth oration of Themistius is a compliment to Peace and the consul Saturninus (A.D. 383).

[2] Ἔθνος τι Σκύθικον πᾶσιν ἄγνωστον. Zosimus, l. iv. [c. 38] p. 252.

[3] I am justified, by reason and example, in applying this Indian name to the μονόξυλα of the barbarians, the single trees hollowed into the shape of a boat, πληθεῖ μονοξύλων ἐμβιβάσαντες. Zosimus, l. iv. [c. 38] p. 253.

> Ausi Danubium quondam tranare Gruthungi
> In lintres fregere nemus: ter mille ruebant
> Per fluvium plenæ cuneis immanibus alni.
>   Claudian, in iv. Cons. Hon. 623.

soldiers; and the women and children securely followed in the
rear.   One of the nights without a moon had been selected for
the execution of their design; and they had almost reached the
southern bank of the Danube, in the firm confidence that they
should find an easy landing and an unguarded camp.   But the
progress of the barbarians was suddenly stopped by an unexpected obstacle—a triple line of vessels, strongly connected with
each other, and which formed an impenetrable chain of two miles
and a half along the river.   While they struggled to force their
way in the unequal conflict, their right flank was overwhelmed
by the irresistible attack of a fleet of galleys, which were urged
down the stream by the united impulse of oars and of the tide.
The weight and velocity of those ships of war broke, and sunk,
and dispersed the rude and feeble canoes of the barbarians:
their valour was ineffectual; and Alatheus, the king or general
of the Ostrogoths, perished, with his bravest troops, either by the
sword of the Romans or in the waves of the Danube.   The last
division of this unfortunate fleet might regain the opposite shore;
but the distress and disorder of the multitude rendered them
alike incapable either of action or counsel; and they soon implored the clemency of the victorious enemy.   On this occasion,
as well as on many others, it is a difficult task to reconcile the
passions and prejudices of the writers of the age of Theodosius.
The partial and malignant historian, who misrepresents every
action of his reign, affirms that the emperor did not appear in
the field of battle till the barbarians had been vanquished by the
valour and conduct of his lieutenant Promotus.[1]   The flattering
poet, who celebrated in the court of Honorius the glory of the
father and of the son, ascribes the victory to the personal prowess
of Theodosius; and almost insinuates that the king of the
Ostrogoths was slain by the hand of the emperor.[2]   The truth of
history might perhaps be found in a just medium between these
extreme and contradictory assertions.

The original treaty, which fixed the settlement of the Goths,
ascertained their privileges, and stipulated their obligations,

---

[1] Zosimus, l. iv. [c. 38] p. 252-255.   He too frequently betrays his poverty
of judgment by disgracing the most serious narratives with trifling and
incredible circumstances.

[2] —— Odothæi Regis *opima*
            Retulit   Ver. 632.

The *opima* were the spoils which a Roman general could only win from
the king, or general, of the enemy, whom he had slain with his own hands:
and no more than three such examples are celebrated in the victorious ages
of Rome.

would illustrate the history of Theodosius and his successors. The series of their history has imperfectly preserved the spirit and substance of this singular agreement.[1] The ravages of war and tyranny had provided many large tracts of fertile but uncultivated land for the use of those barbarians who might not disdain the practice of agriculture. A numerous colony of the Visigoths was seated in Thrace: the remains of the Ostrogoths were planted in Phrygia and Lydia; their immediate wants were supplied by a distribution of corn and cattle; and their future industry was encouraged by an exemption from tribute during a certain term of years. The barbarians would have deserved to feel the cruel and perfidious policy of the Imperial court if they had suffered themselves to be dispersed through the provinces. They required and they obtained the sole possession of the villages and districts assigned for their residence; they still cherished and propagated their native manners and language; asserted, in the bosom of despotism, the freedom of their domestic government; and acknowledged the sovereignty of the emperor, without submitting to the inferior jurisdiction of the laws and magistrates of Rome. The hereditary chiefs of the tribes and families were still permitted to command their followers in peace and war: but the royal dignity was abolished; and the generals of the Goths were appointed and removed at the pleasure of the emperor. An army of forty thousand Goths was maintained for the perpetual service of the empire of the East; and those haughty troops, who assumed the title of *Fœderati*, or allies, were distinguished by their gold collars, liberal pay, and licentious privileges. Their native courage was improved by the use of arms and the knowledge of discipline; and, while the republic was guarded or threatened by the doubtful sword of the barbarians, the last sparks of the military flame were finally extinguished in the minds of the Romans.[2] Theodosius had the address to persuade his allies that the conditions of peace, which had been extorted from him by prudence and necessity, were the voluntary expressions of his sincere friendship for the Gothic

---

[1] See Themistius, Orat. xvi. p. 211. Claudian (in Eutrop. l. ii. 152) mentions the Phrygian colony:—

—— Ostrogothis colitur mistisque Gruthungis
Phryx ager ——

and then proceeds to name the rivers of Lydia, the Pactolus, and Hermus.

[2] Compare Jornandes (c. 21, 28), who marks the condition and number of the Gothic *Fœderati*, with Zosimus (l. iv. p. 258), who mentions their golden collars; and Pacatus (in Panegyr. Vet. xii. 37), who applauds, with false or foolish joy, their bravery and discipline.

nation.[1] A different mode of vindication or apology was opposed to the complaints of the people, who loudly censured these shameful and dangerous concessions.[2] The calamities of the war were painted in the most lively colours; and the first symptoms of the return of order, of plenty, and security were diligently exaggerated. The advocates of Theodosius could affirm, with some appearance of truth and reason, that it was impossible to extirpate so many warlike tribes, who were rendered desperate by the loss of their native country; and that the exhausted provinces would be revived by a fresh supply of soldiers and husbandmen. The barbarians still wore an angry and hostile aspect; but the experience of past times might encourage the hope that they would acquire the habits of industry and obedience; that their manners would be polished by time, education, and the influence of Christianity; and that their posterity would insensibly blend with the great body of the Roman people.[3]

Notwithstanding these specious arguments and these sanguine expectations, it was apparent to every discerning eye that the Goths would long remain the enemies, and might soon become the conquerors, of the Roman empire. Their rude and insolent behaviour expressed their contempt of the citizens and provincials, whom they insulted with impunity.[4] To the zeal and valour of the barbarians Theodosius was indebted for the success of his arms: but their assistance was precarious; and they were sometimes seduced, by a treacherous and inconstant disposition, to abandon his standard at the moment when their service was the most essential. During the civil war against Maximus a great number of Gothic deserters retired into the morasses of Macedonia, wasted the adjacent provinces, and obliged the

---

[1] Amator pacis generisque Gothorum, is the praise bestowed by the Gothic historian (c. xxix.), who represents his nation as innocent, peaceable men, slow to anger and patient of injuries. According to Livy, the Romans conquered the world in their own defence.

[2] Besides the partial invectives of Zosimus (always discontented with the Christian reigns), see the grave representations which Synesius addresses to the emperor Arcadius (de Regno, p. 25, 26, edit. Petav. [Paris, 1612]). The philosophic bishop of Cyrene was near enough to judge; and he was sufficiently removed from the temptation of fear or flattery.

[3] Themistius (Orat. xvi. p. 211, 212) composes an elaborate and rational apology, which is not, however, exempt from the puerilities of Greek rhetoric. Orpheus could *only* charm the wild beasts of Thrace; but Theodosius enchanted the men and women whose predecessors in the same country had torn Orpheus in pieces, etc.

[4] Constantinople was deprived, half a day, of the public allowance of bread, to expiate the murder of a Gothic soldier: κινοῦντες τὸ Σκυθικόν was the guilt of the people. Libanius, Orat. xii. p. 394, edit. Morel.

intrepid monarch to expose his person and exert his power to suppress the rising flame of rebellion.[1]   The public apprehensions were fortified by the strong suspicion that these tumults were not the effect of accidental passion, but the result of deep and premeditated design.   It was generally believed that the Goths had signed the treaty of peace with an hostile and insidious spirit; and that their chiefs had previously bound themselves by a solemn and secret oath never to keep faith with the Romans, to maintain the fairest show of loyalty and friendship, and to watch the favourable moment of rapine, of conquest, and of revenge.   But as the minds of the barbarians were not insensible to the power of gratitude, several of the Gothic leaders sincerely devoted themselves to the service of the empire, or, at least, of the emperor: the whole nation was insensibly divided into two opposite factions, and much sophistry was employed in conversation and dispute to compare the obligations of their first and second engagements.   The Goths who considered themselves as the friends of peace, of justice, and of Rome, were directed by the authority of Fravitta, a valiant and honourable youth, distinguished above the rest of his countrymen by the politeness of his manners, the liberality of his sentiments, and the mild virtues of social life.   But the more numerous faction adhered to the fierce and faithless Priulf, who inflamed the passions and asserted the independence of his warlike followers.   On one of the solemn festivals, when the chiefs of both parties were invited to the Imperial table, they were insensibly heated by wine, till they forgot the usual restraints of discretion and respect, and betrayed in the presence of Theodosius the fatal secret of their domestic disputes.   The emperor, who had been the reluctant witness of this extraordinary controversy, dissembled his fears and resentment, and soon dismissed the tumultuous assembly.   Fravitta, alarmed and exasperated by the insolence of his rival, whose departure from the palace might have been the signal of a civil war, boldly followed him, and, drawing his sword, laid Priulf dead at his feet.   Their companions flew to arms; and the faithful champion of Rome would have been oppressed by superior numbers if he had not been protected by the seasonable interposition of the Imperial guards.[2]   Such were the scenes

---

[1] Zosimus, l. iv. [c. 48] p. 267-271.   He tells a long and ridiculous story of the adventurous prince, who roved the country with only five horsemen, of a spy whom they detected, whipped, and killed in an old woman's cottage, etc.

[2] Compare Eunapius (in Excerpt. Legat. p. 21, 22 [p. 53, 54, ed. Bonn.], with Zosimus (l. iv. [c. 56] p. 279).   The difference of circumstances and

of barbaric rage which disgraced the palace and table of the Roman emperor; and, as the impatient Goths could only be restrained by the firm and temperate character of Theodosius, the public safety seemed to depend on the life and abilities of a single man.[1]

CHAPTER XXVII

Death of Gratian—Ruin of Arianism—St. Ambrose—First Civil War, against Maximus—Character, Administration, and Penance, of Theodosius—Death of Valentinian II.—Second Civil War, against Eugenius—Death of Theodosius

THE fame of Gratian, before he had accomplished the twentieth year of his age, was equal to that of the most celebrated princes. His gentle and amiable disposition endeared him to his private friends, the graceful affability of his manners engaged the affection of the people; the men of letters, who enjoyed the liberality, acknowledged the taste and eloquence, of their sovereign; his valour and dexterity in arms were equally applauded by the soldiers; and the clergy considered the humble piety of Gratian as the first and most useful of his virtues. The victory of Colmar had delivered the West from a formidable invasion, and the grateful provinces of the East ascribed the merits of Theodosius to the author of *his* greatness and of the public safety. Gratian survived those memorable events only four or five years, but he survived his reputation, and, before he fell a victim to rebellion, he had lost, in a great measure, the respect and confidence of the Roman world.

names must undoubtedly be applied to the same story. Fravitta, or Travitta, was afterwards consul (A.D. 401), and still continued his faithful service to the eldest son of Theodosius (Tillemont, Hist. des Empereurs, tom. v. p. 467).

[1] Les Goths ravagèrent tout depuis le Danube jusqu'au Bosphore; exterminèrent Valens et son armée; et ne repassèrent le Danube que pour abandonner l'affreuse solitude qu'ils avoient faite (Œuvres de Montesquieu, tom. iii. p. 479; Considérations sur les *Causes* de la Grandeur et de la Décadence des Romains, c. xvii.). The president Montesquieu seems ignorant that the Goths, after the defeat of Valens, *never* abandoned the Roman territory. It is now thirty years, says Claudian (de Bello Getico, 166, etc., A.D. 404),

> Ex quo jam patrios gens hæc oblita Triones,
> Atque Istrum transvecta semel, vestigia fixit
> Threicio funesta solo——

The error is inexcusable; since it disguises the principal and immediate cause of the fall of the Western empire of Rome.

The remarkable alteration of his character or conduct may not be imputed to the arts of flattery, which had besieged the son of Valentinian from his infancy, nor to the headstrong passion which that gentle youth appears to have escaped. A more attentive view of the life of Gratian may perhaps suggest the true cause of the disappointment of the public hopes. His apparent virtues, instead of being the hardy productions of experience and adversity, were the premature and artificial fruits of a royal education. The anxious tenderness of his father was continually employed to bestow on him those advantages which he might perhaps esteem the more highly as he himself had been deprived of them, and the most skilful masters of every science and of every art had laboured to form the mind and body of the young prince.[1] The knowledge which they painfully communicated was displayed with ostentation and celebrated with lavish praise. His soft and tractable disposition received the fair impression of their judicious precepts, and the absence of passion might easily be mistaken for the strength of reason. His preceptors gradually rose to the rank and consequence of ministers of state,[2] and, as they wisely dissembled their secret authority, he seemed to act with firmness, with propriety, and with judgment on the most important occasions of his life and reign. But the influence of this elaborate instruction did not penetrate beyond the surface, and the skilful preceptors, who so accurately guided the steps of their royal pupil, could not infuse into his feeble and indolent character the vigorous and independent principle of action which renders the laborious pursuit of glory essentially necessary to the happiness and almost to the existence of the hero. As soon as time and accident had removed those faithful counsellors from the throne, the emperor of the West insensibly descended to the level of his natural genius, abandoned the reins of government to the ambitious hands which were stretched forwards to grasp them, and amused his leisure with the most frivolous gratifications. A public sale of favour and injustice was instituted, both in the court and in the provinces, by the worthless delegates of his power, whose merit

---

[1] Valentinian was less attentive to the religion of his son; since he intrusted the education of Gratian to Ausonius, a professed Pagan. (Mém. de l'Académie des Inscriptions, tom. xv. p. 125-138). The poetical fame of Ausonius condemns the taste of his age.

[2] Ausonius was successively promoted to the Prætorian præfecture of Italy (A.D. 377) and of Gaul (A.D. 378); and was at length invested with the consulship (A.D. 379). He expressed his gratitude in a servile and insipid piece of flattery (Actio Gratiarum, p. 699-736 [ed. Toll. Amst. 1671]), which has survived more worthy productions.

it was made *sacrilege* to question.[1] The conscience of the credulous prince was directed by saints and bishops,[2] who procured an
Imperial edict to punish, as a capital offence, the violation, the
neglect, or even the ignorance of the divine law.[3] Among the
various arts which had exercised the youth of Gratian, he had
applied himself, with singular inclination and success, to manage
the horse, to draw the bow, and to dart the javelin; and these
qualifications, which might be useful to a soldier, were prostituted to the viler purposes of hunting. Large parks were enclosed for the Imperial pleasures, and plentifully stocked with
every species of wild beasts, and Gratian neglected the duties
and even the dignity of his rank to consume whole days in the
vain display of his dexterity and boldness in the chase. The
pride and wish of the Roman emperor to excel in an art in which
he might be surpassed by the meanest of his slaves reminded the
numerous spectators of the examples of Nero and Commodus;
but the chaste and temperate Gratian was a stranger to their
monstrous vices, and his hands were stained only with the blood
of animals.[4]

The behaviour of Gratian, which degraded his character in the
eyes of mankind, could not have disturbed the security of his
reign if the army had not been provoked to resent their peculiar
injuries. As long as the young emperor was guided by the
instructions of his masters, he professed himself the friend and
pupil of the soldiers; many of his hours were spent in the
familiar conversation of the camp, and the health, the comforts,
the rewards, the honours of his faithful troops, appeared to be
the object of his attentive concern. But, after Gratian more
freely indulged his prevailing taste for hunting and shooting, he
naturally connected himself with the most dexterous ministers
of his favourite amusement. A body of the Alani was received

---

[1] Disputare de principali judicio non oportet. Sacrilegii enim instar est
dubitare, an is dignus sit, quem elegerit imperator. Codex Justinian. l.
ix. tit. xxix. leg. 2. This convenient law was revived and promulgated,
after the death of Gratian, by the feeble court of Milan.

[2] Ambrose composed, for his instruction, a theological treatise on the
faith of the Trinity: and Tillemont (Hist. des Empereurs, tom. v. p. 158,
169) ascribes to the archbishop the merit of Gratian's intolerant laws.

[3] Qui divinæ legis sanctitatem [aut] nesciendo omittunt, aut negligendo
violant, et offendunt, sacrilegium committunt. Codex Justinian. l. ix.
tit. xxix. leg. 1. Theodosius indeed may claim his share in the merit of
this comprehensive law.

[4] Ammianus (xxxi. 10) and the younger Victor [Epit. c. 47] acknowledge
the virtues of Gratian; and accuse, or rather lament, his degenerate taste.
The odious parallel of Commodus is saved by " licet incruentus; " and
perhaps Philostorgius (l. x. c. 10 [5], and Godefroy, p. 412) had guarded,
with some similar reserve, the comparison of Nero.

into the military and domestic service of the palace, and the admirable skill which they were accustomed to display in the unbounded plains of Scythia was exercised on a more narrow theatre in the parks and enclosures of Gaul. Gratian admired the talents and customs of these favourite guards, to whom alone he intrusted the defence of his person; and, as if he meant to insult the public opinion, he frequently showed himself to the soldiers and people with the dress and arms, the long bow, the sounding quiver, and the fur garments of a Scythian warrior. The unworthy spectacle of a Roman prince who had renounced the dress and manners of his country filled the minds of the legions with grief and indignation.[1] Even the Germans, so strong and formidable in the armies of the empire, affected to disdain the strange and horrid appearance of the savages of the North, who, in the space of a few years, had wandered from the banks of the Volga to those of the Seine. A loud and licentious murmur was echoed through the camps and garrisons of the West; and as the mild indolence of Gratian neglected to extinguish the first symptoms of discontent, the want of love and respect was not supplied by the influence of fear. But the subversion of an established government is always a work of some real, and of much apparent difficulty; and the throne of Gratian was protected by the sanctions of custom, law, religion, and the nice balance of the civil and military powers which had been established by the policy of Constantine. It is not very important to inquire from what causes the revolt of Britain was produced. Accident is commonly the parent of disorder: the seeds of rebellion happened to fall on a soil which was supposed to be more fruitful than any other in tyrants and usurpers;[2] the legions of that sequestered island had been long famous for a spirit of presumption and arrogance;[3] and the name of Maximus was proclaimed by the tumultuary but unanimous voice both of the soldiers and of the provincials. The emperor, or the rebel, for his title was not yet ascertained by fortune, was a native of Spain, the country-

---

[1] Zosimus (l. iv. [c. 35] p. 247) and the younger Victor ascribe the revolution to the favour of the Alani and the discontent of the Roman troops. Dum exercitum negligeret, et paucos ex Alanis, quos ingenti auro ad se transtulerat, anteferret veteri ac Romano militi [Epit. c. 47].

[2] Britannia fertilis provincia tyrannorum, is a memorable expression used by Jerom in the Pelagian controversy, and variously tortured in the disputes of our national antiquaries. The revolutions of the last age appeared to justify the image of the sublime Bossuet, " cette île, plus orageuse que les mers qui l'environment."

[3] Zosimus says of the British soldiers, τῶν ἄλλων ἁπάντων πλέον αὐθαδείᾳ καὶ θυμῷ νικωμένους [l. c.].

man, the fellow-soldier, and the rival of Theodosius, whose elevation he had not seen without some emotions of envy and resentment; the events of his life had long since fixed him in Britain, and I should not be unwilling to find some evidence for the marriage which he is said to have contracted with the daughter of a wealthy lord of Caernarvonshire.[1] But this provincial rank might justly be considered as a state of exile and obscurity, and, if Maximus had obtained any civil or military office, he was not invested with the authority either of governor or general.[2] His abilities and even his integrity are acknowledged by the partial writers of the age, and the merit must indeed have been conspicuous that could extort such a confession in favour of the vanquished enemy of Theodosius. The discontent of Maximus might incline him to censure the conduct of his sovereign, and to encourage, perhaps without any views of ambition, the murmurs of the troops. But in the midst of the tumult he artfully or modestly refused to ascend the throne, and some credit appears to have been given to his own positive declaration that he was compelled to accept the dangerous present of the Imperial purple.[3]

But there was danger likewise in refusing the empire, and, from the moment that Maximus had violated his allegiance to his lawful sovereign, he could not hope to reign, or even to live, if he confined his moderate ambition within the narrow limits of Britain. He boldly and wisely resolved to prevent the designs of Gratian; the youth of the island crowded to his standard, and he invaded Gaul with a fleet and army which were long afterwards remembered as the emigration of a considerable part of the British nation.[4] The emperor, in his peaceful residence

---

[1] Helena the daughter of Eudda. Her chapel may still be seen at Caersegont, now Caer-narvon. (Carte's Hist. of England, vol. i. p. 168, from Rowland's Mona Antiqua.) The prudent reader may not perhaps be satisfied with such Welch evidence.

[2] Camden (vol. i. introduct. p. ci.) appoints him governor of Britain; and the father of our antiquities is followed, as usual, by his blind progeny. Pacatus and Zosimus had taken some pains to prevent this error or fable; and I shall protect myself by their decisive testimonies. Regali habitû *exulem* suum, illi exules orbis induerunt (in Panegyr. Vet. xii. 23), and the Greek historian still less equivocally, αὐτὸς (Maximus) δὲ οὐδὲ εἰς ἀρχὴν ἔντιμον ἔτυχε προελθών (l. iv. [c. 35] p. 248).

[3] Sulpicius Severus, Dialog. ii. 7. Orosius, l. vii. c. 34, p. 556. They both acknowledge (Sulpicius had been his subject) his innocence and merit. It is singular enough that Maximus should be less favourably treated by Zosimus, the partial adversary of his rival.

[4] Archbishop Usher (Antiquitat. Britan. Eccles. p. 107, 108) has diligently collected the legends of the island and the continent. The whole emigration consisted of 30,000 soldiers and 100,000 plebeians, who settled in Bretagne. Their destined brides, St. Ursula with 11,000 noble and

of Paris, was alarmed by their hostile approach, and the darts which he idly wasted on lions and bears might have been employed more honourably against the rebels. But his feeble efforts announced his degenerate spirit and desperate situation, and deprived him of the resources which he still might have found in the support of his subjects and allies. The armies of Gaul, instead of opposing the march of Maximus, received him with joyful and loyal acclamations, and the shame of the desertion was transferred from the people to the prince. The troops whose station more immediately attached them to the service of the palace abandoned the standard of Gratian the first time that it was displayed in the neighbourhood of Paris. The emperor of the West fled towards Lyons with a train of only three hundred horse, and in the cities along the road, where he hoped to find a refuge, or at least a passage, he was taught by cruel experience that every gate is shut against the unfortunate. Yet he might still have reached in safety the dominions of his brother, and soon have returned with the forces of Italy and the East, if he had not suffered himself to be fatally deceived by the perfidious governor of the Lyonnese province. Gratian was amused by protestations of doubtful fidelity, and the hopes of a support which could not be effectual, till the arrival of Andragathius, the general of the cavalry of Maximus, put an end to his suspense. That resolute officer executed, without remorse, the orders or the intentions of the usurper. Gratian, as he rose from supper, was delivered into the hands of the assassin, and his body was denied to the pious and pressing entreaties of his brother Valentinian.[1] The death of the emperor was followed by that of his powerful general Mellobaudes, the king of the Franks, who maintained to the last moment of his life the ambiguous reputation which is the just recompense of obscure and subtle policy.[2] These executions might be necessary to the

60,000 plebeian virgins, mistook their way, landed at Cologne, and were all most cruelly murdered by the Huns. But the plebeian sisters have been defrauded of their equal honours; and, what is still harder, John Trithemius presumes to mention the *children* of these British *virgins*.

[1] Zosimus (l. iv. [c. 35] p. 248, 249) has transported the death of Gratian from Lugdunum in Gaul (Lyons) to Singidunum in Mæsia. Some hints may be extracted from the Chronicles; some lies may be detected in Sozomen (l. vii. c. 13) and Socrates (l. v. c. 11). Ambrose is our most authentic evidence (tom. i. Enarrat. in Psalm lxi. p. 961, tom. ii. Epist. xxiv. p. 888, etc., and de Obitû Valentinian. Consolat. No. 28, p. 1182).

[2] Pacatus (xii. 28) celebrates his fidelity; while his treachery is marked in Prosper's Chronicle as the cause of the ruin of Gratian. Ambrose, who has occasion to exculpate himself, only condemns the death of Vallio, a faithful servant of Gratian (tom. ii. Epist. xxiv. p. 891, edit. Benedict.).

public safety, but the successful usurper, whose power was
acknowledged by all the provinces of the West, had the merit
and the satisfaction of boasting that, except those who had
perished by the chance of war, his triumph was not stained by
the blood of the Romans.[1]

The events of this revolution had passed in such rapid succession that it would have been impossible for Theodosius to march
to the relief of his benefactor before he received the intelligence
of his defeat and death. During the season of sincere grief or
ostentatious mourning the Eastern emperor was interrupted by
the arrival of the principal chamberlain of Maximus; and the
choice of a venerable old man for an office which was usually
exercised by eunuchs announced to the court of Constantinople
the gravity and temperance of the British usurper. The ambassador condescended to justify or excuse the conduct of his
master, and to protest, in specious language, that the murder of
Gratian had been perpetrated, without his knowledge or consent,
by the precipitate zeal of the soldiers. But he proceeded, in a
firm and equal tone, to offer Theodosius the alternative of peace
or war. The speech of the ambassador concluded with a spirited
declaration that, although Maximus, as a Roman and as the
father of his people, would choose rather to employ his forces in
the common defence of the republic, he was armed and prepared,
if his friendship should be rejected, to dispute in a field of battle
the empire of the world. An immediate and peremptory answer
was required, but it was extremely difficult for Theodosius to
satisfy, on this important occasion, either the feelings of his own
mind or the expectations of the public. The imperious voice
of honour and gratitude called aloud for revenge. From the
liberality of Gratian he had received the Imperial diadem; his
patience would encourage the odious suspicion that he was more
deeply sensible of former injuries than of recent obligations; and
if he accepted the friendship, he must seem to share the guilt, of
the assassin. Even the principles of justice and the interest of
society would receive a fatal blow from the impunity of Maximus,
and the example of successful usurpation would tend to dissolve
the artificial fabric of government, and once more to replunge
the empire in the crimes and calamities of the preceding age.
But, as the sentiments of gratitude and honour should invariably
regulate the conduct of an individual, they may be overbalanced

---

[1] He protested, nullum ex adversariis nisi in acie occubuisse. Sulp.
Severus in Vit. B. Martin. c. 23. The orator of Theodosius bestows
reluctant, and therefore weighty, praise on his clemency. Si cui ille, pro
ceteris sceleribus suit, *minus crudelis* fuisse videtur (Panegyr. Vet. xii. 28).

in the mind of a sovereign by the sense of superior duties, and the maxims both of justice and humanity must permit the escape of an atrocious criminal if an innocent people would be involved in the consequences of his punishment.   The assassin of Gratian had usurped, but he actually possessed, the most warlike provinces of the empire; the East was exhausted by the misfortunes, and even by the success, of the Gothic war; and it was seriously to be apprehended that, after the vital strength of the republic had been wasted in a doubtful and destructive contest, the feeble conqueror would remain an easy prey to the barbarians of the north.   These weighty considerations engaged Theodosius to dissemble his resentment and to accept the alliance of the tyrant. But he stipulated that Maximus should content himself with the possession of the countries beyond the Alps.   The brother of Gratian was confirmed and secured in the sovereignty of Italy, Africa, and the Western Illyricum, and some honourable conditions were inserted in the treaty to protect the memory and the laws of the deceased emperor.[1]   According to the custom of the age, the images of the three Imperial colleagues were exhibited to the veneration of the people; nor should it be lightly supposed that, in the moment of a solemn reconciliation, Theodosius secretly cherished the intention of perfidy and revenge.[2]

The contempt of Gratian for the Roman soldiers had exposed him to the fatal effects of their resentment.   His profound veneration for the Christian clergy was rewarded by the applause and gratitude of a powerful order, which has claimed in every age the privilege of dispensing honours, both on earth and in heaven.[3]   The orthodox bishops bewailed his death, and their own irreparable loss; but they were soon comforted by the discovery that Gratian had committed the sceptre of the East to the hands of a prince whose humble faith and fervent zeal were supported by the spirit and abilities of a more vigorous character. Among the benefactors of the church, the fame of Constantine has been rivalled by the glory of Theodosius.   If Constantine had the advantage of erecting the standard of the cross, the emulation of his successor assumed the merit of subduing the Arian heresy, and of abolishing the worship of idols in the Roman

---

[1] Ambrose mentions the laws of Gratian, quas non abrogavit hostis (tom. ii. Epist. xvii. p. 827).

[2] Zosimus, l. iv. [c. 37] p. 251, 252.   We may disclaim his odious suspicions, but we cannot reject the treaty of peace which the friends of Theodosius have absolutely forgotten, or slightly mentioned.

[3] Their oracle, the archbishop of Milan, assigns to his pupil Gratian an high and respectable place in heaven (tom. ii. de Obit. Val. Consol. p. 1193).

world. Theodosius was the first of the emperors baptised in the true faith of the Trinity. Although he was born of a Christian family, the maxims, or at least the practice, of the age encouraged him to delay the ceremony of his initiation till he was admonished of the danger of delay by the serious illness which threatened his life towards the end of the first year of his reign. Before he again took the field against the Goths, he received the sacrament of baptism [1] from Acholius, the orthodox bishop of Thessalonica: [2] and as the emperor ascended from the holy font, still glowing with the warm feelings of regeneration, he dictated a solemn edict, which proclaimed his own faith, and prescribed the religion of his subjects. " It is our pleasure (such is the Imperial style) that all the nations which are governed by our clemency and moderation should stedfastly adhere to the religion which was taught by St. Peter to the Romans, which faithful tradition has preserved, and which is now professed by the pontiff Damasus, and by Peter, bishop of Alexandria, a man of apostolic holiness. According to the discipline of the apostles, and the doctrine of the Gospel, let us believe the sole deity of the Father, the Son, and the Holy Ghost, under an equal majesty and a pious Trinity. We authorise the followers of this doctrine to assume the title of Catholic Christians; and as we judge that all others are extravagant madmen, we brand them with the infamous name of Heretics, and declare that their conventicles shall no longer usurp the respectable appellation of churches. Besides the condemnation of Divine justice, they must expect to suffer the severe penalties which our authority, guided by heavenly wisdom, shall think proper to inflict upon them." [3] The faith of a soldier is commonly the fruit of instruction, rather than of inquiry; but as the emperor always fixed his eyes on the visible landmarks of orthodoxy which he had so prudently constituted, his religious opinions were never affected by the specious texts, the subtle arguments, and the ambiguous creeds of the Arian doctors. Once indeed he expressed a faint inclination to converse with the eloquent and learned Eunomius, who lived in

---

[1] For the baptism of Theodosius, see Sozomen (l. vii. c. 4), Socrates (l. v. c. 6), and Tillemont (Hist. des Empereurs, tom. v. p. 728).

[2] Ascolius, or Acholius, was honoured by the friendship and the praises of Ambrose, who styles him, murus fidei atque sanctitatis (tom. ii. Epist. xv. p. 820); and afterwards celebrates his speed and diligence in running to Constantinople, Italy, etc. (Epist. xvi. p. 822)—a virtue which does not appertain either to a *wall* or a *bishop*.

[3] Codex Theodos. l. xvi. tit. i. leg. 2, with Godefroy's Commentary, tom. vi. p. 5-9. Such an edict deserved the warmest praises of Baronius, auream sanctionem, edictum pium et salutare.—Sic itur ad astra.

retirement at a small distance from Constantinople. But the dangerous interview was prevented by the prayers of the empress Flaccilla, who trembled for the salvation of her husband; and the mind of Theodosius was confirmed by a theological argument adapted to the rudest capacity. He had lately bestowed on his eldest son Arcadius the name and honours of Augustus, and the two princes were seated on a stately throne to receive the homage of their subjects. A bishop, Amphilochius of Iconium, approached the throne, and, after saluting with due reverence the person of his sovereign, he accosted the royal youth with the same familiar tenderness which he might have used towards a plebeian child. Provoked by this insolent behaviour, the monarch gave orders that the rustic priest should be instantly driven from his presence. But while the guards were forcing him to the door, the dexterous polemic had time to execute his design, by exclaiming, with a loud voice, " Such is the treatment, O emperor! which the King of heaven has prepared for those impious men who affect to worship the Father, but refuse to acknowledge the equal majesty of his divine Son." Theodosius immediately embraced the bishop of Iconium, and never forgot the important lesson which he had received from this dramatic parable.[1]

Constantinople was the principal seat and fortress of Arianism; and, in a long interval of forty years,[2] the faith of the princes and prelates who reigned in the capital of the East was rejected in the purer schools of Rome and Alexandria. The archiepiscopal throne of Macedonius, which had been polluted with so much Christian blood, was successively filled by Eudoxus and Damophilus. Their diocese enjoyed a free importation of vice and error from every province of the empire; the eager pursuit of religious controversy afforded a new occupation to the busy idleness of the metropolis: and we may credit the assertion of an intelligent observer, who describes, with some pleasantry, the effects of their loquacious zeal. " This city," says he, " is full of mechanics and slaves, who are all of them profound theologians, and preach in the shops and in the streets. If you

---

[1] Sozomen, l. vii. c. 6. Theodoret, l. v. c. 16. Tillemont is displeased (Mém. Ecclés. tom. vi. p. 627, 628) with the terms of " rustic bishop," " obscure city." Yet I must take leave to think that both Amphilochius and Iconium were objects of inconsiderable magnitude in the Roman empire.

[2] Sozomen, l. vii. c. 5. Socrates, l. v. c. 7. Marcellin. in Chron. The account of forty years must be dated from the election or intrusion of Eusebius, who wisely exchanged the bishopric of Nicomedia for the throne of Constantinople.

desire a man to change a piece of silver, he informs you wherein
the Son differs from the Father; if you ask the price of a loaf,
you are told, by way of reply, that the Son is inferior to the
Father; and if you inquire whether the bath is ready, the answer
is, that the Son was made out of nothing." [1]   The heretics, of
various denominations, subsisted in peace under the protection
of the Arians of Constantinople, who endeavoured to secure the
attachment of those obscure sectaries, while they abused, with
unrelenting severity, the victory which they had obtained over
the followers of the council of Nice.   During the partial reigns of
Constantius and Valens, the feeble remnant of the Homoousians
was deprived of the public and private exercise of their religion;
and it has been observed, in pathetic language, that the scattered
flock was left without a shepherd to wander on the mountains,
or to be devoured by rapacious wolves.[2]   But as their zeal,
instead of being subdued, derived strength and vigour from
oppression, they seized the first moments of imperfect freedom,
which they acquired by the death of Valens, to form themselves
into a regular congregation, under the conduct of an episcopal
pastor.   Two natives of Cappadocia, Basil and Gregory Nazianzen,[3] were distinguished above all their contemporaries [4] by
the rare union of profane eloquence and of orthodox piety.
These orators, who might sometimes be compared, by themselves
and by the public, to the most celebrated of the ancient Greeks,
were united by the ties of the strictest friendship.   They had
cultivated, with equal ardour, the same liberal studies in the
schools of Athens; they had retired, with equal devotion, to the
same solitude in the deserts of Pontus; and every spark of
emulation or envy appeared to be totally extinguished in the

[1] See Jortin's Remarks on Ecclesiastical History, vol. iv. p. 71.   The
thirty-third Oration of Gregory Nazianzen affords indeed some similar
ideas, even some still more ridiculous; but I have not yet found the *words*
of this remarkable passage, which I allege on the faith of a correct and
liberal scholar.

[2] See the thirty-second Oration of Gregory Nazianzen, and the account
of his own life, which he has composed in 1800 iambics.   Yet every physician is prone to exaggerate the inveterate nature of the disease which he
has cured.

[3] I confess myself deeply indebted to the *two* Lives of Gregory Nazianzen,
composed, with very different views. by Tillemont (Mém. Ecclés. tom. ix.
p. 305-560, 692-731), and Le Clerc (Bibliothèque Universelle, tom. xviii.
p. 1-128).

[4] Unless Gregory Nazianzen mistook thirty years in his own age, he was
born, as well as his friend Basil, about the year 329.   The preposterous
chronology of Suidas has been graciously received, because it removes the
scandal of Gregory's father, a saint likewise, begetting children after he
became a bishop (Tillemont, Mém. Ecclés. tom. ix. p. 693-697).

holy and ingenuous breasts of Gregory and Basil. But the exaltation of Basil, from a private life to the archiepiscopal throne of Cæsarea, discovered to the world, and perhaps to himself, the pride of his character; and the first favour which he condescended to bestow on his friend was received, and perhaps was intended, as a cruel insult.[1] Instead of employing the superior talents of Gregory in some useful and conspicuous station, the haughty prelate selected, among the fifty bishoprics of his extensive province, the wretched village of Sasima,[2] without water, without verdure, without society, situate at the junction of three highways, and frequented only by the incessant passage of rude and clamorous waggoners. Gregory submitted with reluctance to this humiliating exile: he was ordained bishop of Sasima; but he solemnly protests that he never consummated his spiritual marriage with this disgusting bride. He afterwards consented to undertake the government of his native church of Nazianzus,[3] of which his father had been bishop above five-and-forty years. But as he was still conscious that he deserved another audience and another theatre, he accepted, with no unworthy ambition, the honourable invitation which was addressed to him from the orthodox party of Constantinople. On his arrival in the capital, Gregory was entertained in the house of a pious and charitable kinsman; the most spacious

---

[1] Gregory's Poem on his own Life contains some beautiful lines (tom. ii.p. 8 [ed. Paris, 1609]), which burst from the heart, and speak the pangs of injured and lost friendship:—

> . . . . . πόνοι κοινοὶ λόγων,
> Ὁμόστεγός τε καὶ συνέστιος βίος,
> Νοῦς εἷς ἐν ἀμφοῖν . . . .
> Διεσκέδασται πάντα, κάρριπται χαμαί.
> Αὗραι φέρουσι τὰς παλαιὰς ἐλπίδας.

In the Midsummer Night's Dream, Helena addresses the same pathetic complaint to her friend Hermia:—

> Is all the counsel that we two have shared,
> The sisters' vows, etc.

Shakspeare had never read the poems of Gregory Nazianzen; he was ignorant of the Greek language; but his mother-tongue, the language of Nature, is the same in Cappadocia and in Britain.

[2] This unfavourable portrait of Sasima is drawn by Gregory Nazianzen (tom. ii. de Vitâ suâ, p. 7, 8). Its precise situation, forty-nine miles from Archelais, and thirty-two from Tyana, is fixed in the Itinerary of Antoninus (p. 144, edit. Wesseling).

[3] The name of Nazianzus has been immortalised by Gregory; but his native town, under the Greek or Roman title of Diocæsarea (Tillemont, Mém. Ecclés. tom. ix. p. 692), is mentioned by Pliny (vi. 3), Ptolemy, and Hierocles (Itinerar. Wesseling, p. 709). It appears to have been situate on the edge of Isauria.

room was consecrated to the uses of religious worship; and the name of *Anastasia* was chosen to express the resurrection of the Nicene faith. This private conventicle was afterwards converted into a magnificent church; and the credulity of the succeeding age was prepared to believe the miracles and visions which attested the presence, or at least the protection, of the Mother of God.[1] The pulpit of the Anastasia was the scene of the labours and triumphs of Gregory Nazianzen; and in the space of two years he experienced all the spiritual adventures which constitute the prosperous or adverse fortunes of a missionary.[2] The Arians, who were provoked by the boldness of his enterprise, represented his doctrine as if he had preached three distinct and equal Deities; and the devout populace was excited to suppress, by violence and tumult, the irregular assemblies of the Athanasian heretics. From the cathedral of St. Sophia there issued a motley crowd "of common beggars, who had forfeited their claim to pity; of monks, who had the appearance of goats or satyrs; and of women, more terrible than so many Jezebels." The doors of the Anastasia were broke open; much mischief was perpetrated, or attempted, with sticks, stones, and firebrands; and as a man lost his life in the affray, Gregory, who was summoned the next morning before the magistrate, had the satisfaction of supposing that he publicly confessed the name of Christ. After he was delivered from the fear and danger of a foreign enemy, his infant church was disgraced and distracted by intestine faction. A stranger, who assumed the name of Maximus[3] and the cloak of a Cynic philosopher, insinuated himself into the confidence of Gregory, deceived and abused his favourable opinion, and, forming a secret connection with some bishops of Egypt, attempted, by a clandestine ordination, to supplant his patron in the episcopal seat of Constantinople. These mortifications might sometimes tempt the Cappadocian missionary to regret his obscure solitude. But his fatigues were rewarded by the daily increase of his fame and his congregation; and he enjoyed the pleasure of observing that the greater part of his numerous audience retired from his sermons

---

[1] See Ducange, Constant. Christiana, l. iv. p. 141, 142. The θεία δύναμις of Sozomen (l. vii. c. 5) is interpreted to mean the Virgin Mary.

[2] Tillemont (Mém. Ecclés. tom. ix. p. 432, etc.) diligently collects, enlarges, and explains, the oratorical and poetical hints of Gregory himself.

[3] He pronounced an oration (tom. i. Orat. xxiii. p. 409) in his praise; but after their quarrel the name of Maximus was changed into that of Heron (see Jerom, tom. i. in Catalog. Script. Eccles. p. 301 [tom. ii. p. 930, ed. Vallars.]). I touch slightly on these obscure and personal squabbles.

satisfied with the eloquence of the preacher,[1] or dissatisfied with the manifold imperfections of their faith and practice.[2]

The catholics of Constantinople were animated with joyful confidence by the baptism and edict of Theodosius; and they impatiently waited the effects of his gracious promise. Their hopes were speedily accomplished; and the emperor, as soon as he had finished the operations of the campaign, made his public entry into the capital at the head of a victorious army. The next day after his arrival he summoned Damophilus to his presence, and offered that Arian prelate the hard alternative of subscribing the Nicene creed, or of instantly resigning, to the orthodox believers, the use and possession of the episcopal palace, the cathedral of St. Sophia, and all the churches of Constantinople. The zeal of Damophilus, which in a catholic saint would have been justly applauded, embraced, without hesitation, a life of poverty and exile,[3] and his removal was immediately followed by the purification of the Imperial city. The Arians might complain, with some appearance of justice, that an inconsiderable congregation of sectaries should usurp the hundred churches which they were insufficient to fill, whilst the far greater part of the people was cruelly excluded from every place of religious worship. Theodosius was still inexorable; but as the angels who protected the catholic cause were only visible to the eyes of faith, he prudently reinforced those heavenly legions with the more effectual aid of temporal and carnal weapons, and the church of St. Sophia was occupied by a large body of the Imperial guards. If the mind of Gregory was susceptible of pride, he must have felt a very lively satisfaction when the emperor conducted him through the streets in solemn triumph, and, with his own hand, respectfully placed him on the archiepiscopal throne of Constantinople. But the saint (who had not subdued the imperfections of human virtue) was deeply affected by the mortifying consideration that his entrance into the fold was that of a wolf rather than of a shepherd; that the glittering arms which surrounded his person were necessary for

---

[1] Under the modest emblem of a dream, Gregory (tom. ii. Carmen ix. p. 78) describes his own success with some human complacency. Yet it should seem, from his familiar conversation with his auditor St. Jerom (tom. i. Epist. ad Nepotian. p. 14 [tom. i. p. 261, ed. Vallars.]), that the preacher understood the true value of popular applause.

[2] Lacrimæ auditorum laudes tuæ sint, is the lively and judicious advice of St. Jerom [loc. cit.].

[3] Socrates (l. v. c. 7) and Sozomen (l. vii. c. 5) relate the evangelical words and actions of Damophilus without a word of approbation. He considered, says Socrates, that it is difficult to *resist* the powerful; but it was easy, and would have been profitable, to *submit*.

his safety; and that he alone was the object of the imprecations of a great party, whom, as men and citizens, it was impossible for him to despise. He beheld the innumerable multitude, of either sex, and of every age, who crowded the streets, the windows, and the roofs of the houses; he heard the tumultuous voice of rage, grief, astonishment, and despair; and Gregory fairly confesses that on the memorable day of his installation the capital of the East wore the appearance of a city taken by storm, and in the hands of a barbarian conqueror.[1] About six weeks afterwards, Theodosius declared his resolution of expelling from all the churches of his dominions the bishops and their clergy who should obstinately refuse to believe, or at least to profess, the doctrine of the council of Nice. His lieutenant Sapor was armed with the ample powers of a general law, a special commission, and a military force;[2] and this ecclesiastical revolution was conducted with so much discretion and vigour, that the religion of the emperor was established, without tumult or bloodshed, in all the provinces of the East. The writings of the Arians, if they had been permitted to exist,[3] would perhaps contain the lamentable story of the persecution which afflicted the church under the reign of the impious Theodosius; and the sufferings of *their* holy confessors might claim the pity of the disinterested reader. Yet there is reason to imagine that the violence of zeal and revenge was in some measure eluded by the want of resistance; and that, in their adversity, the Arians displayed much less firmness than had been exerted by the orthodox party under the reigns of Constantius and Valens. The moral character and conduct of the hostile sects appear to have been governed by the same common principles of nature and religion: but a very material circumstance may be discovered, which tended to distinguish the degrees of their theological faith. Both parties in the schools, as well as in the temples, acknowledged and worshipped the divine majesty of Christ; and, as we are always prone to impute our own sentiments and passions to the Deity, it would be deemed more prudent and respectful to

---

[1] See Gregory Nazianzen, tom. ii. de Vitâ suâ, p. 21, 22. For the sake of posterity, the bishop of Constantinople records a stupendous prodigy. In the month of November, it was a cloudy morning, but the sun broke forth when the procession entered the church.

[2] Of the three ecclesiastical historians, Theodoret alone (l. v. c. 2) has mentioned this important commission of Sapor, which Tillemont (Hist. des Empereurs, tom. v. p. 728), judiciously removes from the reign of Gratian to that of Theodosius.

[3] I do not reckon Philostorgius, though he mentions (l. ix. c. 19) the expulsion of Damophilus. The Eunomian historian has been carefully strained through an orthodox sieve.

exaggerate than to circumscribe the adorable perfections of the Son of God. The disciple of Athanasius exulted in the proud confidence that he had entitled himself to the divine favour, while the follower of Arius must have been tormented by the secret apprehension that he was guilty perhaps of an unpardonable offence by the scanty praise and parsimonious honours which he bestowed on the Judge of the World. The opinions of Arianism might satisfy a cold and speculative mind; but the doctrine of the Nicene Creed, most powerfully recommended by the merits of faith and devotion, was much better adapted to become popular and successful in a believing age.

The hope that truth and wisdom would be found in the assemblies of the orthodox clergy induced the emperor to convene, at Constantinople, a synod of one hundred and fifty bishops, who proceeded, without much difficulty or delay, to complete the theological system which had been established in the council of Nice. The vehement disputes of the fourth century had been chiefly employed on the nature of the Son of God; and the various opinions which were embraced concerning the *Second*, were extended and transferred, by a natural analogy, to the *Third* person of the Trinity.[1] Yet it was found, or it was thought, necessary, by the victorious adversaries of Arianism, to explain the ambiguous language of some respectable doctors; to confirm the faith of the catholics; and to condemn an unpopular and inconsistent sect of Macedonians, who freely admitted that the Son was consubstantial to the Father, while they were fearful of seeming to acknowledge the existence of *Three* Gods. A final and unanimous sentence was pronounced to ratify the equal Deity of the Holy Ghost: the mysterious doctrine has been received by all the nations, and all the churches, of the Christian world; and their grateful reverence has assigned to the bishops of Theodosius the second rank among the general councils.[2] Their knowledge of religious truth may have been preserved by tradition, or it may have been communicated by inspiration; but

---

[1] Le Clerc has given a curious extract (Bibliothèque Universelle, tom. xviii. p. 91-105) of the theological sermons which Gregory Nazianzen pronounced at Constantinople against the Arians, Eunomians, Macedonians, etc. He tells the Macedonians, who deified the Father and the Son, without the Holy Ghost, that they might as well be styled *Tritheists* as *Ditheists*. Gregory himself was almost a Tritheist, and his monarchy of heaven resembles a well-regulated aristocracy.

[2] The first general council of Constantinople now triumphs in the Vatican; but the popes had long hesitated, and their hesitation perplexes and almost staggers the humble Tillemont (Mém. Ecclés. tom. ix. p. 499, 500).

the sober evidence of history will not allow much weight to the personal authority of the Fathers of Constantinople. In an age when the ecclesiastics had scandalously degenerated from the model of apostolical purity, the most worthless and corrupt were always the most eager to frequent and disturb the episcopal assemblies. The conflict and fermentation of so many opposite interests and tempers inflamed the passions of the bishops: and their ruling passions were, the love of gold and the love of dispute. Many of the same prelates who now applauded the orthodox piety of Theodosius had repeatedly changed, with prudent flexibility, their creeds and opinions; and in the various revolutions of the church and state, the religion of their sovereign was the rule of their obsequious faith. When the emperor suspended his prevailing influence, the turbulent synod was blindly impelled by the absurd or selfish motives of pride, hatred, and resentment. The death of Meletius, which happened at the council of Constantinople, presented the most favourable opportunity of terminating the schism of Antioch, by suffering his aged rival, Paulinus, peaceably to end his days in the episcopal chair. The faith and virtues of Paulinus were unblemished. But his cause was supported by the Western churches; and the bishops of the synod resolved to perpetuate the mischiefs of discord, by the hasty ordination of a perjured candidate,[1] rather than to betray the imagined dignity of the East, which had been illustrated by the birth and death of the Son of God. Such unjust and disorderly proceedings forced the gravest members of the assembly to dissent and to secede; and the clamorous majority, which remained masters of the field of battle, could be compared only to wasps or magpies, to a flight of cranes, or to a flock of geese.[2]

A suspicion may possibly arise that so unfavourable a picture of ecclesiastical synods has been drawn by the partial hand of some obstinate heretic or some malicious infidel. But the name of the sincere historian who has conveyed this instructive lesson

---

[1] Before the death of Meletius, six or eight of his most popular ecclesiastics, among whom was Flavian, had *abjured*, for the sake of peace, the bishopric of Antioch (Sozomen, l. vii. c. 3, 11; Socrates, l. v. c. 5). Tillemont thinks it his duty to disbelieve the story; but he owns that there are many circumstances in the life of Flavian which *seem* inconsistent with the praises of Chrysostom and the character of a saint (Mém. Ecclés. tom. x. p. 541).

[2] Consult Gregory Nazianzen, de Vitâ suâ, tom. ii. p. 25-28. His general and particular opinion of the clergy and their assemblies may be seen in verse and prose (tom. i. Orat. i. p. 33; Epist. lv. p. 814, tom. ii.; Carmen x. p. 81). Such passages are faintly marked by Tillemont, and fairly produced by Le Clerc.

to the knowledge of posterity must silence the impotent murmurs of superstition and bigotry. He was one of the most pious and eloquent bishops of the age; a saint, and a doctor of the church; the scourge of Arianism, and the pillar of the orthodox faith; a distinguished member of the council of Constantinople, in which, after the death of Meletius, he exercised the functions of president: in a word—Gregory Nazianzen himself. The harsh and ungenerous treatment which he experienced,[1] instead of derogating from the truth of his evidence, affords an additional proof of the spirit which actuated the deliberations of the synod. Their unanimous suffrage had confirmed the pretensions which the bishop of Constantinople derived from the choice of the people and the approbation of the emperor. But Gregory soon became the victim of malice and envy. The bishops of the East, his strenuous adherents, provoked by his moderation in the affairs of Antioch, abandoned him, without support, to the adverse faction of the Egyptians, who disputed the validity of his election and rigorously asserted the obsolete canon that prohibited the licentious practice of episcopal translations. The pride, or the humility, of Gregory, prompted him to decline a contest which might have been imputed to ambition and avarice; and he publicly offered, not without some mixture of indignation, to renounce the government of a church which had been restored, and almost created, by his labours. His resignation was accepted by the synod, and by the emperor, with more readiness than he seems to have expected. At the time when he might have hoped to enjoy the fruits of his victory, his episcopal throne was filled by the senator Nectarius; and the new archbishop, accidentally recommended by his easy temper and venerable aspect, was obliged to delay the ceremony of his consecration till he had previously despatched the rites of his baptism.[2] After this remarkable experience of the ingratitude of princes and prelates, Gregory retired once more to his obscure solitude of Cappadocia, where he employed the remainder of his life, about eight years, in the exercises of poetry and devotion. The title of Saint has

---

[1] See Gregory, tom. ii. de Vitâ suâ, p. 28-31. The fourteenth, twenty-seventh, and thirty-second Orations were pronounced in the several stages of this business. The peroration of the last (tom. i. p. 528), in which he takes a solemn leave of men and angels, the city and the emperor, the East and the West, etc., is pathetic, and almost sublime.

[2] The whimsical ordination of Nectarius is attested by Sozomen (l. vii. c. 8); but Tillemont observes (Mém. Ecclés. tom. ix. p. 719), Après tout, ce narré de Sozomène est si honteux pour tous ceux qu'il y mêle, et surtout pour Théodose, qu'il vaut mieux travailler à le détruire qu'à le soutenir: an admirable canon of criticism!

been added to his name: but the tenderness of his heart,[1] and the elegance of his genius, reflect a more pleasing lustre on the memory of Gregory Nazianzen.

It was not enough that Theodosius had suppressed the insolent reign of Arianism, or that he had abundantly revenged the injuries which the catholics sustained from the zeal of Constantius and Valens. The orthodox emperor considered every heretic as a rebel against the supreme powers of heaven and of earth; and each of those powers might exercise their peculiar jurisdiction over the soul and body of the guilty. The decrees of the council of Constantinople had ascertained the true standard of the faith; and the ecclesiastics who governed the conscience of Theodosius suggested the most effectual methods of persecution. In the space of fifteen years he promulgated at least fifteen severe edicts against the heretics,[2] more especially against those who rejected the doctrine of the Trinity; and to deprive them of every hope of escape, he sternly enacted that, if any laws or rescripts should be alleged in their favour, the judges should consider them as the illegal productions either of fraud or forgery. The penal statutes were directed against the ministers, the assemblies, and the persons of the heretics; and the passions of the legislator were expressed in the language of declamation and invective. I. The heretical teachers, who usurped the sacred titles of Bishops or Presbyters, were not only excluded from the privileges and emoluments so liberally granted to the orthodox clergy, but they were exposed to the heavy penalties of exile and confiscation, if they presumed to preach the doctrine, or to practise the rites, of their *accursed* sects. A fine of ten pounds of gold (above four hundred pounds sterling) was imposed on every person who should dare to confer, or receive, or promote, an heretical ordination: and it was reasonably expected that, if the race of pastors could be extinguished, their helpless flocks would be compelled, by ignorance and hunger, to return within the pale of the catholic church. II. The rigorous prohibition of conventicles was carefully extended to every possible circumstance in which the heretics could assemble with the intention of worshipping God and Christ according to the dictates of their conscience. Their religious meetings, whether public or secret, by day or by night, in cities

---

[1] I can only be understood to mean that such was his natural temper when it was not hardened or inflamed by religious zeal. From his retirement he exhorts Nectarius to prosecute the heretics of Constantinople.

[2] See the Theodosian Code, l. xvi. tit. v. leg. 6-23, with Godefroy's commentary on each law, and his general summary, or *Paratitlon*, tom. vi. p. 104-110.

or in the country, were equally proscribed by the edicts of Theodosius; and the building, or ground, which had been used for that illegal purpose, was forfeited to the Imperial domain.   III. It was supposed that the error of the heretics could proceed only from the obstinate temper of their minds; and that such a temper was a fit object of censure and punishment.   The anathemas of the church were fortified by a sort of civil excommunication, which separated them from their fellow-citizens by a peculiar brand of infamy; and this declaration of the supreme magistrate tended to justify, or at least to excuse, the insults of a fanatic populace.   The sectaries were gradually disqualified for the possession of honourable or lucrative employments; and Theodosius was satisfied with his own justice, when he decreed that, as the Eunomians distinguished the nature of the Son from that of the Father, they should be incapable of making their wills, or of receiving any advantage from testamentary donations. The guilt of the Manichæan heresy was esteemed of such magnitude that it could be expiated only by the death of the offender; and the same capital punishment was inflicted on the Audians, or *Quartodecimans*,[1] who should dare to perpetrate the atrocious crime of celebrating on an improper day the festival of Easter. Every Roman might exercise the right of public accusation; but the office of *Inquisitors* of the Faith, a name so deservedly abhorred, was first instituted under the reign of Theodosius. Yet we are assured that the execution of his penal edicts was seldom enforced; and that the pious emperor appeared less desirous to punish than to reclaim or terrify his refractory subjects.[2]

The theory of persecution was established by Theodosius, whose justice and piety have been applauded by the saints; but the practice of it, in the fullest extent, was reserved for his rival and colleague, Maximus, the first among the Christian princes who shed the blood of his Christian subjects on account of their religious opinions.   The cause of the Priscillianists,[3]

---

[1] They always kept their Easter, like the Jewish Passover, on the fourteenth day of the first moon after the vernal equinox; and thus pertinaciously opposed the Roman church and Nicene synod, which had *fixed* Easter to a Sunday. Bingham's Antiquities, l. xx. c. 5, vol. ii. p. 309, fol. edit.

[2] Sozomen, l. vii. c. 12.

[3] See the Sacred History of Sulpicius Severus (l. ii. p. 437-452, edit. Lugd. Bat. 1647), a correct and original writer.   Dr. Lardner (Credibility, etc., part ii. vol. ix. p. 256-350) has laboured this article with pure learning, good sense, and moderation. Tillemont (Mém. Ecclés. tom. viii. p. 491-527) has raked together all the dirt of the fathers—an useful scavenger!

a recent sect of heretics who disturbed the provinces of Spain, was transferred, by appeal, from the synod of Bordeaux to the Imperial consistory of Trèves; and by the sentence of the Prætorian præfect, seven persons were tortured, condemned, and executed. The first of these was Priscillian [1] himself, bishop of Avila,[2] in Spain, who adorned the advantages of birth and fortune by the accomplishments of eloquence and learning. Two presbyters and two deacons accompanied their beloved master in his death, which they esteemed as a glorious martyrdom; and the number of religious victims was completed by the execution of Latronian, a poet, who rivalled the fame of the ancients; and of Euchrocia, a noble matron of Bordeaux, the widow of the orator Delphidius.[3] Two bishops, who had embraced the sentiments of Priscillian, were condemned to a distant and dreary exile;[4] and some indulgence was shown to the meaner criminals who assumed the merit of an early repentance. If any credit could be allowed to confessions extorted by fear or pain, and to vague reports, the offspring of malice and credulity, the heresy of the Priscillianists would be found to include the various abominations of magic, of impiety, and of lewdness.[5] Priscillian, who wandered about the world in the company of his spiritual sisters, was accused of praying stark-naked in the midst of the congregation; and it was confidently asserted, that the effects of his criminal intercourse with the daughter of Euchrocia had been suppressed by means still more odious and criminal. But an accurate, or rather a candid inquiry, will discover that, if the Priscillianists violated the laws of nature, it was not by the licentiousness, but by the austerity of their lives. They absolutely condemned the use of the marriage-bed; and the peace of families was often disturbed by indiscreet separations.

---

[1] Sulpicius Severus mentions the arch-heretic with esteem and pity. Felix profecto, si non pravo studio corrupisset optimum ingenium; prorsus multa in eo animi et corporis bona cerneres. (Hist. Sacra, l. ii. p. 439.) Even Jerom (tom. i. in Script. Eccles. p. 302 [tom. ii. p. 934, ed. Vallars.]) speaks with temper of Priscillian and Latronian.

[2] The bishopric (in Old Castile) is now worth 20,000 ducats a-year (Busching's Geography, vol. ii. p. 308), and is therefore much less likely to produce the author of a new heresy.

[3] Exprobrabatur mulieri viduæ nimia religio, et diligentius culta divinitas (Pacat. in Panegyr. Vet. xii. 29). Such was the idea of a humane though ignorant polytheist.

[4] One of them was sent in Syllinam insulam quæ ultra Britanniam est. What must have been the ancient condition of the rocks of Scilly (Camden's Britannia, vol. ii. p. 1519)?

[5] The scandalous calumnies of Augustin, pope Leo, etc., which Tillemont swallows like a child, and Lardner refutes like a man, may suggest some candid suspicions in favour of the older Gnostics.

They enjoined, or recommended, a total abstinence from all animal food; and their continual prayers, fasts, and vigils, inculcated a rule of strict and perfect devotion. The speculative tenets of the sect, concerning the person of Christ and the nature of the human soul, were derived from the Gnostic and Manichæan system; and this vain philosophy, which had been transported from Egypt to Spain, was ill adapted to the grosser spirits of the West. The obscure disciples of Priscillian suffered, languished, and gradually disappeared: his tenets were rejected by the clergy and people, but his death was the subject of a long and vehement controversy; while some arraigned, and others applauded, the justice of his sentence. It is with pleasure that we can observe the humane inconsistency of the most illustrious saints and bishops, Ambrose of Milan [1] and Martin of Tours,[2] who, on this occasion, asserted the cause of toleration. They pitied the unhappy men who had been executed at Trèves; they refused to hold communion with their episcopal murderers; and if Martin deviated from that generous resolution, his motives were laudable, and his repentance was exemplary. The bishops of Tours and Milan pronounced, without hesitation, the eternal damnation of heretics; but they were surprised and shocked by the bloody image of their temporal death, and the honest feelings of nature resisted the artificial prejudices of theology. The humanity of Ambrose and Martin was confirmed by the scandalous irregularity of the proceedings against Priscillian and his adherents. The civil and ecclesiastical ministers had transgressed the limits of their respective provinces. The secular judge had presumed to receive an appeal, and to pronounce a definitive sentence, in a matter of faith and episcopal jurisdiction. The bishops had disgraced themselves by exercising the functions of accusers in a criminal prosecution. The cruelty of Ithacius,[3] who beheld the tortures, and solicited the death of the heretics, provoked the just indignation of mankind; and the vices of that profligate bishop were admitted as a proof that his zeal was instigated by the sordid motives of interest. Since the death of Priscillian, the rude attempts of persecution have been refined and methodised in the holy office, which assigns their distinct parts to the eccle-

---

[1] Ambros. tom. ii. Epist. xxiv. p. 891.

[2] In the Sacred History, and the Life of St. Martin, Sulpicius Severus uses some caution; but he declares himself more freely in the Dialogues (iii. 15). Martin was reproved, however, by his own conscience and by an angel; nor could he afterwards perform miracles with so much ease.

[3] The catholic presbyter (Sulp. Sever. l. ii. p. 448), and the Pagan orator (Pacat. in Panegyr. Vet. xii. 29), reprobate with equal indignation the character and conduct of Ithacius.

siastical and secular powers. The devoted victim is regularly delivered by the priest to the magistrate, and by the magistrate to the executioner; and the inexorable sentence of the church, which declares the spiritual guilt of the offender, is expressed in the mild language of pity and intercession.

Among the ecclesiastics who illustrated the reign of Theodosius, Gregory Nazianzen was distinguished by the talents of an eloquent preacher; the reputation of miraculous gifts added weight and dignity to the monastic virtues of Martin of Tours; [1] but the palm of episcopal vigour and ability was justly claimed by the intrepid Ambrose.[2] He was descended from a noble family of Romans; his father had exercised the important office of Prætorian præfect of Gaul; and the son, after passing through the studies of a liberal education, attained, in the regular gradation of civil honours, the station of consular of Liguria, a province which included the Imperial residence of Milan. At the age of thirty-four, and before he had received the sacrament of baptism, Ambrose, to his own surprise and to that of the world, was suddenly transformed from a governor to an archbishop. Without the least mixture, as it is said, of art or intrigue, the whole body of the people unanimously saluted him with the episcopal title; the concord and perseverance of their acclamations were ascribed to a preternatural impulse; and the reluctant magistrate was compelled to undertake a spiritual office for which he was not prepared by the habits and occupations of his former life. But the active force of his genius soon qualified him to exercise, with zeal and prudence, the duties of his ecclesiastical jurisdiction; and while he cheerfully renounced the vain and splendid trappings of temporal greatness, he condescended, for the good of the church, to direct the conscience of the emperors, and to control the administration of the empire. Gratian loved and revered him as a father; and the elaborate treatise on the faith of the Trinity was designed for the instruction of the young prince. After his tragic death, at a time when the empress Justina trembled for her own safety, and for that of her son Valentinian, the archbishop of Milan was despatched on two different embassies to the court of Trèves. He exercised, with

---

[1] The Life of St. Martin, and the Dialogues concerning his miracles contain facts adapted to the grossest barbarism, in a style not unworthy of the Augustan age. So natural is the alliance between good taste and good sense, that I am always astonished by this contrast.

[2] The short and superficial Life of St. Ambrose, by his deacon Paulinus (Appendix ad edit. Benedict. p. i.-xv.), has the merit of original evidence. Tillemont (Mém. Ecclés. tom. x. p. 78-306) and the Benedictine editor (p. xxxi.-lxiii.) have laboured with their usual diligence.

equal firmness and dexterity, the powers of his spiritual and political characters; and perhaps contributed, by his authority and eloquence, to check the ambition of Maximus, and to protect the peace of Italy.[1] Ambrose had devoted his life and his abilities to the service of the church. Wealth was the object of his contempt; he had renounced his private patrimony; and he sold, without hesitation, the consecrated plate for the redemption of captives. The clergy and people of Milan were attached to their archbishop; and he deserved the esteem, without soliciting the favour, or apprehending the displeasure, of his feeble sovereigns.

The government of Italy, and of the young emperor, naturally devolved to his mother Justina, a woman of beauty and spirit, but who, in the midst of an orthodox people, had the misfortune of professing the Arian heresy, which she endeavoured to instil into the mind of her son. Justina was persuaded that a Roman emperor might claim, in his own dominions, the public exercise of his religion; and she proposed to the archbishop, as a moderate and reasonable concession, that he should resign the use of a single church, either in the city or suburbs of Milan. But the conduct of Ambrose was governed by very different principles.[2] The palaces of the earth might indeed belong to Cæsar, but the churches were the houses of God; and, within the limits of his diocese, he himself, as the lawful successor of the apostles, was the only minister of God. The privileges of Christianity, temporal as well as spiritual, were confined to the true believers; and the mind of Ambrose was satisfied that his own theological opinions were the standard of truth and orthodoxy. The archbishop, who refused to hold any conference or negotiation with the instruments of Satan, declared, with modest firmness, his resolution to die a martyr rather than to yield to the impious sacrilege; and Justina, who resented the refusal as an act of insolence and rebellion, hastily determined to exert the Imperial prerogative of her son. As she desired to perform her public devotions on the approaching festival of Easter, Ambrose was ordered to appear before the council. He obeyed the summons with the respect of a faithful subject, but he was followed, without his consent, by an innumerable people: they pressed, with impetuous

[1] Ambrose himself (tom. ii. Epist. xxiv. p. 888-891) gives the emperor a very spirited account of his own embassy.
[2] His own representation of his principles and conduct (tom. ii. Epist. xx. xxi. xxii. p. 852-880) is one of the curious monuments of ecclesiastical antiquity. It contains two letters to his sister Marcellina, with a petition to Valentinian, and the sermon de Basilicis non tradendis.

zeal, against the gates of the palace; and the affrighted ministers of Valentinian, instead of pronouncing a sentence of exile on the archbishop of Milan, humbly requested that he would interpose his authority to protect the person of the emperor, and to restore the tranquillity of the capital. But the promises which Ambrose received and communicated were soon violated by a perfidious court; and, during six of the most solemn days which Christian piety has set apart for the exercise of religion, the city was agitated by the irregular convulsions of tumult and fanaticism. The officers of the household were directed to prepare, first the Portian, and afterwards the new, *Basilica*, for the immediate reception of the emperor and his mother. The splendid canopy and hangings of the royal seat were arranged in the customary manner; but it was found necessary to defend them, by a strong guard, from the insults of the populace. The Arian ecclesiastics who ventured to show themselves in the streets were exposed to the most imminent danger of their lives; and Ambrose enjoyed the merit and reputation of rescuing his personal enemies from the hands of the enraged multitude.

But while he laboured to restrain the effects of their zeal, the pathetic vehemence of his sermons continually inflamed the angry and seditious temper of the people of Milan. The characters of Eve, of the wife of Job, of Jezebel, of Herodias, were indecently applied to the mother of the emperor; and her desire to obtain a church for the Arians was compared to the most cruel persecutions which Christianity had endured under the reign of Paganism. The measures of the court served only to expose the magnitude of the evil. A fine of two hundred pounds of gold was imposed on the corporate body of merchants and manufacturers: an order was signified, in the name of the emperor, to all the officers and inferior servants of the courts of justice, that, during the continuance of the public disorders, they should strictly confine themselves to their houses: and the ministers of Valentinian imprudently confessed that the most respectable part of the citizens of Milan was attached to the cause of their archbishop. He was again solicited to restore peace to his country, by a timely compliance with the will of his sovereign. The reply of Ambrose was couched in the most humble and respectful terms, which might, however, be interpreted as a serious declaration of civil war. " His life and fortune were in the hands of the emperor; but he would never betray the church of Christ, or degrade the dignity of the episcopal character. In such a cause he was prepared to suffer whatever the malice of the dæmon could inflict; and he only wished to die in the presence of his faithful flock, and at the foot of the altar; *he* had not contributed to excite, but it was in the power of God alone to appease, the rage of the people: he deprecated the scenes of blood and confusion which were likely to ensue; and it was his fervent prayer that he might not survive to behold the ruin of a flourishing city, and perhaps the desolation of all Italy." [1] The obstinate bigotry of Justina would have endangered the empire of her son, if, in this contest with the church and people of Milan, she could have depended on the active obedience of the troops of the palace. A large body of Goths had marched to occupy the *Basilica*, which was the object of the dispute: and it might be expected from the Arian principles and barbarous manners of these foreign mercenaries, that they would not entertain any scruples in the execution of the most sanguinary orders. They were encountered on the sacred threshold by the archbishop, who, thundering against them a sentence of excommunication, asked them, in the tone of a father and a master, Whether it was to invade the house of God that they had implored the hospitable protection of the republic? The suspense of the barbarians allowed some hours for a more effectual negotiation; and the empress was persuaded by the advice of her wisest counsellors to leave the catholics in possession of all the churches of Milan; and to dissemble, till a more convenient season, her intentions of revenge. The mother of Valentinian could never forgive the triumph of Ambrose: and the royal youth uttered a passionate exclamation, that his own servants were ready to betray him into the hands of an insolent priest.

The laws of the empire, some of which were inscribed with the name of Valentinian, still condemned the Arian heresy, and seemed to excuse the resistance of the catholics. By the influence of Justina, an edict of toleration was promulgated in all the provinces which were subject to the court of Milan; the free exercise of their religion was granted to those who professed the faith of Rimini; and the emperor declared that all persons who should infringe this sacred and salutary constitution should be capitally punished, as the enemies of the public peace. [2] The

---

[1] Retz had a similar message from the queen to request that he would appease the tumult of Paris. It was no longer in his power, etc. A quoi j'ajoutai tout ce que vous pouvez vous imaginer de respect, de douleur, de regret, et de soumission, etc. (Mémoires, tom. i. p. 140). Certainly I do not compare either the causes or the men; yet the coadjutor himself had some idea (p. 84) of imitating St. Ambrose.

[2] Sozomen alone (l. vii. c. 13) throws this luminous fact into a dark and perplexed narrative.

character and language of the archbishop of Milan may justify
the suspicion that his conduct soon afforded a reasonable ground,
or at least a specious pretence, to the Arian ministers, who
watched the opportunity of surprising him in some act of disobedience to a law which he strangely represents as a law of
blood and tyranny. A sentence of easy and honourable banishment was pronounced, which enjoined Ambrose to depart from
Milan without delay, whilst it permitted him to choose the place
of his exile and the number of his companions. But the authority
of the saints, who have preached and practised the maxims of
passive loyalty, appeared to Ambrose of less moment than the
extreme and pressing danger of the church. He boldly refused
to obey; and his refusal was supported by the unanimous
consent of his faithful people.[1] They guarded by turns the person
of their archbishop; the gates of the cathedral and the episcopal
palace were strongly secured; and the Imperial troops, who had
formed the blockade, were unwilling to risk the attack of that
impregnable fortress. The numerous poor, who had been relieved
by the liberality of Ambrose, embraced the fair occasion of
signalising their zeal and gratitude; and as the patience of the
multitude might have been exhausted by the length and uni-
formity of nocturnal vigils, he prudently introduced into the
church of Milan the useful institution of a loud and regular
psalmody. While he maintained this arduous contest, he was
instructed, by a dream, to open the earth in a place where the
remains of two martyrs, Gervasius and Protasius,[2] had been
deposited above three hundred years. Immediately under the
pavement of the church two perfect skeletons were found,[3] with
the heads separated from their bodies, and a plentiful effusion
of blood. The holy relics were presented, in solemn pomp, to
the veneration of the people; and every circumstance of this
fortunate discovery was admirably adapted to promote the
designs of Ambrose. The bones of the martyrs, their blood,
their garments, were supposed to contain a healing power; and

[1] Excubabat pia plebs in ecclesiâ mori parata cum episcopo suo . . .
Nos adhuc frigidi excitabamur tamen civitate attonitâ atque turbatâ.
Augustin. Confession. l. ix. c. 7.

[2] Tillemont, Mém. Ecclés. tom. ii. p. 78, 498. Many churches in Italy,
Gaul, etc., were dedicated to these unknown martyrs, of whom St. Gervase
seems to have been more fortunate than his companion.

[3] Invenimus miræ magnitudinis viros duos, ut prisca ætas ferebat, tom.
ii. Epist. xxii. p. 875. The size of these skeletons was fortunately, or
skilfully, suited to the popular prejudice of the gradual decrease of the
human stature, which has prevailed in every age since the time of Homer.

Grandiaque effossis mirabitur ossa sepulchris.

the preternatural influence was communicated to the most distant objects, without losing any part of its original virtue. The extraordinary cure of a blind man,[1] and the reluctant confessions of several dæmoniacs, appeared to justify the faith and sanctity of Ambrose; and the truth of those miracles is attested by Ambrose himself, by his secretary Paulinus, and by his proselyte, the celebrated Augustin, who, at that time, professed the art of rhetoric in Milan. The reason of the present age may possibly approve the incredulity of Justina and her Arian court, who derided the theatrical representations which were exhibited by the contrivance, and at the expense, of the archbishop.[2] Their effect, however, on the minds of the people, was rapid and irresistible; and the feeble sovereign of Italy found himself unable to contend with the favourite of Heaven. The powers likewise of the earth interposed in the defence of Ambrose: the disinterested advice of Theodosius was the genuine result of piety and friendship; and the mask of religious zeal concealed the hostile and ambitious designs of the tyrant of Gaul.[3]

The reign of Maximus might have ended in peace and prosperity, could he have contented himself with the possession of three ample countries, which now constitute the three most flourishing kingdoms of modern Europe. But the aspiring usurper, whose sordid ambition was not dignified by the love of glory and of arms, considered his actual forces as the instruments only of his future greatness, and his success was the immediate cause of his destruction. The wealth which he extorted [4] from the oppressed provinces of Gaul, Spain, and Britain, was employed in levying and maintaining a formidable army of barbarians, collected, for the most part, from the fiercest nations of Germany. The conquest of Italy was the object of his hopes and preparations; and he secretly meditated the ruin of an innocent youth, whose government was abhorred and despised by his catholic subjects. But as Maximus wished to occupy, without resistance,

---

[1] Ambros. tom. ii. Epist. xxii. p. 875. Augustin. Confes. l. ix. c. 7, de Civitat. Dei, l. xxii. c. 8. Paulin. in Vitâ St. Ambros. c. 14, in Append. Benedict. p. 4. The blind man's name was Severus; he touched the holy garment, recovered his sight, and devoted the rest of his life (at least twenty-five years) to the service of the church. I should recommend this miracle to our divines, if it did not prove the worship of relics as well as the Nicene creed.

[2] Paulin. in Vit. St. Ambros. c. 5 [15]. in Append. Benedict. p. 5.

[3] Tillemont, Mém. Ecclés. tom. x. p. 190, 750. He partially allows the mediation of Theodosius, and capriciously rejects that of Maximus, though it is attested by Prosper, Sozomen, and Theodoret.

[4] The modest censure of Sulpicius (Dialog. iii. 15 [p. 576]) inflicts a much deeper wound than the feeble declamation of Pacatus (xii. 25, 26).

the passes of the Alps, he received, with perfidious smiles, Domninus of Syria, the ambassador of Valentinian, and pressed him to accept the aid of a considerable body of troops for the service of a Pannonian war. The penetration of Ambrose had discovered the snares of an enemy under the professions of friendship;[1] but the Syrian Domninus was corrupted or deceived by the liberal favour of the court of Trèves; and the council of Milan obstinately rejected the suspicion of danger with a blind confidence, which was the effect not of courage, but of fear. The march of the auxiliaries was guided by the ambassador; and they were admitted, without distrust, into the fortresses of the Alps. But the crafty tyrant followed, with hasty and silent footsteps, in the rear; and as he diligently intercepted all intelligence of his motions, the gleam of armour and the dust excited by the troops of cavalry first announced the hostile approach of a stranger to the gates of Milan. In this extremity, Justina and her son might accuse their own imprudence and the perfidious arts of Maximus; but they wanted time, and force, and resolution to stand against the Gauls and Germans, either in the field or within the walls of a large and disaffected city. Flight was their only hope; Aquileia their only refuge: and, as Maximus now displayed his genuine character, the brother of Gratian might expect the same fate from the hands of the same assassin. Maximus entered Milan in triumph; and if the wise archbishop refused a dangerous and criminal connection with the usurper, he might indirectly contribute to the success of his arms by inculcating from the pulpit the duty of resignation rather than that of resistance.[2] The unfortunate Justina reached Aquileia in safety; but she distrusted the strength of the fortifications; she dreaded the event of a siege; and she resolved to implore the protection of the great Theodosius, whose power and virtue were celebrated in all the countries of the West. A vessel was secretly provided to transport the Imperial family; they embarked with precipitation in one of the obscure harbours of Venetia, or Istria; traversed the whole extent of the Hadriatic and Ionian seas; turned the extreme promontory of Peloponnesus; and, after a long but successful navigation, reposed themselves in the port of Thessalonica. All the subjects of Valentinian deserted the cause of a prince who, by his abdication, had

---

[1] Esto tutior adversus hominem, pacis involucro [bellum] tegentem, was the wise caution of Ambrose (tom. ii. p. 891) after his return from his second embassy.

[2] Baronius (A.D. 387, No. 63) applies to this season of public distress some of the penitential sermons of the archbishop.

absolved them from the duty of allegiance; and if the little city of Æmona, on the verge of Italy, had not presumed to stop the career of his inglorious victory, Maximus would have obtained without a struggle the sole possession of the Western empire.

Instead of inviting his royal guests to the palace of Constantinople, Theodosius had some unknown reasons to fix their residence at Thessalonica; but these reasons did not proceed from contempt or indifference, as he speedily made a visit to that city, accompanied by the greatest part of his court and senate. After the first tender expressions of friendship and sympathy, the pious emperor of the East gently admonished Justina that the guilt of heresy was sometimes punished in this world as well as in the next; and that the public profession of the Nicene faith would be the most efficacious step to promote the restoration of her son, by the satisfaction which it must occasion both on earth and in heaven. The momentous question of peace or war was referred by Theodosius to the deliberation of his council; and the arguments which might be alleged on the side of honour and justice had acquired, since the death of Gratian, a considerable degree of additional weight. The persecution of the Imperial family, to which Theodosius himself had been indebted for his fortune, was now aggravated by recent and repeated injuries. Neither oaths nor treaties could restrain the boundless ambition of Maximus; and the delay of vigorous and decisive measures, instead of prolonging the blessings of peace, would expose the Eastern empire to the danger of an hostile invasion. The barbarians who had passed the Danube had lately assumed the character of soldiers and subjects, but their native fierceness was yet untamed; and the operations of a war, which would exercise their valour and diminish their numbers, might tend to relieve the provinces from an intolerable oppression. Notwithstanding these specious and solid reasons, which were approved by a majority of the council, Theodosius still hesitated whether he should draw the sword in a contest which could no longer admit any terms of reconciliation; and his magnanimous character was not disgraced by the apprehensions which he felt for the safety of his infant sons, and the welfare of his exhausted people. In this moment of anxious doubt, while the fate of the Roman world depended on the resolution of a single man, the charms of the princess Galla most powerfully pleaded the cause of her brother Valentinian.[1] The heart of Theodosius was softened

---

[1] The flight of Valentinian and the love of Theodosius for his sister are related by Zosimus (l. iv. [c. 43] p. 263, 264). Tillemont produces some

by the tears of beauty; his affections were insensibly engaged by the graces of youth and innocence; the art of Justina managed and directed the impulse of passion; and the celebration of the royal nuptials was the assurance and signal of the civil war. The unfeeling critics, who consider every amorous weakness as an indelible stain on the memory of a great and orthodox emperor, are inclined on this occasion to dispute the suspicious evidence of the historian Zosimus. For my own part, I shall frankly confess that I am willing to find, or even to seek, in the revolutions of the world some traces of the mild and tender sentiments of domestic life; and amidst the crowd of fierce and ambitious conquerors, I can distinguish, with peculiar complacency, a gentle hero who may be supposed to receive his armour from the hands of love. The alliance of the Persian king was secured by the faith of treaties; the martial barbarians were persuaded to follow the standard or to respect the frontiers of an active and liberal monarch; and the dominions of Theodosius, from the Euphrates to the Hadriatic, resounded with the preparations of war both by land and sea. The skilful disposition of the forces of the East seemed to multiply their numbers, and distracted the attention of Maximus. He had reason to fear that a chosen body of troops, under the command of the intrepid Arbogastes, would direct their march along the banks of the Danube, and boldly penetrate through the Rhætian provinces into the centre of Gaul. A powerful fleet was equipped in the harbours of Greece and Epirus, with an apparent design that, as soon as the passage had been opened by a naval victory, Valentinian and his mother should land in Italy, proceed without delay to Rome, and occupy the majestic seat of religion and empire. In the meanwhile Theodosius himself advanced, at the head of a brave and disciplined army, to encounter his unworthy rival, who, after the siege of Æmona, had fixed his camp in the neighbourhood of Siscia, a city of Pannonia, strongly fortified by the broad and rapid stream of the Save.

The veterans, who still remembered the long resistance, and successive resources, of the tyrant Magnentius, might prepare themselves for the labours of three bloody campaigns. But the contest with his successor, who, like him, had usurped the throne of the West, was easily decided in the term of two months,[1] and within the space of two hundred miles. The superior

weak and ambiguous evidence to antedate the second marriage of Theodosius (Hist. des Empereurs, tom. v. p. 740), and consequently to refute ces contes de Zosime qui seroient trop contraires à la piété de Théodose.

[1] See Godefroy's Chronology of the Laws, Cod. Theodos. tom. i. p. cxix.

genius of the emperor of the East might prevail over the feeble Maximus, who in this important crisis showed himself destitute of military skill or personal courage; but the abilities of Theodosius were seconded by the advantage which he possessed of a numerous and active cavalry. The Huns, the Alani, and, after their example, the Goths themselves, were formed into squadrons of archers, who fought on horseback, and confounded the steady valour of the Gauls and Germans by the rapid motions of a Tartar war. After the fatigue of a long march in the heat of summer they spurred their foaming horses into the waters of the Save, swam the river in the presence of the enemy, and instantly charged and routed the troops who guarded the high ground on the opposite side. Marcellinus, the tyrant's brother, advanced to support them with the select cohorts, which were considered as the hope and strength of the army. The action, which had been interrupted by the approach of night, was renewed in the morning; and, after a sharp conflict, the surviving remnant of the bravest soldiers of Maximus threw down their arms at the feet of the conqueror. Without suspending his march, to receive the loyal acclamations of the citizens of Æmona, Theodosius pressed forwards to terminate the war by the death or captivity of his rival, who fled before him with the diligence of fear. From the summit of the Julian Alps he descended with such incredible speed into the plain of Italy that he reached Aquileia on the evening of the first day; and Maximus, who found himself encompassed on all sides, had scarcely time to shut the gates of the city. But the gates could not long resist the effort of a victorious enemy; and the despair, the disaffection, the indifference of the soldiers and people hastened the downfall of the wretched Maximus. He was dragged from his throne, rudely stripped of the Imperial ornaments, the robe, the diadem, and the purple slippers; and conducted, like a malefactor, to the camp and presence of Theodosius, at a place about three miles from Aquileia. The behaviour of the emperor was not intended to insult, and he showed some disposition to pity and forgive the tyrant of the West, who had never been his personal enemy, and was now become the object of his contempt. Our sympathy is the most forcibly excited by the misfortunes to which we are exposed; and the spectacle of a proud competitor now prostrate at his feet could not fail of producing very serious and solemn thoughts in the mind of the victorious emperor. But the feeble emotion of involuntary pity was checked by his regard for public justice and the memory of Gratian; and he abandoned the victim to the pious zeal of the soldiers, who drew him out of the Imperial presence and instantly separated his head from his body. The intelligence of his defeat and death was received with sincere or well-dissembled joy: his son Victor, on whom he had conferred the title of Augustus, died by the order, perhaps by the hand, of the bold Arbogastes; and all the military plans of Theodosius were successfully executed. When he had thus terminated the civil war, with less difficulty and bloodshed than he might naturally expect, he employed the winter months of his residence at Milan to restore the state of the afflicted provinces; and early in the spring he made, after the example of Constantine and Constantius, his triumphal entry into the ancient capital of the Roman empire.[1]

The orator, who may be silent without danger, may praise without difficulty and without reluctance;[2] and posterity will confess that the character of Theodosius[3] might furnish the subject of a sincere and ample panegyric. The wisdom of his laws and the success of his arms rendered his administration respectable in the eyes both of his subjects and of his enemies. He loved and practised the virtues of domestic life, which seldom hold their residence in the palaces of kings. Theodosius was chaste and temperate; he enjoyed, without excess, the sensual and social pleasures of the table, and the warmth of his amorous passions was never diverted from their lawful objects. The proud titles of Imperial greatness were adorned by the tender names of a faithful husband, an indulgent father; his uncle was raised, by his affectionate esteem, to the rank of a second parent; Theodosius embraced, as his own, the children of his brother and sister, and the expressions of his regard were extended to the most distant and obscure branches of his numerous kindred. His familiar friends were judiciously selected from among those persons who, in the equal intercourse of private life, had appeared

---

[1] Besides the hints which may be gathered from chronicles and ecclesiastical history, Zosimus (l. iv. [c. 40, seq.] p. 259-267), Orosius (l. vii. c. 35), and Pacatus (in Panegyr. Vet. xii. 30-47), supply the loose and scanty materials of this civil war. Ambrose (tom. ii. Epist. xl. p. 952, 953) darkly alludes to the well-known events of a magazine surprised, an action at Petovio, a Sicilian, perhaps a naval, victory, etc. Ausonius (p. 236, edit. Toll.) applauds the peculiar merit and good fortune of Aquileia.

[2] Quam promptum laudare principem, tam tutum siluisse de principe (Pacat. in Panegyr. Vet. xii. 2). Latinus Pacatus Drepanius, a native of Gaul, pronounced this oration at Rome (A.D. 388). He was afterwards proconsul of Africa; and his friend Ausonius praises him as a poet second only to Virgil. See Tillemont, Hist. des Empereurs, tom. v. p. 303.

[3] See the fair portrait of Theodosius by the younger Victor; the strokes are distinct and the colours are mixed. The praise of Pacatus is too vague; and Claudian always seems afraid of exalting the father above the son.

before his eyes without a mask; the consciousness of personal and superior merit enabled him to despise the accidental distinction of the purple, and he proved by his conduct that he had forgotten all the injuries, while he most gratefully remembered all the favours and services which he had received before he ascended the throne of the Roman empire. The serious or lively tone of his conversation was adapted to the age, the rank, or the character of his subjects whom he admitted into his society; and the affability of his manners displayed the image of his mind. Theodosius respected the simplicity of the good and virtuous: every art, every talent, of a useful or even of an innocent nature, was rewarded by his judicious liberality; and, except the heretics, whom he persecuted with implacable hatred, the diffusive circle of his benevolence was circumscribed only by the limits of the human race. The government of a mighty empire may assuredly suffice to occupy the time and the abilities of a mortal; yet the diligent prince, without aspiring to the unsuitable reputation of profound learning, always reserved some moments of his leisure for the instructive amusement of reading. History, which enlarged his experience, was his favourite study. The annals of Rome, in the long period of eleven hundred years, presented him with a various and splendid picture of human life; and it has been particularly observed that, whenever he perused the cruel acts of Cinna, of Marius, or of Sylla, he warmly expressed his generous detestation of those enemies of humanity and freedom. His disinterested opinion of past events was usefully applied as the rule of his own actions, and Theodosius has deserved the singular commendation that his virtues always seemed to expand with his fortune; the season of his prosperity was that of his moderation, and his clemency appeared the most conspicuous after the danger and success of the civil war. The Moorish guards of the tyrant had been massacred in the first heat of the victory, and a small number of the most obnoxious criminals suffered the punishment of the law. But the emperor showed himself much more attentive to relieve the innocent than to chastise the guilty. The oppressed subjects of the West, who would have deemed themselves happy in the restoration of their lands, were astonished to receive a sum of money equivalent to their losses; and the liberality of the conqueror supported the aged mother and educated the orphan daughters of Maximus.[1] A character thus accomplished might almost excuse the extra-

---

[1] Ambros. tom. ii. Epist. xl. p. 955. Pacatus, from the want of skill or of courage, omits this glorious circumstance.

vagant supposition of the orator Pacatus that, if the elder Brutus could be permitted to revisit the earth, the stern republican would abjure, at the feet of Theodosius, his hatred of kings; and ingenuously confess that such a monarch was the most faithful guardian of the happiness and dignity of the Roman people.[1]

Yet the piercing eye of the founder of the republic must have discerned two essential imperfections, which might, perhaps, have abated his recent love of despotism. The virtuous mind of Theodosius was often relaxed by indolence,[2] and it was sometimes inflamed by passion.[3] In the pursuit of an important object his active courage was capable of the most vigorous exertions; but as soon as the design was accomplished, or the danger was surmounted, the hero sunk into inglorious repose, and, forgetful that the time of a prince is the property of his people, resigned himself to the enjoyment of the innocent but trifling pleasures of a luxurious court. The natural disposition of Theodosius was hasty and choleric; and, in a station where none could resist and few would dissuade the fatal consequence of his resentment, the humane monarch was justly alarmed by the consciousness of his infirmity and of his power. It was the constant study of his life to suppress or regulate the intemperate sallies of passion; and the success of his efforts enhanced the merit of his clemency. But the painful virtue which claims the merit of victory is exposed to the danger of defeat; and the reign of a wise and merciful prince was polluted by an act of cruelty which would stain the annals of Nero or Domitian. Within the space of three years the inconsistent historian of Theodosius must relate the generous pardon of the citizens of Antioch, and the inhuman massacre of the people of Thessalonica.

The lively impatience of the inhabitants of Antioch was never satisfied with their own situation, or with the character and conduct of their successive sovereigns. The Arian subjects of Theodosius deplored the loss of their churches; and, as three rival bishops disputed the throne of Antioch, the sentence which decided their pretensions excited the murmurs of the two unsuc-

---

[1] Pacat. in Panegyr. Vet. xii. 20.

[2] Zosimus, l. iv. [c. 50] p. 271, 272. His partial evidence is marked by an air of candour and truth. He observes these vicissitudes of sloth and activity, not as a vice but as a singularity in the character of Theodosius.

[3] This choleric temper is acknowledged and excused by Victor [Epit. c. 48]. Sed habes (says Ambrose in decent and manly language to his sovereign) naturæ impetum, quem si quis lenire velit, cito vertes ad misericordiam: si quis stimulet, in magis exsuscitas, ut eum revocare vix possis (tom. ii. Epist. li. p. 998). Theodosius (Claud. in iv. Cons. Hon. 266, etc.) exhorts his son to moderate his anger.

cessful congregations. The exigencies of the Gothic war, and the inevitable expense that accompanied the conclusion of the peace, had constrained the emperor to aggravate the weight of the public impositions; and the provinces of Asia, as they had not been involved in the distress, were the less inclined to contribute to the relief of Europe. The auspicious period now approached of the tenth year of his reign; a festival more grateful to the soldiers, who received a liberal donative, than to the subjects, whose voluntary offerings had been long since converted into an extraordinary and oppressive burden. The edicts of taxation interrupted the repose and pleasures of Antioch; and the tribunal of the magistrate was besieged by a suppliant crowd, who, in pathetic, but at first in respectful language, solicited the redress of their grievances. They were gradually incensed by the pride of their haughty rulers, who treated their complaints as a criminal resistance; their satirical wit degenerated into sharp and angry invectives; and, from the subordinate powers of government, the invectives of the people insensibly rose to attack the sacred character of the emperor himself. Their fury, provoked by a feeble opposition, discharged itself on the images of the Imperial family which were erected, as objects of public veneration, in the most conspicuous places of the city. The statues of Theodosius, of his father, of his wife Flaccilla, of his two sons Arcadius and Honorius, were insolently thrown down from their pedestals, broken in pieces, or dragged with contempt through the streets; and the indignities which were offered to the representations of Imperial majesty sufficiently declared the impious and treasonable wishes of the populace. The tumult was almost immediately suppressed by the arrival of a body of archers; and Antioch had leisure to reflect on the nature and consequences of her crime.[1] According to the duty of his office, the governor of the province despatched a faithful narrative of the whole transaction, while the trembling citizens intrusted the confession of their crime and the assurances of their repentance to the zeal of Flavian their bishop, and to the eloquence of the senator Hilarius, the friend, and most probably the disciple, of Libanius,[2] whose genius on this melancholy occasion was not

---

[1] The Christians and Pagans agreed in believing that the sedition of Antioch was excited by the dæmons. A gigantic woman (says Sozomen, l. vii. c. 23) paraded the streets with a scourge in her hand. An old man, says Libanius (Orat. xii. p. 396), transformed himself into a youth, then a boy, etc.

[2] Zosimus, in his short and disingenuous account (l. iv. [c. 41] p. 258, 259), is certainly mistaken in sending Libanius himself to Constantinople. His own orations fix him at Antioch.

useless to his country. But the two capitals, Antioch and Constantinople, were separated by the distance of eight hundred miles; and, notwithstanding the diligence of the Imperial posts, the guilty city was severely punished by a long and dreadful interval of suspense. Every rumour agitated the hopes and fears of the Antiochians, and they heard with terror that their sovereign, exasperated by the insult which had been offered to his own statues, and more especially to those of his beloved wife, had resolved to level with the ground the offending city, and to massacre, without distinction of age or sex, the criminal inhabitants,[1] many of whom were actually driven, by their apprehensions, to seek a refuge in the mountains of Syria and the adjacent desert. At length, twenty-four days after the sedition, the general Hellebicus, and Cæsarius, master of the offices, declared the will of the emperor and the sentence of Antioch. That proud capital was degraded from the rank of a city; and the metropolis of the East, stripped of its lands, its privileges, and its revenues, was subjected, under the humiliating denomination of a village, to the jurisdiction of Laodicea.[2] The baths, the circus, and the theatres were shut; and, that every source of plenty and pleasure might at the same time be intercepted, the distribution of corn was abolished by the severe instructions of Theodosius. His commissioners then proceeded to inquire into the guilt of individuals—of those who had perpetrated, and of those who had not prevented, the destruction of the sacred statues. The tribunal of Hellebicus and Cæsarius, encompassed with armed soldiers, was erected in the midst of the Forum. The noblest and most wealthy of the citizens of Antioch appeared before them in chains; the examination was assisted by the use of torture, and their sentence was pronounced or suspended, according to the judgment of these extraordinary magistrates. The houses of the criminals were exposed to sale, their wives and children were suddenly reduced from affluence and luxury to the most abject distress, and a bloody execution was expected to conclude the horrors of a day [3] which the preacher of Antioch, the eloquent

---

[1] Libanius (Orat. i. p. 6, edit. Venet.) declares, that under such a reign the fear of a massacre was groundless and absurd, especially in the emperor's absence; for his presence, according to the eloquent slave, might have given a sanction to the most bloody acts.

[2] Laodicea, on the sea-coast, sixty-five miles from Antioch (see Noris, Epoch. Syro-Maced. Dissert. iii. p. 230). The Antiochians were offended that the dependent city of Seleucia should presume to intercede for them.

[3] As the days of the tumult depend on the *movable* festival of Easter, they can only be determined by the previous determination of the year.

Chrysostom, has represented as a lively image of the last and universal judgment of the world. But the ministers of Theodosius performed with reluctance the cruel task which had been assigned them; they dropped a gentle tear over the calamities of the people, and they listened with reverence to the pressing solicitations of the monks and hermits, who descended in swarms from the mountains.[1] Hellebicus and Cæsarius were persuaded to suspend the execution of their sentence; and it was agreed that the former should remain at Antioch, while the latter returned, with all possible speed, to Constantinople, and presumed once more to consult the will of his sovereign. The resentment of Theodosius had already subsided; the deputies of the people, both the bishop and the orator, had obtained a favourable audience; and the reproaches of the emperor were the complaints of injured friendship rather than the stern menaces of pride and power. A free and general pardon was granted to the city and citizens of Antioch; the prison-doors were thrown open; the senators, who despaired of their lives, recovered the possession of their houses and estates; and the capital of the East was restored to the enjoyment of her ancient dignity and splendour. Theodosius condescended to praise the senate of Constantinople, who had generously interceded for their distressed brethren; he rewarded the eloquence of Hilarius with the government of Palestine, and dismissed the bishop of Antioch with the warmest expressions of his respect and gratitude. A thousand new statues arose to the clemency of Theodosius; the applause of his subjects was ratified by the approbation of his own heart; and the emperor confessed that, if the exercise of justice is the most important duty, the indulgence of mercy is the most exquisite pleasure of a sovereign.[2]

The sedition of Thessalonica is ascribed to a more shameful cause, and was productive of much more dreadful consequences. That great city, the metropolis of all the Illyrian provinces, had

The year 387 has been preferred, after a laborious inquiry, by Tillemont (Hist. des Emp. tom. v. p. 741-744) and Montfaucon (Chrysostom, tom. xiii. p. 105-110).

[1] Chrysostom opposes *their* courage, which was not attended with much risk, to the cowardly flight of the Cynics.

[2] The sedition of Antioch is represented in a lively and almost dramatic manner by two orators who had their respective shares of interest and merit. See Libanius (Orat. xiv. xv. [xii. xiii.] p. 389-420, edit. Morel.; Orat. i. p. 1-14, Venet. 1754) and the twenty orations of St. John Chrysostom, *de Statuis* (tom. ii. p. 1-225, edit. Montfaucon). I do not pretend to *much* personal acquaintance with Chrysostom; but Tillemont (Hist. des Empereurs, tom. v. p. 263-283) and Hermant (Vie de St. Chrysostome, tom. i. p. 137-224) had read him with pious curiosity and diligence.

been protected from the dangers of the Gothic war by strong fortifications and a numerous garrison. Botheric, the general of those troops, and, as it should seem from his name, a barbarian, had among his slaves a beautiful boy, who excited the impure desires of one of the charioteers of the circus. The insolent and brutal lover was thrown into prison by the order of Botheric; and he sternly rejected the importunate clamours of the multitude, who, on the day of the public games, lamented the absence of their favourite, and considered the skill of a charioteer as an object of more importance than his virtue. The resentment of the people was embittered by some previous disputes; and, as the strength of the garrison had been drawn away for the service of the Italian war, the feeble remnant, whose numbers were reduced by desertion, could not save the unhappy general from their licentious fury. Botheric and several of his principal officers were inhumanly murdered; their mangled bodies were dragged about the streets; and the emperor, who then resided at Milan, was surprised by the intelligence of the audacious and wanton cruelty of the people of Thessalonica. The sentence of a dispassionate judge would have inflicted a severe punishment on the authors of the crime; and the merit of Botheric might contribute to exasperate the grief and indignation of his master. The fiery and choleric temper of Theodosius was impatient of the dilatory forms of a judicial inquiry; and he hastily resolved that the blood of his lieutenant should be expiated by the blood of the guilty people. Yet his mind still fluctuated between the counsels of clemency and of revenge; the zeal of the bishops had almost extorted from the reluctant emperor the promise of a general pardon; his passion was again inflamed by the flattering suggestions of his minister Rufinus; and, after Theodosius had despatched the messengers of death, he attempted, when it was too late, to prevent the execution of his orders. The punishment of a Roman city was blindly committed to the undistinguishing sword of the barbarians; and the hostile preparations were concerted with the dark and perfidious artifice of an illegal conspiracy. The people of Thessalonica were treacherously invited, in the name of their sovereign, to the games of the circus; and such was their insatiate avidity for those amusements that every consideration of fear or suspicion was disregarded by the numerous spectators. As soon as the assembly was complete, the soldiers, who had secretly been posted round the circus, received the signal, not of the races, but of a general massacre. The promiscuous carnage continued three hours, without discrimination of strangers or natives, of age or sex, of innocence or guilt; the most moderate accounts state the number of the slain at seven thousand; and it is affirmed by some writers that more than fifteen thousand victims were sacrificed to the manes of Botheric. A foreign merchant, who had probably no concern in his murder, offered his own life and all his wealth to supply the place of *one* of his two sons; but while the father hesitated with equal tenderness, while he was doubtful to choose, and unwilling to condemn, the soldiers determined his suspense by plunging their daggers at the same moment into the breasts of the defence-less youths. The apology of the assassins, that they were obliged to produce the prescribed number of heads, serves only to increase, by an appearance of order and design, the horrors of the massacre, which was executed by the commands of Theodosius. The guilt of the emperor is aggravated by his long and frequent residence at Thessalonica. The situation of the unfortunate city, the aspect of the streets and buildings, the dress and faces of the inhabitants, were familiar, and even present, to his imagination; and Theodosius possessed a quick and lively sense of the exist-ence of the people whom he destroyed.[1]

The respectful attachment of the emperor for the orthodox clergy had disposed him to love and admire the character of Ambrose, who united all the episcopal virtues in the most eminent degree. The friends and ministers of Theodosius imitated the example of their sovereign; and he observed, with more surprise than displeasure, that all his secret counsels were immediately communicated to the archbishop, who acted from the laudable persuasion that every measure of civil government may have some connection with the glory of God and the interest of the true religion. The monks and populace of Callinicum, an obscure town on the frontier of Persia, excited by their own fanaticism, and by that of their bishop, had tumultuously burnt a conventicle of the Valentinians and a synagogue of the Jews. The seditious prelate was condemned by the magistrate of the provinces either to rebuild the synagogue or to repay the damage; and this moderate sentence was confirmed by the

---

[1] The original evidence of Ambrose (tom. ii. Epist. li. p. 998), Augustin (de Civitat. Dei, v. 26), and Paulinus (in Vit. Ambros. c. 24), is delivered in vague expressions of horror and pity. It is illustrated by the subsequent and unequal testimonies of Sozomen (l. vii. c. 25), Theodoret (l. v. c. 17), Theophanes (Chronograph. p. 62 [tom. i. p. 113, ed. Bonn.]), Cedrenus (p. 317 [tom. i. p. 556, ed. Bonn.]), and Zonaras (tom. ii. l. xiii. [c. 18] p. 34). Zosimus *alone*, the partial enemy of Theodosius, most unaccount-ably passes over in silence the worst of his actions.

emperor. But it was not confirmed by the archbishop of Milan.[1]
He dictated an epistle of censure and reproach, more suitable
perhaps if the emperor had received the mark of circumcision
and renounced the faith of his baptism. Ambrose considers the
toleration of the Jewish as the persecution of the Christian
religion; boldly declares that he himself and every true believer
would eagerly dispute with the bishop of Callinicum the merit
of the deed and the crown of martyrdom; and laments, in the
most pathetic terms, that the execution of the sentence would be
fatal to the fame and salvation of Theodosius. As this private
admonition did not produce an immediate effect, the archbishop
from his pulpit [2] publicly addressed the emperor on his throne; [3]
nor would he consent to offer the oblation of the altar till he
had obtained from Theodosius a solemn and positive declaration
which secured the impunity of the bishop and monks of Callinicum. The recantation of Theodosius was sincere; [4] and,
during the term of his residence at Milan, his affection for
Ambrose was continually increased by the habits of pious and
familiar conversation.

When Ambrose was informed of the massacre of Thessalonica,
his mind was filled with horror and anguish. He retired into the
country to indulge his grief and to avoid the presence of Theodosius. But as the archbishop was satisfied that a timid silence
would render him the accomplice of his guilt, he represented in
a private letter the enormity of the crime, which could only be
effaced by the tears of penitence. The episcopal vigour of
Ambrose was tempered by prudence; and he contented himself
with signifying [5] an indirect sort of excommunication, by the
assurance that he had been warned in a vision not to offer the
oblation in the name or in the presence of Theodosius, and by the

[1] See the whole transaction in Ambrose (tom. ii. Epist. xl. xli. p. 946-
956), and his biographer Paulinus (c. 23). Bayle and Barbeyrac (Morales
des Pères, c. xvii. p. 325, etc.) have justly condemned the archbishop.
[2] His sermon is a strange allegory of Jeremiah's rod, of an almond-tree,
of the woman who washed and anointed the feet of Christ. But the peroration is direct and personal.
[3] Hodie, Episcope, de me proposuisti. Ambrose modestly confessed it;
but he sternly reprimanded Timesius, general of the horse and foot, who
had presumed to say that the monks of Callinicum deserved punishment.
[4] Yet, five years afterwards, when Theodosius was absent from his
spiritual guide, he tolerated the Jews, and condemned the destruction of
their synagogues. Cod. Theodos. l. xvi. tit. viii. leg. 9, with Godefroy's
Commentary, tom. vi. p. 225.
[5] Ambros. tom. ii. Epist. li. p. 997-1001. His epistle is a miserable
rhapsody on a noble subject. Ambrose could act better than he could
write. His compositions are destitute of taste or genius; without the
spirit of Tertullian, the copious elegance of Lactantius, the lively wit of
Jerom, or the grave energy of Augustin.

advice that he would confine himself to the use of prayer, without presuming to approach the altar of Christ, or to receive the holy eucharist with those hands that were still polluted with the blood of an innocent people. The emperor was deeply affected by his own reproaches and by those of his spiritual father; and after he had bewailed the mischievous and irreparable consequences of his rash fury, he proceeded in the accustomed manner to perform his devotions in the great church of Milan. He was stopped in the porch by the archbishop, who, in the tone and language of an ambassador of Heaven, declared to his sovereign that private contrition was not sufficient to atone for a public fault or to appease the justice of the offended Deity. Theodosius humbly represented that, if he had contracted the guilt of homicide, David, the man after God's own heart, had been guilty not only of murder but of adultery. "You have imitated David in his crime, imitate then his repentance," was the reply of the undaunted Ambrose. The rigorous conditions of peace and pardon were accepted; and the public penance of the emperor Theodosius has been recorded as one of the most honourable events in the annals of the church. According to the mildest rules of ecclesiastical discipline which were established in the fourth century, the crime of homicide was expiated by the penitence of twenty years:[1] and as it was impossible in the period of human life to purge the accumulated guilt of the massacre of Thessalonica, the murderer should have been excluded from the holy communion till the hour of his death. But the archbishop, consulting the maxims of religious policy, granted some indulgence to the rank of his illustrious penitent, who humbled in the dust the pride of the diadem; and the public edification might be admitted as a weighty reason to abridge the duration of his punishment. It was sufficient that the emperor of the Romans, stripped of the ensigns of royalty, should appear in a mournful and suppliant posture; and that, in the midst of the church of Milan, he should humbly solicit, with sighs and tears, the pardon of his sins.[2] In this spiritual

---

[1] According to the discipline of St. Basil (Canon lvi.), the voluntary homicide was *four* years a mourner; *five* an hearer; *seven* in a prostrate state; and *four* in a standing posture. I have the original (Beveridge, Pandect. tom. ii. p. 47-151) and a translation (Chardon, Hist. des Sacremens, tom. iv. p. 219-277) of the Canonical Epistles of St. Basil.

[2] The penance of Theodosius is authenticated by Ambrose (tom. ii. de Obit. Theodos. c. 34, p. 1207), Augustin (de Civitat. Dei, v. 26), and Paulinus (in Vit. Ambros. c. 24). Socrates is ignorant; Sozomen (l. vii. c. 25) concise; and the copious narrative of Theodoret (l. v. c. 18) must be used with precaution.

cure Ambrose employed the various methods of mildness and
severity.   After a delay of about eight months Theodosius was
restored to the communion of the faithful; and the edict, which
interposes a salutary interval of thirty days between the sentence
and the execution, may be accepted as the worthy fruits of his
repentance.[1]   Posterity has applauded the virtuous firmness of
the archbishop: and the example of Theodosius may prove the
beneficial influence of those principles which could force a
monarch, exalted above the apprehension of human punishment,
to respect the laws and ministers of an invisible Judge.   " The
prince," says Montesquieu, " who is actuated by the hopes and
fears of religion, may be compared to a lion, docile only to the
voice, and tractable to the hand, of his keeper." [2]   The motions
of the royal animal will therefore depend on the inclination and
interest of the man who has acquired such dangerous authority
over him; and the priest who holds in his hand the conscience
of a king many inflame or moderate his sanguinary passions.
The cause of humanity and that of persecution have been
asserted by the same Ambrose with equal energy and with equal
success.

After the defeat and death of the tyrant of Gaul, the Roman
world was in the possession of Theodosius.   He derived from the
choice of Gratian his honourable title to the provinces of the
East; he had acquired the West by the right of conquest; and
the three years which he spent in Italy were usefully employed
to restore the authority of the laws and to correct the abuses
which had prevailed with impunity under the usurpation of
Maximus and the minority of Valentinian.   The name of Valentinian was regularly inserted in the public acts, but the tender
age and doubtful faith of the son of Justina appeared to require
the prudent care of an orthodox guardian, and his specious
ambition might have excluded the unfortunate youth, without
a struggle and almost without a murmur, from the administration and even from the inheritance of the empire.   If Theodosius
had consulted the rigid maxims of interest and policy, his conduct would have been justified by his friends, but the generosity
of his behaviour on this memorable occasion has extorted the
applause of his most inveterate enemies.   He seated Valen-

---

[1] Codex Theodos. l. ix. tit. xl. leg. 13.   The date and circumstances of
this law are perplexed with difficulties;   but I feel myself inclined to favour
the honest efforts of Tillemont (Hist. des Emp. tom. v. p. 721) and Pagi
(Critica, tom. i. p. 578).

[2] Un prince qui aime la religion, et qui la craint, est un lion qui cède à
ıa main qui le flatte, ou à la voix qui l'appaise.   Esprit des Loix, l. xxiv. c. 2.

tinian on the throne of Milan, and, without stipulating any present or future advantages, restored him to the absolute dominion of all the provinces from which he had been driven by the arms of Maximus. To the restitution of his ample patrimony Theodosius added the free and generous gift of the countries beyond the Alps which his successful valour had recovered from the assassin of Gratian.[1] Satisfied with the glory which he had acquired by revenging the death of his benefactor and delivering the West from the yoke of tyranny, the emperor returned from Milan to Constantinople, and, in the peaceful possession of the East, insensibly relapsed into his former habits of luxury and indolence. Theodosius discharged his obligation to the brother, he indulged his conjugal tenderness to the sister, of Valentinian; and posterity, which admires the pure and singular glory of his elevation, must applaud his unrivalled generosity in the use of victory.

The empress Justina did not long survive her return to Italy, and, though she beheld the triumph of Theodosius, she was not allowed to influence the government of her son.[2] The pernicious attachment to the Arian sect which Valentinian had imbibed from her example and instructions was soon erased by the lessons of a more orthodox education. His growing zeal for the faith of Nice, and his filial reverence for the character and authority of Ambrose, disposed the catholics to entertain the most favourable opinion of the virtues of the young emperor of the West.[3] They applauded his chastity and temperance, his contempt of pleasure, his application to business, and his tender affection for his two sisters, which would not, however, seduce his impartial equity to pronounce an unjust sentence against the meanest of his subjects. But this amiable youth, before he had accomplished the twentieth year of his age, was oppressed by domestic treason, and the empire was again involved in the horrors of a civil war. Arbogastes,[4] a gallant soldier of the nation of the Franks, held the second rank in the service of

---

[1] Τοῦτο περὶ τοὺς εὐεργέτας καθῆκον ἔδοξεν εἶναι, is the niggard praise of Zosimus himself (l. iv. [c. 48] p. 267). Augustin says, with some happiness of expression, Valentinianum . . . misericordissimâ veneratione restituit.

[2] Sozomen, l. vii. c. 14. His chronology is very irregular.

[3] See Ambrose (tom. ii. de Obit. Valentinian. c. 15, etc., p. 1178, c. 36, etc., p. 1184). When the young emperor gave an entertainment, he fasted himself; he refused to see an handsome actress, etc. Since he ordered his wild beasts to be killed, it is ungenerous in Philostorgius (l. xi. c. 1) to reproach him with the love of that amusement.

[4] Zosimus (l. iv. [c. 53] p. 275) praises the enemy of Theodosius. But he is detested by Socrates (l. v. c. 25) and Orosius (l. vii. c. 35).

Gratian. On the death of his master he joined the standard of Theodosius, contributed, by his valour and military conduct, to the destruction of the tyrant, and was appointed, after the victory, master-general of the armies of Gaul. His real merit and apparent fidelity had gained the confidence both of the prince and people; his boundless liberality corrupted the allegiance of the troops; and, whilst he was universally esteemed as the pillar of the state, the bold and crafty barbarian was secretly determined either to rule or to ruin the empire of the West. The important commands of the army were distributed among the Franks; the creatures of Arbogastes were promoted to all the honours and offices of the civil government; the progress of the conspiracy removed every faithful servant from the presence of Valentinian; and the emperor, without power and without intelligence, insensibly sunk into the precarious and dependent condition of a captive.[1] The indignation which he expressed, though it might arise only from the rash and impatient temper of youth, may be candidly ascribed to the generous spirit of a prince who felt that he was not unworthy to reign. He secretly invited the archbishop of Milan to undertake the office of a mediator, as the pledge of his sincerity and the guardian of his safety. He contrived to apprise the emperor of the East of his helpless situation, and he declared that, unless Theodosius could speedily march to his assistance, he must attempt to escape from the palace, or rather prison, of Vienne, in Gaul, where he had imprudently fixed his residence in the midst of the hostile faction. But the hopes of relief were distant and doubtful; and, as every day furnished some new provocation, the emperor, without strength or counsel, too hastily resolved to risk an immediate contest with his powerful general. He received Arbogastes on the throne, and, as the count approached with some appearance of respect, delivered to him a paper which dismissed him from all his employments. " My authority," replied Arbogastes, with insulting coolness, " does not depend on the smile or the frown of a monarch; " and he contemptuously threw the paper on the ground. The indignant monarch snatched at the sword of one of the guards, which he struggled to draw from its scabbard, and it was not without some degree of violence that he was prevented from using the deadly weapon against his enemy or against himself. A few days after this extraordinary quarrel,

---

[1] Gregory of Tours (l. ii. c. 9, p. 165, in the second volume of the Historians of France) has preserved a curious fragment of Sulpicius Alexander, an historian far more valuable than himself.

in which he had exposed his resentment and his weakness, the unfortunate Valentinian was found strangled in his apartment, and some pains were employed to disguise the manifest guilt of Arbogastes, and to persuade the world that the death of the young emperor had been the voluntary effect of his own despair.[1] His body was conducted with decent pomp to the sepulchre of Milan, and the archbishop pronounced a funeral oration to commemorate his virtue and his misfortunes.[2]   On this occasion the humanity of Ambrose tempted him to make a singular breach in his theological system, and to comfort the weeping sisters of Valentinian by the firm assurance that their pious brother, though he had not received the sacrament of baptism, was introduced, without difficulty, into the mansions of eternal bliss.[3]

The prudence of Arbogastes had prepared the success of his ambitious designs, and the provincials, in whose breasts every sentiment of patriotism or loyalty was extinguished, expected, with tame resignation, the unknown master whom the choice of a Frank might place on the Imperial throne.   But some remains of pride and prejudice still opposed the elevation of Arbogastes himself, and the judicious barbarian thought it more advisable to reign under the name of some dependent Roman. He bestowed the purple on the rhetorician Eugenius,[4] whom he had already raised from the place of his domestic secretary to the rank of master of the offices. In the course both of his private and public service the count had always approved the attachment and abilities of Eugenius; his learning and eloquence, supported by the gravity of his manners, recommended him to the esteem of the people, and the reluctance with which he seemed to ascend the throne may inspire a favourable prejudice of his virtue and moderation.   The ambassadors of the new emperor were immediately despatched to the court of Theodosius, to communicate,

---

[1] Godefroy (Dissertat. ad Philostorg. p. 429-434) has diligently collected all the circumstances of the death of Valentinian II.   The variations and the ignorance of contemporary writers prove that it was secret.

[2] De Obitû Valentinian. tom. ii. p. 1173-1196.   He is forced to speak a discreet and obscure language: yet he is much bolder than any layman, or perhaps any other ecclesiastic, would have dared to be.

[3] See c. 51, p. 1188; c. 75, p. 1193.   Dom Chardon (Hist. des Sacremens, tom. i. p. 86), who owns that St. Ambrose most strenuously maintains the *indispensable* necessity of baptism, labours to reconcile the contradiction.

[4] Quem sibi Germanus famulum delegerat exul,

is the contemptuous expression of Claudian (iv. Cons. Hon. 74).   Eugenius professed Christianity; but his secret attachment to Paganism (Sozomen, l. vii. c. 22; Philostorg. l. xi. c. 2) is probable in a grammarian, and would secure the friendship of Zosimus (l. iv. [c. 54] p. 276, 277).

with affected grief, the unfortunate accident of the death of
Valentinian, and, without mentioning the name of Arbogastes,
to request that the monarch of the East would embrace as his
lawful colleague the respectable citizen who had obtained the
unanimous suffrage of the armies and provinces of the West.[1]
Theodosius was justly provoked that the perfidy of a barbarian
should have destroyed in a moment the labours and the fruit of
his former victory; and he was excited by the tears of his beloved
wife [2] to revenge the fate of her unhappy brother, and once more
to assert by arms the violated majesty of the throne. But as the
second conquest of the West was a task of difficulty and danger,
he dismissed, with splendid presents and an ambiguous answer,
the ambassadors of Eugenius, and almost two years were consumed in the preparations of the civil war. Before he formed
any decisive resolution, the pious emperor was anxious to discover the will of Heaven; and as the progress of Christianity
had silenced the oracles of Delphi and Dodona, he consulted an
Egyptian monk, who possessed, in the opinion of the age, the
gift of miracles and the knowledge of futurity. Eutropius, one
of the favourite eunuchs of the palace of Constantinople, embarked for Alexandria, from whence he sailed up the Nile as far
as the city of Lycopolis, or of Wolves, in the remote province of
Thebais.[3] In the neighbourhood of that city, and on the summit
of a lofty mountain, the holy John [4] had constructed with his own
hands an humble cell, in which he had dwelt above fifty years,
without opening his door, without seeing the face of a woman,
and without tasting any food that had been prepared by fire
or any human art. Five days of the week he spent in prayer and
meditation, but on Saturdays and Sundays he regularly opened
a small window, and gave audience to the crowd of suppliants

---

[1] Zosimus (l. iv. [c. 55] p. 278) mentions this embassy; but he is diverted
by another story from relating the event.

[2] Συνετάραξεν ἡ τούτου γαμετὴ Γάλλα τὰ βασίλεια, τὸν ἀδελφὸν ὀλοφυ-
ρομένη. Zosim. l. iv. [c. 55] p. 277. He afterwards says ([c. 57] p. 280) that
Galla died in childbed [A.D. 394.—S.]; and intimates that the affliction
of her husband was extreme but short.

[3] Lycopolis is the modern Siut, or Osiot, a town of Said, about the size
of St. Denys, which drives a profitable trade with the kingdom of Sennaar,
and has a very convenient fountain, " cujus potû signa virginitatis eripi-
untur." See D'Anville, Description de l'Égypte, p. 181. Abulfeda,
Descript. Egypt. p. 14; and the curious Annotations, p. 25, 92, of his
editor Michaelis.

[4] The Life of John of Lycopolis is described by his two friends, Rufinus
(l. ii. c. i. p. 449) and Palladius (Hist. Lausiac. c. 43, p. 738), in Rosweyde's
great Collection of the Vitæ Patrum. Tillemont (Mém. Ecclés. tom. x.
p. 718, 720) has settled the chronology.

who successively flowed from every part of the Christian world. The eunuch of Theodosius approached the window with respectful steps, proposed his questions concerning the event of the civil war, and soon returned with a favourable oracle, which animated the courage of the emperor by the assurance of a bloody but infallible victory.[1] The accomplishment of the prediction was forwarded by all the means that human prudence could supply. The industry of the two master-generals, Stilicho and Timasius, was directed to recruit the numbers and to revive the discipline of the Roman legions. The formidable troops of barbarians marched under the ensigns of their national chieftains. The Iberian, the Arab, and the Goth, who gazed on each other with mutual astonishment, were enlisted in the service of the same prince; and the renowned Alaric acquired, in the school of Theodosius, the knowledge of the art of war which he afterwards so fatally exerted for the destruction of Rome.[2]

The emperor of the West, or, to speak more properly, his general Arbogastes, was instructed by the misconduct and misfortune of Maximus how dangerous it might prove to extend the line of defence against a skilful antagonist, who was free to press or to suspend, to contract or to multiply, his various methods of attack.[3] Arbogastes fixed his station on the confines of Italy; the troops of Theodosius were permitted to occupy, without resistance, the provinces of Pannonia, as far as the foot of the Julian Alps; and even the passes of the mountains were negligently, or perhaps artfully, abandoned to the bold invader. He descended from the hills, and beheld, with some astonishment, the formidable camp of the Gauls and Germans that covered with arms and tents the open country which extends to the walls

[1] Sozomen, l. vii. c. 22. Claudian (in Eutrop. l. i. 312) mentions the eunuch's journey: but he most contemptuously derives the Egyptian dreams and the oracles of the Nile.

[2] Zosimus, l. iv. [c. 57] p. 280; Socrates, l. vii. 10. Alaric himself (de Bell. Getico, 524) dwells with more complacency on his early exploits against the Romans.

. . . Tot Augustos Hebro qui teste fugavi.

Yet his vanity could scarcely have proved this *plurality* of flying emperors.

[3] Claudian (in iv. Cons. Honor. 77, etc.) contrasts the military plans of the two usurpers:—

. . . Novitas audere priori
Suadebat; cautumque dabant exempla sequentem.
His nova moliri præceps: his quærere tuta
Providus. Hic fusis, collectis viribus ille;
Hic vagus excurrens; hic intra claustra reductus;
Dissimiles, sed morte pares . . .

of Aquileia and the banks of the Frigidus,[1] or Cold River.[2]   This
narrow theatre of the war, circumscribed by the Alps and the
Hadriatic, did not allow much room for the operations of military
skill; the spirit of Arbogastes would have disdained a pardon;
his guilt extinguished the hope of a negotiation; and Theodosius
was impatient to satisfy his glory and revenge by the chastisement of the assassins of Valentinian.   Without weighing the
natural and artificial obstacles that opposed his efforts, the
emperor of the East immediately attacked the fortifications of
his rivals, assigned the post of honourable danger to the Goths,
and cherished a secret wish that the bloody conflict might
diminish the pride and numbers of the conquerors.   Ten thousand of those auxiliaries, and Bacurius, general of the Iberians,
died bravely on the field of battle.   But the victory was not
purchased by their blood; the Gauls maintained their advantage,
and the approach of night protected the disorderly flight, or
retreat, of the troops of Theodosius.   The emperor retired to the
adjacent hills, where he passed a disconsolate night, without
sleep, without provisions, and without hopes,[3] except that strong
assurance which, under the most desperate circumstances, the
independent mind may derive from the contempt of fortune
and of life.   The triumph of Eugenius was celebrated by the
insolent and dissolute joy of his camp, whilst the active and
vigilant Arbogastes secretly detached a considerable body of
troops to occupy the passes of the mountains and to encompass
the rear of the Eastern army.   The dawn of day discovered to
the eyes of Theodosius the extent and the extremity of his danger,
but his apprehensions were soon dispelled by a friendly message
from the leaders of those troops, who expressed their inclination
to desert the standard of the tyrant.   The honourable and
lucrative rewards which they stipulated as the price of their
perfidy were granted without hesitation, and, as ink and paper
could not easily be procured, the emperor subscribed on his own
tablets the ratification of the treaty.   The spirit of his soldiers
was revived by this seasonable reinforcement, and they again

[1] The Frigidus, a small though memorable stream in the country of
Goretz, now called the Vipao, falls into the Sontius, or Lisonzo, above
Aquileia, some miles from the Hadriatic.   See D'Anville's ancient and
modern maps, and the Italia Antiqua of Cluverius (tom. i. p. 188).

[2] Claudian's wit is intolerable: the snow was dyed red; the cold river
smoked; and the channel must have been choked with carcasses if the
current had not been swelled with blood.

[3] Theodoret affirms that St. John and St. Philip appeared to the waking
or sleeping emperor, on horseback, etc.   This is the first instance of apostolic chivalry, which afterwards became so popular in Spain and in the
Crusades.

marched with confidence to surprise the camp of a tyrant whose principal officers appeared to distrust either the justice or the success of his arms. In the heat of the battle a violent tempest,[1] such as is often felt among the Alps, suddenly arose from the East. The army of Theodosius was sheltered by their position from the impetuosity of the wind, which blew a cloud of dust in the faces of the enemy, disordered their ranks, wrested their weapons from their hands, and diverted or repelled their ineffectual javelins. This accidental advantage was skilfully improved: the violence of the storm was magnified by the superstitious terrors of the Gauls, and they yielded without shame to the invisible powers of heaven, who seemed to militate on the side of the pious emperor. His victory was decisive, and the deaths of his two rivals were distinguished only by the difference of their characters. The rhetorician Eugenius, who had almost acquired the dominion of the world, was reduced to implore the mercy of the conqueror, and the unrelenting soldiers separated his head from his body as he lay prostrate at the feet of Theodosius. Arbogastes, after the loss of a battle in which he had discharged the duties of a soldier and a general, wandered several days among the mountains. But when he was convinced that his cause was desperate, and his escape impracticable, the intrepid barbarian imitated the example of the ancient Romans, and turned his sword against his own breast. The fate of the empire was determined in a narrow corner of Italy; and the legitimate successor of the house of Valentinian embraced the archbishop of Milan, and graciously received the submission of the provinces of the West. Those provinces were involved in the guilt of rebellion; while the inflexible courage of Ambrose alone had resisted the claims of successful usurpation. With a manly freedom, which might have been fatal to any other subject, the archbishop rejected the gifts of Eugenius, declined his correspondence, and withdrew himself from Milan to avoid the odious presence of a tyrant whose downfall he predicted in

---

[1] Te propter, gelidis Aquilo de monte procellis
　　Obruit adversas acies; revolutaque tela
　　Vertit in auctores, et turbine reppulit hastas.
　　O nimium dilecte Deo, cui fundit ab antris
　　Æolus armatas hiemes; cui militat Æther,
　　Et conjurati veniunt ad classica venti.

These famous lines of Claudian (in iii. Cons. Honor. 93, etc., A.D. 396) are alleged by his contemporaries, Augustin and Orosius, who suppress the Pagan deity of Æolus, and add some circumstances from the information of eye-witnesses. Within four months after the victory, it was compared by Ambrose to the miraculous victories of Moses and Joshua.

discreet and ambiguous language. The merit of Ambrose was applauded by the conqueror, who secured the attachment of the people by his alliance with the church: and the clemency of Theodosius is ascribed to the humane intercession of the arch-bishop of Milan.[1]

After the defeat of Eugenius, the merit, as well as the authority, of Theodosius was cheerfully acknowledged by all the inhabitants of the Roman world. The experience of his past conduct encouraged the most pleasing expectations of his future reign; and the age of the emperor, which did not exceed fifty years, seemed to extend the prospect of the public felicity. His death, only four months after his victory, was considered by the people as an unforeseen and fatal event, which destroyed in a moment the hopes of the rising generation. But the indulgence of ease and luxury had secretly nourished the principles of disease.[2] The strength of Theodosius was unable to support the sudden and violent transition from the palace to the camp; and the increasing symptoms of a dropsy announced the speedy dissolution of the emperor. The opinion, and perhaps the interest, of the public had confirmed the division of the Eastern and Western empires; and the two royal youths, Arcadius and Honorius, who had already obtained, from the tenderness of their father, the title of Augustus, were destined to fill the thrones of Constantinople and of Rome. Those princes were not permitted to share the danger and glory of the civil war;[3] but as soon as Theodosius had triumphed over his unworthy rivals, he called his younger son, Honorius, to enjoy the fruits of the victory, and to receive the sceptre of the West from the hands of his dying father. The arrival of Honorius at Milan was welcomed by a splendid exhibition of the games of the circus; and the emperor, though he was oppressed by the weight of his disorder, contributed by his presence to the public joy. But the remains

---

[1] The events of this civil war are gathered from Amb ose (tom. ii. Epist. lxii. p. 1022), Paulinus (in Vit. Ambros. c. 26-34), Augustin (de Civitat. Dei, v. 26), Orosius (l. vii. c. 35), Sozomen (l. vii. c. 24), Theodoret (l. v. c. 24), Zosimus (l. iv. [c. 58], p. 281, 282), Claudian (in iii. Cons. Hon. 63-105; in iv. Cons. Hon. 70-117), and the Chronicles published by Scaliger.

[2] This disease, ascribed by Socrates (l. v. c. 26) to the fatigues of war, is represented by Philostorgius (l. xi. c. 2) as the effect of sloth and intemperance; for which Photius calls him an impudent liar (Godefroy, Dissert. p. 438).

[3] Zosimus supposes that the boy Honorius accompanied his father (l. iv. [c. 58] p. 280). Yet the quanto flagrabant pectora voto is all that flattery would allow to a contemporary poet, who clearly describes the emperor's refusal, and the journey of Honorius, *after* the victory (Claudian in iii. Cons. Hon. 78-125).

of his strength were exhausted by the painful effort which he made to assist at the spectacles of the morning. Honorius supplied, during the rest of the day, the place of his father; and the great Theodosius expired in the ensuing night. Notwithstanding the recent animosities of a civil war, his death was universally lamented. The barbarians, whom he had vanquished, and the churchmen, by whom he had been subdued, celebrated with loud and sincere applause the qualities of the deceased emperor which appeared the most valuable in their eyes. The Romans were terrified by the impending dangers of a feeble and divided administration; and every disgraceful moment of the unfortunate reigns of Arcadius and Honorius revived the memory of their irreparable loss.

In the faithful picture of the virtues of Theodosius, his imperfections have not been dissembled; the act of cruelty, and the habits of indolence, which tarnished the glory of one of the greatest of the Roman princes. An historian perpetually adverse to the fame of Theodosius has exaggerated his vices and their pernicious effects; he boldly asserts that every rank of subjects imitated the effeminate manners of their sovereign; that every species of corruption polluted the course of public and private life; and that the feeble restraints of order and decency were insufficient to resist the progress of that degenerate spirit which sacrifices, without a blush, the consideration of duty and interest to the base indulgence of sloth and appetite.[1] The complaints of contemporary writers, who deplore the increase of luxury and depravation of manners, are commonly expressive of their peculiar temper and situation. There are few observers who possess a clear and comprehensive view of the revolutions of society, and who are capable of discovering the nice and secret springs of action which impel, in the same uniform direction, the blind and capricious passions of a multitude of individuals. If it can be affirmed, with any degree of truth, that the luxury of the Romans was more shameless and dissolute in the reign of Theodosius than in the age of Constantine, perhaps, or of Augustus, the alteration cannot be ascribed to any beneficial improvements which had gradually increased the stock of national riches. A long period of calamity or decay must have checked the industry and diminished the wealth of the people; and their profuse luxury must have been the result of that indolent despair which enjoys the present hour and declines the thoughts of futurity. The uncertain condition of their

[1] Zosimus, l. iv. [c. 33] p. 244.

property discouraged the subjects of Theodosius from engaging
in those useful and laborious undertakings which require an
immediate expense, and promise a slow and distant advantage.
The frequent examples of ruin and desolation tempted them not
to spare the remains of a patrimony which might, every hour,
become the prey of the rapacious Goth. And the mad prodigality
which prevails in the confusion of a shipwreck or a siege may
serve to explain the progress of luxury amidst the misfortunes
and terrors of a sinking nation.

The effeminate luxury, which infected the manners of courts
and cities, had instilled a secret and destructive poison into the
camps of the legions; and their degeneracy has been marked by
the pen of a military writer, who had accurately studied the
genuine and ancient principles of Roman discipline. It is the
just and important observation of Vegetius, that the infantry
was invariably covered with defensive armour from the foundation of the city to the reign of the emperor Gratian. The
relaxation of discipline and the disuse of exercise rendered the
soldiers less able and less willing to support the fatigues of the
service; they complained of the weight of the armour, which
they seldom wore; and they successively obtained the permission of laying aside both their cuirasses and their helmets.
The heavy weapons of their ancestors, the short sword and the
formidable *pilum*, which had subdued the world, insensibly
dropped from their feeble hands. As the use of the shield is
incompatible with that of the bow, they reluctantly marched
into the field, condemned to suffer either the pain of wounds or
the ignominy of flight, and always disposed to prefer the more
shameful alternative. The cavalry of the Goths, the Huns, and
the Alani, had felt the benefits and adopted the use of defensive
armour; and, as they excelled in the management of missile
weapons, they easily overwhelmed the naked and trembling
legions, whose heads and breasts were exposed, without defence,
to the arrows of the barbarians. The loss of armies, the destruction of cities, and the dishonour of the Roman name, ineffectually solicited the successors of Gratian to restore the helmets
and cuirasses of the infantry. The enervated soldiers abandoned
their own and the public defence; and their pusillanimous indolence may be considered as the immediate cause of the downfall
of the empire.[1]

---

[1] Vegetius, de Re Militari, l. i. c. 20. The series of calamities, which he
marks, compel us to believe that the *Hero* to whom he dedicates his book
is the last and most inglorious of the Valentinians.

CHAPTER XXVIII

Final Destruction of Paganism—Introduction of the Worship of Saints and Relics among the Christians

THE ruin of Paganism, in the age of Theodosius, is perhaps the only example of the total extirpation of any ancient and popular superstition, and may therefore deserve to be considered as a singular event in the history of the human mind. The Christians, more especially the clergy, had impatiently supported the prudent delays of Constantine and the equal toleration of the elder Valentinian; nor could they deem their conquest perfect or secure as long as their adversaries were permitted to exist. The influence which Ambrose and his brethren had acquired over the youth of Gratian and the piety of Theodosius was employed to infuse the maxims of persecution into the breasts of their Imperial proselytes. Two specious principles of religious juris-prudence were established, from whence they deduced a direct and rigorous conclusion against the subjects of the empire who still adhered to the ceremonies of their ancestors: *that* the magistrate is, in some measure, guilty of the crimes which he neglects to prohibit or to punish; and *that* the idolatrous worship of fabulous deities and real dæmons is the most abominable crime against the supreme majesty of the Creator. The laws of Moses and the examples of Jewish history [1] were hastily, perhaps erroneously, applied by the clergy to the mild and universal reign of Christianity.[2] The zeal of the emperors was excited to vindicate their own honour and that of the Deity; and the temples of the Roman world were subverted about sixty years after the conversion of Constantine.

From the age of Numa to the reign of Gratian, the Romans preserved the regular succession of the several colleges of the sacerdotal order.[3] Fifteen PONTIFFS exercised their supreme

---

[1] St. Ambrose (tom. ii. de Obit. Theodos. p. 1208 [ed. Bened.]) expressly praises and recommends the zeal of Josiah in the destruction of idolatry. The language of Julius Firmicus Maternus on the same subject (de Errore Profan. Relig. p. 467, edit. Gronov. [Rotterod. 1743]) is piously inhuman. Nec filio jubet (the Mosaic Law) parci, nec fratri, et per amatam conjugem gladium vindicem ducit, etc.

[2] Bayle (tom. ii. p. 406, in his Commentaire Philosophique) justifies and limits these intolerant laws by the temporal reign of Jehovah over the Jews. The attempt is laudable.

[3] See the outlines of the Roman hierarchy in Cicero (de Legibus, ii. 7, 8), Livy (i. 20), Dionysius Halicarnassensis (l. ii. [c. 63, *sqq.*] p. 119-129, edit. Hudson), Beaufort (République Romaine, tom. i. p. 1-90), and Moyle vol. i. p. 10-55). The last is the work of an English whig, as well as of a Roman antiquary.

jurisdiction over all things and persons that were consecrated to the service of the gods; and the various questions which perpetually arose in a loose and traditionary system were submitted to the judgment of their holy tribunal. Fifteen grave and learned AUGURS observed the face of the heavens, and prescribed the actions of heroes according to the flight of birds. Fifteen keepers of the Sibylline books (their name of QUINDECEMVIRS was derived from their number) occasionally consulted the history of future, and, as it should seem, of contingent events. Six VESTALS devoted their virginity to the guard of the sacred fire and of the unknown pledges of the duration of Rome, which no mortal had been suffered to behold with impunity.[1] Seven EPULOS prepared the table of the gods, conducted the solemn procession, and regulated the ceremonies of the annual festival. The three FLAMENS of Jupiter, of Mars, and of Quirinus, were considered as the peculiar ministers of the three most powerful deities, who watched over the fate of Rome and of the universe. The KING of the SACRIFICES represented the person of Numa and of his successors in the religious functions, which could be performed only by royal hands. The confraternities of the SALIANS, the LUPERCALS, etc., practised such rites as might extort a smile of contempt from every reasonable man, with a lively confidence of recommending themselves to the favour of the immortal gods. The authority which the Roman priests had formerly obtained in the counsels of the republic was gradually abolished by the establishment of monarchy and the removal of the seat of empire. But the dignity of their sacred character was still protected by the laws and manners of their country; and they still continued, more especially the college of pontiffs, to exercise in the capital, and sometimes in the provinces, the rights of their ecclesiastical and civil jurisdiction. Their robes of purple, chariots of state, and sumptuous entertainments attracted the admiration of the people; and they received, from the consecrated lands and the public revenue, an ample stipend, which liberally supported the splendour of the priesthood and all the expenses of the religious worship of the state. As the service of the altar was not incompatible with the command of

---

[1] These mystic, and perhaps imaginary, symbols have given birth to various fables and conjectures. It seems probable that the Palladium was a small statue (three cubits and a half high) of Minerva, with a lance and distaff; that it was usually inclosed in a *seria*, or barrel; and that a similar barrel was placed by its side to disconcert curiosity or sacrilege. See Mezeriac (Comment. sur les Epitres d'Ovide, tom. i. p. 60-66) and Lipsius (tom. iii. p. 610, de Vestâ, etc., c. 10).

armies, the Romans, after their consulships and triumphs, aspired to the place of pontiff or of augur; the seats of Cicero [1] and Pompey were filled, in the fourth century, by the most illustrious members of the senate; and the dignity of their birth reflected additional splendour on their sacerdotal character. The fifteen priests who composed the college of pontiffs enjoyed a more distinguished rank as the companions of their sovereign; and the Christian emperors condescended to accept the robe and ensigns which were appropriated to the office of supreme pontiff. But when Gratian ascended the throne, more scrupulous or more enlightened, he sternly rejected those profane symbols; [2] applied to the service of the state or of the church the revenues of the priests and vestals; abolished their honours and immunities; and dissolved the ancient fabric of Roman superstition, which was supported by the opinions and habits of eleven hundred years. Paganism was still the constitutional religion of the senate. The hall or temple in which they assembled was adorned by the statue and altar of Victory; [3] a majestic female standing on a globe, with flowing garments, expanded wings, and a crown of laurel in her outstretched hand. [4] The senators were sworn on the altar of the goddess to observe the laws of the emperor and of the empire; and a solemn offering of wine and incense was the ordinary prelude of their public deliberations. [5] The removal of this ancient monument was the only injury which Constantius had offered to the superstition of the Romans. The altar of Victory was again restored by Julian, tolerated by Valentinian, and once more banished from the senate by the zeal of Gratian. [6] But the emperor yet spared the statues of the gods which were exposed to the public veneration: four hundred and twenty-four

---

[1] Cicero frankly (ad Atticum, l. ii. Epist. 5) or indirectly (ad Familiar. l. xv. Epist. 4) confesses that the *Augurate* is the supreme object of his wishes. Pliny is proud to tread in the footsteps of Cicero (l. iv. Epist. 8), and the chain of tradition might be continued from history and marbles.

[2] Zosimus, l. iv. [c. 36] p. 249, 250. I have suppressed the foolish pun about *Pontifex* and *Maximus*.

[With regard to Gibbon's statement that Gratian, when he ascended the throne, sternly rejected the use of the Pagan symbols, and applied them to the service of the Christian Church, this is a mistake. It was at a later period of his life that this occurred.—O. S.]

[3] This statue was transported from Tarentum to Rome, placed in the *Curia Julia* by Cæsar, and decorated by Augustus with the spoils of Egypt.

[4] Prudentius (l. ii. [in Symm.] in initio) has drawn a very awkward portrait of Victory; but the curious reader will obtain more satisfaction from Montfaucon's Antiquities (tom. i. p. 341).

[5] See Suetonius (in August. c. 35) and the Exordium of Pliny's Panegyric.

[6] These facts are mutually allowed by the two advocates Symmachus and Ambrose.

temples, or chapels, still remained to satisfy the devotion of the people, and in every quarter of Rome the delicacy of the Christians was offended by the fumes of idolatrous sacrifice.[1]

But the Christians formed the least numerous party in the senate of Rome;[2] and it was only by their absence that they could express their dissent from the legal, though profane, acts of a Pagan majority. In that assembly the dying embers of freedom were, for a moment, revived and inflamed by the breath of fanaticism. Four respectable deputations were successively voted to the Imperial court,[3] to represent the grievances of the priesthood and the senate, and to solicit the restoration of the altar of Victory. The conduct of this important business was intrusted to the eloquent Symmachus,[4] a wealthy and noble senator, who united the sacred characters of pontiff and augur with the civil dignities of proconsul of Africa and præfect of the city. The breast of Symmachus was animated by the warmest zeal for the cause of expiring Paganism; and his religious antagonists lamented the abuse of his genius and the inefficacy of his moral virtues.[5] The orator, whose petition is extant to the emperor Valentinian, was conscious of the difficulty and danger of the office which he had assumed. He cautiously avoids every topic which might appear to reflect on the religion of his sovereign; humbly declares that prayers and entreaties are his only arms; and artfully draws his arguments from the schools of rhetoric rather than from those of philosophy. Symmachus endeavours to seduce the imagination of a young prince, by displaying the attributes of the goddess of Victory; he insinuates that the confiscation of the revenues which were consecrated to the service of the gods was a measure unworthy of his liberal and disinterested character; and he maintains that the Roman

---

[1] The *Notitia Urbis*, more recent than Constantine, does not find one Christian church worthy to be **named** among the edifices of the city. Ambrose (tom. ii. Epist. xvii. p. 825) deplores the public scandals of Rome, which continually offended the eyes, the ears, and the nostrils of the faithful.

[2] Ambrose repeatedly affirms, in contradiction to common sense (Moyle's Works, vol. ii. p. 147), that the Christians had a majority in the senate.

[3] The *first* (A.D. 382) to Gratian, who refused them audience. The *second* (A.D. 384) to Valentinian, when the field was disputed by Symmachus and Ambrose. The *third* (A.D. 388) to Theodosius; and the *fourth* (A.D. 392) to Valentinian. Lardner (Heathen Testimonies, vol. iv. p. 372-399) fairly represents the whole transaction.

[4] Symmachus, who was invested with all the civil and sacerdotal honours, represented the emperor under the two characters of *Pontifex Maximus* and *Princeps Senatus*. See the proud inscription at the head of his works.

[5] As if any one, says Prudentius (in Symmach. i. 639), should dig in the mud with an instrument of gold and ivory. Even saints, and polemic saints, treat this adversary with respect and civility.

sacrifices would be deprived of their force and energy, if they were no longer celebrated at the expense as well as in the name of the republic. Even scepticism is made to supply an apology for superstition. The great and incomprehensible *secret* of the universe eludes the inquiry of man. Where reason cannot instruct, custom may be permitted to guide; and every nation seems to consult the dictates of prudence, by a faithful attachment to those rites and opinions which have received the sanction of ages. If those ages have been crowned with glory and prosperity—if the devout people has frequently obtained the blessings which they have solicited at the altars of the gods—it must appear still more advisable to persist in the same salutary practice, and not to risk the unknown perils that may attend any rash innovations. The test of antiquity and success was applied with singular advantage to the religion of Numa; and ROME herself, the celestial genius that presided over the fates of the city, is introduced by the orator to plead her own cause before the tribunal of the emperors. " Most excellent princes," says the venerable matron, "fathers of your country! pity and respect my age, which has hitherto flowed in an uninterrupted course of piety. Since I do not repent, permit me to continue in the practice of my ancient rites. Since I am born free, allow me to enjoy my domestic institutions. This religion has reduced the world under my laws. These rites have repelled Hannibal from the city, and the Gauls from the Capitol. Were my grey hairs reserved for such intolerable disgrace? I am ignorant of the new system that I am required to adopt; but I am well assured that the correction of old age is always an ungrateful and ignominious office." [1] The fears of the people supplied what the discretion of the orator had suppressed; and the calamities which afflicted or threatened the declining empire were unanimously imputed by the Pagans to the new religion of Christ and of Constantine.

But the hopes of Symmachus were repeatedly baffled by the firm and dexterous opposition of the archbishop of Milan, who fortified the emperors against the fallacious eloquence of the advocate of Rome. In this controversy Ambrose condescends

---

[1] See the fifty-fourth Epistle of the tenth book of Symmachus [p. 289, ed. Paris, 1604]. In the form and disposition of his ten books of Epistles, he imtiated the younger Pliny, whose rich and florid style he was supposed by his friends to equal or excel (Macrob. Saturnal. l. v. c. i.). But the luxuriancy of Symmachus consists of barren leaves, without fruits, and even without flowers. Few facts and few sentiments can be extracted from his verbose correspondence.

to speak the language of a philosopher, and to ask, with some contempt, why it should be thought necessary to introduce an imaginary and invisible power as the cause of those victories, which were sufficiently explained by the valour and discipline of the legions. He justly derides the absurd reverence for antiquity, which could only tend to discourage the improvements of art and to replunge the human race into their original barbarism. From thence gradually rising to a more lofty and theological tone, he pronounces that Christianity alone is the doctrine of truth and salvation, and that every mode of Polytheism conducts its deluded votaries through the paths of error to the abyss of eternal perdition.[1] Arguments like these, when they were suggested by a favourite bishop, had power to prevent the restoration of the altar of Victory; but the same arguments fell with much more energy and effect from the mouth of a conqueror, and the gods of antiquity were dragged in triumph at the chariot-wheels of Theodosius.[2] In a full meeting of the senate the emperor proposed, according to the forms of the republic, the important question, whether the worship of Jupiter or that of Christ should be the religion of the Romans? The liberty of suffrages, which he affected to allow, was destroyed by

[1] See Ambrose (tom. ii. Epist. xvii. xviii. p. 825-833). The former of these epistles is a short caution; the latter is a formal reply to the petition or *libel* of Symmachus. The same ideas are more copiously expressed in the poetry, if it may deserve that name, of Prudentius, who composed his two books against Symmachus (A.D. 404) while that senator was still alive. It is whimsical enough that Montesquieu (Considérations, etc., c. xix. tom. iii. p. 487) should overlook the two professed antagonists of Symmachus, and amuse himself with descanting on the more remote and indirect confutations of Orosius, St. Augustin, and Salvian.

[2] See Prudentius (in Symmach. l. i. 545, etc.). The Christian agrees with the Pagan Zosimus (l. iv. [c. 59] p. 283) in placing this visit of Theodosius after the *second* civil war, gemini bis victor cæde Tyranni (l. i. 410). But the time and circumstances are better suited to his first triumph.

[The truth of the statement has been questioned that " at a full meeting of the senate the emperor proposed, according to the forms of the republic, whether the worship of Jupiter or of Christ should be the religion of the Romans." It is remarkable that Zosimus and Prudentius concur in asserting the fact of the question being solemnly deliberated by the senate, though with directly opposite results. Zosimus declares that the majority of the assembly adhered to the ancient religion of Rome. Gibbon has taken the authority of Prudentius, who, as a Latin writer, though a poet, deserves more credit than the Greek historian. Both writers concur in placing this scene after the second triumph of Theodosius. But it has been almost demonstrated by Pagi and Tillemont that Theodosius did not visit Rome after the defeat of Eugenius. It is extremely improbable that the Christian emperor would submit such a question to the senate, whose authority was nearly obsolete, except on one occasion, which was almost hailed as an epoch in the restoration of her ancient privileges. The silence of Ambrose on an event so striking and redounding so much to the honour of Christianity is of great weight.—O. S.]

the hopes and fears that his presence inspired; and the arbitrary exile of Symmachus was a recent admonition that it might be dangerous to oppose the wishes of the monarch. On a regular division of the senate, Jupiter was condemned and degraded by the sense of a very large majority; and it is rather surprising that any members should be found bold enough to declare, by their speeches and votes, that they were still attached to the interest of an abdicated deity.[1] The hasty conversion of the senate must be attributed either to supernatural or to sordid motives; and many of these reluctant proselytes betrayed, on every favourable occasion, their secret disposition to throw aside the mask of odious dissimulation. But they were gradually fixed in the new religion, as the cause of the ancient became more hopeless; they yielded to the authority of the emperor, to the fashion of the times, and to the entreaties of their wives and children,[2] who were instigated and governed by the clergy of Rome and the monks of the East. The edifying example of the Anician family was soon imitated by the rest of the nobility: the Bassi, the Paullini, the Gracchi, embraced the Christian religion; and " the luminaries of the world, the venerable assembly of Catos (such are the high-flown expressions of Prudentius), were impatient to strip themselves of their pontifical garment—to cast the skin of the old serpent—to assume the snowy robes of baptismal innocence—and to humble the pride of the consular fasces before the tombs of the martyrs." [3] The citizens, who subsisted by their own industry, and the populace, who were supported by the public liberality, filled the churches of the Lateran and Vatican with an incessant throng of devout proselytes. The decrees of the senate, which pro-

---

[1] Prudentius, after proving that the sense of the senate is declared by a legal majority (609, etc.),

> Adspice quam pleno subsellia nostra Senatû
> Decernant infame Jovis pulvinar, et omne
> Idolum longe purgatâ ex urbe fugandum.
> Qua vocat egregii sententia Principis, illuc
> Libera, tum pedibus, tum corde, frequentia transit.

Zosimus ascribes to the conscript fathers an heathenish courage which few of them are found to possess.

[2] Jerom specifies the pontiff Albinus, who was surrounded with such a believing family of children and grandchildren as would have been sufficient to convert even Jupiter himself—an extraordinary proselyte! (tom. i. ad Lætam, p. 54 [Ep. cvii. tom. i. p. 671, ed. Vallars.]).

[3]
> Exsultare Patres videas, pulcherrima mundi
> Lumina; Conciliumque senûm gestire Catonum
> Candidiore togâ niveum pietatis amictum
> Sumere; et exuvias deponere pontificales.

The fancy of Prudentius is warmed and elevated by victory.

scribed the worship of idols, were ratified by the general consent of the Romans;[1] the splendour of the Capitol was defaced, and the solitary temples were abandoned to ruin and contempt.[2] Rome submitted to the yoke of the Gospel; and the vanquished provinces had not yet lost their reverence for the name and authority of Rome.

The filial piety of the emperors themselves engaged them to proceed with some caution and tenderness in the reformation of the eternal city. Those absolute monarchs acted with less regard to the prejudices of the provincials. The pious labour, which had been suspended near twenty years since the death of Constantius,[3] was vigorously resumed, and finally accomplished, by the zeal of Theodosius. Whilst that warlike prince yet struggled with the Goths, not for the glory, but for the safety of the republic, he ventured to offend a considerable party of his subjects, by some acts which might perhaps secure the protection of Heaven, but which must seem rash and unseasonable in the eye of human prudence. The success of his first experiments against the Pagans encouraged the pious emperor to reiterate and enforce his edicts of proscription: the same laws which had been originally published in the provinces of the East, were applied, after the defeat of Maximus, to the whole extent of the Western empire; and every victory of the orthodox Theodosius contributed to the triumph of the Christian and catholic faith.[4] He attacked superstition in her most vital part, by prohibiting the use of sacrifices,

---

[1] Prudentius, after he has described the conversion of the senate and people, asks, with some truth and confidence,

> Et dubitamus adhuc Romam, tibi, Christe, dicatam
> In leges transîsse tuas?

[2] Jerom exults in the desolation of the Capitol and the other temples of Rome (tom. i. p. 54, tom. ii. p. 95).
[Theodosius seized the funds bestowed by the public for the expense of sacrifices, says Zosimus. This is not so. The public sacrifices ceased not only because they were positively prohibited, but because the public treasury would no longer bear the expense. The public and the private sacrifices in the provinces, which were not under the same regulations with those of the capital, continued to take place. In Rome, however, many Pagan ceremonies, which were without sacrifice, remained in full force. The gods were invoked, the temples were frequented, the pontificates inscribed, according to ancient usage among the family titles of honour, so that it cannot be said that Paganism was completely suppressed by Theodosius.—O. S.]

[3] Libanius (Orat. pro Templis, p. 10, Genev. 1634, published by James Godefroy, and now extremely scarce) accuses Valentinian and Valens of prohibiting sacrifices. Some partial order may have been issued by the Eastern emperor; but the idea of any general law is contradicted by the silence of the Code and the evidence of ecclesiastical history.
[4] See his laws in the Theodosian Code, l. xvi. tit. x. leg. 7-11.

which he declared to be criminal as well as infamous; and if the terms of his edicts more strictly condemned the impious curiosity which examined the entrails of the victims,[1] every subsequent explanation tended to involve in the same guilt the general practice of *immolation*, which essentially constituted the religion of the Pagans. As the temples had been erected for the purpose of sacrifice, it was the duty of a benevolent prince to remove from his subjects the dangerous temptation of offending against the laws which he had enacted. A special commission was granted to Cynegius, the Prætorian præfect of the East, and afterwards to the counts Jovius and Gaudentius, two officers of distinguished rank in the West, by which they were directed to shut the temples, to seize or destroy the instruments of idolatry, to abolish the privileges of the priests, and to confiscate the consecrated property for the benefit of the emperor, of the church, or of the army.[2] Here the desolation might have stopped: and the naked edifices, which were no longer employed in the service of idolatry, might have been protected from the destructive rage of fanaticism. Many of those temples were the most splendid and beautiful monuments of Grecian architecture: and the emperor himself was interested not to deface the splendour of his own cities, or to diminish the value of his own possessions. Those stately edifices might be suffered to remain, as so many lasting trophies of the victory of Christ. In the decline of the arts, they might be usefully converted into magazines, manufactures, or places of public assembly: and perhaps, when the walls of the temple had been sufficiently purified by holy rites, the worship of the true Deity might be allowed to expiate the ancient guilt of idolatry. But as long as they subsisted, the Pagans fondly cherished the secret hope that an auspicious revolution, a second Julian, might again restore the altars of the gods: and the earnestness with which they addressed their unavailing prayers

---

[1] Homer's sacrifices are not accompanied with any inquisition of entrails (see Feithius, Antiquitat. Homer. l. i. c. 10, 16. The Tuscans, who produced the first *Haruspices*, subdued both the Greeks and the Romans (Cicero de Divinatione, ii. 23).

[In opposition to the statement that the Tuscans introduced Pagan worship by divination into Greece and Rome, it may be stated that the Greeks observed the entrails of victims as early as the Persian war. Cf. the famous passage in Æschylus, Prometheus Bound, 493 *sqq.*, where Prometheus is said to have taught mortals the art.—O. S.]

[2] Zosimus, l. iv. [c. 37] p. 245, 249. Theodoret, l. v. c. 21. Idatius in Chron. Prosper. Aquitan. l. iii. c. 38, apud Baronium, Annal. Eccles. A.D. 389, No. 52. Libanius (pro Templis, p. 10) labours to prove that the commands of Theodosius were not direct and positive.

to the throne [1] increased the zeal of the Christian reformers to extirpate, without mercy, the root of superstition. The laws of the emperors exhibit some symptoms of a milder disposition: [2] but their cold and languid efforts were insufficient to stem the torrent of enthusiasm and rapine, which was conducted, or rather impelled, by the spiritual rulers of the church. In Gaul, the holy Martin, bishop of Tours, [3] marched at the head of his faithful monks to destroy the idols, the temples, and the consecrated trees of his extensive diocese; and, in the execution of this arduous task, the prudent reader will judge whether Martin was supported by the aid of miraculous powers or of carnal weapons. In Syria, the divine and excellent Marcellus, [4] as he is styled by Theodoret, a bishop animated with apostolic fervour, resolved to level with the ground the stately temples within the diocese of Apamea. His attack was resisted by the skill and solidity with which the temple of Jupiter had been constructed. The building was seated on an eminence: on each of the four sides the lofty roof was supported by fifteen massy columns, sixteen feet in circumference; and the large stones of which they were composed were firmly cemented with lead and iron. The force of the strongest and sharpest tools had been tried without effect. It was found necessary to undermine the foundations of the columns, which fell down as soon as the temporary wooden props had been consumed with fire; and the difficulties of the enterprise are described under the allegory of a black dæmon, who retarded, though he could not defeat, the operations of the Christian engineers. Elated with victory, Marcellus took the field in person against the powers of darkness; a numerous troop of

[1] Cod. Theodos. l. xvi. tit. x. leg. 8, 18. There is room to believe that this temple of Edessa, which Theodosius wished to save for civil uses, was soon afterwards a heap of ruins (Libanius pro Templis. p. 26, 27, and Godefroy's notes, p. 59).

[Libanius appears to be the best authority for the East where, under Theodosius, the work of devastation was carried on with very different degrees of violence, according to the temper of the local authorities and of the clergy, and more especially the neighbourhood of the more fanatical monks. Neander says that the prohibition of sacrifice would be easily misconstrued into an order for the destruction of the buildings in which sacrifices were performed. (*Geschichte der Christlichen Religion*, vol. ii. p. 156. An abuse of this kind led to this remarkable oration by Libanius. —O. S.]

[2] See this curious oration of Libanius pro Templis, pronounced, or rather composed, about the year 390. I have consulted with advantage Dr. Lardner's version and remarks (Heathen Testimonies, vol. iv. p. 135-163).

[3] See the Life of Martin by Sulpicius Severus, c. 9-14. The saint once mistook (as Don Quixote might have done) an harmless funeral for an idolatrous procession, and imprudently committed a miracle.

[4] Compare Sozomen (l. vii. c. 15) with Theodoret (l. v. c. 21). Between them they relate the crusade and death of Marcellus.

soldiers and gladiators marched under the episcopal banner, and he successively attacked the villages and country temples of the diocese of Apamea. Whenever any resistance or danger was apprehended, the champion of the faith, whose lameness would not allow him either to fight or fly, placed himself at a convenient distance, beyond the reach of darts. But this prudence was the occasion of his death; he was surprised and slain by a body of exasperated rustics; and the synod of the province pronounced, without hesitation, that the holy Marcellus had sacrificed his life in the cause of God. In the support of this cause, the monks, who rushed with tumultuous fury from the desert, distinguished themselves by their zeal and diligence. They deserved the enmity of the Pagans; and some of them might deserve the reproaches of avarice and intemperance—of avarice, which they gratified with holy plunder; and of intemperance, which they indulged at the expense of the people, who foolishly admired their tattered garments, loud psalmody, and artificial paleness.[1] A small number of temples was protected by the fears, the venality, the taste, or the prudence of the civil and ecclesiastical governors. The temple of the Celestial Venus at Carthage, whose sacred precincts formed a circumference of two miles, was judiciously converted into a Christian church;[2] and a similar consecration has preserved inviolate the majestic dome of the Pantheon at Rome.[3] But in almost every province of the Roman world, an army of fanatics, without authority and without discipline, invaded the peaceful inhabitants; and the ruin of the fairest structures of antiquity still displays the ravages of *those* barbarians who alone had time and inclination to execute such laborious destruction.

In this wide and various prospect of devastation, the spectator may distinguish the ruins of the temple of Serapis, at Alexandria.[4] Serapis does not appear to have been one of the

---

[1] Libanius pro Templis, p. 10-13. He rails at these black-garbed men the Christian monks, who eat more than elephants. Poor elephants! *they* are temperate animals.

[2] Prosper. Aquitan. l. iii. c. 38, apud Baronium; Annal. Eccles. A.D. 389, No. 58, etc. The temple had been shut some time, and the access to it was overgrown with brambles.

[3] Donatus, Roma Antiqua et Nova, l. iv. c. 4, p. 468. This consecration was performed by Pope Boniface IV. I am ignorant of the favourable circumstances which had preserved the Pantheon above two hundred years after the reign of Theodosius.

[4] Sophronius composed a recent and separate history (Jerom. in Script. Eccles. tom. i. p. 303), which has furnished materials to Socrates (l. v. c. 16), Theodoret (l. v. c. 22), and Rufinus (l. ii. c. 22). Yet the last, who had been at Alexandria before and after the event, may deserve the credit of an original witness.

native gods, or monsters, who sprung from the fruitful soil of superstitious Egypt.[1] The first of the Ptolemies had been commanded, by a dream, to import the mysterious stranger from the coast of Pontus, where he had been long adored by the inhabitants of Sinope; but his attributes and his reign were so imperfectly understood, that it became a subject of dispute whether he represented the bright orb of day, or the gloomy monarch of the subterraneous regions.[2] The Egyptians, who were obstinately devoted to the religion of their fathers, refused to admit this foreign deity within the walls of their cities.[3] But the obsequious priests, who were seduced by the liberality of the Ptolemies, submitted, without resistance, to the power of the god of Pontus: an honourable and domestic genealogy was provided; and this fortunate usurper was introduced into the throne and bed of Osiris,[4] the husband of Isis, and the celestial monarch of Egypt. Alexandria, which claimed his peculiar protection, gloried in the name of the city of Serapis. His temple,[5] which rivalled the pride and magnificence of the Capitol, was erected on the spacious summit of an artificial mount, raised one hundred steps above the level of the adjacent parts of the city; and the interior cavity was strongly supported by arches, and distributed into vaults and subterraneous apartments. The consecrated buildings were surrounded by a quadrangular portico; the stately halls and exquisite statues displayed the triumph of the arts; and the treasures of ancient learning were preserved in

---

[1] Gerard Vossius (Opera, tom. v. p. 80, and de Idololatriâ, l. i. c. 29) strives to support the strange notion of the Fathers, that the patriarch Joseph was adored in Egypt as the bull Apis and the god Serapis.

[Modern writers are agreed that the worship of Serapis was not so strange to the ancient Egyptians as the narrative of Tacitus would imply. Serapis appears to have been worshipped by the ancient Egyptians as the god of the lower world, and hence to have been identified by the Ptolemies with the Jupiter, Dis, or Pluto of Sinope. He was the Osiris of the lower world, and among the Greeks and Romans took the place of this deity. See Guigniaut, Sérapis et son Origine.—O. S.]

[2] Origo dei nondum nostris celebrata. Ægyptiorum antistites *sic* memorant, etc. Tacit. Hist. iv. 83. The Greeks who had travelled into Egypt were alike ignorant of this new deity.

[3] Macrobius, Saturnal. l. i. c. 7. Such a living fact decisively proves his foreign extraction.

[4] At Rome, Isis and Serapis were united in the same temple. The precedency which the queen assumed may seem to betray her unequal alliance with the stranger of Pontus. But the superiority of the female sex was established in Egypt as a civil and religious institution (Diodor. Sicul. tom. i. l. i. [c. 27] p. 31, edit. Wesseling), and the same order is observed in Plutarch's Treatise of Isis and *Osiris ;* whom he identifies with Serapis.

[5] Ammianus (xxii. 16). The Expositio totius Mundi (p. 8, in Hudson's Geograph. Minor. tom. iii.), and Rufinus (l. ii. c. 22), celebrate the *Serapeum* as one of the wonders of the world.

the famous Alexandrian library, which had arisen with new splendour from its ashes.[1] After the edicts of Theodosius had severely prohibited the sacrifices of the Pagans, they were still tolerated in the city and temple of Serapis; and this singular indulgence was imprudently ascribed to the superstitious terrors of the Christians themselves: as if they had feared to abolish those ancient rites which could alone secure the inundations of the Nile, the harvests of Egypt, and the subsistence of Constantinople.[2]

At that time[3] the archiepiscopal throne of Alexandria was filled by Theophilus,[4] the perpetual enemy of peace and virtue; a bold, bad man, whose hands were alternately polluted with gold and with blood. His pious indignation was excited by the

---

[1] See Mémoires de l'Acad. des Inscriptions, tom. ix. p. 397-416. The *old* library of the Ptolemies was *totally* consumed in Cæsar's Alexandrian war. Marc Antony gave the whole collection of Pergamus (200,000 volumes) to Cleopatra, as the foundation of the *new* library of Alexandria.

[The statements of Gibbon regarding the libraries of Alexandria require some modification. In the Alexandria of the Ptolemies there were two libraries, the larger one in the quarter named the *Bruchium*, and the smaller one was the *Serapeum*—called the daughter of the other, and situated in the quarter called Rhacotis. The former was totally destroyed in the conflagration of the Bruchium during Cæsar's Alexandrian war; but the latter, which was of great value, remained uninjured. It is probable that the collection of Pergamus was placed in the Bruchium after the fire, as that quarter was without a library, and the queen was anxious to repair the ravages occasioned by the Civil War. If this supposition is correct, two Alexandrian libraries continued to exist after the time of Cæsar, and this is rendered still more probable by the fact that, during the first three centuries of the Christian era, the Bruchium was still the literary quarter of Alexandria. But a great change took place in the time of Aurelian. This emperor, in suppressing the revolt of Firmus in Egypt A.D. 273, is said to have destroyed the Bruchium, and though this statement is hardly to be taken literally, the Bruchium ceased from this time to be included within the walls of Alexandria, and was regarded only as a suburb of the city. Whether the great library in the Bruchium with the museum and its other literary establishments perished at this time, we do not know; but the Serapeum for the next century takes its place as the literary quarter of Alexandria, and becomes the chief library of the city. Hence many writers erroneously speak of the Serapeum as if it had been from the beginning the great Alexandrian library.—O. S.]

[2] Libanius (pro Templis, p. 21) indiscreetly provokes his Christian masters by this insulting remark.

[3] We may choose between the date of Marcellinus (A.D. 389) or that of Prosper (A.D. 391). Tillemont (Hist. des. Emp. tom. v. p. 310, 756) prefers the former, and Pagi the latter.

[With regard to "the chapel of Bacchus" which Theophilus overthrew, Sozomen calls it "a temple of Bacchus," but as Dr. Smith says, we may conclude it was a temple of Osiris, as the Greeks gave to this deity the name of Bacchus. Socrates calls the temple a Mithreum.—O. S.]

[4] Tillemont, Mém. Ecclés. tom. xi. p. 441-500. The ambiguous situation of Theophilus—a *saint*, as the friend of Jerom; a *devil*, as the enemy of Chrysostom—produces a sort of impartiality; yet, upon the whole, the balance is justly inclined against him.

honours of Serapis; and the insults which he offered to an ancient
chapel of Bacchus convinced the Pagans that he meditated a
more important and dangerous enterprise. In the tumultuous
capital of Egypt, the slightest provocation was sufficient to
inflame a civil war. The votaries of Serapis, whose strength and
numbers were much inferior to those of their antagonists, rose
in arms at the instigation of the philosopher Olympius,[1] who
exhorted them to die in the defence of the altars of the gods.
These Pagan fanatics fortified themselves in the temple, or rather
fortress, of Serapis; repelled the besiegers by daring sallies and a
resolute defence; and, by the inhuman cruelties which they
exercised on their Christian prisoners, obtained the last consolation of despair. The efforts of the prudent magistrate were
usefully exerted for the establishment of a truce till the answer
of Theodosius should determine the fate of Serapis. The two
parties assembled, without arms, in the principal square; and the
Imperial rescript was publicly read. But when a sentence of
destruction against the idols of Alexandria was pronounced, the
Christians sent up a shout of joy and exultation, whilst the
unfortunate Pagans, whose fury had given way to consternation,
retired with hasty and silent steps, and eluded, by their flight
or obscurity, the resentment of their enemies. Theophilus proceeded to demolish the temple of Serapis, without any other
difficulties than those which he found in the weight and solidity
of the materials; but these obstacles proved so insuperable that
he was obliged to leave the foundations, and to content himself
with reducing the edifice itself to a heap of rubbish, a part of
which was soon afterwards cleared away, to make room for a
church erected in honour of the Christian martyrs. The valuable
library of Alexandria was pillaged or destroyed; and near
twenty years afterwards, the appearance of the empty shelves
excited the regret and indignation of every spectator whose mind
was not totally darkened by religious prejudice.[2] The com-

---

[1] Lardner (Heathen Testimonies, vol. iv. p. 411) has alleged a beautiful
passage from Suidas, or rather from Damascius, which shows the devout
and virtuous Olympius, not in the light of a warrior, but of a prophet.

[2] Nos vidimus armaria librorum, quibus direptis, exinanita ea a nostris
hominibus, nostris temporibus memorent. Orosius, l. vi. c. 15, p. 421,
edit. Havercamp. Though a bigot and a controversial writer, Orosius
seems to blush.

[Gibbon seems to think that the whole of the Serapeum was destroyed,
but this was not the case. It was only the sanctuary of the god that was
levelled with the ground, and the library, the halls and the other
buildings in the consecrated ground remained standing long afterwards.
Moreover, if we credit the story of the destruction of the Alexandrian
library by the Arabs under Amrou, which there seems no good reason to

positions of ancient genius, so many of which have irretrievably perished, might surely have been excepted from the wreck of idolatry, for the amusement and instruction of succeeding ages; and either the zeal or the avarice of the archbishop [1] might have been satiated with the rich spoils which were the reward of his victory. While the images and vases of gold and silver were carefully melted, and those of a less valuable metal were contemptuously broken and cast into the streets, Theophilus laboured to expose the frauds and vices of the ministers of the idols: their dexterity in the management of the loadstone; their secret methods of introducing an human actor into a hollow statue; and their scandalous abuse of the confidence of devout husbands and unsuspecting females.[2] Charges like these may seem to deserve some degree of credit, as they are not repugnant to the crafty and interested spirit of superstition. But the same spirit is equally prone to the base practice of insulting and calumniating a fallen enemy; and our belief is naturally checked by the reflection that it is much less difficult to invent a fictitious story than to support a practical fraud. The colossal statue of Serapis [3] was involved in the ruin of his temple and religion. A great number of plates of different metals, artificially joined together, composed the majestic figure of the deity, who touched on either side the walls of the sanctuary. The aspect of Serapis, his sitting posture, and the sceptre which he bore in his left hand, were extremely similar to the ordinary representations of Jupiter. He was distinguished from Jupiter by the basket, or bushel, which was placed on his head; and by the emblematic monster which he held in his right hand; the head and body of a serpent branching into three tails, which were again terminated by the triple heads of a dog, a lion, and a wolf. It was confidently affirmed that, if any impious hand

doubt, we must conclude that the library in the Serapeum existed down to A.D. 638.—O. S.]

[1] Eunapius, in the Lives of Antoninus and Ædesius, execrates the sacrilegious rapine of Theophilus. Tillemont (Mém. Ecclés. tom. xiii. p. 453) quotes an epistle of Isidore of Pelusium, which reproaches the primate with the *idolatrous* worship of gold, the auri *sacra* fames.

[2] Rufinus names the priest of Saturn who, in the character of the god, familiarly conversed with many pious ladies of quality; till he betrayed himself, in a moment of transport, when he could not disguise the tone of his voice. The authentic and impartial narrative of Æschines (see Bayle, Dictionnaire Critique, SCAMANDRE), and the adventure of Mundus (Joseph. Antiquitat. Judaic. l. xviii. c. 3 [§ 4], p. 877, edit. Havercamp), may prove that such amorous frauds have been practised with success.

[3] See the images of Serapis, in Montfaucon (tom. ii. p. 297): but the description of Macrobius (Saturnal. l. i. c. 20) is much more picturesque and satisfactory.

should dare to violate the majesty of the god, the heavens and
the earth would instantly return to their original chaos. An
intrepid soldier, animated by zeal, and armed with a weighty
battle-axe, ascended the ladder; and even the Christian multitude
expected with some anxiety the event of the combat.[1] He aimed
a vigorous stroke against the cheek of Serapis; the cheek fell
to the ground; the thunder was still silent, and both the heavens
and the earth continued to preserve their accustomed order and
tranquillity. The victorious soldier repeated his blows: the
huge idol was overthrown and broken in pieces; and the limbs
of Serapis were ignominiously dragged through the streets of
Alexandria. His mangled carcase was burnt in the amphitheatre,
amidst the shouts of the populace; and many persons attributed
their conversion to this discovery of the impotence of their
tutelar deity. The popular modes of religion, that propose any
visible and material objects of worship, have the advantage of
adapting and familiarising themselves to the senses of mankind;
but this advantage is counterbalanced by the various and inevitable accidents to which the faith of the idolater is exposed. It
is scarcely possible that, in every disposition of mind, he should
preserve his implicit reverence for the idols, or the relics, which
the naked eye and the profane hand are unable to distinguish
from the most common productions of art or nature; and if,
in the hour of danger, their secret and miraculous virtue does not
operate for their own preservation, he scorns the vain apologies
of his priests, and justly derides the object and the folly of his
superstitious attachment.[2] After the fall of Serapis, some hopes
were still entertained by the Pagans that the Nile would refuse
his annual supply to the impious masters of Egypt; and the
extraordinary delay of the inundation seemed to announce the
displeasure of the river-god. But this delay was soon compensated by the rapid swell of the waters. They suddenly rose to
such an unusual height as to comfort the discontented party
with the pleasing expectation of a deluge; till the peaceful river

---

[1] Sed fortes tremuere manus, motique verendâ
    Majestate loci, si robora sacra ferirent
    In sua credebant redituras membra secures.

(Lucan. iii. 429.) " Is it true " (said Augustus to a veteran of Italy, at
whose house he supped) " that the man who gave the first blow to the
golden statue of Anaitis was instantly deprived of his eyes and of his
life? "—" *I* was that man " (replied the clear-sighted veteran), " and you
now sup on one of the legs of the goddess." (Plin. Hist. Natur. xxxiii. 24.)

[2] The History of the Reformation affords frequent examples of the
sudden change from superstition to contempt.

again subsided to the well-known and fertilising level of sixteen cubits, or about thirty English feet.[1]

The temples of the Roman empire were deserted or destroyed; but the ingenious superstition of the Pagans still attempted to elude the laws of Theodosius, by which all sacrifices had been severely prohibited. The inhabitants of the country, whose conduct was less exposed to the eye of malicious curiosity, disguised their *religious* under the appearance of *convivial* meetings. On the days of solemn festivals they assembled in great numbers under the spreading shade of some consecrated trees; sheep and oxen were slaughtered and roasted; and this rural entertainment was sanctified by the use of incense and by the hymns which were sung in honour of the gods. But it was alleged that, as no part of the animal was made a burnt-offering, as no altar was provided to receive the blood, and as the previous oblation of salt cakes and the concluding ceremony of libations were carefully omitted, these festal meetings did not involve the guests in the guilt or penalty of an illegal sacrifice.[2] Whatever might be the truth of the facts or the merit of the distinction,[3] these vain pretences were swept away by the last edict of Theodosius, which inflicted a deadly wound on the superstition of the Pagans.[4] This prohibitory law is expressed in the most absolute and comprehensive terms. "It is our will and pleasure," says the emperor, "that none of our subjects, whether magistrates or private citizens, however exalted or however humble may be their rank and condition, shall presume in any city or in any place to worship an inanimate idol by the sacrifice of a guiltless victim." The act of sacrificing and the practice of divination by the entrails of the victim are declared (without any regard to the object of the inquiry) a crime of high treason

---

[1] Sozomen, l. vii. c. 20. I have supplied the measure. The same standard of the inundation, and consequently of the cubit, has uniformly subsisted since the time of Herodotus. See Fréret, in the Mém. de l'Académie des Inscriptions, tom. xvi. p. 344-353. Greaves's Miscellaneous Works, vol. i. p. 233. The Egyptian cubit is about twenty-two inches of the English measure.

[2] Libanius (pro Templis, p. 15, 16, 17) pleads their cause with gentle and insinuating rhetoric. From the earliest age such feasts had enlivened the country: and those of Bacchus (Georgic. ii. 380) had produced the theatre of Athens. See Godefroy, ad loc., Liban., and Codex Theodos. tom. vi. p. 284 [ed. Lugd. 1665].

[3] Honorius tolerated these rustic festivals (A.D. 399). "Absque ullo sacrificio, atque ullâ superstitione damnabili." But nine years afterwards he found it necessary to reiterate and enforce the same proviso (Codex Theodos. l. xvi. tit. x. leg. 17, 19).

[4] Cod. Theodos. l. xvi. tit. x. leg. 12. Jortin (Remarks on Eccles. History, vol. iv. p. 134) censures, with becoming asperity, the style and sentiments of this intolerant law.

against the state, which can be expiated only by the death of the guilty. The rites of Pagan superstition which might seem less bloody and atrocious are abolished as highly injurious to the truth and honour of religion; luminaries, garlands, frankincense, and libations of wine are specially enumerated and condemned; and the harmless claims of the domestic genius, of the household gods, are included in this rigorous proscription. The use of any of these profane and illegal ceremonies subjects the offender to the forfeiture of the house or estate where they have been performed; and if he has artfully chosen the property of another for the scene of his impiety, he is compelled to discharge, without delay, a heavy fine of twenty-five pounds of gold, or more than one thousand pounds sterling. A fine not less considerable is imposed on the connivance of the secret enemies of religion who shall neglect the duty of their respective stations, either to reveal or to punish the guilt of idolatry. Such was the persecuting spirit of the laws of Theodosius, which were repeatedly enforced by his sons and grandsons, with the loud and unanimous applause of the Christian world.[1]

In the cruel reigns of Decius and Diocletian Christianity had been proscribed, as a revolt from the ancient and hereditary religion of the empire; and the unjust suspicions which were entertained of a dark and dangerous faction were in some measure countenanced by the inseparable union and rapid conquests of the catholic church. But the same excuses of fear and ignorance cannot be applied to the Christian emperors, who violated the precepts of humanity and of the Gospel. The experience of ages had betrayed the weakness as well as folly of Paganism; the light of reason and of faith had already exposed to the greatest part of mankind the vanity of idols; and the declining sect, which still adhered to their worship, might have been permitted to enjoy in peace and obscurity the religious customs of their ancestors. Had the Pagans been animated by the undaunted zeal which possessed the minds of the primitive believers, the triumph of the church must have been stained with blood; and the martyrs of Jupiter and Apollo might have embraced the glorious opportunity of devoting their lives and

---

[1] Such a charge should not be lightly made; but it may surely be justified by the authority of St. Augustin, who thus addresses the Donatists: " Quis nostrûm, quis vestrûm non laudat leges ab Imperatoribus datas adversus sacrificia Paganorum? Et certe longe ibi pœna severior constituta est; illius quippe impietatis capitale supplicium est." Epist. xciii. No. 10 [tom. ii. p. 308, ed. Bened. 1797], quoted by Le Clerc (Bibliothèque Choisie, tom. viii. p. 277), who adds some judicious reflections on the intolerance of the victorious Christians.

fortunes at the foot of their altars. But such obstinate zeal was not congenial to the loose and careless temper of Polytheism. The violent and repeated strokes of the orthodox princes were broken by the soft and yielding substance against which they were directed; and the ready obedience of the Pagans protected them from the pains and penalties of the Theodosian Code.[1] Instead of asserting that the authority of the gods was superior to that of the emperor, they desisted, with a plaintive murmur, from the use of those sacred rites which their sovereign had condemned. If they were sometimes tempted by a sally of passion, or by the hopes of concealment, to indulge their favourite superstition, their humble repentance disarmed the severity of the Christian magistrate, and they seldom refused to atone for their rashness by submitting, with some secret reluctance, to the yoke of the Gospel. The churches were filled with the increasing multitude of these unworthy proselytes, who had conformed, from temporal motives, to the reigning religion; and whilst they devoutly imitated the postures and recited the prayers of the faithful, they satisfied their conscience by the silent and sincere invocation of the gods of antiquity.[2] If the Pagans wanted patience to suffer, they wanted spirit to resist; and the scattered myriads, who deplored the ruin of the temples, yielded, without a contest, to the fortune of their adversaries. The disorderly opposition [3] of the peasants of Syria and the populace of Alexandria to the rage of private fanaticism was silenced by the name and authority of the emperor. The Pagans of the West, without contributing to the elevation of Eugenius, disgraced by their partial attachment the cause and character of the usurper. The clergy vehemently exclaimed that he aggravated the crime of rebellion by the guilt of apostasy; that, by his permission, the altar of Victory was again restored; and that the idolatrous symbols of Jupiter and Hercules were displayed in the field against the invincible standard of the cross. But the vain hopes of the Pagans were soon annihilated by the defeat of Eugenius; and they were left exposed to the resentment of the conqueror,

---

[1] Orosius, l. vii. c. 28, p. 537. Augustin (Enarrat. in Psalm cxl. apud Lardner, Heathen Testimonies, vol. iv. p. 458) insults their cowardice. " Quis eorum comprehensus est in sacrificio (cum his legibus ista prohiberentur) et non negavit? "

[2] Libanius (pro Templis, p. 17, 18) mentions, without censure, the occasional conformity, and as it were theatrical play, of these hypocrites.

[3] Libanius concludes his apology (p. 32) by declaring to the emperor that, unless he expressly warrants the destruction of the temples, ἴσθι τοὺς τῶν ἀγρῶν δεσπότας, καὶ αὑτοῖς, καὶ τῷ νόμῳ βοηθήσοντας, the proprietors will defend themselves and the laws.

who laboured to deserve the favour of Heaven by the extirpation of idolatry.[1]

A nation of slaves is always prepared to applaud the clemency of their master who, in the abuse of absolute power, does not proceed to the last extremes of injustice and oppression. Theodosius might undoubtedly have proposed to his Pagan subjects the alternative of baptism or of death; and the eloquent Libanius has praised the moderation of a prince who never enacted, by any positive law, that all his subjects should immediately embrace and practise the religion of their sovereign.[2] The profession of Christianity was not made an essential qualification for the enjoyment of the civil rights of society, nor were any peculiar hardships imposed on the sectaries who credulously received the fables of Ovid and obstinately rejected the miracles of the Gospel. The palace, the schools, the army, and the senate were filled with declared and devout Pagans; they obtained, without distinction, the civil and military honours of the empire. Theodosius distinguished his liberal regard for virtue and genius by the consular dignity which he bestowed on Symmachus,[3] and by the personal friendship which he expressed to Libanius;[4] and the two eloquent apologists of Paganism were never required either to change or to dissemble their religious opinions. The Pagans were indulged in the most licentious freedom of speech and writing; the historical and philosophic remains of Eunapius, Zosimus,[5] and the fanatic teachers of the school of Plato, betray the most furious animosity, and contain the sharpest invectives, against the sentiments and conduct of their victorious adversaries.

---

[1] Paulinus, in Vit. Ambros. c. 26.   Augustin de Civitat. Dei, l. v. c. 26. Theodoret, l. v. c. 24.

[2] Libanius suggests the form of a persecuting edict which Theodosius might enact (pro Templis, p. 31): a rash joke and a dangerous experiment. Some princes would have taken his advice.

[3]   Denique pro meritis terrestribus æqua rependens
        Munera, sacricolis summos impertit honores,
        Dux bonus, et certare sinit cum laude suorum:
        Nec pago implicitos per debita culmina mundi
        Ire viros prohibet.
        Ipse magistratum tibi consulis, ipse tribunal
        Contulit.
                                        Prudent. in Symmach. i. 617, etc.

[4] Libanius (pro Templis, p. 32) is proud that Theodosius should thus distinguish a man who even in his *presence* would swear by Jupiter.   Yet this presence seems to be no more than a figure of rhetoric.

[5] Zosimus, who styles himself Count and Ex-advocate of the Treasury, reviles, with partial and indecent bigotry, the Christian princes, and even the father of his sovereign.   His work must have been privately circulated, since it escaped the invectives of the ecclesiastical historians prior to Evagrius (l. iii. c. 40-41), who lived towards the end of the sixth century.

If these audacious libels were publicly known, we must applaud the good sense of the Christian princes, who viewed with a smile of contempt the last struggles of superstition and despair.[1] But the Imperial laws which prohibited the sacrifices and ceremonies of Paganism were rigidly executed; and every hour contributed to destroy the influence of a religion which was supported by custom rather than by argument. The devotion of the poet or the philosopher may be secretly nourished by prayer, meditation, and study; but the exercise of public worship appears to be the only solid foundation of the religious sentiments of the people, which derive their force from imitation and habit. The interruption of that public exercise may consummate, in the period of a few years, the important work of a national revolution. The memory of theological opinions cannot long be preserved without the artificial helps of priests, of temples, and of books.[2] The ignorant vulgar, whose minds are still agitated by the blind hopes and terrors of superstition, will be soon persuaded by their superiors to direct their vows to the reigning deities of the age; and will insensibly imbibe an ardent zeal for the support and propagation of the new doctrine, which spiritual hunger at first compelled them to accept. The generation that arose in the world after the promulgation of the Imperial laws was attracted within the pale of the catholic church: and so rapid, yet so gentle, was the fall of Paganism, that only twenty-eight years after the death of Theodosius the faint and minute vestiges were no longer visible to the eye of the legislator.[3]

The ruin of the Pagan religion is described by the sophists as a dreadful and amazing prodigy, which covered the earth with darkness and restored the ancient dominion of chaos and of night. They relate in solemn and pathetic strains that the temples were converted into sepulchres, and that the holy places, which had been adorned by the statues of the gods, were basely polluted by the relics of Christian martyrs. "The monks" (a race of filthy animals, to whom Eunapius is tempted to refuse the name of men) "are the authors of the new worship,

[1] Yet the Pagans of Africa complained that the times would not allow them to answer with freedom the City of God; nor does St. Augustin (v. 26) deny the charge.

[2] The Moors of Spain, who secretly preserved the Mahometan religion above a century, under the tyranny of the Inquisition, possessed the Koran, with the peculiar use of the Arabic tongue. See the curious and honest story of their expulsion in Geddes (Miscellanies, vol. i. p. 1-198).

[3] Paganos qui supersunt, quanquam jam nullos esse credamus, etc. Cod. Theodos. l. xvi. tit. x. leg. 22, A.D. 423. The younger Theodosius was afterwards satisfied that his judgment had been somewhat premature.

which, in the place of those deities who are conceived by the understanding, has substituted the meanest and most contemptible slaves. The heads, salted and pickled, of those infamous malefactors, who for the multitude of their crimes have suffered a just and ignominious death; their bodies, still marked by the impression of the lash and the scars of those tortures which were inflicted by the sentence of the magistrate; such " (continues Eunapius) " are the gods which the earth produces in our days; such are the martyrs, the supreme arbitrators of our prayers and petitions to the Deity, whose tombs are now consecrated as the objects of the veneration of the people."[1] Without approving the malice, it is natural enough to share the surprise of the sophist, the spectator of a revolution which raised those obscure victims of the laws of Rome to the rank of celestial and invisible protectors of the Roman empire. The grateful respect of the Christians for the martyrs of the faith was exalted, by time and victory, into religious adoration; and the most illustrious of the saints and prophets were deservedly associated to the honours of the martyrs. One hundred and fifty years after the glorious deaths of St. Peter and St. Paul, the Vatican and the Ostian road were distinguished by the tombs, or rather by the trophies, of those spiritual heroes.[2] In the age which followed the conversion of Constantine, the emperors, the consuls, and the generals of armies devoutly visited the sepulchres of a tentmaker and a fisherman;[3] and their venerable bones were deposited under the altars of Christ, on which the bishops of the royal city continually offered the unbloody sacrifice.[4] The new capital of the Eastern world, unable to produce any ancient and domestic trophies, was enriched by the spoils of dependent provinces. The bodies of St. Andrew, St. Luke, and St. Timothy had reposed near three hundred years in the obscure graves from whence they were transported, in solemn pomp, to the church of the apostles, which

---

[1] See Eunapius, in the Life of the sophist Ædesius; in that of Eustathius he foretells the ruin of Paganism, καί τι μυθῶδες, καὶ ἀειδὲς, σκότος τυραννήσει τὰ ἐπὶ γῆς κάλλιστα.

[2] Caius (apud Euseb. Hist. Eccles. l. ii. c. 25), a Roman presbyter, who lived in the time of Zephyrinus (A.D. 202-219), is an early witness of this superstitious practice.

[3] Chrysostom. Quod Christus sit Deus. Tom. i. nov. edit. No. 9. I am indebted for this quotation to Benedict the XIVth's pastoral letter on the Jubilee of the year 1750. See the curious and entertaining letters of M. Chais, tom. iii.

[4] Male facit ergo Romanus episcopus? qui, super mortuorum hominum, Petri and Pauli, secundum nos, ossa veneranda . . . offert Domino sacrificia, et tumulos eorum, Christi arbitratur altaria. Jerom. tom. ii. advers. Vigilant. p. 153. [Tom. ii. p. 395, ed. Vallars.]

the magnificence of Constantine had founded on the banks of the Thracian Bosphorus.[1] About fifty years afterwards the same banks were honoured by the presence of Samuel, the judge and prophet of the people of Israel. His ashes, deposited in a golden vase, and covered with a silken veil, were delivered by the bishops into each other's hands. The relics of Samuel were received by the people with the same joy and reverence which they would have shown to the living prophet; the highways, from Palestine to the gates of Constantinople, were filled with an uninterrupted procession; and the emperor Arcadius himself, at the head of the most illustrious members of the clergy and senate, advanced to meet his extraordinary guest, who had always deserved and claimed the homage of kings.[2] The example of Rome and Constantinople confirmed the faith and discipline of the catholic world. The honours of the saints and martyrs, after a feeble and ineffectual murmur of profane reason,[3] were universally established; and in the age of Ambrose and Jerom something was still deemed wanting to the sanctity of a Christian church, till it had been consecrated by some portion of holy relics, which fixed and inflamed the devotion of the faithful. In the long period of twelve hundred years, which elapsed between the reign of Constantine and the reformation of Luther, the worship of saints and relics corrupted the pure and perfect simplicity of the Christian model; and some symptoms of degeneracy may be observed even in the first generations which adopted and cherished this pernicious innovation.

I. The satisfactory experience that the relics of saints were more valuable than gold or precious stones [4] stimulated the clergy to multiply the treasures of the church. Without much

---

[1] Jerom (tom. ii. p. 122 [contra Vigilant. c. 5, tom. ii. p. 391, ed. Vallars.]) bears witness to these translations, which are neglected by the ecclesiastical historians. The passion of St. Andrew at Patræ is described in an epistle from the clergy of Achaia, which Baronius (Annal. Eccles. A.D. 60, No. 34) wishes to believe, and Tillemont is forced to reject. St. Andrew was adopted as the spiritual founder of Constantinople (Mém. Ecclés. tom. i. p. 317-323, 588-594).

[2] Jerom (tom. ii. p. 122 [l. c. ed. Vallars.]) pompously describes the translation of Samuel, which is noticed in all the chronicles of the times.

[3] The presbyter Vigilantis, the protestant of his age, firmly, though ineffectually, withstood the superstition of monks, relics, saints, fasts, etc., for which Jerom compares him to the Hydra, Cerberus, the Centaurs, etc., and considers him only as the organ of the Dæmon (tom. ii. p. 120-126 [tom. ii. p. 387-402, ed. Vallars.]. Whoever will peruse the controversy of St. Jerom and Vigilantius, and St. Augustin's account of the miracles of St. Stephen, may speedily gain some idea of the spirit of the Fathers.

[4] M. de Beausobre (Hist. du Manichéisme, tom. ii. p. 648) has applied a worldly sense to the pious observation of the clergy of Smyrna, who carefully preserved the relics of St. Polycarp the martyr.

regard for truth or probability, they invented names for
skeletons, and actions for names. The fame of the apostles,
and of the holy men who had imitated their virtues, was darkened
by religious fiction. To the invincible band of genuine and
primitive martyrs they added myriads of imaginary heroes, who
had never existed, except in the fancy of crafty or credulous
legendaries; and there is reason to suspect that Tours might not
be the only diocese in which the bones of a malefactor were
adored instead of those of a saint.[1] A superstitious practice,
which tended to increase the temptations of fraud and credulity,
insensibly extinguished the light of history and of reason in the
Christian world.

II. But the progress of superstition would have been much
less rapid and victorious if the faith of the people had not been
assisted by the seasonable aid of visions and miracles to ascertain
the authenticity and virtue of the most suspicious relics. In
the reign of the younger Theodosius, Lucian,[2] a presbyter of
Jerusalem, and the ecclesiastical minister of the village of Caphargamala, about twenty miles from the city, related a very singular
dream, which, to remove his doubts, had been repeated on three
successive Saturdays. A venerable figure stood before him, in
the silence of the night, with a long beard, a white robe, and a
gold rod; announced himself by the name of Gamaliel; and
revealed to the astonished presbyter, that his own corpse, with
the bodies of his son Abibas, his friend Nicodemus, and the
illustrious Stephen, the first martyr of the Christian faith, were
secretly buried in the adjacent field. He added, with some
impatience, that it was time to release himself and his companions
from their obscure prison; that their appearance would be
salutary to a distressed world; and that they had made choice
of Lucian to inform the bishop of Jerusalem of their situation
and their wishes. The doubts and difficulties which still retarded this important discovery were successively removed by
new visions; and the ground was opened by the bishop, in the

---

[1] Martin of Tours (see his Life, c. 8, by Sulpicius Severus) extorted this
confession from the mouth of the dead man. The error is allowed to be
natural; the discovery is supposed to be miraculous. Which of the two
was likely to happen most frequently?

[2] Lucian composed in Greek his original narrative, which has been translated by Avitus, and published by Baronius (Annal. Eccles. A.D. 415, No.
7-16). The Benedictine editors of St. Augustin have given (at the end of
the work De Civitate Dei) two several copies, with many various readings.
It is the character of falsehood to be loose and inconsistent. The most
incredible parts of the legend are smoothed and softened by Tillemont (Mém.
Ecclés. tom. ii. p. 9, etc.).

presence of an innumerable multitude. The coffins of Gamaliel, of his son, and of his friend, were found in regular order; but when the fourth coffin, which contained the remains of Stephen, was shown to the light, the earth trembled, and an odour such as that of Paradise was smelt, which instantly cured the various diseases of seventy-three of the assistants. The companions of Stephen were left in their peaceful residence of Caphargamala; but the relics of the first martyr were transported, in solemn procession, to a church constructed in their honour on Mount Sion; and the minute particles of those relics, a drop of blood,[1] or the scrapings of a bone, were acknowledged, in almost every province of the Roman world, to possess a divine and miraculous virtue. The grave and learned Augustin,[2] whose understanding scarcely admits the excuse of credulity, has attested the innumerable prodigies which were performed in Africa by the relics of St. Stephen; and this marvellous narrative is inserted in the elaborate work of the City of God, which the bishop of Hippo designed as a solid and immortal proof of the truth of Christianity. Augustin solemnly declares that he has selected those miracles only which were publicly certified by the persons who were either the objects, or the spectators, of the power of the martyr. Many prodigies were omitted or forgotten; and Hippo had been less favourably treated than the other cities of the province. And yet the bishop enumerates above seventy miracles, of which three were resurrections from the dead, in the space of two years, and within the limits of his own diocese.[3] If we enlarge our view to all the dioceses, and all the saints, of the Christian world, it will not be easy to calculate the fables, and the errors, which issued from this inexhaustible source. But we may surely be allowed to observe that a miracle, in that age of superstition and credulity, lost its name and its merit, since it could scarcely be considered as a deviation from the ordinary and established laws of nature.

III. The innumerable miracles, of which the tombs of the

---

[1] A phial of St. Stephen's blood was annually liquefied at Naples till he was superseded by St. Januarius (Ruinart. Hist. Persecut. Vandal. p. 529).

[2] Augustin composed the two-and-twenty books de Civitate Dei in the space of thirteen years, A.D. 413-426. (Tillemont, Mém. Ecclés. tom. xiv. p. 608, etc.) His learning is too often borrowed, and his arguments are too often his own; but the whole work claims the merit of a magnificent design, vigorously, and not unskilfully, executed.

[3] See Augustin de Civitat. Dei, l. xxii. c. 22, and the Appendix, which contains two books of St. Stephen's miracles, by Evodius, bishop of Uzalis. Freculphus (apud Basnage, Hist. des Juifs, tom. viii. p. 249) has preserved a Gallic or Spanish proverb, "Whoever pretends to have read all the miracles of St. Stephen, he lies."

martyrs were the perpetual theatre, revealed to the pious believer the actual state and constitution of the invisible world; and his religious speculations appeared to be founded on the firm basis of fact and experience. Whatever might be the condition of vulgar souls in the long interval between the dissolution and the resurrection of their bodies, it was evident that the superior spirits of the saints and martyrs did not consume that portion of their existence in silent and inglorious sleep.[1] It was evident (without presuming to determine the place of their habitation, or the nature of their felicity) that they enjoyed the lively and active consciousness of their happiness, their virtue, and their powers; and that they had already secured the possession of their eternal reward. The enlargement of their intellectual faculties surpassed the measure of the human imagination; since it was proved by *experience* that they were capable of hearing and understanding the various petitions of their numerous votaries, who, in the same moment of time, but in the most distant parts of the world, invoked the name and assistance of Stephen or of Martin.[2] The confidence of their petitioners was founded on the persuasion that the saints, who reigned with Christ, cast an eye of pity upon earth; that they were warmly interested in the prosperity of the catholic church; and that the individuals who imitated the example of their faith and piety were the peculiar and favourite objects of their most tender regard. Sometimes, indeed, their friendship might be influenced by considerations of a less exalted kind: they viewed with partial affection the places which had been consecrated by their birth, their residence, their death, their burial, or the possession of their relics. The meaner passions of pride, avarice, and revenge, may be deemed unworthy of a celestial breast; yet the saints themselves condescended to testify their grateful approbation of the liberality of their votaries; and the sharpest bolts of punishment were hurled against those impious wretches who

[1] Burnet (de Statû Mortuorum, p. 56-84) collects the opinions of the Fathers, as far as they assert the sleep or repose of human souls till the day of judgment. He afterwards exposes (p. 91, etc.) the inconveniences which must arise if they possessed a more active and sensible existence.

[2] Vigilantius placed the souls of the prophets and martyrs, either in the bosom of Abraham (in loco refrigerii), or else under the altar of God. Nec posse [de] suis tumulis et ubi voluerint adesse præsentes. But Jerom (tom. ii. p. 122 [tom. ii. p. 392, ed. Vallars.]) sternly refutes this *blasphemy*. Tu Deo leges pones? Tu apostolis vincula injicies, ut usque ad diem judicii teneantur custodiâ, nec sint cum Domino suo; de quibus scriptum est, Sequuntur Agnum quocunque vadit. Si Agnus ubique, ergo, et hi, qui cum Agno sunt, ubique esse credendi sunt. Et cum diabolus et dæmones toto vagentur in orbe, etc.

violated their magnificent shrines, or disbelieved their supernatural power.[1] Atrocious, indeed, must have been the guilt, and strange would have been the scepticism, of those men, if they had obstinately resisted the proofs of a divine agency, which the elements, the whole range of the animal creation, and even the subtle and invisible operations of the human mind, were compelled to obey.[2] The immediate, and almost instantaneous, effects, that were supposed to follow the prayer, or the offence, satisfied the Christians of the ample measure of favour and authority which the saints enjoyed in the presence of the Supreme God; and it seemed almost superfluous to inquire whether they were continually obliged to intercede before the throne of grace, or whether they might not be permitted to exercise, according to the dictates of their benevolence and justice, the delegated powers of their subordinate ministry. The imagination, which had been raised by a painful effort to the contemplation and worship of the Universal Cause, eagerly embraced such inferior objects of adoration as were more proportioned to its gross conceptions and imperfect faculties. The sublime and simple theology of the primitive Christians was gradually corrupted: and the MONARCHY of heaven, already clouded by metaphysical subtleties, was degraded by the introduction of a popular mythology which tended to restore the reign of polytheism.[3]

IV. As the objects of religion were gradually reduced to the standard of the imagination, the rites and ceremonies were introduced that seemed most powerfully to affect the senses of the vulgar. If, in the beginning of the fifth century,[4] Tertullian, or Lactantius,[5] had been suddenly raised from the dead, to assist at the festival of some popular saint or martyr,[6] they would

---

[1] Fleury, Discours sur l'Hist. Ecclésiastique, iii. p. 80.

[2] At Minorca, the relics of St. Stephen converted in eight days 540 Jews; with the help, indeed, of some wholesome severities, such as burning the synagogue, driving the obstinate infidels to starve among the rocks, etc. See the original letter of Severus bishop of Minorca (ad calcem St. Augustin. de Civ. Dei), and the judicious remarks of Basnage (tom. viii. p. 245-251).

[3] Mr. Hume (Essays, vol. ii. p. 434) observes, like a philosopher, the natural flux and reflux of polytheism and theism.

[4] D'Aubigné (see his own Mémoires, p. 156-160) frankly offered, with the consent of the Huguenot ministers, to allow the first 400 years as the rule of faith. The Cardinal du Perron haggled for forty years more, which were indiscreetly given. Yet neither party would have found their account in this foolish bargain.

[5] The worship practised and inculcated by Tertullian, Lactantius, Arnobius, etc., is so *extremely* pure and spiritual, that their declamations against the Pagan sometimes glance against the Jewish ceremonies.

[6] Faustus the Manichæan accuses the Catholics of idolatry. Vertitis idola in martyres . . . quos votis similibus colitis. M. de Beausobre (Hist.

have gazed with astonishment and indignation on the profane spectacle which had succeeded to the pure and spiritual worship of a Christian congregation. As soon as the doors of the church were thrown open, they must have been offended by the smoke of incense, the perfume of flowers, and the glare of lamps and tapers, which diffused, at noon-day, a gaudy, superfluous, and, in their opinion, a sacrilegious light. If they approached the balustrade of the altar, they made their way through the prostrate crowd, consisting, for the most part, of strangers and pilgrims, who resorted to the city on the vigil of the feast; and who already felt the strong intoxication of fanaticism, and, perhaps, of wine. Their devout kisses were imprinted on the walls and pavement of the sacred edifice; and their fervent prayers were directed, whatever might be the language of their church, to the bones, the blood, or the ashes of the saint, which were usually concealed, by a linen or silken veil, from the eyes of the vulgar. The Christians frequented the tombs of the martyrs, in the hope of obtaining, from their powerful intercession, every sort of spiritual, but more especially of temporal, blessings. They implored the preservation of their health, or the cure of their infirmities; the fruitfulness of their barren wives, or the safety and happiness of their children. Whenever they undertook any distant or dangerous journey, they requested that the holy martyrs would be their guides and protectors on the road; and if they returned without having experienced any misfortune, they again hastened to the tombs of the martyrs, to celebrate, with grateful thanksgivings, their obligations to the memory and relics of those heavenly patrons. The walls were hung round with symbols of the favours which they had received; eyes, and hands, and feet, of gold and silver: and edifying pictures, which could not long escape the abuse of indiscreet or idolatrous devotion, represented the image, the attributes, and the miracles of the tutelar saint. The same uniform original spirit of superstition might suggest, in the most distant ages and countries, the same methods of deceiving the credulity, and of affecting the senses of mankind:[1] but it must ingenuously be confessed that the ministers of the catholic church

Critique du Manichéisme, tom. ii. p. 629-700), a protestant, but a philosopher, has represented, with candour and learning, the introduction of *Christian idolatry* in the fourth and fifth centuries.

[1] The resemblance of superstition, which could not be imitated, might be traced from Japan to Mexico. Warburton has seized this idea, which he distorts by rendering it too general and absolute (Divine Legation, vol. iv p. 126, etc.).

imitated the profane model which they were impatient to destroy. The most respectable bishops had persuaded themselves that the ignorant rustics would more cheerfully renounce the superstitions of Paganism, if they found some resemblance, some compensation, in the bosom of Christianity. The religion of Constantine achieved, in less than a century, the final conquest of the Roman empire: but the victors themselves were insensibly subdued by the arts of their vanquished rivals.[1]

CHAPTER XXIX

Final Division of the Roman Empire between the Sons of Theodosius—Reign of Arcadius and Honorius—Administration of Rufinus and Stilicho—Revolt and Defeat of Gildo in Africa

THE genius of Rome expired with Theodosius, the last of the successors of Augustus and Constantine who appeared in the field at the head of their armies, and whose authority was universally acknowledged throughout the whole extent of the empire. The memory of his virtues still continued, however, to protect the feeble and inexperienced youth of his two sons. After the death of their father, Arcadius and Honorius were saluted, by the unanimous consent of mankind, as the lawful emperors of the East and of the West; and the oath of fidelity was eagerly taken by every order of the state; the senates of old and new Rome, the clergy, the magistrates, the soldiers, and the people. Arcadius, who then was about eighteen years of age, was born in Spain in the humble habitation of a private family. But he received a princely education in the palace of Constantinople; and his inglorious life was spent in that peaceful and splendid seat of royalty, from whence he appeared to reign over the provinces of Thrace, Asia Minor, Syria, and Egypt, from the Lower Danube to the confines of Persia and Æthiopia. His younger brother, Honorius, assumed, in the eleventh year of his age, the nominal government of Italy, Africa, Gaul, Spain, and Britain; and the troops which guarded the frontiers of his kingdom were opposed, on one side, to the Caledonians, and on the other to the Moors. The great and martial præfecture of Illyricum was divided between the two princes: the defence and

[1] The imitation of Paganism is the subject of Dr. Middleton's agreeable letter from Rome. Warburton's animadversions obliged him to connect (vol. iii. p. 120-132) the history of the two religions, and to prove the antiquity of the Christian copy.

possession of the provinces of Noricum, Pannonia, and Dalmatia, still belonged to the Western empire; but the two large dioceses of Dacia and Macedonia, which Gratian had intrusted to the valour of Theodosius, were for ever united to the empire of the East. The boundary in Europe was not very different from the line which now separates the Germans and the Turks; and the respective advantages of territory, riches, populousness, and military strength, were fairly balanced and compensated in this final and permanent division of the Roman empire. The hereditary sceptre of the sons of Theodosius appeared to be the gift of nature and of their father; the generals and ministers had been accustomed to adore the majesty of the royal infants; and the army and people were not admonished of their rights, and of their power, by the dangerous example of a recent election. The gradual discovery of the weakness of Arcadius and Honorius, and the repeated calamities of their reign, were not sufficient to obliterate the deep and early impressions of loyalty. The subjects of Rome, who still reverenced the persons, or rather the names, of their sovereigns, beheld with equal abhorrence the rebels who opposed, and the ministers who abused, the authority of the throne.

Theodosius had tarnished the glory of his reign by the elevation of Rufinus, an odious favourite, who in an age of civil and religious faction has deserved, from every party, the imputation of every crime. The strong impulse of ambition and avarice [1] had urged Rufinus to abandon his native country, an obscure corner of Gaul,[2] to advance his fortune in the capital of the East: the talent of bold and ready elocution [3] qualified him to succeed in the lucrative profession of the law; and his success in that profession was a regular step to the most honourable and important employments of the state. He was raised, by just degrees, to the station of master of the offices. In the exercise of his various functions, so essentially connected with the whole system of civil government, he acquired the confidence of a monarch who soon discovered his diligence and capacity in business, and who long remained ignorant of the pride, the malice,

---

[1] Alecto, envious of the public felicity, convenes an infernal synod; Megæra recommends her pupil Rufinus, and excites him to deeds of mischief, etc. But there is as much difference between Claudian's fury and that of Virgil, as between the characters of Turnus and Rufinus.

[2] It is evident (Tillemont, Hist. des Emp. tom. v. p. 770), though De Marca is ashamed of his countryman, that Rufinus was born at Elusa, the metropolis of Novempopulania, now a small village of Gascony (D'Anville, Notice de l'Ancienne Gaule, p. 289).

[3] Philostorgius, l. xi. c. 3, with Godefroy's Dissert. p. 440.

and the covetousness of his disposition. These vices were concealed beneath the mask of profound dissimulation; [1] his passions were subservient only to the passions of his master; yet, in the horrid massacre of Thessalonica, the cruel Rufinus inflamed the fury, without imitating the repentance, of Theodosius. The minister, who viewed with proud indifference the rest of mankind, never forgave the appearance of an injury; and his personal enemies had forfeited, in his opinion, the merit of all public services. Promotus, the master-general of the infantry, had saved the empire from the invasion of the Ostrogoths; but he indignantly supported the pre-eminence of a rival whose character and profession he despised; and, in the midst of a public council, the impatient soldier was provoked to chastise with a blow the indecent pride of the favourite. This act of violence was represented to the emperor as an insult which it was incumbent on *his* dignity to resent. The disgrace and exile of Promotus were signified by a peremptory order to repair without delay to a military station on the banks of the Danube; and the death of that general (though he was slain in a skirmish with the barbarians) was imputed to the perfidious arts of Rufinus.[2] The sacrifice of an hero gratified his revenge; the honours of the consulship elated his vanity; but his power was still imperfect and precarious as long as the important posts of præfect of the East, and of præfect of Constantinople, were filled by Tatian [3] and his son Proculus, whose united authority balanced for some time the ambition and favour of the master of the offices. The two præfects were accused of rapine and corruption in the administration of the laws and finances. For the trial of these illustrious offenders the emperor constituted a special commission: several judges were named to share the guilt and reproach of injustice; but the right of pronouncing sentence was reserved to the president alone, and that president was Rufinus himself. The father, stripped of the præfecture of the East, was thrown into a dungeon; but the son, conscious that few ministers can be found innocent where an enemy is their judge, had secretly escaped;

---

[1] A passage of Suidas is expressive of his profound dissimulation; βαθυγνώμων ἄνθρωπος καὶ κρυψίνους.

[2] Zosimus, l. iv. [c. 51] p. 272, 273.

[3] Zosimus, who describes the fall of Tatian and his son (l. iv. [c. 52] p. 273, 74), asserts their innocence; and even *his* testimony may outweigh the charges of their enemies (Cod. Theod. tom. iv. p. 489), who accuse them of oppressing the *Curiæ*. The connection of Tatian with the Arians, while he was præfect of Egypt (A.D. 373), inclines Tillemont to believe that he was guilty of every crime (Hist. des Emp. tom. v. p. 360; Mém. Ecclés. tom. i. p. 589).

and Rufinus must have been satisfied with the least obnoxious victim, if despotism had not condescended to employ the basest and most ungenerous artifice. The prosecution was conducted with an appearance of equity and moderation which flattered Tatian with the hope of a favourable event: his confidence was fortified by the solemn assurances and perfidious oaths of the president, who presumed to interpose the sacred name of Theodosius himself; and the unhappy father was at last persuaded to recall, by a private letter, the fugitive Proculus. He was instantly seized, examined, condemned, and beheaded in one of the suburbs of Constantinople, with a precipitation which disappointed the clemency of the emperor. Without respecting the misfortunes of a consular senator, the cruel judges of Tatian compelled him to behold the execution of his son: the fatal cord was fastened round his own neck; but in the moment when he expected, and perhaps desired, the relief of a speedy death, he was permitted to consume the miserable remnant of his old age in poverty and exile.[1] The punishment of the two præfects might perhaps be excused by the exceptionable parts of their own conduct; the enmity of Rufinus might be palliated by the jealous and unsociable nature of ambition. But he indulged a spirit of revenge, equally repugnant to prudence and to justice, when he degraded their native country of Lycia from the rank of Roman provinces, stigmatised a guiltless people with a mark of ignominy, and declared that the countrymen of Tatian and Proculus should for ever remain incapable of holding any employment of honour or advantage under the Imperial government.[2] The new præfect of the East (for Rufinus instantly succeeded to the vacant honours of his adversary) was not diverted, however, by the most criminal pursuits from the performance of the religious duties which in that age were considered as the most essential to salvation. In the suburb of Chalcedon, surnamed

---

[1] ———Juvenum rorantia colla
Ante patrum vultus strictâ cecidere securi.
Ibat grandævus nato moriente superstes
Post trabeas exsul.   In Rufin. i. 248.

The *facts* of Zosimus explain the *allusions* of Claudian; but his classic interpreters were ignorant of the fourth century. The *fatal cord* I found, with the help of Tillemont, in a sermon of St. Asterius of Amasea.

[2] This odious law is recited and repealed by Arcadius (A.D. 396), in the Theodosian Code, l. ix. tit. xxxviii. leg. 9. The sense, as it is explained by Claudian (in Rufin. i. 232) and Godefroy (tom. iii. p. 279), is perfectly clear.

———Exscindere cives
Funditus, et nomen gentis delere laborat.

The scruples of Pagi and Tillemont can arise only from their zeal for the glory of Theodosius.

the *Oak*, he had built a magnificent villa, to which he devoutly added a stately church consecrated to the apostles St. Peter and St. Paul, and continually sanctified by the prayers and penance of a regular society of monks. A numerous and almost general synod of the bishops of the Eastern empire was summoned to celebrate at the same time the dedication of the church and the baptism of the founder. This double ceremony was performed with extraordinary pomp; and when Rufinus was purified in the holy font from all the sins that he had hitherto committed, a venerable hermit of Egypt rashly proposed himself as the sponsor of a proud and ambitious statesman.[1]

The character of Theodosius imposed on his minister the task of hypocrisy, which disguised, and sometimes restrained, the abuse of power; and Rufinus was apprehensive of disturbing the indolent slumber of a prince still capable of exerting the abilities and the virtue which had raised him to the throne.[2] But the absence, and soon afterwards the death, of the emperor confirmed the absolute authority of Rufinus over the person and dominions of Arcadius, a feeble youth, whom the imperious præfect considered as his pupil, rather than his sovereign. Regardless of the public opinion, he indulged his passions without remorse and without resistance; and his malignant and rapacious spirit rejected every passion that might have contributed to his own glory or the happiness of the people. His avarice,[3] which seems to have prevailed in his corrupt mind over every other sentiment, attracted the wealth of the East by the various arts of

---

[1] Ammonius . . . Rufinum propriis manibus suscepit sacro fonte mundatum. See Rosweyde's Vitæ Patrum, p. 947. [Heraclidis Paradisus in Append. ad Vit. Patr. p. 941 b.] Sozomen (l. viii. c. 17) mentions the church and monastery: and Tillemont (Mém. Ecclés. tom. ix. p. 593) records this synod, in which St. Gregory of Nyssa performed a conspicuous part.

[2] Montesquieu (Esprit des Loix, l. xii. c. 12) praises one of the laws of Theodosius, addressed to the præfect Rufinus (l. ix. tit. iv. leg. unic.), to discourage the prosecution of treasonable or sacrilegious words. A tyrannical statute always proves the existence of tyranny: but a laudable edict may only contain the specious professions or ineffectual wishes of the prince or his ministers. This, I am afraid, is a just though mortifying canon of criticism.

[3] ——————fluctibus auri
Expleri calor ille nequit——————

Congestæ cumulantur opes; orbisque rapinas
Accipit una domus.

This character (Claudian, in Rufin. i. 184-220) is confirmed by Jerom, a disinterested witness (dedecus insatiabilis avaritiæ, tom. i. ad Heliodor. p. 5 [Epist. lx. tom. i. p. 342, ed. Vallars.]), by Zosimus (l. v. [c. 1] p. 286), and by Suidas, who copied the history of Eunapius.

partial and general extortion—oppressive taxes, scandalous bribery, immoderate fines, unjust confiscations, forced or fictitious testaments, by which the tyrant despoiled of their lawful inheritance the children of strangers or enemies; and the public sale of justice, as well as of favour, which he instituted in the palace of Constantinople. The ambitious candidate eagerly solicited, at the expense of the fairest part of his patrimony, the honours and emoluments of some provincial government; the lives and fortunes of the unhappy people were abandoned to the most liberal purchaser; and the public discontent was sometimes appeased by the sacrifice of an unpopular criminal, whose punishment was profitable only to the præfect of the East, his accomplice and his judge. If avarice were not the blindest of the human passions, the motives of Rufinus might excite our curiosity, and we might be tempted to inquire with what view he violated every principle of humanity and justice to accumulate those immense treasures which he could not spend without folly nor possess without danger. Perhaps he vainly imagined that he laboured for the interest of an only daughter, on whom he intended to bestow his royal pupil and the august rank of empress of the East. Perhaps he deceived himself by the opinion that his avarice was the instrument of his ambition. He aspired to place his fortune on a secure and independent basis, which should no longer depend on the caprice of the young emperor; yet he neglected to conciliate the hearts of the soldiers and people by the liberal distribution of those riches which he had acquired with so much toil and with so much guilt. The extreme parsimony of Rufinus left him only the reproach and envy of ill-gotten wealth; his dependents served him without attachment; the universal hatred of mankind was repressed only by the influence of servile fear. The fate of Lucian proclaimed to the East that the præfect, whose industry was much abated in the despatch of ordinary business, was active and indefatigable in the pursuit of revenge. Lucian, the son of the præfect Florentius, the oppressor of Gaul and the enemy of Julian, had employed considerable part of his inheritance, the fruit of rapine and corruption, to purchase the friendship of Rufinus and the high office of count of the East. But the new magistrate imprudently departed from the maxims of the court and of the times, disgraced his benefactor by the contrast of a virtuous and temperate administration, and presumed to refuse an act of injustice which might have tended to the profit of the emperor's uncle. Arcadius was easily persuaded to resent the suppose insult; and the præfect of the East resolved to execute in person the cruel vengeance which he meditated against this ungrateful delegate of his power. He performed with incessant speed the journey of seven or eight hundred miles from Constantinople to Antioch, entered the capital of Syria at the dead of night, and spread universal consternation among a people ignorant of his design, but not ignorant of his character. The count of the fifteen provinces of the East was dragged, like the vilest malefactor, before the arbitrary tribunal of Rufinus. Notwithstanding the clearest evidence of his integrity, which was not impeached even by the voice of an accuser, Lucian was condemned, almost without a trial, to suffer a cruel and ignominious punishment. The ministers of the tyrant, by the order and in the presence of their master, beat him on the neck with leather thongs armed at the extremities with lead; and when he fainted under the violence of the pain, he was removed in a close litter to conceal his dying agonies from the eyes of the indignant city. No sooner had Rufinus perpetrated this inhuman act, the sole object of his expedition, than he returned, amidst the deep and silent curses of a trembling people, from Antioch to Constantinople; and his diligence was accelerated by the hope of accomplishing, without delay, the nuptials of his daughter with the emperor of the East.[1]

But Rufinus soon experienced that a prudent minister should constantly secure his royal captive by the strong, though invisible, chain of habit; and that the merit, and much more easily the favour of the absent, are obliterated in a short time from the mind of a weak and capricious sovereign. While the præfect satiated his revenge at Antioch, a secret conspiracy of the favourite eunuchs, directed by the great chamberlain Eutropius, undermined his power in the palace of Constantinople. They discovered that Arcadius was not inclined to love the daughter of Rufinus, who had been chosen without his consent for his bride, and they contrived to substitute in her place the fair Eudoxia, the daughter of Bauto,[2] a general of the Franks in the service of Rome, and who was educated, since the death of her father, in the family of the sons of Promotus. The young

---

[1] ——Cætera segnis;
   Ad facinus velox; penitus regione remotas
   Impiger ire vias.

This allusion of Claudian (in Rufin. i. 241) is again explained by the circumstantial narrative of Zosimus (l. v. [c. 2] p. 288, 289).
[2] Zosimus (l. iv. [c. 33] p. 243) praises the valour, prudence, and integrity of Bauto the Frank. See Tillemont, Hist. des Empereurs, tom. v. p. 771.

emperor, whose chastity had been strictly guarded by the pious care of his tutor Arsenius,[1] eagerly listened to the artful and flattering descriptions of the charms of Eudoxia; he gazed with impatient ardour on her picture, and he understood the necessity of concealing his amorous designs from the knowledge of a minister who was so deeply interested to oppose the consummation of his happiness. Soon after the return of Rufinus, the approaching ceremony of the royal nuptials was announced to the people of Constantinople, who prepared to celebrate with false and hollow acclamations the fortune of his daughter. A splendid train of eunuchs and officers issued, in hymeneal pomp, from the gates of the palace, bearing aloft the diadem, the robes, and the inestimable ornaments of the future empress. The solemn procession passed through the streets of the city, which were adorned with garlands and filled with spectators; but when it reached the house of the sons of Promotus, the principal eunuch respectfully entered the mansion, invested the fair Eudoxia with the Imperial robes, and conducted her in triumph to the palace and bed of Arcadius.[2] The secrecy and success with which this conspiracy against Rufinus had been conducted imprinted a mark of indelible ridicule on the character of a minister who had suffered himself to be deceived, in a post where the arts of deceit and dissimulation constitute the most distinguished merit. He considered, with a mixture of indignation and fear, the victory of an aspiring eunuch who had secretly captivated the favour of his sovereign; and the disgrace of his daughter, whose interest was inseparably connected with his own, wounded the tenderness, or at least the pride, of Rufinus. At the moment when he flattered himself that he should become the father of a line of kings, a foreign maid, who had been educated in the house of his implacable enemies, was introduced into the Imperial bed; and Eudoxia soon displayed a superiority of sense and spirit to improve the ascendant which her beauty must acquire over the mind of a fond and youthful husband. The emperor would soon be instructed to hate, to fear, and to

[1] Arsenius escaped from the palace of Constantinople, and passed fifty-five years in rigid penance in the monasteries of Egypt. See Tillemont, Mém. Ecclés. tom. xiv. p. 676-702; and Fleury, Hist. Eccles. tom. v. p. 1, etc.; but the latter, for want of authentic materials, has given too much credit to the legend of Metaphrastes.

[2] This story (Zosimus, l. v. [c. 3] p. 290) proves that the hymeneal rites of antiquity were still practised, without idolatry, by the Christians of the East; and the bride was *forcibly* conducted from the house of her parents to that of her husband. Our form of marriage requires, with less delicacy, the express and public consent of a virgin.

destroy the powerful subject whom he had injured; and the consciousness of guilt deprived Rufinus of every hope, either of safety or comfort, in the retirement of a private life. But he still possessed the most effectual means of defending his dignity, and perhaps of oppressing his enemies. The præfect still exercised an uncontrolled authority over the civil and military government of the East: and his treasures, if he could resolve to use them, might be employed to procure proper instruments for the execution of the blackest designs that pride, ambition, and revenge could suggest to a desperate statesman. The character of Rufinus seemed to justify the accusations that he conspired against the person of his sovereign to seat himself on the vacant throne; and that he had secretly invited the Huns and the Goths to invade the provinces of the empire and to increase the public confusion. The subtle præfect, whose life had been spent in the intrigues of the palace, opposed with equal arms the artful measures of the eunuch Eutropius; but the timid soul of Rufinus was astonished by the hostile approach of a more formidable rival, of the great Stilicho, the general, or rather the master, of the empire of the West.[1]

The celestial gift, which Achilles obtained, and Alexander envied, of a poet worthy to celebrate the actions of heroes, has been enjoyed by Stilicho, in a much higher degree than might have been expected from the declining state of genius and of art. The muse of Claudian,[2] devoted to his service, was always prepared to stigmatise his adversaries, Rufinus or Eutropius, with eternal infamy; or to paint, in the most splendid colours, the victories and virtues of a powerful benefactor. In the review of a period indifferently supplied with authentic materials, we cannot refuse to illustrate the annals of Honorius from the invectives, or the panegyrics, of a contemporary writer; but as Claudian appears to have indulged the most ample privilege of a poet and a courtier, some criticism will be requisite to translate the language of fiction or exaggeration into the truth and simplicity of historic prose. His silence concerning the family of Stilicho may be admitted as a proof that his patron was neither able nor desirous to boast of a long series of illustrious progenitors, and the slight mention of his father, an officer of barbarian

---

[1] Zosimus (l. v. [c. 4] p. 290), Orosius (l. vii. c. 37), and the Chronicle of Marcellinus. Claudian (in Rufin. ii. 7-100) paints, in lively colours, the distress and guilt of the præfect.

[2] Stilicho, directly or indirectly, is the perpetual theme of Claudian. The youth and private life of the hero are vaguely expressed in the poem on his first consulship, 35-140.

cavalry in the service of Valens, seems to countenance the assertion that the general who so long commanded the armies of Rome was descended from the savage and perfidious race of the Vandals.[1] If Stilicho had not possessed the external advantages of strength and stature, the most flattering bard, in the presence of so many thousand spectators, would have hesitated to affirm that he surpassed the measure of the demi-gods of antiquity; and that, whenever he moved, with lofty steps, through the streets of the capital, the astonished crowd made room for the stranger, who displayed, in a private condition, the awful majesty of a hero. From his earliest youth he embraced the profession of arms; his prudence and valour were soon distinguished in the field; the horsemen and archers of the East admired his superior dexterity; and in each degree of his military promotions, the public judgment always prevented and approved the choice of the sovereign. He was named by Theodosius to ratify a solemn treaty with the monarch of Persia: he supported, during that important embassy, the dignity of the Roman name; and after his return to Constantinople his merit was rewarded by an intimate and honourable alliance with the Imperial family. Theodosius had been prompted, by a pious motive of fraternal affection, to adopt, for his own, the daughter of his brother Honorius; the beauty and accomplishments of Serena [2] were universally admired by the obsequious court; and Stilicho obtained the preference over a crowd of rivals who ambitiously disputed the hand of the princess, and the favour of her adoptive father.[3] The assurance that the husband of Serena would be faithful to the throne which he was permitted to approach engaged the emperor to exalt the fortunes, and to employ the abilities, of the sagacious and intrepid Stilicho. He rose through the successive steps of master of the horse, and count of the domestics, to the supreme rank of master-general of all the cavalry and infantry of the Roman, or at least of the Western, empire; [4] and his enemies confessed that he invariably

---

[1] Vandalorum imbellis, avaræ, perfidæ, et dolosæ gentis genere editus. Orosius, l. vii. c. 38. Jerom (tom. i. ad Gerontiam, p. 93) calls him a semi-barbarian.

[2] Claudian, in an imperfect poem, has drawn a fair, perhaps a flattering, portrait of Serena. That favourite niece of Theodosius was born, as well as her sister Thermantia, in Spain; from whence, in their earliest youth, they were honourably conducted to the palace of Constantinople.

[3] Some doubt may be entertained whether this adoption was legal, or only metaphorical (see Ducange, Fam. Byzant. p. 75). An old inscription gives Stilicho the singular title of *Pro-gener Divi Theodosii.*

[4] Claudian (Laus Serenæ, 190, 193) expresses, in poetic language, the " dilectus equorum," and the " gemino mox idem culmine duxit agmina."

disdained to barter for gold the rewards of merit, or to defraud the soldiers of the pay and gratifications which they deserved or claimed from the liberality of the state.[1] The valour and conduct which he afterwards displayed in the defence of Italy against the arms of Alaric and Radagaisus may justify the fame of his early achievements; and in an age less attentive to the laws of honour or of pride, the Roman generals might yield the pre-eminence of rank to the ascendant of superior genius.[2] He lamented and revenged the murder of Promotus, his rival and his friend; and the massacre of many thousands of the flying Bastarnæ is represented by the poet as a bloody sacrifice which the Roman Achilles offered to the manes of another Patroclus. The virtues and victories of Stilicho deserved the hatred of Rufinus: and the arts of calumny might have been successful, if the tender and vigilant Serena had not protected her husband against his domestic foes, whilst he vanquished in the field the enemies of the empire.[3] Theodosius continued to support an unworthy minister, to whose diligence he delegated the government of the palace and of the East; but when he marched against the tyrant Eugenius, he associated his faithful general to the labours and glories of the civil war; and in the last moments of his life the dying monarch recommended to Stilicho the care of his sons and of the republic.[4] The ambition and the abilities of Stilicho were not unequal to the important trust; and he claimed the guardianship of the two empires during the minority

The inscription adds, " count of the domestics," an important command, whch Stilicho, in the height of his grandeur, might prudently retain.

[1] The beautiful lines of Claudian (in i. Cons. Stilich. ii. 113) display *his* genius: but the integrity of Stilicho (in the military administration) is much more firmly established by the unwilling evidence of Zosimus (l. v. [c. 34] p. 345).

[2] ——Si bellica nubes
Ingrueret, quamvis annis et jure minori,
Cedere grandævos equitum peditumque magistros
Adspiceres.　　　　　　　Claudian, Laus Seren. v. 196, etc.

A modern general would deem their submission either heroic patriotism or abject servility.

[3] Compare the poem on the first consulship (i. 95-115) with the *Laus Serenæ* (227-237, where it unfortunately breaks off). We may perceive the deep, inveterate malice of Rufinus.

[4] ——Quem *fratribus* ipse
Discedens, clipeum defensoremque dedisti.
　　　　　　　　　　　　　　　　　(iv. Cons. Hon. 432.)

Yet the nomination was private (iii. Cons. Hon. 142—cunctos discedere . . . jubet—and may therefore be suspected. Zosimus and Suidas apply to Stilicho and Rufinus the same equal title of Ἐπίτροποι, guardians, or procurators.

of Arcadius and Honorius.[1] The first measure of his administration, or rather of his reign, displayed to the nations the vigour and activity of a spirit worthy to command. He passed the Alps in the depth of winter; descended the stream of the Rhine, from the fortress of Basel to the marshes of Batavia; reviewed the state of the garrisons; repressed the enterprises of the Germans; and, after establishing along the banks a firm and honourable peace, returned with incredible speed to the palace of Milan.[2] The person and court of Honorius were subject to the master-general of the West; and the armies and provinces of Europe obeyed, without hesitation, a regular authority, which was exercised in the name of their young sovereign. Two rivals only remained to dispute the claims, and to provoke the vengeance, of Stilicho. Within the limits of Africa, Gildo, the Moor, maintained a proud and dangerous independence; and the minister of Constantinople asserted his equal reign over the emperor and the empire of the East.

The impartiality which Stilicho affected, as the common guardian of the royal brothers, engaged him to regulate the equal division of the arms, the jewels, and the magnificent wardrobe and furniture of the deceased emperor.[3] But the most important object of the inheritance consisted of the numerous legions, cohorts, and squadrons, of Romans or barbarians, whom the event of the civil war had united under the standard of Theodosius. The various multitudes of Europe and Asia, exasperated by recent animosities, were overawed by the authority of a single man; and the rigid discipline of Stilicho protected the lands of the citizen from the rapine of the licentious soldier.[4] Anxious, however, and impatient to relieve Italy from the presence of this formidable host, which could be useful only on the frontiers of the empire, he listened to the just requisition of

---

[1] The Roman law distinguishes two sorts of *minority*, which expired at the age of fourteen and of twenty-five. The one was subject to the *tutor*, or guardian, of the person; the other, to the *curator*, or trustee, of the estate (Heineccius, Antiquitat. Rom. ad Jurisprudent. pertinent. l. i. tit. xxii. xxiii. p. 218-232). But these legal ideas were never accurately transferred into the constitution of an elective monarchy.

[2] See Claudian (i. Cons. Stilich. i. 188-242); but he must allow more than fifteen days for the journey and return between Milan and Leyden.

[3] I. Cons. Stilich. ii. 88-94. Not only the robes and diadems of the deceased emperor, but even the helmets, sword-hilts, belts, cuirasses, etc., were enriched with pearls, emeralds, and diamonds.

[4] ——Tantoque remoto
Principe, mutatas orbis non sensit habenas.
This high commendation (i. Cons. Stil. i. 149) may be justified by the fears of the dying emperor (de Bell. Gildon. 292-301), and the peace and good order which were enjoyed after his death (i. Cons. Stil. i. 150-168).

the minister of Arcadius, declared his intention of reconducting in person the troops of the East, and dexterously employed the rumour of a Gothic tumult to conceal his private designs of ambition and revenge.[1] The guilty soul of Rufinus was alarmed by the approach of a warrior and a rival whose enmity he deserved; he computed, with increasing terror, the narrow space of his life and greatness; and, as the last hope of safety, he interposed the authority of the emperor Arcadius. Stilicho, who appears to have directed his march along the sea-coast of the Hadriatic, was not far distant from the city of Thessalonica when he received a peremptory message to recall the troops of the East, and to declare that *his* nearer approach would be considered, by the Byzantine court, as an act of hostility. The prompt and unexpected obedience of the general of the West convinced the vulgar of his loyalty and moderation; and, as he had already engaged the affection of the Eastern troops, he recommended to their zeal the execution of his bloody design, which might be accomplished in his absence, with less danger perhaps, and with less reproach. Stilicho left the command of the troops of the East to Gainas, the Goth, on whose fidelity he firmly relied, with an assurance at least that the hardy barbarian would never be diverted from his purpose by any consideration of fear or remorse. The soldiers were easily persuaded to punish the enemy of Stilicho and of Rome; and such was the general hatred which Rufinus had excited, that the fatal secret, communicated to thousands, was faithfully preserved during the long march from Thessalonica to the gates of Constantinople. As soon as they had resolved his death, they condescended to flatter his pride; the ambitious præfect was seduced to believe that those powerful auxiliaries might be tempted to place the diadem on his head; and the treasures which he distributed with a tardy and reluctant hand were accepted by the indignant multitude as an insult rather than as a gift. At the distance of a mile from the capital, in the field of Mars, before the palace of Hebdomon, the troops halted; and the emperor, as well as his minister, advanced, according to ancient custom, respectfully to salute the power which supported their throne. As Rufinus passed along the ranks, and disguised, with studied courtesy, his innate haughtiness, the wings insensibly wheeled from the right and left, and enclosed the devoted victim within the circle of their

---

[1] Stilicho's march and the death of Rufinus are described by Claudian (in Rufin. l. ii. 101-453), Zosimus (l. v. [c. 7] p. 296, 297), Sozomen (l. viii. c. 1), Socrates (l. vi. c. 1), Philostorgius (l. xi. c. 3, with Godefroy, p. 441), and the Chronicle of Marcellinus.

arms. Before he could reflect on the danger of his situation, Gainas gave the signal of death; a daring and forward soldier plunged his sword into the breast of the guilty præfect, and Rufinus fell, groaned, and expired, at the feet of the affrighted emperor. If the agonies of a moment could expiate the crimes of a whole life, or if the outrages inflicted on a breathless corpse could be the object of pity, our humanity might perhaps be affected by the horrid circumstances which accompanied the murder of Rufinus. His mangled body was abandoned to the brutal fury of the populace of either sex, who hastened in crowds, from every quarter of the city, to trample on the remains of the haughty minister, at whose frown they had so lately trembled. His right hand was cut off, and carried through the streets of Constantinople, in cruel mockery, to extort contributions for the avaricious tyrant, whose head was publicly exposed, borne aloft on the point of a long lance.[1] According to the savage maxims of the Greek republics, his innocent family would have shared the punishment of his crimes. The wife and daughter of Rufinus were indebted for their safety to the influence of religion. *Her* sanctuary protected them from the raging madness of the people; and they were permitted to spend the remainder of their lives in the exercises of Christian devotion in the peaceful retirement of Jerusalem.[2]

The servile poet of Stilicho applauds with ferocious joy this horrid deed, which, in the execution, perhaps of justice, violated every law of nature and society, profaned the majesty of the prince, and renewed the dangerous examples of military licence. The contemplation of the universal order and harmony had satisfied Claudian of the existence of the Deity; but the prosperous impunity of vice appeared to contradict his moral attributes; and the fate of Rufinus was the only event which could dispel the religious doubts of the poet.[3] Such an act might

---

[1] The *dissection* of Rufinus, which Claudian performs with the savage coolness of an anatomist (in Rufin. ii. 405-415), is likewise specified by Zosimus [v. c. 7] and Jerom (tom. i. p. 26 [Epist. lx. tom. i. p. 342, ed. Vallars.]).

[2] The Pagan Zosimus mentions their sanctuary and pilgrimage. The sister of Rufinus, Sylvania, who passed her life at Jerusalem, is famous in monastic history. 1. The studious virgin had diligently, and even repeatedly, perused the commentators on the Bible, Origen, Gregory, Basil, etc., to the amount of five millions of lines. 2. At the age of threescore she could boast that she had never washed her hands, face, or any part of her whole body, except the tips of her fingers, to receive the communion. See the Vitæ Patrum, p. 779, 977.

[3] See the beautiful exordium of his invective against Rufinus, which is curiously discussed by the sceptic Bayle, Dictionnaire Critique, Rufin. Not. E.

vindicate the honour of Providence; but it did not much contribute to the happiness of the people.   In less than three months they were informed of the maxims of the new administration, by a singular edict, which established the exclusive right of the treasury over the spoils of Rufinus; and silenced, under heavy penalties, the presumptuous claims of the subjects of the Eastern empire who had been injured by his rapacious tyranny.[1]   Even Stilicho did not derive from the murder of his rival the fruit which he had proposed; and though he gratified his revenge, his ambition was disappointed.   Under the name of a favourite, the weakness of Arcadius required a master, but he naturally preferred the obsequious arts of the eunuch Eutropius, who had obtained his domestic confidence; and the emperor contemplated with terror and aversion the stern genius of a foreign warrior.   Till they were divided by the jealousy of power, the sword of Gainas, and the charms of Eudoxia, supported the favour of the great chamberlain of the palace: the perfidious Goth, who was appointed master-general of the East, betrayed, without scruple, the interest of his benefactor; and the same troops who had so lately massacred the enemy of Stilicho were engaged to support, against him, the independence of the throne of Constantinople.   The favourites of Arcadius fomented a secret and irreconcilable war against a formidable hero, who aspired to govern and to defend the two empires of Rome and the two sons of Theodosius.   They incessantly laboured, by dark and treacherous machinations, to deprive him of the esteem of the prince, the respect of the people, and the friendship of the barbarians.   The life of Stilicho was repeatedly attempted by the dagger of hired assassins; and a decree was obtained from the senate of Constantinople, to declare him an enemy of the republic, and to confiscate his ample possessions in the provinces of the East.   At a time when the only hope of delaying the ruin of the Roman name depended on the firm union and reciprocal aid of all the nations to whom it had been gradually communicated, the subjects of Arcadius and Honorius were instructed, by their respective masters, to view each other in a foreign and even hostile light; to rejoice in their mutual calamities; and to embrace, as their faithful allies, the barbarians whom they excited to invade the territories of their countrymen.[2]   The

---

[1] See the Theodosian Code, l. ix. tit. xlii. leg. 14, 15.   The new ministers attempted, with inconsistent avarice, to seize the spoils of their predecessor and to provide for their own future security.

[2] See Claudian (i. Cons. Stilich. l. i. 275, 292, 296, l. ii. 83), and Zosimus, l. v. [c. 11] p. 302.

natives of Italy affected to despise the servile and effeminate
Greeks of Byzantium, who presumed to imitate the dress, and to
usurp the dignity, of Roman senators; [1] and the Greeks had not
yet forgot the sentiments of hatred and contempt which their
polished ancestors had so long entertained for the rude inhabitants of the West. The distinction of two governments, which
soon produced the separation of two nations, will justify my
design of suspending the series of the Byzantine history, to prosecute, without interruption, the disgraceful but memorable reign
of Honorius.

The prudent Stilicho, instead of persisting to force the inclinations of a prince and people who rejected his government, wisely
abandoned Arcadius to his unworthy favourites; and his reluctance to involve the two empires in a civil war displayed the
moderation of a minister who had so often signalised his military
spirit and abilities. But if Stilicho had any longer endured the
revolt of Africa, he would have betrayed the security of the
capital, and the majesty of the Western emperor, to the capricious
insolence of a Moorish rebel. Gildo,[2] the brother of the tyrant
Firmus, had preserved and obtained, as the reward of his
apparent fidelity, the immense patrimony which was forfeited
by treason; long and meritorious service in the armies of Rome
raised him to the dignity of a military count; the narrow policy of
the court of Theodosius had adopted the mischievous expedient
of supporting a legal government by the interest of a powerful
family; and the brother of Firmus was invested with the command of Africa. His ambition soon usurped the administration
of justice and of the finances, without account and without
control; and he maintained, during a reign of twelve years, the
possession of an office from which it was impossible to remove
him without the danger of a civil war. During those twelve
years the provinces of Africa groaned under the dominion of a
tyrant who seemed to unite the unfeeling temper of a stranger
with the partial resentments of domestic faction. The forms

---

[1] Claudian turns the consulship of the eunuch Eutropius into a national
reflection (l. ii. 135):

> —— Plaudentem cerne senatum,
> Et Byzantinos proceres, *Graiosque* Quirites:
> O patribus plebes, O digni consule patres.

It is curious to observe the first symptoms of jealousy and schism between
old and new Rome, between the Greeks and Latins.

[2] Claudian may have exaggerated the vices of Gildo; but his Moorish
extraction, his notorious actions, and the complaints of St. Augustin, may
justify the poet's invectives. Baronius (Annal. Eccles. A.D. 398, No. 35-56)
has treated the African rebellion with skill and learning.

of law were often superseded by the use of poison; and if the trembling guests who were invited to the table of Gildo presumed to express their fears, the insolent suspicion served only to excite his fury, and he loudly summoned the ministers of death. Gildo alternately indulged the passions of avarice and lust;[1] and if his *days* were terrible to the rich, his *nights* were not less dreadful to husbands and parents. The fairest of their wives and daughters were prostituted to the embraces of the tyrant; and afterwards abandoned to a ferocious troop of barbarians and assassins, the black or swarthy natives of the desert, whom Gildo considered as the only guardians of his throne. In the civil war between Theodosius and Eugenius, the count, or rather the sovereign of Africa, maintained a haughty and suspicious neutrality; refused to assist either of the contending parties with troops or vessels, expected the declaration of fortune, and reserved for the conqueror the vain professions of his allegiance. Such professions would not have satisfied the master of the Roman world: but the death of Theodosius, and the weakness and discord of his sons, confirmed the power of the Moor, who condescended, as a proof of his moderation, to abstain from the use of the diadem, and to supply Rome with the customary tribute, or rather subsidy, of corn. In every division of the empire, the five provinces of Africa were invariably assigned to the West; and Gildo had consented to govern that extensive country in the name of Honorius; but his knowledge of the character and designs of Stilicho soon engaged him to address his homage to a more distant and feeble sovereign. The ministers of Arcadius embraced the cause of a perfidious rebel; and the delusive hope of adding the numerous cities of Africa to the empire of the East tempted them to assert a claim which they were incapable of supporting either by reason or by arms.[2]

---

[1] Instat terribilis vivis, morientibus hæres,
  Virginibus raptor, thalamis obscenus adulter.
  Nulla quies: oritur prædâ cessante libido,
  Divitibusque dies, et nox metuenda maritis.
    ——— Mauris clarissima quæque
  Fastidita datur.
          De Bello Gildonico, 165, 189.

Baronius condemns, still more severely, the licentiousness of Gildo; as his wife, his daughter, and his sister, were examples of perfect chastity. The adulteries of the African soldiers are checked by one of the Imperial laws.

[2] Inque tuam sortem numerosas transtulit urbes.

Claudian (de Bell. Gildonico, 230-324) has touched, with political delicacy, the intrigues of the Byzantine court, which are likewise mentioned by Zosimus (i. v. [c. 11] p. 302).

When Stilicho had given a firm and decisive answer to the pretensions of the Byzantine court, he solemnly accused the tyrant
of Africa before the tribunal which had formerly judged the kings
and nations of the earth; and the image of the republic was
revived, after a long interval, under the reign of Honorius. The
emperor transmitted an accurate and ample detail of the complaints of the provincials, and the crimes of Gildo, to the Roman
senate; and the members of that venerable assembly were required to pronounce the condemnation of the rebel. Their
unanimous suffrage declared him the enemy of the republic; and
the decree of the senate added a sacred and legitimate sanction
to the Roman arms.[1] A people who still remembered that their
ancestors had been the masters of the world would have applauded,
with conscious pride, the representation of ancient freedom, if
they had not long since been accustomed to prefer the solid assurance of bread to the unsubstantial visions of liberty and greatness.
The subsistence of Rome depended on the harvests of Africa; and
it was evident that a declaration of war would be the signal of
famine. The præfect Symmachus, who presided in the deliberations of the senate, admonished the minister of his just apprehension that, as soon as the revengeful Moor should prohibit the
exportation of corn, the tranquillity, and perhaps the safety, of
the capital would be threatened by the hungry rage of a turbulent multitude.[2] The prudence of Stilicho conceived, and
executed without delay, the most effectual measure for the
relief of the Roman people. A large and seasonable supply of
corn, collected in the inland provinces of Gaul, was embarked
on the rapid stream of the Rhone, and transported by an easy
navigation from the Rhone to the Tiber. During the whole
term of the African war, the granaries of Rome were continually
filled, her dignity was vindicated from the humiliating dependence, and the minds of an immense people were quieted by the
calm confidence of peace and plenty.[3]

The cause of Rome, and the conduct of the African war, were
intrusted by Stilicho to a general active and ardent to avenge
his private injuries on the head of the tyrant. The spirit of
discord which prevailed in the house of Nabal had excited a

[1] Symmachus (l. iv. epist. 4) expresses the judicial forms of the senate;
and Claudian (i. Cons. Stilich. l. i. 325, etc.) seems to feel the spirit of a
Roman.
[2] Claudian finely displays these complaints of Symmachus, in a speech
of the goddess of Rome before the throne of Jupiter (de Bell. Gildon. 28-128).
[3] See Claudian (in Eutrop. l. i. 401, etc.; i. Cons. Stil. l. i. 306, etc.;
ii. Cons. Stilich. 91, etc.).

deadly quarrel between two of his sons, Gildo and Mascezel.[1]
The usurper pursued, with implacable rage, the life of his younger
brother, whose courage and abilities he feared; and Mascezel,
oppressed by superior power, took refuge in the court of Milan;
where he soon received the cruel intelligence that his two innocent
and helpless children had been murdered by their inhuman
uncle. The affliction of the father was suspended only by the
desire of revenge. The viligant Stilicho already prepared to
collect the naval and military forces of the Western empire; and
he had resolved, if the tyrant should be able to wage an equal
and doubtful war, to march against him in person. But as Italy
required his presence, and as it might be dangerous to weaken
the defence of the frontier, he judged it more advisable that
Mascezel should attempt this arduous adventure at the head of
a chosen body of Gallic veterans, who had lately served under
the standard of Eugenius. These troops, who were exhorted
to convince the world that they could subvert, as well as defend,
the throne of an usurper, consisted of the *Jovian*, the *Herculian*,
and the *Augustan* legions; of the *Nervian* auxiliaries; of the
soldiers who displayed in their banners the symbol of a *lion;* and
of the troops which were distinguished by the auspicious names
of *Fortunate* and *Invincible.* Yet such was the smallness of their
establishments, or the difficulty of recruiting, that these *seven*
bands,[2] of high dignity and reputation in the service of Rome,
amounted to no more than five thousand effective men.[3] The
fleet of galleys and transports sailed in tempestuous weather from
the port of Pisa, in Tuscany, and steered their course to the little
island of Capraria, which had borrowed that name from the wild
goats, its original inhabitants, whose place was now occupied by
a new colony of a strange and savage appearance. " The whole
island (says an ingenious traveller of those times) is filled, or
rather defiled, by men who fly from the light. They call themselves *Monks* or solitaries, because they choose to live alone,

---

[1] He was of a mature age, since he had formerly (A.D. 373) served against
his brother Firmus (Ammian. xxix. 5). Claudian, who understood the
court of Milan, dwells on the injuries, rather than the merits, of Mascezel
(de Bell. Gild. 389-414). The Moorish war was not worthy of Honorius or
Stilicho, etc.

[2] Claudian, Bell. Gild. 415-423. The change of discipline allowed him to
use indifferently the names of *Legio, Cohors, Manipulus.* See the *Notitia
Imperii*, S. 38, 40.

[3] Orosius (l. vii. c. 36, p. 565) qualifies this account with an expression of
doubt (ut aiunt); and it scarcely coincides with the δυνάμεις ἀδρὰς of Zosimus
(l. v. [c. 11] p. 303). Yet Claudian, after some declamation about Cadmus's
soldiers, frankly owns that Stilicho sent a small army, lest the rebel should
fly, ne timeare times (i. Cons. Stilich. l. i. 314, etc.).

without any witnesses of their actions. They fear the gifts of fortune, from the apprehension of losing them; and, lest they should be miserable, they embrace a life of voluntary wretchedness. How absurd is their choice! how perverse their understanding! to dread the evils, without being able to support the blessings, of the human condition. Either this melancholy madness is the effect of disease, or else the consciousness of guilt urges these unhappy men to exercise on their own bodies the tortures which are inflicted on fugitive slaves by the hand of justice." [1] Such was the contempt of a profane magistrate for the monks of Capraria, who were revered by the pious Mascezel as the chosen servants of God. [2] Some of them were persuaded, by his entreaties, to embark on board the fleet; and it is observed, to the praise of the Roman general, that his days and nights were employed in prayer, fasting, and the occupation of singing psalms. The devout leader, who with such a reinforcement appeared confident of victory, avoided the dangerous rocks of Corsica, coasted along the eastern side of Sardinia, and secured his ships against the violence of the south wind, by casting anchor in the safe and capacious harbour of Cagliari, at the distance of one hundred and forty miles from the African shores. [3]

Gildo was prepared to resist the invasion with all the forces of Africa. By the liberality of his gifts and promises, he endeavoured to secure the doubtful allegiance of the Roman soldiers, whilst he attracted to his standard the distant tribes of Gætulia and Æthiopia. He proudly reviewed an army of seventy thousand men, and boasted, with the rash presumption which is the forerunner of disgrace, that his numerous cavalry would trample under their horses' feet the troops of Mascezel, and involve, in a cloud of burning sand, the natives of the cold regions of Gaul and Germany. [4] But the Moor who commanded the legions of Honorius was too well acquainted with the manners

---

[1] Claud. Rutil. Numatian. Itinerar. lib. i. 439-448. He afterwards (*ib.* 515-526) mentions a religious madman on the Isle of Gorgona. For such profane remarks, Rutilius and his accomplices are styled, by his commentator Barthius, rabiosi canes diaboli. Tillemont (Mém. Ecclés. tom. xii. p. 471) more calmly observes that the unbelieving poet praises where he means to censure.

[2] Orosius, l. vii. c. 36, p. 564. Augustin commends two of these savage saints of the Isle of Goats (Epist. lxxxi. apud Tillemont, Mém. Ecclés. tom. xiii. p. 317, and Baronius, Annal. Eccles. A.D. 398, No. 51).

[3] Here the first book of the Gildonic war is terminated. The rest of Claudian's poem has been lost; and we are ignorant *how* or *where* the army made good their landing in Africa.

[4] Orosius must be responsible for the account. The presumption of Gildo and his various train of barbarians is celebrated by Claudian (i. Cons. Stil. l. i. 345-355).

of the countrymen to entertain any serious apprehension of a naked and disorderly host of barbarians, whose left arm, instead of a shield, was protected only by a mantle; who were totally disarmed as soon as they had darted their javelin from their right hand; and whose horses had never been taught to bear the control, or to obey the guidance, of the bridle. He fixed his camp of five thousand veterans in the face of a superior enemy, and, after the delay of three days, gave the signal of a general engagement.[1] As Mascezel advanced before the front with fair offers of peace and pardon, he encountered one of the foremost standard-bearers of the Africans, and, on his refusal to yield, struck him on the arm with his sword. The arm and the standard sunk under the weight of the blow, and the imaginary act of submission was hastily repeated by all the standards of the line. At this signal the disaffected cohorts proclaimed the name of their lawful sovereign; the barbarians, astonished by the defection of their Roman allies, dispersed, according to their custom, in tumultuary flight; and Mascezel obtained the honours of an easy and almost bloodless victory.[2] The tyrant escaped from the field of battle to the sea-shore, and threw himself into a small vessel, with the hope of reaching in safety some friendly port of the empire of the East; but the obstinacy of the wind drove him back into the harbour of Tabraca,[3] which had acknowledged, with the rest of the province, the dominion of Honorius, and the authority of his lieutenant. The inhabitants, as a proof of their repentance and loyalty, seized and confined the person of Gildo in a dungeon; and his own despair saved him from the intolerable torture of supporting the presence of an injured and victorious brother.[4] The captives and the spoils of Africa were laid at the feet of the emperor; but Stilicho, whose moderation appeared more conspicuous and more sincere in the midst of prosperity, still affected to consult the laws of the republic, and referred to the senate and people of Rome the judgment of the

---

[1] St. Ambrose, who had been dead about a year, revealed in a vision the time and place of the victory. Mascezel afterwards related his dream to Paulinus, the original biographer of the saint, from whom it might easily pass to Orosius.

[2] Zosimus (l. v. [c. 11] p. 303) supposes an obstinate combat; but the narrative of Orosius appears to conceal a real fact under the disguise of a miracle.

[3] Tabraca lay between the two Hippos (Cellarius, tom. ii. p. 112; D'Anville, tom. iii. p. 84). Orosius has distinctly named the field of battle, but our ignorance cannot define the precise situation.

[4] The death of Gildo is expressed by Claudian (i. Cons. Stil. l. 357) and his best interpreters, Zosimus and Orosius.

most illustrious criminals.[1]   Their trial was public and solemn;
but the judges, in the exercise of this obsolete and precarious
jurisdiction, were impatient to punish the African magistrates
who had intercepted the subsistence of the Roman people.   The
rich and guilty province was oppressed by the Imperial ministers,
who had a visible interest to multiply the number of the accomplices of Gildo; and if an edict of Honorius seems to check the
malicious industry of informers, a subsequent edict, at the distance of ten years, continues and renews the prosecution of the
offences which had been committed in the time of the general
rebellion.[2]   The adherents of the tyrant who escaped the first
fury of the soldiers and the judges might derive some consolation
from the tragic fate of his brother, who could never obtain his
pardon for the extraordinary services which he had performed.
After he had finished an important war in the space of a single
winter, Mascezel was received at the court of Milan with loud
applause, affected gratitude, and secret jealousy;[3] and his death,
which perhaps was the effect of accident, has been considered as
the crime of Stilicho.   In the passage of a bridge, the Moorish
prince, who accompanied the master-general of the West, was
suddenly thrown from his horse into the river; the officious
haste of the attendants was restrained by a cruel and perfidious
smile which they observed on the countenance of Stilicho; and
while they delayed the necessary assistance, the unfortunate
Mascezel was irrecoverably drowned.[4]

The joy of the African triumph was happily connected with
the nuptials of the emperor Honorius, and of his cousin Maria,
the daughter of Stilicho; and this equal and honourable alliance
seemed to invest the powerful minister with the authority of a
parent over his submissive pupil.   The muse of Claudian was

---

[1] Claudian (iii. Cons. Stilich. 99-119) describes their trial (tremuit quos
Africa nuper, cernunt rostra reos), and applauds the restoration of the
ancient constitution.   It is here that he introduces the famous sentence so
familiar to the friends of despotism:

——Nunquam libertas gratior exstat
Quam sub rege pio.

But the freedom which depends on royal piety scarcely deserves that
appellation.

[2] See the Theodosian Code, l. ix. tit. xxxix. leg. 3, tit. xl. leg. 19.

[3] Stilicho, who claimed an equal share in all the victories of Theodosius
and his son, particularly asserts that Africa was recovered by the wisdom
of his counsels (see an inscription produced by Baronius).

[4] I have softened the narrative of Zosimus, which, in its crude simplicity,
is almost incredible (l. v. [c. 11] p. 303).   Orosius damns the victorious
general (p. 538 [lib. vii. c. 36]) for violating the right of sanctuary.

not silent on this propitious day;[1] he sung, in various and lively strains, the happiness of the royal pair, and the glory of the hero who confirmed their union and supported their throne. The ancient fables of Greece, which had almost ceased to be the object of religious faith, were saved from oblivion by the genius of poetry. The picture of the Cyprian grove, the seat of harmony and love; the triumphant progress of Venus over her native seas, and the mild influence which her presence diffused in the palace of Milan, express to every age the natural sentiments of the heart in the just and pleasing language of allegorical fiction. But the amorous impatience which Claudian attributes to the young prince[2] must excite the smiles of the court; and his beauteous spouse (if she deserved the praise of beauty) had not much to fear or to hope from the passions of her lover. Honorius was only in the fourteenth year of his age; Serena, the mother of his bride, deferred, by art or persuasion, the consummation of the royal nuptials; Maria died a virgin, after she had been ten years a wife; and the chastity of the emperor was secured by the coldness, or perhaps the debility, of his constitution.[3] His subjects, who attentively studied the character of their young sovereign, discovered that Honorius was without passions, and consequently without talents; and that his feeble and languid disposition was alike incapable of discharging the duties of his rank, or of enjoying the pleasures of his age. In his early youth he made some progress in the exercises of riding and drawing the bow; but he soon relinquished these fatiguing occupations, and the amusement of feeding poultry became the serious and daily care of the monarch of the West,[4] who resigned the reins of empire to the firm and skilful hand of his guardian Stilicho. The experience of history will countenance the suspicion that a prince

---

[1] Claudian, as the poet laureat, composed a serious and elaborate epithalamium of 340 lines; besides some gay Fescennines, which were sung in a more licentious tone on the wedding night.

[2] —— Calet obvius ire
Jam princeps, tardumque cupit discedere solem.
Nobilis haud aliter *sonipes*—

(de Nuptiis Honor. et Mariæ, 287) and more freely in the Fescennines 112-126 [iv. 14].

Dices, *O quoties*, hoc mihi dulcius
Quam flavos *decies* vincere Sarmatas.
. . . .
Tum victor madido prosilias toro
Nocturni referens vulnera prœlii.

[3] See Zosimus, l. v. [c. 28] p. 333.

[4] Procopius de Bell. Vandal. l. i. c. 2 [tom. i. p. 316, ed. Bonn.]. I have borrowed the general practice of Honorius, without adopting the singular, and, indeed, improbable tale, which is related by the Greek historian.

who was born in the purple received a worse education than the
meanest peasant of his dominions, and that the ambitious
minister suffered him to attain the age of manhood without
attempting to excite his courage or to enlighten his understanding.[1]　The predecessors of Honorius were accustomed to animate
by their example, or at least by their presence, the valour of the
legions; and the dates of their laws attest the perpetual activity
of their motions through the provinces of the Roman world.
But the son of Theodosius passed the slumber of his life a captive
in his palace, a stranger in his country, and the patient, almost
the indifferent, spectator of the ruin of the Western empire,
which was repeatedly attacked, and finally subverted, by the
arms of the barbarians.　In the eventful history of a reign of
twenty-eight years, it will seldom be necessary to mention the
name of the emperor Honorius.

CHAPTER XXX

Revolt of the Goths—They plunder Greece—Two great Invasions of
　　Italy by Alaric and Radagaisus—They are repulsed by Stilicho—
　　The Germans overrun Gaul—Usurpation of Constantine in the West
　　—Disgrace and Death of Stilicho

IF the subjects of Rome could be ignorant of their obligations
to the great Theodosius, they were too soon convinced how
painfully the spirit and abilities of their deceased emperor had
supported the frail and mouldering edifice of the republic.　He
died in the month of January; and before the end of the winter
of the same year, the Gothic nation was in arms.[2]　The barbarian
auxiliaries erected their independent standard, and boldly avowed
the hostile designs which they had long cherished in their
ferocious minds.　Their countrymen, who had been condemned
by the conditions of the last treaty to a life of tranquillity and
labour, deserted their farms at the first sound of the trumpet,
and eagerly resumed the weapons which they had reluctantly
laid down.　The barriers of the Danube were thrown open; the
savage warriors of Scythia issued from their forests; and the
uncommon severity of the winter allowed the poet to remark

---

[1] The lessons of Theodosius, or rather Claudian (iv. Cons Honor. 214-418)
might compose a fine institution for the future prince of a great and free
nation.　It was far above Honorius and his degenerate subjects.

[2] The revolt of the Goths and the blockade of Constantinople are distinctly mentioned by Claudian (in Rufin. l. ii. 7-100), Zosimus (l. v. [c. 5]
p. 292), and Jornandes (de Rebus Geticis, c. 29).

" that they rolled their ponderous waggons over the broad and icy back of the indignant river." [1] The unhappy natives of the provinces to the south of the Danube submitted to the calamities which, in the course of twenty years, were almost grown familiar to their imagination; and the various troops of barbarians who gloried in the Gothic name were irregularly spread from the woody shores of Dalmatia to the walls of Constantinople.[2] The interruption, or at least the diminution, of the subsidy which the Goths had received from the prudent liberality of Theodosius, was the specious pretence of their revolt: the affront was embittered by their contempt for the unwarlike sons of Theodosius; and their resentment was inflamed by the weakness or treachery of the minister of Arcadius. The frequent visits of Rufinus to the camp of the barbarians, whose arms and apparel he affected to imitate, were considered as a sufficient evidence of his guilty correspondence; and the public enemy, from a motive either of gratitude or of policy, was attentive, amidst the general devastation, to spare the private estates of the unpopular præfect. The Goths, instead of being impelled by the blind and headstrong passions of their chiefs, were now directed by the bold and artful genius of Alaric. That renowned leader was descended from the noble race of the Balti,[3] which yielded only to the royal dignity of the Amali: he had solicited the command of the Roman armies; and the Imperial court provoked him to demonstrate the folly of their refusal, and the importance of their loss. Whatever hopes might be entertained of the conquest of Constantinople, the judicious general soon abandoned an impracticable enterprise. In the midst of a divided court and a discontented people, the emperor Arcadius was terrified by the

---

[1] ———— Alii per terga ferocis
    Danubii solidata ruunt; expertaque remos
    Frangunt stagna rotis.   [Claud. ib. v. 24.]
Claudian and Ovid often amuse their fancy by interchanging the metaphors and properties of *liquid* water and *solid* ice. Much false wit has been expended in this easy exercise.

[2] Jerom. tom. i. p. 26 [Epist. lx. tom. i. p. 342, ed. Vallars.]. He endeavours to comfort his friend Heliodorus, bishop of Altinum, for the loss of his nephew Nepotian, by a curious recapitulation of all the public and private misfortunes of the times. See Tillemont, Mém. Ecclés. tom. xii. p. 200, etc.

[3] *Baltha*, or *bold :* origo mirifica, says Jornandes (c. 29). This illustrious race long continued to flourish in France, in the Gothic province of Septimania, or Languedoc, under the corrupted appellation of *Baux :* and a branch of that family afterwards settled in the kingdom of Naples (Grotius in Prolegom. ad Hist. Gothic. p. 53). The lords of Baux, near Arles, and of seventy-nine subordinate places, were independent of the counts of Provence (Longuerue, Description de la France, tom. i. p. 357).

aspect of the Gothic arms: but the want of wisdom and valour was supplied by the strength of the city; and the fortifications, both of the sea and land, might securely brave the impotent and random darts of the barbarians. Alaric disdained to trample any longer on the prostrate and ruined countries of Thrace and Dacia, and he resolved to seek a plentiful harvest of fame and riches in a province which had hitherto escaped the ravages of war.[1]

The character of the civil and military officers on whom Rufinus had devolved the government of Greece confirmed the public suspicion that he had betrayed the ancient seat of freedom and learning to the Gothic invader. The proconsul Antiochus was the unworthy son of a respectable father; and Gerontius, who commanded the provincial troops, was much better qualified to execute the oppressive orders of a tyrant than to defend, with courage and ability, a country most remarkably fortified by the hand of nature. Alaric had traversed, without resistance, the plains of Macedonia and Thessaly, as far as the foot of Mount Oeta, a steep and woody range of hills, almost impervious to his cavalry. They stretched from east to west, to the edge of the sea-shore; and left, between the precipice and the Malian Gulf, an interval of three hundred feet, which in some places was contracted to a road capable of admitting only a single carriage.[2] In this narrow pass of Thermopylæ, where Leonidas and the three hundred Spartans had gloriously devoted their lives, the Goths might have been stopped, or destroyed, by a skilful general; and perhaps the view of that sacred spot might have kindled some sparks of military ardour in the breasts of the degenerate Greeks. The troops which had been posted to defend the straits of Thermopylæ retired, as they were directed, without attempting to disturb the secure and rapid passage of Alaric;[3] and the fertile fields of Phocis and Bœotia were instantly covered by a deluge of barbarians, who massacred the males of an age to bear arms, and drove away the beautiful females, with the spoil and cattle of the flaming villages. The travellers who visited Greece several years afterwards could easily discover the deep and bloody traces of the march of the Goths; and Thebes was

---

[1] Zosimus (l. v. [c. 5] p. 293-295) is our best guide for the conquest of Greece: but the hints and allusion of Claudian are so many rays of historic light.

[2] Compare Herodotus (l. vii. c. 176) and Livy (xxxvi. 15). The narrow entrance of Greece was probably enlarged by each successive ravisher.

[3] He passed, says Eunapius (in Vit. Philosoph. p. 93, edit. Commelin, 1596), through the straits, διὰ τῶν τυλῶν of Thermopylæ) παρῆλθεν, σῶπερ διὰ σταδίου καὶ ἱπποκρότου πεδίου τρέχων.

less indebted for her preservation to the strength of her seven gates than to the eager haste of Alaric, who advanced to occupy the city of Athens and the important harbour of the Piræus. The same impatience urged him to prevent the delay and danger of a siege, by the offer of a capitulation; and as soon as the Athenians heard the voice of the Gothic herald, they were easily persuaded to deliver the greatest part of their wealth, as the ransom of the city of Minerva and its inhabitants. The treaty was ratified by solemn oaths, and observed with mutual fidelity. The Gothic prince, with a small and select train, was admitted within the walls; he indulged himself in the refreshment of the bath, accepted a splendid banquet which was provided by the magistrate, and affected to show that he was not ignorant of the manners of civilised nations.[1] But the whole territory of Attica, from the promontory of Sunium to the town of Megara, was blasted by his baleful presence; and, if we may use the comparison of a contemporary philosopher, Athens itself resembled the bleeding and empty skin of a slaughtered victim. The distance between Megara and Corinth could not much exceed thirty miles; but the *bad road*, an expressive name, which it still bears among the Greeks, was, or mighty easily have been made, impassable for the march of an enemy. The thick and gloomy woods of Mount Cithæron covered the inland country; the Scironian rocks approached the water's edge, and hung over the narrow and winding path, which was confined above six miles along the sea-shore.[2] The passage of those rocks, so infamous in every age, was terminated by the isthmus of Corinth; and a small body of firm and intrepid soldiers might have successfully defended a temporary entrenchment of five or six miles from the Ionian to the Ægean Sea. The confidence of the cities of Peloponnesus in their natural rampart had tempted them to

---

[1] In obedience to Jerom and Claudian (in Rufin. l. ii. 191), I have mixed some darker colours in the mild representation of Zosimus, who wished to soften the calamities of Athens.

Nec fera Cecropias traxissent vincula matres.

Synesius (Epist. cxxxv. p. 272, edit. Petav.) observes that Athens, whose sufferings he imputes to the proconsul's avarice, was at that time less famous for her schools of philosophy than for her trade of honey.

[2] ———— Vallata mari Scironia rupes,
Et duo continuo connectens æquora muro
Isthmos.

Claudian de Bell. Getico, 188.

The Scironian rocks are described by Pausanias (l. i. c. 44, p. 107, edit. Kuhn) and our modern travellers Wheeler (p. 436) and Chandler (p. 298). Hadrian made the road passable for two carriages [Pausan. i. c. 44, § 6, ed. Bekker].

neglect the care of their antique walls; and the avarice of the
Roman governors had exhausted and betrayed the unhappy
province.[1] Corinth, Argos, Sparta, yielded without resistance
to the arms of the Goths; and the most fortunate of the inhabitants were saved by death from beholding the slavery of their
families and the conflagration of their cities.[2] The vases and
statues were distributed among the barbarians, with more regard
to the value of the materials than to the elegance of the workmanship; the female captives submitted to the laws of war;
the enjoyment of beauty was the reward of valour; and the
Greeks could not reasonably complain of an abuse which was
justified by the example of the heroic times.[3] The descendants
of that extraordinary people, who had considered valour and
discipline as the walls of Sparta, no longer remembered the
generous reply of their ancestors to an invader more formidable
than Alaric. " If thou art a god, thou wilt not hurt those who
have never injured thee; if thou art a man, advance—and thou
wilt find men equal to thyself." [4] From Thermopylæ to Sparta
the leader of the Goths pursued his victorious march without
encountering any mortal antagonists; but one of the advocates
of expiring Paganism has confidently asserted that the walls of
Athens were guarded by the goddess Minerva, with her formidable Ægis, and by the angry phantom of Achilles,[5] and that
the conqueror was dismayed by the presence of the hostile deities

---

[1] Claudian (in Rufin. l. ii. 186, and de Bello Getico, 611, etc.) vaguely,
though forcibly, delineates the scene of rapine and destruction.
[With regard to Alaric's invasion of Greece, Prof. Bury points out that
although there is no record that Alaric burnt down the Temple of Eleusis,
it is certain that the invasion of the Goths did coincide with the end of
the Eleusinian mysteries. At the same time we must remember that the
edicts of Theodosius had exercised a repressive influence upon the worship.
Then, as to Athens, there can be no doubt that it surrendered and was
spared by Alaric, also that its glorious art treasures were not pillaged. In
fact, as Gregorovius remarks, Athens suffered less from Alaric than from
the invasion in the time of Dexippus.—O. S.]

[2] Τρὶς μάκαρες Δαναοὶ καὶ τετράκις, etc. These generous lines of Homer
(Odyss. l. v. 306) were transcribed by one of the captive youths of Corinth:
and the tears of Mummius may prove that the rude conqueror, though he
was ignorant of the value of an original picture, possessed the purest source
of good taste, a benevolent heart (Plutarch, Symposiac. l. ix. tom. ii. p. 737,
edit. Wechel. [tom. viii. p. 939, ed. Reiske]).

[3] Homer perpetually describes the exemplary patience of these female
captives, who gave their charms, and even their hearts, to the murderers
of their fathers, brothers, etc. Such a passion (of Eriphile for Achilles) is
touched with admirable delicacy by Racine.

[4] Plutarch (in Pyrrho [c. 26], tom. ii. p. 471, edit. Brian) gives the genuine
answer in the Laconic dialect. Pyrrhus attacked Sparta with 25,000 foot,
2000 horse, and 24 elephants: and the defence of that open town is a fine
comment on the laws of Lycurgus, even in the last stage of decay.

[5] Such, perhaps, as Homer (Iliad, xx. 164) has so nobly painted him.

of Greece. In an age of miracles it would perhaps be unjust to dispute the claim of the historian Zosimus to the common benefit, yet it cannot be dissembled that the mind of Alaric was ill prepared to receive, either in sleeping or waking visions, the impressions of Greek superstition. The songs of Homer and the fame of Achilles had probably never reached the ear of the illiterate *barbarian;* and the *Christian* faith, which he had devoutly embraced, taught him to despise the imaginary deities of Rome and Athens. The invasion of the Goths, instead of vindicating the honour, contributed, at least accidentally, to extirpate the last remains of Paganism; and the mysteries of Ceres, which had subsisted eighteen hundred years, did not survive the destruction of Eleusis and the calamities of Greece.[1]

The last hope of a people who could no longer depend on their arms, their gods, or their sovereign, was placed in the powerful assistance of the general of the West; and Stilicho, who had not been permitted to repulse, advanced to chastise the invaders of Greece.[2] A numerous fleet was equipped in the ports of Italy; and the troops, after a short and prosperous navigation over the Ionian Sea, were safely disembarked on the isthmus, near the ruins of Corinth. The woody and mountainous country of Arcadia, the fabulous residence of Pan and the Dryads, became the scene of a long and doubtful conflict between two generals not unworthy of each other. The skill and perseverance of the Roman at length prevailed; and the Goths, after sustaining a considerable loss from disease and desertion, gradually retreated to the lofty mountain of Pholoe, near the sources of the Peneus, and on the frontiers of Elis—a sacred country, which had formerly been exempted from the calamities of war.[3] The camp of the barbarians was immediately besieged; the waters of the river [4]

[1] Eunapius (in Vit. Philosoph. p. 90-93) intimates that a troop of monks betrayed Greece and followed the Gothic camp.

[2] For Stilicho's Greek war compare the honest narrative of Zosimus (l. v. [c. 7] p. 295, 296) with the curious circumstantial flattery of Claudian (i. Cons. Stilich. l. i. 172-186; iv. Cons. Hon. 459-487). As the event was not glorious, it is artfully thrown into the shade.

[3] The troops who marched through Elis delivered up their arms. This security enriched the Eleans, who were lovers of a rural life. Riches begat pride: they disdained their privilege, and they suffered. Polybius advises them to retire once more within their magic circle. See a learned and judicious discourse on the Olympic games, which Mr. West has prefixed to his translation of Pindar.

[4] Claudian (in iv. Cons. Hon. 480) alludes to the fact without naming the river; perhaps the Alpheus (i. Cons. Stil. l. i. 185).

    —— Et Alpheus Geticis angustus acervis
      Tardior ad Siculos etiamnum pergit amores.

Yet I should prefer the Peneus, a shallow stream in a wide and deep bed

were diverted into another channel; and while they laboured
under the intolerable pressure of thirst and hunger, a strong line
of circumvallation was formed to prevent their escape. After
these precautions Stilicho, too confident of victory, retired to
enjoy his triumph in the theatrical games and lascivious dances
of the Greeks; his soldiers, deserting their standards, spread
themselves over the country of their allies, which they stripped
of all that had been saved from the rapacious hands of the
enemy. Alaric appears to have seized the favourable moment
to execute one of those hardy enterprises in which the abilities
of a general are displayed with more genuine lustre than in the
tumult of a day of battle. To extricate himself from the prison
of Peloponnesus it was necessary that he should pierce the
entrenchments which surrounded his camp; that he should
perform a difficult and dangerous march of thirty miles, as far
as the Gulf of Corinth; and that he should transport his troops,
his captives, and his spoil, over an arm of the sea, which, in the
narrow interval between Rhium and the opposite shore, is at
least half a mile in breadth.[1] The operations of Alaric must
have been secret, prudent, and rapid, since the Roman general
was confounded by the intelligence that the Goths, who had
eluded his efforts, were in full possession of the important
province of Epirus. This unfortunate delay allowed Alaric
sufficient time to conclude the treaty which he secretly negotiated
with the ministers of Constantinople. The apprehension of a
civil war compelled Stilicho to retire, at the haughty mandate of
his rivals, from the dominions of Arcadius; and he respected,
in the enemy of Rome, the honourable character of the ally and
servant of the emperor of the East.

A Grecian philosopher,[2] who visited Constantinople soon after
the death of Theodosius, published his liberal opinions concerning the duties of kings and the state of the Roman republic.
Synesius observes and deplores the fatal abuse which the imprudent bounty of the late emperor had introduced into the

which runs through Elis and falls into the sea below Cyllene. It had been
joined with the Alpheus to cleanse the Augean stable. (Cellarius, tom. i.
p. 760. Chandler's Travels. p. 286.)

[1] Strabo, l. viii. p. 517 [p. 335, ed. Casaub.]. Plin. Hist. Natur. iv. 3.
Wheeler, p. 308. Chandler, p. 275. They measured from different points
the distance between the two lands.

[2] Synesius passed three years (A.D. 397-400) at Constantinople as deputy
from Cyrene to the emperor Arcadius. He presented him with a crown
of gold, and pronounced before him the instructive oration de Regno
(p. 1-32, edit. Petav. Paris, 1612). The philosopher was made bishop of
Ptolemais, A.D. 410, and died about 430. See Tillemont, Mém. Ecclés.
tom. xii. p. 499, 554, 683-685.

military service. The citizens and subjects had purchased an exemption from the indispensable duty of defending their country, which was supported by the arms of barbarian mercenaries. The fugitives of Scythia were permitted to disgrace the illustrious dignities of the empire; their ferocious youth, who disdained the salutary restraint of laws, were more anxious to acquire the riches than to imitate the arts of a people the object of their contempt and hatred; and the power of the Goths was the stone of Tantalus, perpetually suspended over the peace and safety of the devoted state. The measures which Synesius recommends are the dictates of a bold and generous patriot. He exhorts the emperor to revive the courage of his subjects by the example of manly virtue; to banish luxury from the court and from the camp; to substitute, in the place of the barbarian mercenaries, an army of men interested in the defence of their laws and of their property; to force, in such a moment of public danger, the mechanic from his shop and the philosopher from his school; to rouse the indolent citizen from his dream of pleasure; and to arm, for the protection of agriculture, the hands of the laborious husbandman. At the head of such troops, who might deserve the name and would display the spirit of Romans, he animates the son of Theodosius to encounter a race of barbarians who were destitute of any real courage; and never to lay down his arms till he had chased them far away into the solitudes of Scythia, or had reduced them to the state of ignominious servitude which the Lacedæmonians formerly imposed on the captive Helots.[1] The court of Arcadius indulged the zeal, applauded the eloquence, and neglected the advice of Synesius. Perhaps the philosopher, who addresses the emperor of the East in the language of reason and virtue which he might have used to a Spartan king, had not condescended to form a practicable scheme, consistent with the temper and circumstances of a degenerate age. Perhaps the pride of the ministers, whose business was seldom interrupted by reflection, might reject, as wild and visionary, every proposal which exceeded the measure of their capacity, and deviated from the forms and precedents of office. While the oration of Synesius and the downfall of the barbarians were the topics of popular conversation, an edict was published at Constantinople which declared the promotion of Alaric to the rank of master-general of the Eastern Illyricum. The Roman provincials, and the allies who had respected the faith of treaties, were justly indignant that

[1] Synesius de Regno, p. 21-26.

the ruin of Greece and Epirus should be so liberally rewarded. The Gothic conqueror was received as a lawful magistrate in the cities which he had so lately besieged. The fathers whose sons he had massacred, the husbands whose wives he had violated, were subject to his authority; and the success of his rebellion encouraged the ambition of every leader of the foreign mercenaries. The use to which Alaric applied his new command distinguishes the firm and judicious character of his policy. He issued his orders to the four magazines and manufactures of offensive and defensive arms, Margus, Ratiaria, Naissus, and Thessalonica, to provide his troops with an extraordinary supply of shields, helmets, swords, and spears; the unhappy provincials were compelled to forge the instruments of their own destruction; and the barbarians removed the only defect which had sometimes disappointed the efforts of their courage.[1] The birth of Alaric, the glory of his past exploits, and the confidence in his future designs, insensibly united the body of the nation under his victorious standards; and, with the unanimous consent of the barbarian chieftains, the master-general of Illyricum was elevated, according to ancient custom, on a shield, and solemnly proclaimed king of the Visigoths.[2] Armed with this double power, seated on the verge of the two empires, he alternately sold his deceitful promises to the courts of Arcadius and Honorius,[3] till he declared and executed his resolution of invading the dominions of the West. The provinces of Europe which belonged to the Eastern emperor were already exhausted, those of Asia were inaccessible, and the strength of Constantinople had resisted his attack. But he was tempted by the fame, the beauty, the wealth of Italy, which he had twice visited; and he secretly aspired to plant the Gothic standard on the walls of

---

[1] ————— qui fœdera rumpit
  Ditatur: qui servat, eget: vastator Achivæ
  Gentis, et Epirum nuper populatus inultam
  Præsidet Illyrico: jam, quos obsedit, amicos
  Ingreditur muros; illis responsa daturus
  Quorum conjugibus potitur, natosque peremit.

Claudian in Eutrop. l. ii. 212. Alaric applauds his own policy (de Bell. Getic. 533-543) in the use which he had made of this Illyrian jurisdiction.

[2] Jornandes, c. 29, p. 651 [ed. Grot. 1655; p. 81, ed. Lugd. B. 1597]. The Gothic historian adds, with unusual spirit, Cum suis deliberans suasit suo labore quærere regna, quam alienis per otium subjacere.

[Some annotaters think that it was more likely that Alaric was proclaimed king in 395 A.D. after the death of Theodosius.—O. S.]

[3] ——— Discors odiisque anceps civilibus orbis
  Non sua vis tutata diu, dum fœdera fallax
  Ludit, et alternæ perjuria venditat aulæ.

Claudian de Bell. Get. 565.

Rome, and to enrich his army with the accumulated spoils of three hundred triumphs.[1]

The scarcity of facts,[2] and the uncertainty of dates,[3] oppose our attempts to describe the circumstances of the first invasion of Italy by the arms of Alaric. His march, perhaps from Thessalonica, through the warlike and hostile country of Pannonia, as far as the foot of the Julian Alps; his passage of those mountains, which were strongly guarded by troops and entrenchments; the siege of Aquileia, and the conquest of the provinces of Istria and Venetia, appear to have employed a considerable time. Unless his operations were extremely cautious and slow, the length of the interval would suggest a probable suspicion that the Gothic king retreated towards the banks of the Danube, and reinforced his army with fresh swarms of barbarians, before he again attempted to penetrate into the heart of Italy. Since the public and important events escape the diligence of the historian, he may amuse himself with contemplating for a

---

[1] Alpibus Italiæ ruptis penetrabis ad *Urbem*.

This authentic prediction was announced by Alaric, or at least by Claudian (de Bell. Getico, 547), seven years before the event. But as it was not accomplished within the term which has been rashly fixed, the interpreters escaped through an ambiguous meaning.

[Claudian states that a voice had foretold to Alaric that he would plant his standard on the walls of Rome. Cf. Claudian, *De Bello Getico*. 546-7.

> Rumpe omnes, Alarice moras: hoc impiger anno
> Alpibus Italiæ ruptis penetrabis ad urbem.

In Koch's edition of Claudian the fact is indicated that the first and last letters of the two lines spell ROMA.—O. S.]

[2] Our best materials are 970 verses of Claudian, in the poem on the Getic war, and the beginning of that which celebrates the sixth consulship of Honorius. Zosimus is totally silent; and we are reduced to such scraps, or rather crumbs, as we can pick from Orosius and the Chronicles.

[3] Notwithstanding the gross errors of Jornandes, who confounds the Italian wars of Alaric (c. 29), his date of the consulship of Stilicho and Aurelian (A.D. 400) is firm and respectable. It is certain from Claudian (Tillemont, Hist. des Emp. tom. v. p. 804), that the battle of Pollentia was fought A.D. 403; but we cannot easily fill the interval.

[As regards Alaric in Italy, the events which Gibbon supposes to have taken place in 400-402 are uncertain. We know that Alaric crossed the Alps early in the winter of 401 A.D., probably October (Claudian vi. *Cons. Honor*. 440, *Bell. Get*. 471), entered Italy in November of that same year, and fought the battle of Pollentia on Easter Day 402. Alaric was in Istria late in 402 or early in 403, and the battle of Verona was fought in the summer (probably June) of that year, 403. Bury thinks that after Pollentia there must have been another engagement at Asta. The 17th Appendix to Prof. Bury's third volume is worthy of the most careful study by all interested in this question. There is, however, no authority for Gibbon's statement that Honorius on his way to Arles took refuge in Asta. It is (says Dr. W. Smith) simply an hypothesis to account for the presence of Alaric in Liguria, and rests only on Claudian's mention of Asta in conjunction with Pollentia.—O. S.]

moment the influence of the arms of Alaric on the fortunes of two obscure individuals, a presbyter of Aquileia, and an husband-man of Verona. The learned Rufinus, who was summoned by his enemies to appear before a Roman synod,[1] wisely preferred the dangers of a besieged city; and the barbarians, who furiously shook the walls of Aquileia, might save him from the cruel sentence of another heretic, who, at the request of the same bishops, was severely whipped and condemned to perpetual exile on a desert island.[2] The *old man*,[3] who had passed his simple and innocent life in the neighbourhood of Verona, was a stranger to the quarrels both of kings and of bishops; *his* pleasures, his desires, his knowledge, were confined within the little circle of his paternal farm; and a staff supported his aged steps on the same ground where he had sported in his infancy. Yet even this humble and rustic felicity (which Claudian describes with so much truth and feeling) was still exposed to the undistinguishing rage of war. His trees, his old *contemporary* trees,[4] must blaze in the conflagration of the whole country; a detachment of Gothic cavalry might sweep away his cottage and his family; and the power of Alaric could destroy this happiness, which he was not able either to taste or to bestow. " Fame," says the poet, " encircling with terror her gloomy wings, proclaimed the march of the barbarian army, and filled Italy with consternation: " the apprehensions of each individual were increased in just proportion to the measure of his fortune: and the most timid, who had already embarked their valuable effects, meditated their escape to the island of Sicily or the African

---

[1] Tantum Romanæ urbis judicium fugis, ut magis obsidionem barbaricam, quam *pacatæ* urbis judicium velis sustinere. Jerom, tom. ii. p. 239. Rufinus understood his own danger; the *peaceful* city was inflamed by the beldam Marcella and the rest of Jerom's faction.

[2] Jovinian, the enemy of fasts and of celibacy, who was persecuted and insulted by the furious Jerom (Jortin's Remarks, vol. iv. p. 104, etc.). See the original edict of banishment in the Theodosian Code, l. xvi. tit. v. leg. 53.

[3] This epigram (de Sene Veronensi qui suburbium nusquam egressus est) is one of the earliest and most pleasing compositions of Claudian. Cowley's imitation (Hurd's edition, vol. ii. p. 241) has some natural and happy strokes: but it is much inferior to the original portrait, which is evidently drawn from the life.

[4] Ingentem meminit parvo qui germine quercum
    Æquævumque videt consenuisse nemus.

A neighbouring wood born with himself he sees,
And loves his old contemporary trees.

In this passage Cowley is perhaps superior to his original; and the English poet, who was a good botanist, has concealed the *oaks* under a more general expression.

coast. The public distress was aggravated by the fears and reproaches of superstition.[1] Every hour produced some horrid tale of strange and portentous accidents: the Pagans deplored the neglect of omens and the interruption of sacrifices; but the Christians still derived some comfort from the powerful intercession of the saints and martyrs.[2]

The emperor Honorius was distinguished, above his subjects, by the pre-eminence of fear as well as of rank. The pride and luxury in which he was educated had not allowed him to suspect that there existed on the earth any power presumptuous enough to invade the repose of the successor of Augustus. The arts of flattery concealed the impending danger till Alaric approached the palace of Milan. But when the sound of war had awakened the young emperor, instead of flying to arms with the spirit, or even the rashness, of his age, he eagerly listened to those timid counsellors who proposed to convey his sacred person and his faithful attendants to some secure and distant station in the provinces of Gaul. Stilicho alone[3] had courage and authority to resist this disgraceful measure, which would have abandoned Rome and Italy to the barbarians; but as the troops of the palace had been lately detached to the Rhætian frontier, and as the resource of new levies was slow and precarious, the general of the West could only promise that, if the court of Milan would maintain its ground during his absence, he would soon return with an army equal to the encounter of the Gothic king. Without losing a moment (while each moment was so important to the public safety), Stilicho hastily embarked on the Larian lake, ascended the mountains of ice and snow amidst the severity of an Alpine winter, and suddenly repressed, by his unexpected presence, the enemy, who had disturbed the tranquillity of Rhætia.[4] The barbarians, perhaps some tribes of the Alemanni, respected the firmness of a chief who still assumed the language of command; and the choice which he condescended to make of a select number of their bravest youth was considered as a mark of his esteem and favour. The cohorts, who were delivered from

[1] Claudian de Bell. Get. 199-266. He may seem prolix: but fear and superstition occupied as large a space in the minds of the Italians.

[2] From the passages of Paulinus which Baronius has produced (Annal. Eccles. A.D. 403, No. 51) it is manifest that the general alarm had pervaded all Italy, as far as Nola in Campania, where that famous penitent had fixed his abode.

[3] Solus erat Stilicho, etc., is the exclusive commendation which Claudian bestows (de Bell. Get. 267), without condescending to except the emperor. How insignificant must Honorius have appeared in his own court!

[4] The face of the country and the hardiness of Stilicho are finely described (de Bell. Get. 340-363).

the neighbouring foe, diligently repaired to the Imperial standard;
and Stilicho issued his orders to the most remote troops of the
West, to advance, by rapid marches, to the defence of Honorius
and of Italy.   The fortresses of the Rhine were abandoned; and
the safety of Gaul was protected only by the faith of the Germans,
and the ancient terror of the Roman name.   Even the legion
which had been stationed to guard the wall of Britain against
the Caledonians of the North was hastily recalled;[1] and a
numerous body of the cavalry of the Alani was persuaded to
engage in the service of the emperor, who anxiously expected
the return of his general.   The prudence and vigour of Stilicho
were conspicuous on this occasion, which revealed, at the same
time, the weakness of the falling empire.   The legions of Rome,
which had long since languished in the gradual decay of discipline
and courage, were exterminated by the Gothic and civil wars;
and it was found impossible, without exhausting and exposing
the provinces, to assemble an army for the defence of Italy.

When Stilicho seemed to abandon his sovereign in the unguarded palace of Milan, he had probably calculated the term
of his absence, the distance of the enemy, and the obstacles that
might retard their march.   He principally depended on the
rivers of Italy, the Adige, the Mincius, the Oglio, and the Addua,
which, in the winter or spring, by the fall of rains, or by the
melting of the snows, are commonly swelled into broad and impetuous torrents.[2]   But the season happened to be remarkably
dry; and the Goths could traverse, without impediment, the
wide and stony beds, whose centre was faintly marked by the
course of a shallow stream.   The bridge and passage of the
Addua were secured by a strong detachment of the Gothic army;
and as Alaric approached the walls, or rather the suburbs, of
Milan, he enjoyed the proud satisfaction of seeing the emperor of
the Romans fly before him.   Honorius, accompanied by a feeble
train of statesmen and eunuchs, hastily retreated towards the

---

[1] Venit et extremis legio prætenta Britannis
      Quæ Scoto dat frena truci.
                                        De Bell. Get. 416.
Yet the most rapid march from Edinburgh, or Newcastle, to Milan, must
have required a longer space of time than Claudian seems willing to allow
for the duration of the Gothic war.

[2] Every traveller must recollect the face of Lombardy (see Fontenelle,
tom. v. p. 279), which is often tormented by the capricious and irregular
abundance of waters.   The Austrians before Genoa were encamped in the
dry bed of the Polcevera.   " Ne sarebbe " (says Muratori) " mai passato
per mente a que' buoni Alemanni, che quel picciolo torrente potesse, per
cosi dire, in un instante cangiarsi in un terribil gigante."   (Annal. d'Italia,
tom. xvi. p. 443, Milan, 1753, 8vo. edit.)

Alps, with a design of securing his person in the city of Arles,
which had often been the royal residence of his predecessors.
But Honorius [1] had scarcely passed the Po before he was over-
taken by the speed of the Gothic cavalry; [2] since the urgency
of the danger compelled him to seek a temporary shelter within
the fortification of Asta, a town of Liguria or Piemont, situate on
the banks of the Tanarus. [3] The siege of an obscure place, which
contained so rich a prize, and seemed incapable of a long resistance, was instantly formed, and indefatigably pressed, by the
king of the Goths; and the bold declaration, which the emperor
might afterwards make, that his breast had never been susceptible of fear, did not probably obtain much credit even in his
own court. [4] In the last and almost hopeless extremity, after
the barbarians had already proposed the indignity of a capitulation, the Imperial captive was suddenly relieved by the fame,
the approach, and at length the presence, of the hero whom he
had so long expected. At the head of a chosen and intrepid
vanguard, Stilicho swam the stream of the Addua, to gain the
time which he must have lost in the attack of the bridge; the
passage of the Po was an enterprise of much less hazard and
difficulty; and the successful action, in which he cut his way
through the Gothic camp under the walls of Asta, revived the
hopes and vindicated the honour of Rome. Instead of grasping
the fruit of his victory, the barbarian was gradually invested, on
every side, by the troops of the West, who successively issued
through all the passes of the Alps; his quarters were straitened;
his convoys were intercepted; and the vigilance of the Romans
prepared to form a chain of fortifications, and to besiege the lines
of the besiegers. A military council was assembled of the long-
haired chiefs of the Gothic nation; of aged warriors, whose
bodies were wrapped in furs, and whose stern countenances were
marked with honourable wounds. They weighed the glory of
persisting in their attempt against the advantage of securing
their plunder; and they recommended the prudent measure of a

[1] Claudian does not clearly answer our question, Where was Honorius
himself? Yet the flight is marked by the pursuit; and my idea of the
Gothic war is justified by the Italian critics, Sigonius (tom. i. p. ii. p. 369,
de Imp. Occident. l. x.) and Muratori (Annali d'Italia, tom. iv. p. 45).

[2] One of the roads may be traced in the Itineraries (p. 98, 288, 294, with
Wesseling's Notes). Asta lay some miles on the right hand.

[3] Asta, or Asti, a Roman colony, is now the capital of a pleasant county,
which, in the sixteenth century, devolved to the dukes of Savoy (Leandro
Alberti, Descrizzione d'Italia, p. 382).

[4] Nec me timor impulit ullus. He might hold this proud language the
next year at Rome, five hundred miles from the scene of danger (vi. Cons.
Hon. 449).

seasonable retreat. In this important debate, Alaric displayed the spirit of the conqueror of Rome; and after he had reminded his countrymen of their achievements and of their designs, he concluded his animating speech by the solemn and positive assurance that he was resolved to find in Italy either a kingdom or a grave.[1]

The loose discipline of the barbarians always exposed them to the danger of a surprise; but, instead of choosing the dissolute hours of riot and intemperance, Stilicho resolved to attack the *Christian* Goths whilst they were devoutly employed in celebrating the festival of Easter.[2] The execution of the stratagem, or, as it was termed by the clergy, of the sacrilege, was intrusted to Saul, a barbarian and a Pagan, who had served, however, with distinguished reputation among the veteran generals of Theodosius. The camp of the Goths, which Alaric had pitched in the neighbourhood of Pollentia,[3] was thrown into confusion by the sudden and impetuous charge of the Imperial cavalry; but, in a few moments, the undaunted genius of their leader gave them an order and a field of battle; and, as soon as they had recovered from their astonishment, the pious confidence that the God of the Christians would assert their cause added new strength to their native valour. In this engagement, which was long maintained with equal courage and success, the chief of the Alani, whose diminutive and savage form concealed a magnanimous soul, approved his suspected loyalty, by the zeal with which he fought and fell in the service of the republic; and the fame of this gallant barbarian has been imperfectly preserved in the verses of Claudian, since the poet, who celebrates his virtue, has omitted the mention of his name. His death was followed by the flight and dismay of the squadrons which he commanded; and the defeat of the wing of cavalry might have decided the victory of Alaric, if Stilicho had not immediately led the Roman

[1] Hanc ego vel victor regno, vel morte tenebo
      Victus, humum.
The speeches (de Bell. Get. 479-549) of the Gothic Nestor and Achilles are strong, characteristic, adapted to the circumstances, and possibly not less genuine than those of Livy.

[2] Orosius (l. vii. c. 37) is shocked at the impiety of the Romans, who attacked on Easter Sunday such pious Christians. Yet, at the same time, public prayers were offered at the shrine of St. Thomas of Edessa for the destruction of the Arian robber. See Tillemont (Hist. des Emp. tom. v. p. 529), who quotes a homily which has been erroneously ascribed to St. Chrysostom.

[3] The vestiges of Pollentia are twenty-five miles to the south-east of Turin. *Urbs*, in the same neighbourhood, was a royal chace of the kings of Lombardy, and a small river, which excused the prediction, "penetrabis ad urbem." (Cluver. Ital. Antiq. tom. i. p. 83-85.)

and barbarian infantry to the attack. The skill of the general, and the bravery of the soldiers, surmounted every obstacle. In the evening of the bloody day, the Goths retreated from the field of battle; the entrenchments of their camp were forced, and the scene of rapine and slaughter made some atonement for the calamities which they had inflicted on the subjects of the empire.[1] The magnificent spoils of Corinth and Argos enriched the veterans of the West; the captive wife of Alaric, who had impatiently claimed his promise of Roman jewels and Patrician handmaids,[2] was reduced to implore the mercy of the insulting foe; and many thousand prisoners, released from the Gothic chains, dispersed through the provinces of Italy the praises of their heroic deliverer. The triumph of Stilicho[3] was compared by the poet, and perhaps by the public, to that of Marius; who, in the same part of Italy, had encountered and destroyed another army of Northern barbarians. The huge bones and the empty helmets of the Cimbri and of the Goths would easily be confounded by succeeding generations; and posterity might erect a common trophy to the memory of the two most illustrious generals, who had vanquished, on the same memorable ground, the two most formidable enemies of Rome.[4]

The eloquence of Claudian[5] has celebrated, with lavish applause, the victory of Pollentia, one of the most glorious days in the life of his patron; but his reluctant and partial muse bestows more genuine praise on the character of the Gothic king. His name is, indeed, branded with the reproachful epithets of

[1] Orosius wishes, in doubtful words, to insinuate the defeat of the Romans. " Pugnantes vicimus, victores victi sumus." Prosper (in Chron.) makes it an equal and bloody battle; but the Gothic writers, Cassiodorus (in Chron.) and Jornandes (de Reb. Get. c. 30), claim a decisive victory.

[2] Demens Ausonidum gemmata monilia matrum,
Romanasque altâ famulas cervice petebat.
De Bell. Get. 627.
[From these lines of Claudian by no possible stretch of ingenuity can be wrung any authority whereon to base the statement that Alaric's wife fell a captive into the victor's hands.—O. S.]

[3] Claudian (de Bell. Get. 580-647) and Prudentius (in Symmach. l. ii. 694-719) celebrate, without ambiguity, the Roman victory of Pollentia. They are poetical and party writers; yet some credit is due to the most suspicious witnesses who are checked by the recent notoriety of facts.

[4] Claudian's peroration is strong and elegant; but the identity of the Cimbric and Gothic fields must be understood (like Virgil's Philippi, Georgic i. 490) according to the loose geography of a poet. Vercellæ and Pollentia are sixty miles from each other; and the latitude is still greater if the Cimbri were defeated in the wide and barren plain of Verona (Maffei, Verona Illustrata, p. i. p. 54-62).

[5] Claudian and Prudentius must be strictly examined, to reduce the figures and extort the historic sense of those poets.

pirate and robber, to which the conquerors of every age are so justly entitled; but the poet of Stilicho is compelled to acknowledge that Alaric possessed the invincible temper of mind which rises superior to every misfortune, and derives new resources from adversity. After the total defeat of his infantry, he escaped, or rather withdrew, from the field of battle, with the greatest part of his cavalry entire and unbroken. Without wasting a moment to lament the irreparable loss of so many brave companions, he left his victorious enemy to bind in chains the captive images of a Gothic king;[1] and boldly resolved to break through the unguarded passes of the Apennine, to spread desolation over the fruitful face of Tuscany, and to conquer or die before the gates of Rome. The capital was saved by the active and incessant diligence of Stilicho; but he respected the despair of his enemy; and, instead of committing the fate of the republic to the chance of another battle, he proposed to purchase the absence of the barbarians. The spirit of Alaric would have rejected such terms, the permission of a retreat, and the offer of a pension, with contempt and indignation; but he exercised a limited and precarious authority over the independent chieftains who had raised him, for *their* service, above the rank of his equals; they were still less disposed to follow an unsuccessful general, and many of them were tempted to consult their interest by a private negotiation with the minister of Honorius. The king submitted to the voice of his people, ratified the treaty with the empire of the West, and repassed the Po with the remains of the flourishing army which he had led into Italy. A considerable part of the Roman forces still continued to attend his motions: and Stilicho, who maintained a secret correspondence with some of the barbarian chiefs, was punctually apprised of the designs that were formed in the camp and council of Alaric. The king of the Goths, ambitious to signalise his retreat by some splendid achievement, had resolved to occupy the important city of Verona, which commands the principal passage of the Rhætian Alps; and, directing his march through the territories of those German tribes whose alliance would restore his exhausted strength, to invade, on the side of the Rhine, the wealthy and unsuspecting provinces of Gaul. Ignorant of the treason which had already betrayed his bold and judicious enterprise, he advanced towards

---

[1] Et gravant en airain ses frêles avantages
    De mes états conquis enchaîner les images.

The practice of exposing in triumph the images of kings and provinces was familiar to the Romans. The bust of Mithridates himself was twelve feet high, of massy gold (Freinsheᵣᵐ Supplement. Livian. ciii. 47).

the passes of the mountains, already possessed by the Imperial troops; where he was exposed, almost at the same instant, to a general attack in the front, on his flanks, and in the rear. In this bloody action, at a small distance from the walls of Verona, the loss of the Goths was not less heavy than that which they had sustained in the defeat of Pollentia; and their valiant king, who escaped by the swiftness of his horse, must either have been slain or made prisoner, if the hasty rashness of the Alani had not disappointed the measures of the Roman general. Alaric secured the remains of his army on the adjacent rocks; and prepared himself, with undaunted resolution, to maintain a siege against the superior numbers of the enemy, who invested him on all sides. But he could not oppose the destructive progress of hunger and disease; nor was it possible for him to check the continual desertion of his impatient and capricious barbarians. In this extremity he still found resources in his own courage, or in the moderation of his adversary; and the retreat of the Gothic king was considered as the deliverance of Italy.[1] Yet the people, and even the clergy, incapable of forming any rational judgment of the business of peace and war, presumed to arraign the policy of Stilicho, who so often vanquished, so often surrounded, and so often dismissed the implacable enemy of the republic. The first moment of the public safety is devoted to gratitude and joy; but the second is diligently occupied by envy and calumny.[2]

The citizens of Rome had been astonished by the approach of Alaric; and the diligence with which they laboured to restore the walls of the capital confessed their own fears, and the decline of the empire. After the retreat of the barbarians, Honorius was directed to accept the dutiful invitation of the senate, and to celebrate, in the Imperial city, the auspicious era of the Gothic victory, and of his sixth consulship.[3] The suburbs and the streets, from the Milvian bridge to the Palatine mount, were filled by the Roman people, who, in the space of an hundred years, had only thrice been honoured with the presence of their sovereigns. While their eyes were fixed on the chariot where Stilicho was deservedly seated by the side of his royal pupil,

[1] The Getic war and the sixth consulship of Honorius obscurely connect the events of Alaric's retreat and losses.

[2] Taceo de Alarico . . . sæpe victo, sæpe concluso, semperque dimisso. Orosius, l. vii. c. 37, p. 567. Claudian (vi. Cons. Hon. 320) drops the curtain with a fine image.

[3] The remainder of Claudian's poem on the sixth consulship of Honorius describes the journey, the triumph, and the games (330-660).

they applauded the pomp of a triumph which was not stained, like that of Constantine or of Theodosius, with civil blood. The procession passed under a lofty arch, which had been purposely erected: but in less than seven years, the Gothic conquerors of Rome might read, if they were able to read, the superb inscription of that monument, which attested the total defeat and destruction of their nation.[1] The emperor resided several months in the capital, and every part of his behaviour was regulated with care to conciliate the affection of the clergy, the senate, and the people of Rome. The clergy was edified by his frequent visits, and liberal gifts, to the shrines of the apostles. The senate, who, in the triumphal procession, had been excused from the humiliating ceremony of preceding on foot the Imperial chariot, was treated with the decent reverence which Stilicho always affected for that assembly. The people was repeatedly gratified by the attention and courtesy of Honorius in the public games, which were celebrated on that occasion with a magnificence not unworthy of the spectator. As soon as the appointed number of chariot-races was concluded, the decoration of the circus was suddenly changed; the hunting of wild beasts afforded a various and splendid entertainment; and the chase was succeeded by a military dance, which seems, in the lively description of Claudian, to present the image of a modern tournament.

In these games of Honorius, the inhuman combats of gladiators[2] polluted for the last time the amphitheatre of Rome. The first Christian emperor may claim the honour of the first edict which condemned the art and amusement of shedding human blood;[3] but this benevolent law expressed the wishes of the prince, without reforming an inveterate abuse which degraded a civilised nation below the condition of savage cannibals. Several hundred, perhaps several thousand, victims were annually slaughtered in the great cities of the empire; and the month of December, more peculiarly devoted to the combats of gladiators, still exhibited to the eyes of the Roman people a grateful spectacle of blood and cruelty. Amidst the general joy of the victory of Pollentia, a Christian poet exhorted the emperor to extirpate, by his authority, the horrid custom which had so long

---

[1] See the inscription in Mascou's History of the Ancient Germans, viii. 12. The words are positive and indiscreet: Getarum nationem in omne ævum domitam, etc.

[2] On the curious though horrid subject of the gladiators, consult the two books of the Saturnalia of Lipsius, who, as an *antiquarian*, is inclined to excuse the practice of *antiquity* (tom. iii. p. 483-545).

[3] Cod. Theodos. l. xv. tit. xii. leg. 1. The Commentary of Godefroy affords large materials (tom. v. p. 396) for the history of gladiators.

resisted the voice of humanity and religion.[1] The pathetic representations of Prudentius were less effectual than the generous boldness of Telemachus, an Asiatic monk, whose death was more useful to mankind than his life.[2] The Romans were provoked by the interruption of their pleasures; and the rash monk, who had descended into the arena, to separate the gladiators, was overwhelmed under a shower of stones. But the madness of the people soon subsided: they respected the memory of Telemachus, who had deserved the honours of martyrdom; and they submitted, without a murmur, to the laws of Honorius, which abolished for ever the human sacrifices of the amphitheatre. The citizens, who adhered to the manners of their ancestors, might perhaps insinuate that the last remains of a martial spirit were preserved in this school of fortitude, which accustomed the Romans to the sight of blood, and to the contempt of death: a vain and cruel prejudice, so nobly confuted by the valour of ancient Greece and of modern Europe![3]

The recent danger to which the person of the emperor had been exposed in the defenceless palace of Milan urged him to seek a retreat in some inaccessible fortress of Italy, where he might securely remain, while the open country was covered by a deluge of barbarians. On the coast of the Hadriatic, about ten or twelve miles from the most southern of the seven mouths of the Po, the Thessalians had founded the ancient colony of RAVENNA,[4] which they afterwards resigned to the natives of Umbria. Augustus, who had observed the opportunity of the place, prepared, at the distance of three miles from the old town, a capacious harbour for the reception of two hundred and fifty ships of war. This naval establishment, which included the

---

[1] See the peroration of Prudentius (in Symmach. l. ii. 1121-1131), who had doubtless read the eloquent invective of Lactantius (Divin. Institut. l. vi. c. 20). The Christian apologists have not spared these bloody games, which were introduced in the religious festivals of Paganism.

[2] Theodoret, l. v. c. 26. I wish to believe the story of St. Telemachus. Yet no church has been dedicated, no altar has been erected, to the only monk who died a martyr in the cause of humanity.

[3] Crudele gladiatorum spectaculum et inhumanum *nonnullis* videri solet; et *haud scio* an ita sit, ut nunc fit. Cicero Tusculan. ii. 17. He faintly censures the *abuse*, and warmly defends the *use*, of these sports; oculis nulla poterat esse fortior contra dolorem et mortem disciplina. Seneca (Epist. v.) shows the feelings of a man.

[4] This account of Ravenna is drawn from Strabo (l. v. p. 327 [p. 213, ed. Casaub.]), Pliny (iii. 20), Stephen of Byzantium (sub voce 'Ράβεννα, p. 651, edit. Berkel.), Claudian (in vi. Cons. Honor. 494, etc.), Sidonius Apollinaris (l. i. Epist. 5, 8), Jornandes (de Reb. Get. c. 29), Procopius (de Bell. Gothic. l. i. c. i. p. 309, edit. Louvre [tom. ii. p. 8, ed. Bonn]), and Cluverius (Ital. Antiq. tom. i. p. 301-307). Yet I still want a local antiquarian, and a good topographical map.

arsenals and magazines, the barracks of the troops, and the houses of the artificers, derived its origin and name from the permanent station of the Roman fleet; the intermediate space was soon filled with buildings and inhabitants, and the three extensive and populous quarters of Ravenna gradually contributed to form one of the most important cities of Italy. The principal canal of Augustus poured a copious stream of the waters of the Po through the midst of the city, to the entrance of the harbour; the same waters were introduced into the profound ditches that encompassed the walls; they were distributed by a thousand subordinate canals into every part of the city, which they divided into a variety of small islands; the communication was maintained only by the use of boats and bridges; and the houses of Ravenna, whose appearance may be compared to that of Venice, were raised on the foundation of wooden piles. The adjacent country, to the distance of many miles, was a deep and impassable morass; and the artificial causeway which connected Ravenna with the continent might be easily guarded or destroyed on the approach of an hostile army. These morasses were interspersed, however, with vineyards; and though the soil was exhausted by four or five crops, the town enjoyed a more plentiful supply of wine than of fresh water.[1] The air, instead of receiving the sickly and almost pestilential exhalations of low and marshy grounds, was distinguished, like the neighbourhood of Alexandria, as uncommonly pure and salubrious; and this singular advantage was ascribed to the regular tides of the Hadriatic, which swept the canals, interrupted the unwholesome stagnation of the waters, and floated, every day, the vessels of the adjacent country into the heart of Ravenna. The gradual retreat of the sea has left the modern city at the distance of four miles from the Hadriatic, and as early as the fifth or sixth century of the Christian era the port of Augustus was converted into pleasant orchards, and a lonely grove of pines covered the ground where the Roman fleet once rode at anchor.[2] Even this

---

[1] Martial (Epigram iii. 56, 57) plays on the trick of the knave who had sold him wine instead of water; but he seriously declares that a cistern at Ravenna is more valuable than a vineyard. Sidonius complains that the town is destitute of fountains and aqueducts, and ranks the want of fresh water among the local evils, such as the croaking of frogs, the stinging of gnats, etc.

[2] The fable of Theodore and Honoria, which Dryden has so admirably transplanted from Boccaccio (Giornata iii. novell. viii.) was acted in the wood of *Chiassi*, a corrupt word from *Classis*, the naval station, which, with the intermediate road or suburb, the *Via Cæsaris*, constituted the *triple* city of Ravenna.

alteration contributed to increase the natural strength of the place, and the shallowness of the water was a sufficient barrier against the large ships of the enemy.   This advantageous situation was fortified by art and labour; and in the twentieth year of his age the emperor of the West, anxious only for his personal safety, retired to the perpetual confinement of the walls and morasses of Ravenna.   The example of Honorius was imitated by his feeble successors, the Gothic kings, and afterwards the Exarchs, who occupied the throne and palace of the emperors; and till the middle of the eighth century Ravenna was considered as the seat of government and the capital of Italy.[1]

The fears of Honorius were not without foundation, nor were his precautions without effect.   While Italy rejoiced in her deliverance from the Goths, a furious tempest was excited among the nations of Germany, who yielded to the irresistible impulse that appears to have been gradually communicated from the eastern extremity of the continent of Asia.   The Chinese annals, as they have been interpreted by the learned industry of the present age, may be usefully applied to reveal the secret and remote causes of the fall of the Roman empire.   The extensive territory to the north of the great wall was possessed after the flight of the Huns by the victorious Sienpi; who were sometimes broken into independent tribes, and sometimes re-united under a supreme chief; till at length, styling themselves *Topa*, or masters of the earth, they acquired a more solid consistence and a more formidable power.   The Topa soon compelled the pastoral nations of the eastern desert to acknowledge the superiority of their arms; they invaded China in a period of weakness and intestine discord; and these fortunate Tartars, adopting the laws and manners of the vanquished people, founded an Imperial dynasty, which reigned near one hundred and sixty years over the northern provinces of the monarchy. Some generations before they ascended the throne of China, one of the Topa princes had enlisted in his cavalry a slave of the name of Moko, renowned for his valour, but who was tempted, by the fear of punishment, to desert his standard, and to range the desert at the head of an hundred followers.   This gang of robbers and outlaws swelled into a camp, a tribe, a numerous people, distinguished by the appellation of *Geougen ;* and their hereditary chieftains, the posterity of Moko the slave, assumed

---

[1] From the year 404 the dates of the Theodosian Code become sedentary at Constantinople and Ravenna.   See Godefroy's Chronology of the Laws, tom. i. p. cxlviii., etc.

their rank among the Scythian monarchs. The youth of Toulun, the greatest of his descendants, was exercised by those misfortunes which are the school of heroes. He bravely struggled with adversity, broke the imperious yoke of the Topa, and became the legislator of his nation and the conqueror of Tartary. His troops were distributed into regular bands of an hundred and of a thousand men; cowards were stoned to death; the most splendid honours were proposed as the reward of valour; and Toulun, who had knowledge enough to despise the learning of China, adopted only such arts and institutions as were favourable to the military spirit of his government. His tents, which he removed in the winter season to a more southern latitude, were pitched during the summer on the fruitful banks of the Selinga. His conquests stretched from Corea far beyond the river Irtish. He vanquished, in the country to the north of the Caspian sea, the nation of the *Huns ;* and the new title of *Khan,* or *Cagan,* expressed the fame and power which he derived from this memorable victory.[1]

The chain of events is interrupted, or rather is concealed, as it passes from the Volga to the Vistula, through the dark interval which separates the extreme limits of the Chinese and of the Roman geography. Yet the temper of the barbarians, and the experience of successive emigrations, sufficiently declare that the Huns, who were oppressed by the arms of the Geougen, soon withdrew from the presence of an insulting victor. The countries towards the Euxine were already occupied by their kindred tribes; and their hasty flight, which they soon converted into a bold attack, would more naturally be directed towards the rich and level plains through which the Vistula gently flows into the Baltic sea. The North must again have been alarmed and agitated by the invasion of the Huns; and the nations who retreated before them must have pressed with incumbent weight on the confines of Germany.[2] The inhabitants of those regions which the ancients have assigned to the Suevi, the Vandals, and the Burgundians, might embrace the resolution of abandoning to the fugitives of Sarmatia their woods and morasses, or at least of discharging their superfluous numbers on the provinces of the Roman empire.[3] About four years after the victorious

[1] See M. de Guignes, Hist. des Huns, tom. i. p. 179-189, tom. ii. p. 295, 334-338.

[2] Procopius (de Bell. Vandal. l. i. c. iii. p. 182 [ed. Paris; tom. i. p. 319, ed. Bonn]) has observed an emigration from the Palus Mæotis to the north of Germany, which he ascribes to famine. But his views of ancient history are strangely darkened by ignorance and error.

[3] Zosimus (l. v. [c. 26] p. 331) uses the general description of the nations

Toulun had assumed the title of Khan of the Geougen, another barbarian, the haughty Rhodogast, or Radagaisus,[1] marched from the northern extremities of Germany almost to the gates of Rome, and left the remains of his army to achieve the destruction of the West. The Vandals, the Suevi, and the Burgundians, formed the strength of this mighty host; but the Alani, who had found an hospitable reception in their new seats, added their active cavalry to the heavy infantry of the Germans; and the Gothic adventurers crowded so eagerly to the standard of Radagaisus, that, by some historians, he has been styled the King of the Goths. Twelve thousand warriors, distinguished above the vulgar by their noble birth or their valiant deeds, glittered in the van;[2] and the whole multitude, which was not less than two hundred thousand fighting men, might be increased, by the accession of women, of children, and of slaves, to the amount of four hundred thousand persons. This formidable emigration issued from the same coast of the Baltic which had poured forth the myriads of the Cimbri and Teutones to assault Rome and Italy in the vigour of the republic. After the departure of those barbarians, their native country, which was marked by the vestiges of their greatness, long ramparts and gigantic moles,[3] remained, during some ages, a vast and dreary solitude; till the human species was renewed by the powers of generation, and the vacancy was filled by the influx of new inhabitants. The nations who now usurp an extent of land which they are unable to cultivate would soon be assisted by the industrious poverty of their neighbours, if the government of Europe did not protect the claims of dominion and property.

The correspondence of nations was in that age so imperfect and precarious, that the revolutions of the North might escape the knowledge of the court of Ravenna, till the dark cloud, which was collected along the coast of the Baltic, burst in thunder upon the banks of the Upper Danube. The emperor

beyond the Danube and the Rhine. Their situation, and consequently their names, are manifestly shown, even in the various epithets which each ancient writer may have casually added.

[1] The name of Rhadagast was that of a local deity of the Obotrites (in Mecklenburg). A hero might naturally assume the appellation of his tutelar god; but it is not probable that the barbarians should worship an unsuccessful hero. See Mascou, Hist. of the Germans, viii. 14.

[2] Olympiodorus (apud Photium, p. 180 [p. 57, ed. Bekker]) uses the Latin word Ὀπτιμάτοι, which does not convey any precise idea. I suspect that they were the princes and nobles with their faithful companions—the knights with their squires, as they would have been styled some centuries afterwards.

[3] Tacit. de Moribus Germanorum, c. 37.

of the West, if his ministers disturbed his amusements by the news of the impending danger, was satisfied with being the occasion and the spectator of the war.[1] The safety of Rome was intrusted to the counsels and the sword of Stilicho; but such was the feeble and exhausted state of the empire, that it was impossible to restore the fortifications of the Danube, or to prevent by a vigorous effort the invasion of the Germans.[2] The hopes of the vigilant minister of Honorius were confined to the defence of Italy. He once more abandoned the provinces, re-called the troops, pressed the new levies, which were rigorously exacted and pusillanimously eluded; employed the most efficacious means to arrest or allure the deserters; and offered the gift of freedom and of two pieces of gold to all the slaves who would enlist.[3] By these efforts he painfully collected from the subjects of a great empire an army of thirty or forty thousand men, which, in the days of Scipio or Camillus, would have been instantly furnished by the free citizens of the territory of Rome.[4] The thirty legions of Stilicho were reinforced by a large body of barbarian auxiliaries; the faithful Alani were personally attached to his service; and the troops of Huns and of Goths, who marched under the banners of their native princes Huldin and Sarus, were animated by interest and resentment to oppose the ambition of Radagaisus. The king of the confederate Germans passed without resistance the Alps, the Po, and the Apennine; leaving on one hand the inaccessible palace of Honorius securely buried among the marshes of Ravenna, and, on the other, the camp of Stilicho, who had fixed his head-quarters at Ticinum, or Pavia, but who seems to have avoided a decisive battle till he had

---

[1] ———— Cujus agendi
      Spectator vel causa fui,

                    Claudian, vi. Cons. Hon. 439,
is the modest language of Honorius, in speaking of the Gothic war, which he had seen somewhat nearer.

[2] Zosimus (l. v. [c. 26] p. 331) transports the war and the victory of Stilicho beyond the Danube. A strange error, which is awkwardly and imperfectly cured by reading Ἄρνον for Ἴστρον (Tillemont, Hist. des Emp. tom. v. p. 807). In good policy, we must use the service of Zosimus, without esteeming or trusting him.

[3] Codex Theodos. l. vii. tit. xiii. leg. 16. The date of this law (A.D. 406, May 18) satisfies me, as it had done Godefroy (tom. ii. p. 387), of the true year of the invasion of Radagaisus. Tillemont, Pagi, and Muratori, prefer the preceding year; but they are bound, by certain obligations of civility and respect, to St. Paulinus of Nola.

[4] Soon after Rome had been taken by the Gauls, the senate, on a sudden emergency, armed ten legions, 3000 horse and 42,000 foot—a force which the city could not have sent forth under Augustus (Livy, vii. 25). This declaration may puzzle an antiquary, but it is clearly explained by Montesquieu.

assembled his distant forces. Many cities of Italy were pillaged or destroyed; and the siege of Florence [1] by Radagaisus is one of the earliest events in the history of that celebrated republic, whose firmness checked and delayed the unskilful fury of the barbarians. The senate and people trembled at their approach within an hundred and eighty miles of Rome, and anxiously compared the danger which they had escaped with the new perils to which they were exposed. Alaric was a Christian and a soldier, the leader of a disciplined army; who understood the laws of war, who respected the sanctity of treaties, and who had familiarly conversed with the subjects of the empire in the same camps and the same churches. The savage Radagaisus was a stranger to the manners, the religion, and even the language of the civilised nations of the South. The fierceness of his temper was exasperated by cruel superstition; and it was universally believed that he had bound himself by a solemn vow to reduce the city into a heap of stones and ashes, and to sacrifice the most illustrious of the Roman senators on the altars of those gods who were appeased by human blood. The public danger, which should have reconciled all domestic animosities, displayed the incurable madness of religious faction. The oppressed votaries of Jupiter and Mercury respected, in the implacable enemy of Rome, the character of a devout Pagan; loudly declared that they were more apprehensive of the sacrifices than of the arms of Radagaisus; and secretly rejoiced in the calamities of their country, which condemned the faith of their Christian adversaries. [2]

Florence was reduced to the last extremity; and the fainting courage of the citizens was supported only by the authority of St. Ambrose, who had communicated in a dream the promise of a speedy deliverance. [3] On a sudden they beheld from their walls the banners of Stilicho, who advanced with his united force

[1] Machiavel has explained, at least as a philosopher, the origin of Florence, which insensibly descended, for the benefit of trade, from the rock of Fæsulæ to the banks of the Arno (Istoria Florentina, tom. i. l. ii. p. 36; Londra, 1747). The triumvirs sent a colony to Florence, which, under Tiberius (Tacit. Annal. i. 79), deserved the reputation and name of a *flourishing* city. See Cluver. Ital. Antiq. tom. i. p. 507, etc.

[2] Yet the Jupiter of Radagaisus, who worshipped Thor and Woden, was very different from the Olympic or Capitoline Jove. The accommodating temper of polytheism might unite those various and remote deities; but the genuine Romans abhorred the human sacrifices of Gaul and Germany.

[3] Paulinus (in Vit. Ambros. c. 50) relates this story, which he received from the mouth of Pansophia herself, a religious matron of Florence. Yet the archbishop soon ceased to take an active part in the business of the world, and never became a popular saint.

to the relief of the faithful city, and who soon marked that fatal
spot for the grave of the barbarian host.   The apparent con-
tradictions of those writers who variously relate the defeat of
Radagaisus, may be reconciled without offering much violence
to their respective testimonies.   Orosius and Augustin, who were
intimately connected by friendship and religion, ascribe this
miraculous victory to the providence of God rather than to the
valour of man.[1]   They strictly exclude every idea of chance, or
even of bloodshed, and positively affirm that the Romans, whose
camp was the scene of plenty and idleness, enjoyed the distress
of the barbarians slowly expiring on the sharp and barren ridge
of the hills of Fæsulæ, which rise above the city of Florence.
Their extravagant assertion that not a single soldier of the
Christian army was killed, or even wounded, may be dismissed
with silent contempt; but the rest of the narrative of Augustin
and Orosius is consistent with the state of the war and the character of Stilicho.   Conscious that he commanded the *last* army
of the republic, his prudence would not expose it in the open
field to the headstrong fury of the Germans.   The method of
surrounding the enemy with strong lines of circumvallation,
which he had twice employed against the Gothic king, was
repeated on a larger scale and with more considerable effect.
The examples of Cæsar must have been familiar to the most
illiterate of the Roman warriors; and the fortifications of
Dyrrachium, which connected twenty-four castles by a perpetual
ditch and rampart of fifteen miles, afforded the model of an
entrenchment which might confine and starve the most numerous
host of barbarians.[2]   The Roman troops had less degenerated
from the industry than from the valour of their ancestors; and
if the servile and laborious work offended the pride of the soldiers.
Tuscany could supply many thousand peasants who would
labour, though perhaps they would not fight, for the salvation
of their native country.   The imprisoned multitude of horses

---

[1] Augustin de Civitat. Dei, v. 23.   Orosius, l. vii. c. 37, p. 567-571.   The
two friends wrote in Africa ten or twelve years after the victory, and their
authority is implicitly followed by Isidore of Seville (in Chron. p. 713, edit
Grot.).   How many interesting facts might Orosius have inserted in the
vacant space which is devoted to pious nonsense!

[2] Franguntur montes, planumque per ardua Cæsar
Ducit opus: pandit fossas, turritaque summis
Disponit castella jugis, magnoque recessû
Amplexus fines, saltus, nemorosaque tesqua
Et silvas, vastâque feras indagine claudit.

Yet the simplicity of truth (Cæsar, de Bell. Civ. iii. 44) is far greater than
the amplifications of Lucan (Pharsal. l. vi 29-63)

and men [1] was gradually destroyed by famine rather than by the sword; but the Romans were exposed during the progress of such an extensive work to the frequent attacks of an impatient enemy. The despair of the hungry barbarians would precipitate them against the fortifications of Stilicho; the general might sometimes indulge the ardour of his brave auxiliaries, who eagerly pressed to assault the camp of the Germans; and these various incidents might produce the sharp and bloody conflicts which dignify the narrative of Zosimus and the Chronicles of Prosper and Marcellinus.[2] A seasonable supply of men and provisions had been introduced into the walls of Florence, and the famished host of Radagaisus was in its turn besieged. The proud monarch of so many warlike nations, after the loss of his bravest warriors, was reduced to confide either in the faith of a capitulation, or in the clemency of Stilicho.[3] But the death of the royal captive, who was ignominiously beheaded, disgraced the triumph of Rome and of Christianity; and the short delay of his execution was sufficient to brand the conqueror with the guilt of cool and deliberate cruelty.[4] The famished Germans who escaped the fury of the auxiliaries were sold as slaves, at the contemptible price of as many single pieces of gold; but the difference of food and climate swept away great numbers of those unhappy strangers; and it was observed that the inhuman purchasers, instead of reaping the fruits of their labour, were soon obliged to provide the expense of their interment. Stilicho informed the emperor and the senate of his success, and deserved a second time the glorious title of Deliverer of Italy.[5]

The fame of the victory, and more especially of the miracle, has encouraged a vain persuasion that the whole army, or rather

---

[1] The rhetorical expressions of Orosius, " in arido et aspero montis jugo," " in unum ac parvum verticem," are not very suitable to the encampment of a great army. But Fæsulæ, only three miles from Florence, might afford space for the head-quarters of Radagaisus, and would be comprehended within the circuit of the Roman lines.

[2] See Zosimus, l. v. [c. 26] p. 331, and the Chronicles of Prosper and Marcellinus.

[3] Olympiodorus (apud Photium, p. 180 [p. 57, ed. Bekk.]), uses an expression (προσηταιρίσατο) which would denote a strict and friendly alliance, and render Stilicho still more criminal. The pauliper retentus, deinde interfectus, of Orosius [p. 570], is sufficiently odious.

[4] Orosius, piously inhuman, sacrifices the king and people—Agag and the Amalekites—without a symptom of compassion. The bloody actor is less detestable than the cool, unfeeling historian.

[5] And Claudian's muse, was she asleep? had she been ill-paid? Methinks the seventh consulship of Honorius (A.D. 407) would have furnished the subject of a noble poem. Before it was discovered that the state could no longer be saved, Stilicho (after Romulus, Camillus, and Marius) might have been worthily surnamed the fourth founder of Rome.

nation, of Germans who migrated from the shores of the Baltic
miserably perished under the walls of Florence. Such indeed
was the fate of Radagaisus himself, of his brave and faithful
companions, and of more than one-third of the various multitude
of Suèves and Vandals, of Alani and Burgundians, who adhered
to the standard of their general.[1] The union of such an army
might excite our surprise, but the causes of separation are
obvious and forcible: and pride of birth, the insolence of valour,
the jealousy of command, the impatience of subordination, and
the obstinate conflict of opinions, of interests, and of passions,
among so many kings and warriors, who were untaught to yield
or to obey. After the defeat of Radagaisus, two parts of the
German host, which must have exceeded the number of one
hundred thousand men, still remained in arms between the
Apennine and the Alps, or between the Alps and the Danube.
It is uncertain whether they attempted to revenge the death of
their general; but their irregular fury was soon diverted by the
prudence and firmness of Stilicho, who opposed their march and
facilitated their retreat, who considered the safety of Rome and
Italy as the great object of his care, and who sacrificed with too
much indifference the wealth and tranquillity of the distant
provinces.[2] The barbarians acquired, from the junction of some
Pannonian deserters, the knowledge of the country and of the
roads, and the invasion of Gaul, which Alaric had designed, was
executed by the remains of the great army of Radagaisus.[3]

Yet if they expected to derive any assistance from the tribes of
Germany who inhabited the banks of the Rhine, their hopes were
disappointed. The Alemanni preserved a state of inactive
neutrality, and the Franks distinguished their zeal and courage
in the defence of the empire. In the rapid progress down the
Rhine which was the first act of the administration of Stilicho,
he had applied himself with peculiar attention to secure the
alliance of the warlike Franks, and to remove the irreconcilable

---

[1] A luminous passage of Prosper's Chronicle, "*In tres partes, per diversos
principes, divisus exercitus*," reduces the miracle of Florence, and connects
the history of Italy, Gaul, and Germany.

[2] Orosius and Jerom positively charge him with instigating the invasion.
"Excitatæ a Stilichone gentes," etc. They must mean *indirectly*. He
saved Italy at the expense of Gaul.

[3] The Count de Buat is satisfied that the Germans who invaded Gaul were
the *two-thirds* that yet remained of the army of Radagaisus. See the
Histoire Ancienne des Peuples de l'Europe (tom. vii. p. 87, 121, Paris,
1772), an elaborate work, which I had not the advantage of perusing till
the year 1777. As early as 1771, I find the same idea expressed in a rough
draught of the present History. I have since observed a similar intima-
tion in Mascou (viii. 15). Such agreement, without mutual communication, may add some weight to our common sentiment.

enemies of peace and of the republic. Marcomir, one of their kings, was publicly convicted before the tribunal of the Roman magistrate of violating the faith of treaties. He was sentenced to a mild but distant exile in the province of Tuscany; and this degradation of the regal dignity was so far from exciting the resentment of his subjects, that they punished with death the turbulent Sunno, who attempted to revenge his brother, and maintained a dutiful allegiance to the princes who were established on the throne by the choice of Stilicho.[1] When the limits of Gaul and Germany were shaken by the northern emigration, the Franks bravely encountered the single force of the Vandals, who, regardless of the lessons of adversity, had again separated their troops from the standard of their barbarian allies. They paid the penalty of their rashness; and twenty thousand Vandals, with their king Godigisclus, were slain in the field of battle. The whole people must have been extirpated if the squadrons of the Alani, advancing to their relief, had not trampled down the infantry of the Franks, who, after an honourable resistance, were compelled to relinquish the unequal contest. The victorious confederates pursued their march, and on the last day of the year, in a season when the waters of the Rhine were most probably frozen, they entered without opposition the defenceless provinces of Gaul. This memorable passage of the Suevi, the Vandals, the Alani, and the Burgundians, who never afterwards retreated, may be considered as the fall of the Roman empire in the countries beyond the Alps; and the barriers, which had so long separated the savage and the civilised nations of the earth, were from that fatal moment levelled with the ground.[2]

While the peace of Germany was secured by the attachment of the Franks and the neutrality of the Alemanni, the subjects of Rome, unconscious of their approaching calamities, enjoyed the state of quiet and prosperity which had seldom blessed the frontiers of Gaul. Their flocks and herds were permitted to

---

[1] ——— Provincia missos
Expellet citius fasces, quam Francia reges
Quos dederis.

Claudian (i. Cons. Stil. l. i. 235, etc.) is clear and satisfactory. These kings of France are unknown to Gregory of Tours; but the author of the Gesta Francorum mentions both Sunno and Marcomir, and names the latter as the father of Pharamond (in tom. ii. p. 543). He seems to write from good materials, which he did not understand.

[2] See Zosimus (l. vi. [c. 3] p. 373), Orosius (l. vii. c. 40, p. 576), and the Chronicles. Gregory of Tours (l. ii. c. 9, p. 165, in the second volume of the Historians of France) has preserved a valuable fragment of Renatus Profuturus Frigeridus, whose three names denote a Christian, a Roman subject, and a semi-barbarian.

graze in the pastures of the barbarians; their huntsmen penetrated, without fear or danger, into the darkest recesses of the
Hercynian wood.[1]   The banks of the Rhine were crowned, like
those of the Tiber, with elegant houses and well-cultivated farms;
and if a poet descended the river, he might express his doubt on
which side was situated the territory of the Romans.[2]   This
scene of peace and plenty was suddenly changed into a desert;
and the prospect of the smoking ruins could alone distinguish
the solitude of nature from the desolation of man.   The flourishing city of Mentz was surprised and destroyed, and many thousand Christians were inhumanly massacred in the church.
Worms perished after a long and obstinate siege; Strasburg,
Spires, Rheims, Tournay, Arras, Amiens, experienced the cruel
oppression of the German yoke; and the consuming flames of
war spread from the banks of the Rhine over the greatest part
of the seventeen provinces of Gaul.   That rich and extensive
country, as far as the ocean, the Alps, and the Pyrenees, was
delivered to the barbarians, who drove before them in a promiscuous crowd the bishop, the senator, and the virgin, laden with
the spoils of their houses and altars.[3]   The ecclesiastics, to whom
we are indebted for this vague description of the public calamities,
embraced the opportunity of exhorting the Christians to repent
of the sins which had provoked the Divine Justice, and to renounce the perishable goods of a wretched and deceitful world.
But as the Pelagian controversy,[4] which attempts to sound the
abyss of grace and predestination, soon became the serious
employment of the Latin clergy, the Providence which had
decreed, or foreseen, or permitted, such a train of moral and
natural evils, was rashly weighed in the imperfect and fallacious
balance of reason.   The crimes and the misfortunes of the suffer-

---

[1] Claudian (i. Cons. Stil. l. i. 221, etc.; l. ii. 186) describes the peace and
prosperity of the Gallic frontier.   The Abbé Dubos (Hist. Critique, etc.,
tom. i. p. 174) would read *Alba* (a nameless rivulet of the Ardennes)
instead of *Albis ;* and expatiates on the danger of the Gallic cattle grazing
beyond the *Elbe*.   Foolish enough!   In poetical geography, the Elbe and
the Hercynian signify any river or any wood in Germany.   Claudian is not
prepared for the strict examination of our antiquaries.

[2] ——— Geminasque viator
        Cum videat ripas, quæ sit Romana requirat.

[3] Jerom, tom. i. p. 93 [Epist. cxxiii. c. 16, tom. i. p. 908, ed. Vallars.].
See, in the first volume of the Historians of France, p. 777, 782, the proper
extracts from the Carmen de Providentiâ Divinâ, and Salvian.   The
anonymous poet was himself a captive, with his bishop and fellow-citizens.

[4] The Pelagian doctrine, which was first agitated A.D. 405, was condemned, in the space of ten years, at Rome and Carthage.   St. Augustin
fought and conquered; but the Greek church was favourable to his adversaries; and (what is singular enough) the people did not take any part in a
dispute which they could not understand.

ing people were presumptuously compared with those of their ancestors, and they arraigned the Divine Justice, which did not exempt from the common destruction, the feeble the guiltless, the infant portion of the human species. These idle disputants overlooked the invariable laws of nature, which have connected peace with innocence, plenty with industry, and safety with valour. The timid and selfish policy of the court of Ravenna might recall the Palatine legions for the protection of Italy; the remains of the stationary troops might be unequal to the arduous task; and the barbarian auxiliaries might prefer the unbounded licence of spoil to the benefits of a moderate and regular stipend. But the provinces of Gaul were filled with a numerous race of hardy and robust youth, who, in the defence of their houses, their families, and their altars, if they had dared to die, would have deserved to vanquish. The knowledge of their native country would have enabled them to oppose continual and insuperable obstacles to the progress of an invader; and the deficiency of the barbarians in arms as well as in discipline removed the only pretence which excuses the submission of a populous country to the inferior numbers of a veteran army. When France was invaded by Charles the Fifth, he inquired of a prisoner how many *days* Paris might be distant from the frontier; "Perhaps *twelve*, but they will be days of battle:" [1] such was the gallant answer which checked the arrogance of that ambitious prince. The subjects of Honorius and those of Francis I. were animated by a very different spirit; and in less than two years the divided troops of the savages of the Baltic, whose numbers, were they fairly stated, would appear contemptible, advanced without a combat to the foot of the Pyrenæan mountains.

In the early part of the reign of Honorius, the viligance of Stilicho had successfully guarded the remote island of Britain from her incessant enemies of the ocean, the mountains, and the Irish coast.[2] But those restless barbarians could not neglect

---

[1] See the Mémoires de Guillaume du Bellay, l. vi. In French, the original reproof is less obvious and more pointed, from the double sense of the word *journée*, which alike signifies a day's travel or a battle.

[2] Claudian (i. Cons. Stil. l. ii. 250). It is supposed that the Scots of Ireland invaded by sea the whole western coast of Britain; and some slight credit may be given even to Nennius and the Irish traditions (Carte's Hist. of England, vol. i. p. 169). Whitaker's Genuine History of the Britons, p. 199. The sixty-six Lives of St. Patrick, which were extant in the ninth century, must have contained as many thousand lies; yet we may believe that, in one of these Irish inroads, the future apostle was led away captive (Usher, Antiquit. Eccles. Britann. p. 431; and Tillemont, Mém. Ecclés. tom. xvi. p. 456, 782, etc.).

the fair opportunity of the Gothic war, when the walls and stations of the province were stripped of the Roman troops. If any of the legionaries were permitted to return from the Italian expedition, their faithful report of the court and character of Honorius must have tended to dissolve the bonds of allegiance, and to exasperate the seditious temper of the British army. The spirit of revolt, which had formerly disturbed the age of Gallienus, was revived by the capricious violence of the soldiers; and the unfortunate, perhaps the ambitious, candidates, who were the objects of their choice, were the instruments, and at length the victims, of their passion.[1] Marcus was the first whom they placed on the throne, as the lawful emperor of Britain and of the West. They violated, by the hasty murder of Marcus, the oath of fidelity which they had imposed on themselves; and *their* disapprobation of his manners may seem to inscribe an honourable epitaph on his tomb. Gratian was the next whom they adorned with the diadem and the purple; and, at the end of four months, Gratian experienced the fate of his predecessor. The memory of the great Constantine, whom the British legions had given to the church and to the empire, suggested the singular motive of their third choice. They discovered in the ranks a private soldier of the name of Constantine, and their impetuous levity had already seated him on the throne, before they perceived his incapacity to sustain the weight of that glorious appellation.[2] Yet the authority of Constantine was less precarious, and his government was more successful, than the transient reigns of Marcus and of Gratian. The danger of leaving his inactive troops in those camps which had been twice polluted with blood and sedition urged him to attempt the reduction of the Western provinces. He landed at Boulogne with an inconsiderable force; and after he had reposed himself some days, he summoned the cities of Gaul, which had escaped the yoke of the barbarians, to acknowledge their lawful sovereign. They obeyed the summons without reluctance. The neglect of the court of Ravenna had absolved a deserted people from the duty of allegiance; their actual distress encouraged them to accept

---

[1] The British usurpers are taken from Zosimus (l. vi. [c. 2] p. 371-375), Orosius (l. vii. c. 40, p. 576, 577), Olympiodorus (apud Photium, p. 180, 181 [p. 57, ed. Bekker]), the ecclesiastical historians, and the Chronicles. The Latins are ignorant of Marcus.

[2] Cum in Constantino *inconstantiam* . . . execrarentur (Sidonius Apollinaris, l. v. Epist. 9, p. 139, edit. secund. Sirmond.). Yet Sidonius might be tempted, by so fair a pun, to stigmatise a prince who had disgraced his grandfather.

any circumstances of change, without apprehension, and, perhaps, with some degree of hope; and they might flatter themselves that the troops, the authority, and even the name of a Roman emperor, who fixed his residence in Gaul, would protect the unhappy country from the rage of the barbarians. The first successes of Constantine against the detached parties of the Germans were magnified by the voice of adulation into splendid and decisive victories, which the re-union and insolence of the enemy soon reduced to their just value. His negotiations procured a short and precarious truce; and if some tribes of the barbarians were engaged, by the liberality of his gifts and promises, to undertake the defence of the Rhine, these expensive and uncertain treaties, instead of restoring the pristine vigour of the Gallic frontier, served only to disgrace the majesty of the prince, and to exhaust what yet remained of the treasures of the republic. Elated however with this imaginary triumph, the vain deliverer of Gaul advanced into the provinces of the South, to encounter a more pressing and personal danger. Sarus the Goth was ordered to lay the head of the rebel at the feet of the emperor Honorius; and the forces of Britain and Italy were unworthily consumed in this domestic quarrel. After the loss of his two bravest generals, Justinian and Nevigastes, the former of whom was slain in the field of battle, the latter in a peaceful but treacherous interview, Constantine fortified himself within the walls of Vienna. The place was ineffectually attacked seven days; and the Imperial army supported, in a precipitate retreat, the ignominy of purchasing a secure passage from the freebooters and outlaws of the Alps.[1] Those mountains now separated the dominions of two rival monarchs: and the fortifications of the double frontier were guarded by the troops of the empire, whose arms would have been more usefully employed to maintain the Roman limits against the barbarians of Germany and Scythia.

On the side of the Pyrenees, the ambition of Constantine might be justified by the proximity of danger; but his throne was soon established by the conquest, or rather submission, of Spain, which yielded to the influence of regular and habitual subordination, and received the laws and magistrates of the Gallic præfecture. The only opposition which was made to the authority of Constantine proceeded not so much from the powers of government, or the spirit of the people, as from the private zeal and

---

[1] *Bagaudæ* is the name which Zosimus applies to them; perhaps they deserved a less odious character (see Dubos, Hist. Critique, tom. i. p. 203, and this History, vol. ii. p. 69). We shall hear of them again.

interest of the family of Theodosius. Four brothers[1] had
obtained, by the favour of their kinsman, the deceased emperor,
an honourable rank, and ample possessions, in their native
country; and the grateful youths resolved to risk those advantages in the service of his son. After an unsuccessful effort to
maintain their ground at the head of the stationary troops of
Lusitania, they retired to their estates; where they armed and
levied, at their own expense, a considerable body of slaves and
dependents, and boldly marched to occupy the strong posts of
the Pyrenæan mountains. This domestic insurrection alarmed
and perplexed the sovereign of Gaul and Britain; and he was
compelled to negotiate with some troops of barbarian auxiliaries,
for the service of the Spanish war. They were distinguished by
the title of *Honorians*;[2] a name which might have reminded
them of their fidelity to their lawful sovereign; and if it should
candidly be allowed that the *Scots* were influenced by any partial
affection for a British prince, the *Moors* and the *Marcomanni*
could be tempted only by the profuse liberality of the usurper,
who distributed among the barbarians the military, and even
the civil, honours of Spain. The nine bands of *Honorians*, which
may be easily traced on the establishment of the Western empire,
could not exceed the number of five thousand men; yet this inconsiderable force was sufficient to terminate a war which had
threatened the power and safety of Constantine. The rustic
army of the Theodosian family was surrounded and destroyed
in the Pyrenees: two of the brothers had the good fortune to
escape by sea to Italy or the East; the other two, after an interval
of suspense, were executed at Arles; and if Honorius could remain
insensible of the public disgrace, he might perhaps be affected by
the personal misfortunes of his generous kinsmen. Such were
the feeble arms which decided the possession of the Western provinces of Europe, from the wall of Antoninus to the Columns of
Hercules. The events of peace and war have undoubtedly been
diminished by the narrow and imperfect view of the historians
of the times, who were equally ignorant of the causes and of the
effects of the most important revolutions. But the total decay
of the national strength had annihilated even the last resource

[1] Verinianus, Didymus, Theodosius, and Lagodius, who in modern courts
would be styled princes of the blood, were not distinguished by any rank
or privileges above the rest of their fellow-subjects.

[2] These *Honoriani* or *Honoriaci* consisted of two bands of Scots or Atta-
rotti, two of Moors, two of Marcomanni, the Victores, the Ascarii, and the
Gallicani (Notitia Imperii, sect. xxxviii. edit. Lab.). They were part of
the sixty-five *Auxilia Palatina*, and are properly styled ἐν τῇ αὐλῇ τάξεις
by Zosimus (l. vi. [c. 4] p. 374).

of a despotic government; and the revenue of exhausted provinces could no longer purchase the military service of a discontented and pusillanimous people.

The poet, whose flattery has ascribed to the Roman eagle the victories of Pollentia and Verona, pursues the hasty retreat of Alaric from the confines of Italy, with a horrid train of imaginary spectres, such as might hover over an army of barbarians which was almost exterminated by war, famine, and disease.[1] In the course of this unfortunate expedition, the king of the Goths must indeed have sustained a considerable loss; and his harassed forces required an interval of repose to recruit their numbers and revive their confidence. Adversity had exercised and displayed the genius of Alaric; and the fame of his valour invited to the Gothic standard the bravest of the barbarian warriors, who, from the Euxine to the Rhine, were agitated by the desire of rapine and conquest. He had deserved the esteem, and he soon accepted the friendship, of Stilicho himself. Renouncing the service of the emperor of the East, Alaric concluded, with the court of Ravenna, a treaty of peace and alliance, by which he was declared master-general of the Roman armies throughout the præfecture of Illyricum; as it was claimed, according to the true and ancient limits, by the minister of Honorius.[2] The execution of the ambitious design, which was either stipulated or implied in the articles of the treaty, appears to have been suspended by the formidable irruption of Radagaisus; and the neutrality of the Gothic king may perhaps be compared to the indifference of Cæsar, who, in the conspiracy of Catiline, refused either to assist or to oppose the enemy of the republic. After the defeat of the Vandals, Stilicho resumed his pretensions to the provinces of the East; appointed civil magistrates for the administration of justice and of the finances; and declared his impatience to lead to the gates of Constantinople the united armies of the Romans and of the Goths. The prudence, however, of Stilicho, his aversion to civil war, and his perfect knowledge of the weakness of the state, may countenance the suspicion that domestic peace, rather than foreign conquest, was the object of his policy; and that his principal care was to employ the

---

[1] ———— Comitantur euntem
　　Pallor, et atra Fames; et saucia lividus ora
　Luctus; et inferno stridentes agmine Morbi.
　　　　　　　　　Claudian in vi. Cons. Hon. 321, etc.

[2] These dark transactions are investigated by the Count de Buat (Hist. des Peuples de l'Europe, tom. vii. c. iii.-viii. p. 69-206), whose laborious accuracy may sometimes fatigue a superficial reader.

forces of Alaric at a distance from Italy. This design could not
long escape the penetration of the Gothic king, who continued
to hold a doubtful, and perhaps a treacherous, correspondence
with the rival courts; who protracted, like a dissatisfied mercenary, his languid operations of Thessaly and Epirus; and who
soon returned to claim the extravagant reward of his ineffectual
services. From his camp near Æmona,[1] on the confines of Italy,
he transmitted to the emperor of the West a long account of
promises, of expenses, and of demands; called for immediate
satisfaction, and clearly intimated the consequences of a refusal.
Yet, if his conduct was hostile, his language was decent and
dutiful. He humbly professed himself the friend of Stilicho,
and the soldier of Honorius; offered his person and his troops
to march, without delay, against the usurper of Gaul; and
solicited, as a permanent retreat for the Gothic nation, the possession of some vacant province of the Western empire.

The political and secret transactions of two statesmen who
laboured to deceive each other and the world must for ever have
been concealed in the impenetrable darkness of the cabinet,
if the debates of a popular assembly had not thrown some rays
of light on the correspondence of Alaric and Stilicho. The
necessity of finding some artificial support for a government
which, from a principle, not of moderation, but of weakness,
was reduced to negotiate with its own subjects, had insensibly
revived the authority of the Roman senate: and the minister
of Honorius respectfully consulted the legislative council of the
republic. Stilicho assembled the senate in the palace of the
Cæsars; represented, in a studied oration, the actual state of
affairs; proposed the demands of the Gothic king; and submitted to their consideration the choice of peace or war. The
senators, as if they had been suddenly awakened from a dream
of four hundred years, appeared on this important occasion to
be inspired by the courage, rather than by the wisdom, of their
predecessors. They loudly declared, in regular speeches or in
tumultuary acclamations, that it was unworthy of the majesty
of Rome to purchase a precarious and disgraceful truce from a
barbarian king; and that, in the judgment of a magnanimous
people, the chance of ruin was always preferable to the certainty
of dishonour. The minister, whose pacific intentions were

---

[1] See Zosimus, l. v. [c. 29] p. 334, 335. He interrupts his scanty narrative to relate the fable of Æmona, and of the ship Argo, which was drawn
overland from that place to the Hadriatic. Sozomen (l. viii. c. 25; l. ix.
c. 4) and Socrates (l. vii. c. 10) cast a pale and doubtful light, and Orosius
(l. vii. c. 38, p. 571) is abominably partial.

seconded only by the voices of a few servile and venal followers, attempted to allay the general ferment, by an apology for his own conduct, and even for the demands of the Gothic prince. "The payment of a subsidy, which had excited the indignation of the Romans, ought not (such was the language of Stilicho) to be considered in the odious light either of a tribute or of a ransom, extorted by the menaces of a barbarian enemy. Alaric had faithfully asserted the just pretensions of the republic to the provinces which were usurped by the Greeks of Constantinople: he modestly required the fair and stipulated recompense of his services; and if he had desisted from the prosecution of his enterprise, he had obeyed, in his retreat, the peremptory, though private, letters of the emperor himself. These contradictory orders (he would not dissemble the errors of his own family) had been procured by the intercession of Serena. The tender piety of his wife had been too deeply affected by the discord of the royal brothers, the sons of her adopted father; and the sentiments of nature had too easily prevailed over the stern dictates of the public welfare." These ostensible reasons, which faintly disguise the obscure intrigues of the palace of Ravenna, were supported by the authority of Stilicho; and obtained, after a warm debate, the reluctant approbation of the senate. The tumult of virtue and freedom subsided; and the sum of four thousand pounds of gold was granted, under the name of a subsidy, to secure the peace of Italy, and to conciliate the friendship of the king of the Goths. Lampadius alone, one of the most illustrious members of the assembly, still persisted in his dissent; exclaimed with a loud voice, "This is not a treaty of peace, but of servitude;"[1] and escaped the danger of such bold opposition by immediately retiring to the sanctuary of a Christian church.

But the reign of Stilicho drew towards its end; and the proud minister might perceive the symptoms of his approaching disgrace. The generous boldness of Lampadius had been applauded; and the senate, so patiently resigned to a long servitude, rejected with disdain the offer of invidious and imaginary freedom. The troops, who still assumed the name and prerogatives of the Roman legions, were exasperated by the partial affection of Stilicho for the barbarians: and the people imputed to the mischievous policy of the minister the public misfortunes, which were the natural consequence of their own degeneracy. Yet

[1] Zosimus, l. v. [c. 29] p. 338, 339. He repeats the words of Lampadius as they were spoken in Latin, "Non est ista pax, sed pactio servitutis," and then translates them into Greek for the benefit of his readers.

Stilicho might have continued to brave the clamours of the
people, and even of the soldiers, if he could have maintained
his dominion over the feeble mind of his pupil.   But the respectful attachment of Honorius was converted into fear, suspicion,
and hatred.   The crafty Olympius,[1] who concealed his vices
under the mask of Christian piety, had secretly undermined the
benefactor by whose favour he was promoted to the honourable
offices of the Imperial palace.   Olympius revealed to the unsuspecting emperor, who had attained the twenty-fifth year of
his age, that he was without weight or authority in his own
government;   and artfully alarmed his timid and indolent disposition by a lively picture of the designs of Stilicho, who already
meditated the death of his sovereign, with the ambitious hope
of placing the diadem on the head of his son Eucherius.   The
emperor was instigated by his new favourite to assume the tone
of independent dignity;   and the minister was astonished to find
that secret resolutions were formed in the court and council,
which were repugnant to his interest, or to his intentions.
Instead of residing in the palace of Rome, Honorius declared that
it was his pleasure to return to the secure fortress of Ravenna.
On the first intelligence of the death of his brother Arcadius,
he prepared to visit Constantinople, and to regulate, with the
authority of a guardian, the provinces of the infant Theodosius.[2]
The representation of the difficulty and expense of such a distant
expedition checked this strange and sudden sally of active
diligence;   but the dangerous project of showing the emperor
to the camp of Pavia, which was composed of the Roman troops,
the enemies of Stilicho and his barbarian auxiliaries, remained
fixed and unalterable.   The minister was pressed, by the advice
of his confidant, Justinian, a Roman advocate, of a lively and
penetrating genius, to oppose a journey so prejudicial to his
reputation and safety.   His strenuous, but ineffectual, efforts
confirmed the triumph of Olympius;   and the prudent lawyer
withdrew himself from the impending ruin of his patron.

[1] He came from the coast of the Euxine, and exercised a splendid office,
λαμπρᾶς δὲ στρατείας ἐν τοῖς βασιλείοις ἠξιωμένος.   His actions justify his
character, which Zosimus (l. v. [c. 32] p. 340) exposes with visible satisfaction.   Augustin revered the piety of Olympius, whom he styles a true
son of the church (Baronius, Annal. Eccles. A.D. 408, No. 19 etc.; Tillemont, Mém. Ecclés. tom. xiii. p. 467, 468).   But these praises, which the
African saint so unworthily bestows, might proceed as well from ignorance
as from adulation.

[2] Zosimus, l. v. [c. 31] p. 338, 339.   Sozomen, l. ix. c. 4.   Stilicho offered
to undertake the journey to Constantinople, that he might divert Honorius
from the vain attempt.   The Eastern empire would not have obeyed, and
could not have been conquered.

In the passage of the emperor through Bologna a mutiny of the guards was excited and appeased by the secret policy of Stilicho, who announced his instructions to decimate the guilty, and ascribed to his own intercession the merit of their pardon. After this tumult, Honorius embraced, for the last time, the minister whom he now considered as a tyrant, and proceeded on his way to the camp of Pavia, where he was received by the loyal acclamations of the troops who were assembled for the service of the Gallic war. On the morning of the fourth day he pronounced, as he had been taught, a military oration in the presence of the soldiers, whom the charitable visits and artful discourses of Olympius had prepared to execute a dark and bloody conspiracy. At the first signal they massacred the friends of Stilicho, the most illustrious officers of the empire; two Prætorian præfects, of Gaul and of Italy; two masters-general of the cavalry and infantry; the master of the offices, the quæstor, the treasurer, and the count of the domestics. Many lives were lost, many houses were plundered; the furious sedition continued to rage till the close of the evening; and the trembling emperor, who was seen in the streets of Pavia without his robes or diadem, yielded to the persuasions of his favourite, condemned the memory of the slain, and solemnly approved the innocence and fidelity of their assassins. The intelligence of the massacre of Pavia filled the mind of Stilicho with just and gloomy apprehensions, and he instantly summoned, in the camp of Bologna, a council of the confederate leaders who were attached to his service, and would be involved in his ruin. The impetuous voice of the assembly called aloud for arms and for revenge; to march, without a moment's delay, under the banners of a hero whom they had so often followed to victory; to surprise, to oppress, to extirpate the guilty Olympius and his degenerate Romans, and perhaps to fix the diadem on the head of their injured general. Instead of executing a resolution which might have been justified by success, Stilicho hesitated till he was irrecoverably lost. He was still ignorant of the fate of the emperor; he distrusted the fidelity of his own party; and he viewed with horror the fatal consequences of arming a crowd of licentious barbarians against the soldiers and people of Italy. The confederates, impatient of his timorous and doubtful delay, hastily retired with fear and indignation. At the hour of midnight Sarus, a Gothic warrior, renowned among the barbarians themselves for his strength and valour, suddenly invaded the camp of his benefactor, plundered the baggage, cut in pieces the

faithful Huns who guarded his person, and penetrated to the
tent, where the minister, pensive and sleepless, meditated on
the dangers of his situation. Stilicho escaped with difficulty
from the sword of the Goths, and after issuing a last and generous
admonition to the cities of Italy to shut their gates against the
barbarians, his confidence or his despair urged him to throw
himself into Ravenna, which was already in the absolute possession of his enemies. Olympius, who had assumed the dominion
of Honorius, was speedily informed that his rival had embraced,
as a suppliant, the altar of the Christian church. The base and
cruel disposition of the hypocrite was incapable of pity or
remorse; but he piously affected to elude, rather than to violate,
the privilege of the sanctuary. Count Heraclian, with a troop
of soldiers, appeared at the dawn of day before the gates of the
church of Ravenna. The bishop was satisfied by a solemn oath
that the Imperial mandate only directed them to secure the
person of Stilicho: but as soon as the unfortunate minister had
been tempted beyond the holy threshold, he produced the
warrant for his instant execution. Stilicho supported with calm
resignation the injurious names of traitor and parricide; repressed the unseasonable zeal of his followers, who were ready
to attempt an ineffectual rescue; and, with a firmness not unworthy of the last of the Roman generals, submitted his neck
to the sword of Heraclian.[1]

The servile crowd of the palace, who had so long adored the
fortune of Stilicho, affected to insult his fall; and the most
distant connection with the master-general of the West, which
had so lately been a title to wealth and honours, was studiously
denied, and rigorously punished. His family, united by a triple
alliance with the family of Theodosius, might envy the condition
of the meanest peasant. The flight of his son Eucherius was
intercepted; and the death of that innocent youth soon
followed the divorce of Thermantia, who filled the place of her
sister Maria, and who, like Maria, had remained a virgin in the
Imperial bed.[2] The friends of Stilicho who had escaped the
massacre of Pavia were persecuted by the implacable revenge of
Olympius, and the most exquisite cruelty was employed to extort

---

[1] Zosimus (l. v. [c. 30, sqq.] p. 336-345) has copiously, though not clearly,
related the disgrace and death of Stilicho. Olympiodorus (apud Phot.
p. 177 [p. 56, ed. Bekker]), Orosius (l. vii. c. 38, p. 571, 572), Sozomen (l. ix.
c. 4), and Philostorgius (l. xi. c. 3, l. xii. c. 2), afford supplemental hints.

[2] Zosimus, l. v. [c. 28] p. 333. The marriage of a Christian with two
sisters scandalises Tillemont (Hist. des Empereurs, tom. v. p. 557), who
expects, in vain, that Pope Innocent I. should have done something in the
way either of censure or of dispensation.

the confession of a treasonable and sacrilegious conspiracy. They died in silence; their firmness justified the choice,[1] and perhaps absolved the innocence, of their patron; and the despotic power which could take his life without a trial, and stigmatise his memory without a proof, has no jurisdiction over the impartial suffrage of posterity.[2] The services of Stilicho are great and manifest; his crimes, as they are vaguely stated in the language of flattery and hatred, are obscure, at least, and improbable. About four months after his death an edict was published, in the name of Honorius, to restore the free communication of the two empires, which had been so long interrupted by the *public enemy*.[3] The minister, whose fame and fortune depended on the prosperity of the state, was accused of betraying Italy to the barbarians, whom he repeatedly vanquished at Pollentia, at Verona, and before the walls of Florence. His pretended design of placing the diadem on the head of his son Eucherius could not have been conducted without preparations or accomplices; and the ambitious father would not surely have left the future emperor, till the twentieth year of his age, in the humble station of tribune of the notaries. Even the religion of Stilicho was arraigned by the malice of his rival. The seasonable, and almost miraculous, deliverance was devoutly celebrated by the applause of the clergy, who asserted that the restoration of idols and the persecution of the church would have been the first measure of the reign of Eucherius. The son of Stilicho, however, was educated in the bosom of Christianity, which his father had uniformly professed and zealously supported.[4] Serena had borrowed her magnificent necklace from the statue of Vesta;[5] and the Pagans execrated the memory of the sacrilegious minister, by whose order the Sibylline books, the oracles of Rome, had been committed to the flames.[6] The pride and power of Stilicho

---

[1] Two of his friends are honourably mentioned (Zosimus, l. v. [c. 35] p. 346)—Peter, chief of the school of notaries, and the great chamberlain Deuterius. Stilicho had secured the bedchamber; and it is surprising that, under a feeble prince, the bedchamber was not able to secure him.

[2] Orosius (l. vii. c. 38, p. 571, 572) seems to copy the false and furious manifestos which were dispersed through the provinces by the new administration.

[3] See the Theodosian Code, l. vii. tit. xvi. leg. 1: l. ix. tit. xlii. leg. 22. Stilicho is branded with the name of *prædo publicus*, who employed his wealth *ad omnem ditandam, inquietandamque Barbariem*.

[4] Augustin himself is satisfied with the effectual laws which Stilicho had enacted against heretics and idolaters, and which are still extant in the Code. He only applies to Olympius for their confirmation (Baronius, Annal. Eccles. A.D. 408, No. 19).

[5] Zosimus, l. v. [c. 38] p. 351. We may observe the bad taste of the age, in dressing their statues with such awkward finery.

[6] See Rutilius Numatianus (Itinerar. l. ii. 41-60), to whom religious

constituted his real guilt. An honourable reluctance to shed
the blood of his countrymen appears to have contributed to the
success of his unworthy rival; and it is the last humiliation of
the character of Honorius, that posterity has not condescended
to reproach him with his base ingratitude to the guardian of his
youth and the support of his empire.

Among the train of dependents whose wealth and dignity
attracted the notice of their own times, *our* curiosity is excited
by the celebrated name of the poet Claudian, who enjoyed the
favour of Stilicho, and was overwhelmed in the ruin of his patron.
The titular offices of tribune and notary fixed his rank in the
Imperial court: he was indebted to the powerful intercession of
Serena for his marriage with a rich heiress of the province of
Africa; [1] and the statue of Claudian, erected in the forum of
Trajan, was a monument of the taste and liberality of the Roman
senate. [2] After the praises of Stilicho became offensive and
criminal, Claudian was exposed to the enmity of a powerful and
unforgiving courtier whom he had provoked by the insolence of
wit. He had compared, in a lively epigram, the opposite characters of two Prætorian præfects of Italy; he contrasts the
innocent repose of a philosopher, who sometimes resigned the
hours of business to slumber, perhaps to study, with the interested
diligence of a rapacious minister, indefatigable in the pursuit of
unjust or sacrilegious gain. " How happy," continues Claudian,
" how happy might it be for the people of Italy if Mallius could
be constantly awake, and if Hadrian would always sleep!" [3]

enthusiasm has dictated some elegant and forcible lines. Stilicho likewise
stripped the gold plates from the doors of the Capitol, and read a prophetic
sentence which was engraven under them (Zosimus, l. v. [c. 38] p. 352).
These are foolish stories; yet the charge of *impiety* adds weight and credit
to the praise, which Zosimus reluctantly bestows, of his virtues.

[1] At the nuptials of Orpheus (a modest comparison!) all the parts of
animated nature contributed their various gifts, and the gods themselves
enriched their favourite. Claudian had neither flocks, nor herds, nor
vines, nor olives. His wealthy bride was heiress to them all. But he
carried to Africa a recommendatory letter from Serena, his Juno, and was
made happy (Epist. ii. ad Serenam).

[2] Claudian feels the honour like a man who deserved it (in præfat. Bell.
Get.). The original inscription, on marble, was found at Rome, in the
fifteenth century, in the house of Pomponius Lætus. The statue of a poet,
far superior to Claudian, should have been erected, during his lifetime, by
the men of letters, his countrymen and contemporaries. It was a noble
design.

[3] See Epigram xxx.:—

Mallius indulget somno noctesque diesque:
    Insomnis *Pharius* sacra, profana, rapit.
Omnibus, hoc, Italæ gentes, exposcite votis,
    Mallius ut vigilet, dormiat ut Pharius.

Hadrian was a Pharian (of Alexandria). See his public life in Godefroy,

The repose of Mallius was not disturbed by this friendly and gentle admonition; but the cruel vigilance of Hadrian watched the opportunity of revenge, and easily obtained from the enemies of Stilicho the trifling sacrifice of an obnoxious poet. The poet concealed himself, however, during the tumult of the revolution, and, consulting the dictates of prudence rather than of honour, he addressed, in the form of an epistle, a suppliant and humble recantation to the offended præfect. He deplores, in mournful strains, the fatal indiscretion into which he had been hurried by passion and folly; submits to the imitation of his adversary the generous examples of the clemency of god, of heroes, and of lions; and expresses his hope that the magnanimity of Hadrian will not trample on a defenceless and contemptible foe, already humbled by disgrace and poverty, and deeply wounded by the exile, the tortures, and the death of his dearest friends.[1] Whatever might be the success of his prayer or the accidents of his future life, the period of a few years levelled in the grave the minister and the poet: but the name of Hadrian is almost sunk in oblivion, while Claudian is read with pleasure in every country which has retained or acquired the knowledge of the Latin language. If we fairly balance his merits and his defects, we shall acknowledge that Claudian does not either satisfy or silence our reason. It would not be easy to produce a passage that deserves the epithet of sublime or pathetic; to select a verse that melts the heart or enlarges the imagination. We should vainly seek in the poems of Claudian the happy invention and artificial conduct of an interesting fable, or the just and lively representation of the characters and situations of real life. For the service of his patron he published occasional panegyrics and invectives, and the design of these slavish compositions encouraged his propensity to exceed the limits of truth and nature. These imperfections, however, are compensated in some degree by the poetical virtues of Claudian. He was endowed with the rare and precious talent of raising the meanest, of adoring the most barren, and of diversifying the most similar topics; his colouring, more especially in descriptive poetry, is soft and splendid; and he seldom fails to display, and even to abuse, the advantages of a cultivated understanding, a copious fancy, an easy and sometimes forcible expression, and a perpetual

Cod. Theodos. tom. vi. p. 364. Mallius did not always sleep. He composed some elegant dialogues on the Greek systems of natural philosophy (Claud. in Mall. Theodor. Cons. 61-112).

[1] See Claudian's first Epistle. Yet in some places an air of irony and indignation betrays his secret reluctance.

flow of harmonious versification.   To these commendations, independent of any accidents of time and place, we must add the
peculiar merit which Claudian derived from the unfavourable
circumstances of his birth.   In the decline of arts and of empire,
a native of Egypt,[1] who had received the education of a Greek,
assumed in a mature age the familiar use and absolute command
of the Latin language;[2] soared above the heads of his feeble
contemporaries; and placed himself, after an interval of three
hundred years, among the poets of ancient Rome.[3]

CHAPTER XXXI

Invasion of Italy by Alaric—Manners of the Roman Senate and People—
    Rome is thrice besieged, and at length pillaged, by the Goths—
    Death of Alaric—The Goths evacuate Italy—Fall of Constantine—
    Gaul and Spain are occupied by the Barbarians—Independence of
    Britain

THE incapacity of a weak and distracted government may often
assume the appearance and produce the effects of a treasonable
correspondence with the public enemy.   If Alaric himself had
been introduced into the council of Ravenna, he would probably
have advised the same measures which were actually pursued by
the ministers of Honorius.[4]   The king of the Goths would have
conspired, perhaps with some reluctance, to destroy the formidable adversary by whose arms, in Italy as well as in Greece, he
had been twice overthrown.   *Their* active and interested hatred
laboriously accomplished the disgrace and ruin of the great
Stilicho.   The valour of Sarus, his fame in arms, and his personal
or hereditary influence over the confederate barbarians, could

[1] National vanity has made him a Florentine, or a Spaniard.   But the
first Epistle of Claudian proves him a native of Alexandria (Fabricius,
Biblioth. Latin. tom. iii. p. 191-202, edit. Ernest.).

[2] His first Latin verses were composed during the consulship of Probinus,
A.D. 395:—

> Romanos bibimus primum, te consule, fontes,
>   Et Latiæ cessit Graia Thalia togæ.

Besides some Greek epigrams, which are still extant, the Latin poet had
composed, in Greek, the Antiquities of Tarsus, Anazarbus, Berytus, Nice,
etc.   It is more easy to supply the loss of good poetry than of authentic
history.

[3] Strada (Prolusion v. vi.) allows him to contend with the five heroic
poets, Lucretius, Virgil, Ovid, Lucan, and Statius.   His patron is the
accomplished courtier Balthazar Castiglione.   His admirers are numerous
and passionate.   Yet the rigid critics reproach the exotic weeds or flowers
which spring too luxuriantly in his Latian soil.

[4] The series of events, from the death of Stilicho to the arrival of Alaric
before Rome, can only be found in Zosimus, l. v. [c. 35-37] p. 347-350.

recommend him only to the friends of their country who despised or detested the worthless characters of Turpilio, Varanes, and Vigilantius. By the pressing instances of the new favourites, these generals, unworthy as they had shown themselves of the name of soldiers,[1] were promoted to the command of the cavalry, of the infantry, and of the domestic troops. The Gothic prince would have subscribed with pleasure the edict which the fanaticism of Olympius dictated to the simple and devout emperor. Honorius excluded all persons who were adverse to the catholic church from holding any office in the state; obstinately rejected the service of all those who dissented from his religion; and rashly disqualified many of his bravest and most skilful officers who adhered to the Pagan worship or who had imbibed the opinions of Arianism.[2] These measures, so advantageous to an enemy, Alaric would have approved, and might perhaps have suggested; but it may seem doubtful whether the barbarian would have promoted his interest at the expense of the inhuman and absurd cruelty which was perpetrated by the direction, or at least with the connivance, of the Imperial ministers. The foreign auxiliaries who had been attached to the person of Stilicho lamented his death; but the desire of revenge was checked by a natural apprehension for the safety of their wives and children, who were detained as hostages in the strong cities of Italy, where they had likewise deposited their most valuable effects. At the same hour, and as if by a common signal, the cities of Italy were polluted by the same horrid scenes of universal massacre and pillage, which involved in promiscuous destruction the families and fortunes of the barbarians. Exasperated by such an injury, which might have awakened the tamest and most servile spirit, they cast a look of indignation and hope towards the camp of Alaric, and unanimously swore to pursue with just and implacable war the perfidious nation that had so basely violated the laws of hospitality. By the imprudent conduct of the ministers of Honorius the republic lost the assistance, and deserved the enmity, of thirty thousand of her bravest soldiers; and the weight of that formidable army, which alone might have determined the event of the war, was

---

[1] The expression of Zosimus is strong and lively, καταφρόνησιν ἐμποιῆσαι τοῖς πολεμίοις ἀρκοῦντας, sufficient to excite the contempt of the enemy.

[2] Eos qui catholicæ sectæ sunt inimici, intra palatium militare prohibemus. Nullus nobis sit aliquâ ratione conjunctus, qui a nobis fide et religione discordat. Cod. Theodos, l. xvi. tit. v. leg. 42, and Godefroy's Commentary, tom. vi. p. 164. This law was applied in the utmost latitude and rigorously executed. Zosimus, l. v. [c. 46] p. 364.

transferred from the scale of the Romans into that of the Goths.

In the arts of negotiation, as well as in those of war, the Gothic king maintained his superior ascendant over an enemy whose seeming changes proceeded from the total want of counsel and design. From his camp, on the confines of Italy, Alaric attentively observed the revolutions of the palace, watched the progress of faction and discontent, disguised the hostile aspect of a barbarian invader, and assumed the more popular appearance of the friend and ally of the great Stilicho; to whose virtues, when they were no longer formidable, he could pay a just tribute of sincere praise and regret. The pressing invitation of the malcontents, who urged the king of the Goths to invade Italy, was enforced by a lively sense of his personal injuries; and he might speciously complain that the Imperial ministers still delayed and eluded the payment of the four thousand pounds of gold which had been granted by the Roman senate either to reward his services or to appease his fury. His decent firmness was supported by an artful moderation, which contributed to the success of his designs. He required a fair and reasonable satisfaction; but he gave the strongest assurances that, as soon as he had obtained it, he would immediately retire. He refused to trust the faith of the Romans, unless Aëtius and Jason, the sons of two great officers of state, were sent as hostages to his camp: but he offered to deliver in exchange several of the noblest youths of the Gothic nation. The modesty of Alaric was interpreted by the ministers of Ravenna as a sure evidence of his weakness and fear. They disdained either to negotiate a treaty or to assemble an army; and with a rash confidence, derived only from their ignorance of the extreme danger, irretrievably wasted the decisive moments of peace and war. While they expected, in sullen silence, that the barbarians should evacuate the confines of Italy, Alaric, with bold and rapid marches, passed the Alps and the Po; hastily pillaged the cities of Aquileia, Altinum, Concordia, and Cremona, which yielded to his arms; increased his forces by the accession of thirty thousand auxiliaries; and, without meeting a single enemy in the field, advanced as far as the edge of the morass which protected the impregnable residence of the emperor of the West. Instead of attempting the hopeless siege of Ravenna, the prudent leader of the Goths proceeded to Rimini, stretched his ravages along the sea-coast of the Hadriatic, and meditated the conquest of the ancient mistress of the world. An Italian hermit, whose zeal and sanctity were respected by the barbarians themselves, encountered the victorious monarch, and boldly denounced the indignation of Heaven against the oppressors of the earth: but the saint himself was confounded by the solemn asseveration of Alaric that he felt a secret and præternatural impulse, which directed, and even compelled, his march to the gates of Rome. He felt that his genius and his fortune were equal to the most arduous enterprises; and the enthusiasm which he communicated to the Goths insensibly removed the popular and almost superstitious reverence of the nations for the majesty of the Roman name. His troops, animated by the hopes of spoil, followed the course of the Flaminian way, occupied the unguarded passes of the Apennine,[1] descended into the rich plains of Umbria; and, as they lay encamped on the banks of the Clitumnus, might wantonly slaughter and devour the milk-white oxen which had been so long reserved for the use of Roman triumphs.[2] A lofty situation and a seasonable tempest of thunder and lightning preserved the little city of Narni: but the king of the Goths, despising the ignoble prey, still advanced with unabated vigour; and after he had passed through the stately arches, adorned with the spoils of barbaric victories, he pitched his camp under the walls of Rome.[3]

During a period of six hundred and nineteen years the seat of empire had never been violated by the presence of a foreign enemy. The unsuccessful expedition of Hannibal[4] served only to display the character of the senate and people; of a senate degraded, rather than ennobled, by the comparison of an assembly of kings; and of a people to whom the ambassador of

---

[1] Addison (see his Works, vol. ii. p. 54, edit. Baskerville) has given a very picturesque description of the road through the Apennine. The Goths were not at leisure to observe the beauties of the prospect; but they were pleased to find that the Saxa Intercisa, a narrow passage which Vespasian had cut through the rock (Cluver. Italia Antiq. tom. i. p. 618), was totally neglected.

[2]   Hinc albi, Clitumne, greges, et maxima **taurus**
      Victima sæpe, tuo perfusi flumine sacro,
      Romanos ad templa Deum duxere triumphos.
                                    Georg. ii. 147.

Besides Virgil, most of the Latin poets, Propertius, Lucan, Silius Italicus, Claudian, etc., whose passages may be found in Cluverius and Addison, have celebrated the triumphal victims of the Clitumnus.

[3] Some ideas of the march of Alaric are borrowed from the journey of Honorius over the same ground (see Claudian in vi. Cons. Hon. 494-522). The measured distance between Ravenna and Rome was 254 Roman miles. Itinerar. Wesseling. p. 126.

[4] The march and retreat of Hannibal are described by Livy, l. xxvi. c. 7, 8, 9, 10, 11; and the reader is made a spectator of the interesting scene.

Pyrrhus ascribed the inexhaustible resources of the Hydra.[1]
Each of the senators in the time of the Punic war had accomplished his term of military service, either in a subordinate or a
superior station; and the decree which invested with temporary
command all those who had been consuls, or censors, or dictators,
gave the republic the immediate assistance of many brave and
experienced generals. In the beginning of the war the Roman
people consisted of two hundred and fifty thousand citizens of
an age to bear arms.[2] Fifty thousand had already died in the
defence of their country; and the twenty-three legions which
were employed in the different camps of Italy, Greece, Sardinia,
Sicily, and Spain, required about one hundred thousand men.
But there still remained an equal number in Rome and the
adjacent territory who were animated by the same intrepid
courage; and every citizen was trained from his earliest youth
in the discipline and exercises of a soldier. Hannibal was
astonished by the constancy of the senate, who, without raising
the siege of Capua or recalling their scattered forces, expected
his approach. He encamped on the banks of the Anio, at the
distance of three miles from the city: and he was soon informed
that the ground on which he had pitched his tent was sold for an
adequate price at a public auction; and that a body of troops
was dismissed by an opposite road to reinforce the legions of
Spain.[3] He led his Africans to the gates of Rome, where he

[1] These comparisons were used by Cineas, the counsellor of Pyrrhus,
after his return from his embassy, in which he had diligently studied the
discipline and manners of Rome. See Plutarch in Pyrrho [c. 19], tom. ii.
p. 459.

[2] In the three *census* which were made of the Roman people about the
time of the second Punic war, the numbers stand as follows (see Livy,
Epitom. l. xx. Hist. l. xxvii. 36, xxix. 37), 270, 213, 137, 108, 214,000.
The fall of the second and the rise of the third appears so enormous, that
several critics, notwithstanding the unanimity of the MSS., have suspected
some corruption of the text of Livy. (See Drakenborch ad xxvii. 36, and
Beaufort, République Romaine, tom. i. p. 325.) They did not consider
that the second *census* was taken only at Rome, and that the numbers were
diminished, not only by the death, but likewise by the *absence*, of many
soldiers. In the third *census*, Livy expressly affirms that the legions were
mustered by the care of particular commissaries. From the numbers on
the list we must always deduct one-twelfth above threescore and incapable
of bearing arms. See Population de la France, p. 72.

[3] Livy considers these two incidents as the effects only of chance and
courage. I suspect that they were both managed by the admirable policy
of the senate.

[As a parallel instance to what is related of Hannibal, compare the
remarkable transaction in Jerom, xxxii. 6, 44, where the prophet purchases
his uncle's estate at the approach of the Babylonian captivity, in his un-
doubting confidence in the future restoration of the people. In the latter
case it was the triumph of religious faith, in the other of national pride.—
O. S.]

found three armies in order of battle prepared to receive him; but Hannibal dreaded the event of a combat from which he could not hope to escape unless he destroyed the last of his enemies; and his speedy retreat confessed the invincible courage of the Romans.

From the time of the Punic war the uninterrupted succession of senators had preserved the name and image of the republic; and the degenerate subjects of Honorius ambitiously derived their descent from the heroes who had repulsed the arms of Hannibal and subdued the nations of the earth. The temporal honours which the devout Paula [1] inherited and despised are carefully recapitulated by Jerom, the guide of her conscience and the historian of her life. The genealogy of her father, Rogatus, which ascended as high as Agamemnon, might seem to betray a Grecian origin; but her mother, Blæsilla, numbered the Scipios, Æmilius Paulus, and the Gracchi in the list of her ancestors; and Toxotius, the husband of Paula, deduced his royal lineage from Æneas, the father of the Julian line. The vanity of the rich, who desired to be noble, was gratified by these lofty pretensions. Encouraged by the applause of their parasites, they easily imposed on the credulity of the vulgar; and were countenanced in some measure by the custom of adopting the name of their patron, which had always prevailed among the freedmen and clients of illustrious families. Most of those families, however, attacked by so many causes of external violence or internal decay, were gradually extirpated: and it would be more reasonable to seek for a lineal descent of twenty generations among the mountains of the Alps or in the peaceful solitude of Apulia, than on the theatre of Rome, the seat of fortune, of danger, and of perpetual revolutions. Under each successive reign and from every province of the empire a crowd of hardy adventurers, rising to eminence by their talents or their vices, usurped the wealth, the honours, and the palaces of Rome; and oppressed or protected the poor and humble remains of consular families, who were ignorant, perhaps, of the glory of their ancestors.[2]

---

[1] See Jerom, tom. i. p. 169, 170, ad Eustochium [Epist. cviii. tom. i. p. 684, ed. Vallars.]; he bestows on Paula the splendid titles of Gracchorum stirps, soboles Scipionum, Pauli hæres, cujus vocabulum trahit, Martiæ Papyriæ Matris Africani vera et germana propago. This particular description supposes a more solid title than the surname of Julius, which Toxotius shared with a thousand families of the western provinces. See the Index of Tacitus, of Gruter's Inscriptions, etc.

[2] Tacitus (Annal. iii. 55) affirms that, between the battle of Actium and the reign of Vespasian, the senate was gradually filled with *new* families from the Municipia and colonies of Italy.

In the time of Jerom and Claudian the senators unanimously yielded the pre-eminence to the Anician line; and a slight view of *their* history will serve to appreciate the rank and antiquity of the noble families which contended only for the second place.[1]

During the five first ages of the city the name of the Anicians was unknown; they appear to have derived their origin from Præneste; and the ambition of those new citizens was long satisfied with the plebeian honours of tribunes of the people.[2] One hundred and sixty-eight years before the Christian era the family was ennobled by the prætorship of Anicius, who gloriously terminated the Illyrian war by the conquest of the nation and the captivity of their king.[3] From the triumph of that general three consulships in distant periods mark the succession of the Anician name.[4] From the reign of Diocletian to the final extinction of the Western empire that name shone with a lustre which was not eclipsed in the public estimation by the majesty of the Imperial purple.[5] The several branches to whom it was communicated united, by marriage or inheritance, the wealth and titles of the Annian, the Petronian, and the Olybrian houses; and in each generation the number of consulships was multiplied

---

[1] Nec quisquam Procerum tentet (licet ære vetusto
    Floreat, et claro cingatur Roma senatû)
    Se jactare parem; sed primâ sede relictâ
  Aucheniis, de jure licet certare secundo.
                 Claud. in Prob. et Olybrii Coss. 18.

Such a compliment paid to the obscure name of the Auchenii has amazed the critics; but they all agree that, whatever may be the true reading, the sense of Claudian can be applied only to the Anician family.

[2] The earliest date on the annals of Pighius is that of M. Anicius Gallus, Trib. Pl. A.U.C. 506. Another Tribune, Q. Anicius, A.U.C. 508, is distinguished by the epithet of Prænestinus. Livy (xlv. 43) places the Anicii below the great families of Rome.

[3] Livy, xliv. 30, 31, xlv, 3, 26, 43. He fairly appreciates the merit of Anicius, and justly observes that his fame was clouded by the superior lustre of the Macedonian, which preceded the Illyrian, triumph.

[4] The dates of the three consulships are, A.U.C. 593, 818, 967: the two last under the reigns of Nero and Caracalla. The second of these consuls distinguished himself only by his infamous flattery (Tacit. Annal. xv. 74); but even the evidence of crimes, if they bear the stamp of greatness and antiquity, is admitted, without reluctance, to prove the genealogy of a noble house.

[There is still an earlier instance of a member of the family attaining one of the higher offices of the state. Quintus Anicius Prænestinus was curule ædile with Q. Flavius, the celebrated scribe of Appius Claudius Cæcus, B.C. 304. Cf. Pliny, *Hist. Nat.* lib. xxxiii. c. 1, s. 6.—O. S.]

[5] In the sixth century the nobility of the Anician name is mentioned (Cassiodor. Variar. l. x. Ep. 11, 12) with singular respect by the minister of a Gothic king of Italy.

by an hereditary claim.[1] The Anician family excelled in faith and in riches: they were the first of the Roman senate who embraced Christianity; and it is probable that Anicius Julian, who was afterwards consul and præfect of the city, atoned for his attachment to the party of Maxentius by the readiness with which he accepted the religion of Constantine.[2] Their ample patrimony was increased by the industry of Probus, the chief of the Anician family, who shared with Gratian the honours of the consulship, and exercised four times the high office of Prætorian præfect.[3] His immense estates were scattered over the wide extent of the Roman world; and though the public might suspect or disapprove the methods by which they had been acquired, the generosity and magnificence of that fortunate statesman deserved the gratitude of his clients and the admiration of strangers.[4] Such was the respect entertained for his memory, that the two sons of Probus, in their earliest youth and at the request of the senate, were associated in the consular dignity: a memorable distinction, without example in the annals of Rome.[5]

"The marbles of the Anician palace," were used as a proverbial expression of opulence and splendour;[6] but the nobles and senators of Rome aspired in due gradation to imitate that illustrious family. The accurate description of the city, which was composed in the Theodosian age, enumerates one thousand

---

[1] —— Fixus in omnes
Cognatos procedit honos; quemcumque requiras
Hâc de stirpe virum, certum est de Consule nasci.
Per fasces numerantur avi, semperque renatâ
Nobilitate virent, et prolem fata sequuntur.

(Claudian in Prob. et Olyb. Consulat. 12, etc.) The Annii, whose name seems to have merged in the Anician, mark the Fasti with many consulships from the time of Vespasian to the fourth century.

[2] The title of first Christian senator may be justified by the authority of Prudentius (in Symmach. i. 553) and the dislike of the Pagans to the Anician family. See Tillemont, Hist. des Empereurs, tom. iv. p. 183, v. p. 44. Baron. Annal. A.D. 312, No. 78; A.D. 322, No. 2.

[3] Probus . . . claritudine generis et potentiâ et opûm amplitudine cognitus Orbi Romano, per quem universum pœne patrimonia sparsa possedit, juste an secus non judicioli est nostri. Ammian. Marcellin. xxvii. 11. His children and widow erected for him a magnificent tomb in the Vatican, which was demolished in the time of pope Nicholas V. to make room for the new church of St. Peter. Baronius, who laments the ruin of this Christian monument, has diligently preserved the inscriptions and basso-relievos. See Annal. Eccles. A.D. 395, No. 5-17.

[4] Two Persian satraps travelled to Milan and Rome to hear St. Ambrose and to see Probus. (Paulin. in Vit. Ambros.) Claudian (in Cons. Probin. et. Olybr. 30-60) seems at a loss how to express the glory of Probus.

[5] See the poem which Claudian addressed to the two noble youths.

[6] Secundinus, the Manichæan, ap. Baron. Annal. Eccles. A.D. 390, No. 34.

seven hundred and eighty *houses*, the residence of wealthy and
honourable citizens.[1] Many of these stately mansions might
almost excuse the exaggeration of the poet—that Rome contained a multitude of palaces, and that each palace was equal
to a city, since it included within its own precincts everything
which could be subservient either to use or luxury: markets,
hippodromes, temples, fountains, baths, porticos, shady groves,
and artificial aviaries.[2] The historian Olympiodorus, who represents the state of Rome when it was besieged by the Goths,[3]
continues to observe that several of the richest senators received
from their estates an annual income of four thousand pounds of
gold, above one hundred and sixty thousand pounds sterling;
without computing the stated provision of corn and wine, which,
had they been sold, might have equalled in value one-third of
the money. Compared to this immoderate wealth, an ordinary
revenue of a thousand or fifteen hundred pounds of gold might
be considered as no more than adequate to the dignity of the
senatorian rank, which required many expenses of a public
and ostentatious kind. Several examples are recorded in the
age of Honorius of vain and popular nobles who celebrated the
year of their prætorship by a festival which lasted seven days and
cost above one hundred thousand pounds sterling.[4] The estates

---

[1] See Nardini, Roma Antica, p. 89, 498, 500.

[2] Quid loquar inclusas inter laquearia silvas?
     Vernula quâ vario carmine ludit avis?
                    Claud. Rutil. Numatian. Itinerar. ver. 111.
The poet lived at the time of the Gothic invasion. A moderate palace
would have covered Cincinnatus's farm of four acres (Val. Max. iv. 4, 7).
In laxitatem ruris excurrunt, says Seneca, Epist. 114. See a judicious
note of Mr. Hume, Essays, vol. i. p. 562, last 8vo edition.

[3] This curious account of Rome in the reign of Honorius is found in a
fragment of the historian Olympiodorus, ap. Photium, p. 197 [p. 63, ed.
Bekker].

[4] The sons of Alypius [Olympius in Bekker's ed.], of Symmachus, and of
Maximus, spent, during their respective prætorships, twelve, or twenty, or
forty, *centenaries* (or hundredweight of gold). See Olympiodor. ap. Phot.
p. 197 [p. 63, ed. Bekker]. This popular estimation allows some latitude;
but it is difficult to explain a law in the Theodosian Code (l. vi. tit. iv. leg.
5) which fixes the expense of the first prætor at 25,000, of the second at
20,000, and of the third at 15,000 *folles*. The name of *follis* (see Mém. de
l'Académie des Inscriptions, tom. xxviii. p. 727) was equally applied to a
purse of 125 pieces of silver, and to a small copper coin of the value of $\frac{1}{2625}$
part of that purse. In the former sense, the 25,000 *folles* would be equal to
£150,000; in the latter to five or six pounds sterling. The one appears
extravagant, the other is ridiculous. There must have existed some third
and middle value, which is here understood; but ambiguity is an inexcusable fault in the language of laws.

[The centenarium was a hundred pounds weight of gold, and from the
time of Constantine, the pound contained 72 solidi. Supposing the solidus
to be worth only 10s. English, the prætorship of Symmachus cost £72,000,

of the Roman senators, which so far exceed the proportion of modern wealth, were not confined to the limits of Italy. Their possessions extended far beyond the Ionian and Ægean seas to the most distant provinces: the city of Nicopolis, which Augustus had founded as an eternal monument of the Actian victory, was the property of the devout Paula;[1] and it is observed by Seneca, that the rivers which had divided hostile nations now flowed through the lands of private citizens.[2] According to their temper and circumstances, the estates of the Romans were either cultivated by the labour of their slaves, or granted, for a certain and stipulated rent, to the industrious farmer. The economical writers of antiquity strenuously recommend the former method wherever it may be practicable; but if the object should be removed by its distance or magnitude from the immediate eye of the master, they prefer the active care of an old hereditary tenant, attached to the soil and interested in the produce, to the mercenary administration of a negligent, perhaps an unfaithful, steward.[3]

The opulent nobles of an immense capital, who were never excited by the pursuit of military glory, and seldom engaged in the occupations of civil government, naturally resigned their leisure to the business and amusements of private life. At Rome commerce was always held in contempt; but the senators, from the first age of the republic, increased their patrimony and multiplied their clients by the lucrative practice of usury, and

and that of Maximus £144,000. In the passage from the Theodosian Code, quoted by Gibbon, the *follis* means a purse of 125 pieces of silver, and as this *follis* was equal to £5 11s. nearly (according to Mommsen) 25,000 *folles* = £143,750. This sum is prodigious, but it is nearly the same as what was expended by Maximus in his prætorship. Savigny makes the solidus equal to 10s., but Mommsen prefers 12s. as being its approximate value.—O. S.]

[1] Nicopolis . . . in Actiaco littore sita possessionis vestræ nunc pars vel maxima est. Jerom. in præfat. Comment. ad Epistol. ad Titum, tom. ix. p. 243. M. de Tillemont supposes, strangely enough, that it was part of Agamemnon's inheritance. Mém. Ecclés. tom. xii. p. 85.

[2] Seneca, Epist. lxxxix. His language is of the declamatory kind: but declamation could scarcely exaggerate the avarice and luxury of the Romans. The philosopher himself deserved some share of the reproach, if it be true that his rigorous exaction of *Quadringenties*, above three hundred thousand pounds, which he had lent at high interest, provoked a rebellion in Britain. (Dion Cassius, l. lxii. [c. 2] p. 1003.) According to the conjecture of Gale (Antoninus's Itinerary in Britain, p. 92), the same Faustinus possessed an estate near Bury, in Suffolk, and another in the kingdom of Naples.

[3] Volusius, a wealthy senator (Tacit. Annal. iii. 30), always preferred tenants born on the estate. Columella, who received this maxim from him, argues very judiciously on the subject. De Re Rusticâ, l. i. c. 7, p. 408, edit. Gesner. Leipzig, 1735.

the obsolete laws were eluded or violated by the mutual inclinations and interest of both parties.[1] A considerable mass of treasure must always have existed at Rome, either in the current coin of the empire, or in the form of gold and silver plate; and there were many sideboards in the time of Pliny which contained more solid silver than had been transported by Scipio from vanquished Carthage.[2] The greater part of the nobles, who dissipated their fortunes in profuse luxury, found themselves poor in the midst of wealth, and idle in a constant round of dissipation. Their desires were continually gratified by the labour of a thousand hands; of the numerous train of their domestic slaves, who were actuated by the fear of punishment; and of the various professions of artificers and merchants, who were more powerfully impelled by the hopes of gain. The ancients were destitute of many of the conveniences of life which have been invented or improved by the progress of industry; and the plenty of glass and linen has diffused more real comforts among the modern nations of Europe than the senators of Rome could derive from all the refinements of pompous or sensual luxury.[3] Their luxury and their manners have been the subject of minute and laborious disquisition; but as such inquiries would divert me too long from the design of the present work, I shall produce an authentic state of Rome and its inhabitants which is more peculiarly applicable to the period of the Gothic invasion. Ammianus Marcellinus, who prudently chose the capital of the empire as the residence the best adapted to the historian of his own times, has mixed with the narrative of public events a lively representation of the scenes with which he was familiarly conversant. The judicious reader will not always approve the asperity of censure, the choice of circumstances, or the style of

---

[1] Valesius (ad Ammian. xiv. 6) has proved, from Chrysostom and Augustin, that the senators were not allowed to lend money at usury. Yet it appears from the Theodosian Code (see Godefroy ad l. ii. tit. xxxiii. tom. i. p. 230-239) that they were permitted to take six per cent., or one-half of the legal interest; and, what is more singular, this permission was granted to the *young* senators.

[2] Plin. Hist. Natur. xxxiii. 50. He states the silver at only 4380 pounds, which is increased by Livy (xxx. 45) to 100,023; the former seems too little for an opulent city, the latter too much for any private sideboard.

[3] The learned Arbuthnot (Tables of Ancient Coins, etc., p. 153) has observed with humour, and I believe with truth, that Augustus had neither glass to his windows nor a shirt to his back. Under the lower empire the use of linen and glass became somewhat more common.

[This is altogether wrong. The discovery of glass in common use in Pompeii has rather spoilt the point of Arbuthnot's jest. Glass was in general use in the reign of Augustus, and linen became common in that of Tiberius.—O. S.]

expression; he will perhaps detect the latent prejudices and personal resentments which soured the temper of Ammianus himself; but he will surely observe, with philosophic curiosity, the interesting and original picture of the manners of Rome.[1]

" The greatness of Rome (such is the language of the historian) was founded on the rare and almost incredible alliance of virtue and of fortune. The long period of her infancy was employed in a laborious struggle against the tribes of Italy, the neighbours and enemies of the rising city. In the strength and ardour of youth she sustained the storms of war, carried her victorious arms beyond the seas and the mountains, and brought home triumphal laurels from every country of the globe. At length, verging towards old age, and sometimes conquering by the terror only of her name, she sought the blessings of ease and tranquillity. The VENERABLE CITY, which had trampled on the necks of the fiercest nations, and established a system of laws, the perpetual guardians of justice and freedom, was content, like a wise and wealthy parent, to devolve on the Cæsars, her favourite sons, the care of governing her ample patrimony.[2] A secure and profound peace, such as had been once enjoyed in the reign of Numa, succeeded to the tumults of a republic; while Rome was still adored as the queen of the earth, and the subject nations still reverenced the name of the people and the majesty of the senate. But this native splendour (continues Ammianus) is degraded and sullied by the conduct of some nobles, who, unmindful of their own dignity and of that of their country, assume an unbounded licence of vice and folly. They contend with each other in the empty vanity of titles and surnames, and curiously select or invent the most lofty and sonorous appellations— Reburrus or Fabunius, Pagonius or Tarrasius[3]—which may

[1] It is incumbent on me to explain the liberties which I have taken with the text of Ammianus. 1. I have melted down into one piece the sixth chapter of the fourteenth and the fourth of the twenty-eighth book. 2. I have given order and connection to the confused mass of materials. 3. I have softened *some* extravagant hyperboles and pared away some superfluities of the original. 4. I have developed some observations which were insinuated rather than expressed. With these allowances my version will be found, not literal indeed, but faithful and exact.

[2] Claudian, who seems to have read the history of Ammianus, speaks of this great revolution in a much less courtly style:

> Postquam jura ferox in se communia Cæsar
> Transtulit; et lapsi mores; desuetaque priscis
> Artibus, in gremium pacis servile recessi.
>
> De Bell. Gildonico, v. 49.

[3] The minute diligence of antiquarians has not been able to verify these extraordinary names. I am of opinion that they were invented by the historian himself, who was afraid of any personal satire or application.

impress the ears of the vulgar with astonishment and respect.
From a vain ambition of perpetuating their memory, they affect
to multiply their likeness in statues of bronze and marble; nor
are they satisfied unless those statues are covered with plates
of gold; an honourable distinction, first granted to Acilius the
consul, after he had subdued by his arms and counsels the
power of king Antiochus. The ostentation of displaying, of
magnifying perhaps, the rent-roll of the estates which they possess
in all the provinces, from the rising to the setting sun, provokes
the just resentment of every man who recollects that their poor
and invincible ancestors were not distinguished from the meanest
of the soldiers by the delicacy of their food or the splendour of
their apparel.   But the modern nobles measure their rank and
consequence according to the loftiness of their chariots,[1] and the
weighty magnificence of their dress.   Their long robes of silk
and purple float in the wind; and as they are agitated, by art
or accident, they occasionally discover the under garments, the
rich tunics, embroidered with the figures of various animals.[2]
Followed by a train of fifty servants, and tearing up the pavement, they move along the streets with the same impetuous
speed as if they travelled with post-horses; and the example of
the senators is boldly imitated by the matrons and ladies, whose
covered carriages are continually driving round the immense
space of the city and suburbs.   Whenever these persons of high
distinction condescend to visit the public baths, they assume,
on their entrance, a tone of loud and insolent command, and
appropriate to their own use the conveniences which were
designed for the Roman people.   If, in these places of mixed

is certain, however, that the simple denominations of the Romans were
gradually lengthened to the number of four, five, or even seven, pompous
surnames; as for instance, Marcus Mæcius Mæmmius Furius Balburius
Cæcilianus Placidus.   See Noris, Cenotaph. Pisan. Dissert. iv. p. 438.

[1] The *carrucæ*, or coaches of the Romans, were often of solid silver
curiously carved and engraved; and the trappings of the mules or horses
were embossed with gold.   This magnificence continued from the reign of
Nero to that of Honorius; and the Appian way was covered with the
splendid equipages of the nobles, who came out to meet St. Melania when
she returned to Rome six years before the Gothic siege (Seneca, Epist.
lxxxvii.; Plin. Hist. Natur. xxxiii. 49; Paulin. Nolan. apud Baron. Annal.
Eccles. A.D. 397, No. 5).   Yet pomp is well exchanged for convenience;
and a plain modern coach that is hung upon springs is much preferable to
the silver or gold *carts* of antiquity, which rolled on the axletree, and were
exposed, for the most part, to the inclemency of the weather.

[2] In a homily of Asterius, bishop of Amasia, M. de Valois has discovered
(ad Ammian. xiv. 6) that this was a new fashion; that bears, wolves, lions,
and tigers, woods, hunting-matches, etc., were represented in embroidery;
and that the more pious coxcombs substituted the figure or legend of some
favourite saint.

and general resort, they meet any of the infamous ministers of
their pleasures, they express their affection by a tender embrace,
while they proudly decline the salutations of their fellow-citizens,
who are not permitted to aspire above the honour of kissing their
hands or their knees. As soon as they have indulged themselves
in the refreshment of the bath, they resume their rings and the
other ensigns of their dignity, select from their private wardrobe
of the finest linen, such as might suffice for a dozen persons, the
garments the most agreeable to their fancy, and maintain till
their departure the same haughty demeanour, which perhaps
might have been excused in the great Marcellus after the conquest of Syracuse. Sometimes indeed these heroes undertake
more arduous achievements: they visit their estates in Italy,
and procure themselves, by the toil of servile hands, the amusements of the chase.[1] If at any time, but more especially on a
hot day, they have courage to sail in their painted galleys from
the Lucrine lake[2] to their elegant villas on the sea-coast of
Puteoli and Caieta,[3] they compare their own expeditions to the
marches of Cæsar and Alexander. Yet should a fly presume
to settle on the silken folds of their gilded umbrellas, should a
sunbeam penetrate through some unguarded and imperceptible
chink, they deplore their intolerable hardships, and lament in
affected language that they were not born in the land of the
Cimmerians,[4] the regions of eternal darkness. In these journeys
into the country[5] the whole body of the household marches with

---

[1] See Pliny's Epistles, i. 6. Three large wild boars were allured and
taken in the toils without interrupting the studies of the philosophic sportsman.

[2] The change from the inauspicious word *Avernus*, which stands in the
text, is immaterial. The two lakes, Avernus and Lucrinus, communicated
with each other, and were fashioned by the stupendous moles of Agrippa
into the Julian port, which opened through a narrow entrance into the gulf
of Puteoli. Virgil, who resided on the spot, has described (Georgic ii. 161)
this work at the moment of its execution: and his commentators, especially
Catrou, have derived much light from Strabo, Suetonius, and Dion.
Earthquakes and volcanoes have changed the face of the country, and
turned the Lucrine lake, since the year 1538, into the Monte Nuovo. See
Camillo Pellegrino Discorsi della Campania Felice, p. 239, 244, etc. Antonii
Sanfelicii Campania, p. 13, 88.

[3] The regna Cumana et Puteolana; loca cætero quivalde expetenda,
interpellantium autem multitudine pæne fugienda. Cicero ad Attic. xiv.
16.

[4] The proverbial expression of *Cimmerian darkness* was originally
borrowed from the description of Homer (in the eleventh book of the
Odyssey) which he applies to a remote and fabulous country on the shores
of the ocean. See Erasmi Adagia, in his Works, tom. ii. p. 593, the
Leyden edition.

[5] We may learn from Seneca, Epist. cxxiii., three curious circumstances
relative to the journeys of the Romans. 1. They were preceded by a troop

their master.   In the same manner as the cavalry and infantry,
the heavy and the light armed troops, the advanced guard and
the rear, are marshalled by the skill of their military leaders, so the
domestic officers, who bear a rod as an ensign of authority, dis-
tribute and arrange the numerous train of slaves and attendants.
The baggage and wardrobe move in the front, and are immediately followed by a multitude of cooks and inferior ministers
employed in the service of the kitchens and of the table.   The
main body is composed of a promiscuous crowd of slaves,
increased by the accidental concourse of idle or dependent
plebeians.   The rear is closed by the favourite band of eunuchs,
distributed from age to youth, according to the order of seniority.
Their numbers and their deformity excite the horror of the indignant spectators, who are ready to execrate the memory of
Semiramis for the cruel art which she invented of frustrating the
purposes of nature, and of blasting in the bud the hopes of future
generations.   In the exercise of domestic jurisdiction the nobles
of Rome express an exquisite sensibility for any personal injury,
and a contemptuous indifference for the rest of the human
species.   When they have called for warm water, if a slave has
been tardy in his obedience, he is instantly chastised with three
hundred lashes; but should the same slave commit a wilful
murder, the master will mildly observe that he is a worthless
fellow, but that if he repeats the offence he shall not escape
punishment.   Hospitality was formerly the virtue of the
Romans; and every stranger who could plead either merit or
misfortune was relieved or rewarded by their generosity.   At
present, if a foreigner, perhaps of no contemptible rank, is introduced to one of the proud and wealthy senators, he is welcomed
indeed in the first audience with such warm professions and such
kind inquiries, that he retires enchanted with the affability of his
illustrious friend, and full of regret that he had so long delayed
his journey to Rome, the native seat of manners as well as of
empire.   Secure of a favourable reception, he repeats his visit
the ensuing day, and is mortified by the discovery that his person,
his name, and his country are already forgotten.   If he still has
resolution to persevere, he is gradually numbered in the train

of Numidian light-horse, who announced by a cloud of dust the approach
of a great man.   2. Their baggage-mules transported not only the precious
vases but even the fragile vessels of crystal and *murra*, which last is almost
proved, by the learned French translator of Seneca (tom. iii. p. 402-422),
to mean the porcelain of China and Japan.   3. The beautiful faces of the
young slaves were covered with a medicated crust, or ointment, which
secured them against the effects of the sun and frost.

of dependents, and obtains the permission to pay his assiduous and unprofitable court to a haughty patron, incapable of gratitude or friendship, who scarcely deigns to remark his presence, his departure, or his return. Whenever the rich prepare a solemn and popular entertainment,[1] whenever they celebrate with profuse and pernicious luxury their private banquets, the choice of the guests is the subject of anxious deliberation. The modest, the sober, and the learned are seldom preferred; and the nomenclators, who are commonly swayed by interested motives, have the address to insert in the list of invitations the obscure names of the most worthless of mankind. But the frequent and familiar companions of the great are those parasites who practise the most useful of all arts, the art of flattery; who eagerly applaud each word and every action of their immortal patron; gaze with rapture on his marble columns and variegated pavements, and strenuously praise the pomp and elegance which he is taught to consider as a part of his personal merit. At the Roman tables the birds, the *squirrels*,[2] or the fish, which appear of an uncommon size, are contemplated with curious attention; a pair of scales is accurately applied to ascertain their real weight; and, while the more rational guests are disgusted by the vain and tedious repetition, notaries are summoned to attest by an authentic record the truth of such a marvellous event. Another method of introduction into the houses and society of the great is derived from the profession of gaming, or, as it is more politely styled, of play. The confederates are united by a strict and

[1] Distributio solemnium sportularum. The *sportulæ*, or *sportellæ*, were small baskets supposed to contain a quantity of hot provisions of the value of 100 quadrantes, or twelvepence halfpenny, which were ranged in order in the hall, and ostentatiously distributed to the hungry or servile crowd who waited at the door. This indelicate custom is very frequently mentioned in the epigrams of Martial and the satires of Juvenal. See likewise Suetonius, in Claud. c. 21; in Neron. c. 16; in Domitian. c. 4, 7. These baskets of provisions were afterwards converted into large pieces of gold and silver coin, or plate, which were mutually given and accepted even by the persons of the highest rank (see Symmach. Epist. iv. 55, ix. 124, and Miscell. p. 256 [ed. Paris, 1604]), on solemn occasions, of consulships, marriages, etc.

[2] The want of an English name obliges me to refer to the common genus of squirrels, the Latin *glis*, the French *loir*; a little animal who inhabits the woods and remains torpid in cold weather (see Plin. Hist. Natur. viii. 82; Buffon, Hist. Naturelle, tom. viii. 158; Pennant's Synopsis of Quadrupeds, p. 289). The art of rearing and fattening great numbers of *gliers* was practised in Roman villas as a profitable article of rural economy (Varro, de Re Rusticâ, iii. 15). The excessive demand of them for luxurious tables was increased by the foolish prohibitions of the censors; and it is reported that they are still esteemed in modern Rome, and are frequently sent as presents by the Colonna princes (see Brotier, the last editor of Pliny, tom. ii. p. 458, apud Barbou, 1779).

indissoluble bond of friendship, or rather of conspiracy; a superior degree of skill in the *Tesserarian* art (which may be interpreted the game of dice and tables [1]) is a sure road to wealth and reputation. A master of that sublime science, who in a supper or assembly is placed below a magistrate, displays in his countenance the surprise and indignation which Cato might be supposed to feel when he was refused the prætorship by the votes of a capricious people. The acquisition of knowledge seldom engages the curiosity of the nobles, who abhor the fatigue and disdain the advantages of study; and the only books which they peruse are the Satires of Juvenal, and the verbose and fabulous histories of Marius Maximus.[2] The libraries which they have inherited from their fathers are secluded, like dreary sepulchres, from the light of day.[3] But the costly instruments of the theatre, flutes, and enormous lyres, and hydraulic organs, are constructed for their use; and the harmony of vocal and instrumental music is incessantly repeated in the palaces of Rome. In those palaces sound is preferred to sense, and the care of the body to that of the mind. It is allowed as a salutary maxim, that the light and frivolous suspicion of a contagious malady is of sufficient weight to excuse the visits of the most intimate friends; and even the servants who are despatched to make the decent inquiries are not suffered to return home till they have undergone the ceremony of a previous ablution. Yet this selfish and unmanly delicacy occasionally yields to the more imperious passion of avarice. The prospect of gain will urge a rich and gouty senator as far as Spoleto; every sentiment of arrogance and dignity is subdued by the hopes of an inheritance, or even of a legacy; and a wealthy

[1] This game, which might be translated by the more familiar names of *trictrac*, or *backgammon*, was a favourite amusement of the gravest Romans; and old Mucius Scævola, the lawyer, had the reputation of a very skilful player. It was called *ludus duodecim scriptorum*, from the twelve *scripta* or lines which equally divided the *alveolus* or table. On these the two armies, the white and the black, each consisting of fifteen men, or *calculi*, were regularly placed and alternately moved according to the laws of the game and the chances of the *tesseræ* or dice. Dr. Hyde, who diligently traces the history and varieties of the *nerdiludium* (a name of Persic etymology) from Ireland to Japan, pours forth on this trifling subject a copious torrent of classic and Oriental learning. See Syntagma Dissertat. tom. ii. p. 217-405.

[2] Marius Maximus, homo omnium verbosissimus, qui et mythistoricis se voluminibus implicavit. Vopiscus in Hist. August. p. 242 [Vopisc. Firm. c. 1]. He wrote the Lives of the Emperors from Trajan to Alexander Severus. See Gerard Vossius de Historicis Latin. l. ii. c. 3, in his Works, vol. iv. p. 57.

[3] This satire is probably exaggerated. The Saturnalia of Macrobius, and the Epistles of Jerom, afford satisfactory proofs that Christian theology and classic literature were studiously cultivated by several Romans of both sexes and of the highest rank.

childless citizen is the most powerful of the Romans. The art of obtaining the signature of a favourable testament, and sometimes of hastening the moment of its execution, is perfectly understood; and it has happened that in the same house, though in different apartments, a husband and a wife, with the laudable design of overreaching each other, have summoned their respective lawyers, to declare at the same time their mutual but contradictory intentions. The distress which follows and chastises extravagant luxury often reduces the great to the use of the most humiliating expedients. When they desire to borrow, they employ the base and supplicating style of the slave in the comedy; but when they are called upon to pay, they assume the royal and tragic declamation of the grandsons of Hercules. If the demand is repeated, they readily procure some trusty sycophant, instructed to maintain a charge of poison, or magic, against the insolent creditor, who is seldom released from prison till he has signed a discharge of the whole debt. These vices, which degrade the moral character of the Romans, are mixed with a puerile superstition that disgraces their understanding. They listen with confidence to the predictions of haruspices, who pretend to read in the entrails of victims the signs of future greatness and prosperity; and there are many who do not presume either to bathe or to die, or to appear in public, till they have diligently consulted, according to the rules of astrology, the situation of Mercury and the aspect of the moon.[1] It is singular enough that this vain credulity may often be discovered among the profane sceptics who impiously doubt or deny the existence of a celestial power."

In populous cities, which are the seat of commerce and manufactures, the middle ranks of inhabitants, who derive their subsistence from the dexterity or labour of their hands, are commonly the most prolific, the most useful, and, in that sense, the most respectable part of the community. But the plebeians of Rome, who disdained such sedentary and servile arts, had been oppressed from the earliest times by the weight of debt and usury, and the husbandman, during the term of his military service, was obliged to abandon the cultivation of his farm.[2] The lands of Italy,

---

[1] Macrobius, the friend of these Roman nobles, considered the stars as the cause, or at least the signs, of future events (de Somn. Scipion. l. i. c. 19, p. 68).

[2] The histories of Livy (see particularly vi. 36) are full of the extortions of the rich and the sufferings of the poor debtors. The melancholy story of a brave old soldier (Dionys. Hal. l. vi. c. 26, p. 347, edit. Hudson, and Livy, ii. 23) must have been frequently repeated in those primitive times, which have been so undeservedly praised.

which had been originally divided among the families of free and indigent proprietors, were insensibly purchased or usurped by the avarice of the nobles; and in the age which preceded the fall of the republic, it was computed that only two thousand citizens were possessed of any independent substance.[1] Yet as long as the people bestowed by their suffrages the honours of the state, the command of the legions, and the administration of wealthy provinces, their conscious pride alleviated in some measure the hardships of poverty; and their wants were seasonably supplied by the ambitious liberality of the candidates, who aspired to secure a venal majority in the thirty-five tribes, or the hundred and ninety-three centuries, of Rome. But when the prodigal commons had imprudently alienated not only the *use*, but the *inheritance*, of power, they sunk, under the reign of the Cæsars, into a vile and wretched populace, which must, in a few generations, have been totally extinguished, if it had not been continually recruited by the manumission of slaves and the influx of strangers. As early as the time of Hadrian it was the just complaint of the ingenuous natives that the capital had attracted the vices of the universe and the manners of the most opposite nations. The intemperance of the Gauls, the cunning and levity of the Greeks, the savage obstinacy of the Egyptians and Jews, the servile temper of the Asiatics, and the dissolute, effeminate prostitution of the Syrians, were mingled in the various multitude, which, under the proud and false denomination of Romans, presumed to despise their fellow-subjects, and even their sovereigns, who dwelt beyond the precincts of the ETERNAL CITY.[2]

Yet the name of that city was still pronounced with respect: the frequent and capricious tumults of its inhabitants were indulged with impunity; and the successors of Constantine, instead of crushing the last remains of the democracy by the strong arm of military power, embraced the mild policy of

---

[1] Non esse in civitate duo millia hominum qui rem haberent. Cicero, Offic. ii. 21, and Comment. Paul. Manut. in edit. Græv. This vague computation was made A.U.C. 649, in a speech of the tribune Philippus, and it was his object, as well as that of the Gracchi (see Plutarch), to deplore, and perhaps to exaggerate, the misery of the common people.

[2] See the third Satire (60-125) of Juvenal, who indignantly complains,

—— Quamvis quota portio fæcis Achæi!
Jampridem Syrus in Tiberim defluxit Orontes;
Et linguam et mores, etc.

Seneca, when he proposes to comfort his mother (Consolat. ad Helv. c. 6) by the reflection that a great part of mankind were in a state of exile, reminds her how few of the inhabitants of Rome were born in the city.

Augustus, and studied to relieve the poverty and to amuse the idleness of an innumerable people.[1] I. For the convenience of the lazy plebeians, the monthly distributions of corn were converted into a daily allowance of bread; a great number of ovens were constructed and maintained at the public expense; and at the appointed hour, each citizen, who was furnished with a ticket, ascended the flight of steps which had been assigned to his peculiar quarter or division, and received, either as a gift or at a very low price, a loaf of bread of the weight of three pounds for the use of his family. II. The forests of Lucania, whose acorns fattened large droves of wild hogs,[2] afforded, as a species of tribute, a plentiful supply of cheap and wholesome meat. During five months of the year a regular allowance of bacon was distributed to the poorer citizens; and the annual consumption of the capital, at a time when it was much declined from its former lustre, was ascertained, by an edict of Valentinian the Third, at three millions six hundred and twenty-eight thousand pounds.[3] III. In the manners of antiquity the use of oil was indispensable for the lamp as well as for the bath, and the annual tax which was imposed on Africa for the benefit of Rome amounted to the weight of three millions of pounds, to the measure, perhaps, of three hundred thousand English gallons. IV. The anxiety of Augustus to provide the metropolis with sufficient plenty of corn was not extended beyond that necessary article of human subsistence; and when the popular clamour accused the dearness and scarcity of wine, a proclamation was issued by the grave reformer to remind his subjects that no man could reasonably complain of thirst, since the aqueducts of Agrippa had introduced into the city so many copious streams

[1] Almost all that is said of the bread, bacon, oil, wine, etc., may be found in the fourteenth book of the Theodosian Code, which expressly treats of the *police* of the great cities. See particularly the titles iii. iv. xv. xvi. xvii. xxiv. The collateral testimonies are produced in Godefroy's Commentary, and it is needless to transcribe them. According to a law of Theodosius, which appreciates in money the military allowance, a piece of gold (eleven shillings) was equivalent to eighty pounds of bacon, or to eighty pounds of oil, or to twelve modii (or pecks) of salt (Cod. Theod. l. viii. tit. iv. leg. 17). This equation, compared with another of seventy pounds of bacon for an *amphora* (Cod. Theod. l. xiv. tit. iv. leg. 4), fixes the price of wine at about sixteen-pence the gallon.

[2] The anonymous author of the Description of the World (p. 14, in tom. iii. Geograph. Minor. Hudson) observes of Lucania, in his barbarous Latin, Regio obtima, et ipsa omnibus habundans, et lardum multum foras emittit: propter quod est in montibus, cujus æscam animalium variam.

[3] See Novell. ad calcem Cod. Theod. D. Valent. l. i. tit. xv. [tom. vi. App. p. 28, ed. Gothofr.]. This law was published at Rome, June 29th, A.D. 452.

of pure and salubrious water.[1] This rigid sobriety was insensibly relaxed; and, although the generous design of Aurelian[2] does not appear to have been executed in its full extent, the use of wine was allowed on very easy and liberal terms.   The administration of the public cellars was delegated to a magistrate of honourable rank; and a considerable part of the vintage of Campania was reserved for the fortunate inhabitants of Rome.

The stupendous aqueducts, so justly celebrated by the praises of Augustus himself, replenished the *Thermæ*, or baths, which had been constructed in every part of the city with Imperial magnificence.   The baths of Antoninus Caracalla, which were open, at stated hours, for the indiscriminate service of the senators and the people, contained above sixteen hundred seats of marble; and more than three thousand were reckoned in the baths of Diocletian.[3]   The walls of the lofty apartments were covered with curious mosaics, that imitated the art of the pencil in the elegance of design and the variety of colours.   The Egyptian granite was beautifully encrusted with the precious green marble of Numidia; the perpetual stream of hot water was poured into the capacious basins through so many wide mouths of bright and massy silver; and the meanest Roman could purchase, with a small copper coin, the daily enjoyment of a scene of pomp and luxury which might excite the envy of the kings of Asia.[4]   From these stately palaces issued a swarm of dirty and ragged plebeians, without shoes and without a mantle; who loitered away whole days in the street or Forum to hear news and to hold disputes; who dissipated in extravagant gaming the miserable pittance of their wives and children; and spent the hours of the night in obscure taverns and brothels in the indulgence of gross and vulgar sensuality.[5]

But the most lively and splendid amusement of the idle multitude depended on the frequent exhibition of public games and

[1] Sueton. in August. c. 42.   The utmost debauch of the emperor himself, in his favourite wine of Rhætia, never exceeded a *sextarius* (an English pint).   Id. c. 77.   Torrentius ad loc. and Arbuthnot's Tables, p. 86.

[2] His design was to plant vineyards along the sea-coast of Etruria (Vopiscus, in Hist. August. p. 225 [in Aurel. c. 48]), the dreary, unwholesome, uncultivated *Maremme* of modern Tuscany.

[3] Olympiodor. apud Phot. p. 197 [p. 63, ed. Bekker].

[4] Seneca (Epistol. lxxxvi.) compares the baths of Scipio Africanus, at his villa of Liternum, with the magnificence (which was continually increasing) of the public baths of Rome, long before the stately Thermæ of Antoninus and Diocletian were erected.   The *quadrans* paid for admission was the quarter of the *as*, about one-eighth of an English penny.

[5] Ammianus (l. xiv. c. 6, and l. xxviii. c. 4), after describing the luxury and pride of the nobles of Rome, exposes, with equal indignation, the vices and follies of the common people.

spectacles. The piety of Christian princes had suppressed the inhuman combats of gladiators; but the Roman people still considered the Circus as their home, their temple, and the seat of the republic. The impatient crowd rushed at the dawn of day to secure their places, and there were many who passed a sleepless and anxious night in the adjacent porticos. From the morning to the evening, careless of the sun or of the rain, the spectators, who sometimes amounted to the number of four hundred thousand, remained in eager attention; their eyes fixed on the horses and charioteers, their minds agitated with hope and fear for the success of the *colours* which they espoused; and the happiness of Rome appeared to hang on the event of a race.[1] The same immoderate ardour inspired their clamours and their applause as often as they were entertained with the hunting of wild beasts and the various modes of theatrical representation. These representations in modern capitals may deserve to be considered as a pure and elegant school of taste, and perhaps of virtue. But the Tragic and Comic Muse of the Romans, who seldom aspired beyond the imitation of Attic genius,[2] had been almost totally silent since the fall of the republic;[3] and their place was unworthily occupied by licentious farce, effeminate music, and splendid pageantry. The pantomimes,[4] who maintained their reputation from the age of Augustus to the sixth century, expressed, without the use of words, the various fables of the gods and heroes of antiquity; and the perfection of their art, which

---

[1] Juvenal, Satir. xi. 191, etc. The expressions of the historian Ammianus are not less strong and animated than those of the satirist; and both the one and the other painted from the life. The numbers which the great Circus was capable of receiving are taken from the *original Notitiæ* of the city. The differences between them prove that they did not transcribe each other; but the sum may appear incredible, though the country on these occasions flocked to the city.

[2] Sometimes, indeed, they composed original pieces.

——— Vestigia Græca

Ausi deserere et celebrare domestica facta.

Horat. Epistol. ad Pisones, 285, and the learned though perplexed note of Dacier, who might have allowed the name of tragedies to the *Brutus* and the *Decius* of Pacuvius, or to the *Cato* of Maternus. The *Octavia*, ascribed to one of the Senecas, still remains a very unfavourable specimen of Roman tragedy.

[3] In the time of Quintilian and Pliny a tragic poet was reduced to the imperfect method of hiring a great room, and reading his play to the company, whom he invited for that purpose. (See Dialog. de Oratoribus, c. 9, 10, and Plin. Epistol. vii. 17.)

[4] See the dialogue of Lucian, entitled de Saltatione, tom. ii. p. 265-317, edit. Reitz. The pantomimes obtained the honourable name of χειροσόφοι; and it was required that they should be conversant with almost every art and science. Burette (in the Mémoires de l'Académie des Inscriptions, tom. i. p. 127, etc.) has given a short history of the art of pantomimes.

sometimes disarmed the gravity of the philosopher, always excited the applause and wonder of the people. The vast and magnificent theatres of Rome were filled by three thousand female dancers, and by three thousand singers, with the masters of the respective choruses. Such was the popular favour which they enjoyed, that, in a time of scarcity, when all strangers were banished from the city, the merit of contributing to the public pleasures exempted *them* from a law which was strictly executed against the professors of the liberal arts.[1]

It is said that the foolish curiosity of Elagabalus attempted to discover, from the quantity of spiders' webs, the number of the inhabitants of Rome. A more rational method of inquiry might not have been undeserving of the attention of the wisest princes, who could easily have resolved a question so important for the Roman government and so interesting to succeeding ages. The births and deaths of the citizens were duly registered; and if any writer of antiquity had condescended to mention the annual amount, or the common average, we might now produce some satisfactory calculation which would destroy the extravagant assertions of critics, and perhaps confirm the modest and probable conjectures of philosophers.[2] The most diligent researches have collected only the following circumstances, which, slight and imperfect as they are, may tend in some degree to illustrate the question of the populousness of ancient Rome. I. When the capital of the empire was besieged by the Goths, the circuit of the walls was accurately measured by Ammonius, the mathematician, who found it equal to twenty-one miles.[3] It should not be forgotten that the form of the city was almost that of a circle, the geometrical figure which is known to contain the largest space within any given circumference. II. The architect Vitruvius, who flourished in the Augustan age, and whose evidence, on this occasion, has peculiar weight and authority, observes that the

[1] Ammianus, l. xiv. c. 6. He complains, with decent indignation, that the streets of Rome were filled with crowds of females, who might have given children to the state, but whose only occupation was to curl and dress their hair, and jactari volubilibus gyris, dum exprimunt innumera simulacra, quæ finxere fabulæ theatrales.

[2] Lipsius (tom. iii. p. 423, de Magnitud. Romana, l. iii. c. 3) and Isaac Vossius (Observat. Var. p. 26-34) have indulged strange dreams, of four, or eight, or fourteen millions in Rome. Mr. Hume (Essays, vol. i. p. 450-457), with admirable good sense and scepticism, betrays some secret disposition to extenuate the populousness of ancient times.

[3] Olympiodor. ap. Phot. p. 197 [p. 63, ed. Bekker]. See Fabricius, Biblioth. Græc. tom. ix. p. 400.

[The name of the mathematician was Ammon, not Ammonius, and notwithstanding this statement in Olympiodorus, the actual circumference of the walk of Rome could not have exceeded twelve miles.—O. S.]

innumerable habitations of the Roman people would have spread themselves far beyond the narrow limits of the city; and that the want of ground, which was probably contracted on every side by gardens and villas, suggested the common, though inconvenient, practice of raising the houses to a considerable height in the air.[1] But the loftiness of these buildings, which often consisted of hasty work and insufficient materials, was the cause of frequent and fatal accidents; and it was repeatedly enacted by Augustus, as well as by Nero, that the height of private edifices within the walls of Rome should not exceed the measure of seventy feet from the ground.[2] III. Juvenal[3] laments, as it should seem from his own experience, the hardships of the poorer citizens, to whom he addresses the salutary advice of emigrating, without delay, from the smoke of Rome, since they might purchase in the little towns of Italy a cheerful, commodious dwelling at the same price which they annually paid for a dark and miserable lodging. House-rent was therefore immoderately dear: the rich acquired, at an enormous expense, the ground, which they covered with palaces and gardens; but the body of the Roman people was crowded into a narrow space; and the different floors and apartments of the same house were divided, as it is still the custom of Paris and other cities, among several families of plebeians.   IV. The total number of houses in the fourteen regions of the city is accurately stated in the description of Rome composed under the reign of Theodosius, and they amount to forty-eight thousand three hundred and eighty-two.[4]   The two classes of *domus*

---

[1] In eâ autem majestate urbis, et civium infinitâ frequentiâ innumerabiles habitationes opus fuit explicare. Ergo cum recipere non posset area plana tantam multitudinem [ad habitandum] in urbe, ad auxilium altitudinis ædificiorum res ipsa coëgit devenire. Vitruv. ii. 8.   This passage, which I owe to Vossius, is clear, strong, and comprehensive.

[2] The successive testimonies of Pliny, Aristides, Claudian, Rutilius, etc., prove the insufficiency of these restrictive edicts.   See Lipsius, de Magnitud. Romana, l. iii. c. 4.

———— Tabulata tibi jam tertia fumant;
Tu nescis; nam si gradibus trepidatur ab imis
Ultimus ardebit, quem tegula sola tuetur
A pluviâ.   Juvenal, Satir. iii. 199.

[3] Read the whole third Satire, but particularly 166, 223, etc.   The description of a crowded *insula*, or lodging-house, in Petronius (c. 95, 97), perfectly tallies with the complaints of Juvenal; and we learn from legal authority that, in the time of Augustus (Heineccius, Hist. Juris Roman. c. iv. p. 181), the ordinary rent of the several *cœnacula*, or apartments of an *insula*, annually produced forty thousand sesterces, between three and four hundred pounds sterling (Pandect. l. xix. tit. ii. No. 30), a sum which proves at once the large extent and high value of those common buildings.

[4] This sum total is composed of 1780 *domus*, or great houses, of 46,602 *insulæ*, or plebeian habitations (see Nardini, Roma Antica, l. iii. p. 88);

and of *insulæ*, into which they are divided, include all the
habitations of the capital, of every rank and condition, from the
marble palace of the Anicii, with a numerous establishment of
freedmen and slaves, to the lofty and narrow lodging-house
where the poet Codrus and his wife were permitted to hire a
wretched garret immediately under the tiles. If we adopt the
same average which, under similar circumstances, has been
found applicable to Paris,[1] and indifferently allow about twenty-
five persons for each house, of every degree, we may fairly
estimate the inhabitants of Rome at twelve hundred thousand:
a number which cannot be thought excessive for the capital of a
mighty empire, though it exceeds the populousness of the
greatest cities of modern Europe.[2]

Such was the state of Rome under the reign of Honorius, at
the time when the Gothic army formed the siege, or rather the
blockade, of the city.[3] By a skilful disposition of his numerous
and these numbers are ascertained by the agreement of the texts of the
different *Notitiæ*. Nardini, l. viii. p. 498, 500.

[1] See that accurate writer M. de Messance, Recherches sur la Population,
p. 175-187. From probable or certain grounds he assigns to Paris 23,565
houses, 71,114 families, and 576,630 inhabitants.

[2] This computation is not very different from that which M. Brotier, the
last editor of Tacitus (tom. ii. p. 380), has assumed from similar principles;
though he seems to aim at a degree of precision which it is neither possible
nor important to obtain.

[Since the time of Gibbon, the populousness of ancient Rome has been
investigated by several writers, whose names are below. De la Malle has
reduced the population 562,000 souls, and Höck 2,265,000. The estimate
of the former is much too low. The most important datum for estimating
the population is the statement in the Monumentum Ancyranum, that the
plebs urbana in the year 5 B.C. consisted of 320,000 males. This number
contains neither children under 11 years of age (Suetonius, Aug. 41), nor
senators, nor equites, nor slaves. The females and children under eleven
must have been at least double, which would make the plebs urbana
640,000. Höck supposes that as the 320,000 were the persons who received
the *congiaria* from the state, they were only the poorer members of the
plebs urbana, and that the whole number of the latter amounted to
1,250,000. Mommsen, however, has satisfactorily proved that all Roman
citizens received the *congiaria*, with the exception of the senators and the
equites. The latter may have been about 10,000. The number of slaves
was immense, and was at least equal to or double the male population.
In addition to these we must reckon the military and the great mass of
foreigners always resident in Rome, so that the population could not have
been far short of 2,000,000. If this should be considered too large a
number to be distributed among the 1780 domus and the 46,602 insulæ, it
must be remembered that the domus were large palaces, and the insulæ
contained numerous separate dwellings, being divided from other edifices
by a space of at least five feet, whence their name. Besides this, the
slaves were very densely crowded, and lived in cellars and subterranean
dwellings under the public edifices.—O. S.]

[3] For the events of the first siege of Rome, which are often confounded
with those of the second and third, see Zosimus, l. v. [c. 38-42] p. 350-354;
Sozomen, l. ix. c. 6; Olympiodorus, ap. Phot. p. 180 [p. 57, ed. Bekk.];
Philostorgius, l. xii. c. 3; and Godefroy, Dissertat. p. 467-475.

forces, who impatiently watched the moment of an assault, Alaric encompassed the walls, commanded the twelve principal gates, intercepted all communication with the adjacent country, and vigilantly guarded the navigation of the Tiber, from which the Romans derived the surest and most plentiful supply of provisions. The first emotions of the nobles and of the people were those of surprise and indignation, that a vile barbarian should dare to insult the capital of the world; but their arrogance was soon humbled by misfortune; and their unmanly rage, instead of being directed against an enemy in arms, was meanly exercised on a defenceless and innocent victim. Perhaps in the person of Serena the Romans might have respected the niece of Theodosius, the aunt, nay even the adoptive mother, of the reigning emperor; they abhorred the widow of Stilicho; and they listened with credulous passion to the tale of calumny which accused her of maintaining a secret and criminal correspondence with the Gothic invader. Actuated, or overawed, by the same popular frenzy, the senate, without requiring any evidence of her guilt, pronounced the sentence of her death. Serena was ignominiously strangled; and the infatuated multitude were astonished to find that this cruel act of injustice did not immediately produce the retreat of the barbarians and the deliverance of the city. That unfortunate city gradually experienced the distress of scarcity, and at length the horrid calamities of famine. The daily allowance of three pounds of bread was reduced to one-half, to one-third, to nothing; and the price of corn still continued to rise in a rapid and extravagant proportion. The poorer citizens, who were unable to purchase the necessaries of life, solicited the precarious charity of the rich; and for a while the public misery was alleviated by the humanity of Læta, the widow of the emperor Gratian, who had fixed her residence at Rome, and consecrated, to the use of the indigent, the princely revenue which she annually received from the grateful successors of her husband.[1] But these private and temporary donatives were insufficient to appease the hunger of a numerous people; and the progress of famine invaded the marble palaces of the senators themselves. The persons of both sexes, who had been educated in the enjoyment of ease and luxury, discovered how little is requisite to supply the demands of nature; and lavished their unavailing treasures of gold and silver to obtain the coarse and scanty sustenance which they would formerly have rejected with disdain.

---

[1] The mother of Læta was named Pissumena. Her father, family, and country are unknown. Ducange, Fam. Byzantin. p. 59.

The food the most repugnant to sense or imagination, the aliments the most unwholesome and pernicious to the constitution, were eagerly devoured, and fiercely disputed, by the rage of hunger. A dark suspicion was entertained that some desperate wretches fed on the bodies of their fellow-creatures whom they had secretly murdered; and even mothers (such was the horrid conflict of the two most powerful instincts implanted by nature in the human breast), even mothers are said to have tasted the flesh of their slaughtered infants![1] Many thousands of the inhabitants of Rome expired in their houses, or in the streets, for want of sustenance; and as the public sepulchres without the walls were in the power of the enemy, the stench which arose from so many putrid and unburied carcasses infected the air; and the miseries of famine were succeeded and aggravated by the contagion of a pestilential disease. The assurances of speedy and effectual relief, which were repeatedly transmitted from the court of Ravenna, supported, for some time, the fainting resolution of the Romans, till at length the despair of any human aid tempted them to accept the offers of a preternatural deliverance. Pompeianus, præfect of the city, had been persuaded, by the art or fanaticism of some Tuscan diviners, that, by the mysterious force of spells and sacrifices, they could extract the lightning from the clouds, and point those celestial fires against the camp of the barbarians.[2] The important secret was communicated to Innocent, the bishop of Rome; and the successor of St. Peter is accused, perhaps without foundation, of preferring the safety

---

[1] Ad nefandos cibos erupit esurientium rabies, et sua invicem membra aniarunt, dum mater non parcit lactenti infantiæ; et recipit utero, quem paullò ante effuderat. Jerom. ad Principiam, tom. i. p. 121 [Ep. cxxvii. tom. i. p. 953, ed. Vallars.]. The same horrid circumstance is likewise told of the sieges of Jerusalem and Paris. For the latter, compare the tenth book of the Henriade, and the Journal de Henri IV. tom. i. p. 47-83; and observe that a plain narrative of facts is much more pathetic than the most laboured descriptions of epic poetry.

[2] Zosimus (l. v. [c. 41] p. 355, 356) speaks of these ceremonies like a Greek unacquainted with the national superstition of Rome and Tuscany. I suspect that they consisted of two parts, the secret and the public; the former were probably an imitation of the arts and spells by which Numa had drawn down Jupiter and his thunder on Mount Aventine.

———— Quid agant laqueis, quæ carmina dicant,
Quâque trahant superis sedibus arte Jovem,
Scire nefas homini.

The ancilia or shields of Mars, the pignora Imperii, which were carried in solemn procession on the calends of March, derived their origin from this mysterious event (Ovid. Fast. iii. 259-398). It was probably designed to revive this ancient festival, which had been suppressed by Theodosius. In that case we recover a chronological date (March the 1st, A.D. 409) which has not hitherto been observed.

of the republic to the rigid severity of the Christian worship. But when the question was agitated in the senate; when it was proposed, as an essential condition, that those sacrifices should be performed in the Capitol, by the authority and in the presence of the magistrates; the majority of that respectable assembly, apprehensive either of the Divine or of the Imperial displeasure, refused to join in an act which appeared almost equivalent to the public restoration of Paganism.[1]

The last resource of the Romans was in the clemency, or at least in the moderation, of the king of the Goths. The senate, who in this emergency assumed the supreme powers of government, appointed two ambassadors to negotiate with the enemy. This important trust was delegated to Basilius, a senator of Spanish extraction, and already conspicuous in the administration of provinces; and to John, the first tribune of the notaries, who was peculiarly qualified, by his dexterity in business, as well as by his former intimacy with the Gothic prince. When they were introduced into his presence, they declared, perhaps in a more lofty style than became their abject condition, that the Romans were resolved to maintain their dignity, either in peace or war; and that, if Alaric refused them a fair and honourable capitulation, he might sound his trumpets, and prepare to give battle to an innumerable people, exercised in arms and animated by despair. "The thicker the hay, the easier it is mowed," was the concise reply of the barbarian; and this rustic metaphor was accompanied by a loud and insulting laugh, expressive of his contempt for the menaces of an unwarlike populace, enervated by luxury before they were emaciated by famine. He then condescended to fix the ransom which he would accept as the price of his retreat from the walls of Rome: *all* the gold and silver in the city, whether it were the property of the state, or of individuals; *all* the rich and precious movables; and *all* the slaves who could prove their title to the name of *barbarians*. The ministers of the senate presumed to ask, in a modest and suppliant tone, "If such, O king! are your demands, what do you intend to leave us?" "YOUR LIVES," replied the haughty conqueror: they trembled and retired. Yet before they retired, a short suspension of arms was granted, which allowed some time for a more temperate negotiation. The stern features of Alaric were insensibly relaxed; he abated much of the rigour of his

---

[1] Sozomen (l. ix. c. 6) insinuates that the experiment was actually though unsuccessfully made, but he does not mention the name of Innocent; and Tillemont (Mém. Ecclés. tom. x. p. 645) is determined not to believe that a pope could be guilty of such impious condescension.

terms; and at length consented to raise the siege, on the immediate payment of five thousand pounds of gold, of thirty thousand pounds of silver, of four thousand robes of silk, of three thousand pieces of fine scarlet cloth, and of three thousand pounds weight of pepper.[1] But the public treasury was exhausted; the annual rents of the great estates in Italy and the provinces were intercepted by the calamities of war; the gold and gems had been exchanged, during the famine, for the vilest sustenance; the hoards of secret wealth were still concealed by the obstinacy of avarice; and some remains of consecrated spoils afforded the only resource that could avert the impending ruin of the city. As soon as the Romans had satisfied the rapacious demands of Alaric, they were restored, in some measure, to the enjoyment of peace and plenty. Several of the gates were cautiously opened; the importation of provisions from the river and the adjacent country was no longer obstructed by the Goths; the citizens resorted in crowds to the free market which was held during three days in the suburbs; and while the merchants who undertook this gainful trade made a considerable profit, the future subsistence of the city was secured by the ample magazines which were deposited in the public and private granaries. A more regular discipline than could have been expected was maintained in the camp of Alaric; and the wise barbarian justified his regard for the faith of treaties, by the just severity with which he chastised a party of licentious Goths who had insulted some Roman citizens on the road to Ostia. His army, enriched by the contributions of the capital, slowly advanced into the fair and fruitful province of Tuscany, where he proposed to establish his winter-quarters; and the Gothic standard became the refuge of forty thousand barbarian slaves, who had broke their chains, and aspired, under the command of their great deliverer, to revenge the injuries and the disgrace of their cruel servitude. About the same time he received a more honourable reinforcement of Goths and Huns, whom Adolphus,[2]

---

[1] Pepper was a favourite ingredient of the most expensive Roman cookery, and the best sort commonly sold for fifteen denarii, or ten shillings, the pound. See Pliny, Hist. Natur. xii. 14. It was brought from India; and the same country, the coast of Malabar, still affords the greatest plenty; but the improvement of trade and navigation has multiplied the quantity and reduced the price. See Histoire Politique et Philosophique, etc., tom. i. p. 457.

[2] This Gothic chieftain is called, by Jornandes and Isidore, *Athaulphus*; by Zosimus and Orosius, *Ataulphus*; and by Olympiodorus, *Adaoulphus*. I have used the celebrated name of *Adolphus*, which seems to be authorised by the practice of the Swedes, the sons or brothers of the ancient Goths.

the brother of his wife, had conducted, at his pressing invitation, from the banks of the Danube to those of the Tiber, and who had cut their way, with some difficulty and loss, through the superior numbers of the Imperial troops. A victorious leader, who united the daring spirit of a barbarian with the art and discipline of a Roman general, was at the head of an hundred thousand fighting men; and Italy pronounced with terror and respect the formidable name of Alaric.[1]

At the distance of fourteen centuries we may be satisfied with relating the military exploits of the conquerors of Rome, without presuming to investigate the motives of their political conduct. In the midst of his apparent prosperity, Alaric was conscious, perhaps, of some secret weakness, some internal defect; or perhaps the moderation which he displayed was intended only to deceive and disarm the easy credulity of the ministers of Honorius. The king of the Goths repeatedly declared that it was his desire to be considered as the friend of peace and of the Romans. Three senators, at his earnest request, were sent ambassadors to the court of Ravenna, to solicit the exchange of hostages and the conclusion of the treaty; and the proposals which he more clearly expressed during the course of the negotiations could only inspire a doubt of his sincerity, as they might seem inadequate to the state of his fortune. The barbarian still aspired to the rank of master-general of the armies of the West; he stipulated an annual subsidy of corn and money; and he chose the provinces of Dalmatia, Noricum, and Venetia for the seat of his new kingdom, which would have commanded the important communication between Italy and the Danube. If these modest terms should be rejected, Alaric showed a disposition to relinquish his pecuniary demands, and even to content himself with the possession of Noricum; an exhausted and impoverished country, perpetually exposed to the inroads of the barbarians of Germany.[2] But the hopes of peace were disappointed by the weak obstinacy, or interested views, of the minister Olympius. Without listening to the salutary remonstrances of the senate, he dismissed their ambassadors under the conduct of a military escort, too numerous for a retinue of honour, and too feeble for an army of defence. Six thousand Dalmatians, the flower of the Imperial legions, were ordered to march from Ravenna to Rome, through an open country which

---

[1] The treaty between Alaric and the Romans, etc., is taken from Zosimus, l. v. [c. 41, *sqq.*] p. 354, 355, 358, 359, 362, 363. The additional circumstances are too few and trifling to require any other quotation.

[2] Zosimus, l. v. [c. 48] p. 367, 368, 369.

was occupied by the formidable myriads of the barbarians. These brave legionaries, encompassed and betrayed, fell a sacrifice to ministerial folly; their general, Valens, with an hundred soldiers, escaped from the field of battle; and one of the ambassadors, who could no longer claim the protection of the law of nations, was obliged to purchase his freedom with a ransom of thirty thousand pieces of gold. Yet Alaric, instead of resenting this act of impotent hostility, immediately renewed his proposals of peace, and the second embassy of the Roman senate, which derived weight and dignity from the presence of Innocent, bishop of the city, was guarded from the dangers of the road by a detachment of Gothic soldiers.[1]

Olympius[2] might have continued to insult the just resentment of a people who loudly accused him as the author of the public calamities, but his power was undermined by the secret intrigues of the palace. The favourite eunuchs transferred the government of Honorius and the empire to Jovius, the Prætorian præfect—an unworthy servant, who did not atone by the merit of personal attachment for the errors and misfortunes of his administration. The exile, or escape, of the guilty Olympius reserved him for more vicissitudes of fortune: he experienced the adventures of an obscure and wandering life; he again rose to power; he fell a second time into disgrace; his ears were cut off —he expired under the lash—and his ignominious death afforded a grateful spectacle to the friends of Stilicho. After the removal of Olympius, whose character was deeply tainted with religious fanaticism, the Pagans and heretics were delivered from the impolitic proscription which excluded them from the dignities of the state. The brave Gennerid,[3] a soldier of barbarian origin, who still adhered to the worship of his ancestors, had been obliged to lay aside the military belt; and though he was repeatedly assured by the emperor himself that laws were not made for persons of his rank or merit, he refused to accept any partial dis-

---

[1] Zosimus, l. v. [c. 45] p. 360, 361, 362. The bishop, by remaining at Ravenna, escaped the impending calamities of the city. Orosius, l. vii. c. 39, p. 573.

[2] For the adventures of Olympius and his successors in the ministry, see Zosimus, l. v. [c. 46] p. 363, 365, 366; and Olympiodor. ap. Phot. p. 180, 181 [p. 57, ed. Bekk.].

[3] Zosimus (l. v. [c. 46] p. 364) relates this circumstance with visible complacency, and celebrates the character of Gennerid as the last glory of expiring Paganism. Very different were the sentiments of the council of Carthage, who deputed four bishops to the court of Ravenna, to complain of the law which had been just enacted, that all conversions to Christianity should be free and voluntary. See Baronius, Annal. Eccles. A.D. 409, No. 12; A.D. 410, No. 47, 48.

pensation, and persevered in honourable disgrace till he had extorted a general act of justice from the distress of the Roman government. The conduct of Gennerid in the important station to which he was promoted or restored, of master-general of Dalmatia, Pannonia, Noricum, and Rhætia, seemed to revive the discipline and spirit of the republic. From a life of idleness and want his troops were soon habituated to severe exercise and plentiful subsistence, and his private generosity often supplied the rewards which were denied by the avarice or poverty of the court of Ravenna. The valour of Gennerid, formidable to the adjacent barbarians, was the firmest bulwark of the Illyrian frontier; and his vigilant care assisted the empire with a reinforcement of ten thousand Huns, who arrived on the confines of Italy, attended by such a convoy of provisions, and such a numerous train of sheep and oxen, as might have been sufficient not only for the march of an army but for the settlement of a colony. But the court and councils of Honorius still remained a scene of weakness and distraction, of corruption and anarchy. Instigated by the præfect Jovius, the guards rose in furious mutiny and demanded the heads of two generals and of the two principal eunuchs. The generals, under a perfidious promise of safety, were sent on ship-board and privately executed; while the favour of the eunuchs procured them a mild and secure exile at Milan and Constantinople. Eusebius the eunuch and the barbarian Allobich succeeded to the command of the bed-chamber and of the guards; and the mutual jealousy of the subordinate ministers was the cause of their mutual destruction. By the insolent order of the count of the domestics, the great chamberlain was shamefully beaten to death with sticks before the eyes of the astonished emperor; and the subsequent assassination of Allobich, in the midst of a public procession, is the only circumstance of his life in which Honorius discovered the faintest symptom of courage or resentment. Yet before they fell, Eusebius and Allobich had contributed their part to the ruin of the empire by opposing the conclusion of a treaty which Jovius, from a selfish, and perhaps a criminal motive, had negotiated with Alaric, in a personal interview under the walls of Rimini. During the absence of Jovius the emperor was persuaded to assume a lofty tone of inflexible dignity, such as neither his situation nor his character could enable him to support; and a letter, signed with the name of Honorius, was immediately despatched to the Prætorian præfect, granting him a free permission to dispose of the public money, but sternly refusing to prostitute the military honours of Rome to the proud demands of a barbarian. This letter was imprudently communicated to Alaric himself; and the Goth, who in the whole transaction had behaved with temper and decency, expressed in the most outrageous language his lively sense of the insult so wantonly offered to his person and to his nation. The conference of Rimini was hastily interrupted; and the præfect Jovius, on his return to Ravenna, was compelled to adopt, and even to encourage, the fashionable opinions of the court. By his advice and example the principal officers of the state and army were obliged to swear that, without listening in *any* circumstances to *any* conditions of peace, they would still persevere in perpetual and implacable war against the enemy of the republic. This rash engagement opposed an insuperable bar to all future negotiation. The ministers of Honorius were heard to declare that, if they had only invoked the name of the Deity, they would consult the public safety, and trust their souls to the mercy of Heaven: but they had sworn by the sacred head of the emperor himself; they had touched in solemn ceremony that august seat of majesty and wisdom; and the violation of their oath would expose them to the temporal penalties of sacrilege and rebellion.[1]

While the emperor and his court enjoyed with sullen pride the security of the marshes and fortifications of Ravenna, they abandoned Rome, almost without defence, to the resentment of Alaric. Yet such was the moderation which he still preserved, or affected, that as he moved with his army along the Flaminian way he successively despatched the bishops of the towns of Italy to reiterate his offers of peace, and to conjure the emperor that he would save the city and its inhabitants from hostile fire and the sword of the barbarians.[2] These impending calamities were however averted, not indeed by the wisdom of Honorius, but by the prudence or humanity of the Gothic king, who employed a milder, though not less effectual, method of conquest. Instead of assaulting the capital he successfully directed his efforts against the *Port* of Ostia, one of the boldest and most stupendous works

---

[1] Zosimus, l. v. [c. 47-49] p. 367, 368, 369. This custom of swearing by the head, or life, or safety, or genius, of the sovereign, was of the highest antiquity, both in Egypt (Genesis xlii. 15) and Scythia. It was soon transferred, by flattery, to the Cæsars; and Tertullian complains that it was the only oath which the Romans of his time affected to reverence. See an elegant Dissertation of the Abbé Massieu on the Oaths of the Ancients, in the Mém. de l'Académie des Inscriptions, tom. i. p. 208, 209.

[2] Zosimus, l. v. [c. 50] p. 368, 369. I have softened the expressions of Alaric, who expatiates in too florid a manner on the history of Rome.

of Roman magnificence.[1]   The accidents to which the precarious
subsistence of the city was continually exposed in a winter navigation and an open road had suggested to the genius of the first
Cæsar the useful design which was executed under the reign of
Claudius.   The artificial moles which formed the narrow entrance
advanced far into the sea, and firmly repelled the fury of the
waves, while the largest vessels securely rode at anchor within
three deep and capacious basins which received the northern
branch of the Tiber about two miles from the ancient colony of
Ostia.[2]   The Roman *Port* insensibly swelled to the size of an
episcopal city,[3] where the corn of Africa was deposited in spacious
granaries for the use of the capital.   As soon as Alaric was in
possession of that important place he summoned the city to
surrender at discretion; and his demands were enforced by the
positive declaration that a refusal, or even a delay, should be
instantly followed by the destruction of the magazines on which
the life of the Roman people depended.   The clamours of that
people and the terror of famine subdued the pride of the senate;
they listened without reluctance to the proposal of placing a

---

[1] See Sueton. in Claud. c. 20; Dion Cassius, l. lx. [c. 11] p. 949, edit.
Reimar; and the lively description of Juvenal, Satir. xii. 75, etc.   In the
sixteenth century, when the remains of this Augustan port were still visible,
the antiquarians sketched the plan (see D'Anville, Mém. de l'Académie des
Inscriptions, tom. xxx. p. 198), and declared with enthusiasm that all the
monarchs of Europe would be unable to execute so great a work (Bergier,
Hist. des Grands Chemins des Romains, tom. ii. p. 356).

[2] The *Ostia Tiberina* (see Cluver. Italia Antiq. l. iii. p. 870-879), in the
plural number, the two mouths of the Tiber, were separated by the Holy
Island, an equilateral triangle, whose sides were each of them computed at
about two miles.   The colony of Ostia was founded immediately beyond
the left, or southern, and the *Port* immediately beyond the right, or
northern, branch of the river; and the distance between their remains
measures something more than two miles on Cingolani's map.   In the
time of Strabo the sand and mud deposited by the Tiber had choked the
harbour of Ostia; the progress of the same cause has added much to the
size of the Holy Island, and gradually left both Ostia and the Port at a
considerable distance from the shore.   The dry channels (fiumi morti) and
the large estuaries (stagno di Ponente, di Levante) mark the changes of
the river and the efforts of the sea.   Consult, for the present state of this
dreary and desolate tract, the excellent map of the ecclesiastical state by
the mathematicians of Benedict XIV.; an actual survey of the *Agro
Romano*, in six sheets, by Cingolani, which contains 113,819 *rubbia* (about
570,000 acres); and the large topographical map of Ameti, in eight sheets.

[3] As early as the third (Lardner's Credibility of the Gospel, part ii. vol.
iii. p. 89-92), or at least the fourth century (Carol. a Sancto Paulo, Notit.
Eccles. p. 47), the Port of Rome was an episcopal city, which was demolished, as it should seem, in the ninth century, by pope Gregory IV.,
during the incursions of the Arabs.   It is now reduced to an inn, a church,
and the house or palace of the bishop, who ranks as one of six cardinal
bishops of the Roman church.   See Eschinard, Descrizione di Roma et
dell' Agro Romano, p. 328.

new emperor on the throne of the unworthy Honorius; and the suffrage of the Gothic conqueror bestowed the purple on Attalus, præfect of the city. The grateful monarch immediately acknowledged his protector as master-general of the armies of the West; Adolphus, with the rank of count of the domestics, obtained the custody of the person of Attalus; and the two hostile nations seemed to be united in the closest bands of friendship and alliance.[1]

The gates of the city were thrown open, and the new emperor of the Romans, encompassed on every side by the Gothic arms, was conducted in tumultuous procession to the palace of Augustus and Trajan. After he had distributed the civil and military dignities among his favourites and followers, Attalus convened an assembly of the senate, before whom, in a formal and florid speech, he asserted his resolution of restoring the majesty of the republic, and of uniting to the empire the provinces of Egypt and the East which had once acknowledged the sovereignty of Rome. Such extravagant promises inspired every reasonable citizen with a just contempt for the character of an unwarlike usurper, whose elevation was the deepest and most ignominious wound which the republic had yet sustained from the insolence of the barbarians. But the populace, with their usual levity, applauded the change of masters. The public discontent was favourable to the rival of Honorius; and the sectaries, oppressed by his persecuting edicts, expected some degree of countenance, or at least of toleration, from a prince who, in his native country of Ionia, had been educated in the Pagan superstition, and who had since received the sacrament of baptism from the hands of an Arian bishop.[2] The first days of the reign of Attalus were fair and prosperous. An officer of confidence was sent with an inconsiderable body of troops to secure the obedience of Africa; the greatest part of Italy submitted to the terror of the Gothic powers; and though the city of Bologna made a vigorous and effectual resistance, the people of Milan, dissatisfied perhaps with the absence of Honorius, accepted with loud acclamations the choice of the Roman senate. At the head of a formidable army, Alaric conducted his royal captive almost to the gates of Ravenna;

---

[1] For the elevation of Attalus, consult Zosimus, l. vi. [c. 6, 7] p. 377-380; Sozomen, l. ix. c. 8, 9; Olympiodor. ap. Phot. p. 180, 181 [p. 57, ed. Bekk.]; Philostorg. l. xii. c. 3, and Godefroy, Dissertat. p. 470.

[2] We may admit the evidence of Sozomen for the Arian baptism, and that of Philostorgius for the Pagan education, of Attalus. The visible joy of Zosimus, and the discontent which he imputes to the Anician family, are very unfavourable to the Christianity of the new emperor.

and a solemn embassy of the principal ministers—of Jovius the
Prætorian præfect, of Valens, master of the cavalry and infantry,
of the quæstor Potamius, and of Julian, the first of the notaries
—was introduced with martial pomp into the Gothic camp. In
the name of their sovereign they consented to acknowledge the
lawful election of his competitor, and to divide the provinces of
Italy and the West between the two emperors. Their proposals
were rejected with disdain; and the refusal was aggravated by
the insulting clemency of Attalus, who condescended to promise
that if Honorius would instantly resign the purple he should be
permitted to pass the remainder of his life in the peaceful exile
of some remote island.[1] So desperate indeed did the situation
of the son of Theodosius appear to those who were the best
acquainted with his strength and resources, that Jovius and
Valens, his minister and his general, betrayed their trust, in-
famously deserted the sinking cause of their benefactor, and
devoted their treacherous allegiance to the service of his more
fortunate rival. Astonished by such examples of domestic
treason, Honorius trembled at the approach of every servant,
at the arrival of every messenger. He dreaded the secret enemies
who might lurk in his capital, his palace, his bed-chamber; and
some ships lay ready in the harbour of Ravenna to transport the
abdicated monarch to the dominions of his infant nephew, the
emperor of the East.

But there *is* a Providence (such at least was the opinion of the
historian Procopius[2]) that watches over innocence and folly,
and the pretensions of Honorius to its peculiar care cannot
reasonably be disputed. At the moment when his despair,
incapable of any wise or manly resolution, meditated a shameful
flight, a seasonable reinforcement of four thousand veterans
unexpectedly landed in the port of Ravenna. To these valiant
strangers, whose fidelity had not been corrupted by the factions
of the court, he committed the walls and gates of the city, and
the slumbers of the emperor were no longer disturbed by the
apprehension of imminent and internal danger. The favourable
intelligence which was received from Africa suddenly changed
the opinions of men and the state of public affairs. The troops
and officers whom Attalus had sent into that province were

---

[1] He carried his insolence so far as to declare that he should mutilate
Honorius before he sent him into exile. But this assertion of Zosimus [l. vi.
c. 8] is destroyed by the more impartial testimony of Olympiodorus, who
attributes the ungenerous proposal (which was absolutely rejected by
Attalus) to the baseness and perhaps the treachery of Jovius.
[2] Procop. de Bell. Vandal. l. i. c. 2 [tom. i. p. 318, ed. Bonn].

defeated and slain, and the active zeal of Heraclian maintained his own allegiance and that of his people. The faithful count of Africa transmitted a large sum of money, which fixed the attachment of the Imperial guards; and his vigilance in preventing the exportation of corn and oil introduced famine, tumult, and discontent into the walls of Rome. The failure of the African expedition was the source of mutual complaint and recrimination in the party of Attalus, and the mind of his protector was insensibly alienated from the interest of a prince who wanted spirit to command or docility to obey. The most imprudent measures were adopted, without the knowledge or against the advice of Alaric, and the obstinate refusal of the senate to allow in the embarkation the mixture even of five hundred Goths, betrayed a suspicious and distrustful temper which in their situation was neither generous nor prudent. The resentment of the Gothic king was exasperated by the malicious arts of Jovius, who had been raised to the rank of patrician, and who afterwards excused his double perfidy by declaring without a blush that he had only *seemed* to abandon the service of Honorius more effectually to ruin the cause of the usurper. In a large plain near Rimini, and in the presence of an innumerable multitude of Romans and barbarians, the wretched Attalus was publicly despoiled of the diadem and purple; and those ensigns of royalty were sent by Alaric as the pledge of peace and friendship to the son of Theodosius.[1] The officers who returned to their duty were reinstated in their employments, and even the merit of a tardy repentance was graciously allowed; but the degraded emperor of the Romans, desirous of life and insensible of disgrace, implored the permission of following the Gothic camp in the train of a haughty and capricious barbarian.[2]

The degradation of Attalus removed the only real obstacle to the conclusion of the peace, and Alaric advanced within three miles of Ravenna to press the irresolution of the Imperial ministers, whose insolence soon returned with the return of fortune. His indignation was kindled by the report that a rival chieftain, that Sarus, the personal enemy of Adolphus, and the hereditary foe of the house of Balti, had been received into

---

[1] See the cause and circumstances of the fall of Attalus in Zosimus, l. vi. [c. 9-12], p. 380-383. Sozomen, l. ix. c. 8. Philostorg. l. xii. c. 3. The two acts of indemnity in the Theodosian Code, l. ix. tit. xxxviii. leg. 11, 12, which were published the 12th of February and the 8th of August, A.D. 410, evidently relate to this usurper.

[2] In hoc, Alaricus, imperatore, facto, infecto, refecto, ac defecto . . mimum risit, et ludum spectavit imperii. Orosius, l. vii. c. 42, p. 582.

the palace. At the head of three hundred followers that fearless barbarian immediately sallied from the gates of Ravenna, surprised and cut in pieces a considerable body of Goths, re-entered the city in triumph, and was permitted to insult his adversary by the voice of a herald, who publicly declared that the guilt of Alaric had for ever excluded him from the friendship and alliance of the emperor.[1] The crime and folly of the court of Ravenna was expiated a third time by the calamities of Rome. The king of the Goths, who no longer dissembled his appetite for plunder and revenge, appeared in arms under the walls of the capital; and the trembling senate, without any hopes of relief, prepared by a desperate resistance to delay the ruin of their country. But they were unable to guard against the secret conspiracy of their slaves and domestics, who either from birth or interest were attached to the cause of the enemy. At the hour of midnight the Salarian gate was silently opened, and the inhabitants were awakened by the tremendous sound of the Gothic trumpet. Eleven hundred and sixty-three years after the foundation of Rome, the Imperial city, which had subdued and civilised so considerable a part of mankind, was delivered to the licentious fury of the tribes of Germany and Scythia.[2]

The proclamation of Alaric, when he forced his entrance into a vanquished city, discovered, however, some regard for the laws of humanity and religion. He encouraged his troops boldly to seize the rewards of valour, and to enrich themselves with the spoils of a wealthy and effeminate people; but he exhorted them at the same time to spare the lives of the unresisting citizens, and to respect the churches of the apostles St. Peter and St. Paul as holy and inviolable sanctuaries. Amidst the horrors of a nocturnal tumult several of the Christian Goths displayed the fervour of a recent conversion; and some instances of their

---

[1] Zosimus, l. vi. [c. 13] p. 384. Sozomen, l. ix. c. 9. Philostorgius. l. xii. c. 3. In this place the text of Zosimus is mutilated, and we have lost the remainder of his sixth and last book, which ended with the sack of Rome. Credulous and partial as he is, we must take our leave of that historian with some regret.

[2] Adest Alaricus, trepidam Romam obsidet, turbat, irrumpit. Orosius, vii. c. 39, p. 573. He despatches this great event in seven words; but he employs whole pages in celebrating the devotion of the Goths. I have extracted from an improbable story of Procopius the circumstances which had an air of probability. Procop. de Bell. Vandal. l. i. c. 2 [tom. i. p. 315, ed. Bonn]. He supposes that the city was surprised while the senators slept in the afternoon; but Jerom, with more authority and more reason, affirms that it was in the night, nocte Moab capta est; nocte cecidit murus ejus, tom. i. p. 121, ad Principiam [Epist. cxxvii. c. 12, tom. i. p. 953, ed. Vallars.].

uncommon piety and moderation are related, and perhaps adorned, by the zeal of ecclesiastical writers.[1] While the barbarians roamed through the city in quest of prey, the humble dwelling of an aged virgin, who had devoted her life to the service of the altar, was forced open by one of the powerful Goths. He immediately demanded, though in civil language, all the gold and silver in her possession, and was astonished at the readiness with which she conducted him to a splendid hoard of massy plate of the richest materials and the most curious workmanship. The barbarian viewed with wonder and delight this valuable acquisition, till he was interrupted by a serious admonition, addressed to him in the following words: "These," said she, "are the consecrated vessels belonging to St. Peter: if you presume to touch them, the sacrilegious deed will remain on your conscience. For my part, I dare not keep what I am unable to defend." The Gothic captain, struck with reverential awe, despatched a messenger to inform the king of the treasure which he had discovered, and received a peremptory order from Alaric, that all the consecrated plate and ornaments should be transported, without damage or delay, to the church of the apostle. From the extremity, perhaps, of the Quirinal hill to the distant quarter of the Vatican, a numerous detachment of Goths, marching in order of battle through the principal streets, protected with glittering arms the long train of their devout companions who bore aloft on their heads the sacred vessels of gold and silver, and the martial shouts of the barbarians were mingled with the sound of religious psalmody. From all the adjacent houses a crowd of Christians hastened to join this edifying procession, and a multitude of fugitives, without distinction of age or rank, or even of sect, had the good fortune to escape to the secure and hospitable sanctuary of the Vatican. The learned work concerning the *City of God* was professedly composed by St. Augustin, to justify the ways of Providence in the destruction of the Roman greatness. He celebrates with peculiar satisfaction this memorable triumph of Christ, and insults his adversaries by challenging them to produce some similar example of a town

---

[1] Orosius (l. vii. c. 39, p. 573-576) applauds the piety of the Christian Goths without seeming to perceive that the greatest part of them were Arian heretics. Jornandes (c. 30, p. 653 [p. 86, ed. Lugd. B. 1597]) and Isidore of Seville (Chron. p. 714, edit. Grot.), who were both attached to the Gothic cause, have repeated and embellished these edifying tales. According to Isidore, Alaric himself was heard to say that he waged war with the Romans, and not with the Apostles. Such was the style of the seventh century; two hundred years before, the fame and merit had been ascribed, not to the Apostles, but to Christ.

taken by storm, in which the fabulous gods of antiquity had been able to protect either themselves of their deluded votaries.[1]

In the sack of Rome some rare and extraordinary examples of barbarian virtue have been deservedly applauded. But the holy precincts of the Vatican and the apostolic churches could receive a very small proportion of the Roman people: many thousand warriors, more especially of the Huns who served under the standard of Alaric, were strangers to the name, or at least to the faith, of Christ, and we may suspect, without any breach of charity or candour, that in the hour of savage licence, when every passion was inflamed and every restraint was removed, the precepts of the Gospel seldom influenced the behaviour of the Gothic Christians. The writers the best disposed to exaggerate their clemency have freely confessed that a cruel slaughter was made of the Romans,[2] and that the streets of the city were filled with dead bodies, which remained without burial during the general consternation. The despair of the citizens was some-times converted into fury; and whenever the barbarians were provoked by opposition, they extended the promiscuous massacre to the feeble, the innocent, and the helpless. The private revenge of forty thousand slaves was exercised without pity or remorse; and the ignominious lashes which they had formerly received were washed away in the blood of the guilty or obnoxious families. The matrons and virgins of Rome were exposed to injuries more dreadful, in the apprehension of chastity, than death itself; and the ecclesiastical historian has selected an example of female virtue for the admiration of future ages.[3] A

[1] See Augustin, de Civitat. Dei, l. i. c. 1-6. He particularly appeals to the examples of Troy, Syracuse, and Tarentum.

[2] Jerom (tom. i. p. 121, ad Principiam [Ep. cxxvii. tom. i. p. 953, ed. Vallars.]) has applied to the sack of Rome all the strong expressions of Virgil:—

> Quis cladem illius noctis, quis funera fando,
> Explicet, etc

Procopius (l. i. c. 2 [tom. i. p. 316, ed. Bonn]) positively affirms that great numbers were slain by the Goths. Augustin (de Civ. Dei, l. i. c. 12, 13) offers Christian comfort for the death of those whose bodies (*multa corpora*) had remained (*in tantâ strage*) unburied. Baronius, from the different writings of the Fathers, has thrown some light on the sack of Rome. Annal. Eccles. A.D. 410, No. 16-44.

[3] Sozomen, l. ix. c. 10. Augustin (de Civitat. Dei, l. i. c. 17) intimates that some virgins or matrons actually killed themselves to escape viola-tion; and though he admires their spirit, he is obliged, by his theology, to condemn their rash presumption. Perhaps the good bishop of Hippo was too easy in the belief, as well as too rigid in the censure, of this act of female heroism. The twenty maidens (if they ever existed) who threw them-selves into the Elbe when Magdeburg was taken by storm, have been multi-plied to the number of twelve hundred. See Harte's History of Gustavus Adolphus, vol. i. p. 308.

Roman lady, of singular beauty and orthodox faith, had excited
the impatient desires of a young Goth, who, according to the
sagacious remark of Sozomen, was attached to the Arian heresy.
Exasperated by her obstinate resistance, he drew his sword, and,
with the anger of a lover, slightly wounded her neck. The
bleeding heroine still continued to brave his resentment and to
repel his love, till the ravisher desisted from his unavailing
efforts, respectfully conducted her to the sanctuary of the
Vatican, and gave six pieces of gold to the guards of the church
on condition that they should restore her inviolate to the arms of
her husband. Such instances of courage and generosity were
not extremely common. The brutal soldiers satisfied their
sensual appetites without consulting either the inclination or the
duties of their female captives; and a nice question of casuistry
was seriously agitated, Whether those tender victims, who had
inflexibly refused their consent to the violation which they sustained, had lost, by their misfortune, the glorious crown of
virginity.[1] There were other losses indeed of a more substantial
kind and more general concern. It cannot be presumed that
all the barbarians were at all times capable of perpetrating such
amorous outrages; and the want of youth, or beauty, or chastity,
protected the greatest part of the Roman women from the danger
of a rape. But avarice is an insatiate and universal passion;
since the enjoyment of almost every object that can afford
pleasure to the different tastes and tempers of mankind may be
procured by the possession of wealth. In the pillage of Rome
a just preference was given to gold and jewels, which contain
the greatest value in the smallest compass and weight; but,
after these portable riches had been removed by the more
diligent robbers, the palaces of Rome were rudely stripped of their
splendid and costly furniture. The sideboards of massy plate,
and the variegated wardrobes of silk and purple, were irregularly piled in the waggons that always followed the march of a
Gothic army. The most exquisite works of art were roughly
handled or wantonly destroyed: many a statue was melted for
the sake of the precious materials; and many a vase, in the

---

[1] See Augustin, de Civitat. Dei. l. i. c. 16-18. He treats the subject with
remarkable accuracy: and after admitting that there cannot be any crime
where there is no consent, he adds, Sed quia non solum quod ad dolorem,
verum etiam quod ad libidinem, pertinet, in corpore alieno perpetrari
potest; quicquid tale factum fuerit, etsi retentam constantissimo animo
pudicitiam non excutit, pudorem tamen incutit, ne credatur factum cum
mentis etiam voluntate, quod fieri fortasse sine carnis aliquâ voluptate non
potuit. In c. 18 he makes some curious distinctions between moral and
physical virginity.

division of the spoil, was shivered into fragments by the stroke of a battle-axe. The acquisition of riches served only to stimulate the avarice of the rapacious barbarians, who proceeded by threats, by blows, and by tortures, to force from their prisoners the confession of hidden treasure.[1] Visible splendour and expense were alleged as the proof of a plentiful fortune; the appearance of poverty was imputed to a parsimonious disposition; and the obstinacy of some misers, who endured the most cruel torments before they would discover the secret object of their affection, was fatal to many unhappy wretches, who expired under the lash for refusing to reveal their imaginary treasures. The edifices of Rome, though the damage has been much exaggerated, received some injury from the violence of the Goths. At their entrance through the Salarian gate they fired the adjacent houses to guide their march and to distract the attention of the citizens; the flames, which encountered no obstacle in the disorder of the night, consumed many private and public buildings, and the ruins of the palace of Sallust[2] remained in the age of Justinian a stately monument of the Gothic conflagration.[3] Yet a contemporary historian has observed that fire could scarcely consume the enormous beams of solid brass, and that the strength of man was insufficient to subvert the foundations of ancient structures. Some truth may possibly be concealed in his devout assertion, that the wrath of Heaven supplied the imperfections of hostile rage, and that the proud Forum of Rome, decorated with the statues of so many gods and heroes, was levelled in the dust by the stroke of lightning.[4]

[1] Marcella, a Roman lady, equally respectable for her rank, her age, and her piety, was thrown on the ground and cruelly beaten and whipped, cæsam fustibus flagellisque, etc. Jerom, tom. i. p. 121, ad Principiam Ep. cxxvii. c. 13, tom. i. p. 953, ed. Vallars.]. See Augustin, de Civ. Dei, l. i. c. 10. The modern Sacco di Roma, p. 208, gives an idea of the various methods of torturing prisoners for gold.

[2] The historian Sallust, who usefully practised the vices which he has so eloquently censured, employed the plunder of Numidia to adorn his palace and gardens on the Quirinal hill. The spot where the house stood is now marked by the church of St. Susanna, separated only by a street from the baths of Diocletian, and not far distant from the Salarian gate. See Nardini, Roma Antica, p. 192, 193, and the great Plan of Modern Rome, by Nolli.

[3] The expressions of Procopius are distinct and moderate (de Bell. Vandal. l. i. c. 2 [tom. i. p. 316, ed. Bonn]). The chronicle of Marcellinus speaks too strongly, partem urbis Romæ cremavit; and the words of Philostorgius (ἐν ἐρειπίοις δὲ τῆς πόλεως κειμένης, l. xii. c. 3) convey a false and exaggerated idea. Bargæus has composed a particular dissertation (see tom. iv. Antiquit. Rom. Græv.) to prove that the edifices of Rome were not subverted by the Goths and Vandals.

[4] Orosius, l. ii. c. 19, p. 143. He speaks as if he disapproved all statues; vel Deum vel hominem mentiuntur. They consisted of the kings of Alba

Whatever might be the numbers of equestrian or plebeian rank who perished in the massacre of Rome, it is confidently affirmed that only one senator lost his life by the sword of the enemy.[1] But it was not easy to compute the multitudes who, from an honourable station and a prosperous fortune, were suddenly reduced to the miserable condition of captives and exiles. As the barbarians had more occasion for money than for slaves, they fixed at a moderate price the redemption of their indigent prisoners; and the ransom was often paid by the benevolence of their friends, or the charity of strangers.[2] The captives, who were regularly sold, either in open market or by private contract, would have legally regained their native freedom, which it was impossible for a citizen to lose or to alienate.[3] But as it was soon discovered that the vindication of their liberty would endanger their lives, and that the Goths, unless they were tempted to sell, might be provoked to murder their useless prisoners, the civil jurisprudence had been already qualified by a wise regulation, that they should be obliged to serve the moderate term of five years, till they had discharged by their labour the price of their redemption.[4] The nations who invaded the Roman empire had driven before them, into Italy, whole troops of hungry and affrighted provincials, less apprehensive of servitude than of famine. The calamities of Rome and Italy dispersed the inhabitants to the most lonely, the most secure, the most distant places of refuge. While the Gothic cavalry spread terror and desolation along the sea-coast of Campania and Tuscany, the little island of Igilium, separated by a narrow channel from the Argentarian promontory, repulsed, or

and Rome from Æneas, the Romans illustrious either in arms or arts, and the deified Cæsars. The expression which he uses of *Forum* is somewhat ambiguous, since there existed *five* principal *Fora*; but as they were all contiguous and adjacent, in the plain which is surrounded by the Capitoline, the Quirinal, the Esquiline, and the Palatine hills, they might fairly be considered as *one*. See the Roma Antiqua of Donatus, p. 162-201, and the Roma Antica of Nardini, p. 212-273. The former is more useful for the ancient descriptions, the latter for the actual topography.

[1] Orosius (l. ii. c. 19, p. 142) compares the cruelty of the Gauls and the clemency of the Goths. Ibi vix quemquam inventum senatorem, qui vel absens evaserit; hic vix quemquam requiri, qui forte ut latens perierit. But there is an air of rhetoric, and perhaps of falsehood, in this antithesis; and Socrates (l. vii. c. 10) affirms, perhaps by an opposite exaggeration, that *many* senators were put to death with various and exquisite tortures.

[2] Multi . . . Christiani captivi ducti sunt. Augustin, de Civ. Dei, l. i. c. 14; and the Christians experienced no peculiar hardships.

[3] See Heineccius, Antiquitat. Juris Roman. tom. i. p. 96.

[4] Appendix Cod. Theodos. xvi. in Sirmond. Opera, tom. i. p. 735. This edict was published on the 11th of December, A.D. 408, and is more reasonable than properly belonged to the ministers of Honorius.

eluded, their hostile attempts; and at so small a distance from Rome, great numbers of citizens were securely concealed in the thick woods of that sequestered spot.[1] The ample patrimonies which many senatorian families possessed in Africa invited them, if they had time and prudence to escape from the ruin of their country, to embrace the shelter of that hospitable province. The most illustrious of these fugitives was the noble and pious Proba,[2] the widow of the præfect Petronius. After the death of her husband, the most powerful subject of Rome, she had remained at the head of the Anician family, and successively supplied, from her private fortune, the expense of the consulships of her three sons. When the city was besieged and taken by the Goths, Proba supported with Christian resignation the loss of immense riches; embarked in a small vessel, from whence she beheld, at sea, the flames of her burning palace; and fled with her daughter Læta, and her grand-daughter, the celebrated virgin Demetrias, to the coast of Africa. The benevolent profusion with which the matron distributed the fruits or the price of her estates contributed to alleviate the misfortunes of exile and captivity. But even the family of Proba herself was not exempt from the rapacious oppression of Count Heraclian, who basely sold, in matrimonial prostitution, the noblest maidens of Rome to the lust or avarice of the Syrian merchants. The Italian fugitives were dispersed through the provinces, along the coast of Egypt and Asia, as far as Constantinople and Jerusalem; and the village of Bethlem, the solitary residence of St. Jerom and his female

---

[1] Eminus Igilii sylvosa cacumina miror;
    Quem fraudare nefas laudis honore suæ.
Hæc proprios nuper tutata est insula saltus;
    Sive loci ingenio, seu domini genio.
Gurgite cum modico victricibus obstitit armis,
    Tanquam longinquo dissociata mari.
Hæc multos laterâ suscepit ab urbe fugatos,
    Hic fessis posito certa timore salus.
Plurima terreno populaverat æquora bello,
    Contra naturam classe timendus eques:
Unum, mira fides, vario discrimine portum!
    Tam prope Romanis, tam procul esse Getis.
                                   Rutilius, in Itinerar. l. i. 325.
The island is now called Giglio. See Cluver. Ital. Antiq. l. ii. p. 502.

[2] As the adventures of Proba and her family are connected with the life of St. Augustin, they are diligently illustrated by Tillemont, Mém. Eccles. tom. xiii. p. 620-635. Some time after their arrival in Africa, Demetrias took the veil and made a vow of virginity; an event which was considered as of the highest importance to Rome and to the world. All the *Saints* wrote congratulatory letters to her; that of Jerom is still extant (tom. i. p. 62-73, ad Demetriad. de servandâ Virginitat. [Epist. cxxx. tom. i. p. 969, ed. Vallars.]), and contains a mixture of absurd reasoning, spirited declamation, and curious facts, some of which relate to the siege and sack of Rome.

converts, was crowned with illustrious beggars, of either sex and every age, who excited the public compassion by the remembrance of their past fortune.[1] This awful catastrophe of Rome filled the astonished empire with grief and terror. So interesting a contrast of greatness and ruin disposed the fond credulity of the people to deplore, and even to exaggerate, the afflictions of the queen of cities. The clergy, who applied to recent events the lofty metaphors of Oriental prophecy, were sometimes tempted to confound the destruction of the capital and the dissolution of the globe.

There exists in human nature a strong propensity to depreciate the advantages, and to magnify the evils, of the present times. Yet, when the first emotions had subsided, and a fair estimate was made of the real damage, the more learned and judicious contemporaries were forced to confess that infant Rome had formerly received more essential injury from the Gauls than she had now sustained from the Goths in her declining age.[2] The experience of eleven centuries has enabled posterity to produce a much more singular parallel; and to affirm with confidence, that the ravages of the barbarians whom Alaric had led from the banks of the Danube were less destructive than the hostilities exercised by the troops of Charles the Fifth, a catholic prince, who styled himself Emperor of the Romans.[3] The Goths evacuated the city at the end of six days, but Rome remained above nine months in the possession of the Imperialists; and every hour was stained by some atrocious act of cruelty, lust, and rapine. The authority of Alaric preserved some order and moderation among the ferocious multitude which acknowledged him for their leader and king; but the constable of Bourbon had gloriously fallen in the attack of the walls; and the death of

---

[1] See the pathetic complaint of Jerom (tom. v. p. 400) in his preface to the second book of his Commentaries on the Prophet Ezekiel.

[2] Orosius, though with some theological partiality, states this comparison, l. ii. c. 19, p. 142, l. vii. c. 39, p. 575. But, in the history of the taking of Rome by the Gauls, everything is uncertain, and perhaps fabulous. See Beaufort sur l'Incertitude, etc., de l'Histoire Romaine, p. 356; and Melot, in the Mém. de l'Académie des Inscript. tom. xv. p. 1-21.

[3] The reader who wishes to inform himself of the circumstances of this famous event may peruse an admirable narrative in Dr. Robertson's History of Charles V. vol. ii. p. 283; or consult the Annali d'Italia of the learned Muratori, tom. xiv. p. 230-244, octavo edition. If he is desirous of examining the originals, he may have recourse to the eighteenth book of the great, but unfinished, history of Guicciardini. But the account which most truly deserves the name of authentic and original is a little book, entitled Il Sacco di Roma, composed, within less than a month after the assault of the city, by the *brother* of the historian Guicciardini, who appears to have been an able magistrate and a dispassionate writer.

the general removed every restraint of discipline from an army which consisted of three independent nations, the Italians, the Spaniards, and the Germans. In the beginning of the sixteenth century the manners of Italy exhibited a remarkable scene of the depravity of mankind. They united the sanguinary crimes that prevail in an unsettled state of society, with the polished vices which spring from the abuse of art and luxury; and the loose adventurers, who had violated every prejudice of patriotism and superstition to assault the palace of the Roman pontiff, must deserve to be considered as the most profligate of the *Italians*. At the same era the *Spaniards* were the terror both of the Old and New World; but their high-spirited valour was disgraced by gloomy pride, rapacious avarice, and unrelenting cruelty. Indefatigable in the pursuit of fame and riches, they had improved, by repeated practice, the most exquisite and effectual methods of torturing their prisoners: many of the Castilians who pillaged Rome were familiars of the holy inquisition; and some volunteers, perhaps, were lately returned from the conquest of Mexico. The *Germans* were less corrupt than the Italians, less cruel than the Spaniards; and the rustic, or even savage, aspect of those *Tramontane* warriors, often disguised a simple and merciful disposition. But they had imbibed, in the first fervour of the Reformation, the spirit, as well as the principles, of Luther. It was their favourite amusement to insult, or destroy, the consecrated objects of catholic superstition; they indulged, without pity or remorse, a devout hatred against the clergy of every denomination and degree who form so considerable a part of the inhabitants of modern Rome; and their fanatic zeal might aspire to subvert the throne of Antichrist, to purify, with blood and fire, the abominations of the spiritual Babylon.[1]

The retreat of the victorious Goths, who evacuated Rome on the sixth day,[2] might be the result of prudence, but it was not surely the effect of fear.[3] At the head of an army encumbered with rich and weighty spoils, their intrepid leader advanced along the Appian Way into the southern provinces of Italy, destroying

---

[1] The furious spirit of Luther, the effect of temper and enthusiasm, has been forcibly attacked (Bossuet, Hist. des Variations des Eglises Protestantes, livre i. p. 20-36) and feebly defended (Seckendorf, Comment. de Lutheranismo, especially l. i. No. 78, p. 120, and l. iii. No. 122, p. 556).

[2] Marcellinus, in Chron. Orosius (l. vii. c. 39, p. 575), asserts that he left Rome on the *third* day; but this difference is easily reconciled by the successive motions of great bodies of troops.

[3] Socrates (l. vii. c. 10) pretends, without any colour of truth or reason, that Alaric fled on the report that the armies of the Eastern empire were in full march to attack him.

whatever dared to oppose his passage, and contenting himself
with the plunder of the unresisting country. The fate of Capua,
the proud and luxurious metropolis of Campania, and which was
respected, even in its decay, as the eighth city of the empire,[1]
is buried in oblivion; whilst the adjacent town of Nola [2] has been
illustrated, on this occasion, by the sanctity of Paulinus,[3] who
was successively a consul, a monk, and a bishop. At the age
of forty he renounced the enjoyment of wealth and honour, of
society and literature, to embrace a life of solitude and penance;
and the loud applause of the clergy encouraged him to despise the
reproaches of his worldly friends, who ascribed this desperate act
to some disorder of the mind or body.[4] An early and passionate
attachment determined him to fix his humble dwelling in one of
the suburbs of Nola, near the miraculous tomb of St. Felix, which
the public devotion had already surrounded with five large and
populous churches. The remains of his fortune, and of his understanding, were dedicated to the service of the glorious martyr;
whose praise, on the day of his festival, Paulinus never failed to
celebrate by a solemn hymn; and in whose name he erected
a sixth church, of superior elegance and beauty, which was
decorated with many curious pictures from the history of the
Old and New Testament. Such assiduous zeal secured the
favour of the saint,[5] or at least of the people; and, after fifteen
years' retirement, the Roman consul was compelled to accept the
bishopric of Nola, a few months before the city was invested
by the Goths. During the siege, some religious persons were
satisfied that they had seen, either in dreams or visions, the divine
form of their tutelar patron; yet it soon appeared by the event,
that Felix wanted power, or inclination, to preserve the flock of

---

[1] Ausonius de Claris Urbibus, p. 233, edit. Toll. The luxury of Capua
had formerly surpassed that of Sybaris itself. See Athenæus Deipno-
sophist. l. xii. [c. 36] p. 528, edit. Casaubon.

[2] Forty-eight years before the foundation of Rome (about 800 before the
Christian era) the Tuscans built Capua and Nola, at the distance of twenty-
three miles from each other: but the latter of the two cities never emerged
from a state of mediocrity.

[3] Tillemont (Mém. Ecclés. tom. xiv. p. 1-146) has compiled, with his
usual diligence, all that relates to the life and writings of Paulinus, whose
retreat is celebrated by his own pen and by the praises of St. Ambrose,
St. Jerom, St. Augustin, Sulpicius Severus, etc., his Christian friends and
contemporaries.

[4] See the affectionate letters of Ausonius (Epist. xix.-xxv. p. 650-698,
edit. Toll.) to his colleague, his friend, and his disciple, Paulinus. The
religion of Ausonius is still a problem (see Mém. de l'Académie des Inscriptions, tom. xv. p. 123-138). I believe that it was such in his own time, and
consequently that in his heart he was a Pagan.

[5] The humble Paulinus once presumed to say that he believed St. Felix
did love him; at least, as a master loves his little dog.

which he had formerly been the shepherd. Nola was not saved from the general devastation;[1] and the captive bishop was protected only by the general opinion of his innocence and poverty. Above four years elapsed from the successful invasion of Italy by the arms of Alaric, to the voluntary retreat of the Goths under the conduct of his successor Adolphus; and, during the whole time, they reigned without control over a country which, in the opinion of the ancients, had united all the various excellences of nature and art. The prosperity, indeed, which Italy had attained in the auspicious age of the Antonines, had gradually declined with the decline of the empire. The fruits of a long peace perished under the rude grasp of the barbarians; and they themselves were incapable of tasting the more elegant refinements of luxury which had been prepared for the use of the soft and polished Italians. Each soldier, however, claimed an ample portion of the substantial plenty, the corn and cattle, oil and wine, that was daily collected, and consumed, in the Gothic camp; and the principal warriors insulted the villas and gardens, once inhabited by Lucullus and Cicero, along the beauteous coast of Campania. Their trembling captives, the sons and daughters of Roman senators, presented, in goblets of gold and gems, large draughts of Falernian wine to the haughty victors, who stretched their huge limbs under the shade of plane-trees,[2] artificially disposed to exclude the scorching rays, and to admit the genial warmth, of the sun. These delights were enhanced by the memory of past hardships: the comparison of their native soil, the bleak and barren hills of Scythia, and the frozen banks of the Elbe and Danube, added new charms to the felicity of the Italian climate.[3]

---

[1] See Jornandes, de Reb. Get. c. 30, p. 653. Philostorgius, l. xii. c. 3. Augustin, de Civ. Dei, l. i. c. 10. Baronius, Annal. Eccles. A.D. 410, No. 45, 46.

[2] The *platanus*, or plane-tree, was a favourite of the ancients, by whom it was propagated, for the sake of shade, from the East to Gaul. Pliny, Hist. Natur. xii. 3, 4, 5. He mentions several of an enormous size; one in the Imperial villa at Velitræ, which Caligula called his nest, as the branches were capable of holding a large table, the proper attendants, and the emperor himself, whom Pliny quaintly styles *pars umbræ*; an expression which might, with equal reason, be applied to Alaric.

[3]   The prostrate South to the destroyer yields
        Her boasted titles and her golden fields;
        With grim delight the brood of winter view
        A brighter day, and skies of azure hue;
        Scent the new fragrance of the opening rose,
        And quaff the pendent vintage as it grows.

See Gray's Poems, published by Mr. Mason, p. 197. Instead of compiling tables of chronology and natural history, why did not Mr. Gray apply the

Whether fame, or conquest, or riches were the object of Alaric, he pursued that object with an indefatigable ardour which could neither be quelled by adversity nor satiated by success. No sooner had he reached the extreme land of Italy than he was attracted by the neighbouring prospect of a fertile and peaceful island. Yet even the possession of Sicily he considered only as an intermediate step to the important expedition which he already meditated against the continent of Africa. The straits of Rhegium and Messina [1] are twelve miles in length, and in the narrowest passage about one mile and a half broad; and the fabulous monsters of the deep, the rocks of Scylla and the whirlpool of Charybdis, could terrify none but the most timid and unskilful mariners. Yet as soon as the first division of the Goths had embarked, a sudden tempest arose, which sunk or scattered many of the transports; their courage was daunted by the terrors of a new element; and the whole design was defeated by the premature death of Alaric, which fixed, after a short illness, the fatal term of his conquests. The ferocious character of the barbarians was displayed in the funeral of a hero whose valour and fortune they celebrated with mournful applause. By the labour of a captive multitude they forcibly diverted the course of the Busentinus, a small river that washes the walls of Consentia. The royal sepulchre, adorned with the splendid spoils and trophies of Rome, was constructed in the vacant bed; the waters were then restored to their natural channel; and the secret spot where the remains of Alaric had been deposited was for ever concealed by the inhuman massacre of the prisoners who had been employed to execute the work. [2]

The personal animosities and hereditary feuds of the barbarians were suspended by the strong necessity of their affairs; and the brave Adolphus, the brother-in-law of the deceased monarch, was unanimously elected to succeed to his throne. The character and political system of the new king of the Goths may be best understood from his own conversation with an illustrious citizen of Narbonne, who afterwards, in a pilgrimage to the Holy Land, related it to St. Jerom, in the presence of the historian Orosius. " In the full confidence of valour and victory, I once

powers of his genius to finish the philosophic poem of which he has left such an exquisite specimen?

[1] For the perfect description of the Straits of Messina, Scylla, Charybdis, etc., see Cluverius (Ital. Antiq. l. iv. p. 1293, and Sicilia Antiq. l. i. p. 60-76), who had diligently studied the ancients and surveyed with a curious eye the actual face of the country.

[2] Jornandes, de Reb. Get. c. 30, p. 654 [p. 87, ed. Lugd. B. 1597].

aspired (said Adolphus) to change the face of the universe; to obliterate the name of Rome; to erect on its ruins the dominion of the Goths; and to acquire, like Augustus, the immortal fame of the founder of a new empire. By repeated experiments I was gradually convinced that laws are essentially necessary to maintain and regulate a well-constituted state; and that the fierce untractable humour of the Goths was incapable of bearing the salutary yoke of laws and civil government. From that moment I proposed to myself a different object of glory and ambition; and it is now my sincere wish that the gratitude of future ages should acknowledge the merit of a stranger, who employed the sword of the Goths, not to subvert, but to restore and maintain, the prosperity of the Roman empire." [1] With these pacific views the successor of Alaric suspended the operations of war, and seriously negotiated with the Imperial court a treaty of friendship and alliance. It was the interest of the ministers of Honorius, who were now released from the obligation of their extravagant oath, to deliver Italy from the intolerable weight of the Gothic powers; and they readily accepted their service against the tyrants and barbarians who infested the provinces beyond the Alps. [2] Adolphus, assuming the character of a Roman general, directed his march from the extremity of Campania to the southern provinces of Gaul. His troops, either by force or agreement, immediately occupied the cities of Narbonne, Toulouse, and Bordeaux; and though they were repulsed by Count Boniface from the walls of Marseilles, they soon extended their quarters from the Mediterranean to the ocean. The oppressed provincials might exclaim that the miserable remnant which the enemy had spared was cruelly ravished by their pretended allies; yet some specious colours were not wanting to palliate or justify the violence of the Goths. The cities of Gaul which they attacked might perhaps be considered as in a state of rebellion against the government of Honorius: the articles of the treaty or the secret instructions of the court might sometimes be alleged in favour of the seeming usurpations of Adolphus; and the guilt of any irregular unsuccessful act of hostility might always be imputed, with an appearance of truth, to the ungovern-

[1] Orosius, l. vii. c. 43, p. 584, 585. He was sent by St. Augustin, in the year 415, from Africa to Palestine, to visit St. Jerom and to consult with him on the subject of the Pelagian controversy.

[2] Jornandes supposes, without much probability, that Adolphus visited and plundered Rome a second time (more locustarum erasit). Yet he agrees with Orosius in supposing that a treaty of peace was concluded between the Gothic prince and Honorius. See Oros. l. vii. c. 43, p. 584, 585. Jornandes, de Reb. Geticis, c. 31, p. 654, 655 [p. 88, ed. Lugd. B.].

able spirit of a barbarian host impatient of peace or discipline. The luxury of Italy had been less effectual to soften the temper than to relax the courage of the Goths; and they had imbibed the vices, without imitating the arts and institutions, of civilised society.[1]

The professions of Adolphus were probably sincere, and his attachment to the cause of the republic was secured by the ascendant which a Roman princess had acquired over the heart and understanding of the barbarian king. Placidia,[2] the daughter of the great Theodosius, and of Galla, his second wife, had received a royal education in the palace of Constantinople; but the eventful story of her life is connected with the revolutions which agitated the Western empire under the reign of her brother Honorius. When Rome was first invested by the arms of Alaric, Placidia, who was then about twenty years of age, resided in the city; and her ready consent to the death of her cousin Serena has a cruel and ungrateful appearance, which, according to the circumstances of the action, may be aggravated or excused by the consideration of her tender age.[3] The victorious barbarians detained, either as a hostage or a captive,[4] the sister of Honorius; but while she was exposed to the disgrace of following round Italy the motions of a Gothic camp, she experienced, however, a decent and respectful treatment. The authority of Jornandes, who praises the beauty of Placidia, may perhaps be counterbalanced by the silence, the expressive silence, of her flatterers: yet the splendour of her birth, the bloom of youth, the elegance of manners, and the dexterous insinuations which she condescended to employ, made a deep impression on the mind of Adolphus; and the Gothic king aspired to call himself the brother of the emperor. The ministers of Honorius rejected with disdain the proposal of an alliance so injurious to every sentiment of Roman pride; and repeatedly urged the restitution of Placidia as an indispensable condition of the treaty of peace. But the daughter of Theodosius submitted without reluctance to the desires of the conqueror, a young and valiant prince, who yielded

[1] The retreat of the Goths from Italy and their first transactions in Gaul are dark and doubtful. I have derived much assistance from Mascou (Hist. of the Ancient Germans, l. viii. c. 29, 35, 36, 37), who has illustrated and connected the broken chronicles and fragments of the times.

[2] See an account of Placidia in Ducange, Fam. Byzant. p. 72; and Tillemont, Hist. des Empereurs, tom. v. p. 260, 386, etc., tom. vi. p. 240.

[3] Zosim. l. v. [c. 38] p. 350.

[4] Zosim. l. vi. [c. 12] p. 383. Orosius (l. vii. c. 40, p. 576) and the Chronicles of Marcellinus and Idatius seem to suppose that the Goths did not carry away Placidia till after the last siege of Rome.

to Alaric in loftiness of stature, but who excelled in the more attractive qualities of grace and beauty. The marriage of Adolphus and Placidia [1] was consummated before the Goths retired from Italy; and the solemn, perhaps the anniversary, day of their nuptials was afterwards celebrated in the house of Ingenuus, one of the most illustrious citizens of Narbonne in Gaul. The bride, attired and adorned like a Roman empress, was placed on a throne of state; and the king of the Goths, who assumed on this occasion the Roman habit, contented himself with a less honourable seat by her side. The nuptial gift, which, according to the custom of his nation,[2] was offered to Placidia, consisted of the rare and magnificent spoils of her country. Fifty beautiful youths, in silken robes, carried a basin in each hand; and one of these basins was filled with pieces of gold, the other with precious stones of an inestimable value. Attalus, so long the sport of fortune and of the Goths, was appointed to lead the chorus of the Hymeneal song; and the degraded emperor might aspire to the praise of a skilful musician. The barbarians enjoyed the insolence of their triumph; and the provincials rejoiced in this alliance, which tempered, by the mild influence of love and reason, the fierce spirit of their Gothic lord.[3]

The hundred basins of gold and gems presented to Placidia at her nuptial feast formed an inconsiderable portion of the Gothic treasures; of which some extraordinary specimens may be selected from the history of the successors of Adolphus. Many curious and costly ornaments of pure gold, enriched with jewels, were found in their palace of Narbonne when it was pillaged in

---

[1] See the pictures of Adolphus and Placidia, and the account of their marriage, in Jornandes, de Reb. Geticis, c. 31, p. 654, 655 [p. 88, ed. Lugd. B.]. With regard to the place where the nuptials were stipulated, or consummated, or celebrated, the MSS. of Jornandes vary between two neighbouring cities, Forli and Imola (Forum Livii and Forum Cornelii). It is fair and easy to reconcile the Gothic historian with Olympiodorus (see Mascou, l. viii. c. 36): but Tillemont grows peevish, and swears that it is not worth while to try to conciliate Jornandes with any good authors.

[2] The Visigoths (the subjects of Adolphus) restrained, by subsequent laws, the prodigality of conjugal love. It was illegal for a husband to make any gift or settlement for the benefit of his wife during the first year of their marriage; and his liberality could not at any time exceed the tenth part of his property. The Lombards were somewhat more indulgent: they allowed the *morgingcap* immediately after the wedding night; and this famous gift, the reward of virginity, might equal the fourth part of the husband's substance. Some cautious maidens, indeed, were wise enough to stipulate beforehand a present which they were too sure of not deserving. See Montesquieu, Esprit des Loix, l. xix. c. 25. Muratori, delle Antichità Italiane, tom. i. Dissertazione xx. p. 243.

[3] We owe the curious detail of this nuptial feast to the historian Olympiodorus, ap. Photium, p. 185, 188 [p. 59, ed. Bekk.].

the sixth century by the Franks: sixty cups or chalices; fifteen *patens*, or plates, for the use of the communion; twenty boxes, or cases, to hold the books of the gospels: this consecrated wealth [1] was distributed by the son of Clovis among the churches of his dominions, and his pious liberality seems to upbraid some former sacrilege of the Goths. They possessed, with more security of conscience, the famous *missorium*, or great dish for the service of the table, of massy gold, of the weight of five hundred pounds, and of far superior value, from the precious stones, the exquisite workmanship, and the tradition that it had been presented by Aëtius, the patrician, to Torismond, king of the Goths. One of the successors of Torismond purchased the aid of the French monarch by the promise of this magnificent gift. When he was seated on the throne of Spain, he delivered it with reluctance to the ambassadors of Dagobert; despoiled them on the road; stipulated, after a long negotiation, the inadequate ransom of two hundred thousand pieces of gold; and preserved the *missorium* as the pride of the Gothic treasury.[2] When that treasury, after the conquest of Spain, was plundered by the Arabs, they admired and they have celebrated another object still more remarkable; a table of considerable size, of one single piece of solid emerald,[3] encircled with three rows of fine pearls, supported by three hundred and sixty-five feet of gems and massy gold, and estimated at the price of five hundred thousand pieces of gold.[4] Some portion of the Gothic treasures might be the gift of friendship or the tribute of obedience; but the far

[1] See in the great collection of the Historians of France by Dom Bouquet, tom. ii. Greg. Turonens. l. iii. c. 10, p. 191. Gesta Regum Francorum, c. 23, p. 557. The anonymous writer, with an ignorance worthy of his times, supposes that these instruments of Christian worship had belonged to the temple of Solomon. If he has any meaning, it must be that they were found in the sack of Rome.

[2] Consult the following original testimonies in the Historians of France, tom. ii. Fredegarii Scholastici Chron. c. 73, p. 441. Fredegar. Fragment. iii. p. 463. Gesta Regis Dagobert. c. 29, p. 587. The accession of Sisenand to the throne of Spain happened A.D. 631. The 200,000 pieces of gold were appropriated by Dagobert to the foundation of the church of St. Denys.

[3] The president Goguet (Origine des Loix, etc., tom. ii. p. 239) is of opinion that the stupendous pieces of emerald, the statues and columns which antiquity has placed in Egypt, at Gades, at Constantinople, were in reality artificial compositions of coloured glass. The famous emerald dish which is shown at Genoa is supposed to countenance the suspicion.

[4] Elmacin. Hist. Saracenica, l. i. p. 85; Roderic. Tolet. Hist. Arab. c. 9. Cardonne, Hist. de l'Afrique et de l'Espagne sous les Arabes, tom. i. p. 83. It was called the Table of Solomon, according to the custom of the Orientals, who ascribe to that prince every ancient work of knowledge or magnificence.

greater part had been the fruits of war and rapine, the spoils of the empire, and perhaps of Rome.

After the deliverance of Italy from the oppression of the Goths, some secret counsellor was permitted, amidst the factions of the palace, to heal the wounds of that afflicted country.[1] By a wise and humane regulation the eight provinces which had been the most deeply injured—Campania, Tuscany, Picenum, Samnium, Apulia, Calabria, Bruttium, and Lucania—obtained an indulgence of five years; the ordinary tribute was reduced to one-fifth, and even that fifth was destined to restore and support the useful institution of the public posts. By another law the lands which had been left without inhabitants or cultivation were granted, with some diminution of taxes, to the neighbours who should occupy or the strangers who should solicit them; and the new possessors were secured against the future claims of the fugitive proprietors. About the same time a general amnesty was published in the name of Honorius, to abolish the guilt and memory of all the *involuntary* offences which had been committed by his unhappy subjects during the term of the public disorder and calamity. A decent and respectful attention was paid to the restoration of the capital; the citizens were encouraged to rebuild the edifices which had been destroyed or damaged by hostile fire; and extraordinary supplies of corn were imported from the coast of Africa. The crowds that so lately fled before the sword of the barbarians were soon recalled by the hopes of plenty and pleasure; and Albinus, præfect of Rome, informed the court, with some anxiety and surprise, that in a single day he had taken an account of the arrival of fourteen thousand strangers.[2] In less than seven years the vestiges of the Gothic invasion were almost obliterated, and the city appeared to resume its former splendour and tranquillity. The venerable matron replaced her crown of laurel, which had been ruffled by the storms of war, and was still amused in the last moment of her decay with the prophecies of revenge, of victory, and of eternal dominion.[3]

---

[1] His three laws are inserted in the Theodosian Code, l. xi. tit. xxviii. leg. 7; l. xiii. tit. xi. leg. 12; l. xv. tit. xiv. leg. 14. The expressions of the last are very remarkable, since they contain not only a pardon, but an apology.

[2] Olympiodorus ap. Phot. p. 188 [p. 59, ed. Bekk.]. Philostorgius (l. xii. c. 5) observes, that when Honorius made his triumphal entry he encouraged the Romans, with his hand and voice (χειρὶ καὶ γλώττῃ), to rebuild their city; and the Chronicle of Prosper commends Heraclian, qui in Romanæ urbis reparationem strenuum exhibuerat ministerium.

[3] The date of the voyage of Claudius Rutilius Numatianus is clogged with some difficulties; but Scaliger has deduced from astronomical char-

This apparent tranquillity was soon disturbed by the approach of an hostile armament from the country which afforded the daily subsistence of the Roman people. Heraclian, count of Africa, who under the most difficult and distressful circumstances had supported with active loyalty the cause of Honorius, was tempted in the year of his consulship to assume the character of a rebel and the title of emperor. The ports of Africa were immediately filled with the naval forces, at the head of which he prepared to invade Italy; and his fleet, when it cast anchor at the mouth of the Tiber, indeed surpassed the fleets of Xerxes and Alexander, if *all* the vessels, including the royal galley and the smallest boat, did actually amount to the incredible number of three thousand two hundred.[1] Yet with such an armament, which might have subverted or restored the greatest empires of the earth, the African usurper made a very faint and feeble impression on the provinces of his rival. As he marched from the port along the road which leads to the gates of Rome, he was encountered, terrified, and routed by one of the Imperial captains; and the lord of this mighty host, deserting his fortune and his friends, ignominiously fled with a single ship.[2] When Heraclian landed in the harbour of Carthage, he found that the whole province, disdaining such an unworthy ruler, had returned to their allegiance. The rebel was beheaded in the ancient temple of Memory, his consulship was abolished,[3] and the remains of his private fortune, not exceeding the moderate sum of four thousand pounds of gold, were granted to the brave Constantius, who had already defended the throne which he afterwards shared with his feeble sovereign. Honorious viewed with supine indifference the calamities of Rome and Italy,[4] but he rebellious

acters that he left Rome the 24th of September, and embarked at Porto the 9th of October, A.D. 416. See Tillemont, Hist. des Empereurs, tom. v. p. 820. In this poetical Itinerary, Rutilius (l. i. 115, etc.) addresses Rome in a high strain of congratulation:

> Erige crinales lauros, seniumque sacrati
> Verticis in virides, Roma, recinge comas, etc.

[1] Orosius composed his history in Africa only two years after the event; yet his authority seems to be overbalanced by the improbability of the fact. The Chronicle of Marcellinus gives Heraclian 700 ships and 3000 men: the latter of these numbers is ridiculously corrupt; but the former would please me very much.

[2] The Chronicle of Idatius affirms, without the least appearance of truth, that he advanced as far as Otriculum, in Umbria, where he was overthrown in a great battle, with the loss of fifty thousand men.

[3] See Cod. Theod. l. xv. tit. xiv. leg. 13. The legal acts performed in his name, even the manumission of slaves, were declared invalid till they had been formally repealed.

[4] I have disdained to mention a very foolish, and probably a false, report (Procop. de Bell. Vandal. l. i. c. 2 [tom. i. p. 316, ed. Bonn]), that Honorius

attempts of Attalus and Heraclian against his personal safety awakened for a moment the torpid instinct of his nature. He was probably ignorant of the causes and events which preserved him from these impending dangers; and as Italy was no longer invaded by any foreign or domestic enemies, he peaceably existed in the palace of Ravenna, while the tyrants beyond the Alps were repeatedly vanquished in the name and by the lieutenants of the son of Theodosius.[1] In the course of a busy and interesting narrative I might possibly forget to mention the death of such a prince, and I shall therefore take the precaution of observing in this place that he survived the last siege of Rome about thirteen years.

The usurpation of Constantine, who received the purple from the legions of Britain, had been successful, and seemed to be secure. His title was acknowledged from the wall of Antoninus to the Columns of Hercules, and, in the midst of the public disorder, he shared the dominion and the plunder of Gaul and Spain with the tribes of barbarians whose destructive progress was no longer checked by the Rhine or Pyrenees. Stained with the blood of the kinsmen of Honorius, he extorted from the court of Ravenna, with which he secretly corresponded, the ratification of his rebellious claims. Constantine engaged himself by a solemn promise to deliver Italy from the Goths, advanced as far as the banks of the Po, and, after alarming rather than assisting his pusillanimous ally, hastily returned to the palace of Arles, to celebrate with intemperate luxury his vain and ostentatious triumph. But this transient prosperity was soon interrupted and destroyed by the revolt of Count Gerontius, the bravest of his generals, who, during the absence of his son Constans, a prince already invested with the Imperial purple, had been left to command in the provinces of Spain. For some reason of which we are ignorant, Gerontius, instead of assuming the diadem, placed it on the head of his friend Maximus, who fixed his residence at Tarragona, while the active count pressed forwards,

was alarmed by the *loss* of Rome till he understood that it was not a favourite chicken of that name, but *only* the capital of the world, which had been lost. Yet even this story is some evidence of the public opinion.

[1] The materials for the lives of all these tyrants are taken from six contemporary historians, two Latins and four Greeks: Orosius, l. vii. c. 42, p. 581, 582, 583; Renatus Profuturus Frigeridus, apud Gregor. Turon. l. ii. c. 9, in the Historians of France, tom. ii. p. 165, 166; Zosimus, l. vi. [c. 2] p. 370, 371; Olympiodorus, apud Phot. p. 180, 181, 184, 185 [p. 57 *sqq.*, ed Bekk.]; Sozomen, l. ix. c. 12, 13, 14, 15; and Philostorgius, l. xii. c. 5, 6, with Godefroy's Dissertations, p. 477-481; besides the four Chronicles of Prosper Tyro, Prosper of Aquitain, Idatius, and Marcellinus.

through the Pyrenees to surprise the two emperors Constantine and Constans before they could prepare for their defence. The son was made prisoner at Vienne, and immediately put to death; and the unfortunate youth had scarcely leisure to deplore the elevation of his family, which had tempted or compelled him sacrilegiously to desert the peaceful obscurity of the monastic life. The father maintained a siege within the walls of Arles; but those walls must have yielded to the assailants had not the city been unexpectedly relieved by the approach of an Italian army. The name of Honorius, the proclamation of a lawful emperor, astonished the contending parties of the rebels. Gerontius, abandoned by his own troops, escaped to the confines of Spain, and rescued his name from oblivion by the Roman courage which appeared to animate the last moments of his life. In the middle of the night a great body of his perfidious soldiers surrounded and attacked his house, which he had strongly barricaded. His wife, a valiant friend of the nation of the Alani, and some faithful slaves, were still attached to his person; and he used with so much skill and resolution a large magazine of darts and arrows, that above three hundred of the assailants lost their lives in the attempt. His slaves, when all the missile weapons were spent, fled at the dawn of day; and Gerontius, if he had not been restrained by conjugal tenderness, might have imitated their example; till the soldiers, provoked by such obstinate resistance, applied fire on all sides to the house. In this fatal extremity he complied with the request of his barbarian friend and cut off his head. The wife of Gerontius, who conjured him not to abandon her to a life of misery and disgrace, eagerly presented her neck to his sword: and the tragic scene was terminated by the death of the count himself, who, after three ineffectual strokes, drew a short dagger and sheathed it in his heart.[1] The unprotected Maximus, whom he had invested with the purple, was indebted for his life to the contempt that was entertained of his power and abilities. The caprice of the barbarians, who ravaged Spain, once more seated this Imperial phantom on the throne: but they soon resigned him to the justice of Honorius; and the tyrant Maximus, after he had been shown to the people of Ravenna and Rome, was publicly executed.

---

[1] The praises which Sozomen has bestowed on this act of despair appear strange and scandalous in the mouth of an ecclesiastical historian. He observes (p. 379 [ed. Cantab. 1720]) that the wife of Gerontius was a *Christian*; and that her death was worthy of her religion, and of immortal fame.

The general, Constantius was his name, who raised by his approach the siege of Arles and dissipated the troops of Gerontius, was born a Roman; and this remarkable distinction is strongly expressive of the decay of military spirit among the subjects of the empire. The strength and majesty which were conspicuous in the person of that general [1] marked him in the popular opinion as a candidate worthy of the throne which he afterwards ascended. In the familiar intercourse of private life his manners were cheerful and engaging: nor would he sometimes disdain, in the licence of convivial mirth, to vie with the pantomimes themselves in the exercises of their ridiculous profession. But when the trumpet summoned him to arms; when he mounted his horse, and, bending down (for such was his singular practice) almost upon the neck, fiercely rolled his large animated eyes round the field, Constantius then struck terror into his foes and inspired his soldiers with the assurance of victory. He had received from the court of Ravenna the important commission of extirpating rebellion in the provinces of the West; and the pretended emperor Constantine, after enjoying a short and anxious respite, was again besieged in his capital by the arms of a more formidable enemy. Yet this interval allowed time for a successful negotiation with the Franks and Alemanni; and his ambassador, Edobic, soon returned at the head of an army to disturb the operations of the siege of Arles. The Roman general, instead of expecting the attack in his lines, boldly, and perhaps wisely, resolved to pass the Rhone and to meet the barbarians. His measures were conducted with so much skill and secrecy, that, while they engaged the infantry of Constantius in the front, they were suddenly attacked, surrounded, and destroyed by the cavalry of his lieutenant Ulphilas, who had silently gained an advantageous post in their rear. The remains of the army of Edobic were preserved by flight or submission, and their leader escaped from the field of battle to the house of a faithless friend, who too clearly understood that the head of his obnoxious guest would be an acceptable and lucrative present for the Imperial general. On this occasion Constantius behaved with the magnanimity of a genuine Roman. Subduing or suppressing every sentiment of jealousy, he publicly acknowledged the merit and services of Ulphilas; but he turned with horror from the assassin

---

[1] Εἶδος ἄξιον τυραννίδος, is the expression of Olympiodorus, which he seems to have borrowed from Æolus, a tragedy of Euripides, of which some fragments only are now extant (Euripid. Barnes, tom. ii. p. 443, ver. 38). This allusion may prove that the ancient tragic poets were still familiar to the Greeks of the fifth century.

of Edobic, and sternly intimated his commands that the camp
should no longer be polluted by the presence of an ungrateful
wretch who had violated the laws of friendship and hospitality.
The usurper, who beheld from the walls of Arles the ruin of his
last hopes, was tempted to place some confidence in so generous
a conqueror. He required a solemn promise for his security;
and after receiving, by the imposition of hands, the sacred character of a Christian presbyter, he ventured to open the gates
of the city. But he soon experienced that the principles of
honour and integrity, which might regulate the ordinary conduct of Constantius, were superseded by the loose doctrines of
political morality. The Roman general indeed refused to sully
his laurels with the blood of Constantine; but the abdicated
emperor and his son Julian were sent, under a strong guard, into
Italy; and before they reached the palace of Ravenna they met
the ministers of death.

At a time when it was universally confessed that almost every
man in the empire was superior in personal merit to the princes
whom the accident of their birth had seated on the throne, a
rapid succession of usurpers, regardless of the fate of their predecessors, still continued to arise. This mischief was peculiarly
felt in the provinces of Spain and Gaul, where the principles of
order and obedience had been extinguished by war and rebellion.
Before Constantine resigned the purple, and in the fourth month
of the siege of Arles, intelligence was received in the Imperial
camp that Jovinus had assumed the diadem at Mentz, in the
Upper Germany, at the instigation of Goar, king of the Alani, and
of Guntiarius, king of the Burgundians; and that the candidate
on whom they had bestowed the empire advanced with a formidable host of barbarians from the banks of the Rhine to those of
the Rhone. Every circumstance is dark and extraordinary in
the short history of the reign of Jovinus. It was natural to
expect that a brave and skilful general, at the head of a victorious
army, would have asserted, in a field of battle, the justice of the
cause of Honorius. The hasty retreat of Constantius might be
justified by weighty reasons; but he resigned without a struggle
the possession of Gaul; and Dardanus, the Prætorian præfect,
is recorded as the only magistrate who refused to yield obedience
to the usurper.[1] When the Goths, two years after the siege of

---

[1] Sidonius Apollinaris (l. v. Epist. 9, p. 139, and Not. Sirmond. p. 58),
after stigmatising the *inconstancy* of Constantine, the *facility* of Jovinus,
the *perfidy* of Gerontius, continues to observe that *all* the vices of these
tyrants were united in the person of Dardanus. Yet the præfect supported
a respectable character in the world, and even in the church; held a devout

Rome, established their quarters in Gaul, it was natural to suppose that their inclinations could be divided only between the emperor Honorius, with whom they had formed a recent alliance, and the degraded Attalus, whom they reserved in their camp for the occasional purpose of acting the part of a musician or a monarch. Yet in a moment of disgust (for which it is not easy to assign a cause or a date) Adolphus connected himself with the usurper of Gaul; and imposed on Attalus the ignominious task of negotiating the treaty which ratified his own disgrace. We are again surprised to read, that, instead of considering the Gothic alliance as the firmest support of his throne, Jovinus upbraided, in dark and ambiguous language, the officious importunity of Attalus; that, scorning the advice of his great ally, he invested with the purple his brother Sebastian; and that he most imprudently accepted the service of Sarus, when that gallant chief, the soldier of Honorius, was provoked to desert the court of a prince who knew not how to reward or punish. Adolphus, educated among a race of warriors, who esteemed the duty of revenge as the most precious and sacred portion of their inheritance, advanced with a body of ten thousand Goths to encounter the hereditary enemy of the house of Balti. He attacked Sarus at an unguarded moment, when he was accompanied only by eighteen or twenty of his valiant followers. United by friendship, animated by despair, but at length oppressed by multitudes, this band of heroes deserved the esteem, without exciting the compassion, of their enemies; and the lion was no sooner taken in the toils [1] than he was instantly despatched. The death of Sarus dissolved the loose alliance which Adolphus still maintained with the usurpers of Gaul. He again listened to the dictates of love and prudence; and soon satisfied the brother of Placidia, by the assurance that he would immediately transmit to the palace of Ravenna the heads of the two tyrants, Jovinus and Sebastian. The king of the Goths executed his promise without difficulty or delay: the helpless brothers, unsupported by any personal merit, were abandoned by their barbarian auxiliaries; and the short opposition of Valentia was expiated

correspondence with St. Augustin and St. Jerom; and was complimented by the latter (tom. iii. p. 66) with the epithets of Christianorum Nobilissime and Nobilium Christianissime.

[1] The expression may be understood almost literally: Olympiodorus says, μόλις σάκκοις ἐζώγρησαν. Σάκκος (or σάκος) may signify a sack or a loose garment; and this method of entangling and catching an enemy, laciniis contortis, was much practised by the Huns (Ammian. xxxi. 2). Il fut pris vif avec des filets, is the translation of Tillemont, Hist. des Empereurs, tom. v. p. 608.

by the ruin of one of the oldest cities of Gaul. The emperor chosen by the Roman senate, who had been promoted, degraded, insulted, restored, again degraded, and again insulted, was finally abandoned to his fate; but when the Gothic king withdrew his protection, he was restrained, by pity or contempt, from offering any violence to the person of Attalus. The unfortunate Attalus, who was left without subjects or allies, embarked in one of the ports of Spain, in search of some secure and solitary retreat; but he was intercepted at sea, conducted to the presence of Honorius, led in triumph through the streets of Rome or Ravenna, and publicly exposed to the gazing multitude, on the second step of the throne of his *invincible* conqueror. The same measure of punishment with which, in the days of his prosperity, he was accused of menacing his rival, was inflicted on Attalus himself: he was condemned, after the amputation of two fingers, to a perpetual exile in the isle of Lipari, where he was supplied with the decent necessaries of life. The remainder of the reign of Honorius was undisturbed by rebellion; and it may be observed that in the space of five years seven usurpers had yielded to the fortune of a prince who was himself incapable either of counsel or of action.

The situation of Spain, separated on all sides from the enemies of Rome, by the sea, by the mountains, and by intermediate provinces, had secured the long tranquillity of that remote and sequestered country; and we may observe, as a sure symptom of domestic happiness, that, in a period of four hundred years, Spain furnished very few materials to the history of the Roman empire. The footsteps of the barbarians, who, in the reign of Gallienus, had penetrated beyond the Pyrenees, were soon obliterated by the return of peace; and in the fourth century of the Christian era, the cities of Emerita or Merida, of Corduba, Seville, Bracara, and Tarragona, were numbered with the most illustrious of the Roman world. The various plenty of the animal, the vegetable, and the mineral kingdoms, was improved and manufactured by the skill of an industrious people; and the peculiar advantages of naval stores contributed to support an extensive and profitable trade.[1] The arts and sciences flourished

---

[1] Without recurring to the more ancient writers, I shall quote three respectable testimonies which belong to the fourth and seventh centuries: the Expositio totius Mundi (p. 16, in the third volume of Hudson's Minor Geographers), Ausonius (de Claris Urbibus, p. 242, edit. Toll.), and Isidore of Seville (Præfat. ad Chron. ap Grotium, Hist. Goth. p. 707). Many particulars relative to the fertility and trade of Spain may be found in Nonnius, Hispania, Illustrata; and in Huet, Hist. du Commerce des Anciens, c. 40, p. 228-234.

under the protection of the emperors; and if the character of
the Spaniards was enfeebled by peace and servitude, the hostile
approach of the Germans, who had spread terror and desolation
from the Rhine to the Pyrenees, seemed to rekindle some sparks
of military ardour. As long as the defence of the mountains was
intrusted to the hardy and faithful militia of the country, they
successfully repelled the frequent attempts of the barbarians.
But no sooner had the national troops been compelled to resign
their post to the Honorian bands in the service of Constantine,
than the gates of Spain were treacherously betrayed to the
public enemy, about ten months before the sack of Rome by
the Goths.[1] The consciousness of guilt, and the thirst of rapine,
prompted the mercenary guards of the Pyrenees to desert their
station; to invite the arms of the Suevi, the Vandals, and the
Alani; and to swell the torrent which was poured with irresistible
violence from the frontiers of Gaul to the sea of Africa. The
misfortunes of Spain may be described in the language of its
most eloquent historian, who has concisely expressed the passionate, and perhaps exaggerated, declamations of contemporary
writers.[2] " The irruption of these nations was followed by the
most dreadful calamities: as the barbarians exercised their
indiscriminate cruelty on the fortunes of the Romans and the
Spaniards, and ravaged with equal fury the cities and the open
country. The progress of famine reduced the miserable inhabitants to feed on the flesh of their fellow-creatures; and even the
wild beasts, who multiplied, without control, in the desert, were
exasperated by the taste of blood and the impatience of hunger
boldly to attack and devour their human prey. Pestilence soon
appeared, the inseparable companion of famine; a large proportion of the people was swept away; and the groans of the dying
excited only the envy of their surviving friends. At length the
barbarians, satiated with carnage and rapine, and afflicted by
the contagious evils which they themselves had introduced, fixed
their permanent seats in the depopulated country. The ancient
Gallicia, whose limits included the kingdom of Old Castille, was
divided between the Suevi and the Vandals; the Alani were
scattered over the provinces of Carthagena and Lusitania, from
the Mediterranean to the Atlantic Ocean; and the fruitful terri-

[1] The date is accurately fixed in the Fasti and the Chronicle of Idatius.
Orosius (l. vii. c. 40, p. 578) imputes the loss of Spain to the treachery of
the Honorians; while Sozomen (l. ix. c. 12) accuses only their negligence.
[2] Idatius wishes to apply the prophecies of Daniel to these national
calamities, and is therefore obliged to accommodate the circumstances of
the event to the terms of the prediction.

tory of Bætica was allotted to the Silingi, another branch of the Vandalic nation. After regulating this partition, the conquerors contracted with their new subjects some reciprocal engagements of protection and obedience: the lands were again cultivated; and the towns and villages were again occupied by a captive people. The greatest part of the Spaniards was even disposed to prefer this new condition of poverty and barbarism to the severe oppressions of the Roman government; yet there were many who still asserted their native freedom, and who refused, more especially in the mountains of Gallicia, to submit to the barbarian yoke." [1]

The important present of the heads of Jovinus and Sebastian had approved the friendship of Adolphus, and restored Gaul to the obedience of his brother Honorius. Peace was incompatible with the situation and temper of the king of the Goths. He readily accepted the proposal of turning his victorious arms against the barbarians of Spain; the troops of Constantius intercepted his communication with the seaports of Gaul, and gently pressed his march towards the Pyrenees: [2] he passed the mountains, and surprised, in the name of the emperor, the city of Barcelona. The fondness of Adolphus for his Roman bride was not abated by time or possession; and the birth of a son, surnamed, from his illustrious grandsire, Theodosius, appeared to fix him for ever in the interest of the republic. The loss of that infant, whose remains were deposited in a silver coffin in one of the churches near Barcelona, afflicted his parents; but the grief of the Gothic king was suspended by the labours of the field; and the course of his victories was soon interrupted by domestic treason. He had imprudently received into his service one of the followers of Sarus, a barbarian of a daring spirit, but of a diminutive stature, whose secret desire of revenging the death of his beloved patron was continually irritated by the sarcasms of his insolent master. Adolphus was assassinated in the palace of Barcelona; the laws of the succession were violated by a tumultuous faction; [3] and a stranger to the royal

[1] Mariana de Rebus Hispanicis, l. v. c. 1, tom. i. p. 148. Hag. Comit. 1733. He had read in Orosius (l. vii. c. 41, p. 579) that the barbarians had turned their swords into ploughshares; and that many of the provincials preferred inter Barbaros pauperem libertatem, quam inter Romanos tributariam solicitudinem, sustinere.

[2] This mixture of force and persuasion may be fairly inferred from comparing Orosius and Jornandes, the Roman and the Gothic historian.

[3] According to the system of Jornandes (c. 33, p. 659 [ed. Grot.]), the true hereditary right to the Gothic sceptre was vested in the Amali; but those princes, who were the vassals of the Huns, commanded the tribes of the Ostrogoths in some distant parts of Germany or Scythia.

race, Singeric, the brother of Sarus himself, was seated on the Gothic throne. The first act of his reign was the inhuman murder of the six children of Adolphus, the issue of a former marriage, whom he tore, without pity, from the feeble arms of a venerable bishop.[1] The unfortunate Placidia, instead of the respectful compassion which she might have excited in the most savage breasts, was treated with cruel and wanton insult. The daughter of the emperor Theodosius, confounded among a crowd of vulgar captives, was compelled to march on foot above twelve miles, before the horse of a barbarian, the assassin of an husband whom Placidia loved and lamented.[2]

But Placidia soon obtained the pleasure of revenge; and the view of her ignominious sufferings might rouse an indignant people against the tyrant, who was assassinated on the seventh day of his usurpation. After the death of Singeric, the free choice of the nation bestowed the Gothic sceptre on Wallia, whose warlike and ambitious temper appeared, in the beginning of his reign, extremely hostile to the republic. He marched in arms from Barcelona to the shores of the Atlantic Ocean, which the ancients revered and dreaded as the boundary of the world. But when he reached the southern promontory of Spain,[3] and, from the rock now covered by the fortress of Gibraltar, contemplated the neighbouring and fertile coast of Africa, Wallia resumed the designs of conquest which had been interrupted by the death of Alaric. The winds and waves again disappointed the enterprise of the Goths; and the minds of a superstitious people were deeply affected by the repeated disasters of storms and shipwrecks. In this disposition, the successor of Adolphus no longer refused to listen to a Roman ambassador, whose proposals were enforced by the real, or supposed, approach of a numerous army, under the conduct of the brave Constantius. A solemn treaty was stipulated and observed: Placidia was honourably restored to her brother; six hundred thousand

---

[1] The murder is related by Olympiodorus; but the number of the children is taken from an epitaph of suspected authority.

[2] The death of Adolphus was celebrated at Constantinople with illuminations and Circensian games. (See Chron. Alexandrin.) It may seem doubtful whether the Greeks were actuated on this occasion by their hatred of the barbarians or of the Latins.

[3] Quòd *Tartessiacis* avus hujus Vallia *terris*
Vandalicas turmas, et juncti Martis Alanos
Stravit, et occiduam texêre cadavera *Calpen*.
Sidon. Appollinar. in Panegyr. Anthem. 363,
p. 300, edit Sirmond.

measures of wheat were delivered to the hungry Goths;[1] and
Wallia engaged to draw his sword in the service of the empire.
A bloody war was instantly excited among the barbarians of
Spain; and the contending princes are said to have addressed
their letters, their ambassadors, and their hostages, to the throne
of the Western emperor, exhorting him to remain a tranquil
spectator of their contest, the events of which must be favourable
to the Romans by the mutual slaughter of their common enemies.[2]
The Spanish war was obstinately supported, during three campaigns, with desperate valour and various success; and the
martial achievements of Wallia diffused through the empire the
superior renown of the Gothic hero. He exterminated the
Silingi, who had irretrievably ruined the elegant plenty of the
province of Bætica. He slew, in battle, the king of the Alani;
and the remains of those Scythian wanderers who escaped from
the field, instead of choosing a new leader, humbly sought a
refuge under the standard of the Vandals, with whom they were
ever afterwards confounded. The Vandals themselves, and the
Suevi, yielded to the efforts of the invincible Goths. The promiscuous multitude of barbarians, whose retreat had been intercepted, were driven into the mountains of Gallicia; where
they still continued, in a narrow compass and on a barren soil,
to exercise their domestic and implacable hostilities. In the
pride of victory, Wallia was faithful to his engagements: he
restored his Spanish conquests to the obedience of Honorius; and
the tyranny of the Imperial officers soon reduced an oppressed
people to regret the time of their barbarian servitude. While
the event of the war was still doubtful, the first advantages obtained by the arms of Wallia had encouraged the court of
Ravenna to decree the honours of a triumph to their feeble
sovereign. He entered Rome like the ancient conquerors of
nations; and if the monuments of servile corruption had not
long since met with the fate which they deserved, we should
probably find that a crowd of poets and orators, of magistrates
and bishops, applauded the fortune, the wisdom, and the invincible courage of the emperor Honorius.[3]

[1] This supply was very acceptable: the Goths were insulted by the
Vandals of Spain with the epithet of *Truli*, because in their extreme distress
they had given a piece of gold for a *trula*, or about half a pound of flour.
Olympiod. apud Phot. p. 189 [p. 60, ed. Bekk.].

[2] Orosius inserts a copy of these pretended letters. Tu cum omnibus
pacem habe, omniumque obsides accipe; nos nobis confligimus, nobis
perimus, tibi vincimus; immortalis vero quæstus erit Reipublicæ tuæ, si
utrique pereamus [p. 586]. The idea is just; but I cannot persuade
myself that it was entertained or expressed by the barbarians.

[3] Romam triumphans ingreditur is the formal expression of Prosper's

Such a triumph might have been justly claimed by the ally of Rome, if Wallia, before he repassed the Pyrenees, had extirpated the seeds of the Spanish war. His victorious Goths, forty-three years after they had passed the Danube, were established, according to the faith of treaties, in the possession of the second Aquitain, a maritime province between the Garonne and the Loire, under the civil and ecclesiastical jurisdiction of Bourdeaux. That metropolis, advantageously situated for the trade of the ocean, was built in a regular and elegant form; and its numerous inhabitants were distinguished among the Gauls by their wealth, their learning, and the politeness of their manners. The adjacent province, which has been fondly compared to the garden of Eden, is blessed with a fruitful soil and a temperate climate; the face of the country displayed the arts and the rewards of industry; and the Goths, after their martial toils, luxuriously exhausted the rich vineyards of Aquitain.[1] The Gothic limits were enlarged by the additional gift of some neighbouring dioceses; and the successors of Alaric fixed their royal residence at Toulouse, which included five populous quarters, or cities, within the spacious circuit of its walls. About the same time, in the last years of the reign of Honorius, the GOTHS, the BURGUNDIANS, and the FRANKS, obtained a permanent seat and dominion in the provinces of Gaul. The liberal grant of the usurper Jovinus to his Burgundian allies was confirmed by the lawful emperor; the lands of the First, or Upper, Germany, were ceded to those formidable barbarians; and they gradually occupied, either by conquest or treaty, the two provinces which still retain, with the titles of *Duchy* and of *County*, the national appellation of Burgundy.[2] The Franks, the valiant and faithful allies of the Roman republic, were soon tempted to imitate the invaders whom they had so bravely resisted. Trèves, the capital of Gaul, was pillaged by their lawless bands; and the humble colony which they so long maintained in the

Chronicle. The facts which relate to the death of Adolphus and the exploits of Wallia are related from Olympiodorus (ap Phot. p. 188 [p. 59, 60, ed. Bekk.]), Orosius (l. vii. c. 43, p. 584-587), Jornandes (de Rebus Geticis, c. 31, 32), and the Chronicles of Idatius and Isidore.

[1] Ausonius (de Claris Urbibus, p. 257-262 [No. 14]) celebrates Bourdeaux with the partial affection of a native. See in Salvian (de Gubern. Dei, p. 228, Paris, 1608) a florid description of the provinces of Aquitain and Novempopulania.

[2] Orosius (l. vii. c. 32, p. 550) commends the mildness and modesty of these Burgundians, who treated their subjects of Gaul as their Christian brethren. Mascou has illustrated the origin of their kingdom in the four first annotations at the end of his laborious History of the Ancient Germans, vol. ii. p. 555-572 of the English translation.

district of Toxandria, in Brabant, insensibly multiplied along the banks of the Meuse and Scheld, till their independent power filled the whole extent of the Second, or Lower, Germany. These facts may be sufficiently justified by historic evidence; but the foundation of the French monarchy by Pharamond, the conquests, the laws, and even the existence of that hero, have been justly arraigned by the impartial severity of modern criticism.[1]

The ruin of the opulent provinces of Gaul may be dated from the establishment of these barbarians, whose alliance was dangerous and oppressive, and who were capriciously impelled, by interest or passion, to violate the public peace. A heavy and partial ransom was imposed on the surviving provincials who had escaped the calamities of war; the fairest and most fertile lands were assigned to the rapacious strangers, for the use of their families, their slaves, and their cattle; and the trembling natives relinquished with a sigh the inheritance of their fathers. Yet these domestic misfortunes, which are seldom the lot of a vanquished people, had been felt and inflicted by the Romans themselves, not only in the insolence of foreign conquest, but in the madness of civil discord. The Triumvirs proscribed eighteen of the most flourishing colonies of Italy, and distributed their lands and houses to the veterans who revenged the death of Cæsar, and oppressed the liberty of their country. Two poets, of unequal fame, have deplored, in similar circumstances, the loss of their patrimony; but the legionaries of Augustus appear to have surpassed, in violence and injustice, the barbarians who invaded Gaul under the reign of Honorius. It was not without the utmost difficulty that Virgil escaped from the sword of the centurion who had usurped his farm in the neighbourhood of Mantua;[2] but Paulinus of Bourdeaux received

---

[1] See Mascou, l. viii. c. 43, 44, 45. Except in a short and suspicious line of the Chronicle of Prosper (in tom. i. p. 638), the name of Pharamond is never mentioned before the seventh century. The author of the Gesta Francorum (in tom. ii. p. 543) suggests, probably enough, that the choice of Pharamond, or at least of a king, was recommended to the Franks by his father Marcomir, who was an exile in Tuscany.

[2] O Lycida, vivi pervenimus: advena nostri
(Quod nunquam veriti sumus) ut possessor agelli
Diceret: Hæc mea sunt; veteres migrate coloni.
Nunc victi tristes, etc.

See the whole of the ninth eclogue, with the useful Commentary of Servius. Fifteen miles of the Mantuan territory were assigned to the veterans, with a reservation in favour of the inhabitants of three miles round the city. Even in this favour they were cheated by Alfenus Varus, a famous lawyer and one of the commissioners, who measured eight hundred paces of water and morass.

a sum of money from his Gothic purchaser, which he accepted
with pleasure and surprise; and, though it was much inferior
to the real value of his estate, this act of rapine was disguised
by some colours of moderation and equity.[1] The odious name
of conquerors was softened into the mild and friendly appellation
of the *guests* of the Romans; and the barbarians of Gaul, more
especially the Goths, repeatedly declared that they were bound
to the people by the ties of hospitality, and to the emperor by
the duty of allegiance and military service. The title of Honorius
and his successors, their laws and their civil magistrates, were
still respected in the provinces of Gaul, of which they had resigned
the possession to the barbarian allies; and the kings, who exercised a supreme and independent authority over their native
subjects, ambitiously solicited the more honourable rank of
master-generals of the Imperial armies.[2] Such was the involuntary reverence which the Roman name still impressed on the
minds of those warriors who had borne away in triumph the
spoils of the Capitol.

Whilst Italy was ravaged by the Goths, and a succession of
feeble tyrants oppressed the provinces beyond the Alps, the
British island separated itself from the body of the Roman
empire. The regular forces which guarded that remote province
had been gradually withdrawn; and Britain was abandoned,
without defence, to the Saxon pirates and the savages of Ireland
and Caledonia. The Britons, reduced to this extremity, no
longer relied on the tardy and doubtful aid of a declining
monarchy. They assembled in arms, repelled the invaders,
and rejoiced in the important discovery of their own strength.[3]
Afflicted by similar calamities, and actuated by the same spirit,
the Armorican provinces (a name which comprehended the
maritime countries of Gaul between the Seine and the Loire) [4]
resolved to imitate the example of the neighbouring island.
They expelled the Roman magistrates, who acted under the

[1] See the remarkable passage of the Eucharisticon of Paulinus, 575, apud
Mascou, l. viii. c. 42.
[2] This important truth is established by the accuracy of Tillemont (Hist.
des Emp. tom. v. p. 641) and by the ingenuity of the Abbé Dubos (Hist. de
l'Etablissement de la Monarchie Françoise dans les Gaules, tom. i. p. 259).
[3] Zosimus (l. vi. [c. 5] 376 [c. 10], 383) relates in a few words the revolt of
Britain and Armorica. Our antiquarians, even the great Camden himself,
have been betrayed into many gross errors by their imperfect knowledge
of the history of the continent.
[4] The limits of Armorica are defined by two national geographers,
Messieurs de Valois and d'Anville, in their *Notitias* of Ancient Gaul. The
word had been used in a more extensive, and was afterwards contracted to
a much narrower, signification.

authority of the usurper Constantine; and a free government
was established among a people who had so long been subject
to the arbitrary will of a master. The independence of Britain
and Armorica was soon confirmed by Honorius himself, the lawful
emperor of the West; and the letters by which he committed
to the new states the care of their own safety might be interpreted as an absolute and perpetual abdication of the exercise
and rights of sovereignty. This interpretation was, in some
measure, justified by the event. After the usurpers of Gaul
had successively fallen, the maritime provinces were restored
to the empire. Yet their obedience was imperfect and precarious: the vain, inconstant, rebellious disposition of the people,
was incompatible either with freedom or servitude;[1] and
Armorica, though it could not long maintain the form of a
republic,[2] was agitated by frequent and destructive revolts.
Britain was irrecoverably lost.[3] But as the emperors wisely
acquiesced in the independence of a remote province, the separation was not embittered by the reproach of tyranny or rebellion;
and the claims of allegiance and protection were succeeded by
the mutual and voluntary offices of national friendship.[4]

This revolution dissolved the artificial fabric of civil and
military government; and the independent country, during a
period of forty years, till the descent of the Saxons, was ruled by

> [1] Gens inter geminos notissima clauditur amnes,
>   Armoricana prius veteri cognomine dicta.
>   Torva, ferox, ventosa, procax, incauta, rebellis;
>   Inconstans, disparque sibi novitatis amore;
>   Prodiga verborum, sed non et prodiga facti.

Erricus, Monach. in Vit. St. Germani, l. v. apud Vales. Notit. Galliarum,
p. 43. Valesius alleges several testimonies to confirm this character; to
which I shall add the evidence of the presbyter Constantine (A.D. 488), who,
in the Life of St. Germain, calls the Armorican rebels mobilem et indis-
ciplinatum populum.   See the Historians of France, tom. i. p. 643.

[2] I thought it necessary to enter my protest against this part of the
system of the Abbé Dubos, which Montesquieu has so vigorously opposed.
See Esprit des Loix, l. xxx. c. 24.

[3] Βρεταννίαν μέντοι Ῥωμαῖοι ἀνασώσασθαι οὐκέτι ἔσχον, are the words of
Procopius (de Bell. Vandal. l. i. c. 2, p. 181, Louvre edition [tom. i. p. 318,
ed. Bonn]), in a very important passage which has been too much neglected.
Even Bede (Hist. Gent. Anglican. l. i. c. 12, p. 50, edit. Smith) acknowledges that the Romans finally left Britain in the reign of Honorius.   Yet
our modern historians and antiquaries extend the term of their dominion;
and there are some who allow only the interval of a few months between
their departure and the arrival of the Saxons.

[4] Bede has not forgot the occasional aid of the legions against the Scots
and Picts; and more authentic proof will hereafter be produced that the
independent Britons raised 12,000 men for the service of the emperor
Anthemius in Gaul.

the authority of the clergy, the nobles, and the municipal towns.[1]
I. Zosimus, who alone has preserved the memory of this singular
transaction, very accurately observes that the letters of Honorius
were addressed to the *cities* of Britain.[2] Under the protection
of the Romans, ninety-two considerable towns had arisen in the
several parts of that great province; and, among these, thirty-
three cities were distinguished above the rest by their superior
privileges and importance.[3] Each of these cities, as in all the
other provinces of the empire, formed a legal corporation, for the
purpose of regulating their domestic policy; and the powers of
municipal government were distributed among annual magistrates, a select senate, and the assembly of the people, according
to the original model of the Roman constitution.[4] The management of a common revenue, the exercise of civil and criminal
jurisdiction, and the habits of public counsel and command,
were inherent to these petty republics; and when they asserted
their independence, the youth of the city, and of the adjacent
districts, would naturally range themselves under the standard
of the magistrate. But the desire of obtaining the advantages,
and of escaping the burthens, of political society, is a perpetual
and inexhaustible source of discord; nor can it reasonably be
presumed that the restoration of British freedom was exempt
from tumult and faction. The pre-eminence of birth and fortune
must have been frequently violated by bold and popular citizens;
and the haughty nobles, who complained that they were become
the subjects of their own servants,[5] would sometimes regret the
reign of an arbitrary monarch. II. The jurisdiction of each
city over the adjacent country was supported by the patrimonial
influence of the principal senators; and the smaller towns, the
villages, and the proprietors of land, consulted their own safety
by adhering to the shelter of these rising republics. The sphere

---

[1] I owe it to myself and to historic truth to declare that some *circumstances* in this paragraph are founded only on conjecture and analogy.
The stubbornness of our language has sometimes forced me to deviate
from the *conditional* into the *indicative* mood.

[2] Πρὸς τὰς ἐν Βρεταννίᾳ πόλεις. Zosimus, l. vi. [c. 10] p. 383.

[3] Two cities of Britain were *municipia*, nine *colonies*, ten *Latii jure
donatæ*, twelve *stipendiariæ* of eminent note. This detail is taken from
Richard of Cirencester, de Sitû Britanniæ, p. 36; and though it may not
seem probable that he wrote from the MSS. of a Roman general, he shows
a genuine knowledge of antiquity, very extraordinary for a monk of the
fourteenth century.

[4] See Maffei, Verona Illustrata, part. i. l. v. p. 83-106.

[5] Leges restituit, libertatemque reducit,
  Et servos famulis non sinit esse suis.
                                        Itinerar Rutil. l. i 215.

of their attraction was proportioned to the respective degrees of their wealth and populousness; but the hereditary lords of ample possessions, who were not oppressed by the neighbourhood of any powerful city, aspired to the rank of independent princes, and boldly exercised the rights of peace and war. The gardens and villas, which exhibited some faint imitation of Italian elegance, would soon be converted into strong castles, the refuge, in time of danger, of the adjacent country: [1] the produce of the land was applied to purchase arms and horses; to maintain a military force of slaves, of peasants, and of licentious followers: and the chieftain might assume, within his own domain, the powers of a civil magistrate. Several of these British chiefs might be the genuine posterity of ancient kings; and many more would be tempted to adopt this honourable genealogy, and to vindicate their hereditary claims, which had been suspended by the usurpation of the Cæsars. [2] Their situation and their hopes would dispose them to affect the dress, the language, and the customs of their ancestors. If the *princes* of Britain relapsed into barbarism, while the *cities* studiously preserved the laws and manners of Rome, the whole island must have been gradually divided by the distinction of two national parties; again broken into a thousand subdivisions of war and faction by the various provocations of interest and resentment. The public strength, instead of being united against a foreign enemy, was consumed in obscure and intestine quarrels; and the personal merit which had placed a successful leader at the head of his equals might enable him to subdue the freedom of some neighbouring cities, and to claim a rank among the *tyrants* [3] who infested Britain after the dissolution of the Roman government. III. The British church might be composed of thirty or forty bishops, [4] with an adequate proportion of the inferior clergy; and

---

[1] An inscription (apud Sirmond, Not. ad Sidon. Appollinar. p. 59) describes a castle, cum muris et portis, tuitioni omnium, erected by Dardanus on his own estate near Sisteron in the second Narbonnese, and named by him Theopolis.

[2] The establishment of their power would have been easy indeed if we could adopt the impracticable scheme of a lively and learned antiquarian, who supposes that the British monarchs of the several tribes continued to reign, though with subordinate jurisdiction, from the time of Claudius to that of Honorius. See Whitaker's History of Manchester, vol. i. p. 247-257.

[3] Ἀλλ' οὖσα ὑπὸ τυράννοις ἀπ' αὐτοῦ ἔμενε. Procopius, de Bell. Vandal. l. i. c. 2, p. 181 [ed. Paris; tom. i. p. 318, ed. Bonn]. Britannia fertilis provincia tyrannorum, was the expression of Jerom in the year 415 (tom. ii. p. 255, ad Ctesiphont. [Epist. cxxxiii. c. 9, tom. i. p. 1032, ed. Vallars.]). By the pilgrims who resorted every year to the Holy Land, the monk of Bethlem received the earliest and most accurate intelligence.

[4] See Bingham's Eccles. Antiquities, vol. i. l. ix. c. 6, p. 394.

the want of riches (for they seem to have been poor)[1] would compel them to deserve the public esteem by a decent and exemplary behaviour. The interest, as well as the temper, of the clergy, was favourable to the peace and union of their distracted country: those salutary lessons might be frequently inculcated in their popular discourses; and the episcopal synods were the only councils that could pretend to the weight and authority of a national assembly. In such councils, where the princes and magistrates sat promiscuously with the bishops, the important affairs of the state, as well as of the church, might be freely debated, differences reconciled, alliances formed, contributions imposed, wise resolutions often concerted, and sometimes executed; and there is reason to believe, that, in moments of extreme danger, a *Pendragon*, or Dictator, was elected by the general consent of the Britons. These pastoral cares, so worthy of the episcopal character, were interrupted, however, by zeal and superstition; and the British clergy incessantly laboured to eradicate the Pelagian heresy, which they abhorred as the peculiar disgrace of their native country.[2]

It is somewhat remarkable, or rather it is extremely natural, that the revolt of Britain and Armorica should have introduced an appearance of liberty into the obedient provinces of Gaul. In a solemn edict,[3] filled with the strongest assurances of that paternal affection which princes so often express, and so seldom feel, the emperor Honorius promulgated his intention of convening an annual assembly of the *seven provinces*: a name peculiarly appropriated to Aquitain and the ancient Narbonnese, which had long since exchanged their Celtic rudeness for the useful and elegant arts of Italy.[4] Arles, the seat of government and commerce, was appointed for the place of the assembly, which regularly continued twenty-eight days, from the fifteenth of August to the thirteenth of September of every year. It con-

---

[1] It is reported of *three* British bishops who assisted at the council of Rimini, A.D. 359, tam pauperes fuisse ut nihil [proprium] haberent. Sulpicius Severus, Hist. Sacra, l. ii. p. 420. Some of their brethren, however, were in better circumstances.

[2] Consult Usher, de Antiq. Eccles. Britannicar. c. 8-12.

[3] See the correct text of this edict, as published by Sirmond (Not. ad Sidon. Apollin. p. 147). Hincmar of Rheims, who assigns a place to the *bishops*, had probably seen (in the ninth century) a more perfect copy. Dubos, Hist. Critique de la Monarchie Françoise, tom. i. p. 241-255.

[4] It is evident from the *Notitia* that the seven provinces were the Viennensis, the maritime Alps, the first and second Narbonnese, Novempopulania, and the first and second Aquitain. In the room of the first Aquitain, the Abbé Dubos, on the authority of Hincmar, desires to introduce the first Lugdunensis or Lyonnese.

sisted of the Prætorian præfect of the Gauls; of seven provincial
governors, one consular, and six presidents; of the magistrates,
and perhaps the bishops, of about sixty cities; and of a com-
petent, though indefinite, number of the most honourable and
opulent *possessors* of land, who might justly be considered as the
representatives of their country.   They were empowered to interpret and communicate the laws of their sovereign; to expose the
grievances and wishes of their constituents; to moderate the
excessive or unequal weight of taxes; and to deliberate on every
subject of local or national importance that could tend to the
restoration of the peace and prosperity of the seven provinces.
If such an institution, which gave the people an interest in their
own government, had been universally established by Trajan or
the Antonines, the seeds of public wisdom and virtue might have
been cherished and propagated in the empire of Rome.   The
privileges of the subject would have secured the throne of the
monarch; the abuses of an arbitrary administration might have
been prevented, in some degree, or corrected, by the interposition
of these representative assemblies; and the country would have
been defended against a foreign enemy by the arms of natives
and freemen.   Under the mild and generous influence of liberty,
the Roman empire might have remained invincible and immortal;
or if its excessive magnitude, and the instability of human
affairs, had opposed such perpetual continuance, its vital and
constituent members might have separately preserved their
vigour and independence.   But in the decline of the empire,
when every principle of health and life had been exhausted, the
tardy application of this partial remedy was incapable of
producing any important or salutary effects.   The emperor
Honorius expresses his surprise that he must compel the reluctant provinces to accept a privilege which they should ardently
have solicited.   A fine of three, or even five, pounds of gold was
imposed on the absent representatives, who seem to have declined
this imaginary gift of a free constitution, as the last and most
cruel insult of their oppressors.

CHAPTER XXXII

Arcadius Emperor of the East—Administration and Disgrace of Eutropius—
    Revolt of Gainas—Persecution of St. John Chrysostom—Theodosius
    II. Emperor of the East—His Sister Pulcheria—His Wife Eudocia—
    The Persian War, and Division of Armenia

THE division of the Roman world between the sons of Theodosius marks the final establishment of the empire of the East,
which, from the reign of Arcadius to the taking of Constantinople
by the Turks, subsisted one thousand and fifty-eight years in a
state of premature and perpetual decay. The sovereign of that
empire assumed and obstinately retained the vain, and at length
fictitious, title of Emperor of the ROMANS; and the hereditary
appellations of CÆSAR and AUGUSTUS continued to declare that
he was the legitimate successor of the first of men, who had
reigned over the first of nations. The palace of Constantinople
rivalled, and perhaps excelled, the magnificence of Persia; and
the eloquent sermons of St. Chrysostom [1] celebrate, while they
condemn, the pompous luxury of the reign of Arcadius. " The
emperor," says he, " wears on his head either a diadem or a crown
of gold, decorated with precious stones of inestimable value.
These ornaments and his purple garments are reserved for his
sacred person alone; and his robes of silk are embroidered with
the figures of golden dragons. His throne is of massy gold.
Whenever he appears in public he is surrounded by his courtiers,
his guards, and his attendants. Their spears, their shields, their
cuirasses, the bridles and trappings of their horses, have either
the substance or the appearance of gold; and the large splendid
boss in the midst of their shield is encircled with smaller bosses,
which represent the shape of the human eye. The two mules
that draw the chariot of the monarch are perfectly white, and
shining all over with gold. The chariot itself, of pure and solid
gold, attracts the admiration of the spectators, who contemplate
the purple curtains, the snowy carpet, the size of the precious
stones, and the resplendent plates of gold, that glitter as they are
agitated by the motion of the carriage. The Imperial pictures
are white, on a blue ground; the emperor appears seated on his

[1] Father Montfaucon, who, by the command of his Benedictine superiors,
was compelled (see Longueruana, tom. i. p. 205) to execute the laborious
edition of St. Chrysostom, in thirteen volumes in folio (Paris, 1738), amused
himself with extracting from that immense collection of morals some
curious *antiquities*, which illustrate the manners of the Theodosian age
(see Chrysostom, Opera, tom. xiii. p. 192-196), and his French Dissertation,
in the Mémoires de l'Acad. des Inscriptions, tom. xiii. p. 474-490.

throne, with his arms, his horses, and his guards beside him; and
his vanquished enemies in chains at his feet." The successors
of Constantine established their perpetual residence in the royal
city which he had erected on the verge of Europe and Asia.
Inaccessible to the menaces of their enemies, and perhaps to the
complaints of their people, they received with each wind the
tributary productions of every climate; while the impregnable
strength of their capital continued for ages to defy the hostile
attempts of the barbarians. Their dominions were bounded by
the Hadriatic and the Tigris; and the whole interval of twenty-
five days' navigation, which separated the extreme cold of
Scythia from the torrid zone of Æthiopia,[1] was comprehended
within the limits of the empire of the East. The populous
countries of that empire were the seat of art and learning, of
luxury and wealth; and the inhabitants, who had assumed the
language and manners of Greeks, styled themselves, with some
appearance of truth, the most enlightened and civilised portion
of the human species. The form of government was a pure and
simple monarchy; the name of the ROMAN REPUBLIC, which so
long preserved a faint tradition of freedom, was confined to the
Latin provinces; and the princes of Constantinople measured
their greatness by the servile obedience of their people. They
were ignorant how much this passive disposition enervates and
degrades every faculty of the mind. The subjects who had
resigned their will to the absolute commands of a master were
equally incapable of guarding their lives and fortunes against
the assaults of the barbarians, or of defending their reason from
the terrors of superstition.

The first events of the reign of Arcadius and Honorius are so
intimately connected, that the rebellion of the Goths and the fall
of Rufinus have already claimed a place in the history of the West.
It has already been observed that Eutropius,[2] one of the prin-

[1] According to the loose reckoning, that a ship could sail with a fair wind
1000 stadia, or 125 miles, in the revolution of a day and night, Diodorus
Siculus computes ten days from the Palus Mæotis to Rhodes, and four days
from Rhodes to Alexandria. The navigation of the Nile, from Alexandria
to Syene, under the tropic of Cancer, required, as it was against the stream,
ten days more. Diodor. Sicul. tom. i. l. iii. [c. 33] p. 200, edit. Wesseling.
He might, without much impropriety, measure the extreme heat from the
verge of the torrid zone; but he speaks of the Mæotis, in the 47th degree
of northern latitude, as if it lay within the polar circle.

[2] Barthius, who adored his author with the blind superstition of a commentator, gives the preference to the two books which Claudian composed
against Eutropius, above all his other productions (Baillet, Jugemens des
Savans, tom. iv. p. 227). They are indeed a very elegant and spirited
satire, and would be more valuable in an historical light, if the invective
were less vague and more temperate.

cipal eunuchs of the palace of Constantinople, succeeded the haughty minister whose ruin he had accomplished and whose vices he soon imitated. Every order of the state bowed to the new favourite; and their tame and obsequious submission encouraged him to insult the laws, and, what is still more difficult and dangerous, the manners of his country. Under the weakest of the predecessors of Arcadius the reign of the eunuchs had been secret and almost invisible. They insinuated themselves into the confidence of the prince; but their ostensible functions were confined to the menial service of the wardrobe and Imperial bed-chamber. They might direct in a whisper the public counsels, and blast by their malicious suggestions the fame and fortunes of the most illustrious citizens; but they never presumed to stand forward in the front of empire,[1] or to profane the public honours of the state. Eutropius was the first of his artificial sex who dared to assume the character of a Roman magistrate and general.[2] Sometimes, in the presence of the blushing senate, he ascended the tribunal to pronounce judgment or to repeat elaborate harangues; and sometimes appeared on horseback, at the head of his troops, in the dress and armour of a hero. The disregard of custom and decency always betrays a weak and ill-regulated mind; nor does Eutropius seem to have compensated for the folly of the design by any superior merit or ability in the execution. His former habits of life had not introduced him to the study of the laws or the exercises of the field; his awkward and unsuccessful attempts provoked the secret contempt of the spectators; the Goths expressed their wish that *such* a general might always command the armies of Rome; and the name of the minister was branded with ridicule, more pernicious, perhaps, than hatred to a public character. The subjects of Arcadius

---

[1] After lamenting the progress of the eunuchs in the Roman palace, and defining their proper functions, Claudian adds,

> ———— A fronte recedant
>   Imperii.

In Eutrop. i. 422.

Yet it does not appear that the eunuch had assumed any of the efficient offices of the empire, and he is styled only Præpositus sacri cubiculi in the edict of his banishment. See Cod. Theod. l. ix. tit. xl. leg. 17.

[2] Jamque oblita sui, nec sobria divitiis mens
> In miseras leges hominumque negotia ludit:
> Judicat eunuchus . . .
> Arma etiam violare parat. . . .

Claudian (in Eutrop. i. 229-270), with that mixture of indignation and humour which always pleases in a satiric poet, describes the insolent folly of the eunuch, the disgrace of the empire, and the joy of the Goths.

> ———— Gaudet, cum viderit, hostis,
> Et sentit jam deesse viros.

were exasperated by the recollection that this deformed and
decrepit eunuch,[1] who so perversely mimicked the actions of a
man, was born in the most abject condition of servitude; that
before he entered the Imperial palace he had been successively
sold and purchased by an hundred masters, who had exhausted
his youthful strength in every mean and infamous office, and at
length dismissed him in his old age to freedom and poverty.[2]
While these disgraceful stories were circulated, and perhaps
exaggerated, in private conversations, the vanity of the favourite
was flattered with the most extraordinary honours. In the
senate, in the capital, in the provinces, the statues of Eutropius
were erected, in brass or marble, decorated with the symbols of
his civil and military virtues, and inscribed with the pompous
title of the third founder of Constantinople. He was promoted
to the rank of *patrician*, which began to signify, in a popular and
even legal acceptation, the father of the emperor: and the last
year of the fourth century was polluted by the *consulship* of
an eunuch and a slave. This strange and inexpiable prodigy[3]
awakened, however, the prejudices of the Romans. The
effeminate consul was rejected by the West as an indelible stain
to the annals of the republic; and without invoking the shades
of Brutus and Camillus, the colleague of Eutropius, a learned
and respectable magistrate,[4] sufficiently represented the different
maxims of the two administrations.

The bold and vigorous mind of Rufinus seems to have been

---

[1] The poet's lively description of his deformity (i. 110-125) is confirmed
by the authentic testimony of Chrysostom (tom. iii. [in Eutrop. i. c. 3]
p. 384, edit. Montfaucon), who observes that, when the paint was washed
away, the face of Eutropius appeared more ugly and wrinkled than that
of an old woman. Claudian remarks (i. 469), and the remark must have
been founded on experience, that there was scarcely any interval between
the youth and the decrepit age of a eunuch.

[2] Eutropius appears to have been a native of Armenia or Assyria. His
three services, which Claudian more particularly describes, were these:—
1. He spent many years as the catamite of Ptolemy, a groom or soldier of
the Imperial stables. 2. Ptolemy gave him to the old general Arintheus,
for whom he very skilfully exercised the profession of a pimp. 3. He was
given, on her marriage, to the daughter of Arintheus; and the future consul
was employed to comb her hair, to present the silver ewer, to wash and to
fan his mistress in hot weather. See l. i. 31-137.

[3] Claudian (l. i. in Eutrop. 1-22), after enumerating the various prodigies
of monstrous births, speaking animals, showers of blood or stones, double
suns, etc., adds, with some exaggeration,
              Omnia cesserunt eunucho consule monstra.
The first book concludes with a noble speech of the goddess of Rome to her
favourite Honorius, deprecating the *new* ignominy to which she was
exposed.

[4] Fl. Mallius Theodorus, whose civil honours and philosophical works
have been celebrated by Claudian in a very elegant panegyric.

actuated by a more sanguinary and revengeful spirit; but the avarice of the eunuch was not less insatiate than that of the præfect.[1] As long as he despoiled the oppressors who had enriched themselves with the plunder of the people, Eutropius might gratify his covetous disposition without much envy or injustice: but the progress of his rapine soon invaded the wealth which had been acquired by lawful inheritance or laudable industry. The usual methods of extortion were practised and improved; and Claudian has sketched a lively and original picture of the public auction of the state. " The impotence of the eunuch " (says that agreeable satirist) " has served only to stimulate his avarice: the same hand which, in his servile condition, was exercised in petty thefts to unlock the coffers of his master, now grasps the riches of the world; and this infamous broker of the empire appreciates and divides the Roman provinces from Mount Hæmus to the Tigris. One man, at the expense of his villa, is made proconsul of Asia; a second purchases Syria with his wife's jewels; and a third laments that he has exchanged his paternal estate for the government of Bithynia. In the antechamber of Eutropius a large tablet is exposed to public view, which marks the respective prices of the provinces. The different value of Pontus, of Galatia, of Lydia is accurately distinguished. Lycia may be obtained for so many thousand pieces of gold; but the opulence of Phrygia will require a more considerable sum. The eunuch wishes to obliterate by the general disgrace his personal ignominy; and as he has been sold himself, he is desirous of selling the rest of mankind. In the eager contention, the balance, which contains the fate and fortunes of the province, often trembles on the beam; and till one of the scales is inclined by a superior weight, the mind of the impartial judge remains in anxious suspense.[2] Such " (continues the indignant poet) " are the fruits of Roman valour, of the defeat of Antiochus, and of the triumph of Pompey." This venal prostitution of public honours secured the impunity of *future* crimes; but the riches which Eutropius derived from

---

[1] Μεθύων δέ ἤδη τῷ πλούτῳ, drunk with riches, is the forcible expression of Zosimus (l. v. [c. 10] p. 301); and the avarice of Eutropius is equally execrated in the Lexicon of Suidas and the Chronicle of Marcellinus. Chrysostom had often admonished the favourite of the vanity and danger of immoderate wealth, tom. iii. p. 381 [in Eutrop. i. c. 1].

[2] ——— certantum sæpe duorum
Diversum suspendit onus· cum pondere judex
Vergit, et in geminas nutat provincia lances.

Claudian (i. 192-209) so curiously distinguishes the circumstances of the sale that they all seem to allude to particular anecdotes.

confiscation were *already* stained with injustice; since it was decent to accuse and to condemn the proprietors of the wealth which he was impatient to confiscate. Some noble blood was shed by the hand of the executioner; and the most inhospitable extremities of the empire were filled with innocent and illustrious exiles. Among the generals and consuls of the East, Abundantius [1] had reason to dread the first effects of the resentment of Eutropius. He had been guilty of the unpardonable crime of introducing that abject slave to the palace of Constantinople; and some degree of praise must be allowed to a powerful and ungrateful favourite who was satisfied with the disgrace of his benefactor. Abundantius was stripped of his ample fortunes by an Imperial rescript, and banished to Pityus, on the Euxine, the last frontier of the Roman world; where he subsisted by the precarious mercy of the barbarians till he could obtain, after the fall of Eutropius, a milder exile at Sidon in Phœnicia. The destruction of Timasius [2] required a more serious and regular mode of attack. That great officer, the master-general of the armies of Theodosius, had signalised his valour by a decisive victory which he obtained over the Goths of Thessaly; but he was too prone, after the example of his sovereign, to enjoy the luxury of peace and to abandon his confidence to wicked and designing flatterers. Timasius had despised the public clamour by promoting an infamous dependent to the command of a cohort; and he deserved to feel the ingratitude of Bargus, who was secretly instigated by the favourite to accuse his patron of a treasonable conspiracy. The general was arraigned before the tribunal of Arcadius himself; and the principal eunuch stood by the side of the throne to suggest the questions and answers of his sovereign. But as this form of trial might be deemed partial and arbitrary, the further inquiry into the crimes of Timasius was delegated to Saturninus and Procopius; the former of consular rank, the latter still respected as the father-in-law

---

[1] Claudian (in Eutrop. i. 154-170) mentions the *guilt* and exile of Abundantius; nor could he fail to quote the example of the artist who made the first trial of the brazen bull which he presented to Phalaris. See Zosimus l. v. [c. 10] p. 302; Jerom, tom. i. p. 26 [Ep. lx. c. 16, tom. i. p. 342, ed. Vallars.]. The difference of place is easily reconciled; but the decisive authority of Asterius of Amasia (Orat. iv. p. 76, apud Tillemont, Hist. de Empereurs, tom. v. p. 435) must turn the scale in favour of Pityus.

[2] Suidas (most probably from the history of Eunapius) has given a very unfavourable picture of Timasius. The account of his accuser, the judge, trial, etc., is perfectly agreeable to the practice of ancient and modern courts. (See Zosimus, l. v. [c. 9] p. 298, 299, 300.) I am almost tempted to quote the romance of a great master (Fielding's Works, vol. iv. p. 49, etc., 8vo. edit.), which may be considered as the history of human nature.

of the emperor Valens. The appearances of a fair and legal proceeding were maintained by the blunt honesty of Procopius; and he yielded with reluctance to the obsequious dexterity of his colleague, who pronounced a sentence of condemnation against the unfortunate Timasius. His immense riches were confiscated in the name of the emperor and for the benefit of the favourite; and he was doomed to perpetual exile at Oasis, a solitary spot in the midst of the sandy deserts of Libya.[1] Secluded from all human converse, the master-general of the Roman armies was lost for ever to the world; but the circumstances of his fate have been related in a various and contradictory manner. It is insinuated that Eutropius despatched a private order for his secret execution.[2] It was reported that in attempting to escape from Oasis he perished in the desert of thirst and hunger, and that his dead body was found on the sands of Libya.[3] It has been asserted with more confidence that his son Syagrius, after successfully eluding the pursuit of the agents and emissaries of the court, collected a band of African robbers; that he rescued Timasius from the place of his exile; and that both the father and the son disappeared from the knowledge of mankind.[4] But the ungrateful Bargus, instead of being suffered to possess the reward of guilt, was soon afterwards circumvented and destroyed by the more powerful villainy of the minister himself, who retained sense and spirit enough to abhor the instrument of his own crimes.

The public hatred and the despair of individuals continually threatened, or seemed to threaten, the personal safety of Eutropius, as well as of the numerous adherents who were attached to his fortune and had been promoted by his venal favour. For their mutual defence he contrived the safeguard of a law which violated every principle of humanity and justice.[5] I. It

---

[1] The great Oasis was one of the spots in the sands of Libya, watered with springs, and capable of producing wheat, barley, and palm-trees. It was about three days' journey from north to south, about half a day in breadth, and at the distance of about five days' march to the west of Abydus, on the Nile. See D'Anville, Description de l'Egypte, p. 186, 187, 188. The barren desert which encompasses Oasis (Zosimus l. v. [c. 9] p. 300) has suggested the idea of comparative fertility, and even the epithet of the *happy island* (Herodot. iii. 26).

[2] The line of Claudian, in Eutrop. l. i. 180,

> Marmaricus claris violatur cædibus Hammon,

evidently alludes to *his* persuasion of the death of Timasius.

[3] Sozomen, l. viii. c. 7. He speaks from report, ὡς τινος ἐπυθόμην.

[4] Zosimus, l. v. [c. 9] p. 300. Yet he seems to suspect that this rumour was spread by the friends of Eutropius.

[5] See the Theodosian Code, l. ix. tit. 14, ad legem Corneliam de Sicariis, leg. 3, and the Code of Justinian, l. ix. tit. viii. ad legem Juliam de Majestate, leg. 5 The alteration of the *title*, from murder to treason, was an

is enacted, in the name and by the authority of Arcadius, that all those who shall conspire, either with subjects or with strangers, against the lives of any of the persons whom the emperor considers as the members of his own body, shall be punished with death and confiscation. This species of fictitious and metaphorical treason is extended to protect not only the *illustrious* officers of the state and army who are admitted into the sacred consistory, but likewise the principal domestics of the palace, the senators of Constantinople, the military commanders, and the civil magistrates of the provinces: a vague and indefinite list, which, under the successors of Constantine, included an obscure and numerous train of subordinate ministers. II. This extreme severity might perhaps be justified, had it been only directed to secure the representatives of the sovereign from any actual violence in the execution of their office. But the whole body of Imperial dependents claimed a privilege, or rather impunity, which screened them in the loosest moments of their lives from the hasty, perhaps the justifiable, resentment of their fellow-citizens: and, by a strange perversion of the laws, the same degree of guilt and punishment was applied to a private quarrel and to a deliberate conspiracy against the emperor and the empire. The edict of Arcadius most positively and most absurdly declares that in such cases of treason, *thoughts* and *actions* ought to be punished with equal severity; that the knowledge of a mischievous intention, unless it be instantly revealed, becomes equally criminal with the intention itself;[1] and that those rash men who shall presume to solicit the pardon of traitors shall themselves be branded with public and perpetual infamy. III. "With regard to the sons of the traitors" (continues the emperor), "although they ought to share the punishment, since they will probably imitate the guilt of their parents, yet, by the special effect of our Imperial lenity, we grant them their lives; but, at the same time, we declare them incapable of inheriting, either on the father's or on the mother's side, or of receiving any gift or legacy from the testament either of

improvement of the subtle Tribonian. Godefroy, in a formal dissertation which he has inserted in his Commentary, illustrates this law of Arcadius and explains all the difficult passages which had been perverted by the jurisconsults of the darker ages. See tom. iii. p. 88-111.

[1] Bartolus understands a simple and naked consciousness, without any sign of approbation or concurrence. For this opinion, says Baldus, he is now roasting in hell. For my own part, continues the discreet Heineccius (Element. Jur. Civil. l. iv. p. 411), I must approve the theory of Bartolus but in practice I should incline to the sentiment of Baldus. Yet Bartolus was gravely quoted by the lawyers of Cardinal Richelieu; and Eutropius was indirectly guilty of the murder of the virtuous De Thou.

kinsmen or of strangers. Stigmatised with hereditary infamy, excluded from the hopes of honours or fortune, let them endure the pangs of poverty and contempt till they shall consider life as a calamity and death as a comfort and relief." In such words, so well adapted to insult the feelings of mankind, did the emperor, or rather his favourite eunuch, applaud the moderation of a law which transferred the same unjust and inhuman penalties to the children of all those who had seconded or who had not disclosed these fictitious conspiracies. Some of the noblest regulations of Roman jurisprudence have been suffered to expire; but this edict, a convenient and forcible engine of ministerial tyranny, was carefully inserted in the codes of Theodosius and Justinian; and the same maxims have been revived in modern ages to protect the electors of Germany and the cardinals of the church of Rome.[1]

Yet these sanguinary laws, which spread terror among a disarmed and dispirited people, were of too weak a texture to restrain the bold enterprise of Tribigild [2] the Ostrogoth. The colony of that warlike nation, which had been planted by Theodosius in one of the most fertile districts of Phrygia,[3] impatiently compared the slow returns of laborious husbandry with the successful rapine and liberal rewards of Alaric; and their leader resented, as a personal affront, his own ungracious reception in the palace of Constantinople. A soft and wealthy province in the heart of the empire was astonished by the sound of war, and the faithful vassal who had been disregarded or oppressed was again respected as soon as he resumed the hostile character of a barbarian. The vineyards and fruitful fields between the rapid Marsyas and the winding Mæander [4] were consumed with

---

[1] Godefroy, tom. iii. p. 89. It is, however, suspected that this law, so repugnant to the maxims of Germanic freedom, has been surreptitiously added to the golden bull.

[2] A copious and circumstantial narrative (which he might have reserved for more important events) is bestowed by Zosimus (l. v. [c. 10, sqq.] p. 304-312) on the revolt of Tribigild and Gainas. See likewise Socrates, l. vi. c. 6, and Sozomen, l. viii. c. 4. The second book of Claudian against Eutropius is a fine though imperfect piece of history.

[3] Claudian (in Eutrop. l. ii. 237-250) very accurately observes that the ancient name and nation of the Phrygians extended very far on every side, till their limits were contracted by the colonies of the Bithynians of Thrace, of the Greeks, and at last of the Gauls. His description (ii. 257-272) of the fertility of Phrygia, and of the four rivers that produced gold, is just and picturesque.

[4] Xenophon, Anabasis, l. i. [c. 2, § 8] p. 11, 12, edit. Hutchinson; Strabo, l. xii. p. 865, edit. Amstel. [p. 577, ed. Casaub.]; Q. Curt. l. iii. c. 1. Claudian compares the junction of the Marsyas and Mæander to that of the Saone and the Rhône, with this difference, however, that the smaller of the Phrygian rivers is not accelerated but retarded by the larger.

fire; the decayed walls of the cities crumbled into dust at the first stroke of an enemy; the trembling inhabitants escaped from a bloody massacre to the shores of the Hellespont; and a considerable part of Asia Minor was desolated by the rebellion of Tribigild. His rapid progress was checked by the resistance of the peasants of Pamphylia; and the Ostrogoths, attacked in a narrow pass between the city of Selgæ,[1] a deep morass, and the craggy cliffs of Mount Taurus, were defeated with the loss of their bravest troops. But the spirit of their chief was not daunted by misfortune, and his army was continually recruited by swarms of barbarians and outlaws who were desirous of exercising the profession of robbery under the more honourable names of war and conquest. The rumours of the success of Tribigild might for some time be suppressed by fear, or disguised by flattery; yet they gradually alarmed both the court and the capital. Every misfortune was exaggerated in dark and doubtful hints, and the future designs of the rebels became the subject of anxious conjecture. Whenever Tribigild advanced into the inland country, the Romans were inclined to suppose that he meditated the passage of Mount Taurus and the invasion of Syria. If he descended towards the sea, they imputed, and perhaps suggested, to the Gothic chief the more dangerous project of arming a fleet in the harbours of Ionia, and of extending his depredations along the maritime coast, from the mouth of the Nile to the port of Constantinople. The approach of danger and the obstinacy of Tribigild, who refused all terms of accommodation, compelled Eutropius to summon a council of war.[2] After claiming for himself the privilege of a veteran soldier, the eunuch intrusted the guard of Thrace and the Hellespont to Gainas the Goth, and the command of the Asiatic army to his favourite Leo; two generals who differently but effectually promoted the cause of the rebels. Leo,[3] who from the bulk of his body and the dulness of his mind was surnamed the Ajax of the East, had deserted his original trade of a woolcomber, to exercis-

[1] Selgæ, a colony of the Lacedæmonians, had formerly numbered twenty thousand citizens; but in the age of Zosimus it was reduced to a πολίχνη or small town. See Cellarius, Geograph. Antiq. tom. ii. p. 117.

[2] The council of Eutropius, in Claudian, may be compared to that of Domitian in the fourth Satire of Juvenal. The principal members of the former were, juvenes protervi lascivique senes; one of them had been a cook, a second a woolcomber. The language of their original profession exposes their assumed dignity; and their trifling conversation about tragedies, dancers, etc., is made still more ridiculous by the importance of the debate.

[3] Claudian (l. ii. 376-461) has branded him with infamy; and Zosimus in more temperate language, confirms his reproaches. L. v. [c. 14] p. 30.

with much less skill and success the military profession; and his uncertain operations were capriciously framed and executed with an ignorance of real difficulties and a timorous neglect of every favourable opportunity. The rashness of the Ostrogoths had drawn them into a disadvantageous position between the rivers Melas and Eurymedon, where they were almost besieged by the peasants of Pamphylia; but the arrival of an Imperial army, instead of completing their destruction, afforded the means of safety and victory. Tribigild surprised the unguarded camp of the Romans in the darkness of the night, seduced the faith of the greater part of the barbarian auxiliaries, and dissipated without much effort the troops which had been corrupted by the relaxation of discipline and the luxury of the capital. The discontent of Gainas, who had so boldly contrived and executed the death of Rufinus, was irritated by the fortune of his unworthy successor; he accused his own dishonourable patience under the servile reign of an eunuch; and the ambitious Goth was convicted, at least in the public opinion, of secretly fomenting the revolt of Tribigild, with whom he was connected by a domestic as well as by a national alliance.[1] When Gainas passed the Hellespont, to unite under his standard the remains of the Asiatic troops, he skilfully adapted his motions to the wishes of the Ostrogoths, abandoning by his retreat the country which they desired to invade, or facilitating by his approach the desertion of the barbarian auxiliaries. To the Imperial court he repeatedly magnified the valour, the genius, the inexhaustible resources of Tribigild, confessed his own inability to prosecute the war, and extorted the permission of negotiating with his invincible adversary. The conditions of peace were dictated by the haughty rebel; and the peremptory demand of the head of Eutropius revealed the author and the design of this hostile conspiracy.

The bold satirist, who has indulged his discontent by the partial and passionate censure of the Christian emperors, violates the dignity rather than the truth of history by comparing the son of Theodosius to one of those harmless and simple animals who scarcely feel that they are the property of their shepherd. Two passions, however—fear and conjugal affection—awakened the languid soul of Arcadius: he was terrified by the threats of a victorious barbarian, and he yielded to the tender

---

[1] The *conspiracy* of Gainas and Tribigild, which is attested by the Greek historian, had not reached the ears of Claudian, who attributes the revolt of the Ostrogoth to his own *martial spirit* and the advice of his wife.

eloquence of his wife Eudoxia, who, with a flood of artificial tears, presenting her infant children to their father, implored his justice for some real or imaginary insult which she imputed to the audacious eunuch.[1] The emperor's hand was directed to sign the condemnation of Eutropius; the magic spell, which during four years had bound the prince and the people, was instantly dissolved; and the acclamations that so lately hailed the merit and fortune of the favourite were converted into the clamours of the soldiers and people, who reproached his crimes and pressed his immediate execution. In this hour of distress and despair his only refuge was in the sanctuary of the church, whose privileges he had wisely, or profanely, attempted to circumscribe; and the most eloquent of the saints, John Chrysostom, enjoyed the triumph of protecting a prostrate minister, whose choice had raised him to the ecclesiastical throne of Constantinople. The archbishop, ascending the pulpit of the cathedral that he might be distinctly seen and heard by an innumerable crowd of either sex and of every age, pronounced a seasonable and pathetic discourse on the forgiveness of injuries and the instability of human greatness. The agonies of the pale and affrighted wretch, who lay grovelling under the table of the altar, exhibited a solemn and instructive spectacle; and the orator, who was afterwards accused of insulting the misfortunes of Eutropius, laboured to excite the contempt, that he might assuage the fury, of the people.[2] The powers of humanity, of superstition, and of eloquence prevailed. The empress Eudoxia was restrained, by her own prejudices or by those of her subjects, from violating the sanctuary of the church; and Eutropius was tempted to capitulate, by the milder arts of persuasion, and by an oath that his life should be spared.[3] Careless of the dignity of

---

[1] This anecdote, which Philostorgius alone has preserved (l. xi. c. 6, and Gothofred, Dissertat. p. 451-456), is curious and important, since it connects the revolt of the Goths with the secret intrigues of the palace.

[2] See the Homily [i. in Eutrop.] of Chrysostom, tom. iii. p. 381-386, of which the exordium is particularly beautiful; Socrates, l. vi. c. 5; Sozomen, l. viii. c. 7. Montfaucon (in his Life of Chrysostom, tom. xiii. p. 135) too hastily supposes that Tribigild was *actually* in Constantinople, and that he commanded the soldiers who were ordered to seize Eutropius. Even Claudian, a Pagan poet (Præfat. ad. l. ii. in Eutrop. 27), has mentioned the flight of the eunuch to the sanctuary.

> Suppliciterque pias humilis prostratus ad aras
> Mitigat iratas voce tremente nurus.

[3] Chrysostom, in another homily [in Eutr. ii. c. 1] (tom. iii. p. 386), affects to declare that Eutropius would not have been taken, had he not deserted the church. Zosimus (l. v. [c. 18] p. 313), on the contrary, pretends that his enemies forced him (ἐξαρπάσαντες αὐτὸν) from the sanctuary. Yet the

their sovereign, the new ministers of the palace immediately published an edict, to declare that his late favourite had disgraced the names of consul and patrician, to abolish his statues, to confiscate his wealth, and to inflict a perpetual exile in the island of Cyprus.[1] A despicable and decrepit eunuch could no longer alarm the fears of his enemies; nor was he capable of enjoying what yet remained—the comforts of peace, of solitude, and of a happy climate. But their implacable revenge still envied him the last moments of a miserable life, and Eutropius had no sooner touched the shores of Cyprus than he was hastily recalled. The vain hope of eluding, by a change of place, the obligation of an oath, engaged the empress to transfer the scene of his trial and execution from Constantinople to the adjacent suburb of Chalcedon. The consul Aurelian pronounced the sentence; and the motives of that sentence expose the jurisprudence of a despotic government. The crimes which Eutropius had committed against the people might have justified his death; but he was found guilty of harnessing to his chariot the *sacred* animals, who, from their breed or colour, were reserved for the use of the emperor alone.[2]

While this domestic revolution was transacted, Gainas [3] openly revolted from his allegiance, united his forces at Thyatira in Lydia with those of Tribigild, and still maintained his superior ascendant over the rebellious leader of the Ostrogoths. The confederate armies advanced without resistance to the straits of the Hellespont and the Bosphorus, and Arcadius was instructed to prevent the loss of his Asiatic dominions by resigning his authority and his person to the faith of the barbarians. The church of the holy martyr Euphemia, situate on a lofty eminence near Chalcedon,[4] was chosen for the place of the interview.

promise is an evidence of some treaty; and the strong assurance of Claudian (Præfat. ad. l. ii. 46),

> Sed tamen exemplo non feriere tuo,

may be considered as an evidence of some promise.

[1] Cod. Theod. l. ix. tit. xl. leg. 14 [leg. 17]. The date of that law (Jan. 17, A.D. 399) is erroneous and corrupt, since the fall of Eutropius could not happen till the autumn of the same year. See Tillemont, Hist. des Empereurs, tom. v. p. 780.

[2] Zosimus, l. v. [c. 18] p. 313. Philostorgius, l. xi. c. 6.

[3] Zosimus (l. v. [c. 18-22] p. 313-323), Socrates (l. vi. c. 4 [6]), Sozomen (l. viii. c. 4), and Theodoret (l. v. c. 32, 33), represent, though with some various circumstances, the conspiracy, defeat, and death of Gainas.

[4] Ὁσίας Εὐφημίας μαρτύριον is the expression of Zosimus himself (l. v. [c. 18] p. 314), who inadvertently uses the fashionable language of the Christians. Evagrius describes (l. ii. c. 3) the situation, architecture, relics, and miracles of that celebrated church, in which the general council of Chalcedon was afterwards held.

Gainas bowed with reverence at the feet of the emperor, whilst he required the sacrifice of Aurelian and Saturninus, two ministers of consular rank; and their naked necks were exposed by the haughty rebel to the edge of the sword, till he condescended to grant them a precarious and disgraceful respite. The Goths, according to the terms of the agreement, were immediately transported from Asia into Europe; and their victorious chief, who accepted the title of master-general of the Roman armies, soon filled Constantinople with his troops, and distributed among his dependents the honours and rewards of the empire. In his early youth Gainas had passed the Danube as a suppliant and a fugitive: his elevation had been the work of valour and fortune, and his indiscreet or perfidious conduct was the cause of his rapid downfall. Notwithstanding the vigorous opposition of the archbishop, he importunately claimed for his Arian sectaries the possession of a peculiar church, and the pride of the catholics was offended by the public toleration of heresy.[1] Every quarter of Constantinople was filled with tumult and disorder; and the barbarians gazed with such ardour on the rich shops of the jewellers and the tables of the bankers which were covered with gold and silver, that it was judged prudent to remove those dangerous temptations from their sight. They resented the injurious precaution; and some alarming attempts were made during the night to attack and destroy with fire the Imperial palace.[2] In this state of mutual and suspicious hostility, the guards and the people of Constantinople shut the gates, and rose in arms to prevent or to punish the conspiracy of the Goths. During the absence of Gainas his troops were surprised and oppressed; seven thousand barbarians perished in this bloody massacre. In the fury of the pursuit the catholics uncovered the roof, and continued to throw down flaming logs of wood till they overwhelmed their adversaries, who had retreated to the church or conventicle of the Arians. Gainas was either innocent of the design or too confident of his success; he was astonished by the intelligence that the flower of his army had been ingloriously destroyed; that he himself was declared a public

---

[1] The pious remonstrances of Chrysostom, which do not appear in his own writings, are strongly urged by Theodoret; but his insinuation that they were successful is disproved by facts. Tillemont (Hist. des Empereurs, tom. v. p. 383) has discovered that the emperor, to satisfy the rapacious demands of Gainas, was obliged to melt the plate of the church of the Apostles.

[2] The ecclesiastical historians, who sometimes guide and sometimes follow the public opinion, most confidently assert that the palace of Constantinople was guarded by legions of angels.

enemy; and that his countryman Fravitta, a brave and loyal confederate, had assumed the management of the war by sea and land. The enterprises of the rebel against the cities of Thrace were encountered by a firm and well-ordered defence: his hungry soldiers were soon reduced to the grass that grew on the margin of the fortifications; and Gainas, who vainly regretted the wealth and luxury of Asia, embraced a desperate resolution of forcing the passage of the Hellespont. He was destitute of vessels, but the woods of the Chersonesus afforded materials for rafts, and his intrepid barbarians did not refuse to trust themselves to the waves. But Fravitta attentively watched the progress of their undertaking. As soon as they had gained the middle of the stream, the Roman galleys,[1] impelled by the full force of oars, of the current, and of a favourable wind, rushed forwards in compact order and with irresistible weight, and the Hellespont was covered with the fragments of the Gothic shipwreck. After the destruction of his hopes and the loss of many thousands of his bravest soldiers, Gainas, who could no longer aspire to govern or to subdue the Romans, determined to resume the independence of a savage life. A light and active body of barbarian horse, disengaged from their infantry and baggage, might perform in eight or ten days a march of three hundred miles from the Hellespont to the Danube;[2] the garrisons of that important frontier had been gradually annihilated; the river in the month of December would be deeply frozen; and the unbounded prospect of Scythia was open to the ambition of Gainas. This design was secretly communicated to the national troops, who devoted themselves to the fortunes of their leader; and before the signal of departure was given, a great number of provincial auxiliaries, whom he suspected of an attachment to their native country, were perfidiously massacred. The Goths advanced by rapid marches through the plains of Thrace, and they were soon delivered

---

[1] Zosimus (l. v. [c. 20] p. 319) mentions these galleys by the name of *Liburnians*, and observes that they were as swift (without explaining the difference between them) as the vessels with fifty oars; but that they were far inferior in speed to the *triremes*, which had been long disused. Yet he reasonably concludes, from the testimony of Polybius, that galleys of a still larger size had been constructed in the Punic wars. Since the establishment of the Roman empire over the Mediterranean, the useless art of building large ships of war had probably been neglected, and at length forgotten.

[2] Chishull (Travels, p. 61-63, 72-76) proceeded from Gallipoli, through Hadrianople, to the Danube, in about fifteen days. He was in the train of an English ambassador, whose baggage consisted of seventy-one waggons. That learned traveller has the merit of tracing a curious and unfrequented route.

from the fear of a pursuit by the vanity of Fravitta, who, instead
of extinguishing the war, hastened to enjoy the popular applause,
and to assume the peaceful honours of the consulship.   But a
formidable ally appeared in arms to vindicate the majesty of the
empire, and to guard the peace and liberty of Scythia.[1] The
superior forces of Uldin, king of the Huns, opposed the progress
of Gainas; an hostile and ruined country prohibited his retreat;
he disdained to capitulate; and after repeatedly attempting to
cut his way through the ranks of the enemy, he was slain, with
his desperate followers, in the field of battle.   Eleven days after
the naval victory of the Hellespont, the head of Gainas, the
inestimable gift of the conqueror, was received at Constantinople with the most liberal expressions of gratitude; and the
public deliverance was celebrated by festivals and illuminations.
The triumphs of Arcadius became the subject of epic poems;[2]
and the monarch, no longer oppressed by any hostile terrors,
resigned himself to the mild and absolute dominion of his wife,
the fair and artful Eudoxia, who has sullied her fame by the
persecution of St. John Chrysostom.

After the death of the indolent Nectarius, the successor of
Gregory Nazianzen, the church of Constantinople was distracted
by the ambition of rival candidates, who were not ashamed to
solicit, with gold or flattery, the suffrage of the people or of the
favourite.   On this occasion Eutropius seems to have deviated
from his ordinary maxims; and his uncorrupted judgment was
determined only by the superior merit of a stranger.   In a late
journey into the East he had admired the sermons of John, a
native and presbyter of Antioch, whose name has been distinguished by the epithet of Chrysostom, or the Golden Mouth.[3]

[1] The narrative of Zosimus, who actually leads Gainas beyond the
Danube, must be corrected by the testimony of Socrates [l. vi. c. 6] and
Sozomen [l. viii. c. 4], that he was killed in *Thrace*, and by the precise and
authentic dates of the Alexandrian or Paschal Chronicle, p. 307 [ed. Paris;
tom. i. p. 567, ed. Bonn].   The naval victory of the Hellespont is fixed to
the month Apellæus, the tenth of the calends of January (December 23);
the head of Gainas was brought to Constantinople the third of the nones
of January (January 3), in the month Audynæus.

[2] Eusebius Scholasticus acquired much fame by his poem on the Gothic
war, in which he had served.   Near forty years afterwards, Ammonius
recited another poem on the same subject, in the presence of the emperor
Theodosius.   See Socrates, l. vi. c. 6.

[3] The sixth book of Socrates, the eighth of Sozomen, and the fifth of
Theodoret, afford curious and authentic materials for the Life of John
Chrysostom.   Besides those general historians, I have taken for my guides
the four principal biographers of the saint:—1. The author of a partial and
passionate Vindication of the Archbishop of Constantinople, composed in
the form of a dialogue, and under the name of his zealous partisan, Palladius, bishop of Helenopolis (Tillemont, Mém. Ecclés. tom. xi. p. 500-533).

A private order was despatched to the governor of Syria; and as the people might be unwilling to resign their favourite preacher, he was transported, with speed and secrecy, in a post-chariot, from Antioch to Constantinople. The unanimous and unsolicited consent of the court, the clergy, and the people ratified the choice of the minister; and, both as a saint and as an orator, the new archbishop surpassed the sanguine expectations of the public. Born of a noble and opulent family in the capital of Syria, Chrysostom had been educated, by the care of a tender mother, under the tuition of the most skilful masters. He studied the art of rhetoric in the school of Libanius; and that celebrated sophist, who soon discovered the talents of his disciple, ingenuously confessed that John would have deserved to succeed him had he not been stolen away by the Christians. His piety soon disposed him to receive the sacrament of baptism; to renounce the lucrative and honourable profession of the law; and to bury himself in the adjacent desert, where he subdued the lusts of the flesh by an austere penance of six years. His infirmities compelled him to return to the society of mankind; and the authority of Meletius devoted his talents to the service of the church: but in the midst of his family, and afterwards on the archiepiscopal throne, Chrysostom still persevered in the practice of the monastic virtues. The ample revenues, which his predecessors had consumed in pomp and luxury, he diligently applied to the establishment of hospitals; and the multitudes who were supported by his charity preferred the eloquent and edifying discourses of their archbishop to the amusements of the theatre or the circus. The monuments of that eloquence, which was admired near twenty years at Antioch and Constantinople, have been carefully preserved; and the possession of near one thousand sermons or homilies has authorised the critics [1] of suc-

---

It is inserted among the works of Chrysostom, tom. xiii. p. 1-90, edit. Montfaucon. 2. The moderate Erasmus (tom. iii. Epist. MCL. p. 1331-1347, edit. Lugd. Bat.). His vivacity and good sense were his own; his errors, in the uncultivated state of ecclesiastical antiquity, were almost inevitable. 3. The learned Tillemont (Mém. Ecclésiastiques, tom. xi. p. 1-405, 547-626, etc. etc.), who compiles the Lives of the saints with incredible patience and religious accuracy. He has minutely searched the voluminous works of Chrysostom himself. 4. Father Montfaucon, who has perused those works with the curious diligence of an editor, discovered several new homilies, and again reviewed and composed the Life of Chrysostom (Opera Chrysostom. tom. xiii. p. 91-177).

[1] As I am *almost* a stranger to the voluminous sermons of Chrysostom, I have given my confidence to the two most judicious and moderate of the ecclesiastical critics, Erasmus (tom. iii. p. 1344) and Dupin (Bibliothèque Ecclésiastique, tom. iii. p. 38); yet the good taste of the former is sometimes vitiated by an excessive love of antiquity, and the good sense of the latter is always restrained by prudential considerations.

ceeding times to appreciate the genuine merit of Chrysostom. They unanimously attribute to the Christian orator the free command of an elegant and copious language; the judgment to conceal the advantages which he derived from the knowledge of rhetoric and philosophy; an inexhaustible fund of metaphors and similitudes, of ideas and images, to vary and illustrate the most familiar topics; the happy art of engaging the passions in the service of virtue, and of exposing the folly as well as the turpitude of vice almost with the truth and spirit of a dramatic representation.

The pastoral labours of the archbishop of Constantinople provoked and gradually united against him two sorts of enemies; the aspiring clergy, who envied his success, and the obstinate sinners, who were offended by his reproofs. When Chrysostom thundered from the pulpit of St. Sophia against the degeneracy of the Christians, his shafts were spent among the crowd, without wounding or even marking the character of any individual. When he declaimed against the peculiar vices of the rich, poverty might obtain a transient consolation from his invectives: but the guilty were still sheltered by their numbers; and the reproach itself was dignified by some ideas of superiority and enjoyment. But as the pyramid rose towards the summit, it insensibly diminished to a point; and the magistrates, the ministers, the favourite eunuchs, the ladies of the court,[1] the empress Eudoxia herself, had a much larger share of guilt to divide among a smaller proportion of criminals. The personal applications of the audience were anticipated or confirmed by the testimony of their own conscience; and the intrepid preacher assumed the dangerous right of exposing both the offence and the offender to the public abhorrence. The secret resentment of the court encouraged the discontent of the clergy and monks of Constantinople, who were too hastily reformed by the fervent zeal of their archbishop. He had condemned from the pulpit the domestic females of the clergy of Constantinople, who, under the name of servants or sisters, afforded a perpetual occasion either of sin or of scandal. The silent and solitary ascetics, who had secluded

[1] The females of Constantinople distinguished themselves by their enmity or their attachment to Chrysostom. Three noble and opulent widows—Marsa, Castricia, and Eugraphia—were the leaders of the persecution (Pallad. Dialog. tom. xiii. p. 14 [c. 4, p. 35, ed. Paris, 1680]). It was impossible that they should forgive a preacher who reproached their affectation to conceal, by the ornaments of dress, their age and ugliness (Pallad. p. 27). Olympias, by equal zeal, displayed in a more pious cause, has obtained the title of saint. See Tillemont, Mém. Ecclés. tom. xi. p. 416-440.

themselves from the world, were entitled to the warmest approbation of Chrysostom; but he despised and stigmatised, as the
disgrace of their holy profession, the crowd of degenerate monks,
who, from some unworthy motives of pleasure or profit, so frequently infested the streets of the capital. To the voice of
persuasion the archbishop was obliged to add the terrors of
authority; and his ardour in the exercise of ecclesiastical jurisdiction was not always exempt from passion; nor was it always
guided by prudence. Chrysostom was naturally of a choleric
disposition.[1] Although he struggled, according to the precepts
of the Gospel, to love his private enemies, he indulged himself
in the privilege of hating the enemies of God and of the church;
and his sentiments were sometimes delivered with too much
energy of countenance and expression. He still maintained,
from some considerations of health or abstinence, his former
habits of taking his repasts alone; and this inhospitable custom,[2]
which his enemies imputed to pride, contributed at least to
nourish the infirmity of a morose and unsocial humour.
Separated from that familiar intercourse which facilitates the
knowledge and the despatch of business, he reposed an unsuspecting confidence in his deacon Serapion; and seldom applied
his speculative knowledge of human nature to the particular
characters either of his dependents or of his equals. Conscious of
the purity of his intentions, and perhaps of the superiority of his
genius, the archbishop of Constantinople extended the jurisdiction of the Imperial city, that he might enlarge the sphere of
his pastoral labours; and the conduct which the profane imputed
to an ambitious motive, appeared to Chrysostom himself in
the light of a sacred and indispensable duty. In his visitation
through the Asiatic provinces he deposed thirteen bishops of
Lydia and Phrygia; and indiscreetly declared that a deep corruption of simony and licentiousness had infected the whole
episcopal order.[3] If those bishops were innocent, such a rash and

---

[1] Sozomen, and more especially Socrates, have defined the real character
of Chrysostom with a temperate and impartial freedom very offensive to
his blind admirers. Those historians lived in the next generation, when
party violence was abated, and had conversed with many persons intimately acquainted with the virtues and imperfections of the saint.

[2] Palladius (tom. xiii. p. 40, etc. [c. xii. p. 102, ed. Paris, 1680]) very
seriously defends the archbishop. 1. He never tasted wine. 2. The
weakness of his stomach required a peculiar diet. 3. Business, or study,
or devotion, often kept him fasting till sunset. 4. He detested the noise
and levity of great dinners. 5. He saved the expense for the use of the
poor. 6. He was apprehensive, in a capital like Constantinople, of the
envy and reproach of partial invitations.

[3] Chrysostom declares his free opinion (tom. ix. hom. iii. in Act. Apostol.

unjust condemnation must excite a well-grounded discontent.
If they were guilty, the numerous associates of their guilt would
soon discover that their own safety depended on the ruin of the
archbishop, whom they studied to represent as the tyrant of the
Eastern church.

This ecclesiastical conspiracy was managed by Theophilus,[1]
archbishop of Alexandria, an active and ambitious prelate, who
displayed the fruits of rapine in monuments of ostentation.   His
national dislike to the rising greatness of a city which degraded
him from the second to the third rank in the Christian world was
exasperated by some personal disputes with Chrysostom himself.[2]
By the private invitation of the empress, Theophilus landed at
Constantinople, with a stout body of Egyptian mariners, to
encounter the populace; and a train of dependent bishops, to
secure by their voices the majority of a synod. The synod [3]
was convened in the suburb of Chalcedon, surnamed the *Oak*,
where Rufinus had erected a stately church and monastery;
and their proceedings were continued during fourteen days or
sessions. A bishop and a deacon accused the archbishop of
Constantinople; but the frivolous or improbable nature of the
forty-seven articles which they presented against him may justly
be considered as a fair and unexceptionable panegyric. Four
successive summons were signified to Chrysostom; but he still
refused to trust either his person or his reputation in the hands of
his implacable enemies, who, prudently declining the examination of any particular charges, condemned his contumacious
disobedience, and hastily pronounced a sentence of deposition.
The synod of the *Oak* immediately addressed the emperor to
ratify and execute their judgment, and charitably insinuated
that the penalties of treason might be inflicted on the audacious
preacher, who had reviled, under the name of Jezebel, the
empress Eudoxia herself. The archbishop was rudely arrested,

p. 29) that the number of bishops who might be saved bore a very small
proportion to those who would be damned.

[1] See Tillemont, Mém. Ecclés. tom. xi. p. 441-500.

[2] I have purposely omitted the controversy which arose among the
monks of Egypt concerning Origenism and Anthropomorphism, the dissimulation and violence of Theophilus, his artful management of the simplicity of Epiphanius, the persecution and flight of the *long* or tall brothers,
the ambiguous support which they received at Constantinople from
Chrysostom, etc. etc.

[3] Photius (p. 53-60 [p. 17, *sqq.* ed. Bekk.]) has preserved the original acts
of the synod of the Oak, which destroy the false assertion that Chrysostom
was condemned by no more than thirty-six bishops, of whom twenty-nine
were Egyptians. Forty-five bishops subscribed his sentence. See Tillemont, Mém. Ecclés. tom. xi. p. 595.

and conducted through the city, by one of the Imperial
messengers, who landed him, after a short navigation, near the
entrance of the Euxine; from whence, before the expiration of
two days, he was gloriously recalled.

The first astonishment of his faithful people had been mute
and passive: they suddenly rose with unanimous and irresistible
fury. Theophilus escaped, but the promiscuous crowd of monks
and Egyptian mariners was slaughtered without pity in the
streets of Constantinople.[1] A seasonable earthquake justified
the interposition of Heaven; the torrent of sedition rolled forwards to the gates of the palace; and the empress, agitated by
fear or remorse, threw herself at the feet of Arcadius, and confessed that the public safety could be purchased only by the
restoration of Chrysostom. The Bosphorus was covered with
innumerable vessels; the shores of Europe and Asia were profusely illuminated; and the acclamations of a victorious people
accompanied, from the port to the cathedral, the triumph of the
archbishop, who too easily consented to resume the exercise
of his functions, before his sentence had been legally reversed
by the authority of an ecclesiastical synod. Ignorant, or careless, of the impending danger, Chrysostom indulged his zeal,
or perhaps his resentment; declaimed with peculiar asperity
against *female* vices; and condemned the profane honours which
were addressed, almost in the precincts of St. Sophia, to the
statue of the empress. His imprudence tempted his enemies
to inflame the haughty spirit of Eudoxia, by reporting, or perhaps
inventing, the famous exordium of a sermon, " Herodias is again
furious; Herodias again dances; she once more requires the head
of John: " an insolent allusion, which, as a woman and a sovereign, it was impossible for her to forgive.[2] The short interval
of a perfidious truce was employed to concert more effectual
measures for the disgrace and ruin of the archbishop. A
numerous council of the Eastern prelates, who were guided from

---

[1] Palladius owns (p. 30 [c. 8, p. 75]) that if the people of Constantinople
had found Theophilus, they would certainly have thrown him into the sea.
Socrates mentions (l. vi. c. 17) a battle between the mob and the sailors of
Alexandria, in which many wounds were given, and some lives were lost.
The massacre of the monks is observed only by the Pagan Zosimus (l. v.
[c. 23] p. 324), who acknowledges that Chrysostom had a singular talent
to lead the illiterate multitude, ἦν γὰρ ὁ ἄνθρωπος ἄλογον ὄχλον ὑπαγαγέσθαι
δεινός,

[2] See Socrates, l. vi. c. 18. Sozomen, l. viii. c. 20. Zosimus (l. v. [c. 24]
p. 324, 327) mentions, in general terms, his invectives against Eudoxia.
The homily which begins with those famous words is rejected as spurious.
Montfaucon, tom. xiii. p. 151. Tillemont, Mém. Ecclés. tom. xi. p. 603.

a distance by the advice of Theophilus, confirmed the validity, without examining the justice, of the former sentence; and a detachment of barbarian troops was introduced into the city, to suppress the emotions of the people. On the vigil of Easter the solemn administration of baptism was rudely interrupted by the soldiers, who alarmed the modesty of the naked catechumens, and violated, by their presence, the awful mysteries of the Christian worship. Arsacius occupied the church of St. Sophia and the archiepiscopal throne. The catholics retreated to the baths of Constantine, and afterwards to the fields, where they were still pursued and insulted by the guards, the bishops, and the magistrates. The fatal day of the second and final exile of Chrysostom was marked by the conflagration of the cathedral, of the senate-house, and of the adjacent buildings; and this calamity was imputed, without proof, but not without probability, to the despair of a persecuted faction.[1]

Cicero might claim some merit if his voluntary banishment preserved the peace of the republic;[2] but the submission of Chrysostom was the indispensable duty of a Christian and a subject. Instead of listening to his humble prayer that he might be permitted to reside at Cyzicus or Nicomedia, the inflexible empress assigned for his exile the remote and desolate town of Cucusus, among the ridges of Mount Taurus, in the Lesser Armenia. A secret hope was entertained that the archbishop might perish in a difficult and dangerous march of seventy days in the heat of summer, through the provinces of Asia Minor, where he was continually threatened by the hostile attacks of the Isaurians, and the more implacable fury of the monks. Yet Chrysostum arrived in safety at the place of his confinement; and the three years which he spent at Cucusus, and the neighbouring town of Arabissus, were the last and most glorious of his life. His character was consecrated by absence and persecution; the faults of his administration were no longer remembered; but every tongue repeated the praises of his genius and virtue: and the respectful attention of the Christian world was fixed on a desert spot among the mountains of Taurus. From that solitude the archbishop, whose active mind was invigorated by misfortunes, maintained a strict and

---

[1] We might naturally expect such a charge from Zosimus (l. v. [c. 24] p. 327); but it is remarkable enough that it should be confirmed by Socrates, l. vi. c. 18, and the Paschal Chronicle, p. 307 [ed. Paris; tom. i. p. 568, ed. Bonn].

[2] He displays those specious motives (Post Reditum, c. 13, 14) in the language of an orator and a politician.

frequent correspondence [1] with the most distant provinces;
exhorted the separate congregation of his faithful adherents to
persevere in their allegiance; urged the destruction of the temples
of Phœnicia, and the extirpation of heresy in the isle of Cyprus;
extended his pastoral care to the missions of Persia and Scythia;
negotiated, by his ambassadors, with the Roman pontiff and the
emperor Honorius; and boldly appealed, from a partial synod,
to the supreme tribunal of a free and general council. The
mind of the illustrious exile was still independent; but his
captive body was exposed to the revenge of the oppressors, who
continued to abuse the name and authority of Arcadius.[2] An
order was despatched for the instant removal of Chrysostom to
the extreme desert of Pityus: and his guards so faithfully
obeyed their cruel instructions, that, before he reached the sea-
coast of the Euxine, he expired at Comana, in Pontus, in the
sixtieth year of his age. The succeeding generation acknowledged his innocence and merit. The archbishops of the East,
who might blush that their predecessors had been the enemies of
Chrysostom, were gradually disposed, by the firmness of the
Roman pontiff, to restore the honours of that venerable name.[3]
At the pious solicitation of the clergy and people of Constantinople, his relics, thirty years after his death, were transported
from their obscure sepulchre to the royal city.[4] The emperor
Theodosius advanced to receive them as far as Chalcedon; and,

[1] Two hundred and forty-two of the epistles of Chrysostom are still
extant (Opera, tom. iii. p. 528-736 [ed. Bened.]). They are addressed to a
great variety of persons, and show a firmness of mind much superior to
that of Cicero in his exile. The fourteenth epistle contains a curious
narrative of the dangers of his journey.

[2] After the exile of Chrysostom, Theophilus published an *enormous* and
horrible volume against him, in which he perpetually repeats the polite
expressions of hostem humanitatis, sacrilegorum principem, immundum
dæmonem; he affirms that John Chrysostom had delivered his soul to be
adulterated by the devil; and wishes that some farther punishment,
adequate (if possible) to the magnitude of his crimes, may be inflicted on
him. St. Jerom, at the request of his friend Theophilus, translated this
edifying performance from Greek into Latin. See Facundus Hermian.
Defens. pro iii. Capitul. l. vi. c. 5 [p. 260, ed. Paris, 1629], published by
Sirmond, Opera, tom. ii. p. 595, 596, 597.

[3] His name was inserted by his successor Atticus in the dyptics of the
church of Constantinople, A.D. 418. Ten years afterwards he was revered
as a saint. Cyril, who inherited the place and the passions of his uncle
Theophilus, yielded with much reluctance. See Facund. Hermian. l. iv. c.
1 [p. 142, ed. Par. 1629]; Tillemont, Mém. Ecclés. tom. xiv. p. 277-283.

[4] Socrates, l. vii. c. 45; Theodoret, l. v. c. 36. This event reconciled the
Joanites, who had hitherto refused to acknowledge his successors. During
his lifetime the Joannites were respected by the catholics as the true and
orthodox communion of Constantinople. Their obstinacy gradually
drove them to the brink of schism.

falling prostrate on the coffin, implored, in the name of his guilty
parents, Arcadius and Eudoxia, the forgiveness of the injured
saint.[1]

Yet a reasonable doubt may be entertained whether any
stain of hereditary guilt could be derived from Arcadius to his
successor.   Eudoxia was a young and beautiful woman, who
indulged her passions and despised her husband: Count John
enjoyed, at least, the familiar confidence of the empress; and
the public named him as the real father of Theodosius the
younger.[2]   The birth of a son was accepted, however, by the
pious husband as an event the most fortunate and honourable
to himself, to his family, and to the Eastern world: and the royal
infant, by an unprecedented favour, was invested with the titles
of Cæsar and Augustus.   In less than four years afterwards,
Eudoxia, in the bloom of youth, was destroyed by the consequences of a miscarriage; and this untimely death confounded
the prophecy of a holy bishop,[3] who, amidst the universal joy,
had ventured to foretell that she should behold the long and
auspicious reign of her glorious son.   The catholics applauded
the justice of Heaven, which avenged the persecution of St.
Chrysostom; and perhaps the emperor was the only person who
sincerely bewailed the loss of the haughty and rapacious Eudoxia.
Such a domestic misfortune afflicted *him* more deeply than the
public calamities of the East [4]—the licentious excursions, from
Pontus to Palestine, of the Isaurian robbers, whose impunity
accused the weakness of the government; and the earthquakes,
the conflagrations, the famine, and the flights of locusts,[5] which
the popular discontent was equally disposed to attribute to the
incapacity of the monarch.   At length, in the thirty-first year

---

[1] According to some accounts (Baronius, Annal. Eccles. A.D. 438, No. 9,
10), the emperor was forced to send a letter of invitation and excuses before
the body of the ceremonious saint could be moved from Comana.

[2] Zosimus, l. v. [c. 18] p. 315.   The chastity of an empress should not be
impeached without producing a witness; but it is astonishing that the
witness should write and live under a prince whose legitimacy he dared to
attack.   We must suppose that his history was a party libel, privately
read and circulated by the Pagans.   Tillemont (Hist. des Empereurs,
tom. v. p. 782) is not averse to brand the reputation of Eudoxia.

[3] Porphyry of Gaza.   His zeal was transported by the order which he
had obtained for the destruction of eight Pagan temples of that city.   See
the curious details of his life (Baronius, A.D. 401, No. 17-51), originally
written in Greek, or perhaps in Syriac, by a monk, one of his favourite
deacons.

[4] Philostorg. l. xi. c. 8, and Godefroy, Dissertat. p. 457.

[5] Jerom (tom. vi. p. 73, 76) describes in lively colours the regular and
destructive march of the locusts, which spread a dark cloud between
heaven and earth over the land of Palestine.   Seasonable winds scattered
them, partly into the Dead Sea and partly into the Mediterranean.

of his age, after a reign (if we may abuse that word) of thirteen years, three months, and fifteen days, Arcadius expired in the palace of Constantinople. It is impossible to delineate his character; since, in a period very copiously furnished with historical materials, it has not been possible to remark one action that properly belongs to the son of the great Theodosius.

The historian Procopius [1] has indeed illuminated the mind of the dying emperor with a ray of human prudence, or celestial wisdom. Arcadius considered, with anxious foresight, the helpless condition of his son Theodosius, who was no more than seven years of age, the dangerous factions of a minority, and the aspiring spirit of Jezdegerd, the Persian monarch. Instead of tempting the allegiance of an ambitious subject by the participation of supreme power, he boldly appealed to the magnanimity of a king, and placed, by a solemn testament, the sceptre of the East in the hands of Jezdegerd himself. The royal guardian accepted and discharged this honourable trust with unexampled fidelity; and the infancy of Theodosius was protected by the arms and councils of Persia. Such is the singular narrative of Procopius; and his veracity is not disputed by Agathias, [2] while he presumes to dissent from his judgment, and to arraign the wisdom of a Christian emperor, who so rashly, though so fortunately, committed his son and his dominions to the unknown faith of a stranger, a rival, and a heathen. At the distance of one hundred and fifty years, this political question might be debated in the court of Justinian; but a prudent historian will refuse to examine the *propriety*, till he has ascertained the *truth*, of the testament of Arcadius. As it stands without a parallel in the history of the world, we may justly require that it should be attested by the positive and unanimous evidence of contemporaries. The strange novelty of the event, which excites our distrust, must have attracted their notice; and their universal silence annihilates the vain tradition of the succeeding age.

The maxims of Roman jurisprudence, if they could fairly be transferred from private property to public dominion, would have adjudged to the emperor Honorius the guardianship of his nephew, till he had attained, at least, the fourteenth year of his

---

[1] Procopius, de Bell. Persic. l. i. c. 2, p. 8, edit. Louvre [tom. i. p. 14, ed. Bonn].

[2] Agathias, l. iv. [c. 26] p. 136, 137 [p. 264, ed. Bonn]. Although he confesses the prevalence of the tradition, he asserts that Procopius was the first who had committed it to writing. Tillemont (Hist. des Empereurs, tom. vi. p. 597) argues very sensibly on the merits of this fable. His criticism was not warped by any ecclesiastical authority: both Procopius and Agathias are half Pagans.

age. But the weakness of Honorius, and the calamities of his reign, disqualified him from prosecuting this natural claim; and such was the absolute separation of the two monarchies, both in interest and affection, that Constantinople would have obeyed with less reluctance the orders of the Persian, than those of the Italian court. Under a prince whose weakness is disguised by the external signs of manhood and discretion, the most worthless favourites may secretly dispute the empire of the palace, and dictate to submissive provinces the commands of a master whom they direct and despise. But the ministers of a child, who is incapable of arming them with the sanction of the royal name, must acquire and exercise an independent authority. The great officers of the state and army, who had been appointed before the death of Arcadius, formed an aristocracy which might have inspired them with the idea of a free republic; and the government of the Eastern empire was fortunately assumed by the præfect Anthemius,[1] who obtained, by his superior abilities, a lasting ascendant over the minds of his equals. The safety of the young emperor proved the merit and integrity of Anthemius; and his prudent firmness sustained the force and reputation of an infant reign. Uldin, with a formidable host of barbarians, was encamped in the heart of Thrace; he proudly rejected all terms of accommodation; and, pointing to the rising sun, declared to the Roman ambassadors that the course of that planet should alone terminate the conquests of the Huns. But the desertion of his confederates, who were privately convinced of the justice and liberality of the Imperial ministers, obliged Uldin to repass the Danube: the tribe of the Scyrri, which composed his rear-guard, was almost extirpated; and many thousand captives were dispersed, to cultivate, with servile labour, the fields of Asia.[2] In the midst of the public triumph, Constantinople was protected by a strong enclosure of new and more extensive walls; the same vigilant care was applied to restore the fortifications of the Illyrian cities; and a plan was judiciously conceived, which, in the space of seven years, would have secured the command of the Danube, by establishing on

[1] Socrates, l. vii. c. 1. Anthemius was the grandson of Philip, one of the ministers of Constantius, and the grandfather of the emperor Anthemius. After his return from the Persian embassy, he was appointed consul and Prætorian præfect of the East, in the year 405; and held the præfecture about ten years. See his honours and praises in Godefroy, Cod. Theod. tom. vi. p. 350; Tillemont, Hist. des Emp. tom. vi. p. 1, etc.

[2] Sozomen, l. ix. c. 5. He saw some Scyrri at work near Mount Olympus, in Bithynia, and cherished the vain hope that those captives were the last of the nation.

that river a perpetual fleet of two hundred and fifty armed vessels.[1]

But the Romans had so long been accustomed to the authority of a monarch, that the first, even among the females of the Imperial family, who displayed any courage or capacity, was permitted to ascend the vacant throne of Theodosius. His sister Pulcheria,[2] who was only two years older than himself, received at the age of sixteen the title of *Augusta ;* and though her favour might be sometimes clouded by caprice or intrigue, she continued to govern the Eastern empire near forty years; during the long minority of her brother, and after his death in her own name, and in the name of Marcian, her nominal husband. From a motive either of prudence or religion, she embraced a life of celibacy; and notwithstanding some aspersions on the chastity of Pulcheria,[3] this resolution, which she communicated to her sisters Arcadia and Marina, was celebrated by the Christian world as the sublime effort of heroic piety. In the presence of the clergy and people the three daughters of Arcadius [4] dedicated their virginity to God; and the obligation of their solemn vow was inscribed on a tablet of gold and gems, which they publicly offered in the great church of Constantinople. Their palace was converted into a monastery, and all males—except the guides of their conscience, the saints who had forgotten the distinction of sexes—were scrupulously excluded from the holy threshold. Pulcheria, her two sisters, and a chosen train of favourite damsels, formed a religious community: they renounced the vanity of dress, interrupted by frequent fasts their simple and frugal diet, allotted a portion of their time to works of embroidery, and devoted several hours of the day and night to the exercises of prayer and psalmody. The piety of a Christian virgin was adorned by the zeal and liberality of an empress. Ecclesiastical history describes the splendid churches which were built at the expense of Pulcheria in all the provinces of the East, her charit-

---

[1] Cod. Theod. l. vii. tit. xviii.; l. xv. tit. i. leg. 49.

[2] Sozomen has filled three chapters with a magnificent panegyric of Pulcheria (l. ix. c. 1, 2, 3); and Tillemont (Mémoires Ecclés. tom. xv. p. 171-184) has dedicated a separate article to the honour of St. Pulcheria, virgin and empress.

[3] Suidas (Excerpta, p. 68, in Script. Byzant.) pretends, on the credit of the Nestorians, that Pulcheria was exasperated against their founder, because he censured her connection with the beautiful Paulinus, and her incest with her brother Theodosius.

[4] See Ducange, Famil. Byzantin. p. 70. Flaccilla, the eldest daughter, either died before Arcadius, or, if *she* lived till the year 431 (Marcellin. Chron.), some defect of mind or body must have excluded her from the honours of her rank.

able foundations for the benefit of strangers and the poor, the ample donations which she assigned for the perpetual maintenance of monastic societies, and the active severity with which she laboured to suppress the opposite heresies of Nestorius and Eutyches. Such virtues were supposed to deserve the peculiar favour of the Deity: and the relics of martyrs, as well as the knowledge of future events, were communicated in visions and revelations to the Imperial saint.[1] Yet the devotion of Pulcheria never diverted her indefatigable attention from temporal affairs; and she alone, among all the descendants of the great Theodosius, appears to have inherited any share of his manly spirit and abilities. The elegant and familiar use which she had acquired both of the Greek and Latin languages was readily applied to the various occasions of speaking or writing on public business: her deliberations were maturely weighed; her actions were prompt and decisive; and while she moved without noise or ostentation the wheel of government, she discreetly attributed to the genius of the emperor the long tranquillity of his reign. In the last years of his peaceful life Europe was indeed afflicted by the arms of Attila; but the more extensive provinces of Asia still continued to enjoy a profound and permanent repose. Theodosius the younger was never reduced to the disgraceful necessity of encountering and punishing a rebellious subject: and since we cannot applaud the vigour, some praise may be due to the mildness and prosperity, of the administration of Pulcheria.

The Roman world was deeply interested in the education of its master. A regular course of study and exercise was judiciously instituted; of the military exercises of riding, and shooting with the bow; of the liberal studies of grammar, rhetoric, and philosophy: the most skilful masters of the East ambitiously solicited the attention of their royal pupil, and several noble youths were introduced into the palace to animate his diligence by the emulation of friendship. Pulcheria alone discharged the important task of instructing her brother in the arts of government; but her precepts may countenance some suspicion of the extent of her capacity or of the purity of her intentions. She

---

[1] She was admonished, by repeated dreams, of the place where the relics of the forty martyrs had been buried. The ground had successively belonged to the house and garden of a woman of Constantinople, to a monastery of Macedonian monks, and to a church of St. Thyrsus, erected by Cæsarius, who was consul A.D. 397; and the memory of the relics was almost obliterated. Notwithstanding the charitable wishes of Dr. Jortin (Remarks, tom. iv. p. 234), it is not easy to acquit Pulcheria of some share in the pious fraud, which must have been transacted when she was more than five-and-thirty years of age.

taught him to maintain a grave and majestic deportment; to walk, to hold his robes, to seat himself on his throne in a manner worthy of a great prince; to abstain from laughter, to listen with condescension, to return suitable answers; to assume by turns a serious or a placid countenance; in a word, to represent with grace and dignity the external figure of a Roman emperor. But Theodosius [1] was never excited to support the weight and glory of an illustrious name; and, instead of aspiring to imitate his ancestors, he degenerated (if we may presume to measure the degrees of incapacity) below the weakness of his father and his uncle. Arcadius and Honorius had been assisted by the guardian care of a parent, whose lessons were enforced by his authority and example. But the unfortunate prince who is born in the purple must remain a stranger to the voice of truth; and the son of Arcadius was condemned to pass his perpetual infancy encompassed only by a servile train of women and eunuchs. The ample leisure which he acquired by neglecting the essential duties of his high office was filled by idle amusements and unprofitable studies. Hunting was the only active pursuit that could tempt him beyond the limits of the palace; but he most assiduously laboured, sometimes by the light of a midnight lamp, in the mechanic occupations of painting and carving; and the elegance with which he transcribed religious books entitled the Roman emperor to the singular epithet of *Calligraphes*, or a fair writer. Separated from the world by an impenetrable veil, Theodosius trusted the persons whom he loved; he loved those who were accustomed to amuse and flatter his indolence; and as he never perused the papers that were presented for the royal signature, the acts of injustice the most repugnant to his character were frequently perpetrated in his name. The emperor himself was chaste, temperate, liberal, and merciful; but these qualities—which can only deserve the name of virtues when they are supported by courage and regulated by discretion—were seldom beneficial, and they sometimes proved mischievous, to

[1] There is a remarkable difference between the two ecclesiastical historians who in general bear so close a resemblance. Sozomen (l. ix. c. 1) ascribes to Pulcheria the government of the empire and the education of her brother, whom he scarcely condescends to praise. Socrates, though he affectedly disclaims all hopes of favour or fame, composes an elaborate panegyric on the emperor, and cautiously suppresses the merits of his sister (l. vii. c. 22, 42). Philostorgius (l. xii. c. 7) expresses the influence of Pulcheria in gentle and courtly language, τὰς βασιλικὰς σημειώσεις ὑπηρε-ουμένη καὶ διευθύνουσα. Suidas (Excerpt. p. 53) gives a true character of Theodosius; and I have followed the example of Tillemont (tom. vi. p. 25) in borrowing some strokes from the modern Greeks.

mankind. His mind, enervated by a royal education, was oppressed and degraded by abject superstition: he fasted, he sung psalms, he blindly accepted the miracles and doctrines with which his faith was continually nourished. Theodosius devoutly worshipped the dead and living saints of the catholic church; and he once refused to eat till an insolent monk, who had cast an excommunication on his sovereign, condescended to heal the spiritual wound which he had inflicted.[1]

The story of a fair and virtuous maiden, exalted from a private condition to the Imperial throne, might be deemed an incredible romance, if such a romance had not been verified in the marriage of Theodosius. The celebrated Athenais[2] was educated by her father Leontius in the religion and sciences of the Greeks; and so advantageous was the opinion which the Athenian philosopher entertained of his contemporaries, that he divided his patrimony between his two sons, bequeathing to his daughter a small legacy of one hundred pieces of gold, in the lively confidence that her beauty and merit would be a sufficient portion. The jealousy and avarice of her brothers soon compelled Athenais to seek a refuge at Constantinople, and with some hopes, either of justice or favour, to throw herself at the feet of Pulcheria. That sagacious princess listened to her eloquent complaint, and secretly destined the daughter of the philosopher Leontius for the future wife of the emperor of the East, who had now attained the twentieth year of his age. She easily excited the curiosity of her brother by an interesting picture of the charms of Athenais: large eyes, a well-proportioned nose, a fair complexion, golden locks, a slender person, a graceful demeanour, an understanding improved by study, and a virtue tried by distress. Theodosius, concealed behind a curtain in the apartment of his sister, was permitted to behold the Athenian virgin: the modest youth immediately declared his pure and honourable love, and the

---

[1] Theodoret, l. v. c. 37. The bishop of Cyrrhus, one of the first men of his age for his learning and piety, applauds the obedience of Theodosius to the divine laws.

[2] Socrates (l. vii. c. 21) mentions her name (Athenais, the daughter of Leontius, an Athenian sophist), her baptism, marriage, and poetical genius. The most ancient account of her history is in John Malala (part ii. p. 20, 21, edit. Venet. 1733 [p. 354, 355, ed. Bonn]) and in the Paschal Chronicle (p. 311, 312 [ed. Paris; tom. i. p. 576, 577, ed. Bonn]). Those authors had probably seen original pictures of the empress Eudocia. The modern Greeks, Zonaras, Cedrenus, etc., have displayed the love, rather than the talent, of fiction. From Nicephorus, indeed, I have ventured to assume her age. The writer of a romance would not have *imagined* that Athenais was near twenty-eight years old when she inflamed the heart of a young emperor.

royal nuptials were celebrated amidst the acclamations of the capital and the provinces. Athenais, who was easily persuaded to renounce the errors of Paganism, received at her baptism the Christian name of Eudocia: but the cautious Pulcheria withheld the title of Augusta till the wife of Theodosius had approved her fruitfulness by the birth of a daughter, who espoused fifteen years afterwards the emperor of the West. The brothers of Eudocia obeyed, with some anxiety, her Imperial summons; but as she could easily forgive their fortunate unkindness, she indulged the tenderness, or perhaps the vanity, of a sister, by promoting them to the rank of consuls and præfects. In the luxury of the palace she still cultivated those ingenuous arts which had contributed to her greatness, and wisely dedicated her talents to the honour of religion and of her husband. Eudocia composed a poetical paraphrase of the first eight books of the Old Testament and of the prophecies of Daniel and Zechariah; a cento of the verses of Homer, applied to the life and miracles of Christ, the legend of St. Cyprian, and a panegyric on the Persian victories of Theodosius: and her writings, which were applauded by a servile and superstitious age, have not been disdained by the candour of impartial criticism.[1] The fondness of the emperor was not abated by time and possession; and Eudocia, after the marriage of her daughter, was permitted to discharge her grateful vows by a solemn pilgrimage to Jerusalem. Her ostentatious progress through the East may seem inconsistent with the spirit of Christian humility: she pronounced from a throne of gold and gems an eloquent oration to the senate of Antioch, declared her royal intention of enlarging the walls of the city, bestowed a donative of two hundred pounds of gold to restore the public baths, and accepted the statues which were decreed by the gratitude of Antioch. In the Holy Land her alms and pious foundations exceeded the munificence of the great Helena; and though the public treasure might be impoverished by this excessive liberality, she enjoyed the conscious satisfaction of returning to Constantinople with the chains of St. Peter, the right arm of St. Stephen, and an undoubted picture of the Virgin, painted by St. Luke.[2]

---

[1] Socrates, l. vii. c. 21. Photius, p. 413-420 [p. 128, 129, ed. Bekk.]. The Homeric cento is still extant, and has been repeatedly printed; but the claim of Eudocia to that insipid performance is disputed by the critics. See Fabricius, Biblioth. Græc. tom. i. p. 357. The *Ionia*, a miscellaneous dictionary of history and fable, was compiled by another empress of the name of Eudocia who lived in the eleventh century: and the work is still extant in manuscript.

[2] Baronius (Annal. Eccles. A.D. 438, 439) is copious and florid; but he is accused of placing the lies of different ages on the same level of authenticity.

But this pilgrimage was the fatal term of the glories of Eudocia. Satiated with empty pomp, and unmindful perhaps of her obligations to Pulcheria, she ambitiously aspired to the government of the Eastern empire: the palace was distracted by female discord; but the victory was at last decided by the superior ascendant of the sister of Theodosius. The execution of Paulinus, master of the offices, and the disgrace of Cyrus, Prætorian præfect of the East, convinced the public that the favour of Eudocia was insufficient to protect her most faithful friends, and the uncommon beauty of Paulinus encouraged the secret rumour that his guilt was that of a successful lover.[1]   As soon as the empress perceived that the affection of Theodosius was irretrievably lost, she requested the permission of retiring to the distant solitude of Jerusalem. She obtained her request, but the jealousy of Theodosius, or the vindictive spirit of Pulcheria, pursued her in her last retreat; and Saturninus, count of the domestics, was directed to punish with death two ecclesiastics, her most favoured servants. Eudocia instantly revenged them by the assassination of the count: the furious passions which she indulged on this suspicious occasion seemed to justify the severity of Theodosius; and the empress, ignominiously stripped of the honours of her rank,[2] was disgraced, perhaps unjustly, in the eyes of the world. The remainder of the life of Eudocia, about sixteen years, was spent in exile and devotion; and the approach of age, the death of Theodosius, the misfortunes of her only daughter, who was led a captive from Rome to Carthage, and the society of the Holy Monks of Palestine, insensibly confirmed the religious temper of her mind. After a full experience of the vicissitudes of human life, the daughter of the philosopher Leontius expired at Jerusalem, in the sixty-seventh year of her age; protesting with her dying breath that she had never transgressed the bounds of innocence and friendship.[3]

[1] In this short view of the disgrace of Eudocia I have imitated the caution of Evagrius (l. i. c. 21) and Count Marcellinus (in Chron. A.D. 440 and 444 [p. 26]). The two authentic dates assigned by the latter overturn a great part of the Greek fictions; and the celebrated story of the *apple*, etc., is fit only for the Arabian Nights, where something not very unlike it may be found.

[2] Priscus (in Excerpt. Legat. p. 69 [ed. Paris; p. 208, ed. Bonn]), a contemporary and a courtier, drily mentions her Pagan and Christian names without adding any title of honour or respect.

[3] For the *two* pilgrimages of Eudocia, and her long residence at Jerusalem, her devotion, alms, etc., see Socrates (l. vii. c. 47) and Evagrius (l. i. c. 20, 21, 22). The Paschal Chronicle may sometimes deserve regard; and, in the domestic history of Antioch, John Malala becomes a writer of good authority. The Abbé Guenée, in a memoir on the fertility of Pales-

The gentle mind of Theodosius was never inflamed by the ambition of conquest or military renown; and the slight alarm of a Persian war scarcely interrupted the tranquillity of the East. The motives of this war were just and honourable. In the last year of the reign of Jezdegerd, the supposed guardian of Theodosius, a bishop, who aspired to the crown of martyrdom, destroyed one of the fire-temples of Susa.[1] His zeal and obstinacy were revenged on his brethren: the Magi excited a cruel persecution; and the intolerant zeal of Jezdegerd was imitated by his son Varanes, or Bahram, who soon afterwards ascended the throne. Some Christian fugitives, who escaped to the Roman frontier, were sternly demanded, and generously refused; and the refusal, aggravated by commercial disputes, soon kindled a war between the rival monarchies. The mountains of Armenia, and the plains of Mesopotamia, were filled with hostile armies; but the operations of two successive campaigns were not productive of any decisive or memorable events. Some engagements were fought, some towns were besieged, with various and doubtful success: and if the Romans failed in their attempt to recover the long-lost possession of Nisibis, the Persians were repulsed from the walls of a Mesopotamian city by the valour of a martial bishop, who pointed his thundering engine in the name of St. Thomas the Apostle. Yet the splendid victories which the incredible speed of the messenger Palladius repeatedly announced to the palace of Constantinople were celebrated with festivals and panegyrics. From these panegyrics the historians [2] of the age might borrow their extraordinary, and perhaps fabulous, tales; of the proud challenge of a Persian hero, who was entangled by the net, and despatched by the sword, of Areobindus the Goth; of the ten thousand *Immortals*, who were slain in the attack of the Roman camp; and of the hundred thousand Arabs, or Saracens, who were impelled by a panic terror to throw themselves headlong into the Euphrates. Such events may be disbelieved or disregarded; but the charity of a bishop, Acacius of Amida, whose name might have dignified the saintly calendar,

tine, of which I have only seen an extract, calculates the gifts of Eudocia at 20,488 pounds of gold, above 800,000 pounds sterling.

[1] Theodoret, l. v. c. 39. Tillemont, Mém. Ecclés. tom. xii. p. 356-364. Assemanni, Bibliot. Oriental. tom. iii. p. 396, tom. iv. p. 61. Theodoret blames the rashness of Abdas, but extols the constancy of his martyrdom. Yet I do not clearly understand the casuistry which prohibits our repairing the damage which we have unlawfully committed.

[2] Socrates (l. vii. c. 18, 19, 20, 21) is the best author for the Persian war. We may likewise consult the three Chronicles, the Paschal, and those of Marcellinus and Malala.

shall not be lost in oblivion.   Boldly declaring that vases of gold
and silver are useless to a God who neither eats nor drinks, the
generous prelate sold the plate of the church of Amida; employed
the price in the redemption of seven thousand Persian captives;
supplied their wants with affectionate liberality; and dismissed
them to their native country, to inform their king of the true
spirit of the religion which he persecuted.   The practice of
benevolence in the midst of war must always tend to assuage
the animosity of contending nations; and I wish to persuade
myself that Acacius contributed to the restoration of peace.   In
the conference which was held on the limits of the two empires,
the Roman ambassadors degraded the personal character of
their sovereign, by a vain attempt to magnify the extent of his
power, when they seriously advised the Persians to prevent, by a
timely accommodation, the wrath of a monarch who was yet
ignorant of this distant war.   A truce of one hundred years
was solemnly ratified; and although the revolutions of Armenia
might threaten the public tranquillity, the essential conditions
of this treaty were respected near fourscore years by the successors of Constantine and Artaxerxes.

Since the Roman and Parthian standards first encountered on
the banks of the Euphrates, the kingdom of Armenia[1] was
alternately oppressed by its formidable protectors; and in the
course of this History, several events, which inclined the balance
of peace and war, have been already related.   A disgraceful
treaty had resigned Armenia to the ambition of Sapor; and the
scale of Persia appeared to preponderate.   But the royal race
of Arsaces impatiently submitted to the house of Sassan; the
turbulent nobles asserted, or betrayed, their hereditary independence; and the nation was still attached to the *Christian*
princes of Constantinople.   In the beginning of the fifth century
Armenia was divided by the progress of war and faction;[2] and

---

[1] This account of the ruin and division of the kingdom of Armenia is
taken from the third book of the Armenian history of Moses of Chorene.
Deficient as he is in every qualification of a good historian, his local information, his passions, and his prejudices are strongly expressive of a
native and contemporary.   Procopius (de Ædificiis, l. iii. c. 1-5) relates the
same facts in a very different manner; but I have extracted the circumstances, the most probable in themselves and the least inconsistent with
Moses of Chorene.

[2] The western Armenians used the Greek language and characters in
their religious offices; but the use of that hostile tongue was prohibited
by the Persians in the eastern provinces, which were obliged to use the
Syriac, till the invention of the Armenian letters by Mesrobes in the beginning of the fifth century, and the subsequent version of the Bible into the
Armenian language; an event which relaxed the connection of the church
and nation with Constantinople.

the unnatural division precipitated the downfall of that ancient monarchy. Chosroes, the Persian vassal, reigned over the eastern and most extensive portion of the country; while the western province acknowledged the jurisdiction of Arsaces, and the supremacy of the emperor Arcadius. After the death of Arsaces, the Romans suppressed the regal government, and imposed on their allies the condition of subjects. The military command was delegated to the count of the Armenian frontier; the city of Theodosiopolis [1] was built and fortified in a strong situation, on a fertile and lofty ground, near the sources of the Euphrates; and the dependent territories were ruled by five satraps, whose dignity was marked by a peculiar habit of gold and purple. The less fortunate nobles, who lamented the loss of their king, and envied the honours of their equals, were provoked to negotiate their peace and pardon at the Persian court; and, returning with their followers to the palace of Artaxata, acknowledged Chosroes for their lawful sovereign. About thirty years afterwards, Artasires, the nephew and successor of Chosroes, fell under the displeasure of the haughty and capricious nobles of Armenia; and they unanimously desired a Persian governor in the room of an unworthy king. The answer of the archbishop Isaac, whose sanction they earnestly solicited, is expressive of the character of a superstitious people. He deplored the manifest and inexcusable vices of Artasires; and declared that he should not hesitate to accuse him before the tribunal of a Christian emperor, who would punish, without destroying, the sinner. " Our king," continued Isaac, " is too much addicted to licentious pleasures, but he has been purified in the holy waters of baptism. He is a lover of women, but he does not adore the fire or the elements. He may deserve the reproach of lewdness, but he is an undoubted catholic; and his faith is pure, though his manners are flagitious. I will never consent to abandon my sheep to the rage of devouring wolves; and you would soon repent your rash exchange of the infirmities of a believer, for the specious virtues of an heathen." [2] Exasperated by the firmness of Isaac, the factious nobles accused both the king and the archbishop as the secret adherents of the

---

[1] Moses Choren. l. iii. c. 59, p. 309 and p. 358 [ed. Whiston, Lond. 1736]. Procopius, de Ædificiis, l. iii. c. 5. Theodosiopolis stands, or rather stood, about thirty-five miles to the east of Arzeroum, the modern capital of Turkish Armenia. See D'Anville, Géographie Ancienne, tom. ii. p. 99, 100.

[2] Moses Choren. l. iii. c. 63, p. 316. According to the institution of St. Gregory, the Apostle of Armenia, the archbishop was always of the royal family; a circumstance which, in some degree, corrected the influence of the sacerdotal character, and united the mitre with the crown.

emperor; and absurdly rejoiced in the sentence of condemnation, which, after a partial hearing, was solemnly pronounced by Bahram himself. The descendants of Arsaces were degraded from the royal dignity,[1] which they had possessed above five hundred and sixty years;[2] and the dominions of the unfortunate Artasires, under the new and significant appellation of Persarmenia, were reduced into the form of a province. This usurpation excited the jealousy of the Roman government; but the rising disputes were soon terminated by an amicable, though unequal, partition of the ancient kingdom of Armenia; and a territorial acquisition, which Augustus might have despised, reflected some lustre on the declining empire of the younger Theodosius.

CHAPTER XXXIII

Death of Honorius—Valentinian III. Emperor of the West—Administration of his Mother Placidia—Aëtius and Boniface—Conquest of Africa by the Vandals

DURING a long and disgraceful reign of twenty-eight years, Honorius, emperor of the West, was separated from the friendship of his brother, and afterwards of his nephew, who reigned over the East; and Constantinople beheld, with apparent indifference and secret joy, the calamities of Rome. The strange adventures of Placidia gradually renewed and cemented the alliance of the two empires. The daughter of the great Theodosius had been the captive and the queen of the Goths; she lost an affectionate husband; she was dragged in chains by his insulting assassin; she tasted the pleasure of revenge, and was exchanged, in the treaty of peace, for six hundred thousand measures of wheat. After her return from Spain to Italy, Placidia experienced a new persecution in the bosom of her

---

[1] A branch of the royal house of Arsaces still subsisted with the rank and possessions (as it should seem) of Armenian satraps. See Moses Choren. l. iii. c. 65, p. 321.

[2] Valarsaces was appointed king of Armenia by his brother the Parthian monarch, immediately after the defeat of Antiochus Sidetes (Moses Choren. l. ii. c. 2, p. 85), one hundred and thirty years before Christ. Without depending on the various and contradictory periods of the reigns of the last kings, we may be assured that the ruin of the Armenian kingdom happened after the council of Chalcedon, A.D. 431 (l. iii. c. 61, p. 312); and under Varanes, or Bahram, king of Persia (l. iii. c. 64, p. 317), who reigned from A.D. 420 to 440. See Assemanni, Bibliot. Oriental. tom. iii. p. 396.

family. She was averse to a marriage which had been stipulated without her consent; and the brave Constantius, as a noble reward for the tyrants whom he had vanquished, received, from the hand of Honorius himself, the struggling and reluctant hand of the widow of Adolphus. But her resistance ended with the ceremony of the nuptials; nor did Placidia refuse to become the mother of Honoria and Valentinian the Third, or to assume and exercise an absolute dominion over the mind of her grateful husband. The generous soldier, whose time had hitherto been divided between social pleasure and military service, was taught new lessons of avarice and ambition: he extorted the title of Augustus; and the servant of Honorius was associated to the empire of the West. The death of Constantius, in the seventh month of his reign, instead of diminishing, seemed to increase, the power of Placidia; and the indecent familiarity [1] of her brother, which might be no more than the symptoms of a childish affection, were universally attributed to incestuous love. On a sudden, by some base intrigues of a steward and a nurse, this excessive fondness was converted into an irreconcilable quarrel: the debates of the emperor and his sister were not long confined within the walls of the palace; and as the Gothic soldiers adhered to their queen, the city of Ravenna was agitated with bloody and dangerous tumults, which could only be appeased by the forced or voluntary retreat of Placidia and her children. The royal exiles landed at Constantinople, soon after the marriage of Theodosius, during the festival of the Persian victories. They were treated with kindness and magnificence; but as the statues of the emperor Constantius had been rejected by the Eastern court, the title of Augusta could not decently be allowed to his widow. Within a few months after the arrival of Placidia a swift messenger announced the death of Honorius, the consequence of a dropsy; but the important secret was not divulged till the necessary orders had been despatched for the march of a large body of troops to the sea-coast of Dalmatia. The shops and the gates of Constantinople remained shut during seven days; and the loss of a foreign prince, who could neither be

---

[1] Τὰ συνεχῆ κατὰ στόμα φιλήματα, is the expression of Olympiodorus (apud Photium, p. 196 [p. 62 b, ed. Bekk.]); who means, perhaps, to describe the same caresses which Mahomet bestowed on his *daughter* Phatemah. Quando (says the prophet himself), quando subit mihi desiderium Paradisi, osculor eam, et ingero linguam meam in os ejus. But this sensual indulgence was justified by miracle and mystery; and the anecdote has been communicated to the public by the Reverend Father Maracci, in his Version and Confutation of the Koran, tom. i. p. 32.

esteemed nor regretted, was celebrated with loud and affected demonstrations of the public grief.

While the ministers of Constantinople deliberated, the vacant throne of Honorius was usurped by the ambition of a stranger. The name of the rebel was John; he filled the confidential office of *Primicerius,* or principal secretary; and history has attributed to his character more virtues than can easily be reconciled with the violation of the most sacred duty. Elated by the submission of Italy, and the hope of an alliance with the Huns, John presumed to insult, by an embassy, the majesty of the Eastern emperor; but when he understood that his agents had been banished, imprisoned, and at length chased away with deserved ignominy, John prepared to assert by arms the injustice of his claims. In such a cause the grandson of the great Theodosius should have marched in person; but the young emperor was easily diverted by his physicians from so rash and hazardous a design; and the conduct of the Italian expedition was prudently intrusted to Ardaburius and his son Aspar, who had already signalised their valour against the Persians. It was resolved that Ardaburius should embark with the infantry; whilst Aspar, at the head of the cavalry, conducted Placidia, and her son Valentinian, along the sea-coast of the Hadriatic. The march of the cavalry was performed with such active diligence, that they surprised, without resistance, the important city of Aquileia; when the hopes of Aspar were unexpectedly confounded by the intelligence that a storm had dispersed the Imperial fleet, and that his father, with only two galleys, was taken and carried a prisoner into the port of Ravenna. Yet this incident, unfortunate as it might seem, facilitated the conquest of Italy. Ardaburius employed, or abused, the courteous freedom which he was permitted to enjoy, to revive among the troops a sense of loyalty and gratitude; and, as soon as the conspiracy was ripe for execution, he invited, by private messages, and pressed the approach of Aspar. A shepherd, whom the popular credulity transformed into an angel, guided the Eastern cavalry, by a secret, and, it was thought, an impassable road, through the morasses of the Po: the gates of Ravenna, after a short struggle, were thrown open; and the defenceless tyrant was delivered to the mercy, or rather to the cruelty, of the conquerors. His right hand was first cut off; and after he had been exposed, mounted on an ass, to the public derision, John was beheaded in the circus of Aquileia. The emperor Theodosius, when he received the news of the victory, interrupted the horse-races; and singing, as he marched through the streets, a suitable psalm, conducted his people from the Hippodrome to the church, where he spent the remainder of the day in grateful devotion.[1]

In a monarchy which, according to various precedents, might be considered as elective, or hereditary, or patrimonial, it was impossible that the intricate claims of female and collateral succession should be clearly defined;[2] and Theodosius, by the right of consanguinity or conquest, might have reigned the sole legitimate emperor of the Romans. For a moment, perhaps, his eyes were dazzled by the prospect of unbounded sway; but his indolent temper gradually acquiesced in the dictates of sound policy. He contented himself with the possession of the East; and wisely relinquished the laborious task of waging a distant and doubtful war against the barbarians beyond the Alps, or of securing the obedience of the Italians and Africans, whose minds were alienated by the irreconcilable difference of language and interest. Instead of listening to the voice of ambition, Theodosius resolved to imitate the moderation of his grandfather, and to seat his cousin Valentinian on the throne of the West. The royal infant was distinguished at Constantinople by the title of *Nobilissimus*: he was promoted, before his departure from Thessalonica, to the rank and dignity of *Cæsar*: and, after the conquest of Italy, the patrician Helion, by the authority of Theodosius, and in the presence of the senate, saluted Valentinian the Third by the name of Augustus, and solemnly invested him with the diadem and the Imperial purple.[3] By the agreement of the three females who governed the Roman world, the son of Placidia was betrothed to Eudoxia, the daughter of Theodosius and Athenais; and, as soon as the lover and his bride had attained the age of puberty, this honourable alliance was faithfully accomplished. At the same time, as a compensation, perhaps, for the expenses of the war, the Western Illyricum was

---

[1] For these revolutions of the Western empire consult Olympiodor. apud Phot. p. 192, 193, 196, 197, 200 [p. 61-63, ed. Bekk.]; Sozomen, l. ix. c. 16; Socrates, l. vii. 23, 24; Philostorgius, l. xii. c. 10, 11 [12-14], and Godefroy, Dissertat. p. 486; Procopius, de Bell. Vandal. l. i. c. 3, p. 182, 183 [ed. Paris; tom. i. p. 319 *seqq.* ed. Bonn]; Theophanes, in Chronograph. p. 72, 73 [ed. Par.; tom. i. p. 129-131, ed. Bonn]; and the Chronicles.

[2] See Grotius de Jure Belli et Pacis, l. ii. c. 7. He has laboriously, but vainly, attempted to form a reasonable system of jurisprudence from the various and discordant modes of royal succession, which have been introduced by fraud or force, by time or accident.

[3] The original writers are not agreed (see Muratori, Annali d'Italia, tom. iv. p. 139) whether Valentinian received the Imperial diadem at Rome or Ravenna. In this uncertainty, I am willing to believe that some respect was shown to the senate.

detached from the Italian dominions, and yielded to the throne
of Constantinople.[1]   The emperor of the East acquired the useful
dominion of the rich and maritime province of Dalmatia, and the
dangerous sovereignty of Pannonia and Noricum, which had been
filled and ravaged above twenty years by a promiscuous crowd
of Huns, Ostrogoths, Vandals, and *Bavarians*.   Theodosius and
Valentinian continued to respect the obligations of their public
and domestic alliance; but the unity of the Roman government
was finally dissolved.   By a positive declaration, the validity of
all future laws was limited to the dominions of their peculiar
author; unless he should think proper to communicate them,
subscribed with his own hand, for the approbation of his independent colleague.[2]

Valentinian, when he received the title of Augustus, was no
more than six years of age; and his long minority was intrusted
to the guardian care of a mother who might assert a female claim
to the succession of the Western empire.   Placidia envied, but
she could not equal, the reputation and virtues of the wife and
sister of Theodosius; the elegant genius of Eudocia, the wise
and successful policy of Pulcheria.   The mother of Valentinian
was jealous of the power which she was incapable of exercising:[3]
she reigned twenty-five years, in the name of her son; and the
character of that unworthy emperor gradually countenanced
the suspicion that Placidia had enervated his youth by a dissolute
education, and studiously diverted his attention from every
manly and honourable pursuit.   Amidst the decay of military
spirit, her armies were commanded by two generals, Aëtius[4] and

---

[1] The Count de Buat (Hist. des Peuples de l'Europe, tom. vii. p. 292-300)
has established the reality, explained the motives, and traced the consequences, of this remarkable cession.

[2] See the first *Novel* of Theodosius, by which he ratifies and communicates (A.D. 438) the Theodosian Code.   About 40 years before that time
the unity of legislation had been proved by an exception.   The Jews, who
were numerous in the cities of Apulia and Calabria, produced a law of the
East to justify their exemption from municipal offices (Cod. Theod. l. xvi.
tit. viii. leg. 13); and the Western emperor was obliged to invalidate, by a
special edict, the law, quam constat meis partibus esse damnosam.   Cod.
Theod. l. xi. [xii.] tit. i. leg. 158.

[3] Cassiodorus (Variar. l. xi. Epist. i. p. 238 [p. 161, ed. Venet.]) has compared the regencies of Placidia and Amalasuntha.   He arraigns the weakness of the mother of Valentinian, and praises the virtues of his royal
mistress.   On this occasion flattery seems to have spoken the language of
truth.

[4] Philostorgius, l. xii. c. 12 [14], and Godefroy's Dissertat. p. 493, etc.;
and Renatus Frigeridus, apud Gregor. Turon. l. ii. c. 8, in tom. ii. p. 163.
The father of Aëtius was Gaudentius, an illustrious citizen of the province
of Scythia and master-general of the cavalry; his mother was a rich and
noble Italian.   From his earliest youth, Aëtius, as a soldier and a hostage,
had conversed with the barbarians.

Boniface,[1] who may be deservedly named as the last of the Romans. Their union might have supported a sinking empire; their discord was the fatal and immediate cause of the loss of Africa. The invasion and defeat of Attila has immortalised the fame of Aëtius; and though time has thrown a shade over the exploits of his rival, the defence of Marseilles, and the deliverance of Africa, attest the military talents of Count Boniface. In the field of battle, in partial encounters, in single combats, he was still the terror of the barbarians: the clergy, and particularly his friend Augustin, were edified by the Christian piety which had once tempted him to retire from the world; the people applauded his spotless integrity; the army dreaded his equal and inexorable justice, which may be displayed in a very singular example. A peasant, who complained of the criminal intimacy between his wife and a Gothic soldier, was directed to attend his tribunal the following day: in the evening the count, who had diligently informed himself of the time and place of the assignation, mounted his horse, rode ten miles into the country, surprised the guilty couple, punished the soldier with instant death, and silenced the complaints of the husband, by presenting him, the next morning, with the head of the adulterer. The abilities of Aëtius and Boniface might have been usefully employed against the public enemies in separate and important commands; but the experience of their past conduct should have decided the real favour and confidence of the empress Placidia. In the melancholy season of her exile and distress, Boniface alone had maintained her cause with unshaken fidelity; and the troops and treasures of Africa had essentially contributed to extinguish the rebellion. The same rebellion had been supported by the zeal and activity of Aëtius, who brought an army of sixty thousand Huns from the Danube to the confines of Italy, for the service of the usurper. The untimely death of John compelled him to accept an advantageous treaty; but he still continued, the subject and the soldier of Valentinian, to entertain a secret, perhaps a treasonable, correspondence with his barbarian allies, whose retreat had been purchased by liberal gifts and more liberal promises. But Aëtius possessed an advantage of singular moment in a female reign: he was present: he besieged with

---

[1] For the character of Boniface see Olympiodorus, apud Phot. p. 196 [p. 62 b, ed. Bekk.]; and St. Augustin, apud Tillemont, Mémoires Ecclés. tom. xiii. p. 712-715, 886. The bishop of Hippo at length deplored the fall of his friend, who, after a solemn vow of chastity, had married a second wife of the Arian sect, and who was suspected of keeping several concubines in his house.

artful and assiduous flattery the palace of Ravenna; disguise
his dark designs with the mask of loyalty and friendship; an
at length deceived both his mistress and his absent rival, by
subtle conspiracy which a weak woman and a brave man could nc
easily suspect. He secretly persuaded [1] Placidia to recall Bon
face from the government of Africa; he secretly advised Bonifac
to disobey the Imperial summons: to the one, he represente
the order as a sentence of death; to the other, he stated th
refusal as a signal of revolt; and when the credulous and unsus
pectful count had armed the province in his defence, Aëtiu
applauded his sagacity in foreseeing the rebellion which his ow
perfidy had excited. A temperate inquiry into the real motive
of Boniface would have restored a faithful servant to his dut
and to the republic; but the arts of Aëtius still continued t
betray and to inflame, and the count was urged by persecutio
to embrace the most desperate counsels. The success wit
which he eluded or repelled the first attacks could not inspire
vain confidence that, at the head of some loose disorderl
Africans, he should be able to withstand the regular forces of th
West, commanded by a rival whose military character it wa
impossible for him to despise. After some hesitation, the las
struggles of prudence and loyalty, Boniface despatched a trust
friend to the court, or rather to the camp, of Gonderic, king of th
Vandals, with the proposal of a strict alliance, and the offer of a
advantageous and perpetual settlement.

After the retreat of the Goths the authority of Honorius hac
obtained a precarious establishment in Spain, except only ir
the province of Gallicia, where the Suevi and the Vandals hac
fortified their camps in mutual discord and hostile independ
ence. The Vandals prevailed, and their adversaries were be
sieged in the Nervasian hills, between Leon and Oviedo, till th
approach of Count Asterius compelled, or rather provoked, th
victorious barbarians to remove the scene of the war to th
plains of Bætica. The rapid progress of the Vandals soor
required a more effectual opposition, and the master-genera
Castinus marched against them with a numerous army o
Romans and Goths. Vanquished in battle by an inferior enemy
Castinus fled with dishonour to Tarragona; and this memorable

---

[1] Procopius (de Bell. Vandal. l. i. c. 3, 4, p. 182-186 [tom. i. p. 319-528
ed. Bonn]) relates the fraud of Aëtius, the revolt of Boniface, and the los
of Africa. This anecdote, which is supported by some collateral testimony
(see Ruinart, Hist. Persecut. Vandal. p. 420, 421) seems agreeable to the
practice of ancient and modern courts, and would be naturally revealed by
the repentance of Boniface.

defeat, which has been represented as the punishment, was most probably the effect, of his rash presumption.[1] Seville and Carthagena became the reward, or rather the prey, of the ferocious conquerors; and the vessels which they found in the harbour of Carthagena might easily transport them to the isles of Majorca and Minorca, where the Spanish fugitives, as in a secure recess, had vainly concealed their families and their fortunes. The experience of navigation, and perhaps the prospect of Africa, encouraged the Vandals to accept the invitation which they received from Count Boniface, and the death of Gonderic served only to forward and animate the bold enterprise. In the room of a prince not conspicuous for any superior powers of the mind or body, they acquired his bastard brother, the terrible Genseric;[2] a name which in the destruction of the Roman empire has deserved an equal rank with the names of Alaric and Attila. The king of the Vandals is described to have been of a middle stature, with a lameness in one leg, which he had contracted by an accidental fall from his horse. His slow and cautious speech seldom declared the deep purposes of his soul: he disdained to imitate the luxury of the vanquished, but he indulged the sterner passions of anger and revenge. The ambition of Genseric was without bounds and without scruples, and the warrior could dexterously employ the dark engines of policy to solicit the allies who might be useful to his success, or to scatter among his enemies the seeds of hatred and contention. Almost in the moment of his departure he was informed that Hermanric, king of the Suevi, had presumed to ravage the Spanish territories which he was resolved to abandon. Impatient of the insult, Genseric pursued the hasty retreat of the Suevi as far as Merida, precipitated the king and his army into the river Anas, and calmly returned to the sea-shore to embark his victorious troops. The vessels which transported the Vandals over the modern Straits of Gibraltar, a channel only twelve miles in breadth, were furnished by the Spainards, who

[1] See the Chronicles of Prosper and Idatius [Sirmond, Op. tom. ii. p. 298]. Salvian (de Gubernat. Dei, l. vii. p. 246, Paris, 1608) ascribes the victory of the Vandals to their superior piety. They fasted, they prayed, they carried a Bible in the front of the Host, with the design, perhaps, of reproaching the perfidy and sacrilege of their enemies.

[2] Gizericus (his name is variously expressed) staturâ mediocris et equi casû claudicans, animo profundus, sermone rarus, luxuriæ contemptor, irâ turbidus, habendi cupidus, ad solicitandas gentes providentissimus, semina contentionum jacere, odia miscere paratus. Jornandes, de Rebus Geticis, c. 33, p. 657. This portrait, which is drawn with some skill and a strong likeness, must have been copied from the Gothic history of Cassiodorus.

anxiously wished their departure, and by the African general, who had implored their formidable assistance.[1]

Our fancy, so long accustomed to exaggerate and multiply the martial swarms of barbarians that seemed to issue from the North, will perhaps be surprised by the account of the army which Genseric mustered on the coast of Mauritania. The Vandals, who in twenty years had penetrated from the Elbe to Mount Atlas, were united under the command of their warlike king; and he reigned with equal authority over the Alani, who had passed within the term of human life from the cold of Scythia to the excessive heat of an African climate. The hopes of the bold enterprise had excited many brave adventurers of the Gothic nation, and many desperate provincials were tempted to repair their fortunes by the same means which had occasioned their ruin. Yet this various multitude amounted only to fifty thousand effective men; and though Genseric artfully magnified his apparent strength by appointing eighty *chiliarchs*, or commanders of thousands, the fallacious increase of old men, of children, and of slaves, would scarcely have swelled his army to the number of fourscore thousand persons.[2] But his own dexterity and the discontents of Africa soon fortified the Vandal powers by the accession of numerous and active allies. The parts of Mauritania which border on the great desert and the Atlantic ocean were filled with a fierce and untractable race of men, whose savage temper had been exasperated rather than reclaimed by their dread of the Roman arms. The wandering Moors,[3] as they gradually ventured to approach the sea-shore and the camp of the Vandals, must have viewed with terror and

---

[1] See the Chronicle of Idatius. That bishop, a Spaniard and a contemporary, places the passage of the Vandals in the month of May, of the year of Abraham (which commences in October) 2444. This date, which coincides with A.D. 429, is confirmed by Isidore, another Spanish bishop, and is justly preferred to the opinion of those writers who have marked for that event one of the two preceding years. See Pagi Critica, tom. ii. p. 205, etc.

[2] Compare Procopius (de Bell. Vandal. l. i. c. 5, p. 190 [tom. i. p. 334, ed. Bonn]) and Victor Vitensis (de Persecutione Vandal. l. i. c. 1, p. 3, edit. Ruinart). We are assured by Idatius that Genseric evacuated Spain, cum Vandalis *omnibus* eorumque familiis [Sirm. Op. tom. ii. p. 299]; and Possidius (in Vit. Augustin. c. 28, apud Ruinart, p. 427) describes his army as manus ingens immanium gentium Vandalorum et Alanorum, commixtam secum habens Gothorum gentem, aliarumque diversarum personas.

[3] For the manners of the Moors see Procopius (de Bell. Vandal. l. ii. c. 6, p. 249 [tom. i. p. 434, ed. Bonn]); for their figure and complexion, M. de Buffon (Histoire Naturelle, tom. iii. p. 430). Procopius says in general that the Moors had joined the Vandals before the death of Valentinian (de Bell. Vandal. l. i. c. 5, p. 190 [tom. i. p. 334, ed. Bonn]); and it is probable that the independent tribes did not embrace any uniform system of policy.

astonishment the dress, the armour, the martial pride and discipline of the unknown strangers who had landed on their coast; and the fair complexions of the blue-eyed warriors of Germany formed a very singular contrast with the swarthy or olive hue which is derived from the neighbourhood of the torrid zone. After the first difficulties had in some measure been removed which arose from the mutual ignorance of their respective language, the Moors, regardless of any future consequence, embraced the alliance of the enemies of Rome, and a crowd of naked savages rushed from the woods and valleys of Mount Atlas, to satiate their revenge on the polished tyrants who had injuriously expelled them from the native sovereignty of the land.

The persecution of the Donatists[1] was an event not less favourable to the designs of Genseric. Seventeen years before he landed in Africa, a public conference was held at Carthage by the order of the magistrate. The catholics were satisfied that, after the invincible reasons which they had alleged, the obstinacy of the schismatics must be inexcusable and voluntary, and the emperor Honorius was persuaded to inflict the most rigorous penalties on a faction which had so long abused his patience and clemency. Three hundred bishops,[2] with many thousands of the inferior clergy, were torn from their churches, stripped of their ecclesiastical possessions, banished to the islands, and proscribed by the laws, if they presumed to conceal themselves in the provinces of Africa. Their numerous congregations, both in cities and in the country, were deprived of the rights of citizens and of the exercise of religious worship. A regular scale of fines, from ten to two hundred pounds of silver, was curiously ascertained, according to the distinctions of rank and fortune, to punish the crime of assisting at a schismatic conventicle; and if the fine had been levied five times without subduing the obstinacy of the offender, his future punishment was referred to the discretion of the Imperial court.[3] By these severities, which obtained the warmest approbation of St. Augustin,[4] great numbers of

---

[1] See Tillemont, Mémoires Ecclés. tom. xiii. p. 516-558; and the whole series of the persecution, in the original monuments, published by Dupin at the end of Optatus, p. 323-515.

[2] The Donatist bishops, at the conference of Carthage, amounted to 279; and they asserted that their whole number was not less than 400. The Catholics had 286 present, 120 absent, besides sixty-four vacant bishoprics.

[3] The fifth title of the sixteenth book of the Theodosian Code exhibits a series of the Imperial laws against the Donatists, from the year 400 to the year 428. Of these the 54th law, promulgated by Honorius, A.D. 414, is the most severe and effectual.

[4] St. Augustin altered his opinion with regard to the proper treatment of heretics. His pathetic declaration of pity and indulgence for the Mani-

Donatists were reconciled to the catholic church; but the fanatics who still persevered in their opposition were provoked to madness and despair; the distracted country was filled with tumult and bloodshed; the armed troops of Circumcellions alternately pointed their rage against themselves or against their adversaries; and the calendar of martyrs received on both sides a considerable augmentation.[1] Under these circumstances Genseric, a Christian, but an enemy of the orthodox communion, showed himself to the Donatists as a powerful deliverer, from whom they might reasonably expect the repeal of the odious and oppressive edicts of the Roman emperors.[2] The conquest of Africa was facilitated by the active zeal or the secret favour of a domestic faction; the wanton outrages against the churches and the clergy, of which the Vandals are accused, may be fairly imputed to the fanaticism of their allies; and the intolerant spirit which disgraced the triumph of Christianity contributed to the loss of the most important province of the West.[3]

The court and the people were astonished by the strange intelligence that a virtuous hero, after so many favours and so many services, had renounced his allegiance and invited the barbarians to destroy the province intrusted to his command. The friends of Boniface, who still believed that his criminal behaviour might be excused by some honourable motive, solicited, during the absence of Aëtius, a free conference with the Count of Africa; and Darius, an officer of high distinction, was named for the important embassy.[4] In their first interview

chæans has been inserted by Mr. Locke (vol. iii. p. 469) among the choice specimens of his commonplace book. Another philosopher, the celebrated Bayle (tom. ii. p. 445-496), has refuted, with superfluous diligence and ingenuity, the arguments by which the bishop of Hippo justified, in his old age, the persecution of the Donatists.

[1] See Tillemont, Mém. Ecclés. tom. xiii. p. 586-592, 806. The Donatists boasted of *thousands* of these voluntary martyrs. Augustin asserts, and probably with truth, that these numbers were much exaggerated; but he sternly maintains that it was better that *some* should burn themselves in this world than that *all* should burn in hell flames.

[2] According to St. Augustin and Theodoret, the Donatists were inclined to the principles, or at least to the party, of the Arians, which Genseric supported. Tillemont, Mém. Ecclés. tom. vi. p. 68.

[3] See Baronius, Annal. Eccles. A.D. 428, No. 7, A.D. 439, No. 35. The cardinal, though more inclined to seek the cause of great events in heaven than on the earth, has observed the apparent connection of the Vandals and the Donatists. Under the reign of the barbarians, the schismatics of Africa enjoyed an obscure peace of one hundred years; at the end of which we may again trace them by the light of the Imperial persecutions. See Tillemont, Mém. Ecclés. tom. vi. p. 192, etc.

[4] In a confidential letter to Count Boniface, St. Augustin, without examining the grounds of the quarrel, piously exhorts him to discharge the duties of a Christian and a subject; to extricate himself without delay

at Carthage the imaginary provocations were mutually explained, the opposite letters of Aëtius were produced and compared, and the fraud was easily detected. Placidia and Boniface lamented their fatal error, and the count had sufficient magnanimity to confide in the forgiveness of his sovereign, or to expose his head to her future resentment. His repentance was fervent and sincere; but he soon discovered that it was no longer in his power to restore the edifice which he had shaken to its foundations. Carthage and the Roman garrisons returned with their general to the allegiance of Valentinian, but the rest of Africa was still distracted with war and faction; and the inexorable king of the Vandals, disdaining all terms of accommodation, sternly refused to relinquish the possession of his prey. The band of veterans who marched under the standard of Boniface, and his hasty levies of provincial troops, were defeated with considerable loss; the victorious barbarians insulted the open country; and Carthage, Cirta, and Hippo Regius, were the only cities that appeared to rise above the general inundation.

The long and narrow tract of the African coast was filled with frequent monuments of Roman art and magnificence; and the respective degrees of improvement might be accurately measured by the distance from Carthage and the Mediterranean. A simple reflection will impress every thinking mind with the clearest idea of fertility and cultivation: the country was extremely populous; the inhabitants reserved a liberal subsistence for their own use; and the annual exportation, particularly of wheat, was so regular and plentiful, that Africa deserved the name of the common granary of Rome and of mankind. On a sudden the seven fruitful provinces, from Tangier to Tripoli, were overwhelmed by the invasion of the Vandals, whose destructive rage has perhaps been exaggerated by popular animosity, religious zeal, and extravagant declamation. War in its fairest form implies a perpetual violation of humanity and justice; and the hostilities of barbarians are inflamed by the fierce and lawless spirit which incessantly disturbs their peaceful and domestic society. The Vandals, where they found resistance, seldom gave quarter; and the deaths of their valiant countrymen were expiated by the ruin of the cities under whose walls they had fallen. Careless of the distinction of age, or sex, or rank, they employed every species of indignity and torture to

from his dangerous and guilty situation; and even, if he could obtain the consent of his wife, to embrace a life of celibacy and penance (Tillemont. Mém. Ecclés. tom. xiii. p. 890). The bishop was intimately connected with Darius, the minister of peace (id. tom. xiii. p. 928).

force from the captives a discovery of their hidden wealth. The stern policy of Genseric justified his frequent examples of military execution: he was not always the master of his own passions or of those of his followers; and the calamities of war were aggravated by the licentiousness of the Moors and the fanaticism of the Donatists. Yet I shall not easily be persuaded that it was the common practice of the Vandals to extirpate the olives and other fruit trees of a country where they intended to settle: nor can I believe that it was a usual stratagem to slaughter great numbers of their prisoners before the walls of a besieged city, for the sole purpose of infecting the air and producing a pestilence, of which they themselves must have been the first victims.[1]

The generous mind of Count Boniface was tortured by the exquisite distress of beholding the ruin which he had occasioned, and whose rapid progress he was unable to check. After the loss of a battle he retired into Hippo Regius, where he was immediately besieged by an enemy who considered him as the real bulwark of Africa. The maritime colony of *Hippo*,[2] about two hundred miles westward of Carthage, had formerly acquired the distinguishing epithet of *Regius* from the residence of Numidian kings; and some remains of trade and populousness still adhere to the modern city, which is known in Europe by the corrupted name of Bona. The military labours and anxious reflections of Count Boniface were alleviated by the edifying conversation of his friend St. Augustin;[3] till that bishop, the light and pillar of the catholic church, was gently released, in the third month of the siege and in the seventy-sixth year of his age, from the actual and the impending calamities of his country. The youth of Augustin had been stained by the vices and errors which he

[1] The original complaints of the desolation of Africa are contained—1. In a letter from Capreolus, bishop of Carthage, to excuse his absence from the council of Ephesus (ap. Ruinart, p. 428). 2. In the Life of St. Augustin by his friend and colleague Possidius (ap. Ruinart, p. 427). 3. In the History of the Vandalic Persecution, by Victor Vitensis (l. i. c. 1, 2, 3, edit. Ruinart). The last picture, which was drawn sixty years after the event, is more expressive of the author's passions than of the truth of facts.

[2] See Cellarius, Geograph. Antiq. tom. ii. part ii. p. 112. Leo African. in Ramusio, tom. i. fol. 70. L'Afrique de Marmol, tom. ii. p. 434, 437. Shaw's Travels, p. 46, 47. The old Hippo Regius was finally destroyed by the Arabs in the seventh century; but a new town, at the distance of two miles, was built with the materials; and it contained in the sixteenth century about three hundred families of industrious, but turbulent, manufacturers. The adjacent territory is renowned for a pure air, a fertile soil, and plenty of exquisite fruits.

[3] The Life of St. Augustin, by Tillemont, fills a quarto volume (Mém. Ecclés. tom. xiii.) of more than one thousand pages; and the diligence of that learned Jansenist was excited, on this occasion, by factious and devout zeal for the founder of his sect.

so ingenuously confesses; but from the moment of his conversion to that of his death the manners of the bishop of Hippo were pure and austere, and the most conspicuous of his virtues was an ardent zeal against heretics of every denomination—the Manichæans, the Donatists, and the Pelagians, against whom he waged a perpetual controversy. When the city, some months after his death, was burnt by the Vandals, the library was fortunately saved which contained his voluminous writings—two hundred and thirty-two separate books or treatises on theological subjects, besides a complete exposition of the psalter and the gospel, and a copious magazine of epistles and homilies.[1] According to the judgment of the most impartial critics, the superficial learning of Augustin was confined to the Latin language;[2] and his style, though sometimes animated by the eloquence of passion, is usually clouded by false and affected rhetoric. But he possessed a strong, capacious, argumentative mind; he boldly sounded the dark abyss of grace, predestination, free-will, and original sin; and the rigid system of Christianity which he framed or restored[3] has been entertained with public applause and secret reluctance by the Latin church.[4]

By the skill of Boniface, and perhaps by the ignorance of the Vandals, the siege of Hippo was protracted above fourteen months: the sea was continually open; and when the adjacent

[1] Such at least is the account of Victor Vitensis (de Persecut. Vandal. l i. c. 3); though Gennadius seems to doubt whether any person had read, or even collected, all the works of St. Augustin (see Hieronym. Opera, tom. i. p. 319, in Catalog. Scriptor. Eccles.). They have been repeatedly printed; and Dupin (Bibliothèque Ecclés. tom. iii. p. 158-257) has given a large and satisfactory abstract of them as they stand in the last edition of the Benedictines. My personal acquaintance with the bishop of Hippo does not extend beyond the *Confessions* and the *City of God*.

[2] In his early youth (Confess. i. 14) St. Augustin disliked and neglected the study of Greek; and he frankly owns that he read the Platonists in a Latin version (Confess. vii. 9). Some modern critics have thought that his ignorance of Greek disqualified him from expounding the Scriptures; and Cicero or Quintilian would have required the knowledge of that language in a professor of rhetoric.

[3] These questions were seldom agitated from the time of St. Paul to that of St. Augustin. I am informed that the Greek fathers maintain the natural sentiments of the Semi-Pelagians; and that the orthodoxy of St. Augustin was derived from the Manichæan school.

[4] The church of Rome has canonised Augustin and reprobated Calvin. Yet, as the *real* difference between them is invisible even to a theological microscope, the Molinists are oppressed by the authority of the saint, and the Jansenists are disgraced by their resemblance to the heretic. In the meanwhile the Protestant Arminians stand aloof and deride the mutual perplexity of the disputants (see a curious Review of the Controversy by Le Clerc, Bibliothèque Universelle, tom. xiv. p. 144-398). Perhaps a reasoner still more independent may smile in *his* turn when he peruses an Arminian Commentary on the Epistle to the Romans.

country had been exhausted by irregular rapine, the besiegers themselves were compelled by famine to relinquish their enterprise. The importance and danger of Africa were deeply felt by the regent of the West. Placidia implored the assistance of her Eastern ally; and the Italian fleet and army were reinforced by Aspar, who sailed from Constantinople with a powerful armament. As soon as the force of the two empires was united under the command of Boniface, he boldly marched against the Vandals; and the loss of a second battle irretrievably decided the fate of Africa. He embarked with the precipitation of despair, and the people of Hippo were permitted, with their families and effects, to occupy the vacant place of the soldiers, the greatest part of whom were either slain or made prisoners by the Vandals. The count, whose fatal credulity had wounded the vitals of the republic, might enter the palace of Ravenna with some anxiety, which was soon removed by the smiles of Placidia. Boniface accepted with gratitude the rank of patrician and the dignity of master-general of the Roman armies; but he must have blushed at the sight of those medals in which he was represented with the name and attributes of victory.[1] The discovery of his fraud, the displeasure of the empress, and the distinguished favour of his rival, exasperated the haughty and perfidious soul of Aëtius. He hastily returned from Gaul to Italy, with a retinue, or rather with an army, of barbarian followers; and such was the weakness of the government, that the two generals decided their private quarrel in a bloody battle. Boniface was successful; but he received in the conflict a mortal wound from the spear of his adversary, of which he expired within a few days, in such Christian and charitable sentiments that he exhorted his wife, a rich heiress of Spain, to accept Aëtius for her second husband. But Aëtius could not derive any immediate advantage from the generosity of his dying enemy: he was proclaimed a rebel by the justice of Placidia; and though he attempted to defend some strong fortresses, erected on his patrimonial estate, the Imperial power soon compelled him to retire into Pannonia, to the tents of his faithful Huns. The

---

[1] Ducange, Fam. Byzant. p. 67. On one side, the head of Valentinian; on the reverse, Boniface with a scourge in one hand and a palm in the other, standing in a triumphal car, which is drawn by four horses, or, in another medal, by four stags; an unlucky emblem! I should doubt whether another example can be found of the head of a subject on the reverse of an Imperial medal. See Science des Médailles, by the Père Jobert, tom. i. p. 132-150, edit. of 1739, by the Baron de la Bastie.

republic was deprived by their mutual discord of the service of her two most illustrious champions.[1]

It might naturally be expected, after the retreat of Boniface, that the Vandals would achieve without resistance or delay the conquest of Africa. Eight years however elapsed from the evacuation of Hippo to the reduction of Carthage. In the midst of that interval the ambitious Genseric, in the full tide of apparent prosperity, negotiated a treaty of peace, by which he gave his son Hunneric for an hostage, and consented to leave the Western emperor in the undisturbed possession of the three Mauritanias.[2] This moderation, which cannot be imputed to the justice, must be ascribed to the policy, of the conqueror. His throne was encompassed with domestic enemies, who accused the baseness of his birth, and asserted the legitimate claims of his nephews, the sons of Gonderic. Those nephews, indeed, he sacrificed to his safety; and their mother, the widow of the deceased king, was precipitated by his order into the river Ampsaga. But the public discontent burst forth in dangerous and frequent conspiracies; and the warlike tyrant is supposed to have shed more Vandal blood by the hand of the executioner than in the field of battle.[3] The convulsions of Africa, which had favoured his attack, opposed the firm establishment of his power; and the various seditions of the Moors and Germans, the Donatists and catholics, continually disturbed or threatened the unsettled reign of the conqueror. As he advanced towards Carthage he was forced to withdraw his troops from the Western provinces; the sea-coast was exposed to the naval enterprises of the Romans of Spain and Italy; and, in the heart of Numidia, the strong inland city of Cirta still persisted in obstinate independence.[4] These difficulties were gradually subdued by the spirit, the perseverance, and the cruelty of Genseric; who alternately applied the arts of peace and war to the establishment of his African

---

[1] Procopius (de Bell. Vandal. l. i. c. 3, p. 185 [tom. i. p. 325, ed. Bonn]) continues the history of Boniface no farther than his return to Italy. His death is mentioned by Prosper [Ann. 432] and Marcellinus; the expression of the latter, that Aëtius the day before had provided himself with a *longer* spear, implies something like a regular duel.

[2] See Procopius, de Bell. Vandal. l. i. c. 4, p. 186 [tom. i. p. 327, ed Bonn]. Valentinian published several humane laws to relieve the distress of his Numidian and Mauritanian subjects; he discharged them in a great measure from the payment of their debts, reduced their tribute to one-eighth, and gave them a right of appeal from their provincial magistrates to the præfect of Rome. Cod. Theod. tom. vi. Novell. p. 11, 12.

[3] Victor Vitensis, de Persecut. Vandal. l. ii. c. 5, p. 26. The cruelties of Genseric towards his subjects are strongly expressed in Prosper's Chronicle, A.D. 442.

[4] Possidius, in Vit. Augustin. c. 28, apud Ruinart, p. 428.

kingdom. He subscribed a solemn treaty, with the hope of deriving some advantage from the term of its continuance and the moment of its violation. The vigilance of his enemies was relaxed by the protestations of friendship which concealed his hostile approach; and Carthage was at length surprised by the Vandals, five hundred and eighty-five years after the destruction of the city and republic by the younger Scipio.[1]

A new city had arisen from its ruins, with the title of a colony; and though Carthage might yield to the royal prerogatives of Constantinople, and perhaps to the trade of Alexandria, or the splendour of Antioch, she still maintained the second rank in the West; as the *Rome* (if we may use the style of contemporaries) of the African world. That wealthy and opulent metropolis [2] displayed, in a dependent condition, the image of a flourishing republic. Carthage contained the manufactures, the arms, and the treasures of the six provinces. A regular subordination of civil honours gradually ascended from the procurators of the streets and quarters of the city to the tribunal of the supreme magistrate, who, with the title of proconsul, represented the state and dignity of a consul of ancient Rome. Schools and *gymnasia* were instituted for the education of the African youth; and the liberal arts and manners, grammar, rhetoric, and philosophy, were publicly taught in the Greek and Latin languages. The buildings of Carthage were uniform and magnificent: a shady grove was planted in the midst of the capital; the *new* port, a secure and capacious harbour, was subservient to the commercial industry of citizens and strangers; and the splendid games of the circus and theatre were exhibited almost in the presence of the barbarians. The reputation of the Carthaginians was not equal to that of their country, and the reproach of Punic faith still adhered to their subtle and faithless character.[3] The habits of trade and the abuse of luxury had corrupted their manners; but their impious contempt of monks and the shameless practice of unnatural lusts are the two abominations which excite the

[1] See the Chronicles of Idatius, Isidore, Prosper, and Marcellinus. They mark the same year, but different days, for the surprisal of Carthage.

[2] The picture of Carthage, as it flourished in the fourth and fifth centuries, is taken from the Expositio totius Mundi, p. 17, 18, in the third volume of Hudson's Minor Geographers; from Ausonius de Claris Urbibus, p. 228, 229; and principally from Salvian, de Gubernatione Dei, l. vii. p. 257, 258. I am surprised that the *Notitia* should not place either a mint or an arsenal at Carthage, but only a gynecæum, or female manufacture.

[3] The anonymous author of the Expositio totius Mundi compares, in his barbarous Latin, the country and the inhabitants; and, after stigmatising their want of faith, he coolly concludes, Difficile autem inter eos invenitur bonus, tamen in multis pauci boni esse possunt. P. 18.

pious vehemence of Salvian, the preacher of the age.[1] The king of the Vandals severely reformed the vices of a voluptuous people; and the ancient, noble, ingenuous freedom of Carthage (these expressions of Victor are not without energy) was reduced by Genseric into a state of ignominious servitude. After he had permitted his licentious troops to satiate their rage and avarice, he instituted a more regular system of rapine and oppression. An edict was promulgated, which enjoined all persons, without fraud or delay, to deliver their gold, silver, jewels, and valuable furniture or apparel to the royal officers; and the attempt to secrete any part of their patrimony was inexorably punished with death and torture as an act of treason against the state. The lands of the proconsular province, which formed the immediate district of Carthage, were accurately measured and divided among the barbarians; and the conqueror reserved for his peculiar domain the fertile territory of Byzacium and the adjacent parts of Numidia and Gætulia.[2]

It was natural enough that Genseric should hate those whom he had injured: the nobility and senators of Carthage were exposed to his jealousy and resentment; and all those who refused the ignominious terms which their honour and religion forbade them to accept were compelled by the Arian tyrant to embrace the condition of perpetual banishment. Rome, Italy, and the provinces of the East, were filled with a crowd of exiles, of fugitives, and of ingenuous captives, who solicited the public compassion: and the benevolent epistles of Theodoret still preserve the names and misfortunes of Cælestian and Maria.[3] The Syrian bishop deplores the misfortunes of Cælestian, who, from the state of a noble and opulent senator of Carthage, was reduced, with his wife, and family, and servants, to beg his bread in a foreign country; but he applauds the resignation of the Christian exile, and the philosophic temper which, under the pressure of such calamities, could enjoy more real happiness than was the ordinary lot of wealth and prosperity. The story

[1] He declares that the peculiar vices of each country were collected in the sink of Carthage (l. vii. p. 257). In the indulgence of vice the Africans applauded their manly virtue. Et illi se magis virilis fortitudinis esse crederent, qui maxime viros feminei usûs probrositate fregissent (p. 268). The streets of Carthage were polluted by effeminate wretches, who publicly assumed the countenance, the dress, and the character, of women (p. 264). If a monk appeared in the city, the holy man was pursued with impious scorn and ridicule; detestantibus ridentium cachinnis (p. 289).

[2] Compare Procopius, de Bell. Vandal. l. i. c. 5, p. 189, 190 [tom. i. p. 332 sqq., ed. Bonn]; and Victor Vitensis, de Persecut. Vandal. l. i. c. 4.

[3] Ruinart (p. 444-457) has collected from Theodoret and other authors the misfortunes, real and fabulous, of the inhabitants of Carthage.

of Maria, the daughter of the magnificent Eudæmon, is singular and interesting. In the sack of Carthage she was purchased from the Vandals by some merchants of Syria, who afterwards sold her as a slave in their native country. A female attendant, transported in the same ship, and sold in the same family, still continued to respect a mistress whom fortune had reduced to the common level of servitude; and the daughter of Eudæmon received from her grateful affection the domestic services which she had once required from her obedience. This remarkable behaviour divulged the real condition of Maria, who, in the absence of the bishop of Cyrrhus, was redeemed from slavery by the generosity of some soldiers of the garrison. The liberality of Theodoret provided for her decent maintenance; and she passed ten months among the deaconesses of the church, till she was unexpectedly informed that her father, who had escaped from the ruin of Carthage, exercised an honourable office in one of the Western provinces. Her filial impatience was seconded by the pious bishop: Theodoret, in a letter still extant, recommends Maria to the bishop of Ægæ, a maritime city of Cilicia, which was frequented, during the annual fair, by the vessels of the West; most earnestly requesting that his colleague would use the maiden with a tenderness suitable to her birth; and that he would intrust her to the care of such faithful merchants as would esteem it a sufficient gain if they restored a daughter, lost beyond all human hope, to the arms of her afflicted parent.

Among the insipid legends of ecclesiastical history, I am tempted to distinguish the memorable fable of the Seven Sleepers;[1] whose imaginary date corresponds with the reign of the younger Theodosius, and the conquest of Africa by the Vandals.[2] When the emperor Decius persecuted the Christians, seven noble youths of Ephesus concealed themselves in a spacious

[1] The choice of fabulous circumstances is of small importance; yet I have confined myself to the narrative which was translated from the Syriac by the care of Gregory of Tours (de Gloriâ Martyrûm, l. i. c. 95, in Max. Bibliothecâ Patrum, tom. xi. p. 856), to the Greek acts of their martyrdom (apud Photium, p. 1400, 1401 [p. 467, ed. Bekk.]), and to the Annals of the Patriarch Eutychius (tom. i. p. 391, 531, 532, 535, vers. Pocock [Oxon. 1658]).

[2] Two Syriac writers, as they are quoted by Assemanni (Bibliot. Oriental. tom. i. p. 336, 338), place the resurrection of the Seven Sleepers in the year 736 (A.D. 425) or 748 (A.D. 437) of the era of the Seleucides. Their Greek acts, which Photius had read, assign the date of the thirty-eighth year of the reign of Theodosius, which may coincide either with A.D. 439 or 446. The period which had elapsed since the persecution of Decius is easily ascertained; and nothing less than the ignorance of Mahomet or the legendaries could suppose an interval of three or four hundred years.

cavern in the side of an adjacent mountain; where they were doomed to perish by the tyrant, who gave orders that the entrance should be firmly secured with a pile of huge stones. They immediately fell into a deep slumber, which was miraculously prolonged, without injuring the powers of life, during a period of one hundred and eighty-seven years. At the end of that time, the slaves of Adolius, to whom the inheritance of the mountain had descended, removed the stones, to supply materials for some rustic edifice: the light of the sun darted into the cavern, and the Seven Sleepers were permitted to awake. After a slumber, as they thought of a few hours, they were pressed by the calls of hunger; and resolved that Jamblichus, one of their number, should secretly return to the city to purchase bread for the use of his companions. The youth (if we may still employ that appellation) could no longer recognise the once familiar aspect of his native country; and his surprise was increased by the appearance of a large cross, triumphantly erected over the principal gate of Ephesus. His singular dress and obsolete language confounded the baker, to whom he offered an ancient medal of Decius as the current coin of the empire; and Jamblichus, on the suspicion of a secret treasure, was dragged before the judge. Their mutual inquiries produced the amazing discovery that two centuries were almost elapsed since Jamblichus and his friends had escaped from the rage of a Pagan tyrant. The bishop of Ephesus, the clergy, the magistrates, the people, and, as it is said, the emperor Theodosius himself, hastened to visit the cavern of the Seven Sleepers; who bestowed their benediction, related their story, and at the same instant peaceably expired. The origin of this marvellous fable cannot be ascribed to the pious fraud and credulity of the *modern* Greeks, since the authentic tradition may be traced within half a century of the supposed miracle. James of Sarug, a Syrian bishop, who was born only two years after the death of the younger Theodosius, has devoted one of his two hundred and thirty homilies to the praise of the young men of Ephesus.[1] Their legend, before the end of the sixth century, was translated from the Syriac into the Latin language, by the care of Gregory of Tours. The hostile

---

[1] James, one of the orthodox fathers of the Syrian church, was born A.D. 452; he began to compose his sermons A.D. 474; he was made bishop of Batnæ, in the district of Sarug and province of Mesopotamia, A.D. 519, and died A.D. 521. (Assemanni, tom. i. p. 288, 289.) For the homily *de Pueris Ephesinis*, see p. 335-339: though I could wish that Assemanni had translated the text of James of Sarug instead of answering the objections of Baronius.

communions of the East preserve their memory with equal reverence; and their names are honourably inscribed in the Roman, the Abyssinian, and the Russian calendar.[1] Nor has their reputation been confined to the Christian world. This popular tale, which Mahomet might learn when he drove his camels to the fairs of Syria, is introduced, as a divine revelation, into the Koran.[2] The story of the Seven Sleepers has been adopted and adorned by the nations, from Bengal to Africa, who profess the Mahometan religion;[3] and some vestiges of a similar tradition have been discovered in the remote extremities of Scandinavia.[4] This easy and universal belief, so expressive of the sense of mankind, may be ascribed to the genuine merit of the fable itself. We imperceptibly advance from youth to age without observing the gradual, but incessant, change of human affairs; and even in our larger experience of history, the imagination is accustomed, by a perpetual series of causes and effects, to unite the most distant revolutions. But if the interval between two memorable eras could be instantly annihilated; if it were possible, after a momentary slumber of two hundred years, to display the *new* world to the eyes of a spectator who still retained a lively and recent impression of the *old*, his surprise and his reflections would furnish the pleasing subject of a philosophical romance. The scene could not be more advantageously placed than in the two centuries which elapsed between the reigns of Decius and of Theodosius the Younger. During this period the seat of government had been transported from Rome to a new city on the banks of the Thracian Bosphorus; and the

[1] See the *Acta Sanctorum* of the Bollandists (Mensis Julii, tom. vi. p. 375-397). This immense calendar of Saints, in one hundred and twenty-six years (1644-1770), and in fifty volumes in folio, has advanced no farther than the 7th day of October. The suppression of the Jesuits has most probably checked an undertaking which, through the medium of fable and superstition, communicates much historical and philosophical instruction.

[2] See Maracci Alcoran. Sura xviii. tom. ii. p. 420-427, and tom. i. part iv. p. 103. With such an ample privilege Mahomet has not shown much taste or ingenuity. He has invented the dog (Al Rakim) of the Seven Sleepers; the respect of the sun, who altered his course twice a day that he might not shine into the cavern; and the care of God himself, who preserved their bodies from putrefaction by turning them to the right and left.

[3] See D'Herbelot, Bibliothèque Orientale, p. 139; and Renaudot, Hist. Patriarch. Alexandrin, p. 39, 40.

[4] Paul, the deacon of Aquileia (de Gestis Langobardorum, l. i. c. 4, p. 745, 746, edit. Grot.), who lived towards the end of the eighth century, has placed in a cavern under a rock on the shore of the ocean the Seven Sleepers of the North, whose long repose was respected by the barbarians. Their dress declared them to be Romans; and the deacon conjectures that they were reserved by Providence as the future apostles of those unbelieving countries.

abuse of military spirit had been suppressed by an artificial system of tame and ceremonious servitude. The throne of the persecuting Decius was filled by a succession of Christian and orthodox princes, who had extirpated the fabulous gods of antiquity: and the public devotion of the age was impatient to exalt the saints and martyrs of the catholic church on the altars of Diana and Hercules. The union of the Roman empire was dissolved; its genius was humbled in the dust; and armies of unknown barbarians, issuing from the frozen regions of the North, had established their victorious reign over the fairest provinces of Europe and Africa.

CHAPTER XXXIV

The Character, Conquests, and Court of Attila, King of the Huns—Death of Theodosius the Younger—Elevation of Marcian to the Empire of the East

THE Western world was oppressed by the Goths and Vandals, who fled before the Huns; but the achievements of the Huns themselves were not adequate to their power and prosperity. Their victorious hordes had spread from the Volga to the Danube; but the public force was exhausted by the discord of independent chieftains; their valour was idly consumed in obscure and predatory excursions; and they often degraded their national dignity, by condescending, for the hopes of spoil, to enlist under the banners of their fugitive enemies. In the reign of ATTILA [1] the Huns again became the terror of the world;

[1] The authentic materials for the history of Attila may be found in Jornandes (de Rebus Geticis, c. 34-50, p. 660-688, edit. Grot.) and Priscus (Excerpta de Legationibus, p. 33-76, Paris, 1648 [p. 140-220, ed. Bonn]). I have not seen the Lives of Attila, composed by Juvencus Cælius Calanus Dalmatinus, in the twelfth century, or by Nicolas Olahus, archbishop of Gran, in the sixteenth. See Mascou's History of the Germans, ix. 23, and Maffei Osservazioni Litterarie, tom. i. p. 88, 89. Whatever the modern Hungarians have added must be fabulous; and they do not seem to have excelled in the art of fiction. They suppose that when Attila invaded Gaul and Italy, married innumerable wives, etc., he was one hundred and twenty years of age. Thevrocz Chron. p. i. c. 22, in Script. Hungar. tom. i. p. 76.

[Attila is the outstanding figure in this chapter, and under his German name, Etzel, is the hero of many well-known Scandinavian and German poems, of which the most perfect is the celebrated *Nibelungen Lied*. This poem and others reveal the impression which Attila made on his contemporaries and succeeding ages, and therefore deserve mention in connection with the history of the king of the Huns. In these poems Etzel or Attila appears in conflict with the Burgundians and Franks, and the destruction of Gundicarius, king of the Burgundians, by the Huns in 436 is supposed to and I shall now describe the character and actions of that formidable barbarian, who alternately insulted and invaded the East and the West, and urged the rapid downfall of the Roman Empire.

In the tide of emigration which impetuously rolled from the confines of China to those of Germany, the most powerful and populous tribes may commonly be found on the verge of the Roman provinces. The accumulated weight was sustained for a while by artificial barriers; and the easy condescension of the emperors invited, without satisfying, the insolent demands of the barbarians, who had acquired an eager appetite for the luxuries of civilised life. The Hungarians, who ambitiously insert the name of Attila among their native kings, may affirm with truth that the hordes which were subject to his uncle Roas, or Rugilas, had formed their encampments within the limits of modern Hungary,[1] in a fertile country which liberally supplied the wants of a nation of hunters and shepherds. In this advantageous situation, Rugilas, and his valiant brothers, who continually added to their power and reputation, commanded the alternative of peace or war with the two empires. His alliance with the Romans of the West was cemented by his personal friendship for the great Aëtius, who was always secure of finding in the barbarian camp an hospitable reception and a powerful support. At his solicitation, and in the name of John the usurper, sixty thousand Huns advanced to the confines of Italy; their march and their retreat were alike expensive to the state; and the grateful policy of Aëtius abandoned the possession of Pannonia to his faithful confederates. The Romans of the East were not less apprehensive of the arms of Rugilas, which

be represented by the catastrophe of the *Nibelungen Lied*. Theodoric, the Ostrogoth, under the name of Dietrich of Bern, that is, Theodoric of Verona, is represented as the contemporary of Attila, though he was not born till two years after the death of Attila; and Siegfried, whose adventures form so prominent a part of the poem, is identified with much probability with Sigebert, king of Austrasia, who was assassinated in 575. See the Fall of the Nibelungers, London, 1850; Grimm, Die Deutsche Heldensage, p. 63.—O. S.]

[1] Hungary has been successively occupied by three Scythian colonies:— 1. The Huns of Attila; 2. The Abares, in the sixth century; and, 3. The Turks or Magyars, A.D. 889, the immediate and genuine ancestors of the modern Hungarians, whose connection with the two former is extremely faint and remote. The *Prodromus* and *Notitia* of Matthew Belius appear to contain a rich fund of information concerning ancient and modern Hungary. I have seen the extracts in Bibliothèque Ancienne et Moderne, tom. xxii. p. 1-51, and Bibliothèque Raisonée, tom. xvi. p. 127-175.

[The modern Hungarians cannot claim to be the descendants of Attila and his Huns. The Magyars are a Finnish race, while the Huns were certainly Turks.—O. S.]

threatened the provinces, or even the capital. Some ecclesiastical historians have destroyed the barbarians with lightning and pestilence;[1] but Theodosius was reduced to the more humble expedient of stipulating an annual payment of three hundred and fifty pounds of gold, and of disguising this dishonourable tribute by the title of general, which the king of the Huns condescended to accept. The public tranquillity was frequently interrupted by the fierce impatience of the barbarians and the perfidious intrigues of the Byzantine court. Four dependent nations, among whom we may distinguish the Bavarians, disclaimed the sovereignty of the Huns; and their revolt was encouraged and protected by a Roman alliance; till the just claims and formidable power of Rugilas were effectually urged by the voice of Eslaw, his ambassador. Peace was the unanimous wish of the senate: their decree was ratified by the emperor; and two ambassadors were named—Plinthas, a general of Scythian extraction, but of consular rank; and the quæstor Epigenes, a wise and experienced statesman, who was recommended to that office by his ambitious colleague.

The death of Rugilas suspended the progress of the treaty. His two nephews, Attila and Bleda, who succeeded to the throne of their uncle, consented to a personal interview with the ambassadors of Constantinople; but as they proudly refused to dismount, the business was transacted on horseback, in a spacious plain near the city of Margus, in the Upper Mæsia. The kings of the Huns assumed the solid benefits, as well as the vain honours, of the negotiation. They dictated the conditions of peace, and each condition was an insult on the majesty of the empire. Besides the freedom of a safe and plentiful market on the banks of the Danube, they required that the annual contribution should be augmented from three hundred and fifty to seven hundred pounds of gold; that a fine or ransom, of eight pieces of gold, should be paid for every Roman captive who had escaped from his barbarian master; that the emperor should renounce all treaties and engagements with the enemies of the Huns; and that all the fugitives who had taken refuge in the court or provinces of Theodosius should be delivered to the justice of their offended sovereign. This justice was rigorously inflicted on some unfortunate youths of a royal race. They were crucified on the territories of the empire, by the command of

---

[1] Socrates, l. vii. c. 43; Theodoret, l. v. c. 37. Tillemont, who always depends on the faith of his ecclesiastical authors, strenuously contends (Hist. des Emp. tom. vi. p. 136, 607) that the wars and personages were not the same.

Attila: and, as soon as the king of the Huns had impressed the Romans with the terror of his name, he indulged them in a short and arbitrary respite, whilst he subdued the rebellious or independent nations of Scythia and Germany.[1]

Attila, the son of Mundzuk, deduced his noble, perhaps his regal, descent[2] from the ancient Huns, who had formerly contended with the monarchs of China. His features, according to the observation of a Gothic historian, bore the stamp of his national origin; and the portrait of Attila exhibits the genuine deformity of a modern Calmuck;[3] a large head, a swarthy complexion, small deep-seated eyes, a flat nose, a few hairs in the place of a beard, broad shoulders, and a short square body, of nervous strength, though of a disproportioned form. The haughty step and demeanour of the king of the Huns expressed the consciousness of his superiority above the rest of mankind; and he had a custom of fiercely rolling his eyes, as if he wished to enjoy the terror which he inspired. Yet this savage hero was not inaccessible to pity; his suppliant enemies might confide in the assurance of peace or pardon; and Attila was considered by his subjects as a just and indulgent master. He delighted in war; but, after he had ascended the throne in a mature age, his head, rather than his hand, achieved the conquest of the North; and the fame of an adventurous soldier was usefully exchanged for that of a prudent and successful general. The effects of personal valour are so inconsiderable, except in poetry or romance, that victory, even among barbarians, must depend on the degree of skill with which the passions of the multitude are combined and guided for the service of a single man. The Scythian conquerors, Attila and Zingis, surpassed their rude countrymen in art, rather than in courage; and it may be observed that the monarchies, both of the Huns and of the Moguls, were erected by their founders on the basis of popular superstition. The miraculous conception, which fraud and credulity ascribed to the virgin-mother of Zingis, raised him above the level of human nature; and the naked prophet, who, in the name of the Deity, invested

---

[1] See Priscus, p. 47, 48 [ed. Par.; pp. 166-170, ed. Bonn], and Hist. des Peuples de l'Europe, tom. vii. c. xii. xiii. xiv. xv.

[2] Priscus, p. 39 [p. 150, ed. Bonn]. The modern Hungarians have deduced his genealogy, which ascends, in the thirty-fifth degree, to Ham the son of Noah; yet they are ignorant of his father's real name. (De Guignes, Hist. des Huns, tom. ii. p. 297.)

[3] Compare Jornandes (c. 35, p. 661) with Buffon, Hist. Naturelle, tom. iii. p. 380. The former had a right to observe, originis suæ signa restituens. The character and portrait of Attila are probably transcribed from Cassiodorus.

him with the empire of the earth, pointed the valour of the Moguls with irresistible enthusiasm.[1] The religious arts of Attila were not less skilfully adapted to the character of his age and country. It was natural enough that the Scythians should adore, with peculiar devotion, the god of war; but as they were incapable of forming either an abstract idea or a corporeal representation, they worshipped their tutelar deity under the symbol of an iron cimeter.[2] One of the shepherds of the Huns perceived that a heifer, who was grazing, had wounded herself in the foot, and curiously followed the track of the blood, till he discovered, among the long grass, the point of an ancient sword, which he dug out of the ground, and presented to Attila. That magnanimous, or rather that artful, prince accepted, with pious gratitude, this celestial favour; and, as the rightful possessor of the *sword of Mars*, asserted his divine and indefeasible claim to the dominion of the earth.[3] If the rites of Scythia were practised on this solemn occasion, a lofty altar, or rather pile of faggots, three hundred yards in length and in breadth, was raised in a spacious plain; and the sword of Mars was placed erect on the summit of this rustic altar, which was annually consecrated by the blood of sheep, horses, and of the hundredth captive.[4] Whether human sacrifices formed any part of the worship of Attila, or whether he propitiated the god of war with the victims which he continually offered in the field of battle, the favourite of Mars soon acquired a sacred character, which rendered his conquests more easy and more permanent; and the barbarian princes confessed, in the language of devotion or flattery, that they could not presume to gaze, with a steady eye, on the divine

---

[1] Abulpharag. Dynast. vers. Pocock, p. 281 [ed. Oxon. 1663]; Genealogical History of the Tartars, by Abulghazi Bahader Khan, part iii. c. 15, part iv. c. 3; Vie de Gengiscan, par Petit de la Croix, l. i. c. 1, 6. The relations of the missionaries who visited Tartary in the thirteenth century (see the seventh volume of the Histoire des Voyages) express the popular language and opinions; Zingis is styled the son of God, etc. etc.

[2] Nec templum apud eos visitur, aut delubrum, ne tugurium quidem culmo tectum cerni usquam potest; sed *gladius* barbarico ritû humi figitur nudus, eumque ut Martem regionum quas circumcircant præsulem verecundius colunt. Ammian. Marcellin. xxxi. 2, and the learned Notes of Lindenbrogius and Valesius.

[3] Priscus relates this remarkable story, both in his own text (p. 65 [p. 201, ed. Bonn]) and in the quotation made by Jornandes (c. 35, p. 662). He might have explained the tradition, or fable, which characterised this famous sword, and the name as well as attributes of the Scythian deity whom he has translated into the Mars of the Greeks and Romans.

[4] Herodot. l. iv. c. 62. For the sake of economy, I have calculated by the smallest stadium. In the human sacrifices, they cut off the shoulder and arm of the victim, which they threw up into the air, and drew omens and presages from the manner of their falling on the pile.

majesty of the king of the Huns.[1] His brother Bleda, who reigned over a considerable part of the nation, was compelled to resign his sceptre and his life. Yet even this cruel act was attributed to a supernatural impulse; and the vigour with which Attila wielded the sword of Mars convinced the world that it had been reserved alone for his invincible arm.[2] But the extent of his empire affords the only remaining evidence of the number and importance of his victories; and the Scythian monarch, however ignorant of the value of science and philosophy, might perhaps lament that his illiterate subjects were destitute of the art which could perpetuate the memory of his exploits.

If a line of separation were drawn between the civilised and the savage climates of the globe; between the inhabitants of cities, who cultivated the earth, and the hunters and shepherds, who dwelt in tents, Attila might aspire to the title of supreme and sole monarch of the barbarians.[3] He alone, among the conquerors of ancient and modern times, united the two mighty kingdoms of Germany and Scythia; and those vague appellations, when they are applied to his reign, may be understood with an ample latitude. Thuringia, which stretched beyond its actual limits as far as the Danube, was in the number of his provinces; he interposed, with the weight of a powerful neighbour, in the domestic affairs of the Franks; and one of his lieutenants chastised, and almost exterminated, the Burgundians of the Rhine. He subdued the islands of the ocean, the kingdoms of Scandinavia, encompassed and divided by the waters of the Baltic; and the Huns might derive a tribute of furs from that northern region, which has been protected from all other conquerors by the severity of the climate and the courage of the natives. Towards the East, it is difficult to circumscribe the dominion of Attila over the Scythian deserts; yet we may be assured that he reigned on the banks of the Volga; that the king of the Huns was dreaded, not only as a warrior, but as a

---

[1] Priscus, p. 55 [p. 182, ed. Bonn]. A more civilised hero, Augustus himself, was pleased if the person on whom he fixed his eyes seemed unable to support their divine lustre. Sueton. in August. c. 79.

[2] The Count de Buat (Hist. des Peuples de l'Europe, tom. vii. p. 428, 429) attempts to clear Attila from the murder of his brother, and is almost inclined to reject the concurrent testimony of Jornandes and the contemporary Chronicles.

[3] Fortissimarum gentium dominus, qui inauditâ ante se potentiâ, solus Scythica et Germanica regna possedit. Jornandes, c. 49, p. 684; Priscus, p. 64, 65 [p. 199-201, ed. Bonn]. M. de Guignes, by his knowledge of the Chinese, has acquired (tom. ii. p. 295-301) an adequate idea of the empire of Attila.

magician;[1] that he insulted and vanquished the khan of the
formidable Geougen; and that he sent ambassadors to negotiate
an equal alliance with the empire of China.   In the proud review
of the nations who acknowledged the sovereignty of Attila, and
who never entertained, during his lifetime, the thought of a
revolt, the Gepidæ and the Ostrogoths were distinguished by their
numbers, their bravery, and the personal merit of their chiefs.
The renowned Ardaric, king of the Gepidæ, was the faithful and
sagacious counsellor of the monarch, who esteemed his intrepid
genius, whilst he loved the mild and discreet virtues of the noble
Walamir, king of the Ostrogoths.   The crowd of vulgar kings,
the leaders of so many martial tribes, who served under the
standard of Attila, were ranged in the submissive order of
guards and domestics round the person of their master.   They
watched his nod; they trembled at his frown; and at the first
signal of his will, they executed, without murmur or hesitation,
his stern and absolute commands.   In time of peace, the dependent princes, with their national troops, attended the royal
camp in regular succession; but when Attila collected his
military force, he was able to bring into the field an army of five,
or, according to another account, of seven hundred thousand
barbarians.[2]

The ambassadors of the Huns might awaken the attention of
Theodosius, by reminding him that they were his neighbours
both in Europe and Asia; since they touched the Danube on
one hand, and reached with the other as far as the Tanais.   In
the reign of his father Arcadius, a band of adventurous Huns
had ravaged the provinces of the East, from whence they brought
away rich spoils and innumerable captives.   They advanced,
by a secret path, along the shores of the Caspian Sea; traversed
the snowy mountains of Armenia; passed the Tigris, the
Euphrates, and the Halys; recruited their weary cavalry with

[1] See Hist. des Huns, tom. ii. p. 296.   The Geougen believed that the
Huns could excite at pleasure storms of wind and rain.   This phenomenon
was produced by the stone *Gezi*, to whose magic power the loss of a battle
was ascribed by the Mahometan Tartars of the fourteenth century.   See
Cherefeddin Ali, Hist. de Timur Bec, tom. i. p. 82, 83.

[2] Jornandes, c. 35, p. 661; c. 37, p. 667.   See Tillemont, Hist. des
Empereurs, tom. vi. p. 129, 138.   Corneille has represented the pride of
Attila to his subject kings, and his tragedy opens with these two ridiculous
lines:—

Ils ne sont pas venus, nos deux rois! qu'on leur die
Qu'ils se font trop attendre, et qu'Attila s'ennuie.

The two kings of the Gepidæ and the Ostrogoths are profound politicians
and sentimental lovers; and the whole piece exhibits the defects, without
the genius, of the poet.

the generous breed of Cappadocian horses; occupied the hilly
country of Cilicia; and disturbed the festal songs and dances
of the citizens of Antioch.[1] Egypt trembled at their approach;
and the monks and pilgrims of the Holy Land prepared to escape
their fury by a speedy embarkation. The memory of this
invasion was still recent in the minds of the Orientals. The
subjects of Attila might execute, with superior forces, the design
which these adventurers had so boldly attempted; and it soon
became the subject of anxious conjecture whether the tempest
would fall on the dominions of Rome or of Persia. Some of the
great vassals of the king of the Huns, who were themselves in the
rank of powerful princes, had been sent to ratify an alliance and
society of arms with the emperor, or rather with the general, of
the West. They related, during their residence at Rome, the
circumstances of an expedition which they had lately made into
the East. After passing a desert and a morass supposed by the
Romans to be the lake Mæotis, they penetrated through the
mountains, and arrived, at the end of fifteen days' march, on the

---

[1] ———— alii per Caspia claustra
Armeniasque nives, inopino tramite ducti
Invadunt Orientis opes: jam pascua fumant
Cappadocum, volucrumque parens Argæus equorum.
Jam rubet altus Halys, nec se defendit iniquo
Monte Cilix; Syriæ tractus vastantur amœni;
Assuetumque choris, et lætâ plebe canorum,
Proterit imbellem sonipes hostilis Orontem.

                      Claudian, in Rufin. l. ii. 28-35.

See likewise, in Eutrop. l. i. 243-251, and the strong description of Jerom,
who wrote from his feelings, tom. i. p. 26, ad Heliodor. p. 200, ad Ocean.
[p. 342 and 460 ed. Vallars.]. Philostorgius (l. ix. c. 8 [17]) mentions this
irruption.

[Niebuhr, in his "Lectures on the History of Rome," says that
"Gibbon's description of Attila's power is one of the weak parts of his
work," and there are strong reasons for believing that the extent of
Attila's power and dominions has been overstated. It must be remembered that the halo of fiction and romance around Attila is exclusively
German, and as Attila was the conqueror of the Germans, there was a
natural tendency on the part of that people to exaggerate the might of the
monarch by whom they had been subdued. Our chief authority for the
extent of Attila is Jornandes, who was himself a Goth. It is possible that
many of the people mentioned in the list of Attila's hosts may have been
simple confederates, or a portion of them may have been incorporated in
his army as he passed through their country. Some notion may be formed
of the real magnitude of Attila's kingdom by the extent of the kingdoms
which were formed out of his dominions after his death. Suffice it to say
that the area out of which they grew was limited to Pannonia, Western
Dacia, Eastern Rhætia, and North Mœsia. It is probable that the sovereign sway of Attila was bounded by the eastern frontier of Bohemia on
the west, and by the Mæotes, or thereabouts on the east. The northern
boundary was uncertain, but it certainly did not extend as far north as
Jornandes would lead us to suppose.—O. S.]

confines of Media, where they advanced as far as the unknown cities of Basic and Cursic.[1] They encountered the Persian army in the plains of Media; and the air, according to their own expression, was darkened by a cloud of arrows. But the Huns were obliged to retire before the numbers of the enemy. Their laborious retreat was affected by a different road; they lost the greatest part of their booty; and at length returned to the royal camp, with some knowledge of the country, and an impatient desire of revenge. In the free conversation of the Imperial ambassadors, who discussed, at the court of Attila, the character and designs of their formidable enemy, the ministers of Constantinople expressed their hope that his strength might be diverted and employed in a long and doubtful contest with the princes of the house of Sassan. The more sagacious Italians admonished their Eastern brethren of the folly and danger of such a hope; and convinced them, *that* the Medes and Persians were incapable of resisting the arms of the Huns; and *that* the easy and important acquisition would exalt the pride, as well as power, of the conqueror. Instead of contenting himself with a moderate contribution and a military title, which equalled him only to the generals of Theodosius, Attila would proceed to impose a disgraceful and intolerable yoke of the necks on the prostrate and captive Romans, who would then be encompassed on all sides by the empire of the Huns.[2]

While the powers of Europe and Asia were solicitous to avert the impending danger, the alliance of Attila maintained the Vandals in the possession of Africa. An enterprise had been concerted between the courts of Ravenna and Constantinople for the recovery of that valuable province; and the ports of Sicily were already filled with the military and naval forces of Theodosius. But the subtle Genseric, who spread his negotiations round the world, prevented their designs, by exciting the king of the Huns to invade the Eastern empire; and a trifling incident soon became the motive, or pretence, of a destructive war.[3] Under the faith of the treaty of Margus, a free market

---

[1] [" The unknown cities of Basic and Cursic." Gibbon has fallen into a curious error here. Basic and Cursic are not the names of cities, but the names of the two commanders who were over the respective bands of Huns who invaded Persia.—O. S.]

[2] See the original conversation in Priscus, p. 64, 65 [ed. Par.; p. 198-201, ed. Bonn].

[3] Priscus, p. 331. His history contained a copious and elegant account of the war (Evagrius, l. i. c. 17); but the extracts which relate to the embassies are the only parts that have reached our times. The original work was accessible, however, to the writers from whom we borrow our

was held on the northern side of the Danube, which was protected by a Roman fortress surnamed Constantia. A troop of barbarians violated the commercial security; killed, or dispersed, the unsuspecting traders; and levelled the fortress with the ground. The Huns justified this outrage as an act of reprisal; alleged that the bishop of Margus had entered their territories, to discover and steal a secret treasure of their kings; and sternly demanded the guilty prelate, the sacrilegious spoil, and the fugitive subjects, who had escaped from the justice of Attila. The refusal of the Byzantine court was the signal of war; and the Mæsians at first applauded the generous firmness of their sovereign. But they were soon intimidated by the destruction of Viminiacum and the adjacent towns; and the people was persuaded to adopt the convenient maxim, that a private citizen, however innocent or respectable, may be justly sacrificed to the safety of his country. The bishop of Margus, who did not possess the spirit of a martyr, resolved to prevent the designs which he suspected. He boldly treated with the princes of the Huns; secured, by solemn oaths, his pardon and reward; posted a numerous detachment of barbarians, in silent ambush, on the banks of the Danube; and, at the appointed hour, opened, with his own hand, the gates of his episcopal city. This advantage, which had been obtained by treachery, served as a prelude to more honourable and decisive victories. The Illyrian frontier was covered by a line of castles and fortresses; and though the greatest part of them consisted only of a single tower, with a small garrison, they were commonly sufficient to repel, or to intercept, the inroads of an enemy who was ignorant of the art, and impatient of the delay, of a regular siege. But these slight obstacles were instantly swept away by the inundation of the Huns.[1] They destroyed, with fire and sword, the populous cities of Sirmium and Singidunum, of Ratiaria and Marcianopolis, of Naissus and Sardica; where every circumstance in the discipline of the people and the construction of the buildings had been gradually adapted to the sole purpose of defence. The whole breadth of Europe, as it extends above five hundred miles

imperfect knowledge, Jornandes, Theophanes, Count Marcellinus, Prosper-Tyro, and the author of the Alexandrian, or Paschal, Chronicle. M. de Buat (Hist. des Peuples de l'Europe, tom. vii. c. xv.) has examined the cause, the circumstances, and the duration of this war; and will not allow it to extend beyond the year four hundred and forty-four.

[1] Procopius, de Ædificiis, l. iv. c. 5 [tom. iii. p. 286, ed. Bonn]. These fortresses were afterwards restored, strengthened, and enlarged by the emperor Justinian; but they were soon destroyed by the Abares, who succeeded to the power and possessions of the Huns.

from the Euxine to the Hadriatic, was at once invaded, and occupied, and desolated, by the myriads of barbarians whom Attila led into the field. The public danger and distress could not, however, provoke Theodosius to interrupt his amusements and devotion, or to appear in person at the head of the Roman legions. But the troops which had been sent against Genseric were hastily recalled from Sicily; the garrisons, on the side of Persia, were exhausted; and a military force was collected in Europe, formidable by their arms and numbers, if the generals had understood the science of command, and their soldiers the duty of obedience. The armies of the Eastern empire were vanquished in three successive engagements; and the progress of Attila may be traced by the fields of battle. The two former, on the banks of the Utus, and under the walls of Marcianopolis, were fought in the extensive plains between the Danube and Mount Hæmus. As the Romans were pressed by a victorious enemy, they gradually, and unskilfully, retired towards the Chersonesus of Thrace; and that narrow peninsula, the last extremity of the land, was marked by their third and irreparable defeat. By the destruction of this army, Attila acquired the indisputable possession of the field. From the Hellespont to Thermopylæ and the suburbs of Constantinople he ravaged, without resistance and without mercy, the provinces of Thrace and Macedonia. Heraclea and Hadrianople might, perhaps, escape this dreadful irruption of the Huns; but the words the most expressive of total extirpation and erasure are applied to the calamities which they inflicted on seventy cities of the Eastern empire.[1] Theodosius, his court, and the unwarlike people, were protected by the walls of Constantinople; but those walls had been shaken by a recent earthquake, and the fall of fifty-eight towers had opened a large and tremendous breach. The damage indeed was speedily repaired; but this accident was aggravated by a superstitious fear that Heaven itself had delivered the Imperial city to the shepherds of Scythia, who were strangers to the laws, the language, and the religion of the Romans.[2]

In all their invasions of the civilised empires of the South, the

---

[1] Septuaginta civitates (says Prosper-Tyro) deprædatione vastatæ. The language of Count Marcellinus is still more forcible. Pene totam Europam, invasis *excisisque* civitatibus atque castellis, *conrasit.*

[2] Tillemont (Hist. des Empereurs, tom. vi. p. 106, 107) has paid great attention to this memorable earthquake, which was felt as far from Constantinople as Antioch and Alexandria, and is celebrated by all the ecclesiastical writers. In the hands of a popular preacher, an earthquake is an engine of admirable effect.

Scythian shepherds have been uniformly actuated by a savage and destructive spirit. The laws of war, that restrain the exercise of national rapine and murder, are founded on two principles of substantial interest: the knowledge of the permanent benefits which may be obtained by a moderate use of conquest, and a just apprehension lest the desolation which we inflict on the enemy's country may be retaliated on our own. But these considerations of hope and fear are almost unknown in the pastoral state of nations. The Huns of Attila may without injustice be compared to the Moguls and Tartars before their primitive manners were changed by religion and luxury; and the evidence of Oriental history may reflect some light on the short and imperfect annals of Rome. After the Moguls had subdued the northern provinces of China, it was seriously proposed, not in the hour of victory and passion, but in calm deliberate council, to exterminate all the inhabitants of that populous country, that the vacant land might be converted to the pasture of cattle. The firmness of a Chinese mandarin,[1] who insinuated some principles of rational policy into the mind of Zingis, diverted him from the execution of this horrid design. But in the cities of Asia which yielded to the Moguls, the inhuman abuse of the rights of war was exercised with a regular form of discipline, which may, with equal reason though not with equal authority, be imputed to the victorious Huns. The inhabitants who had submitted to their discretion were ordered to evacuate their houses and to assemble in some plain adjacent to the city, where a division was made of the vanquished into three parts. The first class consisted of the soldiers of the garrison and of the young men capable of bearing arms; and their fate was instantly decided: they were either enlisted among the Moguls, or they were massacred on the spot by the troops, who, with pointed spears and bended bows, had formed a circle round the captive multitude. The second class, composed of the young and beautiful women, of the artificers of every rank and profession, and of the more wealthy or honourable citizens, from whom a private ransom might be expected, was distributed in equal or proportionable lots. The remainder, whose life or

---

[1] He represented to the emperor of the Moguls that the four provinces (Petcheli, Chantong, Chansi, and Leaotong) which he already possessed might annually produce, under a mild administration, 500,000 ounces of silver, 400,000 measures of rice, and 800,000 pieces of silk. Gaubil, Hist. de la Dynastie des Mongous, p. 58, 59. Yelutchousay (such was the name of the mandarin) was a wise and virtuous minister, who saved his country and civilised the conquerors. See p. 102, 103.

death was alike unless to the conquerors, were permitted to return to the city, which in the meanwhile had been stripped of its valuable furniture; and a tax was imposed on those wretched inhabitants for the indulgence of breathing their native air. Such was the behaviour of the Moguls when they were not conscious of any extraordinary rigour.[1] But the most casual provocation, the slightest motive of caprice or convenience, often provoked them to involve a whole people in an indiscriminate massacre; and the ruin of some flourishing cities was executed with such unrelenting perseverance, that, according to their own expression, horses might run without stumbling over the ground where they had once stood. The three great capitals of Khorasan, Maru, Neisabour, and Herat, were destroyed by the armies of Zingis; and the exact account which was taken of the slain amounted to four millions three hundred and forty-seven thousand persons.[1] Timur, or Tamerlane, was educated in a less barbarous age and in the profession of the Mahometan religion; yet, if Attila equalled the hostile ravages of Tamerlane,[3] either the Tartar or the Hun might deserve the epithet of the Scourge of God.[4]

It may be affirmed with bolder assurance that the Huns depopulated the provinces of the empire by the number of Roman subjects whom they led away into captivity. In the hands of a wise legislator such an industrious colony might have contributed to diffuse through the deserts of Scythia the rudiments of the useful and ornamental arts; but these captives, who had

---

[1] Particular instances would be endless; but the curious reader may consult the Life of Gengiscan, by Petit de la Croix, the Histoire des Mongous, and the fifteenth book of the History of the Huns.

[2] At Maru, 1,300,000; at Herat, 1,600,000; at Neisabour, 1,747,000. D'Herbelot, Bibliothèque Orientale, p. 380, 381. I use the orthography of D'Anville's maps. It must, however, be allowed, that the Persians were disposed to exaggerate their losses, and the Moguls to magnify their exploits.

[3] Cherefeddin Ali, his servile panegyrist, would afford us many horrid examples. In his camp before Delhi, Timur massacred 100,000 Indian prisoners, who had *smiled* when the army of their countrymen appeared in sight (Hist. de Timur Bec, tom. iii. p. 90). The people of Ispahan supplied 70,000 human skulls for the structure of several lofty towers (id. tom. i. p. 434). A similar tax was levied on the revolt of Bagdad (tom. iii. p. 370); and the exact account, which Cherefeddin was not able to procure from the proper officers, is stated by another historian (Ahmed Arabsiada, tom. ii. p. 175, vers. Manger) at 90,000 heads.

[4] The ancients, Jornandes, Priscus, etc., are ignorant of this epithet. The modern Hungarians have imagined that it was applied, by a hermit of Gaul, to Attila, who was pleased to insert it among the titles of his royal dignity. Mascou, ix. 23, and Tillemont, Hist. des Empereurs, tom. vi. p. 143.

been taken in war, were accidentally dispersed among the hordes
that obeyed the empire of Attila. The estimate of their respective value was formed by the simple judgment of unenlightened
and unprejudiced barbarians. Perhaps they might not understand the merit of a theologian profoundly skilled in the con-
troversies of the Trinity and the Incarnation; yet they respected
the ministers of every religion; and the active zeal of the
Christian missionaries, without approaching the person or the
palace of the monarch, successfully laboured in the propagation
of the gospel.[1] The pastoral tribes, who were ignorant of the
distinction of landed property, must have disregarded the use
as well as the abuse of civil jurisprudence; and the skill of an
eloquent lawyer could excite only their contempt or their
abhorrence.[2] The perpetual intercourse of the Huns and the
Goths had communicated the familiar knowledge of the two
national dialects; and the barbarians were ambitious of con-
versing in Latin, the military idiom even of the Eastern empire.[3]
But they disdained the language and the sciences of the Greeks;
and the vain sophist or grave philosopher who had enjoyed the
flattering applause of the schools, was mortified to find that his
robust servant was a captive of more value and importance than
himself. The mechanic arts were encouraged and esteemed, as
they tended to satisfy the wants of the Huns. An architect in
the service of Onegesius, one of the favourites of Attila, was
employed to construct a bath: but this work was a rare example
of private luxury; and the trades of the smith, the carpenter,
the armourer, were much more adapted to supply a wandering
people with the useful instruments of peace and war. But the
merit of the physician was received with universal favour and
respect: the barbarians, who despised death, might be apprehensive of disease; and the haughty conqueror trembled in
the presence of a captive to whom he ascribed perhaps an

[1] The missionaries of St. Chrysostom had converted great numbers of
the Scythians, who dwelt beyond the Danube in tents and waggons. Theodoret, l. v. c. 31; Photius, p. 1517 [p. 508 b, ed. Bekk.]. The Mahometans,
the Nestorians, and the Latin Christians, thought themselves secure of
gaining the sons and grandsons of Zingis, who treated the rival missionaries
with impartial favour.

[2] The Germans, who exterminated Varus and his legions, had been particularly offended with the Roman laws and lawyers. One of the barbarians,
after the effectual precautions of cutting out the tongue of an advocate,
and sewing up his mouth, observed with much satisfaction that the viper
could no longer hiss. Florus, iv. 12.

[3] Priscus, p. 59 [p. 190, ed. Bonn]. It should seem that the Huns preferred the Gothic and Latin languages to their own, which was probably a
harsh and barren idiom.

imaginary power of prolonging or preserving his life.[1] The Huns might be provoked to insult the misery of their slaves, over whom they exercised a despotic command;[2] but their manners were not susceptible of a refined system of oppression, and the efforts of courage and diligence were often recompensed by the gift of freedom. The historian Priscus, whose embassy is a source of curious instruction, was accosted in the camp of Attila by a stranger, who saluted him in the Greek language, but whose dress and figure displayed the appearance of a wealthy Scythian. In the siege of Viminiacum he had lost, according to his own account, his fortune and liberty: he became the slave of Onegesius; but his faithful services against the Romans and the Acatzires had gradually raised him to the rank of the native Huns, to whom he was attached by the domestic pledges of a new wife and several children. The spoils of war had restored and improved his private property; he was admitted to the table of his former lord; and the apostate Greek blessed the hour of his captivity, since it had been the introduction to a happy and independent state, which he held by the honourable tenure of military service. This reflection naturally produced a dispute on the advantages and defects of the Roman government, which was severely arraigned by the apostate, and defended by Priscus in a prolix and feeble declamation. The freedman of Onegesius exposed, in true and lively colours, the vices of a declining empire of which he had so long been the victim; the cruel absurdity of the Roman princes, unable to protect their subjects against the public enemy, unwilling to trust them with arms for their own defence; the intolerable weight of taxes, rendered still more oppressive by the intricate or arbitrary modes of collection; the obscurity of numerous and contradictory laws; the tedious and expensive forms of judicial proceedings; the partial administration of justice; and the universal corruption which increased the influence of the rich and aggravated the misfortunes of the poor. A sentiment of patriotic sympathy was at length revived in the breast of the

---

[1] Philip de Comines, in his admirable picture of the last moments of Lewis XI. (Mémoires, l. vi. c. 12), represents the insolence of his physician, who, in five months, extorted 54,000 crowns and a rich bishopric from the stern avaricious tyrant.

[2] Priscus (p. 61 [p. 194, ed. Bonn]) extols the equity of the Roman laws, which protected the life of a slave. Occidere solent (says Tacitus of the Germans) non disciplinâ et severitate, sed impetu et irâ, ut inimicum, nisi quòd impune. De Moribus Germ. c. 25. The Heruli, who were the subjects of Attila, claimed and exercised the power of life and death over their slaves. See a remarkable instance in the second book of Agathias.

fortunate exile, and he lamented with a flood of tears the guilt or weakness of those magistrates who had perverted the wisest and most salutary institutions.[1]

The timid or selfish policy of the Western Romans had abandoned the Eastern empire to the Huns.[2]   The loss of armies and the want of discipline or virtue were not supplied by the personal character of the monarch.   Theodosius might still affect the style as well as the title of *Invincible Augustus*, but he was reduced to solicit the clemency of Attila, who imperiously dictated these harsh and humiliating conditions of peace.   I. The emperor of the East resigned, by an express or tacit convention, an extensive and important territory which stretched along the southern banks of the Danube, from Singidunum, or Belgrade, as far as Novæ, in the diocese of Thrace.   The breadth was defined by the vague computation of fifteen days' journey; but, from the proposal of Attila to remove the situation of the national market, it soon appeared that he comprehended the ruined city of Naissus within the limits of his dominions.   II. The king of the Huns required and obtained that his tribute or subsidy should be augmented from seven hundred pounds of gold to the annual sum of two thousand one hundred; and he stipulated the immediate payment of six thousand pounds of gold to defray the expenses, or to expiate the guilt, of the war.   One might imagine that such a demand, which scarcely equalled the measure of private wealth, would have been readily discharged by the opulent empire of the East; and the public distress affords a remarkable proof of the improverished, or at least of the disorderly, state of the finances.   A large proportion of the taxes extorted from the people was detained and intercepted in their passage through the foulest channels to the treasury of Constantinople.   The revenue was dissipated by Theodosius and his favourites in wasteful and profuse luxury, which was disguised by the names of Imperial magnificence or Christian charity.   The immediate supplies had been exhausted by the unforeseen necessity of military preparations.   A personal contribution, rigorously but capriciously imposed on the members of the senatorian order, was the only expedient that could disarm without loss of time the impatient avarice of Attila: and the poverty of the nobles compelled them to adopt the scandalous resource of exposing to public auction the jewels of their wives and the hereditary ornaments of their

---

[1] See the whole conversation in Priscus, p. 59-62 [p. 189-197, ed. Bonn].
[2] Nova iterum Orienti assurgit ruina . . . quum nulla ab Occidentalibus ferrentur auxilia.   Prosper-Tyro composed his Chronicle in the West; and his observation implies a censure.

palaces.[1] III. The king of the Huns appears to have established as a principle of national jurisprudence, that he could never lose the property which he had once acquired in the persons who had yielded either a voluntary or reluctant submission to his authority. From this principle he concluded, and the conclusions of Attila were irrevocable laws, that the Huns who had been taken prisoners in war should be released without delay and without ransom; that every Roman captive who had presumed to escape should purchase his right to freedom at the price of twelve pieces of gold; and that all the barbarians who had deserted the standard of Attila should be restored without any promise or stipulation of pardon. In the execution of this cruel and ignominious treaty the Imperial officers were forced to massacre several loyal and noble deserters who refused to devote themselves to certain death; and the Romans forfeited all reasonable claims to the friendship of any Scythian people by this public confession that they were destitute either of faith or power to protect the suppliant who had embraced the throne of Theodosius.[2]

The firmness of a single town, so obscure that except on this occasion it has never been mentioned by any historian or geographer, exposed the disgrace of the emperor and empire. Azimus, or Azimuntium, a small city of Thrace on the Illyrian borders,[3] had been distinguished by the martial spirit of its youth, the skill and reputation of the leaders whom they had chosen, and their daring exploits against the innumerable host of the barbarians. Instead of tamely expecting their approach, the Azimuntines attacked, in frequent and successful sallies, the troops of the Huns, who gradually declined the dangerous

[1] According to the description, or rather invective, of Chrysostom, an auction of Byzantine luxury must have been very productive. Every wealthy house possessed a semicircular table of massy silver, such as two men could scarcely lift; a vase of solid gold of the weight of forty pounds; cups, dishes, of the same metal, etc.

[2] The articles of the treaty, expressed without much order or precision, may be found in Priscus (p. 34, 35, 36, 37, 53, etc. [ed. Par.; p. 142-148, 178, etc., ed. Bonn]). Count Marcellinus dispenses some comfort by observing—1. *That* Attila himself solicited the peace and presents which he had formerly refused; and, 2. *That*, about the same time, the ambassadors of India presented a fine large tame tiger to the emperor Theodosius.

[3] Priscus, p. 35, 36 [p. 143, 144, ed. Bonn]. Among the hundred and eighty-two forts or castles of Thrace enumerated by Procopius (de Ædificiis, l. iv. c. xi. tom. ii. p. 92, edit. Paris [tom. iii. p. 306, ed. Bonn]). there is one of the name of *Esimontou*, whose position is doubtfully marked, in the neighbourhood of Anchialus and the Euxine Sea. The name and walls of Azimuntium might subsist till the reign of Justinian; but the race of its brave defenders had been carefully extirpated by the jealousy of the Roman princes.

neighbourhood, rescued from their hands the spoil and the captives, and recruited their domestic force by the voluntary association of fugitives and deserters. After the conclusion of the treaty Attila still menaced the empire with implacable war, unless the Azimuntines were persuaded or compelled to comply with the conditions which their sovereign had accepted. The ministers of Theodosius confessed, with shame and with truth, that they no longer possessed any authority over a society of men who so bravely asserted their natural independence; and the king of the Huns condescended to negotiate an equal exchange with the citizens of Azimus. They demanded the restitution of some shepherds, who with their cattle had been accidentally surprised. A strict though fruitless inquiry was allowed; but the Huns were obliged to swear that they did not detain any prisoners belonging to the city before they could recover two surviving countrymen whom the Azimuntines had reserved as pledges for the safety of their lost companions. Attila, on his side, was satisfied and deceived by their solemn asseveration that the rest of the captives had been put to the sword; and that it was their constant practice immediately to dismiss the Romans and the deserters who had obtained the security of the public faith. This prudent and officious dissimulation may be condemned or excused by the casuists as they incline to the rigid decree of St. Augustin, or to the milder sentiment of St. Jerom and St. Chrysostom: but every soldier, every statesman, must acknowledge that, if the race of the Azimuntines had been encouraged and multiplied, the barbarians would have ceased to trample on the majesty of the empire.[1]

It would have been strange, indeed, if Theodosius had purchased, by the loss of honour, a secure and solid tranquillity, or if his tameness had not invited the repetition of injuries. The Byzantine court was insulted by five or six successive embassies;[2] and the ministers of Attila were uniformly instructed to press the tardy or imperfect execution of the last treaty; to produce

---

[1] The peevish dispute of St. Jerom and St. Augustin, who laboured by different expedients to reconcile the *seeming* quarrel of the two apostles, St. Peter and St. Paul, depends on the solution of an important question (Middleton's Works, vol. ii. p. 5-10), which has been frequently agitated by catholic and protestant divines, and even by lawyers and philosophers of every age.

[2] Montesquieu (Considérations sur la Grandeur, etc., c. xix.) has delineated, with a bold and easy pencil, some of the most striking circumstances of the pride of Attila and the disgrace of the Romans. He deserves the praise of having read the Fragments of Priscus, which have been too much disregarded.

the names of fugitives and deserters who were still protected by the empire; and to declare, with seeming moderation, that, unless their sovereign obtained complete and immediate satisfaction, it would be impossible for him, were it even his wish, to check the resentment of his warlike tribes. Besides the motives of pride and interest which might prompt the king of the Huns to continue this train of negotiation, he was influenced by the less honourable view of enriching his favourites at the expense of his enemies. The Imperial treasury was exhausted to procure the friendly offices of the ambassadors and their principal attendants, whose favourable report might conduce to the maintenance of peace. The barbarian monarch was flattered by the liberal reception of his ministers; he computed with pleasure the value and splendour of their gifts, rigorously exacted the performance of every promise which would contribute to their private emolument, and treated as an important business of state the marriage of his secretary Constantius.[1] That Gallic adventurer, who was recommended by Aëtius to the king of the Huns, had engaged his service to the ministers of Constantinople for the stipulated reward of a wealthy and noble wife; and the daughter of Count Saturninus was chosen to discharge the obligations of her country. The reluctance of the victim, some domestic troubles, and the unjust confiscation of her fortune, cooled the ardour of her interested lover; but he still demanded, in the name of Attila, an equivalent alliance; and, after many ambiguous delays and excuses, the Byzantine court was compelled to sacrifice to this insolent stranger the widow of Armatius, whose birth, opulence, and beauty placed her in the most illustrious rank of the Roman matrons. For these importunate and oppressive embassies Attila claimed a suitable return: he weighed, with suspicious pride, the character and station of the Imperial envoys; but he condescended to promise that he would advance as far as Sardica to receive any ministers who had been invested with the consular dignity. The council of Theodosius eluded this proposal by representing the desolate and ruined condition of Sardica; and even ventured to insinuate that every officer of the army or household was qualified to treat with the

---

[1] See Priscus, p. 69, 71, 72, etc. [p. 208, 213, ed. Bonn]. I would fain believe that this adventurer was afterwards crucified by the order of Attila, on a suspicion of treasonable practices; but Priscus (p. 57 [p. 185, 186, ed. Bonn]) has too plainly distinguished *two* persons of the name of Constantius, who, from the similar events of their lives, might have been easily confounded.

most powerful princes of Scythia.   Maximin,[1] a respectable
courtier, whose abilities had been long exercised in civil and
military employments, accepted with reluctance the trouble-
some, and perhaps dangerous, commission of reconciling the
angry spirit of the king of the Huns.   His friend, the historian
Priscus,[2] embraced the opportunity of observing the barbarian
hero in the peaceful and domestic scenes of life: but the secret
of the embassy, a fatal and guilty secret, was intrusted only to
the interpreter Vigilius.   The two last ambassadors of the Huns,
Orestes, a noble subject of the Pannonian province, and Edecon,
a valiant chieftain of the tribe of the Scyrri, returned at the same
time from Constantinople to the royal camp.   Their obscure
names were afterwards illustrated by the extraordinary fortune
and the contrast of their sons: the two servants of Attila became
the fathers of the last Roman emperor of the West, and of the
first barbarian king of Italy.

The ambassadors, who were followed by a numerous train of
men and horses, made their first halt at Sardica, at the distance
of three hundred and fifty miles, or thirteen days' journey, from
Constantinople.   As the remains of Sardica were still included
within the limits of the empire, it was incumbent on the Romans
to exercise the duties of hospitality.   They provided, with the
assistance of the provincials, a sufficient number of sheep and
oxen, and invited the Huns to a splendid, or, at least, a plentiful
supper.   But the harmony of the entertainment was soon disturbed by mutual prejudice and indiscretion.   The greatness
of the emperor and the empire was warmly maintained by their
ministers; the Huns, with equal ardour, asserted the superiority
of their victorious monarch: the dispute was inflamed by the
rash and unseasonable flattery of Vigilius, who passionately
rejected the comparison of a mere mortal with the divine Theodosius; and it was with extreme difficulty that Maximin and
Priscus were able to divert the conversation or to soothe the

---

[1] In the Persian treaty, concluded in the year 422, the wise and eloquent
Maximin had been the assessor of Ardaburius (Socrates, l. vii. c. 20).
When Marcian ascended the throne, the office of Great Chamberlain was
bestowed on Maximin, who is ranked in a public edict among the four principal ministers of state (Novell. ad Calc. Cod. Theod. p. 31 [tit. ii.]).   He
executed a civil and military commission in the eastern provinces; and his
death was lamented by the savages of Æthiopia, whose incursions he had
repressed.   See Priscus, p. 40, 41 [p. 153, 154, ed. Bonn].

[2] Priscus was a native of Panium in Thrace, and deserved by his eloquence an honourable place among the sophists of the age.   His Byzantine
history, which related to his own times, was comprised in seven books.
See Fabricius Biblioth. Græc. tom. vi. p. 235, 236.   Notwithstanding the
charitable judgment of the critics, I suspect that Priscus was a Pagan.

angry minds of the barbarians. When they rose from table the Imperial ambassador presented Edecon and Orestes with rich gifts of silk robes and Indian pearls, which they thankfully accepted. Yet Orestes could not forbear insinuating that *he* had not always been treated with such respect and liberality: and the offensive distinction which was implied between his civil office and the hereditary rank of his colleague seems to have made Edecon a doubtful friend and Orestes an irreconcilable enemy. After this entertainment they travelled about one hundred miles from Sardica to Naissus. That flourishing city, which had given birth to the great Constantine, was levelled with the ground; the inhabitants were destroyed or dispersed; and the appearance of some sick persons, who were still permitted to exist among the ruins of the churches, served only to increase the horror of the prospect. The surface of the country was covered with the bones of the slain; and the ambassadors, who directed their course to the north-west, were obliged to pass the hills of modern Servia before they descended into the flat and marshy grounds which are terminated by the Danube. The Huns were masters of the great river: their navigation was performed in large canoes, hollowed out of the trunk of a single tree; the ministers of Theodosius were safely landed on the opposite bank; and their barbarian associates immediately hastened to the camp of Attila, which was equally prepared for the amusements of hunting or of war. No sooner had Maximin advanced about two miles from the Danube than he began to experience the fastidious insolence of the conqueror. He was sternly forbid to pitch his tents in a pleasant valley, lest he should infringe the distant awe that was due to the royal mansion. The ministers of Attila pressed him to communicate the business and the instructions which he reserved for the ear of their sovereign. When Maximin temperately urged the contrary practice of nations, he was still more confounded to find that the resolutions of the Sacred Consistory, those secrets (says Priscus) which should not be revealed to the gods themselves, had been treacherously disclosed to the public enemy. On his refusal to comply with such ignominious terms, the Imperial envoy was commanded instantly to depart; the order was recalled; it was again repeated; and the Huns renewed their ineffectual attempts to subdue the patient firmness of Maximin. At length, by the intercession of Scotta, the brother of Onegesius, whose friendship had been purchased by a liberal gift, he was admitted to the royal presence; but, instead of obtaining a decisive answer, he was compelled to undertake a remote journey towards the North, that Attila might enjoy the proud satisfaction of receiving in the same camp the ambassadors of the Eastern and Western empires. His journey was regulated by the guides, who obliged him to halt, to hasten his march, or to deviate from the common road, as it best suited the convenience of the king. The Romans who traversed the plains of Hungary suppose that they passed *several* navigable rivers, either in canoes or portable boats; but there is reason to suspect that the winding stream of the Theiss, or Tibiscus, might present itself in different places under different names. From the contiguous villages they received a plentiful and regular supply of provisions; mead instead of wine, millet in the place of bread, and a certain liquor named *camus*, which, according to the report of Priscus, was distilled from barley.[1] Such fare might appear coarse and indelicate to men who had tasted the luxury of Constantinople; but, in their accidental distress, they were relieved by the gentleness and hospitality of the same barbarians, so terrible and so merciless in war. The ambassadors had encamped on the edge of a large morass. A violent tempest of wind and rain, of thunder and lightning, overturned their tents, immersed their baggage and furniture in the water, and scattered their retinue, who wandered in the darkness of the night, uncertain of their road and apprehensive of some unknown danger, till they awakened by their cries the inhabitants of a neighbouring village, the property of the widow of Bleda. A bright illumination, and, in a few moments, a comfortable fire of reeds, was kindled by their officious benevolence: the wants, and even the desires, of the Romans were liberally satisfied; and they seem to have been embarrassed by the singular politeness of Bleda's widow, who added to her other favours the gift, or at least the loan, of a sufficient number of beautiful and obsequious damsels. The sunshine of the succeeding day was dedicated to repose, to collect and dry the baggage, and to the refreshment of the men and horses; but, in the evening, before they pursued their journey, the ambassadors expressed their gratitude to the bounteous lady of the village by a very acceptible present of silver cups, red fleeces,

---

The Huns themselves still continued to despise the labours of agriculture: they abused the privilege of a victorious nation; and the Goths, their industrious subjects, who cultivated the earth, dreaded their neighbourhood, like that of so many ravenous wolves (Priscus, p. 45 [p. 163, ed. Bonn]). In the same manner the Sarts and Tadgics provide for their own subsistence, and for that of the Usbec Tartars, their lazy and rapacious sovereigns. See Genealogical History of the Tartars, p. 423, 455, etc.

dried fruits, and Indian pepper.   Soon after this adventure they rejoined the march of Attila, from whom they had been separated about six days; and slowly proceeded to the capital of an empire which did not contain, in the space of several thousand miles, a single city.

As far as we may ascertain the vague and obscure geography of Priscus, this capital appears to have been seated between the Danube, the Theiss, and the Carpathian hills, in the plains of Upper Hungary, and most probably in the neighbourhood of Jazberin, Agria, or Tokay.[1]   In its origin it could be no more than an accidental camp, which, by the long and frequent residence of Attila, had insensibly swelled into a huge village, for the reception of his court, of the troops who followed his person, and of the various multitude of idle or industrious slaves and retainers.[2]   The baths, constructed by Onegesius, were the only edifice of stone;   the materials had been transported from Pannonia; and since the adjacent country was destitute even of large timber, it may be presumed that the meaner habitations of the royal village consisted of straw, of mud, or of canvas.   The wooden houses of the more illustrious Huns were built and adorned with rude magnificence, according to the rank, the fortune, or the taste of the proprietors.   They seem to have been distributed with some degree of order and symmetry; and each spot became more honourable as it approached the person of the sovereign.   The palace of Attila, which surpassed all other houses in his dominions, was built entirely of wood, and covered an ample space of ground.   The outward enclosure was a lofty

[1] It is evident that Priscus passed the Danube and the Theiss, and that he did not reach the foot of the Carpathian hills.   Agria, Tokay, and Jazberin are situate in the plains circumscribed by this definition.   M. de Buat (Histoire des Peuples, etc., tom. vii. p. 461) has chosen Tokay; Otrokosci (p. 180, apud Mascou, ix. 23), a learned Hungarian, has preferred Jazberin, a place about thirty-six miles westward of Buda and the Danube. [M. St. Martin considers the narrative of Priscus, the only authority of Count de Buat and of Gibbon, too vague to fix the position of Attila's camp.   " It is worthy of remark that in the Hungarian traditions collected by Thevrocz, l. 2, c. 17, precisely on the left branch of the Danube, where Attila's residence was situated, in the same parallel stands the present city of Buda, in Hungarian Buduvur.   It is for this reason that this city has retained for a long time among the Germans of Hungary the name of Etzelnburg or Etzelaburg, viz., the city of Attila.   St. Martin sees no reason for not accepting the narration of the Hungarian historians.—O. S.]
[2] The royal village of Attila may be compared to the city of Karacorum, the residence of the successors of Zingis, which, though it appears to have been a more stable habitation, did not equal the size or splendour of the town and abbey of St. Denys in the 13th century (see Rubruquis, in the Histoire Générale des Voyages, tom. vii. p. 286).   The camp of Aurengzebe, as it is so agreeably described by Bernier (tom. ii. p. 217-235), blended the manners of Scythia with the magnificence and luxury of Hindostan.

wall, or palisade, of smooth square timber, intersected with high towers, but intended rather for ornament than defence. This wall, which seems to have encircled the declivity of a hill, comprehended a great variety of wooden edifices, adapted to the uses of royalty. A separate house was assigned to each of the numerous wives of Attila; and, instead of the rigid and illiberal confinement imposed by Asiatic jealousy, they politely admitted the Roman ambassadors to their presence, their table, and even to the freedom of an innocent embrace. When Maximin offered his presents to Cerca the principal queen, he admired the singular architecture of her mansion, the height of the round columns, the size and beauty of the wood, which was curiously shaped or turned, or polished or carved; and his attentive eye was able to discover some taste in the ornaments, and some regularity in the proportions. After passing through the guards who watched before the gate, the ambassadors were introduced into the private apartment of Cerca. The wife of Attila received their visit sitting, or rather lying, on a soft couch; the floor was covered with a carpet; the domestics formed a circle round the queen; and her damsels, seated on the ground, were employed in working the variegated embroidery which adorned the dress of the barbaric warriors. The Huns were ambitious of displaying those riches which were the fruit and evidence of their victories; the trappings of their horses, their swords, and even their shoes, were studded with gold and precious stones; and their tables were profusely spread with plates, and goblets, and vases of gold and silver, which had been fashioned by the labour of Grecian artists. The monarch alone assumed the superior pride of still adhering to the simplicity of his Scythian ancestors.[1] The dress of Attila, his arms, and the furniture of his horse, were plain, without ornament, and of a single colour. The royal table was served in wooden cups and platters; flesh was his only food; and the conqueror of the North never tasted the luxury of bread.

When Attila first gave audience to the Roman ambassadors on the banks of the Danube, his tent was encompassed with a formidable guard. The monarch himself was seated in a wooden chair. His stern countenance, angry gestures, and impatient tone astonished the firmness of Maximin; but Vigilius had more reason to tremble, since he distinctly understood the menace, that if Attila did not respect the law of nations, he would nail the

---

[1] When the Moguls displayed the spoils of Asia in the diet of Toncal, the throne of Zingis was still covered with the original black felt carpet on which he had been seated when he was raised to the command of his warlike countrymen. See Vie de Gengiscan, l. iv. c. 9.

deceitful interpreter to a cross, and leave his body to the vultures. The barbarians condescended, by producing an accurate list, to expose the bold falsehood of Vigilius, who had affirmed that no more than seventeen deserters could be found. But he arrogantly declared that he apprehended only the disgrace of contending with his fugitive slaves; since he despised their impotent efforts to defend the provinces which Theodosius had intrusted to their arms: " For what fortress " (added Attila), " what city, in the wide extent of the Roman empire, can hope to exist, secure and impregnable, if it is our pleasure that it should be erased from the earth? " He dismissed, however, the interpreter, who returned to Constantinople with his peremptory demand of more complete restitution, and a more splendid embassy. His anger gradually subsided, and his domestic satisfaction in a marriage which he celebrated on the road with the daughter of Eslam might perhaps contribute to mollify the native fierceness of his temper. The entrance of Attila into the royal village was marked by a very singular ceremony. A numerous troop of women came out to meet their hero and their king. They marched before him, distributed into long and regular files: the intervals between the files were filled by white veils of thin linen, which the women on either side bore aloft in their hands, and which formed a canopy for a chorus of young virgins, who chanted hymns and songs in the Scythian language. The wife of his favourite Onegesius, with a train of female attendants, saluted Attila at the door of her own house, on his way to the palace; and offered, according to the custom of the country, her respectful homage, by entreating him to taste the wine and meat which she had prepared for his reception. As soon as the monarch had graciously accepted her hospitable gift, his domestics lifted a small silver table to a convenient height, as he sat on horseback; and Attila, when he had touched the goblet with his lips, again saluted the wife of Onegesius, and continued his march. During his residence at the seat of empire his hours were not wasted in the recluse idleness of a seraglio; and the king of the Huns could maintain his superior dignity without concealing his person from the public view. He frequently assembled his council, and gave audience to the ambassadors of the nations; and his people might appeal to the supreme tribunal, which he held at stated times, and, according to the Eastern custom, before the principal gate of his wooden palace. The Romans, both of the East and of the West, were twice invited to the banquets where Attila feasted with the princes and nobles of Scythia. Maximin and his colleagues were stopped on the threshold, till they had made a devout libation to the health and prosperity of the king of the Huns; and were conducted, after this ceremony, to their respective seats in a spacious hall. The royal table and couch, covered with carpets and fine linen, was raised by several steps in the midst of the hall; and a son, an uncle, or perhaps a favourite king, were admitted to share the simple and homely repast of Attila. Two lines of small tables, each of which contained three or four guests, were ranged in order on either hand; the right was esteemed the most honourable, but the Romans ingenuously confess that they were placed on the left; and that Beric, an unknown chieftain, most probably of the Gothic race, preceded the representatives of Theodosius and Valentinian. The barbarian monarch received from his cupbearer a goblet filled with wine, and courteously drank to the health of the most distinguished guest, who rose from his seat and expressed, in the same manner, his loyal and respectful vows. This ceremony was successively performed for all, or at least for the illustrious persons of the assembly; and a considerable time must have been consumed, since it was thrice repeated as each course or service was placed on the table. But the wine still remained after the meat had been removed; and the Huns continued to indulge their intemperance long after the sober and decent ambassadors of the two empires had withdrawn themselves from the nocturnal banquet. Yet before they retired they enjoyed a singular opportunity of observing the manners of the nation in their convivial amusements. Two Scythians stood before the couch of Attila, and recited the verses which they had composed to celebrate his valour and his victories. A profound silence prevailed in the hall; and the attention of the guests was captivated by the vocal harmony, which revived and perpetuated the memory of their own exploits: a martial ardour flashed from the eyes of the warriors, who were impatient for battle; and the tears of the old men expressed their generous despair that they could no longer partake the danger and glory of the field.[1] This entertainment, which might be considered as a school of military virtue, was succeeded by a farce that debased the dignity of human nature. A Moorish and a Scythian buffoon successively excited the mirth of the rude spectators, by their deformed figure,

---

[1] If we may believe Plutarch (in Demetrio, tom. v. [c. 19] p. 24), it was the custom of the Scythians, when they indulged in the pleasures of the table, to awaken their languid courage by the martial harmony of twanging their bow-strings.

ridiculous dress, antic gestures, absurd speeches, and the strange unintelligible confusion of the Latin, the Gothic, and the Hunnic languages; and the hall resounded with loud and licentious peals of laughter. In the midst of this intemperate riot, Attila alone, without a change of countenance, maintained his steadfast and inflexible gravity, which was never relaxed, except on the entrance of Irnac, the youngest of his sons: he embraced the boy with a smile of paternal tenderness, gently pinched him by the cheek, and betrayed a partial affection, which was justified by the assurance of his prophets that Irnac would be the future support of his family and empire. Two days afterwards the ambassadors received a second invitation; and they had reason to praise the politeness, as well as the hospitality, of Attila. The king of the Huns held a long and familiar conversation with Maximin; but his civility was interrupted by rude expressions and haughty reproaches; and he was provoked, by a motive of interest, to support, with unbecoming zeal, the private claims of his secretary Constantius. "The emperor" (said Attila) "has long promised him a rich wife: Constantius must not be disappointed; nor should a Roman emperor deserve the name of liar." On the third day the ambassadors were dismissed; the freedom of several captives was granted, for a moderate ransom, to their pressing entreaties; and, besides the royal presents, they were permitted to accept from each of the Scythian nobles the honourable and useful gift of a horse. Maximin returned, by the same road, to Constantinople; and though he was involved in an accidental dispute with Beric, the new ambassador of Attila, he flattered himself that he had contributed, by the laborious journey, to confirm the peace and alliance of the two nations.[1]

But the Roman ambassador was ignorant of the treacherous design which had been concealed under the mask of the public faith. The surprise and satisfaction of Edecon, when he contemplated the splendour of Constantinople, had encouraged the interpreter Vigilius to procure for him a secret interview with the eunuch Chrysaphius,[2] who governed the emperor and the

---

[1] The curious narrative of this embassy, which required few observations, and was not susceptible of any collateral evidence, may be found in Priscus, p. 49-70 [ed. Par.; p. 170-209, ed. Bonn]. But I have not confined myself to the same order; and I had previously extracted the historical circumstances, which were less intimately connected with the journey and business of the Roman ambassadors.

[2] M. de Tillemont has very properly given the succession of chamberlains who reigned in the name of Theodosius. Chrysaphius was the last, and, according to the unanimous evidence of history, the worst of these favourites

empire. After some previous conversation, and a mutual oath of secrecy, the eunuch, who had not, from his own feelings or experience, imbibed any exalted notions of ministerial virtue, ventured to propose the death of Attila, as an important service, by which Edecon might deserve a liberal share of the wealth and luxury which he admired. The ambassador of the Huns listened to the tempting offer; and professed, with apparent zeal, his ability, as well as readiness, to execute the bloody deed: the design was communicated to the master of the offices, and the devout Theodosius consented to the assassination of his invincible enemy. But this perfidious conspiracy was defeated by the dissimulation, or the repentance, of Edecon; and though he might exaggerate his inward abhorrence for the treason which he seemed to approve, he dexterously assumed the merit of an early and voluntary confession. If we *now* review the embassy of Maximin and the behaviour of Attila, we must applaud the barbarian, who respected the laws of hospitality, and generously entertained and dismissed the minister of a prince who had conspired against his life. But the rashness of Vigilius will appear still more extraordinary, since he returned, conscious of his guilt and danger, to the royal camp accompanied by his son, and carrying with him a weighty purse of gold, which the favourite eunuch had furnished, to satisfy the demands of Edecon and to corrupt the fidelity of the guards. The interpreter was instantly seized and dragged before the tribunal of Attila, where he asserted his innocence with specious firmness, till the threat of inflicting instant death on his son extorted from him a sincere discovery of the criminal transaction. Under the name of ransom, or confiscation, the rapacious king of the Huns accepted two hundred pounds of gold for the life of a traitor whom he disdained to punish. He pointed his just indignation against a nobler object. His ambassadors, Eslaw and Orestes, were immediately despatched to Constantinople with a peremptory instruction, which it was much safer for them to execute than to disobey. They boldly entered the Imperial presence with the fatal purse hanging down from the neck of Orestes, who interrogated the eunuch Chrysaphius, as he stood beside the throne, whether he recognised the evidence of his guilt. But the office of reproof was reserved for the superior dignity of his colleague Eslaw, who gravely addressed the emperor of the East in the following words:

(see Hist. des Empereurs, tom. vi. p. 117-119; Mém. Ecclés. tom. xv. p. 438). His partiality for his godfather, the heresiarch Eutyches, engaged him to persecute the orthodox party.

"Theodosius is the son of an illustrious and respectable parent: Attila likewise is descended from a noble race; and *he* has supported, by his actions, the dignity which he inherited from his father Mundzuk. But Theodosius has forfeited his paternal honours, and, by consenting to pay tribute, has degraded himself to the condition of a slave. It is therefore just that he should reverence the man whom fortune and merit have placed above him, instead of attempting, like a wicked slave, clandestinely to conspire against his master." The son of Arcadius, who was accustomed only to the voice of flattery, heard with astonishment the severe language of truth: he blushed and trembled; nor did he presume directly to refuse the head of Chrysaphius, which Eslaw and Orestes were instructed to demand. A solemn embassy, armed with full powers and magnificent gifts, was hastily sent to deprecate the wrath of Attila; and his pride was gratified by the choice of Nomius and Anatolius, two ministers of consular or patrician rank, of whom the one was great treasurer, and the other was master-general of the armies of the East. He condescended to meet these ambassadors on the banks of the river Drenco; and though he at first affected a stern and haughty demeanour, his anger was insensibly mollified by their eloquence and liberality. He condescended to pardon the emperor, the eunuch, and the interpreter; bound himself by an oath to observe the conditions of peace; released a great number of captives; abandoned the fugitives and deserters to their fate; and resigned a large territory, to the south of the Danube, which he had already exhausted of its wealth and inhabitants. But this treaty was purchased at an expense which might have supported a vigorous and successful war; and the subjects of Theodosius were compelled to redeem the safety of a worthless favourite by oppressive taxes which they would more cheerfully have paid for his destruction.[1]

The emperor Theodosius did not long survive the most humiliating circumstance of an inglorious life. As he was riding or hunting in the neighbourhood of Constantinople, he was thrown from his horse into the river Lycus: the spine of his back was injured by the fall; and he expired some days afterwards, in the

---

[1] This secret conspiracy, and its important consequences, may be traced in the fragments of Priscus, p. 37, 38, 39, 54, 70, 71, 72 [p. 146-150, 180, 210-214, ed. Bonn]. The chronology of that historian is not fixed by any precise date; but the series of negotiations between Attila and the Eastern empire must be included within the three or four years which are terminated, A.D. 450, by the death of Theodosius.

fiftieth year of his age, and the forty-third of his reign.[1] His sister Pulcheria, whose authority had been controlled both in civil and ecclesiastical affairs by the pernicious influence of the eunuchs, was unanimously proclaimed empress of the East; and the Romans, for the first time, submitted to a female reign.   No sooner had Pulcheria ascended the throne than she indulged her own and the public resentment by an act of popular justice. Without any legal trial, the eunuch Chrysaphius was executed before the gates of the city; and the immense riches which had been accumulated by the rapacious favourite served only to hasten and to justify his punishment.[2] Amidst the general acclamations of the clergy and people, the empress did not forget the prejudice and disadvantage to which her sex was exposed; and she wisely resolved to prevent their murmurs by the choice of a colleague who would always respect the superior rank and virgin chastity of his wife.   She gave her hand to Marcian, a senator, about sixty years of age, and the nominal husband of Pulcheria was solemnly invested with the Imperial purple.   The zeal which he displayed for the orthodox creed, as it was established by the council of Chalcedon, would alone have inspired the grateful eloquence of the catholics.   But the behaviour of Marcian in a private life, and afterwards on the throne, may support a more rational belief that he was qualified to restore and invigorate an empire which had been almost dissolved by the successive weakness of two hereditary monarchs.   He was born in Thrace, and educated to the profession of arms; but Marcian's youth had been severely exercised by poverty and misfortune, since his only resource, when he first arrived at Constantinople, consisted in two hundred pieces of gold which he had borrowed of a friend.   He passed nineteen years in the domestic and military service of Aspar and his son Ardaburius; followed those powerful generals to the Persian and African wars; and obtained, by their influence, the honourable rank of tribune and senator.   His mild disposition and useful talents, without alarming the jealousy, recommended Marcian to the esteem and favour of his patrons; he had seen, perhaps he had felt, the

---

[1] Theodorus the Reader (see Vales. Hist. Eccles. tom. iii. p. 563) and the Paschal Chronicle mention the fall without specifying the injury; but the consequence was so likely to happen, and so unlikely to be invented, that we may safely give credit to Nicephorus Callistus, a Greek of the fourteenth century.

[2] Pulcheriæ nutû (says Count Marcellinus) suâ cum avaritiâ interemptus est.   She abandoned the eunuch to the pious revenge of a son whose father had suffered at his instigation.

abuses of a venal and oppressive administration; and his own example gave weight and energy to the laws which he promulgated for the reformation of manners.[1]

CHAPTER XXXV

Invasion of Gaul by Attila—He is repulsed by Aëtius and the Visigoths—Attila invades and evacuates Italy—The Deaths of Attila, Aëtius, and Valentinian the Third

IT was the opinion of Marcian, that war should be avoided as long as it is possible to preserve a secure and honourable peace; but it was likewise his opinion that peace cannot be honourable or secure, if the sovereign betrays a pusillanimous aversion to war. This temperate courage dictated his reply to the demands of Attila, who insolently pressed the payment of the annual tribute. The emperor signified to the barbarians that they must no longer insult the majesty of Rome by the mention of a tribute; that he was disposed to reward, with becoming liberality, the faithful friendship of his allies; but that, if they presumed to violate the public peace, they should feel that he possessed troops, and arms, and resolution, to repel their attacks. The same language, even in the camp of the Huns, was used by his ambassador Apollonius, whose bold refusal to deliver the presents, till he had been admitted to a personal interview, displayed a sense of dignity, and a contempt of danger, which Attila was not prepared to expect from the degenerate Romans.[2] He threatened to chastise the rash successor of Theodosius; but he hesitated, whether he should first direct his invincible arms against the Eastern or the Western empire. While mankind awaited his decision with awful suspense, he sent an equal defiance to the courts of Ravenna and Constantinople; and his ministers saluted the two emperors with the same haughty declaration. "Attila, *my* lord, and *thy* lord, commands thee to provide a palace for his immediate reception."[3] But as the barbarian despised, or

[1] Procopius, de Bell. Vandal. l. i. c. 4 [tom. i. p. 325, *sqq.* ed Bonn]; Evagrius, l. ii. c. 1; Theophanes, p. 90, 91 [ed. Par.; tom. i. p. 161-164, ed. Bonn]; Novell, ad Calcem Cod. Theod. tom. vi. p. 30. The praises which St. Leo and the catholics have bestowed on Marcian are diligently transcribed by Baronius, as an encouragement for future princes.

[2] See Priscus, p. 39, 72 [p. 213, 214, ed. Bonn].

[3] The Alexandrian or Paschal Chronicle, which introduces this haughty message during the lifetime of Theodosius, may have anticipated the date; but the dull annalist was incapable of inventing the original and genuine style of Attila.

affected to despise, the Romans of the East, whom he had so often vanquished, he soon declared his resolution of suspending the easy conquest till he had achieved a more glorious and important enterprise. In the memorable invasions of Gaul and Italy, the Huns were naturally attracted by the wealth and fertility of those provinces; but the particular motives and provocations of Attila can only be explained by the state of the Western empire under the reign of Valentinian, or, to speak more correctly, under the administration of Aëtius.[1]

After the death of his rival Boniface, Aëtius had prudently retired to the tents of the Huns; and he was indebted to their alliance for his safety and his restoration. Instead of the suppliant language of a guilty exile, he solicited his pardon at the head of sixty thousand barbarians; and the empress Placidia confessed, by a feeble resistance, that the condescension which might have been ascribed to clemency was the effect of weakness or fear. She delivered herself, her son Valentinian, and the Western empire, into the hands of an insolent subject; nor could Placidia protect the son-in-law of Boniface, the virtuous and faithful Sebastian,[2] from the implacable persecution which urged him from one kingdom to another, till he miserably perished in the service of the Vandals. The fortunate Aëtius, who was immediately promoted to the rank of patrician, and thrice invested with the honours of the consulship, assumed, with the title of master of the cavalry and infantry, the whole military power of the state; and he is sometimes styled, by contemporary writers, the duke, or general, of the Romans of the West. His prudence, rather than his virtue, engaged him to leave the grandson of Theodosius in the possession of the purple; and Valentinian was permitted to enjoy the peace and luxury of Italy, while the patrician appeared in the glorious light of a hero and a patriot, who supported near twenty years the ruins of the Western empire. The Gothic historian ingenuously confesses

---

[1] The second book of the Histoire Critique de l'Etablissement de la Monarchie Françoise, tom. i. p. 189-424, throws great light on the state of Gaul when it was invaded by Attila; but the ingenious author, the Abbé Dubos, too often bewilders himself in system and conjecture.

[2] Victor Vitensis (de Persecut. Vandal. l. i. c. 6, p. 8, edit. Ruinart) calls him, acer consilio et strenuus in bello: but his courage, when he became unfortunate, was censured as desperate rashness; and Sebastian deserved, or obtained, the epithet of *præceps* (Sidon. Apollinar. Carmen ix. 281). His adventures at Constantinople, in Sicily, Gaul, Spain, and Africa, are faintly marked in the Chronicles of Marcellinus and Idatius. In his distress he was always followed by a numerous train; since he could ravage the Hellespont and Propontis and seize the city of Barcelona.

that Aëtius was born for the salvation of the Roman republic;[1] and the following portrait, though it is drawn in the fairest colours, must be allowed to contain a much larger proportion of truth than of flattery.[2] " His mother was a wealthy and noble Italian, and his father Gaudentius, who held a distinguished rank in the province of Scythia, gradually rose from the station of a military *domestic* to the dignity of master of the cavalry. Their son, who was enrolled almost in his infancy in the guards, was given as a hostage, first to Alaric, and afterwards to the Huns; and he successively obtained the civil and military honours of the palace, for which he was equally qualified by superior merit. The graceful figure of Aëtius was not above the middle stature; but his manly limbs were admirably formed for strength, beauty, and agility; and he excelled in the martial exercises of managing a horse, drawing the bow, and darting the javelin. He could patiently endure the want of food or of sleep; and his mind and body were alike capable of the most laborious efforts. He possessed the genuine courage that can despise not only dangers, but injuries: and it was impossible either to corrupt, or deceive, or intimidate the firm integrity of his soul." [3] The barbarians, who had seated themselves in the Western provinces, were insensibly taught to respect the faith and valour of the patrician Aëtius. He soothed their passions, consulted their prejudices, balanced their interests, and checked their ambition. A seasonable treaty which he concluded with Genseric protected Italy from the depredations of the Vandals; the independent Britons implored and acknowledged his salutary aid; the Imperial authority was restored and maintained in Gaul and Spain; and he compelled the Franks and the Suevi, whom he had vanquished in the field, to become the useful confederates of the republic.

From a principle of interest, as well as gratitude, Aëtius

[1] Reipublicæ Romanæ singulariter natus, qui superbiam Suevorum, Francorumque barbariem immensis cædibus servire Imperio Romano coegisset. Jornandes de Rebus Geticis, c. 34, p. 660.

[2] [Some valuable fragments of a poetical panegyric on Aëtius by Merobaudes, a Spaniard, were recovered from a palimpsest MS. by the industry and sagacity of Niebuhr, and were reprinted in the edition of the Byzantine historians. The poet speaks in glowing terms of the long peace enjoyed under the administration of Aëtius. The poet was rewarded by a statue publicly dedicated to his honour in Rome.—O. S.]

[3] This portrait is drawn by Renatus Profuturus Frigeridus, a contemporary historian, known only by some extracts which are preserved by Gregory of Tours (l. ii. c. 8, in tom. ii. p. 163). It was probably the duty, or at least the interest, of Renatus, to magnify the virtues of Aëtius; but he would have shown more dexterity if he had not insisted on his patient, *forgiving* disposition.

assiduously cultivated the alliance of the Huns. While he resided in their tents as a hostage or an exile, he had familiarly conversed with Attila himself, the nephew of his benefactor; and the two famous antagonists appear to have been connected by a personal and military friendship, which they afterwards confirmed by mutual gifts, frequent embassies, and the education of Carpilio, the son of Aëtius, in the camp of Attila. By the specious professions of gratitude and voluntary attachment, the patrician might disguise his apprehensions of the Scythian conqueror, who pressed the two empires with his innumerable armies. His demands were obeyed or eluded. When he claimed the spoils of a vanquished city, some vases of gold, which had been fraudulently embezzled, the civil and military governors of Noricum were immediately despatched to satisfy his complaints:[1] and it is evident, from their conversation with Maximin and Priscus in the royal village, that the valour and prudence of Aëtius had not saved the Western Romans from the common ignominy of tribute. Yet his dexterous policy prolonged the advantages of a salutary peace; and a numerous army of Huns and Alani, whom he had attached to his person, was employed in the defence of Gaul. Two colonies of these barbarians were judiciously fixed in the territories of Valence and Orleans;[2] and their active cavalry secured the important passages of the Rhône and of the Loire. These savage allies were not indeed less formidable to the subjects than to the enemies of Rome. Their original settlement was enforced with the licentious violence of conquest; and the province through which they marched was exposed to all the calamities of an hostile invasion.[3] Strangers

---

[1] The embassy consisted of Count Romulus; of Promotus, president of Noricum; and of Romanus, the military duke. They were accompanied by Tatullus, an illustrious citizen of Petovio, in the same province, and father of Orestes, who had married the daughter of Count Romulus. See Priscus, p. 57, 65 [p. 185, 198, ed. Bonn]. Cassiodorus (Variar. i. 4) mentions another embassy which was executed by his father and Carpilio, the son of Aëtius; and, as Attila was no more, he could safely boast of their manly, intrepid behaviour in his presence.

[2] Deserta Valentinæ urbis rura Alanis partienda traduntur. Prosper. Tyronis Chron. in Historiens de France, tom. i. p. 639. A few lines afterwards, Prosper observes that lands in the *ulterior* Gaul were assigned to the Alani. Without admitting the correction of Dubos (tom. i. p. 300), the reasonable supposition of *two* colonies or garrisons of Alani will confirm his arguments and remove his objections.

[3] See Prosper, Tyro, p. 639. Sidonius (Panegyr. Avit. 246) complains, in the name of Auvergne, his native country--

> Litorius Scythicos equites tunc forte, subacto
> Celsus Aremorico, Geticum rapiebat in agmen
> Per terras, Arverne, tuas : qui proxima quæque

to the emperor or the republic, the Alani of Gaul were devoted to the ambition of Aëtius; and though he might suspect that, in a contest with Attila himself, they would revolt to the standard of their national king, the patrician laboured to restrain, rather than to excite, their zeal and resentment against the Goths, the Burgundians, and the Franks.

The kingdom established by the Visigoths in the southern provinces of Gaul had gradually acquired strength and maturity; and the conduct of those ambitious barbarians, either in peace or war, engaged the perpetual vigilance of Aëtius. After the death of Wallia, the Gothic sceptre devolved to Theodoric, the son of the great Alaric;[1] and his prosperous reign of more than thirty years over a turbulent people may be allowed to prove that his prudence was supported by uncommon vigour, both of mind and body. Impatient of his narrow limits, Theodoric aspired to the possession of Arles, the wealthy seat of government and commerce; but the city was saved by the timely approach of Aëtius; and the Gothic king, who had raised the siege with some loss and disgrace, was persuaded, for an adequate subsidy, to divert the martial valour of his subjects in a Spanish war. Yet Theodoric still watched, and eagerly seized, the favourable moment of renewing his hostile attempts. The Goths besieged Narbonne, while the Belgic provinces were invaded by the Burgundians; and the public safety was threatened on every side by the apparent union of the enemies of Rome. On every side, the activity of Aëtius and his Scythian cavalry opposed a firm and successful resistance. Twenty thousand Burgundians were slain in battle; and the remains of the nation humbly accepted a dependent seat in the mountains of Savoy.[2] The walls of

Discursu, flammis, ferro, feritate, rapinis,
Delebant; pacis fallentes nomen inane.
Another poet, Paulinus of Perigord, confirms the complaint:
Nam socium vix ferre queas, qui durior hoste.
See Dubos, tom. i. p. 330.

[1] Theodoric II., the son of Theodoric I., declares to Avitus his resolution of repairing, or expiating, the fault which his *grandfather* had committed.
Quæ *noster* peccavit *avus*, quem fuscat id unum,
Quod te, Roma, capit.
Sidon. Panegyric. Avit. 505.
This character, applicable only to the great Alaric, establishes the genealogy of the Gothic kings, which has hitherto been unnoticed.

[2] The name of *Sapaudia*, the origin of *Savoy*, is first mentioned by Ammianus Marcellinus [l. xv. c. 11]; and two military posts are ascertained by the Notitia within the limits of that province; a cohort was stationed at Grenoble in Dauphiné; and Ebredunum, or Iverdun, sheltered a fleet of small vessels which commanded the lake of Neufchâtel. See Valesius, Notit. Galliarum, p. 503. D'Anville, Notice de l'Ancienne Gaule, p. 284, 579.

Narbonne had been shaken by the battering engines, and the inhabitants had endured the last extremities of famine, when Count Litorius, approaching in silence, and directing each horseman to carry behind him two sacks of flour, cut his way through the entrenchments of the besiegers. The siege was immediately raised; and the more decisive victory, which is ascribed to the personal conduct of Aëtius himself, was marked with the blood of eight thousand Goths. But in the absence of the patrician, who was hastily summoned to Italy by some public or private interest, Count Litorius succeeded to the command ; and his presumption soon discovered that far different talents are required to lead a wing of cavalry, or to direct the operations of an important war. At the head of an army of Huns, he rashly advanced to the gates of Toulouse, full of careless contempt for an enemy whom his misfortunes had rendered prudent, and his situation made desperate. The predictions of the augurs had inspired Litorius with the profane confidence that he should enter the Gothic capital in triumph; and the trust which he reposed in his Pagan allies encouraged him to reject the fair conditions of peace which were repeatedly proposed by the bishops in the name of Theodoric. The king of the Goths exhibited in his distress the edifying contrast of Christian piety and moderation; nor did he lay aside his sackcloth and ashes till he was prepared to arm for the combat. His soldiers, animated with martial and religious enthusiasm, assaulted the camp of Litorius. The conflict was obstinate; the slaughter was mutual. The Roman general, after a total defeat, which could be imputed only to his unskilful rashness, was actually led through the streets of Toulouse, not in his own, but in a hostile triumph; and the misery which he experienced, in a long and ignominious captivity, excited the compassion of the barbarians themselves.[1] Such a loss, in a country whose spirit and finances were long since exhausted, could not easily be repaired; and the Goths, assuming, in their turn, the sentiments of ambition and revenge, would have planted their victorious standards on the banks of the Rhône, if the presence of Aëtius had not restored strength and discipline to the Romans.[2]

---

[1] Salvian has attempted to explain the moral government of the Deity; a task which may be readily performed by supposing that the calamities of the wicked are *judgments*, and those of the righteous, *trials*.

[2] —————— Capto terrarum damna patebant
   Litorio: in Rhodanum proprios producere fines,
   Theudoridæ fixum; nec erat pugnare necesse,
   Sed migrare Getis. Rabidam trux asperat iram
   Victor; quòd sensit Scythicum sub mœnibus hostem

The two armies expected the signal of a decisive action; but the generals, who were conscious of each other's force, and doubtful of their own superiority, prudently sheathed their swords in the field of battle; and their reconciliation was permanent and sincere. Theodoric, king of the Visigoths, appears to have deserved the love of his subjects, the confidence of his allies, and the esteem of mankind. His throne was surrounded by six valiant sons, who were educated with equal care in the exercises of the barbarian camp, and in those of the Gallic schools: from the study of the Roman jurisprudence they acquired the theory, at least, of law and justice; and the harmonious sense of Virgil contributed to soften the asperity of their native manners.[1] The two daughters of the Gothic king were given in marriage to the eldest sons of the kings of the Suevi and of the Vandals, who reigned in Spain and Africa; but these illustrious alliances were pregnant with guilt and discord. The queen of the Suevi bewailed the death of an husband, inhumanly massacred by her brother. The princess of the Vandals was the victim of a jealous tyrant, whom she called her father. The cruel Genseric suspected that his son's wife had conspired to poison him; the supposed crime was punished by the amputation of her nose and ears; and the unhappy daughter of Theodoric was ignominiously returned to the court of Toulouse in that deformed and mutilated condition. This horrid act, which must seem incredible to a civilised age, drew tears from every spectator; but Theodoric was urged, by the feelings of a parent and a king, to revenge such irreparable injuries. The Imperial ministers, who always cherished the discord of the barbarians, would have supplied the Goths with arms, and ships, and treasures, for the African war; and the cruelty of Genseric might have been fatal to himself, if the artful Vandal had not armed, in his cause, the formidable power of the Huns. His rich gifts and pressing solicitations

Imputat, et nihil est gravius, si forsitan unquam
Vincere contingat, trepido.

Panegyr. Avit. 300, etc.

Sidonius then proceeds, according to the duty of a panegyrist, to transfer the whole merit from Aëtius to his minister Avitus.

[1] Theodoric II., revered, in the person of Avitus, the character of his preceptor.

——— Mihi Romula dudum
Per te jura placent; parvumque ediscere jussit
Ad tua verba pater, docili quo prisca *Maronis*
Carmine molliret Scythicos mihi pagina mores.

Sidon. Panegyric. Avit. 495, etc.

inflamed the ambition of Attila; and the designs of Aëtius and Theodoric were prevented by the invasion of Gaul.[1]

The Franks, whose monarchy was still confined to the neighbourhood of the Lower Rhine, had wisely established the right of hereditary succession in the noble family of the Merovingians.[2] These princes were elevated on a buckler, the symbol of military command; [3] and the royal fashion of long hair was the ensign of their birth and dignity. Their flaxen locks, which they combed and dressed with singular care, hung down in flowing ringlets on their back and shoulders; while the rest of the nation were obliged, either by law or custom, to shave the hinder part of their head, to comb their hair over the forehead, and to content themselves with the ornament of two small whiskers.[4] The lofty stature of the Franks and their blue eyes denoted a Germanic origin; their close apparel accurately expressed the figure of their limbs; a weighty sword was suspended from a broad belt; their bodies were protected by a large shield: and these warlike barbarians were trained from their earliest youth to run, to leap, to swim; to dart the javelin or battle-axe with unerring aim; to advance without hesitation against a superior enemy; and to maintain, either in life or death, the invincible reputation of their ancestors.[5] Clodion, the first of their long-haired kings

[1] Our authorities for the reign of Theodoric I. are, Jornandes de Rebus Geticis, c. 34, 36, and the Chronicles of Idatius and the two Prospers, inserted in the Historians of France, tom. i. p. 612-640. To these we may add Salvian de Gubernatione Dei, l. vii. p. 243, 244, 245, and the Panegyric of Avitus by Sidonius.

[2] Reges *Crinitos* [super] se creavisse de primâ, et ut ita dicam, nobiliori suorum familiâ (Greg. Turon. l. ii. c. 9, p. 166, of the second volume of the Historians of France). Gregory himself does not mention the *Merovingian* name, which may be traced, however, to the beginning of the seventh century, as the distinctive appellation of the royal family, and even of the French monarchy. An ingenious critic has deduced the Merovingians from the great Maroboduus; and he has clearly proved that the prince who gave his name to the first race was more ancient than the father of Childeric. See Mémoires de l'Académie des Inscriptions, tom. xx. p. 52-90, tom. xxx. p. 557-587.

[3] This German custom, which may be traced from Tacitus to Gregory of Tours, was at length adopted by the emperors of Constantinople. From a MS. of the tenth century, Montfaucon has delineated the representation of a similar ceremony, which the ignorance of the age had applied to king David. See Monumens de la Monarchie Françoise, tom. i. Discours Préliminaire.

[4] Cæsaries prolixa . . . crinium flagellis per terga dismissis, etc. See the Preface to the third volume of the Historians of France and the Abbé Le Bœuf (Dissertat. tom. iii. p. 47-79). This peculiar fashion of the Merovingians has been remarked by natives and strangers; by Priscus (tom. i. p. 608 [p. 152, ed. Bonn]), by Agathias (tom. ii. p. 49 [l. i. c. 3, p. 19, ed. Bonn]), and by Gregory of Tours (l. iii. 18, vi. 24, viii. 10, tom. ii. p. 196, 278, 316).

[5] See an original picture of the figure, dress, arms, and temper of the

whose name and actions are mentioned in authentic history, held his residence at Dispargum,[1] a village or fortress, whose place may be assigned between Louvain and Brussels.   From the report of his spies the king of the Franks was informed that the defenceless state of the second Belgic must yield, on the slightest attack, to the valour of his subjects.   He boldly penetrated through the thickets and morasses of the Carbonarian forest;[2] occupied Tournay and Cambray, the only cities which existed in the fifth century;   and extended his conquests as far as the river Somme, over a desolate country whose cultivation and populousness are the effects of more recent industry.[3]   While Clodion lay encamped in the plains of Artois,[4] and celebrated with vain and ostentatious security the marriage perhaps of his son, the nuptial feast was interrupted by the unexpected and unwelcome presence of Aëtius, who had passed the Somme at the head of his light cavalry.   The tables, which had been spread under the shelter of a hill along the banks of a pleasant stream, were rudely overturned; the Franks were oppressed before they could recover their arms or their ranks, and their unavailing valour was fatal only to themselves.   The loaded waggons which had followed their march afforded a rich booty; and the virgin-bride with her female attendants submitted to the new lovers who were imposed on them by the chance of war.   This advantage, which had been obtained by the skill and activity of Aëtius, might reflect some disgrace on the military prudence of Clodion; but the king of the Franks soon regained his strength and reputation, and still maintained the possession of his Gallic kingdom from the Rhine to

ancient Franks, in Sidonius Apollinaris (Panegyr. Majorian. 238-254); and such pictures, though coarsely drawn, have a real and intrinsic value. Father Daniel (Hist. de la Milice Françoise, tom. i. p. 2-7) has illustrated the description.

[1] Dubos, Hist. Critique, etc., tom. i. p. 271, 272.   Some geographers have placed Dispargum on the German side of the Rhine.   See a note of the Benedictine Editors to the Historians of France, tom. ii. p. 166.

[2] The Carbonarian wood was that part of the great forest of the Ardennes which lay between the Escaut, or Scheldt, and the Meuse.   Vales. Notit. Gall. p. 126.

[3] Gregor. Turon. l. ii. c. 9, in tom. ii. p. 166, 167; Fredegar. Epitom. c. 9, p. 395; Gesta Reg. Francor. c. 5, in tom. ii. p. 544; Vit. St. Remig. ab Hincmar, in tom. iii. p. 373.

[4] —— Francus quâ Cloio patentes
    Atrebatum terras pervaserat.
                                   Panegyr. Majorian. 212.

The precise spot was a town or village called Vicus *Helena*; and both the name and the place are discovered by modern geographers at Lens.   See Vales. Notit. Gall. p. 246.   Longuerue, Description de la France, tom. ii. p. 88.

the Somme.[1] Under his reign, and most probably from the enterprising spirit of his subjects, the three capitals, Mentz, Trèves, and Cologne, experienced the effects of hostile cruelty and avarice. The distress of Cologne was prolonged by the perpetual dominion of the same barbarians who evacuated the ruins of Trèves; and Trèves, which in the space of forty years had been four times besieged and pillaged, was disposed to lose the memory of her afflictions in the vain amusements of the circus.[2] The death of Clodion, after a reign of twenty years, exposed his kingdom to the discord and ambition of his two sons. Meroveus, the younger,[3] was persuaded to implore the protection of Rome; he was received at the Imperial court as the ally of Valentinian and the adopted son of the patrician Aëtius, and dismissed to his native country with splendid gifts and the strongest assurances of friendship and support. During his absence his elder brother had solicited with equal ardour the formidable aid of Attila; and the king of the Huns embraced an alliance which facilitated the passage of the Rhine, and justified by a specious and honourable pretence the invasion of Gaul.[4]

When Attila declared his resolution of supporting the cause of his allies the Vandals and the Franks, at the same time, and almost in the spirit of romantic chivalry, the savage monarch professed himself the lover and the champion of the princess Honoria. The sister of Valentinian was educated in the palace of Ravenna; and as her marriage might be productive of some

[1] See a vague account of the action in Sidonius, Panegyr. Majorian. 212-230. The French critics, impatient to establish their monarchy in Gaul, have drawn a strong argument from the silence of Sidonius, who dares not insinuate that the vanquished Franks were compelled to repass the Rhine. Dubos, tom. i. p. 322.

[2] Salvian (de Gubernat. Dei, l. vi.) has expressed, in vague and declamatory language, the misfortunes of these three cities, which are distinctly ascertained by the learned Mascou, Hist. of the Ancient Germans, ix. 21.

[3] Priscus in relating the contest does not name the two brothers; the second of whom he had seen at Rome, a beardless youth, with long flowing hair (Historians of France, tom. i. p. 607, 608 [p. 152, ed. Bonn]). The Benedictine Editors are inclined to believe that they were the sons of some unknown king of the Franks who reigned on the banks of the Neckar; but the arguments of M. de Foncemagne (Mém. de l'Académie, tom. viii. p. 464) seem to prove that the succession of Clodion was disputed by his two sons, and that the younger was Meroveus, the father of Childeric.

[What the relation was of Meroveus to Clodion is extremely doubtful. By some writers he is spoken of as a son, by others as an illegitimate son, by a third set as merely belonging to his race. Cf. Sismondi, *Histoire des Français*, i. 117.—O. S.]

[4] Under the Merovingian race the throne was hereditary; but all the sons of the deceased monarch were equally entitled to their share of his treasures and territories. See the Dissertations of M. de Foncemagne, in the sixth and eighth volumes of the Mémoires de l'Académie.

danger to the state, she was raised, by the title of *Augusta*,[1] above the hopes of the most presumptuous subject. But the fair Honoria had no sooner attained the sixteenth year of her age than she detested the importunate greatness which must for ever exclude her from the comforts of honourable love: in the midst of vain and unsatisfactory pomp Honoria sighed, yielded to the impulse of nature, and threw herself into the arms of her chamberlain Eugenius. Her guilt and shame (such is the absurd language of imperious man) were soon betrayed by the appearances of pregnancy: but the disgrace of the royal family was published to the world by the imprudence of the empress Placidia, who dismissed her daughter, after a strict and shameful confinement, to a remote exile at Constantinople. The unhappy princess passed twelve or fourteen years in the irksome society of the sisters of Theodosius and their chosen virgins, to whose *crown* Honoria could no longer aspire, and whose monastic assiduity of prayer, fasting, and vigils she reluctantly imitated. Her impatience of long and hopeless celibacy urged her to embrace a strange and desperate resolution. The name of Attila was familiar and formidable at Constantinople, and his frequent embassies entertained a perpetual intercourse between his camp and the Imperial palace. In the pursuit of love, or rather of revenge, the daughter of Placidia sacrificed every duty and every prejudice, and offered to deliver her person into the arms of a barbarian of whose language she was ignorant, whose figure was scarcely human, and whose religion and manners she abhorred. By the ministry of a faithful eunuch she transmitted to Attila a ring, the pledge of her affection, and earnestly conjured him to claim her as a lawful spouse to whom he had been secretly betrothed. These indecent advances were received, however, with coldness and disdain; and the king of the Huns continued to multiply the number of his wives till his love was awakened by the more forcible passions of ambition and avarice. The invasion of Gaul was preceded and justified by a formal demand of the princess Honoria, with a just and equal share of the Imperial patrimony. His predecessors, the ancient Tanjous, had often addressed in the same hostile and peremptory manner the daughters of China; and the pretensions of Attila were not less offensive to the majesty of Rome. A firm but temperate refusal was communicated to his ambassadors. The right of

---

[1] A medal is still extant which exhibits the pleasing countenance of Honoria, with the title of Augusta; and on the reverse, the improper legend of *Salus Reipublicæ* round the monogram of Christ. See Ducange, Famil. Byzantin. p. 67, 73.

female succession, though it might derive a specious argument from the recent examples of Placidia and Pulcheria, was strenuously denied, and the indissoluble engagements of Honoria were opposed to the claims of her Scythian lover.[1]   On the discovery of her connection with the king of the Huns, the guilty princess had been sent away, as an object of horror, from Constantinople to Italy: her life was spared, but the ceremony of her marriage was performed with some obscure and nominal husband before she was immured in a perpetual prison, to bewail those crimes and misfortunes which Honoria might have escaped had she not been born the daughter of an emperor.[2]

A native of Gaul and a contemporary, the learned and eloquent Sidonius, who was afterwards bishop of Clermont, had made a promise to one of his friends that he would compose a regular history of the war of Attila. If the modesty of Sidonius had not discouraged him from the prosecution of this interesting work,[3] the historian would have related with the simplicity of truth those memorable events to which the poet, in vague and doubtful metaphors, has concisely alluded.[4] The kings and nations of Germany and Scythia, from the Volga perhaps to the Danube, obeyed the warlike summons of Attila. From the royal village in the plains of Hungary his standard moved towards the West, and after a march of seven or eight hundred miles he reached the conflux of the Rhine and the Neckar, where he was joined by the Franks who adhered to his ally, the elder of the sons of Clodion. A troop of light barbarians

---

[1] See Priscus, p. 39, 40 [p. 151, 152, ed. Bonn]. It might be fairly alleged that, if females could succeed to the throne, Valentinian himself, who had married the daughter and heiress of the younger Theodosius, would have asserted her right to the Eastern empire.

[2] The adventures of Honoria are imperfectly related by Jornandes, de Successione Regn. c. 97, and de Reb. Get. c. 42, p. 674; and in the Chronicles of Prosper and Marcellinus; but they cannot be made consistent or probable, unless we separate, by an interval of time and place, her intrigue with Eugenius and her invitation of Attila.

[3] Exegeras mihi, ut promitterem tibi Attilæ bellum stylo me posteris intimaturum . . . cœperam scribere, sed operis arrepti fasce perspecto, tæduit inchoasse. Sidon. Apoll. l. viii. Epist. 15, p. 246.

[4] ——— Subito cum rupta tumultu
Barbaries totas in te transfuderat Arctos,
Gallia. Pugnacem Rugum comitante Gelono,
Gepida trux sequitur; Scyrum Burgundio cogit:
Chunus, Bellonotus, Neurus, Basterna, *Toringus*,
Bructerus, ulvosâ vel quem Nicer abluit undâ
Prorumpit Francus. Cecidit cito secta bipenni
Hercynia in lintres, et Rhenum texuit alno.
Et jam terrificis diffuderat Attila turmis
In campos se, Belga, tuos.
                    Panegyr. Avit. 319, etc.

who roamed in quest of plunder might choose the winter for the convenience of passing the river on the ice, but the innumerable cavalry of the Huns required such plenty of forage and provisions as could be procure only in a milder season; the Hercynian forest supplied materials for a bridge of boats, and the hostile myriads were poured with resistless violence into the Belgic provinces.[1] The consternation of Gaul was universal, and the various fortunes of its cities have been adorned by tradition with martyrdoms and miracles.[2] Troyes was saved by the merits of St. Lupus; St. Servatius was removed from the world that he might not behold the ruin of Tongres; and the prayers of St. Genevieve diverted the march of Attila from the neighbourhood of Paris. But as the greatest part of the Gallic cities were alike destitute of saints and soldiers, they were besieged and stormed by the Huns, who practised, in the example of Metz,[3] their customary maxims of war. They involved in a promiscuous massacre the priests who served at the altar and the infants who, in the hour of danger, had been providently baptised by the bishop; the flourishing city was delivered to the flames, and a solitary chapel of St. Stephen marked the place where it formerly stood. From the Rhine and the Moselle, Attila advanced into the heart of Gaul, crossed the Seine at Auxerre, and after a long and laborious march fixed his camp under the walls of Orleans. He was desirous of

[1] The most authentic and circumstantial account of this war is contained in Jornandes (de Reb. Geticis, c. 36-41, p. 662-672), who has sometimes abridged, and sometimes transcribed, the larger history of Cassiodorus. Jornandes, a quotation which it would be superfluous to repeat, may be corrected and illustrated by Gregory of Tours, l. ii. c. 5, 6, 7, and the Chronicles of Idatius, Isidore, and the two Prospers. All the ancient testimonies are collected and inserted in the Historians of France; but the reader should be cautioned against a supposed extract from the Chronicle of Idatius (among the fragments of Fredegarius, tom. ii. p. 462), which often contradicts the genuine text of the Gallician bishop.

[2] The *ancient* legendaries deserve some regard, as they are obliged to connect their fables with the real history of their own times. See the Lives of St. Lupus, St. Anianus, the bishops of Metz, Ste. Genevieve, etc., in the Historians of France, tom. i. p. 644, 645, 649, tom. iii. p. 369.

[3] The scepticism of the Count de Buat (Hist. des Peuples, tom. vii. p. 539 540) cannot be reconciled with any principles of reason or criticism. Is not Gregory of Tours precise and positive in his account of the destruction of Metz? At the distance of no more than an hundred years could he be ignorant, could the people be ignorant, of the fate of a city, the actual residence of his sovereigns, the kings of Austrasia? The learned Count, who seems to have undertaken the apology of Attila and the barbarians, appeals to the false Idatius, *parcens* civitatibus Germaniæ et Galliæ, and forgets that the true Idatius had explicitly affirmed, plurimæ civitates *effractæ*, among which he enumerates Metz.

securing his conquests by the possession of an advantageous
post which commanded the passage of the Loire; and he
depended on the secret invitation of Sangiban, king of the
Alani, who had promised to betray the city and to revolt from
the service of the empire.   But this treacherous conspiracy was
detected and disappointed: Orleans had been strengthened
with recent fortifications, and the assaults of the Huns were
vigorously repelled by the faithful valour of the soldiers or
citizens who defended the place.   The pastoral diligence of
Anianus, a bishop of primitive sanctity and consummate
prudence, exhausted every art of religious policy to support
their courage till the arrival of the expected succours.   After
an obstinate siege the walls were shaken by the battering rams;
the Huns had already occupied the suburbs, and the people
who were incapable of bearing arms lay prostrate in prayer.
Anianus, who anxiously counted the days and hours, despatched
a trusty messenger to observe from the rampart the face of the
distant country.   He returned twice without any intelligence
that could inspire hope or comfort; but in his third report he
mentioned a small cloud which he had faintly descried at the
extremity of the horizon.   " It is the aid of God! " exclaimed
the bishop in a tone of pious confidence; and the whole multitude
repeated after him " It is the aid of God."   The remote object,
on which every eye was fixed, became each moment larger and
more distinct: the Roman and Gothic banners were gradually
perceived; and a favourable wind, blowing aside the dust, discovered, in deep array, the impatient squadrons of Aëtius and
Theodoric, who pressed forwards to the relief of Orleans.

The facility with which Attila had penetrated into the heart
of Gaul may be ascribed to his insidious policy as well as to
the terror of his arms.   His public declarations were skilfully
mitigated by his private assurances; he alternately soothed and
threatened the Romans and the Goths; and the courts of
Ravenna and Toulouse, mutually suspicious of each other's
intentions, beheld with supine indifference the approach of their
common enemy.   Aëtius was the sole guardian of the public
safety; but his wisest measures were embarrassed by a faction
which, since the death of Placidia, infested the Imperial palace:
the youth of Italy trembled at the sound of the trumpet; and
the barbarians, who from fear or affection were inclined to the
cause of Attila, awaited with doubtful and venal faith the event
of the war.   The patrician passed the Alps at the head of some
troops whose strength and numbers scarcely deserved the name

of an army.[1] But on his arrival at Arles or Lyons he was
confounded by the intelligence that the Visigoths, refusing to
embrace the defence of Gaul, had determined to expect within
their own territories the formidable invader whom they professed to despise. The senator Avitus, who after the honourable
exercise of the Prætorian præfecture had retired to his estate
in Auvergne, was persuaded to accept the important embassy,
which he executed with ability and success. He represented
to Theodoric that an ambitious conqueror who aspired to the
dominion of the earth could be resisted only by the firm and
unanimous alliance of the powers whom he laboured to oppress.
The lively eloquence of Avitus inflamed the Gothic warriors
by the description of the injuries which their ancestors had
suffered from the Huns, whose implacable fury still pursued
them from the Danube to the foot of the Pyrenees. He strenuously urged that it was the duty of every Christian to save from
sacrilegious violation the churches of God and the relics of the
saints; that it was the interest of every barbarian who had
acquired a settlement in Gaul to defend the fields and vineyards,
which were cultivated for his use, against the desolation of the
Scythian shepherds. Theodoric yielded to the evidence of
truth, adopted the measure at once the most prudent and the
most honourable, and declared that as the faithful ally of
Aëtius and the Romans he was ready to expose his life and
kingdom for the common safety of Gaul.[2] The Visigoths, who
at that time were in the mature vigour of their fame and power,
obeyed with alacrity the signal of war, prepared their arms and
horses, and assembled under the standard of their aged king,
who was resolved, with his two eldest sons, Torismond and
Theodoric, to command in person his numerous and valiant
people. The example of the Goths determined several tribes
or nations that seemed to fluctuate between the Huns and the
Romans. The indefatigable diligence of the patrician gradually
collected the troops of Gaul and Germany, who had formerly

---

[1] ——— Vix liquerat Alpes
Aëtius, tenue, et rarum sine milite ducens
Robur, in auxiliis Geticum male credulus agmen
Incassum propriis præsumens adfore castris.
                              Panegyr. Avit. 328, etc.

[2] The policy of Attila, of Aëtius, and of the Visigoths, is imperfectly described in the Panegyric of Avitus and the thirty-sixth chapter of Jornandes.
The poet and the historian were both biassed by personal or national prejudices. The former exalts the merit and importance of Avitus; orbis,
Avite, salus, etc.! The latter is anxious to show the Goths in the most
favourable light.   Yet their agreement, when they are fairly interpreted,
is a proof of their veracity.

acknowledged themselves the subjects or soldiers of the republic, but who now claimed the rewards of voluntary service and the rank of independent allies; the Læti, the Armoricans, the Breones, the Saxons, the Burgundians, the Sarmatians or Alani, the Ripuarians, and the Franks who followed Meroveus as their lawful prince. Such was the various army which, under the conduct of Aëtius and Theodoric, advanced by rapid marches to relieve Orleans, and to give battle to the innumerable host of Attila.[1]

On their approach the king of the Huns immediately raised the siege, and sounded a retreat to recall the foremost of his troops from the pillage of a city which they had already entered.[2] The valour of Attila was always guided by his prudence; and as he foresaw the fatal consequences of a defeat in the heart of Gaul, he repassed the Seine, and expected the enemy in the plains of Châlons, whose smooth and level surface was adapted to the operations of his Scythian cavalry. But in this tumultuary retreat the vanguard of the Romans and their allies continually pressed, and sometimes engaged, the troops whom Attila had posted in the rear; the hostile columns, in the darkness of the night and the perplexity of the roads, might encounter each other without design; and the bloody conflict of the Franks and Gepidæ, in which fifteen thousand[3] barbarians were slain, was a prelude to a more general and decisive action. The Catalaunian fields[4] spread themselves round Châlons, and extend, according to the vague measurement of Jornandes, to the length of one hundred and fifty, and the breadth of one hundred miles, over the whole province, which is entitled to

---

[1] The review of the army of Aëtius is made by Jornandes, c. 36, p. 664, edit. Grot. tom. ii. p. 23, of the Historians of France, with the notes of the Benedictine editor. The *Læti* were a promiscuous race of barbarians, born or naturalised in Gaul; and the Riparii, or *Ripuarii*, derived their name from their posts on the three rivers, the Rhine, the Meuse, and the Moselle; the *Armoricans* possessed the independent cities between the Seine and the Loire. A colony of *Saxons* had been planted in the diocese of Bayeux; the *Burgundians* were settled in Savoy; and the *Breones* were a warlike tribe of Rhætians, to the east of the lake of Constance.

[2] Aurelianensis urbis obsidio, oppugnatio, irruptio, nec direptio. Sidon. Apollin. l. viii. Epist. 15, p. 246. The preservation of Orleans might easily be turned into a miracle, obtained and foretold by the holy bishop.

[3] The common editions read XCM; but there is some authority of manuscripts (and almost any authority is sufficient) for the more reasonable number of XVM.

[4] Châlons, or Duro-Catalaunum, afterwards *Catalauni*, had formerly made a part of the territory of Rheims, from whence it is distant only twenty-seven miles. See Vales. Notit. Gall. p. 136; D'Anville, Notice de l'Ancienne Gaule, p. 212, 279.

the appellation of a *champaign* country.[1] This spacious plain
was distinguished, however, by some inequalities of ground;
and the importance of an height which commanded the camp
of Attila was understood and disputed by the two generals.
The young and valiant Torismond first occupied the summit;
the Goths rushed with irresistible weight on the Huns, who
laboured to ascend from the opposite side: and the possession
of this advantageous post inspired both the troops and their
leaders with a fair assurance of victory. The anxiety of Attila
prompted him to consult his priests and haruspices. It was
reported that, after scrutinising the entrails of victims and
scraping their bones, they revealed, in mysterious language, his
own defeat, with the death of his principal adversary; and that
the barbarian, by accepting the equivalent, expressed his involuntary esteem for the superior merit of Aëtius. But the
unusual despondency which seemed to prevail among the Huns
engaged Attila to use the expedient, so familiar to the generals
of antiquity, of animating his troops by a military oration;
and his language was that of a king who had often fought and
conquered at their head.[2] He pressed them to consider their
past glory, their actual danger, and their future hopes. The
same fortune which opened the deserts and morasses of Scythia
to their unarmed valour, which had laid so many warlike nations
prostrate at their feet, had reserved the *joys* of this memorable
field for the consummation of their victories. The cautious steps
of their enemies, their strict alliance, and their advantageous
posts, he artfully represented as the effects, not of prudence,
but of fear. The Visigoths alone were the strength and nerves
of the opposite army, and the Huns might securely trample on
the degenerate Romans, whose close and compact order betrayed
their apprehensions, and who were equally incapable of supporting the dangers or the fatigues of a day of battle. The doctrine
of predestination, so favourable to martial virtue, was carefully
inculcated by the king of the Huns; who assured his subjects
that the warriors, protected by Heaven, were safe and in-
vulnerable amidst the darts of the enemy; but that the unerring
Fates would strike their victims in the bosom of inglorious peace.

[1] The name of Campania, or Champagne, is frequently mentioned by
Gregory of Tours; and that great province, of which Rheims was the
capital, obeyed the command of a duke. Vales. Notit. p. 120-123.
[2] I am sensible that these military orations are usually composed by the
historian; yet the old Ostrogoths, who had served under Attila, might
repeat his discourse to Cassiodorus; the ideas, and even the expressions,
have an original Scythian cast; and I doubt whether an Italian of the sixth
century would have thought of the hujus certaminis *gaudia*.

" I myself," continued Attila, " will throw the first javelin, and the wretch who refuses to imitate the example of his sovereign is devoted to inevitable death." The spirit of the barbarians was rekindled by the presence, the voice, and the example of their intrepid leader; and Attila, yielding to their impatience, immediately formed his order of battle. At the head of his brave and faithful Huns, he occupied in person the centre of the line. The nations subject to his empire, the Rugians, the Heruli, the Thuringians, the Franks, the Burgundians, were extended, on either hand, over the ample space of the Catalaunian fields; the right wing was commanded by Ardaric, king of the Gepidæ; and the three valiant brothers who reigned over the Ostrogoths were posted on the left to oppose the kindred tribes of the Visigoths. The disposition of the allies was regulated by a different principle. Sangiban, the faithless king of the Alani, was placed in the centre: where his motions might be strictly watched, and his treachery might be instantly punished. Aëtius assumed the command of the left, and Theodoric of the right wing; while Torismond still continued to occupy the heights which appear to have stretched on the flank, and perhaps the rear, of the Scythian army. The nations from the Volga to the Atlantic were assembled on the plain of Châlons; but many of these nations had been divided by faction, or conquest, or emigration; and the appearance of similar arms and ensigns, which threatened each other, presented the image of a civil war.

The discipline and tactics of the Greeks and Romans form an interesting part of their national manners. The attentive study of the military operations of Xenophon, or Cæsar, or Frederic, when they are described by the same genius which conceived and executed them, may tend to improve (if such improvement can be wished) the art of destroying the human species. But the battle of Châlons can only excite our curiosity by the magnitude of the object; since it was decided by the blind impetuosity of barbarians, and has been related by partial writers, whose civil or ecclesiastical profession secluded them from the knowledge of military affairs. Cassiodorus, however, had familiarly conversed with many Gothic warriors who served in that memorable engagement; " a conflict," as they informed him, " fierce, various, obstinate, and bloody; such as could not be paralleled either in the present or in past ages." The number of the slain amounted to one hundred and sixty-two thousand, or, according to another account, three hundred thousand persons; [1] and these incredible exaggerations suppose a real and effective loss, sufficient to justify the historian's remark that whole generations may be swept away by the madness of kings in the space of a single hour. After the mutual and repeated discharge of missile weapons, in which the archers of Scythia might signalise their superior dexterity, the cavalry and infantry of the two armies were furiously mingled in closer combat. The Huns, who fought under the eyes of their king, pierced through the feeble and doubtful centre of the allies, separated their wings from each other, and wheeling, with a rapid effort, to the left, directed their whole force against the Visigoths. As Theodoric rode along the ranks to animate his troops, he received a mortal stroke from the javelin of Andages, a noble Ostrogoth, and immediately fell from his horse. The wounded king was oppressed in the general disorder and trampled under the feet of his own cavalry; and this important death served to explain the ambiguous prophecy of the haruspices. Attila already exulted in the confidence of victory, when the valiant Torismond descended from the hills, and verified the remainder of the prediction. The Visigoths, who had been thrown into confusion by the flight, or defection, of the Alani, gradually restored their order of battle; and the Huns were undoubtedly vanquished, since Attila was compelled to retreat. He had exposed his person with the rashness of a private soldier; but the intrepid troops of the centre had pushed forwards beyond the rest of the line; their attack was faintly supported; their flanks were unguarded; and the conquerors of Scythia and Germany were saved by the approach of the night from a total defeat. They retired within the circle of waggons that fortified their camp; and the dismounted squadrons prepared themselves for a defence to which neither their arms nor their temper were adapted. The event was doubtful: but Attila had secured a last and honourable resource. The saddles and rich furniture of the cavalry were collected by his order into a funeral pile; and the magnanimous barbarian had resolved, if his entrenchments should be forced, to rush

---

[1] The expressions of Jornandes, or rather of Cassiodorus, are extremely strong. Bellum atrox, multiplex, immane, pertinax, cui simile nulle usquam narrat antiquitas: ubi talia gesta referuntur, ut nihil esset quod in vitâ suâ conspicere potuisset egregius, qui hujus miraculi privaretur aspectû [c. 40, p. 668]. Dubos (Hist. Critique, tom. i. p. 392, 393) attempts to reconcile the 162,000 of Jornandes with the 300,000 of Idatius and Isidore, by supposing that the larger number included the total destruction of the war, the effects of disease, the slaughter of the unarmed people, etc.

headlong into the flames, and to deprive his enemies of the glory which they might have acquired by the death or captivity of Attila.[1]

But his enemies had passed the night in equal disorder and anxiety. The inconsiderate courage of Torismond was tempted to urge the pursuit, till he unexpectedly found himself, with a few followers, in the midst of the Scythian waggons. In the confusion of a nocturnal combat he was thrown from his horse; and the Gothic prince must have perished like his father, if his youthful strength and the intrepid zeal of his companions had not rescued him from this dangerous situation. In the same manner, but on the left of the line, Aëtius himself, separated from his allies, ignorant of their victory, and anxious for their fate, encountered and escaped the hostile troops that were scattered over the plains of Châlons; and at length reached the camp of the Goths, which he could only fortify with a slight rampart of shields till the dawn of day. The Imperial general was soon satisfied of the defeat of Attila, who still remained inactive within his entrenchments; and when he contemplated the bloody scene, he observed, with secret satisfaction, that the loss had principally fallen on the barbarians. The body of Theodoric, pierced with honourable wounds, was discovered under a heap of the slain: his subjects bewailed the death of their king and father; but their tears were mingled with songs and acclamations, and his funeral rites were performed in the face of a vanquished enemy. The Goths, clashing their arms, elevated on a buckler his eldest son Torismond, to whom they justly ascribed the glory of their success; and the new king accepted the obligation of revenge as a sacred portion of his paternal inheritance. Yet the Goths themselves were astonished by the fierce and undaunted aspect of their formidable antagonist; and their historian has compared Attila to a lion encompassed in his den and threatening his hunters with redoubled fury. The kings and nations who might have deserted his standard in the hour of distress were made sensible that the displeasure of their monarch was the most imminent and inevitable danger. All his instruments of martial music incessantly sounded a loud and animating strain of defiance; and the foremost troops, who advanced to the assault, were checked or destroyed by showers

---

[1] The Count de Buat (Hist. des Peuples, etc., tom. vii. p. 554-573), still depending on the *false*, and again rejecting the *true*, Idatius, has divided the defeat of Attila into two great battles; the former near Orleans, the latter in Champagne: in the one, Theodoric was slain; in the other, he was revenged.

of arrows from every side of the entrenchments. It was determined in a general council of war to besiege the king of the Huns in his camp, to intercept his provisions, and to reduce him to the alternative of a disgraceful treaty or an unequal combat. But the impatience of the barbarians soon disdained these cautious and dilatory measures: and the mature policy of Aëtius was apprehensive that, after the extirpation of the Huns, the republic would be oppressed by the pride and power of the Gothic nation. The patrician exerted the superior ascendant of authority and reason to calm the passions which the son of Theodoric considered as a duty; represented, with seeming affection and real truth, the dangers of absence and delay; and persuaded Torismond to disappoint, by his speedy return, the ambitious designs of his brothers, who might occupy the throne and treasures of Toulouse.[1] After the departure of the Goths, and the separation of the allied army, Attila was surprised at the vast silence that reigned over the plains of Châlons: the suspicion of some hostile stratagem detained him several days within the circle of his waggons, and his retreat beyond the Rhine confessed the last victory which was achieved in the name of the Western empire. Meroveus and his Franks, observing a prudent distance, and magnifying the opinion of their strength by the numerous fires which they kindled every night, continued to follow the rear of the Huns till they reached the confines of Thuringia. The Thuringians served in the army of Attila: they traversed, both in their march and in their return, the territories of the Franks; and it was perhaps in this war that they exercised the cruelties which, about fourscore years afterwards, were revenged by the son of Clovis. They massacred their hostages, as well as their captives: two hundred young maidens were tortured with exquisite and unrelenting rage; their bodies were torn asunder by wild horses, or their bones were crushed under the weight of rolling waggons; and their unburied limbs were abandoned on the public roads as a prey to dogs and vultures. Such were those savage ancestors whose imaginary virtues have sometimes excited the praise and envy of civilised ages![2]

---

[1] Jornandes de Rebus Geticis, c. 41, p. 671. The policy of Aëtius and the behaviour of Torismond are extremely natural; and the patrician, according to Gregory of Tours (l. ii. c. 7, p. 163), dismissed the prince of the Franks by suggesting to him a similar apprehension. The false Idatius ridiculously pretends that Aëtius paid a clandestine nocturnal visit to the kings of the Huns and of the Visigoths; from each of whom he obtained a bribe of ten thousand pieces of gold as the price of an undisturbed retreat.

[2] These cruelties, which are passionately deplored by Theodoric, the son

Neither the spirit, nor the forces, nor the reputation of Attila were impaired by the failure of the Gallic expedition. In the ensuing spring he repeated his demand of the princess Honoria and her patrimonial treasures. The demand was again rejected or eluded; and the indignant lover immediately took the field, passed the Alps, invaded Italy, and besieged Aquileia with an innumerable host of barbarians. Those barbarians were unskilled in the methods of conducting a regular siege, which, even among the ancients, required some knowledge, or at least some practice, of the mechanic arts. But the labour of many thousand provincials and captives, whose lives were sacrificed without pity, might execute the most painful and dangerous work. The skill of the Roman artists might be corrupted to the destruction of their country. The walls of Aquileia were assaulted by a formidable train of battering rams, movable turrets, and engines that threw stones, darts, and fire; [1] and the monarch of the Huns employed the forcible impulse of hope, fear, emulation, and interest, to subvert the only barrier which delayed the conquest of Italy. Aquileia was at that period one of the richest, the most populous, and the strongest of the maritime cities of the Hadriatic coast. The Gothic auxiliaries, who appear to have served under their native princes, Alaric and Antala, communicated their intrepid spirit; and the citizens still remembered the glorious and successful resistance which their ancestors had opposed to a fierce, inexorable barbarian, who disgraced the majesty of the Roman purple. Three months were consumed without effect in the siege of Aquileia; till the want of provisions and the clamours of his army compelled Attila to relinquish the enterprise, and reluctantly to issue his orders that the troops should strike their tents the next morning, and begin their retreat. But as he rode round the walls, pensive, angry, and disappointed, he observed a stork preparing to leave

of Clovis (Gregory of Tours, l. iii. c. 10, p. 190), suit the time and circumstances of the invasion of Attila. His residence in Thuringia was long attested by popular tradition; and he is supposed to have assembled a *couroultai*, or diet, in the territory of Eisenach. See Mascou, ix. 30, who settles with nice accuracy the extent of ancient Thuringia, and derives its name from the Gothic tribe of the Thervingi.

[1] Machinis constructis, omnibusque tormentorum generibus adhibitis. Jornandes, c. 42, p. 673. In the thirteenth century the Moguls battered the cities of China with large engines constructed by the Mahometans or Christians in their service, which threw stones from 150 to 300 pounds weight. In the defence of their country the Chinese used gunpowder, and even bombs, above an hundred years before they were known in Europe; yet even those celestial, or infernal, arms were insufficient to protect a pusillanimous nation. See Gaubil, Hist. des Mongous, p. 70, 71, 155, 157, etc.

her nest in one of the towers, and to fly with her infant family towards the country. He seized, with the ready penetration of a statesman, this trifling incident which chance had offered to superstition; and exclaimed, in a loud and cheerful tone, that such a domestic bird, so constantly attached to human society, would never have abandoned her ancient seats unless those towers had been devoted to impending ruin and solitude.[1] The favourable omen inspired an assurance of victory; the siege was renewed, and prosecuted with fresh vigour; a large breach was made in the part of the wall from whence the stork had taken her flight; the Huns mounted to the assault with irresistible fury; and the succeeding generation could scarcely discover the ruins of Aquileia.[2] After this dreadful chastisement, Attila pursued his march; and as he passed, the cities of Altinum, Concordia, and Padua were reduced into heaps of stones and ashes. The inland towns, Vicenza, Verona, and Bergamo, were exposed to the rapacious cruelty of the Huns. Milan and Pavia submitted, without resistance, to the loss of their wealth; and applauded the unusual clemency which preserved from the flames the public as well as private buildings, and spared the lives of the captive multitude. The popular traditions of Comum, Turin, or Modena may justly be suspected; yet they concur with more authentic evidence to prove that Attila spread his ravages over the rich plains of modern Lombardy, which are divided by the Po, and bounded by the Alps and Apennine.[3] When he took possession of the royal palace of Milan, he was surprised and offended at the sight of a picture which represented the Cæsars seated on their throne, and the princes of Scythia prostrate at their feet. The revenge which Attila inflicted on this monument of Roman vanity was harmless and ingenious. He commanded a painter to reverse the figures and the attitudes; and the emperors were delineated on the same canvas approach-

---

[1] The same story is told by Jornandes and by Procopius (de Bell. Vandal. l. i. c. 4, p. 187, 188 [tom. i. p. 330, ed. Bonn]): nor is it easy to decide which is the original. But the Greek historian is guilty of an inexcusable mistake in placing the siege of Aquileia *after* the death of Aëtius.

[2] Jornandes, about an hundred years afterwards, affirms that Aquileia was so completely ruined, ita ut vix ejus vestigia, ut appareant, reliquerint. See Jornandes de Reb. Geticis, c. 42, p. 673. Paul. Diacon. l. ii. c. 14, p. 785 [Grot. Hist. Goth.]. Liutprand, Hist. l. iii. c. 2. The name of Aquileia was sometimes applied to Forum Julii (Cividad del Friuli), the more recent capital of the Venetian province.

[3] In describing this war of Attila, so famous but so imperfectly known, I have taken for my guides two learned Italians who considered the subject with some peculiar advantages: Sigonius, de Imperio Occidentali, l. xiii. in his Works. tom. i. p. 495-502; and Muratori, Annali d'Italia, tom. iv. p. 229-236, 8vo edition.

ing in a suppliant posture to empty their bags of tributary gold before the throne of the Scythian monarch.[1] The spectators must have confessed the truth and propriety of the alteration; and were perhaps tempted to apply, on this singular occasion, the well-known fable of the dispute between the lion and the man.[2]

It is a saying worthy of the ferocious pride of Attila, that the grass never grew on the spot where his horse had trod. Yet the savage destroyer undesignedly laid the foundations of a republic which revived, in the feudal state of Europe, the art and spirit of commercial industry. The celebrated name of Venice, or Venetia,[3] was formerly diffused over a large and fertile province of Italy, from the confines of Pannonia to the river Addua, and from the Po to the Rhætian and Julian Alps. Before the irruption of the barbarians, fifty Venetian cities flourished in peace and prosperity: Aquileia was placed in the most conspicuous station: but the ancient dignity of Padua was supported by agriculture and manufactures; and the property of five hundred citizens, who were entitled to the equestrian rank, must have amounted, at the strictest computation, to one million seven hundred thousand pounds. Many families of Aquileia, Padua, and the adjacent towns, who fled from the sword of the Huns, found a safe, though obscure, refuge in the neighbouring islands.[4] At the extremity of the Gulf, where the Hadriatic feebly imitates the tides of the ocean, near an hundred small islands are separated by shallow water from the continent,

---

[1] This anecdote may be found under two different articles (μεδιόλανον and κόρυκος) of the miscellaneous compilation of Suidas.

[2] Leo respondit, humanâ hoc pictum manû:
    Videres hominem dejectum, si pingere
    Leones scirent.

                    Appendix ad Phædrum, Fab. xxv.

The lion in Phædrus very foolishly appeals from pictures to the amphitheatre; and I am glad to observe that the native taste of La Fontaine (l. iii. fable x.) has omitted this most lame and impotent conclusion.

[3] Paul the Deacon (de Gestis Langobard. l. ii. c. 14 [seqq.], p. 784) describes the provinces of Italy about the end of the eighth century. *Venetia* non solum in paucis insulis quas nunc Venetias dicimus, constat; sed ejus terminus a Pannoniæ finibus usque Adduam fluvium protelatur. The history of that province till the age of Charlemagne forms the first and most interesting part of the Verona Illustrata (p. 1-388), in which the Marquis Scipio Maffei has shown himself equally capable of enlarged views and minute disquisitions.

[4] This emigration is not attested by any contemporary evidence; but the fact is proved by the event, and the circumstances might be preserved by tradition. The citizens of Aquileia retired to the Isle of Gradus, those of Padua to Rivus Altus, or Rialto, where the city of Venice was afterwards built, etc.

and protected from the waves by several long slips of land, which admit the entrance of vessels through some secret and narrow channels.[1] Till the middle of the fifth century these remote and sequestered spots remained without cultivation, with few inhabitants, and almost without a name. But the manners of the Venetian fugitives, their arts and their government, were gradually formed by their new situation; and one of the epistles of Cassiodorus,[2] which describes their condition about seventy years afterwards, may be considered as the primitive monument of the republic.[3] The minister of Theodoric compares them, in his quaint declamatory style, to waterfowl, who had fixed their nests on the bosom of the waves; and though he allows that the Venetian provinces had formerly contained many noble families, he insinuates that they were now reduced by misfortune to the same level of humble poverty. Fish was the common, and almost the universal, food of every rank: their only treasure consisted in the plenty of salt which they extracted from the sea: and the exchange of that commodity, so essential to human life, was substituted in the neighbouring markets to the currency of gold and silver. A

---

[1] The topography and antiquities of the Venetian islands, from Gradus to Clodia, or Chioggia, are accurately stated in the Dissertatio Chorographica de Italiâ Medii Ævi, p. 151-155.

[2] Cassiodor. Variar. l. xii. Epist. 24. Maffei (Verona Illustrata, part i. p. 240-254) has translated and explained this curious letter, in the spirit of a learned antiquarian and a faithful subject, who considered Venice as the only legitimate offspring of the Roman republic. He fixes the date of the epistle, and consequently the præfecture, of Cassiodorus, A.D. 523; and the Marquis's authority has the more weight as he had prepared an edition of his works and actually published a dissertation on the true orthography of his name. See Osservazioni Letterarie, tom. ii. p. 290-339.

[3] [Count Figliasi was the first to prove, in his *Memoirs of the Veneti*, that, from the most remote period, this nation, which occupied the country which has since been called the Venetian States, likewise inhabited the islands scattered upon the coast, and that from thence arose the names *Venetia prima* and *secunda*, of which the first applied to the mainland and the second to the islands and lagoons. From the time of the Pelasgi and of the Etrurians, the first Veneti inhabiting a fertile and pleasant country devoted themselves to agriculture; the second, placed in the midst of canals at the mouth of several rivers, conveniently situated with regard to the islands of Greece, as well as the fertile plains of Italy, applied themselves to navigation and commerce. Both submitted to the Romans a short time before the second Punic war; yet it was not till after the victory of Marius over the Cimbri that their country was reduced to a Roman province. Under the emperors, Venetia Prima obtained more than once, by its calamities, a place in history. But the maritime province was occupied with fisheries, salt works, and commerce. The Romans have considered the inhabitants of this part as beneath the dignity of history, and have left them in obscurity. They dwelt there until their islands afforded a retreat to their ruined and fugitive compatriots. Cf. Sismondi, *Hist. des Repub. Italiennes*, vol. i. p. 313.—O. S.]

people whose habitations might be doubtfully assigned to the
earth or water soon became alike familiar with the two elements;
and the demands of avarice succeeded to those of necessity.
The islanders, who, from Grado to Chiozza, were intimately
connected with each other, penetrated into the heart of Italy,
by the secure, though laborious, navigation of the rivers and
inland canals. Their vessels, which were continually increasing
in size and number, visited all the harbours of the Gulf; and the
marriage which Venice annually celebrates with the Hadriatic
was contracted in her early infancy. The epistle of Cassiodorus,
the Prætorian præfect, is addressed to the maritime tribunes;
and he exhorts them, in a mild tone of authority, to animate
the zeal of their countrymen for the public service, which
required their assistance to transport the magazines of wine
and oil from the province of Istria to the royal city of Ravenna.
The ambiguous office of these magistrates is explained by the
tradition, that, in the twelve principal islands, twelve tribunes,
or judges, were created by an annual and popular election. The
existence of the Venetian republic under the Gothic kingdom
of Italy is attested by the same authentic record which annihilates their lofty claim of original and perpetual independence.[1]

The Italians, who had long since renounced the exercise of
arms, were surprised, after forty years' peace, by the approach
of a formidable barbarian, whom they abhorred as the enemy
of their religion as well as of their republic. Amidst the general
consternation, Aëtius alone was incapable of fear; but it was
impossible that he should achieve alone and unassisted any
military exploits worthy of his former renown. The barbarians
who had defended Gaul refused to march to the relief of Italy;
and the succours promised by the Eastern emperor were distant
and doubtful. Since Aëtius, at the head of his domestic troops,
still maintained the field, and harassed or retarded the march of
Attila, he never showed himself more truly great than at the
time when his conduct was blamed by an ignorant and ungrateful
people.[2] If the mind of Valentinian had been susceptible of

---

[1] See, in the second volume of Amelot de la Houssaie, Histoire du
Gouvernement de Venise, a translation of the famous *Squittenio*. This
book, which has been exalted far above its merits, is stained in every line
with the disingenuous malevolence of party: but the principal evidence,
genuine and apocryphal, is brought together, and the reader will easily
choose the fair medium.

[2] Sirmond (Not. ad Sidon. Apollin. p. 19) has published a curious passage
from the Chronicle of Prosper. Attila, redintegratis viribus, quas in Gallia
amiserat, Italiam ingredi per Pannonias intendit; nihil duce nostro Aëtio
secundum prioris belli opera prospiciente, etc. He reproaches Aëtius with

any generous sentiments, he would have chosen such a general for his example and his guide. But the timid grandson of Theodosius, instead of sharing the dangers, escaped from the sound, of war; and his hasty retreat from Ravenna to Rome, from an impregnable fortress to an open capital, betrayed his secret intention of abandoning Italy as soon as the danger should approach his Imperial person. This shameful abdication was suspended, however, by the spirit of doubt and delay which commonly adheres to pusillanimous counsels, and sometimes corrects their pernicious tendency. The Western emperor, with the senate and people of Rome, embraced the more salutary resolution of deprecating, by a solemn and suppliant embassy, the wrath of Attila. This important commission was accepted by Avienus, who, from his birth and riches, his consular dignity, the numerous train of his clients, and his personal abilities, held the first rank in the Roman senate. The specious and artful character of Avienus [1] was admirably qualified to conduct a negotiation either of public or private interest: his colleague Trigetius had exercised the Prætorian præfecture of Italy; and Leo, bishop of Rome, consented to expose his life for the safety of his flock. The genius of Leo [2] was exercised and displayed in the public misfortunes; and he has deserved the appellation of *Great* by the successful zeal with which he laboured to establish his opinions and his authority, under the venerable names of orthodox faith and ecclesiastical discipline. The Roman ambassadors were introduced to the tent of Attila, as he lay encamped at the place where the slow-winding Mincius is lost in the foaming waves of the lake Benacus,[3] and trampled, with his Scythian cavalry, the farms of Catullus and Virgil.[4] The

neglecting to guard the Alps and with a design to abandon Italy; but this rash censure may at least be counterbalanced by the favourable testimonies of Idatius and Isidore.

[1] See the original portraits of Avienus and his rival Basilius delineated and contrasted in the epistles (i. 9, p. 22) of Sidonius. He had studied the characters of the two chiefs of the senate; but he attached himself to Basilius as the more solid and disinterested friend.

[2] The character and principles of Leo may be traced in one hundred and forty-one original epistles, which illustrate the ecclesiastical history of his long and busy pontificate, from A.D. 440 to 461. See Dupin, Bibliothèque Ecclésiastique, tom. iii. part i. p. 120-165.

[3] ——— tardis ingens ubi flexibus errat
Mincius, et tenerâ prætexit arundine ripas

Anne lacus tantos, te Lari maxime, teque
Fluctibus, et fremitu assurgens *Benace* marino.

[4] The Marquis Maffei (Verona Illustrata, part i. p. 95, 129, 221, part ii. p. 2, 6) has illustrated with taste and learning this interesting topography. He places the interview of Attila and St. Leo near Ariolica, or Ardelica,

barbarian monarch listened with favourable, and even respectful, attention; and the deliverance of Italy was purchased by the immense ransom or dowry of the princess Honoria. The state of his army might facilitate the treaty and hasten his retreat. Their martial spirit was relaxed by the wealth and indolence of a warm climate. The shepherds of the North, whose ordinary food consisted of milk and raw flesh, indulged themselves too freely in the use of bread, of wine, and of meat prepared and seasoned by the arts of cookery; and the progress of disease revenged in some measure the injuries of the Italians.[1] When Attila declared his resolution of carrying his victorious arms to the gates of Rome, he was admonished by his friends, as well as by his enemies, that had Alaric not long survived the conquest of the eternal city. His mind, superior to real danger, was assaulted by imaginary terrors; nor could he escape the influence of superstition, which had so often been subservient to his designs.[2] The pressing eloquence of Leo, his majestic aspect and sacerdotal robes, excited the veneration of Attila for the spiritual father of the Christians. The apparition of the two apostles of St. Peter and St. Paul, who menaced the barbarian with instant death if he rejected the prayer of their successor, is one of the noblest legends of ecclesiastical tradition. The safety of Rome might deserve the interposition of celestial beings; and some indulgence is due to a fable which has been represented by the pencil of Raphael and the chisel of Algardi.[3]

Before the king of the Huns evacuated Italy, he threatened to return more dreadful, and more implacable, if his bride, the princess Honoria, were not delivered to his ambassadors within the term stipulated by the treaty. Yet, in the meanwhile,

now Peschiera, at the conflux of the lake and river; ascertains the villa of Catullus, in the delightful peninsula of Sirmio, and discovers the Andes of Virgil in the village of Bandes, precisely situate, quâ se subducere colles incipiunt, where the Veronese hills imperceptibly slope down into the plain of Mantua.

[1] Si statim infesto agmine urbem petiissent, grande discrimen esset: sed in Venetiâ quo fere tractu Italia mollissima est, ipsâ soli cœlique clementiâ robur elanguit. Ad hoc panis usû carnisque coctæ, et dulcedine vini mitigatos, etc. This passage of Florus (iii. 3) is still more applicable to the Huns than to the Cimbri, and it may serve as a commentary on the *celestial* plague with which Idatius and Isidore have afflicted the troops of Attila.

[2] The historian Priscus had positively mentioned the effect which this example produced on the mind of Attila. Jornandes, c. 42, p. 673.

[3] The picture of Raphael is in the Vatican; the basso (or perhaps the alto) relievo of Algardi on one of the altars of St. Peter's (see Dubos, Réflexions sur la Poésie et sur la Peinture, tom. i. p. 519, 520). Baronius (Annal. Eccles. A.D. 452, No. 57, 58) bravely sustains the truth of the apparition; which is rejected, however, by the most learned and pious Catholics.

Attila relieved his tender anxiety, by adding a beautiful maid,
whose name was Ildico, to the list of his innumerable wives.[1]
Their marriage was celebrated with barbaric pomp and festivity,
at his wooden palace beyond the Danube; and the monarch,
oppressed with wine and sleep, retired at a late hour from the
banquet to the nuptial bed. His attendants continued to respect
his pleasures or his repose the greatest part of the ensuing day,
till the unusual silence alarmed their fears and suspicions; and,
after attempting to awaken Attila by loud and repeated cries,
they at length broke into the royal apartment. They found
the trembling bride sitting by the bedside, hiding her face with
her veil, and lamenting her own danger, as well as the death of
the king, who had expired during the night.[2] An artery had
suddenly burst: and as Attila lay in a supine posture, he was
suffocated by a torrent of blood, which, instead of finding a
passage through the nostrils, regurgitated into the lungs and
stomach. His body was solemnly exposed in the midst of the
plain, under a silken pavilion; and the chosen squadrons of the
Huns, wheeling round in measured evolutions, chanted a funeral
song to the memory of a hero, glorious in his life, invincible in
his death, the father of his people, the scourge of his enemies,
and the terror of the world. According to their national custom,
the barbarians cut off a part of their hair, gashed their faces
with unseemly wounds, and bewailed their valiant leader as he
deserved, not with the tears of women, but with the blood of
warriors. The remains of Attila were enclosed within three
coffins of gold, of silver, and of iron, and privately buried in the
night: the spoils of nations were thrown into his grave; the
captives who had opened the ground were inhumanly massacred;
and the same Huns, who had indulged such excessive grief,

[1] Attila, ut Priscus historicus refert, extinctionis suæ tempore, puellam
Ildico nomine, decoram valde, sibi [in] matrimonium post innumerabiles
uxores . . . socians. Jornandes, c. 49, p. 683, 684. He afterwards adds
(c. 50, p. 686) Filii Attilæ, quorum per licentiam libidinis pœne populus
fuit. Polygamy has been established among the Tartars of every age.
The rank of plebeian wives is regulated only by their personal charms: and
the faded matron prepares, without a murmur, the bed which is destined
for her blooming rival. But in royal families the daughters of Khans
communicate to their sons a prior right of inheritance. See Genealogical
History, p. 406, 407, 408.

[2] The report of her *guilt* reached Constantinople, where it obtained a very
different name; and Marcellinus observes, that the tyrant of Europe was
slain in the night by the hand and the knife of a woman. Corneille, who
has adapted the genuine account to his tragedy, describes the irruption of
blood in forty bombast lines, and Attila exclaims, with ridiculous fury,

——————— S'il ne veut s'arrêter (*his blood*),
(Dit-il) on.me.payera ce qui m'en va coûter.

feasted, with dissolute and intemperate mirth, about the recent sepulchre of their king. It was reported at Constantinople that, on the fortunate night in which he expired, Marcian beheld in a dream the bow of Attila broken asunder: and the report may be allowed to prove how seldom the image of that formidable barbarian was absent from the mind of a Roman emperor.[1]

The revolution which subverted the empire of the Huns established the fame of Attila, whose genius alone had sustained the huge and disjointed fabric. After his death the boldest chieftains aspired to the rank of kings; the most powerful kings refused to acknowledge a superior; and the numerous sons whom so many various mothers bore to the deceased monarch divided and disputed like a private inheritance the sovereign command of the nations of Germany and Scythia. The bold Ardaric felt and represented the disgrace of this servile partition; and his subjects, the warlike Gepidæ, with the Ostrogoths, under the conduct of three valiant brothers, encouraged their allies to vindicate the rights of freedom and royalty. In a bloody and decisive conflict on the banks of the river Netad in Pannonia, the lance of the Gepidæ, the sword of the Goths, the arrows of the Huns, the Suevic infantry, the light arms of the Heruli, and the heavy weapons of the Alani, encountered or supported each other; and the victory of Ardaric was accompanied with the slaughter of thirty thousand of his enemies. Ellac, the eldest son of Attila, lost his life and crown in the memorable battle of Netad: his early valour had raised him to the throne of the Acatzires, a Scythian people, whom he subdued; and his father, who loved the superior merit, would have envied the death, of Ellac.[2] His brother Dengisich, with an army of Huns still formidable in their flight and ruin, maintained his ground above fifteen years on the banks of the Danube. The palace of Attila, with the old country of Dacia, from the Carpathian hills to the Euxine, became the seat of a new power which was erected by Ardaric, king of the Gepidæ. The Pannonian conquests, from Vienna to Sirmium, were occupied by the Ostrogoths; and the

---

[1] The curious circumstances of the death and funeral of Attila are related by Jornandes (c. 49, p. 683, 684, 685), and were probably transcribed from Priscus.

[2] See Jornandes, de Rebus Geticis, c. 50, p. 685, 686, 687, 688. His distinction of the national arms is curious and important. Nam ibi admirandum reor fuisse spectaculum, ubi cernere erat cunctis, pugnantem Gothum ense furentem, Gepidam in vulnere suorum cuncta tela frangentem, Suevum pede, Hunnum sagittâ præsumere, Alanum gravi, Herulum levi, armaturâ, aciem instruere. I am not precisely informed of the situation of the river Netad.

settlements of the tribes who had so bravely asserted their native freedom were irregularly distributed according to the measure of their respective strength. Surrounded and oppressed by the multitude of his father's slaves, the kingdom of Dengisich was confined to the circle of his waggons; his desperate courage urged him to invade the Eastern empire: he fell in battle, and his head, ignominiously exposed in the Hippodrome, exhibited a grateful spectacle to the people of Constantinople. Attila had fondly or superstitiously believed that Irnac, the youngest of his sons, was destined to perpetuate the glories of his race. The character of that prince, who attempted to moderate the rashness of his brother Dengisich, was more suitable to the declining condition of the Huns; and Irnac, with his subject hordes, retired into the heart of the Lesser Scythia. They were soon overwhelmed by a torrent of new barbarians, who followed the same road which their own ancestors had formerly discovered. The *Geougen*, or Avares, whose residence is assigned by the Greek writers to the shores of the ocean, impelled the adjacent tribes; till at length the Igours of the North, issuing from the cold Siberian regions which produce the most valuable furs, spread themselves over the desert as far as the Borysthenes and the Caspian gates, and finally extinguished the empire of the Huns.[1]

Such an event might contribute to the safety of the Eastern empire under the reign of a prince who conciliated the friendship, without forfeiting the esteem, of the barbarians. But the emperor of the West, the feeble and dissolute Valentinian, who had reached his thirty-fifth year without attaining the age of reason or courage, abused this apparent security to undermine the foundations of his own throne by the murder of the patrician Aëtius. From the instinct of a base and jealous mind, he hated the man who was universally celebrated as the terror of the barbarians and the support of the republic; and his new favourite, the eunuch Heraclius, awakened the emperor from the supine lethargy which might be disguised during the life of Placidia [2] by the excuse of filial piety. The fame of Aëtius,

[1] Two modern historians have thrown much new light on the ruin and division of the empire of Attila—M. de Buat, by his laborious and minute diligence (tom. viii. p. 3-31, 68-94); and M. de Guignes, by his extraordinary knowledge of the Chinese language and writers. See Hist. des Huns, tom. ii. p. 315-319.

[2] Placidia died at Rome, November 27, A.D. 450. She was buried at Ravenna, where her sepulchre, and even her corpse, seated in a chair of cypress-wood, were preserved for ages. The empress received many compliments from the orthodox clergy; and St. Peter Chrysologus assured her that her zeal for the Trinity had been recompensed by an august trinity of children. See Tillemont, Hist. des Emp. tom. vi. p. 240.

his wealth and dignity, the numerous and martial train of
barbarian followers, his powerful dependents who filled the civil
offices of the state, and the hopes of his son Gaudentius, who
was already contracted to Eudoxia, the emperor's daughter,
had raised him above the rank of a subject. The ambitious
designs, of which he was secretly accused, excited the fears as
well as the resentment of Valentinian. Aëtius himself, supported
by the consciousness of his merit, his services, and perhaps his
innocence, seems to have maintained a haughty and indiscreet
behaviour. The patrician offended his sovereign by an hostile
declaration; he aggravated the offence by compelling him to
ratify with a solemn oath a treaty of reconciliation and alliance;
he proclaimed his suspicions, he neglected his safety; and from a
vain confidence that the enemy whom he despised was incapable
even of a manly crime, he rashly ventured his person in the
palace of Rome. Whilst he urged, perhaps with intemperate
vehemence, the marriage of his son, Valentinian, drawing his
sword—the first sword he had ever drawn—plunged it in the
breast of a general who had saved his empire: his courtiers and
eunuchs ambitiously struggled to imitate their master; and
Aëtius, pierced with an hundred wounds, fell dead in the royal
presence. Boethius, the Prætorian præfect, was killed at the
same moment; and before the event could be divulged, the
principal friends of the patrician were summoned to the palace
and separately murdered. The horrid deed, palliated by the
specious names of justice and necessity, was immediately communicated by the emperor to his soldiers, his subjects, and his
allies. The nations who were strangers or enemies to Aëtius
generously deplored the unworthy fate of a hero; the barbarians
who had been attached to his service dissembled their grief and
resentment; and the public contempt which had been so long
entertained for Valentinian was at once converted into deep and
universal abhorrence. Such sentiments seldom pervade the
walls of a palace; yet the emperor was confounded by the
honest reply of a Roman whose approbation he had not disdained to solicit. "I am ignorant, sir, of your motives or
provocations; I only know that you have acted like a man who
cuts off his right hand with his left." [1]

The luxury of Rome seems to have attracted the long and

---

[1] Aëtium Placidus mactavit semivir amens, is the expression of Sidonius
(Panegyr. Avit. 359). The poet knew the world, and was not inclined to
flatter a minister who had injured or disgraced Avitus and Majorian, the
successive heroes of his song.

frequent visits of Valentinian, who was consequently more despised at Rome than in any other part of his dominions. A republican spirit was insensibly revived in the senate, as their authority, and even their supplies, became necessary for the support of his feeble government. The stately demeanour of an hereditary monarch offended their pride, and the pleasures of Valentinian were injurious to the peace and honour of noble families. The birth of the empress Eudoxia was equal to his own, and her charms and tender affection deserved those testimonies of love which her inconstant husband dissipated in vague and unlawful amours. Petronius Maximus, a wealthy senator of the Anician family, who had been twice consul, was possessed of a chaste and beautiful wife: her obstinate resistance served only to irritate the desires of Valentinian, and he resolved to accomplish them either by stratagem or force. Deep gaming was one of the vices of the court; the emperor, who, by chance or contrivance, had gained from Maximus a considerable sum, uncourteously exacted his ring as a security for the debt, and sent it by a trusty messenger to his wife, with an order in her husband's name that she should immediately attend the empress Eudoxia. The unsuspecting wife of Maximus was conveyed in her litter to the Imperial palace; the emissaries of her impatient lover conducted her to a remote and silent bed-chamber; and Valentinian violated, without remorse, the laws of hospitality. Her tears when she returned home, her deep affliction, and the bitter reproaches against a husband whom she considered as the accomplice of his own shame, excited Maximus to a just revenge; the desire of revenge was stimulated by ambition; and he might reasonably aspire, by the free suffrage of the Roman senate, to the throne of a detested and despicable rival. Valentinian, who supposed that every human breast was devoid like his own of friendship and gratitude, had imprudently admitted among his guards several domestics and followers of Aëtius. Two of these, of barbarian race, were persuaded to execute a sacred and honourable duty by punishing with death the assassin of their patron; and their intrepid courage did not long expect a favourable moment. Whilst Valentinian amused himself in the field of Mars with the spectacle of some military sports, they suddenly rushed upon him with drawn weapons, despatched the guilty Heraclius, and stabbed the emperor to the heart, without the least opposition from his numerous train, who seemed to rejoice in the tyrant's death. Such was the fate of Valentinian the Third,[1] the last Roman emperor of the family of Theodosius. He faithfully imitated the hereditary weakness of his cousin and his two uncles, without inheriting the gentleness, the purity, the innocence, which alleviate in their characters the want of spirit and ability. Valentinian was less excusable, since he had passions without virtues: even his religion was questionable; and though he never deviated into the paths of heresy, he scandalised the pious Christians by his attachment to the profane arts of magic and divination.

As early as the time of Cicero and Varro it was the opinion of the Roman augurs that the *twelve vultures* which Romulus had seen, represented the *twelve centuries* assigned for the fatal period of his city.[2] This prophecy, disregarded perhaps in the season of health and prosperity, inspired the people with gloomy apprehensions when the twelfth century, clouded with disgrace and misfortune, was almost elapsed;[3] and even posterity must acknowledge with some surprise that the arbitrary interpretation of an accidental or fabulous circumstance has been seriously verified in the downfall of the Western empire. But its fall was announced by a clearer omen than the flight of vultures: the Roman government appeared every day less formidable to its enemies, more odious and oppressive to its subjects.[4] The taxes were multiplied with the public distress; economy was neglected

---

[1] With regard to the cause and circumstances of the deaths of Aëtius and Valentinian, our information is dark and imperfect. Procopius (de Bell. Vandal. l. i. c. 4, p. 186, 187, 188 [tom. i. p. 327-331, ed. Bonn]) is a fabulous writer for the events which precede his own memory. His narrative must therefore be supplied and corrected by five or six Chronicles, none of which were composed in Rome or Italy, and which can only express, in broken sentences, the popular rumours as they were conveyed to Gaul, Spain, Africa, Constantinople, or Alexandria.

[2] This interpretation of Vettius, a celebrated augur, was quoted by Varro in the xviiith book of his Antiquities. Censorinus, de Die Natali, c. 17, p. 90, 91, edit. Havercamp.

[3] According to Varro, the twelfth century would expire A.D. 447; but the uncertainty of the true era of Rome might allow some latitude of anticipation or delay. The poets of the age, Claudian (de Bell. Getico, 265) and Sidonius (in Panegyr. Avit. 357), may be admitted as fair witnesses of the popular opinion.

Tunc reputant annos, interceptoque volatû
Vulturis, incidunt properatis sæcula metis.
. . . .
Jam prope fata tui bissenas Vulturis alas
Implebant; scis namque tuos, scis, Roma, labores.

See Dubos, Hist. Critique, tom. i. p. 340-346.

[4] The fifth book of Salvian is filled with pathetic lamentations and vehement invectives. His immoderate freedom serves to prove the weakness, as well as the corruption, of the Roman government. His book was published after the loss of Africa (A.D. 439), and before Attila's war (A.D. 451).

in proportion as it became necessary; and the injustice of the rich shifted the unequal burden from themselves to the people, whom they defrauded of the *indulgences* that might sometimes have alleviated their misery. The severe inquisition, which confiscated their goods and tortured their persons, compelled the subjects of Valentinian to prefer the more simple tyranny of the barbarians, to fly to the woods and mountains, or to embrace the vile and abject condition of mercenary servants. They abjured and abhorred the name of Roman citizens, which had formerly excited the ambition of mankind. The Armorican provinces of Gaul and the greatest part of Spain were thrown into a state of disorderly independence by the confederations of the Bagaudæ, and the Imperial ministers pursued with proscriptive laws and ineffectual arms the rebels whom they had made.[1] If all the barbarian conquerors had been annihilated in the same hour, their total destruction would not have restored the empire of the West: and if Rome still survived, she survived the loss of freedom, of virtue, and of honour.

CHAPTER XXXVI

Sack of Rome by Genseric, King of the Vandals—His Naval Depredations
—Succession of the last Emperors of the West, Maximus, Avitus,
Majorian, Severus, Anthemius, Olybrius, Glycerius, Nepos, Augustulus—Total Extinction of the Western Empire—Reign of Odoacer,
the first Barbarian King of Italy

THE loss or desolation of the provinces from the Ocean to the Alps impaired the glory and greatness of Rome: her internal prosperity was irretrievably destroyed by the separation of Africa. The rapacious Vandals confiscated the patrimonial estates of the senators, and intercepted the regular subsidies which relieved the poverty and encouraged the idleness of the plebeians. The distress of the Romans was soon aggravated by an unexpected attack; and the province, so long cultivated for

[1] The Bagaudæ of Spain, who fought pitched battles with the Roman troops, are repeatedly mentioned in the Chronicle of Idatius. Salvian has described their distress and rebellion in very forcible language. Itaque nomen civium Romanorum . . . nunc ultro repudiatur ac fugitur, nec vile tamen [tantum] sed etiam abominabile pœne habetur . . . Et hinc est ut etiam hi qui ad barbaros non confugiunt, barbari tamen esse coguntur, scilicet ut est pars magna Hispanorum, et non minima Gallorum . . . De Bagaudis nunc mihi sermo est, qui per malos judices et cruentos spoliati, afflicti, necati postquam jus Romanæ libertatis amiserant, etiam honorem Romani nominis perdiderunt . . . Vocamus rebelles, vocamus perditos quos esse compulimus criminosos. De Gubernat. Dei, l. v. p. 158, 159.

their use by industrious and obedient subjects, was armed against them by an ambitious barbarian. The Vandals and Alani, who followed the successful standard of Genseric, had acquired a rich and fertile territory, which stretched along the coast above ninety days' journey from Tangier to Tripoli; but their narrow limits were pressed and confined, on either side, by the sandy desert and the Mediterranean. The discovery and conquest of the Black nations, that might dwell beneath the torrid zone, could not tempt the rational ambition of Genseric; but he cast his eyes towards the sea; he resolved to create a naval power, and his bold resolution was executed with steady and active perseverance. The woods of Mount Atlas afforded an inexhaustible nursery of timber; his new subjects were skilled in the arts of navigation and shipbuilding; he animated his daring Vandals to embrace a mode of warfare which would render every maritime country accessible to their arms; the Moors and Africans were allured by the hopes of plunder; and, after an interval of six centuries, the fleets that issued from the port of Carthage again claimed the empire of the Mediterranean. The success of the Vandals, the conquest of Sicily, the sack of Palermo, and the frequent descents on the coast of Lucania, awakened and alarmed the mother of Valentinian and the sister of Theodosius. Alliances were formed; and armaments, expensive and ineffectual, were prepared for the destruction of the common enemy, who reserved his courage to encounter those dangers which his policy could not prevent or elude. The designs of the Roman government were repeatedly baffled by his artful delays, ambiguous promises, and apparent concessions; and the interposition of his formidable confederate, the king of the Huns, recalled the emperors from the conquest of Africa to the care of their domestic safety. The revolutions of the palace, which left the Western empire without a defender and without a lawful prince, dispelled the apprehensions and stimulated the avarice of Genseric. He immediately equipped a numerous fleet of Vandals and Moors, and cast anchor at the mouth of the Tiber, about three months after the death of Valentinian and the elevation of Maximus to the Imperial throne.

The private life of the senator Petronius Maximus [1] was often alleged as a rare example of human felicity. His birth was noble

---

[1] Sidonius Apollinaris composed the thirteenth epistle of the second book to refute the paradox of his friend Serranus, who entertained a singular though generous enthusiasm for the deceased emperor. This epistle, with some indulgence, may claim the praise of an elegant composition; and it throws much light on the character of Maximus.

and illustrious, since he descended from the Anician family; his dignity was supported by an adequate patrimony in land and money; and these advantages of fortune were accompanied with liberal arts and decent manners, which adorn or imitate the inestimable gifts of genius and virtue. The luxury of his palace and table was hospitable and elegant. Whenever Maximus appeared in public, he was surrounded by a train of grateful and obsequious clients;[1] and it is possible that among these clients he might deserve and possess some real friends. His merit was rewarded by the favour of the prince and senate: he thrice exercised the office of Prætorian præfect of Italy; he was twice invested with the consulship, and he obtained the rank of patrician. These civil honours were not incompatible with the enjoyment of leisure and tranquillity; his hours, according to the demands of pleasure or reason, were accurately distributed by a water-clock; and this avarice of time may be allowed to prove the sense which Maximus entertained of his own happiness. The injury which he received from the emperor Valentinian appears to excuse the most bloody revenge. Yet a philosopher might have reflected, that, if the resistance of his wife had been sincere, her chastity was still inviolate, and that it could never be restored if she had consented to the will of the adulterer. A patriot would have hesitated before he plunged himself and his country into those inevitable calamities which must follow the extinction of the royal house of Theodosius.

The imprudent Maximus disregarded these salutary considerations: he gratified his resentment and ambition; he saw the bleeding corpse of Valentinian at his feet; and he heard himself saluted Emperor by the unanimous voice of the senate and people. But the day of his inauguration was the last day of his happiness. He was imprisoned (such is the lively expression of Sidonius) in the palace; and after passing a sleepless night, he sighed that he had attained the summit of his wishes, and aspired only to descend from the dangerous elevation. Oppressed by the weight of the diadem, he communicated his anxious thoughts to his friend and quæstor Fulgentius; and when he looked back with unavailing regret on the secure pleasures of his former life, the emperor exclaimed, " O fortunate Damocles, thy reign began and ended with the same dinner: " a well-known allusion,

---

[1] Clientum prævia, pedisequa, circumfusa, populositas, is the train which Sidonius himself (l. i. Epist. 9) assigns to another senator of consular rank.

which Fulgentius afterwards repeated as an instructive lesson for princes and subjects.[1]

The reign of Maximus continued about three months. His hours, of which he had lost the command, were disturbed by remorse, or guilt, or terror; and his throne was shaken by the seditions of the soldiers, the people, and the confederate barbarians. The marriage of his son Palladius with the eldest daughter of the late emperor might tend to establish the hereditary succession of his family; but the violence which he offered to the empress Eudoxia could proceed only from the blind impulse of lust or revenge. His own wife, the cause of these tragic events, had been seasonably removed by death; and the widow of Valentinian was compelled to violate her decent mourning, perhaps her real grief, and to submit to the embraces of a presumptuous usurper, whom she suspected as the assassin of her deceased husband. These suspicions were soon justified by the indiscreet confession of Maximus himself; and he wantonly provoked the hatred of his reluctant bride, who was still conscious that she descended from a line of emperors. From the East, however, Eudoxia could not hope to obtain any effectual assistance: her father and her aunt Pulcheria were dead; her mother languished at Jerusalem in disgrace and exile; and the sceptre of Constantinople was in the hands of a stranger. She directed her eyes towards Carthage; secretly implored the aid of the king of the Vandals; and persuaded Genseric to improve the fair opportunity of disguising his rapacious designs by the specious names of honour, justice, and compassion.[2] Whatever abilities Maximus might have shown in a subordinate station, he was found incapable of administering an empire: and though he might easily have been informed of the naval preparations which were made on the opposite shores of Africa, he expected with supine indifference the approach of the enemy, without

[1] Districtus ensis cui super impiâ
   Cervice pendet. non *Siculæ dapes*
   Dulcem elaborabunt saporem:
   Non avium citharæque cantus
   Somnum reducent.
                              Horat. Carm. iii. 1.
Sidonius concludes his letter with the story of Damocles, which Cicero (Tusculan. v. 20, 21) had so inimitably told.
[2] Notwithstanding the evidence of Procopius, Evagrius, Idatius, Marcellinus, etc., the learned Muratori (Annali d'Italia, tom. iv. p. 249) doubts the reality of this invitation, and observes, with great truth, " Non si può dir quanto sia facile il popolo a sognare e spacciar voci false." But his argument, from the interval of time and place, is extremely feeble. The figs which grew near Carthage were produced to the senate of Rome on the third day.

adopting any measures of defence, of negotiation, or of a timely retreat. When the Vandals disembarked at the mouth of the Tiber, the emperor was suddenly roused from his lethargy by the clamours of a trembling and exasperated multitude. The only hope which presented itself to his astonished mind was that of a precipitate flight, and he exhorted the senators to imitate the example of their prince. But no sooner did Maximus appear in the streets than he was assaulted by a shower of stones: a Roman or a Burgundian soldier claimed the honour of the first wound; his mangled body was ignominiously cast into the Tiber; the Roman people rejoiced in the punishment which they had inflicted on the author of the public calamities; and the domestics of Eudoxia signalised their zeal in the service of their mistress.[1]

On the third day after the tumult, Genseric boldly advanced from the port of Ostia to the gates of the defenceless city. Instead of a sally of the Roman youth, there issued from the gates an unarmed and venerable procession of the bishop at the head of his clergy.[2] The fearless spirit of Leo, his authority and eloquence, *again* mitigated the fierceness of a barbarian conqueror: the king of the Vandals promised to spare the unresisting multitude, to protect the buildings from fire, and to exempt the captives from torture; and although such orders were neither seriously given, nor strictly obeyed, the mediation of Leo was glorious to himself, and in some degree beneficial to his country. But Rome and its inhabitants were delivered to the licentiousness of the Vandals and Moors, whose blind passions revenged the injuries of Carthage. The pillage lasted fourteen days and nights; and all that yet remained of public or private wealth, of sacred or profane treasure, was diligently transported to the vessels of Genseric. Among the spoils, the splendid relics of two temples, or rather of two religions, exhibited a memorable example of the vicissitudes of human and divine things. Since the abolition of Paganism, the Capitol had been violated and abandoned; yet the statues of the gods and heroes were still respected, and the curious roof of gilt bronze was reserved for

---

[1] . . . Infidoque tibi Burgundio ductu
Extorquet trepidas mactandi principis iras.
Sidon. in Panegyr. Avit. 442.

A remarkable line, which insinuates that Rome and Maximus were betrayed by their Burgundian mercenaries.

[2] The apparent success of pope Leo may be justified by Prosper, and the *Historia Miscellan.*; but the improbable notion of Baronius (A.D. 455, No. 13) that Genseric spared the three apostolical churches is not countenanced even by the doubtful testimony of the *Liber Pontificalis*.

the rapacious hands of Genseric.[1] The holy instruments of the
Jewish worship,[2] the gold table, and the gold candlestick with
seven branches, originally framed according to the particular
instructions of God himself, and which were placed in the
sanctuary of his temple, had been ostentatiously displayed to
the Roman people in the triumph of Titus. They were afterwards deposited in the temple of Peace; and at the end of four
hundred years, the spoils of Jerusalem were transferred from
Rome to Carthage, by a barbarian who derived his origin from
the shores of the Baltic. These ancient monuments might
attract the notice of curiosity as well as of avarice. But the
Christian churches, enriched and adorned by the prevailing
superstition of the times, afforded more plentiful materials for
sacrilege; and the pious liberality of pope Leo, who melted six
silver vases, the gift of Constantine, each of an hundred pounds
weight, is an evidence of the damage which he attempted to
repair. In the forty-five years that had elapsed since the Gothic
invasion, the pomp and luxury of Rome were in some measure
restored; and it was difficult either to escape, or to satisfy, the
avarice of a conqueror who possessed leisure to collect, and
ships to transport, the wealth of the capital. The Imperial
ornaments of the palace, the magnificent furniture and wardrobe,
the sideboards of massy plate, were accumulated with disorderly
rapine: the gold and silver amounted to several thousand
talents; yet even the brass and copper were laboriously removed.
Eudoxia herself, who advanced to meet her friend and deliverer,
soon bewailed the imprudence of her own conduct. She was
rudely stripped of her jewels; and the unfortunate empress, with
her two daughters, the only surviving remains of the great
Theodosius, was compelled, as a captive, to follow the haughty
Vandal, who immediately hoisted sail, and returned with a
prosperous navigation to the port of Carthage.[3] Many thousand

[1] The profusion of Catulus, the first who gilt the roof of the Capitol, was
not universally approved (Plin. Hist. Natur. xxxiii. 18); but it was far
exceeded by the emperor's, and the external gilding of the temple cost
Domitian 12,000 talents (£2,400,000). The expressions of Claudian and
Rutilius (*luce metalli æmula . . . fastigia astris*, and *confunduntque vagos
delubra micantia visus*) manifestly prove that this splendid covering was
not removed either by the Christians or the Goths (see Donatus, Roma
Antiqua, l. ii. c. 6, p. 125). It should seem that the roof of the Capitol was
decorated with gilt statues, and chariots drawn by four horses.
[2] The curious reader may consult the learned and accurate treatise of
Hadrian Reland, de Spoliis Templi Hierosolymitani in Arcû Titiano Romæ
conspicuis, in 12mo. Trajecti ad Rhenum, 1716.
[3] The vessel which transported the relics of the Capitol was the only one
of the whole fleet that suffered shipwreck. If a bigoted sophist, a Pagan

Romans of both sexes, chosen for some useful or agreeable qualifications, reluctantly embarked on board the fleet of Genseric; and their distress was aggravated by the unfeeling barbarians, who, in the division of the booty, separated the wives from their husbands, and the children from their parents. The charity of Deogratias, bishop of Carthage,[1] was their only consolation and support. He generously sold the gold and silver plate of the church to purchase the freedom of some, to alleviate the slavery of others, and to assist the wants and infirmities of a captive multitude, whose health was impaired by the hardships which they had suffered in the passage from Italy to Africa. By his order, two spacious churches were converted into hospitals: the sick were distributed in convenient beds, and liberally supplied with food and medicines; and the aged prelate repeated his visits both in the day and night, with an assiduity that surpassed his strength, and a tender sympathy which enhanced the value of his services. Compare this scene with the field of Cannæ; and judge between Hannibal and the successor of St. Cyprian.[2]

The deaths of Aëtius and Valentinian had relaxed the ties which held the barbarians of Gaul in peace and subordination. The sea-coast was infested by the Saxons; the Alemanni and the Franks advanced from the Rhine to the Seine; and the ambition of the Goths seemed to meditate more extensive and permanent conquests. The emperor Maximus relieved himself, by a judicious choice, from the weight of these distant cares; he silenced the solicitations of his friends, listened to the voice of fame, and promoted a stranger to the general command of the forces in Gaul. Avitus,[3] the stranger whose merit was so nobly rewarded, descended from a wealthy and honourable family in the diocese of Auvergne. The convulsions of the times urged him to embrace, with the same ardour, the civil

bigot, had mentioned the accident, he might have rejoiced that this cargo of sacrilege was lost in the sea.

[1] See Victor Vitensis, de Persecut. Vandal. l. i. c. 8, p. 11, 12, edit. Ruinart. Deogratias governed the church of Carthage only three years. If he had not been privately buried, his corpse would have been torn piecemeal by the mad devotion of the people.

[2] The general evidence for the death of Maximus, and the sack of Rome by the Vandals, is comprised in Sidonius (Panegyr. Avit. 441-450), Procopius (de Bell. Vandal. l. i. c. 4, 5, p. 188, 189 [tom. i. p. 332, ed. Bonn], and l. ii. c. 9, p. 255 [tom. i. p. 445, sq., ed. Bo]), Evagrius (l. ii. c. 7), Jornandes (de Reb. Geticis, c. 45, p. 677), and the Chronicles of Idatius, Prosper, Marcellinus, and Theophanes, under the proper year.

[3] The private life and elevation of Avitus must be deduced, with becoming suspicion, from the panegyric pronounced by Sidonius Apollinaris, his subject, and his son-in-law.

and military professions; and the indefatigable youth blended the studies of literature and jurisprudence with the exercise of arms and hunting. Thirty years of his life were laudably spent in the public service; he alternately displayed his talents in war and negotiation; and the soldier of Aëtius, after executing the most important embassies, was raised to the station of Prætorian præfect of Gaul. Either the merit of Avitus excited envy, or his moderation was desirous of repose, since he calmly retired to an estate which he possessed in the neighbourhood of Clermont. A copious stream, issuing from the mountain, and falling head-long in many a loud and foaming cascade, discharged its waters into a lake about two miles in length, and the villa was pleasantly seated on the margin of the lake. The baths, the porticoes, the summer and winter apartments, were adapted to the purposes of luxury and use; and the adjacent country afforded the various prospects of woods, pastures, and meadows.[1] In this retreat, where Avitus amused his leisure with books, rural sports, the practice of husbandry, and the society of his friends,[2] he received the Imperial diploma, which constituted him master-general of the cavalry and infantry of Gaul. He assumed the military command; the barbarians suspended their fury; and whatever means he might employ, whatever concessions he might be forced to make, the people enjoyed the benefits of actual tranquillity. But the fate of Gaul depended on the Visigoths; and the Roman general, less attentive to his dignity than to the public interest, did not disdain to visit Toulouse in the character of an ambassador. He was received with courteous hospitality by Theodoric, the king of the Goths; but while Avitus laid the foundations of a solid alliance with that powerful nation, he was astonished by the intelligence that the emperor Maximus was slain, and that Rome had been pillaged by the Vandals. A vacant throne, which he might ascend without guilt or danger,

---

[1] After the example of the younger Pliny, Sidonius (l. ii. Epist. 2) has laboured the florid, prolix, and obscure description of his villa, which bore the name (*Avitacum*), and had been the property, of Avitus. The precise situation is not ascertained. Consult, however, the notes of Savaron and Sirmond.

[2] Sidonius (l. ii. Epist. 9) has described the country life of the Gallic nobles, in a visit which he made to his friends, whose estates were in the neighbourhood of Nismes. The morning hours were spent in the *sphæristerium* or tennis-court, or in the library, which was furnished with *Latin* authors, profane and religious—the former for the men, the latter for the ladies. The table was twice served, at dinner and supper, with hot meat (boiled and roast) and wine. During the intermediate time, the company slept, took the air on horseback, and used the warm bath.

tempted his ambition:[1] and the Visigoths were easily persuaded to support his claim by their irresistible suffrage. They loved the person of Avitus; they respected his virtues; and they were not insensible of the advantage, as well as honour, of giving an emperor to the West. The season was now approaching in which the annual assembly of the seven provinces was held at Arles; their deliberations might perhaps be influenced by the presence of Theodoric and his martial brothers; but their choice would naturally incline to the most illustrious of their countrymen. Avitus, after a decent resistance, accepted the Imperial diadem from the representatives of Gaul; and his election was ratified by the acclamations of the barbarians and provincials. The formal consent of Marcian, emperor of the East, was solicited and obtained; but the senate, Rome, and Italy, though humbled by their recent calamities, submitted with a secret murmur to the presumption of the Gallic usurper.

Theodoric, to whom Avitus was indebted for the purple, had acquired the Gothic sceptre by the murder of his elder brother Torismond; and he justified this atrocious deed by the design which his predecessor had formed of violating his alliance with the empire.[2] Such a crime might not be incompatible with the virtues of a barbarian; but the manners of Theodoric were gentle and humane; and posterity may contemplate without terror the original picture of a Gothic king, whom Sidonius had intimately observed in the hours of peace and of social intercourse. In an epistle, dated from the court of Toulouse, the orator satisfies the curiosity of one of his friends, in the following description:[3] " By the majesty of his appearance, Theodoric would command the respect of those who are ignorant of his merit; and although he is born a prince, his merit would dignify a private station. He is of a middle stature, his body appears rather plump than fat, and in his well-proportioned limbs agility is united with muscular strength.[4] If you examine his coun-

[1] Seventy lines of panegyric (505-575) which describe the importunity of Theodoric and of Gaul, struggling to overcome the modest reluctance of Avitus, are blown away by three words of an honest historian. Romanum *ambisset* Imperium (Greg. Turon. l. ii. c. 11, in tom. ii. p. 168).

[2] Isidore, archbishop of Seville, who was himself of the blood-royal of the Goths, acknowledges and almost justifies (Hist. Goth. p. 718) the crime which their slave Jornandes had basely dissembled (c. 43, p. 675).

[3] This elaborate description (l. i. Ep. i. p. 2-7) was dictated by some political motive. It was designed for the public eye, and had been shown by the friends of Sidonius before it was inserted in the collection of his epistles. The first book was published separately. See Tillemont, Mémoires Ecclés. tom. xvi. p. 264.

[4] I have suppressed, in this portrait of Theodoric, several minute circumstances and technical phrases, which could be tolerable, or indeed intelli-

tenance, you will distinguish a high forehead, large shaggy eye-brows, an equiline nose, thin lips, a regular set of white teeth, and a fair complexion, that blushes more frequently from modesty than from anger. The ordinary distribution of his time, as far as it is exposed to the public view, may be concisely represented. Before daybreak he repairs, with a small train, to his domestic chapel, where the service is performed by the Arian clergy; but those who presume to interpret his secret sentiments consider this assiduous devotion as the effect of habit and policy. The rest of the morning is employed in the administration of his kingdom. His chair is surrounded by some military officers of decent aspect and behaviour: the noisy crowd of his barbarian guards occupies the hall of audience, but they are not permitted to stand within the veils or curtains that conceal the council-chamber from vulgar eyes. The ambassadors of the nations are successively introduced: Theodoric listens with attention, answers them with discreet brevity, and either announces or delays, according to the nature of their business, his final resolution. About eight (the second hour) he rises from his throne, and visits either his treasury or his stables. If he chooses to hunt, or at least to exercise himself on horseback, his bow is carried by a favourite youth; but when the game is marked, he bends it with his own hand, and seldom misses the object of his aim: as a king, he disdains to bear arms in such ignoble warfare; but as a soldier, he would blush to accept any military service which he could perform himself. On common days his dinner is not different from the repast of a private citizen; but every Saturday many honourable guests are invited to the royal table, which, on these occasions, is served with the elegance of Greece, the plenty of Gaul, and the order and diligence of Italy.[1] The gold or silver plate is less remark-able for its weight than for the brightness and curious workman-ship: the taste is gratified without the help of foreign and costly luxury; the size and number of the cups of wine are regulated with a strict regard to the laws of temperance; and the respectful silence that prevails is interrupted only by grave and instructive conversation. After dinner Theodoric sometimes indulges him-self in a short slumber; and as soon as he wakes he calls for the dice and tables, encourages his friends to forget the royal

gible, to those only who, like the contemporaries of Sidonius, had frequented the markets where naked slaves were exposed to sale (Dubos, Hist. Critique, tom. i. p. 404).

[1] Videas ibi elegantiam Græcam, abundantiam Gallicanam; celeritatem Italam; publicam pompam, privatam diligentiam, regiam disciplinam.

majesty, and is delighted when they freely express the passions which are excited by the incidents of play. At this game, which he loves as the image of war, he alternately displays his eagerness, his skill, his patience, and his cheerful temper. If he loses, he laughs: he is modest and silent if he wins. Yet, notwithstanding this seeming indifference, his courtiers choose to solicit any favour in the moments of victory; and I myself, in my applications to the king, have derived some benefit from my losses.[1] About the ninth hour (three o'clock) the tide of business again returns, and flows incessantly till after sunset, when the signal of the royal supper dismisses the weary crowd of suppliants and pleaders. At the supper, a more familiar repast, buffoons and pantomimes are sometimes introduced, to divert, not to offend, the company by their ridiculous wit: but female singers, and the soft effeminate modes of music, are severely banished, and such martial tunes as animate the soul to deeds of valour are alone grateful to the ear of Theodoric. He retires from table; and the nocturnal guards are immediately posted at the entrance of the treasury, the palace, and the private apartments."

When the king of the Visigoths encouraged Avitus to assume the purple, he offered his person and his forces as a faithful soldier of the republic.[2] The exploits of Theodoric soon convinced the world that he had not degenerated from the warlike virtues of his ancestors. After the establishment of the Goths in Aquitain, and the passage of the Vandals into Africa, the Suevi, who had fixed their kingdom in Gallicia, aspired to the conquest of Spain, and threatened to extinguish the feeble remains of the Roman dominion. The provincials of Carthagena and Tarragona, afflicted by an hostile invasion, represented their injuries and their apprehensions. Count Fronto was despatched, in the name of the emperor Avitus, with advantageous offers of peace and alliance; and Theodoric interposed his weighty mediation to declare that, unless his brother-in-law, the king of the Suevi, immediately retired, he should be obliged to arm in the cause of justice and of Rome. "Tell him,"

---

[1] Tunc etiam ego aliquid obsecraturus feliciter vincor, et mihi tabula perit ut causa salvetur [p. 6]. Sidonius of Auvergne was not a subject of Theodoric; but he might be compelled to solicit either justice or favour at the court of Toulouse.

[2] Theodoric himself had given a solemn and voluntary promise of fidelity, which was understood both in Gaul and Spain:—

—— Romæ sum, te duce, Amicus,
    Principe te, MILES.

Sidon. Panegyr. Avit. 511

replied the haughty Rechiarius, "that I despise his friendship and his arms; but that I shall soon try whether he will dare to expect my arrival under the walls of Toulouse." Such a challenge urged Theodoric to prevent the bold designs of his enemy: he passed the Pyrenees at the head of the Visigoths; the Franks and Burgundians served under his standard; and though he professed himself the dutiful servant of Avitus, he privately stipulated, for himself and his successors, the absolute possession of his Spanish conquests. The two armies, or rather the two nations, encountered each other on the banks of the river Urbicus, about twelve miles from Astorga; and the decisive victory of the Goths appeared for a while to have extirpated the name and kingdom of the Suevi. From the field of battle Theodoric advanced to Braga, their metropolis, which still retained the splendid vestiges of its ancient commerce and dignity.[1] His entrance was not polluted with blood; and the Goths respected the chastity of their female captives, more especially of the consecrated virgins: but the greatest part of the clergy and people were made slaves, and even the churches and altars were confounded in the universal pillage. The unfortunate king of the Suevi had escaped to one of the ports of the ocean; but the obstinacy of the winds opposed his flight: he was delivered to his implacable rival; and Rechiarius, who neither desired nor expected mercy, received, with manly constancy, the death which he would probably have inflicted. After this bloody sacrifice to policy or resentment, Theodoric carried his victorious arms as far as Merida, the principal town of Lusitania, without meeting any resistance, except from the miraculous powers of St. Eulalia; but he was stopped in the full career of success, and recalled from Spain before he could provide for the security of his conquests. In his retreat towards the Pyrenees he revenged his disappointment on the country through which he passed; and, in the sack of Polentia and Astorga, he showed himself a faithless ally, as well as a cruel enemy. Whilst the king of the Visigoths fought and vanquished in the name of Avitus, the reign of Avitus had expired; and both the honour and the interest of Theodoric were deeply

---

[1] Quæque sinû pelagi jactat se Bracara dives.
    Auson. de Claris Urbibus, p. 245 [Emerita, ix.].

From the design of the king of the Suevi, it is evident that the navigation from the ports of Gallicia to the Mediterranean was known and practised. The ships of Bracara, or Braga, cautiously steered along the coast, without daring to lose themselves in the Atlantic.

wounded by the disgrace of a friend whom he had seated on the throne of the Western empire.[1]

The pressing solicitations of the senate and people persuaded the emperor Avitus to fix his residence at Rome, and to accept the consulship for the ensuing year. On the first day of January, his son-in-law, Sidonius Apollinaris, celebrated his praises in a panegyric of six hundred verses; but this composition, though it was rewarded with a brass statue,[2] seems to contain a very moderate proportion either of genius or of truth. The poet, if we may degrade that sacred name, exaggerates the merit of a sovereign and a father; and his prophecy of a long and glorious reign was soon contradicted by the event. Avitus, at a time when the Imperial dignity was reduced to a pre-eminence of toil and danger, indulged himself in the pleasures of Italian luxury: age had not extinguished his amorous inclinations; and he is accused of insulting, with indiscreet and ungenerous raillery, the husbands whose wives he had seduced or violated.[3] But the Romans were not inclined either to excuse his faults or to acknowledge his virtues. The several parts of the empire became every day more alienated from each other; and the stranger of Gaul was the object of popular hatred and contempt. The senate asserted their legitimate claim in the election of an emperor; and their authority, which had been originally derived from the old constitution, was again fortified by the actual weakness of a declining monarchy. Yet even such a monarchy might have resisted the votes of an unarmed senate, if their discontent had not been supported, or perhaps inflamed, by Count Ricimer, one of the principal commanders of the barbarian troops who formed the military defence of Italy. The daughter of Wallia, king of the Visigoths, was the mother of Ricimer; but he was descended, on the father's side, from the nation of the Suevi:[4] his pride or patriotism might be exasperated by the misfortunes

---

[1] This Suevic war is the most authentic part of the Chronicle of Idatius, who, as bishop of Iria Flavia, was himself a spectator and a sufferer. Jornandes (c. 44, p. 675, 676, 677) has expatiated with pleasure on the Gothic victory.

[2] In one of the porticoes or galleries belonging to Trajan's library, among the statues of famous writers and orators. Sidon. Apoll. l. ix. Epist. 16, p. 284; Carm. viii. p. 350.

[3] Luxuriose agere volens a senatoribus projectus est, is the concise expression of Gregory of Tours (l. ii. c. xi. in tom. ii. p. 168). An old Chronicle (in tom. ii. p. 649) mentions an indecent jest of Avitus, which seems more applicable to Rome than to Trèves.

[4] Sidonius (Panegyr. Anthem. 302 [360], etc.) praises the royal birth of Ricimer, the lawful heir, as he chooses to insinuate, both of the Gothic and Suevic kingdoms.

of his countrymen; and he obeyed with reluctance an emperor
in whose elevation he had not been consulted. His faithful
and important services against the common enemy rendered
him still more formidable;[1] and, after destroying on the coast
of Corsica a fleet of Vandals, which consisted of sixty galleys,
Ricimer returned in triumph with the appellation of the Deliverer
of Italy. He chose that moment to signify to Avitus that his
reign was at an end; and the feeble emperor, at a distance from
his Gothic allies, was compelled, after a short and unavailing
struggle, to abdicate the purple. By the clemency, however,
or the contempt of Ricimer,[2] he was permitted to descend from
the throne to the more desirable station of bishop of Placentia:
but the resentment of the senate was still unsatisfied; and their
inflexible severity pronounced the sentence of his death. He
fled towards the Alps, with the humble hope, not of arming the
Visigoths in his cause, but of securing his person and treasures
in the sanctuary of Julian, one of the tutelar saints of Auvergne.[3]
Disease, or the hand of the executioner, arrested him on the road;
yet his remains were decently transported to Brivas, or Brioude,
in his native province, and he reposed at the feet of his holy
patron.[4] Avitus left only one daughter, the wife of Sidonius
Apollinaris, who inherited the patrimony of his father-in-law;
lamenting, at the same time, the disappointment of his public
and private expectations. His resentment prompted him to
join, or at least to countenance, the measures of a rebellious
faction in Gaul; and the poet had contracted some guilt, which
it was incumbent on him to expiate by a new tribute of flattery
to the succeeding emperor.[5]

The successor of Avitus presents the welcome discovery of a

---

[1] See the Chronicle of Idatius. Jornandes (c. xliv. p. 676 [c. 45, p. 678])
styles him, with some truth, virum egregium, et pene tunc in Italiâ ad
exercitum singularem.

[2] Parcens innocentiæ Aviti, is the compassionate but contemptuous
language of Victor Tunnunensis (in Chron. apud Scaliger Euseb.). In
another place he calls him vir totius simplicitatis. This commendation is
more humble, but it is more solid and sincere, than the praises of Sidonius.

[3] He suffered, as it is supposed, in the persecution of Diocletian (Tillemont, Mém. Ecclés. tom. v. p. 279, 696). Gregory of Tours, his peculiar
votary, has dedicated to the glory of Julian the Martyr an entire book (de
Gloriâ Martyrum, l. ii. in Max. Bibliot. Patrum, tom. xi. p. 861-871), in
which he relates about fifty foolish miracles performed by his relics.

[4] Gregory of Tours (l. ii. c. xi. p. 168) is concise, but correct, in the reign
of his countryman. The words of Idatius, "caret imperio, caret et vitâ"
[Hist. de France, i. p. 621], seem to imply that the death of Avitus was
violent; but it must have been secret, since Evagrius (l. ii. c. 7) could
suppose that he died of the plague.

[5] After a modest appeal to the examples of his brethren, Virgil and
Horace, Sidonius honestly confesses the debt, and promises payment:—

great and heroic character, such as sometimes arise, in a degenerate age, to vindicate the honour of the human species. The emperor Majorian has deserved the praises of his contemporaries and of posterity; and these praises may be strongly expressed in the words of a judicious and disinterested historian: "That he was gentle to his subjects; that he was terrible to his enemies; and that he excelled in *every* virtue *all* his predecessors who had reigned over the Romans." [1] Such a testimony may justify at least the panegyric of Sidonius; and we may acquiesce in the assurance that, although the obsequious orator would have flattered with equal zeal the most worthless of princes, the extraordinary merit of his object confined him, on this occasion, within the bounds of truth. [2] Majorian derived his name from his maternal grandfather, who, in the reign of the great Theodosius, had commanded the troops of the Illyrian frontier. He gave his daughter in marriage to the father of Majorian, a respectable officer, who administered the revenues of Gaul with skill and integrity; and generously preferred the friendship of Aëtius to the tempting offers of an insidious court. His son, the future emperor, who was educated in the profession of arms, displayed, from his early youth, intrepid courage, premature wisdom, and unbounded liberality in a scanty fortune. He followed the standard of Aëtius, contributed to his success, shared, and sometimes eclipsed, his glory, and at last excited the jealousy of the patrician, or rather of his wife, who forced him to retire from the service. [3] Majorian, after the death of Aëtius, was recalled and

---

Sic mihi diverso nuper sub Marte cadenti
Jussisti placido victor ut essem animo.
Serviat ergo tibi servati lingua poetæ,
Atque meæ vitæ laus tua sit pretium.
                          Sidon. Apoll. Carm. iv. p. 308.

See Dubos, Hist. Critique, tom. i. p. 448, etc.

[1] The words of Procopius deserve to be transcribed: οὗτος γὰρ ὁ Μᾱιορῖνος ξύμπαντας τοὺς πώποτε 'Ρωμαίων βεβασιλευκότας ὑπεραίρων ἀρετῇ πάσῃ ; and afterwards, ἀνὴρ τὰ μὲν εἰς τοὺς ὑπηκόους μέτριος γεγονώς, φοβερὸς δὲ τὰ ἐς τοὺς παλεμίους (de Bell. Vandal. l. i. c. 7, p. 194 [tom. i. p. 340 and 342, ed. Bonn])—a concise but comprehensive definition of royal virtue.

[2] The Panegyric was pronounced at Lyons before the end of the year 458, while the emperor was still consul. It has more art than genius, and more labour than art. The ornaments are false or trivial; the expression is feeble and prolix; and Sidonius wants the skill to exhibit the principal figure in a strong and distinct light. The private life of Majorian occupies about two hundred lines, 107-305.

[3] She pressed his immediate death, and was scarcely satisfied with his disgrace. It should seem that Aëtius, like Belisarius and Marlborough, was governed by his wife, whose fervent piety, though it might work miracles (Gregor. Turon. l. ii. c. 7, p. 162), was not incompatible with base and sanguinary counsels.

promoted: and his intimate connection with Count Ricimer was
the immediate step by which he ascended the throne of the
Western empire. During the vacancy that succeeded the
abdication of Avitus, the ambitious barbarian, whose birth
excluded him from the Imperial dignity, governed Italy, with the
title of Patrician; resigned to his friend the conspicuous station
of master-general of the cavalry and infantry, and, after an
interval of some months, consented to the unanimous wish of
the Romans, whose favour Majorian had solicited by a recent
victory over the Alemanni.[1] He was invested with the purple at
Ravenna: and the epistle which he addressed to the senate will
best describe his situation and his sentiments. " Your election,
Conscript Fathers! and the ordinance of the most valiant army,
have made me your emperor.[2] May the propitious Deity direct
and prosper the counsels and events of my administration to
your advantage and to the public welfare! For my own part,
I did not aspire, I have submitted, to reign; nor should I have
discharged the obligations of a citizen if I had refused, with base
and selfish ingratitude, to support the weight of those labours
which were imposed by the republic. Assist, therefore, the
prince whom you have made; partake the duties which you have
enjoined; and may our common endeavours promote the happiness of an empire which I have accepted from your hands. Be
assured that, in our times, justice shall resume her ancient vigour,
and that virtue shall become not only innocent but meritorious.
Let none, except the authors themselves, be apprehensive of
delations,[3] which, as a subject, I have always condemned, and,
as a prince, will severely punish. Our own vigilance, and that
of our father, the patrician Ricimer, shall regulate all military
affairs and provide for the safety of the Roman world, which we

---

[1] The Alemanni had passed the Rhætian Alps, and were defeated in the
Campi Canini, or Valley of Bellinzone, through which the Ticino flows, in
its descent from Mount Adula, to the Lago Maggiore (Cluver. Italia Antiq.
tom. i. p. 100, 101). This boasted victory over *nine hundred* barbarians
(Panegyr. Majorian. 373, etc.) betrays the extreme weakness of Italy.

[2] Imperatorem me factum, P. C. electionis vestræ arbitrio, et fortissimi
exercitûs ordinatione agnoscite (Novell. Majorian. tit. iii. p. 34, ad Calcem
Cod. Theodos.). Sidonius proclaims the unanimous voice of the empire:—

—— Postquam ordine vobis
Ordo omnis regnum dederat; *plebs, curia, miles,*
Et *collega* simul.   [Carm. v.] 386.

This language is ancient and constitutional; and we may observe that the
clergy were not yet considered as a distinct order of the state.

[3] Either *dilationes*, or *delationes*, would afford a tolerable reading; but
there is much more sense and spirit in the latter, to which I have therefore
given the preference.

have saved from foreign and domestic enemies.[1] You now understand the maxims of my government: you may confide in the faithful love and sincere assurances of a prince who has formerly been the companion of your life and dangers, who still glories in the name of senator, and who is anxious that you should never repent of the judgment which you have pronounced in his favour." The emperor, who, amidst the ruins of the Roman world, revived the ancient language of law and liberty, which Trajan would not have disclaimed, must have derived those generous sentiments from his own heart, since they were not suggested to his imitation by the customs of his age or the example of his predecessors.[2]

The private and public actions of Majorian are very imperfectly known: but his laws, remarkable for an original cast of thought and expression, faithfully represent the character of a sovereign who loved his people, who sympathised in their distress, who had studied the causes of the decline of the empire, and who was capable of applying (as far as such reformation was practicable) judicious and effectual remedies to the public disorders.[3] His regulations concerning the finances manifestly tended to remove, or at least to mitigate, the most intolerable grievances. I. From the first hour of his reign he was solicitous (I translate his own words) to relieve the *weary* fortunes of the provincials, oppressed by the accumulated weight of indictions and superindictions.[4] With this view, he granted an universal amnesty, a final and absolute discharge of all arrears of tribute, of all debts which, under any pretence, the fiscal officers might demand from the people. This wise dereliction of obsolete, vexatious, and unprofitable claims, improved and purified the sources of the public revenue; and the subject, who could now look back without despair, might labour with hope and gratitude for himself and for his country. II. In the assessment and

---

[1] Ab externo hoste et a domesticâ clade liberavimus: by the latter, Majorian must understand the tyranny of Avitus, whose death he consequently avowed as a meritorious act. On this occasion Sidonius is fearful and obscure; he describes the twelve Cæsars, the nations of Africa, etc., that he may escape the dangerous name of Avitus (305-369).

[2] See the whole edict or epistle of Majorian to the senate (Novell. tit. iv. p. 34). Yet the expression *regnum nostrum* bears some taint of the age, and does not mix kindly with the word *respublica*, which he frequently repeats.

[3] See the laws of Majorian (they are only nine in number, but very long and various), at the end of the Theodosian Code, Novell. l. iv. p. 32-37. Godefroy has not given any commentary on these additional pieces.

[4] Fessas provincialium variâ atque multiplici tributorum exactione fortunas, et extraordinariis fiscalium solutionum oneribus attritas, etc. Novell. Majorian. tit. iv. p. 34.

collection of taxes Majorian restored the ordinary jurisdiction of the provincial magistrates, and suppressed the extraordinary commissions which had been introduced in the name of the emperor himself or of the Prætorian præfects. The favourite servants who obtained such irregular powers were insolent in their behaviour and arbitrary in their demands: they affected to despise the subordinate tribunals, and they were discontented if their fees and profits did not twice exceed the sum which they condescended to pay into the treasury. One instance of their extortion would appear incredible were it not authenticated by the legislator himself. They exacted the whole payment in gold: but they refused the current coin of the empire, and would accept only such ancient pieces as were stamped with the names of Faustina or the Antonines. The subject who was unprovided with these curious medals had recourse to the expedient of compounding with their rapacious demands; or, if he succeeded in the research, his imposition was doubled according to the weight and value of the money of former times.[1] III. "The municipal corporations (says the emperor), the lesser senates (so antiquity has justly styled them), deserve to be considered as the heart of the cities and the sinews of the republic. And yet so low are they now reduced, by the injustice of magistrates and the venality of collectors, that many of their members, renouncing their dignity and their country, have taken refuge in distant and obscure exile." He urges, and even compels, their return to their respective cities; but he removes the grievance which had forced them to desert the exercise of their municipal functions. They are directed, under the authority of the provincial magistrates, to resume their office of levying the tribute; but, instead of being made responsible for the whole sum assessed on their district, they are only required to produce a regular account of

---

[1] The learned Greaves (vol. i. p. 329, 330, 331) has found, by a diligent inquiry, that *aurei* of the Antonines weighed one hundred and eighteen, and those of the fifth century only sixty-eight English grains. Majorian gives currency to all gold coin, excepting only the *Gallic solidus*, from its deficiency, not in the weight, but in the standard.

[Until about the time of Constantine, "Defensor" was the title of persons who were employed in municipal matters of merely a temporary kind. But about the first half or the middle of the fourth century the Defensores appear as regularly established functionaries. Their title is Defensor Civitatis, Plebis, Loci. They were elected by the whole town, and not merely by the decurions, and, unlike the magistrates, who were chosen from the decurions, they could not be taken from the latter body. The office was, at its origin, held for five years, but after the time of Justinian only for two. The principal business of the decurion was to protect the town against the oppression of the governor. Cf. Savigny, *Geschichte des Romischen Rechts*, vol. i. p. 88.—O. S.]

the payments which they have actually received, and of the defaulters who are still indebted to the public. IV. But Majorian was not ignorant that these corporate bodies were too much inclined to retaliate the injustice and oppression which they had suffered, and he therefore revives the useful office of the *defenders of cities*. He exhorts the people to elect, in a full and free assembly, some man of discretion and integrity who would dare to assert their privileges, to represent their grievances, to protect the poor from the tyranny of the rich, and to inform the emperor of the abuses that were committed under the sanction of his name and authority.

The spectator who casts a mournful view over the ruins of ancient Rome is tempted to accuse the memory of the Goths and Vandals for the mischief which they had neither leisure, nor power, nor perhaps inclination, to perpetrate. The tempest of war might strike some lofty turrets to the ground; but the destruction which undermined the foundations of those massy fabrics was prosecuted, slowly and silently, during a period of ten centuries; and the motives of interest, that afterwards operated without shame or control, were severely checked by the taste and spirit of the emperor Majorian. The decay of the city had gradually impaired the value of the public works. The circus and theatres might still excite, but they seldom gratified, the desires of the people: the temples which had escaped the zeal of the Christians were no longer inhabited either by gods or men; the diminished crowds of the Romans were lost in the immense space of their baths and porticoes; and the stately libraries and halls of justice became useless to an indolent generation whose repose was seldom disturbed either by study or business. The monuments of consular or Imperial greatness were no longer revered as the immortal glory of the capital: they were only esteemed as an inexhaustible mine of materials, cheaper, and more convenient, than the distant quarry. Specious petitions were continually addressed to the easy magistrates of Rome which stated the want of stones or bricks for some necessary service: the fairest forms of architecture were rudely defaced for the sake of some paltry or pretended repairs; and the degenerate Romans, who converted the spoil to their own emolument, demolished, with sacrilegious hands, the labours of their ancestors. Majorian, who had often sighed over the desolation of the city, applied a severe remedy to the growing evil.[1] He

---

[1] The whole edict (Novell. Majorian. tit. vi. p. 35) is curious. " Antiquarum ædium dissipatur speciosa constructio; et ut [earum] aliquid

reserved to the prince and senate the sole cognisance of the
extreme cases which might justify the destruction of an ancient
edifice; imposed a fine of fifty pounds of gold (two thousand
pounds sterling) on every magistrate who should presume to
grant such illegal and scandalous licence; and threatened to
chastise the criminal obedience of their subordinate officers by
a severe whipping and the amputation of both their hands.   In
the last instance the legislator might seem to forget the proportion of guilt and punishment; but his zeal arose from a generous
principle, and Majorian was anxious to protect the monuments
of those ages in which he would have desired and deserved to live.
The emperor conceived that it was his interest to increase the
number of his subjects; that it was his duty to guard the purity
of the marriage-bed: but the means which he employed to accomplish these salutary purposes are of an ambiguous, and perhaps
exceptionable, kind.   The pious maids who consecrated their
virginity to Christ were restrained from taking the veil till they
had reached their fortieth year.   Widows under that age were
compelled to form a second alliance within the term of five years,
by the forfeiture of half their wealth to their nearest relations or
to the state.   Unequal marriages were condemned or annulled.
The punishment of confiscation and exile was deemed so inadequate to the guilt of adultery, that, if the criminal returned to
Italy, he might, by the express declaration of Majorian, be slain
with impunity.[1]

While the emperor Majorian assiduously laboured to restore
the happiness and virtue of the Romans, he encountered the
arms of Genseric, from his character and situation their most
formidable enemy.   A fleet of Vandals and Moors landed at
the mouth of the Liris or Garigliano; but the Imperial troops
surprised and attacked the disorderly barbarians, who were
encumbered with the spoils of Campania; they were chased
with slaughter to their ships, and their leader, the king's brother-

reparetur, magna diruuntur. Hinc jam occasio nascitur, ut etiam unus-
quisque privatum ædificium construens, per gratiam judicum . . . præsumere de publicis locis necessaria, et transferre non dubitet," etc. With
equal zeal, but with less power, Petrarch, in the fourteenth century,
repeated the same complaints (Vie de Petrarque, tom. i. p. 326, 327). If I
prosecute this History, I shall not be unmindful of the decline and fall of
the *city* of Rome—an interesting object, to which my plan was originally
confined.

[1] The emperor chides the lenity of Rogatian, consular of Tuscany, in a
style of acrimonious reproof, which sounds almost like personal resentment
(Novell. tit. ix. p. 37). The law of Majorian which punished obstinate
widows was soon afterwards repealed by his successor Severus (Novell.
Sever. tit. i. p. 37).

in-law, was found in the number of the slain.[1] Such vigilance might announce the character of the new reign, but the strictest vigilance and the most numerous forces were insufficient to protect the long-extended coast of Italy from the depredations of a naval war. The public opinion had imposed a nobler and more arduous task on the genius of Majorian. Rome expected from him alone the restitution of Africa, and the design which he formed of attacking the Vandals in their new settlements was the result of bold and judicious policy. If the intrepid emperor could have infused his own spirit into the youth of Italy; if he could have revived in the field of Mars the manly exercises in which he had always surpassed his equals; he might have marched against Genseric at the head of a *Roman* army. Such a reformation of national manners might be embraced by the rising generation; but it is the misfortune of those princes who laboriously sustain a declining monarchy, that, to obtain some immediate advantage, or to avert some impending danger, they are forced to countenance, and even to multiply, the most pernicious abuses. Majorian, like the weakest of his predecessors, was reduced to the disgraceful expedient of substituting barbarian auxiliaries in the place of his unwarlike subjects: and his superior abilities could only be displayed in the vigour and dexterity with which he wielded a dangerous instrument, so apt to recoil on the hand that used it. Besides the confederates who were already engaged in the service of the empire, the fame of his liberality and valour attracted the nations of the Danube, the Borysthenes, and perhaps of the Tanais. Many thousands of the bravest subjects of Attila, the Gepidæ, the Ostrogoths, the Rugians, the Burgundians, the Suevi, the Alani, assembled in the plains of Liguria, and their formidable strength was balanced by their mutual animosities.[2] They passed the Alps in a severe winter. The emperor led the way on foot and in complete armour, sounding with his long staff the depth of the ice or snow, and encouraging the Scythians, who complained of the extreme cold, by the cheerful assurance that they should be satisfied with the heat of Africa. The citizens of Lyons had presumed to shut their gates: they soon implored, and experienced, the clemency of Majorian. He vanquished Theodoric in the field, and admitted to his friendship and alliance a

---

[1] Sidon. Panegyr. Majorian. 385-440.
[2] The review of the army, and passage of the Alps, contain the most tolerable passages of the Panegyric (470-552). M. de Buat (Hist. des Peuples, etc., tom. viii. p. 49-55) is a more satisfactory commentator than either Savaron or Sirmond.

king whom he had found not unworthy of his arms. The
beneficial though precarious reunion of the greatest part of
Gaul and Spain was the effect of persuasion as well as of force; [1]
and the independent Bagaudæ, who had escaped or resisted the
oppression of former reigns, were disposed to confide in the
virtues of Majorian. His camp was filled with barbarian allies;
his throne was supported by the zeal of an affectionate people;
but the emperor had foreseen that it was impossible without a
maritime power to achieve the conquest of Africa. In the first
Punic war the republic had exerted such incredible diligence
that, within sixty days after the first stroke of the axe had been
given in the forest, a fleet of one hundred and sixty galleys
proudly rode at anchor in the sea. [2] Under circumstances much
less favourable, Majorian equalled the spirit and perseverance
of the ancient Romans. The woods of the Apennine were felled;
the arsenals and manufactures of Ravenna and Misenum were
restored; Italy and Gaul vied with each other in liberal contributions to the public service; and the Imperial navy of three
hundred large galleys, with an adequate proportion of transports and smaller vessels, was collected in the secure and
capacious harbour of Carthagena in Spain. [3] The intrepid
countenance of Majorian animated his troops with a confidence
of victory; and if we might credit the historian Procopius, his
courage sometimes hurried him beyond the bounds of prudence.
Anxious to explore with his own eyes the state of the Vandals,
he ventured, after disguising the colour of his hair, to visit
Carthage in the character of his own ambassador: and Genseric
was afterwards mortified by the discovery that he had entertained and dismissed the emperor of the Romans. Such an
anecdote may be rejected as an improbable fiction, but it is a

---

[1] Τὰ μὲν ὅπλοις, τὰ δὲ λόγοις, is the just and forcible distinction of Priscus
(Excerpt. Legat. p. 42 [p. 156, ed. Bonn]), in a short fragment which
throws much light on the history of Majorian. Jornandes has suppressed
the defeat and alliance of the Visigoths, which were solemnly proclaimed
in Gallicia, and are marked in the Chronicle of Idatius.

[2] Florus, l. ii. c. 2. He amuses himself with the poetical fancy that the
trees had been transformed into ships; and, indeed, the whole transaction,
as it is related in the first book of Polybius, deviates too much from the
probable course of human events.

[3]   Interea duplici texis dum littore classem
      Inferno superoque mari, cadit omnis in æquor
      Silva tibi, etc.
                              Sidon. Panegyr. Majorian. 441-461.

The number of ships, which Priscus fixes at 300, is magnified by an indefinite comparison with the fleets of Agamemnon, Xerxes, and Augustus.

fiction which would not have been imagined unless in the life of a hero.[1]

Without the help of a personal interview, Genseric was sufficiently acquainted with the genius and designs of his adversary. He practised his customary arts of fraud and delay, but he practised them without success. His applications for peace became each hour more submissive, and perhaps more sincere; but the inflexible Majorian had adopted the ancient maxim that Rome could not be safe as long as Carthage existed in a hostile state. The king of the Vandals distrusted the valour of his native subjects, who were enervated by the luxury of the South;[2] he suspected the fidelity of the vanquished people, who abhorred him as an Arian tyrant; and the desperate measure which he executed of reducing Mauritania into a desert[3] could not defeat the operations of the Roman emperor, who was at liberty to land his troops on any part of the African coast. But Genseric was saved from impending and inevitable ruin by the treachery of some powerful subjects, envious or apprehensive of their master's success. Guided by their secret intelligence, he surprised the unguarded fleet in the bay of Carthagena: many of the ships were sunk, or taken, or burnt; and the preparations of three years were destroyed in a single day.[4] After this event the behaviour of the two antagonists showed them superior to their fortune. The Vandal, instead of being elated by this accidental victory, immediately renewed his solicitations for peace. The emperor of the West, who was capable of forming great designs and of supporting heavy disappointments, consented to a treaty, or rather to a suspension of arms, in the full assurance that before he could restore his

---

[1] Procopius de Bell. Vandal. l. i. c. 7, p. 194 [tom. i. p. 341, ed. Bonn]. When Genseric conducted his unknown guest into the arsenal of Carthage, the arms clashed of their own accord. Majorian had tinged his yellow locks with a black colour.

[2] Spoliisque potitus
    Immensis, robur luxû jam perdidit omne,
    Quo valuit dum pauper erat.
                  Panegyr. Majorian. 330.
He afterwards applies to Genseric, unjustly as it should seem, the vices of his subjects.

[3] He burnt the villages and poisoned the springs (Priscus, p. 42 [p. 156, ed. Bonn]). Dubos (Hist. Critique, tom. i. p. 475) observes that the magazines which the Moors buried in the earth might escape his destructive search. Two or three hundred pits are sometimes dug in the same place, and each pit contains at least four hundred bushels of corn. Shaw's Travels, p. 139.

[4] Idatius, who was safe in Gallicia from the power of Ricimer, boldly and honestly declares, Vandali per proditores admoniti, etc.: he dissembles, however, the name of the traitor.

navy he should be supplied with provocations to justify a second war. Majorian returned to Italy to prosecute his labours for the public happiness; and as he was conscious of his own integrity, he might long remain ignorant of the dark conspiracy which threatened his throne and his life. The recent misfortune of Carthagena sullied the glory which had dazzled the eyes of the multitude: almost every description of civil and military officers were exasperated against the Reformer, since they all derived some advantage from the abuses which he endeavoured to suppress; and the patrician Ricimer impelled the inconstant passions of the barbarians against a prince whom he esteemed and hated. The virtues of Majorian could not protect him from the impetuous sedition which broke out in the camp near Tortona at the foot of the Alps. He was compelled to abdicate the Imperial purple; five days after his abdication it was reported that he died of a dysentery;[1] and the humble tomb which covered his remains was consecrated by the respect and gratitude of succeeding generations.[2] The private character of Majorian inspired love and respect. Malicious calumny and satire excited his indignation, or, if he himself were the object, his contempt; but he protected the freedom of wit, and in the hours which the emperor gave to the familiar society of his friends he could indulge his taste for pleasantry without degrading the majesty of his rank.[3]

It was not perhaps without some regret that Ricimer sacrificed his friend to the interest of his ambition: but he resolved in a second choice to avoid the imprudent preference of superior virtue and merit. At his command the obsequious senate of Rome bestowed the Imperial title on Libius Severus, who ascended the throne of the West without emerging from the

---

[1] Procop. de Bell. Vandal. l. i. c. 7, p. 194 [tom. i. p. 342, ed. Bonn]. The testimony of Idatius is fair and impartial: " Maj rianum de Galliis Romam redeuntem, et Romano imperio vel nomini res necessarias ordinantem, Richimer livore percitus, et *invidorum* consilio fultus, fraude interficit circumventum " [Sirmondi Op. tom. ii. p. 311]. Some read *Suevorum*, and I am unwilling to efface either of the words, as they express the different accomplices who united in the conspiracy against Majorian.

[2] See the Epigrams of Ennodius, No. cxxxv. inter Sirmond. Opera, tom. i. p. 1903. It is flat and obscure; but Ennodius was made bishop of Pavia fifty years after the death of Majorian, and his praise deserves credit and regard.

[3] Sidonius gives a tedious account (l. i. Epist. xi. p. 25-31) of a supper at Arles, to which he was invited by Majorian a short time before his death. He had no intention of praising a deceased emperor; but a casual disinterested remark, " Subrisit Augustus; ut erat, auctoritate servatâ, cum se communioni dedisset, joci plenus," outweighs the six hundred lines of his venal panegyric.

obscurity of a private condition. History has scarcely deigned to notice his birth, his elevation, his character, or his death. Severus expired as soon as his life became inconvenient to his patron;[1] and it would be useless to discriminate his nominal reign in the vacant interval of six years between the death of Majorian and the elevation of Anthemius. During that period the government was in the hands of Ricimer alone; and although the modest barbarian disclaimed the name of king, he accumulated treasures, formed a separate army, negotiated private alliances, and ruled Italy with the same independent and despotic authority which was afterwards exercised by Odoacer and Theodoric. But his dominions were bounded by the Alps; and two Roman generals, Marcellinus and Ægidius, maintained their allegiance to the republic, by rejecting with disdain the phantom which he styled an emperor. Marcellinus still adhered to the old religion; and the devout Pagans, who secretly disobeyed the laws of the church and state, applauded his profound skill in the science of divination. But he possessed the more valuable qualifications of learning, virtue, and courage;[2] the study of the Latin literature had improved his taste, and his military talents had recommended him to the esteem and confidence of the great Aëtius, in whose ruin he was involved. By a timely flight Marcellinus escaped the rage of Valentinian, and boldly aserted his liberty amidst the convulsions of the Western empire. His voluntary or reluctant submission to the authority of Majorian was rewarded by the government of Sicily and the command of an army stationed in that island to oppose or to attack the Vandals; but his barbarian mercenaries, after the emperor's death, were tempted to revolt by the artful liberality of Ricimer. At the head of a band of faithful followers the intrepid Marcellinus occupied the province of Dalmatia, assumed the title of patrician of the West, secured the love of his subjects by a mild and equitable reign, built a fleet which claimed the dominion of the Hadriatic, and alternately alarmed

---

[1] Sidonius (Panegyr. Anthem. 317) dismisses him to heaven:—

> Auxerat Augustus naturæ lege Severus
> Divorum numerum.

And an old list of the emperors, composed about the time of Justinian, praises his piety, and fixes his residence at Rome (Sirmond. Not. ad Sidon, p. 111, 112).

[2] Tillemont, who is always scandalised by the virtues of infidels, attributes this advantageous portrait of Marcellinus (which Suidas has preserved) to the partial zeal of some Pagan historian (Hist. des Empereurs. tom. vi. p. 330).

the coasts of Italy and of Africa.[1] Ægidius, the master-general of Gaul, who equalled, or at least who imitated, the heroes of ancient Rome,[2] proclaimed his immortal resentment against the assassins of his beloved master. A brave and numerous army was attached to his standard: and though he was prevented by the arts of Ricimer and the arms of the Visigoths from marching to the gates of Rome, he maintained his independent sovereignty beyond the Alps and rendered the name of Ægidius respectable both in peace and war. The Franks, who had punished with exile the youthful follies of Childeric, elected the Roman general for their king; his vanity rather than his ambition was gratified by that singular honour; and when the nation at the end of four years repented of the injury which they had offered to the Merovingian family, he patiently acquiesced in the restoration of the lawful prince. The authority of Ægidius ended only with his life, and the suspicions of poison and secret violence, which derived some countenance from the character of Ricimer, were eagerly entertained by the passionate credulity of the Gauls.[3]

The kingdom of Italy, a name to which the Western empire was gradually reduced, was afflicted, under the reign of Ricimer, by the incessant depredations of the Vandal pirates.[4] In the spring of each year they equipped a formidable navy in the port of Carthage, and Genseric himself, though in a very advanced age, still commanded in person the most important expeditions.

---

[1] Procopius de Bell. Vandal. l. i. c. 6, p. 191 [tom. i. p. 336, ed. Bonn]. In various circumstances of the life of Marcellinus, it is not easy to reconcile the Greek historian with the Latin Chronicles of the times.

[2] I must apply to Ægidius the praises which Sidonius (Panegyr. Majorian. 553) bestows on a nameless master-general, who commanded the rearguard of Majorian. Idatius, from public report, commends his Christian piety; and Priscus mentions (p. 42 [p. 156, 157, ed. Bonn]) his military virtues.

[3] Greg. Turon. l. ii. c. 12, in tom. ii. p. 168. The Père Daniel, whose ideas were superficial and modern, has started some objections against the story of Childeric (Hist. de France, tom. i. Préface Historique, p. lxxviii. etc.); but they have been fairly satisfied by Dubos (Hist. Critique, tom. i. p. 460-510), and by two authors who disputed the prize of the Academy of Soissons (p. 131-177, 310-339). With regard to the term of Childeric's exile, it is necessary either to prolong the life of Ægidius beyond the date assigned by the Chronicle of Idatius, or to correct the text of Gregory, by reading *quarto* anno, instead of *octavo*.

[4] The naval war of Genseric is described by Priscus (Excerpta Legation. p. 42 [p. 157, ed. Bonn]), Procopius (de Bell. Vandal. l. i. c. 5, p. 189, 190, and c. 22, p. 228 [tom. i. p. 332, *sqq.*, and p. 399, ed. Bonn]), Victor Vitensis (de Persecut. Vandal. l. i. c. 17, and Ruinart, p. 467-481), and in the three panegyrics of Sidonius, whose chronological order is absurdly transposed in the editions both of Savaron and Sirmond. (Avit. Carm. vii. 441-451. Majorian. Carm. v. 327-350, 385-440. Anthem. Carm. ii. 348-386.) In

His designs were concealed with impenetrable secrecy till the moment that he hoisted sail. When he was asked by his pilot what course he should steer, " Leave the determination to the winds (replied the barbarian, with pious arrogance): *they* will transport us to the guilty coast whose inhabitants have provoked the divine justice; " but if Genseric himself deigned to issue more precise orders, he judged the most wealthy to be the most criminal. The Vandals repeatedly visited the coasts of Spain, Liguria, Tuscany, Campania, Lucania, Bruttium, Apulia, Calabria, Venetia, Dalmatia, Epirus, Greece, and Sicily: they were tempted to subdue the island of Sardinia, so advantageously placed in the centre of the Mediterranean; and their arms spread desolation or terror from the Columns of Hercules to the mouth of the Nile. As they were more ambitious of spoil than of glory, they seldom attacked any fortified cities, or engaged any regular troops in the open field. But the celerity of their motions enabled them almost at the same time to threaten and to attack the most distant objects which attracted their desires; and as they always embarked a sufficient number of horses, they had no sooner landed than they swept the dismayed country with a body of light cavalry. Yet, notwithstanding the example of their king, the native Vandals and Alani insensibly declined this toilsome and perilous warfare; the hardy generation of the first conquerors was almost extinguished, and their sons, who were born in Africa, enjoyed the delicious baths and gardens which had been acquired by the valour of their fathers. Their place was readily supplied by a various multitude of Moors and Romans, of captives and outlaws; and those desperate wretches, who had already violated the laws of their country, were the most eager to promote the atrocious acts which disgrace the victories of Genseric. In the treatment of his unhappy prisoners he sometimes consulted his avarice, and sometimes indulged his cruelty; and the massacre of five hundred noble citizens of Zante or Zacynthus, whose mangled bodies he cast into the Ionian Sea, was imputed by the public indignation to his latest posterity.

Such crimes could not be excused by any provocations, but the

one passage the poet seems inspired by his subject, and expresses a strong idea by a lively image:—

——— Hinc Vandalus hostis
Urget; et in nostrum numerosâ classe quotannis
Militat excidium; conversoque ordine fati
Torrida Caucaseos infert mihi Byrsa furores.

[Carm. ii. 347.]

war which the king of the Vandals prosecuted against the Roman
empire was justified by a specious and reasonable motive. The
widow of Valentinian, Eudoxia, whom he had led captive from
Rome to Carthage, was the sole heiress of the Theodosian house;
her elder daughter, Eudocia, became the reluctant wife of
Hunneric, his eldest son; and the stern father, asserting a legal
claim which could not easily be refuted or satisfied, demanded
a just proportion of the Imperial patrimony. An adequate, or
at least a valuable, compensation was offered by the Eastern
emperor to purchase a necessary peace. Eudoxia, and her
younger daughter Placidia, were honourably restored, and the
fury of the Vandals was confined to the limits of the Western
empire. The Italians, destitute of a naval force, which alone
was capable of protecting their coasts, implored the aid of the
more fortunate nations of the East, who had formerly acknowledged in peace and war the supremacy of Rome. But the perpetual division of the two empires had alienated their interest
and their inclinations; the faith of a recent treaty was alleged;
and the Western Romans, instead of arms and ships, could only
obtain the assistance of a cold and ineffectual mediation. The
haughty Ricimer, who had long struggled with the difficulties of
his situation, was at length reduced to address the throne of
Constantinople in the humble language of a subject; and Italy
submitted, as the price and security of the alliance, to accept a
master from the choice of the emperor of the East.[1] It is not
the purpose of the present chapter, or even of the present volume,
to continue the distinct series of the Byzantine history; but a
concise view of the reign and character of the emperor Leo may
explain the last efforts that were attempted to save the falling
empire of the West.[2]

Since the death of the younger Theodosius, the domestic repose
of Constantinople had never been interrupted by war or faction.
Pulcheria had bestowed her hand, and the sceptre of the East, on

---

[1] The poet himself is compelled to acknowledge the distress of Ricimer:—

> Præterea invictus Ricimer, quem publica fata
> Respiciunt, *proprio* solus vix *Marte* repellit
> Piratam per rura vagum.

[Carm. ii. 352.]

Italy addresses her complaint to the Tiber; and Rome, at the solicitation
of the river-god, transports herself to Constantinople, renounces her
ancient claims, and implores the friendship of Aurora, the goddess of the
East. This fabulous machinery, which the genius of Claudian had used
and abused, is the constant and miserable resource of the muse of Sidonius.

[2] The original authors of the reigns of Marcian, Leo, and Zeno, are
reduced to some imperfect fragments, whose deficiencies must be supplied
from the more recent compilations of Theophanes, Zonaras, and Cedrenus.

the modest virtue of Marcian: he gratefully reverenced her august rank and virgin chastity; and, after her death, he gave his people the example of the religious worship that was due to the memory of the Imperial saint.[1] Attentive to the prosperity of his own dominions, Marcian seemed to behold with indifference the misfortunes of Rome; and the obstinate refusal of a brave and active prince to draw his sword against the Vandals was ascribed to a secret promise which had formerly been exacted from him when he was a captive in the power of Genseric.[2] The death of Marcian, after a reign of seven years, would have exposed the East to the danger of a popular election, if the superior weight of a single family had not been able to incline the balance in favour of the candidate whose interest they supported. The patrician Aspar might have placed the diadem on his own head, if he would have subscribed the Nicene creed.[3] During three generations the armies of the East were successively commanded by his father, by himself, and by his son Ardaburius; his barbarian guards formed a military force that overawed the palace and the capital; and the liberal distribution of his immense treasures rendered Aspar as popular as he was powerful. He recommended the obscure name of Leo of Thrace, a military tribune, and the principal steward of his household. His nomination was unanimously ratified by the senate; and the servant of Aspar received the Imperial crown from the hands of the patriarch or bishop, who was permitted to express, by this unusual ceremony, the suffrage of the Deity.[4] This emperor, the first of the name of Leo, has been distinguished by the title of the *Great*, from a succession of princes who gradually fixed in the opinion of the Greeks a very humble standard of heroic, or at least of royal, perfection. Yet the temperate firmness with which Leo resisted the oppression of his benefactor showed that he was conscious of his duty and of his prerogative. Aspar was astonished to find that his influence could no longer appoint a præfect of Constantinople: he presumed to reproach his sovereign

---

[1] St. Pulcheria died A.D. 453, four years before her nominal husband; and her festival is celebrated on the 10th of September by the modern Greeks: she bequeathed an immense patrimony to pious, or at least to ecclesiastical uses. See Tillemont. Mémoires Ecclés. tom. xv. p. 181-184.

[2] See Procopius de Bell. Vandal. l. i. c. 4, p. 185 [tom. i. p. 325, ed. Bonn].

[3] From this disability of Aspar to ascend the throne, it may be inferred that the stain of *Heresy* was perpetual and indelible, while that of *Barbarism* disappeared in the second generation.

[4] Theophanes, p. 95 [ed. Par.; tom. i. p. 170, ed. Bonn]. This appears to be the first origin of a ceremony which all the Christian princes of the world have since adopted; and from which the clergy have deduced the most formidable consequences.

with a breach of promise, and, insolently shaking his purple, " It is not proper (said he) that the man who is invested with this garment should be guilty of lying." " Nor is it proper (replied Leo) that a prince should be compelled to resign his own judgment, and the public interest, to the will of a subject." [1] After this extraordinary scene, it was impossible that the reconciliation of the emperor and the patrician could be sincere; or, at least, that it could be solid and permanent. An army of Isaurians [2] was secretly levied and introduced into Constantinople; and while Leo undermined the authority, and prepared the disgrace, of the family of Aspar, his mild and cautious behaviour restrained them from any rash and desperate attempts, which might have been fatal to themselves or their enemies. The measures of peace and war were affected by this internal revolution. As long as Aspar degraded the majesty of the throne, the secret correspondence of religion and interest engaged him to favour the cause of Genseric. When Leo had delivered himself from that ignominious servitude, he listened to the complaints of the Italians; resolved to extirpate the tyranny of the Vandals; and declared his alliance with his colleague Anthemius, whom he solemnly invested with the diadem and purple of the West.

The virtues of Anthemius have perhaps been magnified, since the Imperial descent, which he could only deduce from the usurper Procopius, has been swelled into a line of emperors.[3] But the merit of his immediate parents, their honours, and their riches, rendered Anthemius one of the most illustrious subjects of the East. His father, Procopius, obtained, after his Persian embassy, the rank of general and patrician; and the name of Anthemius was derived from his maternal grandfather, the celebrated præfect, who protected, with so much ability and success, the infant reign of Theodosius. The grandson of the præfect

---

[1] Cedrenus (p. 346 [ed. Par.; tom. i. p. 607, ed. Bonn]), who was conversant with the writers of better days, has preserved the remarkable words of Aspar, Βασιλεῦ, τὸν ταύτην τὴν ἀλουργίδα περιβεβλημένον οὐ χρῆ διαψεύδεσθαι.

[2] The power of the Isaurians agitated the Eastern empire in the two succeeding reigns of Zeno and Anastasius; but it ended in the destruction of those barbarians, who maintained their fierce independence about two hundred and thirty years.

[3] ――― Tali tu civis ab urbe
Procopio genitore micas; cui prisca propago
    Augustis venit a proavis.

The poet (Sidon. Panegyr. Anthem. 67-306) then proceeds to relate the private life and fortunes of the future emperor, with which he must have been very imperfectly acquainted.

was raised above the condition of a private subject by his
marriage with Euphemia, the daughter of the emperor Marcian.
This splendid alliance, which might supersede the necessity of
merit, hastened the promotion of Anthemius to the successive
dignities of count, of master-general, of consul, and of patrician;
and his merit or fortune claimed the honours of a victory which
was obtained on the banks of the Danube over the Huns.   Without indulging an extravagant ambition, the son-in-law of
Marcian might hope to be his successor; but Anthemius supported the disappointment with courage and patience; and his
subsequent elevation was universally approved by the public,
who esteemed him worthy to reign till he ascended the throne.[1]
The emperor of the West marched from Constantinople, attended
by several counts of high distinction, and a body of guards
almost equal to the strength and numbers of a regular army: he
entered Rome in triumph, and the choice of Leo was confirmed
by the senate, the people, and the barbarian confederates of
Italy.[2]   The solemn inauguration of Anthemius was followed
by the nuptials of his daughter and the patrician Ricimer; a
fortunate event, which was considered as the firmest security of
the union and happiness of the state.   The wealth of two
empires was ostentatiously displayed; and many senators completed their ruin, by an expensive effort to disguise their poverty.
All serious business was suspended during this festival; the
courts of justice were shut; the streets of Rome, the theatres,
the places of public and private resort, resounded with hymenæal
songs and dances: and the royal bride, clothed in silken robes,
with a crown on her head, was conducted to the palace of Ricimer,
who had changed his military dress for the habit of a consul and
a senator.   On this memorable occasion, Sidonius, whose early
ambition had been so fatally blasted, appeared as the orator of
Auvergne, among the provincial deputies who addressed the
throne with congratulations or complaints.[3]   The calends of
January were now approaching, and the venal poet, who had
loved Avitus and esteemed Majorian, was persuaded by his

---

[1] Sidonius discovers, with tolerable ingenuity, that this disappointment
added new lustre to the virtues of Anthemius (210, etc.), who declined one
sceptre, and reluctantly accepted another (22, etc.).

[2] The poet again celebrates the unanimity of all orders of the state
(15-22); and the Chronicle of Idatius mentions the forces which attended
his march.

[3] Interveni etenim nuptiis Patricii Ricimeris, cui filia perennis Augusti
in spem publicæ securitatis copulabatur.   The journey of Sidonius fr i.
Lyons, and the festival of Rome, are described with some spirit
Epist. 5, p. 9-13;   Epist. 9, p. 21.

friends to celebrate, in heroic verse, the merit, the felicity, the second consulship, and the future triumphs of the emperor Anthemius. Sidonius pronounced, with assurance and success, a panegyric which is still extant; and whatever might be the imperfections, either of the subject or of the composition, the welcome flatterer was immediately rewarded with the præfecture of Rome; a dignity which placed him among the illustrious personages of the empire, till he wisely preferred the more respectable character of a bishop and a saint.[1]

The Greeks ambitiously commend the piety and catholic faith of the emperor whom they gave to the West; nor do they forget to observe that, when he left Constantinople, he converted his palace into the pious foundation of a public bath, a church, and an hospital for old men.[2] Yet some suspicious appearances are found to sully the theological fame of Anthemius. From the conversation of Philotheus, a Macedonian sectary, he had imbibed the spirit of religious toleration; and the heretics of Rome would have assembled with impunity, if the bold and vehement censure which pope Hilary pronounced in the church of St. Peter had not obliged him to abjure the unpopular indulgence.[3] Even the Pagans, a feeble and obscure remnant, conceived some vain hopes, from the indifference, or partiality, of Anthemius; and his singular friendship for the philosopher Severus, whom he promoted to the consulship, was ascribed to a secret project of reviving the ancient worship of the gods.[4] These idols were crumbled into dust: and the mythology which had once been the creed of nations was so universally disbelieved, that it might be employed without scandal, or at least without

---

[1] Sidonius (l. i. Epist. 9, p. 23, 24) very fairly states his motive, his labour, and his reward. "Hic ipse Panegyricus, si non judicium, certe eventum, boni operis, accepit." He was made bishop of Clermont A.D. 471. Tillemont, Mém. Ecclés. tom. xvi. p. 750.

[2] The palace of Anthemius stood on the banks of the Propontis. In the ninth century, Alexius, the son-in-law of the emperor Theophilus, obtained permission to purchase the ground, and ended his days in a monastery which he founded on that delightful spot. Ducange, Constantinopolis Christiana, p. 117, 152.

[3] Papa Hilarius . . . apud beatum Petrum Apostolum, palam ne id fieret, clarâ voce constrinxit, in tantum ut non ea facienda cum interpositione juramenti idem promitteret Imperator. Gelasius Epistol. ad Andronicum, apud Baron. A.D. 467, No. 3. The cardinal observes, with some complacency, that it was much easier to plant heresies at Constantinople than at Rome.

[4] Damascius, in the Life of the philosopher Isidore, apud Photium, post 10 [p. 340a, ed. Bekk.]. Damascius, who lived under Justinian, comdæmons, their work, consisting of 570 præternatural stories of souls, tions, the dotage of Platonic Paganism.

suspicion, by Christian poets.[1]   Yet the vestiges of superstition were not absolutely obliterated, and the festival of the Lupercalia, whose origin had preceded the foundation of Rome, was still celebrated under the reign of Anthemius.   The savage and simple rites were expressive of an early state of society before the invention of arts and agriculture.   The rustic deities who presided over the toils and pleasures of the pastoral life, Pan, Faunus, and their train of satyrs, were such as the fancy of shepherds might create, sportive, petulant, and lascivious; whose power was limited, and whose malice was inoffensive.   A goat was the offering the best adapted to their character and attributes; the flesh of the victim was roasted on willow spits; and the riotous youths, who crowded to the feast, ran naked about the fields, with leather thongs in their hands, communicating, as it was supposed, the blessing of fecundity to the women whom they touched.[2]   The altar of Pan was erected, perhaps by Evander the Arcadian, in a dark recess in the side of the Palatine hill, watered by a perpetual fountain, and shaded by a hanging grove.   A tradition that, in the same place, Romulus and Remus were suckled by the wolf, rendered it still more sacred and venerable in the eyes of the Romans; and this sylvan spot was gradually surrounded by the stately edifices of the Forum.[3]   After the conversion of the Imperial city, the Christians still continued, in the month of February, the annual celebration of the Lupercalia; to which they ascribed a secret and mysterious influence on the genial powers of the animal and vegetable world.   The bishops of Rome were solicitous to abolish a profane custom so repugnant to the spirit of Christianity; but their zeal was not supported by the authority of the civil magistrate: the inveterate abuse subsisted till the end of the fifth century, and pope Gelasius, who purified the capital from the last stain of idolatry, appeased, by a formal apology, the murmurs of the senate and people.[4]

---

[1] In the poetical works of Sidonius, which he afterwards condemned (l. ix. Epist. 16, p. 285), the fabulous deities are the principal actors.   If Jerom was scourged by the angels for only reading Virgil, the bishop of Clermont, for such a vile imitation, deserved an additional whipping from the Muses.

[2] Ovid (Fast. l. ii. 267-452) has given an amusing description of the follies of antiquity, which still inspired so much respect, that a grave magistrate, running naked through the streets, was not an object of astonishment or laughter.

[3] See Dionys. Halicarn. l. i. [c. 79] p. 25, 65, edit. Hudson.   The Roman antiquaries, Donatus (l. ii. c. 18, p. 173, 174) and Nardini (p. 386, 387), have laboured to ascertain the true situation of the Lupercal.

[4] Baronius published, from the MSS. of the Vatican, this epistle of Pope Gelasius (A.D. 496, No. 28-45), which is entitled Adversus Andromachum

In all his public declarations the emperor Leo assumes the
authority, and professes the affection of a father for his son
Anthemius, with whom he had divided the administration of the
universe.[1]   The situation, and perhaps the character, of Leo
dissuaded him from exposing his person to the toils and dangers
of an African war.   But the powers of the Eastern empire were
strenuously exerted to deliver Italy and the Mediterranean from
the Vandals; and Genseric, who had so long oppressed both the
land and sea, was threatened from every side with a formidable
invasion.   The campaign was opened by a bold and successful
enterprise of the præfect Heraclius.[2]   The troops of Egypt,
Thebais, and Libya were embarked under this command: and
the Arabs, with a train of horses and camels, opened the roads of
the desert.   Heraclius landed on the coast of Tripoli, surprised
and subdued the cities of that province, and prepared, by a
laborious march, which Cato had formerly executed,[3] to join the
Imperial army under the walls of Carthage.   The intelligence of
this loss extorted from Genseric some insidious and ineffectual
propositions of peace: but he was still more seriously alarmed by
the reconciliation of Marcellinus with the two empires.   The
independent patrician had been persuaded to acknowledge the
legitimate title of Anthemius, whom he accompanied in his
journey to Rome; the Dalmatian fleet was received into the
harbours of Italy; the active valour of Marcellinus expelled the
Vandals from the island of Sardinia; and the languid efforts of
the West added some weight to the immense preparations of the
Eastern Romans.   The expense of the naval armament which

Senatorem, cæterosque Romanos, qui Lupercalia secundum morem pris-
tinum colenda constituebant. Gelasius always supposes that his adversaries are nominal Christians, and, that he may not yield to them in absurd
prejudice, he imputes to this harmless festival all the *calamities* of the age.
    [1] Itaque nos quibus totius mundi regimen commisit superna provisio. . . .
Pius et triumphator semper Augustus filius noster Anthemius, licet Divina
Majestas et nostra creatio pietati ejus plenam Imperii commiserit potes-
tatem, etc. . . . Such is the dignified style of Leo, whom Anthemius
respectfully names Dominus et Pater meus Princeps sacratissimus Leo.
See Novell. Anthem. tit. ii. iii. p. 38, ad calcem Cod. Theod.
    [2] The expedition of Heraclius is clouded with difficulties (Tillemont, Hist.
des Empereurs, tom. vi. p. 640), and it requires some dexterity to use the
circumstances afforded by Theophanes, without injury to the more respectable evidence of Procopius.
    [3] The march of Cato from Berenice, in the province of Cyrene, was much
longer than that of Heraclius from Tripoli. He passed the deep sandy
desert in thirty days, and was found necessary to provide, besides the
ordinary supplies, a great number of skins filled with water, and several
Psylli, who were supposed to possess the art of sucking the wounds which
had been made by the serpents of their native country. See Plutarch in
Caton. Uticens. [c. 56] tom. iv. p. 275; Strabon. Geograph. l. xvii. p. 1193
[p. 836, ed. Casaub.].

Leo sent against the Vandals has been distinctly ascertained;
and the curious and instructive account displays the wealth of
the declining empire. The Royal demesnes, or private patrimony of the prince, supplied seventeen thousand pounds of gold;
forty-seven thousand pounds of gold, and seven hundred thousand of silver, were levied and paid into the treasury by the
Prætorian præfects. But the cities were reduced to extreme
poverty; and the diligent calculation of fines and forfeitures, as
a valuable object of the revenue, does not suggest the idea of a
just, or merciful, administration. The whole expense, by what-
soever means it was defrayed, of the African campaign, amounted
to the sum of one hundred and thirty thousand pounds of gold,
about five millions two hundred thousand pounds sterling, at a
time when the value of money appears, from the comparative
price of corn, to have been somewhat higher than in the present
age.[1] The fleet that sailed from Constantinople to Carthage
consisted of eleven hundred and thirteen ships, and the number
of soldiers and mariners exceeded one hundred thousand men.
Basiliscus, the brother of the empress Verina, was intrusted with
this important command. His sister, the wife of Leo, had exaggerated the merit of his former exploits against the Scythians.
But the discovery of his guilt, or incapacity, was reserved for the
African war; and his friends could only save his military reputation by asserting that he had conspired with Aspar to spare
Genseric, and to betray the last hope of the Western empire.

Experience has shown that the success of an invader most
commonly depends on the vigour and celerity of his operations.
The strength and sharpness of the first impression are blunted by
delay; the health and spirit of the troops insensibly languish in
a distant climate; the naval and military force, a mighty effort
which perhaps can never be repeated, is silently consumed; and
every hour that is wasted in negotiation accustoms the enemy

---

[1] The principal sum is clearly expressed by Procopius (de Bell. Vandal.
l. i. c. 6, p. 191 [tom. i. p. 335, ed. Bonn]); the smaller constituent parts,
which Tillemont (Hist. des Empereurs, tom. vi. p. 396) has laboriously
collected from the Byzantine writers, are less certain and less important.
The historian Malchus laments the public misery (Excerpt. ex Suida in
Corp. Hist. Byzant. p. 58); but he is surely unjust when he charges Leo
with hoarding the treasures which he extorted from the people [p. 270, ed.
Bonn].

[John Lydus, in his work, De Magistratibus, estimates the expenditure
at 65,000 pounds of gold and 700,000 pounds of silver, and regards this
proceeding, the blame of which he lays on Basiliscus, as bringing about the
shipwreck of the state. On this point Milman says, " From that time all
the revenues of the empire were anticipated, and the finances fell into
inextricable confusion."—O. S.]

to contemplate and examine those hostile terrors which, on their first appearance, he deemed irresistible. The formidable navy of Basiliscus pursued its prosperous navigation from the Thracian Bosphorus to the coast of Africa. He landed his troops at Cape Bona, or the promontory of Mercury, about forty miles from Carthage.[1] The army of Heraclius, and the fleet of Marcellinus, either joined or seconded the Imperial lieutenant; and the Vandals who opposed his progress by sea or land were successively vanquished.[2] If Basiliscus had seized the moment of consternation, and boldly advanced to the capital, Carthage must have surrendered, and the kingdom of the Vandals was extinguished. Genseric beheld the danger with firmness, and eluded it with his veteran dexterity. He protested, in the most respectful language, that he was ready to submit his person and his dominions to the will of the emperor; but he requested a truce of five days to regulate the terms of his submission; and it was universally believed that his secret liberality contributed to the success of this public negotiation. Instead of obstinately refusing whatever indulgence his enemy so earnestly solicited, the guilty, or the credulous, Basiliscus consented to the fatal truce; and his imprudent security seemed to proclaim that he already considered himself as the conqueror of Africa. During this short interval the wind became favourable to the designs of Genseric. He manned his largest ships of war with the bravest of the Moors and Vandals; and they towed after them many large barks filled with combustible materials. In the obscurity of the night, these destructive vessels were impelled against the unguarded and unsuspecting fleet of the Romans, who were awakened by the sense of their instant danger. Their close and crowded order assisted the progress of the fire, which was communicated with rapid and irresistible violence; and the noise of the wind, the crackling of the flames, the dissonant cries of the soldiers and mariners, who could neither command nor obey, increased the horror of the nocturnal tumult. Whilst they laboured to extricate themselves from the fire-ships, and to save at least a part of the navy the galleys of Genseric assaulted them with temperate and disciplined valour; and many of the Romans,

---

[1] This promontory is forty miles from Carthage (Procop. l. i. c. 6, p. 192 [De Bell. Vandal. tom. i. p. 377, ed. Bonn]), and twenty leagues from Sicily (Shaw's Travels, p. 89). Scipio landed farther in the bay, at the fair promontory; see the animated description of Livy, xxix. 26, 27.

[2] Theophanes (p. 100 [tom. i. p. 179, ed. Bonn]) affirms that many ships of the Vandals were sunk. The assertion of Jornandes (de Successione Regn.), that Basiliscus attacked Carthage, must be understood in a very qualified sense.

who escaped the fury of the flames, were destroyed or taken by the victorious Vandals. Among the events of that disastrous night, the heroic, or rather desperate, courage of John, one of the principal officers of Basiliscus, has rescued his name from oblivion. When the ship which he had bravely defended was almost consumed, he threw himself in his armour into the sea, disdainfully rejected the esteem and pity of Genso, the son of Genseric, who pressed him to accept honourable quarter, and sunk under the waves; exclaiming, with his last breath, that he would never fall alive into the hands of those impious dogs. Actuated by a far different spirit, Basiliscus, whose station was the most remote from danger, disgracefully fled in the beginning of the engagement, returned to Constantinople with the loss of more than half of his fleet and army, and sheltered his guilty head in the sanctuary of St. Sophia, till his sister, by her tears and entreaties, could obtain his pardon from the indignant emperor. Heraclius effected his retreat through the desert; Marcellinus retired to Sicily, where he was assassinated, perhaps at the instigation of Ricimer, by one of his own captains; and the king of the Vandals expressed his surprise and satisfaction that the Romans themselves should remove from the world his most formidable antagonists.[1] After the failure of this great expedition, Genseric again became the tyrant of the sea: the coasts of Italy, Greece, and Asia, were again exposed to his revenge and avarice; Tripoli and Sardinia returned to his obedience; he added Sicily to the number of his provinces; and, before he died, in the fulness of years and of glory, he beheld the final extinction of the empire of the West.[2]

During his long and active reign the African monarch had studiously cultivated the friendship of the barbarians of Europe, whose arms he might employ in a seasonable and effectual diversion against the two empires. After the death of Attila he renewed his alliance with the Visigoths of Gaul; and the sons of the elder Theodoric, who successively reigned over that warlike nation, were easily persuaded, by the sense of interest, to forget the cruel affront which Genseric had inflicted on their

---

[1] Damascius in Vit. Isidor. apud Phot. p. 1048 [p. 342, ed. Bekk.]. It will appear, by comparing the three short chronicles of the times, that Marcellinus had fought near Carthage, and was killed in Sicily.

[2] For the African war see Procopius (de Bell. Vandal. l. i. c. 6, p. 191, 192, 193 [tom. i. p. 335 *sqq.*, ed. Bonn]), Theophanes (p. 99, 100, 101 [ed Par.; tom. i. p. 179 *sqq.*, ed. Bonn]), Cedrenus (p. 349, 350 [tom. i. p. 613. ed. Bonn]), and Zonaras (tom. ii. l. xiv. p. 50, 51). Montesquieu (Considérations sur la Grandeur, etc., c. xx. tom. iii. p. 497) has made a judicious observation on the failure of these great naval armaments.

sister.[1] The death of the emperor Majorian delivered Theodoric
the Second from the restraint of fear, and perhaps of honour;
he violated his recent treaty with the Romans; and the ample
territory of Narbonne, which he firmly united to his dominions,
became the immediate reward of his perfidy.   The selfish policy
of Ricimer encouraged him to invade the provinces which were
in the possession of Ægidius, his rival; but the active count, by
the defence of Arles and the victory of Orleans, saved Gaul,
and checked during his lifetime the progress of the Visigoths.
Their ambition was soon rekindled; and the design of extinguishing the Roman empire in Spain and Gaul was conceived
and almost completed in the reign of Euric, who assassinated
his brother Theodoric, and displayed, with a more savage temper,
superior abilities both in peace and war.   He passed the Pyrenees
at the head of a numerous army, subdued the cities of Saragossa
and Pampeluna, vanquished in battle the martial nobles of the
Tarragonese province, carried his victorious arms into the heart
of Lusitania, and permitted the Suevi to hold the kingdom of
Gallicia under the Gothic monarchy of Spain.[2] The efforts of
Euric were not less vigorous or less successful in Gaul; and
throughout the country that extends from the Pyrenees to the
Rhône and the Loire, Berry and Auvergne were the only cities
or dioceses which refused to acknowledge him as their master.[3]
In the defence of Clermont, their principal town, the inhabitants
of Auvergne sustained with inflexible resolution the miseries of
war, pestilence, and famine; and the Visigoths, relinquishing the
fruitless siege, suspended the hopes of that important conquest.
The youth of the province were animated by the heroic and almost
incredible valour of Ecdicius, the son of the emperor Avitus,[4]
who made a desperate sally with only eighteen horsemen, boldly
attacked the Gothic army, and, after maintaining a flying
skirmish, retired safe and victorious within the walls of Clermont.

  [1] Jornandes is our best guide through the reigns of Theodoric II. and
Euric (de Rebus Geticis, c. 44, 45, 46, 47, p. 675-681). Idatius ends too
soon, and Isidore is too sparing of the information which he might have
given on the affairs of Spain.   The events that relate to Gaul are laboriously illustrated in the third book of the Abbé Dubos, Hist. Critique, tom. i.
p. 424-620.
  [2] See Mariana, Hist. Hispan. tom. i. l. v. c. 5, p. 162.
  [3] An imperfect, but original, picture of Gaul, more especially of Auvergne,
is shown by Sidonius; who, as a senator and afterwards as a bishop, was
deeply interested in the fate of his country.   See l. v. [vii.] Epist. 1, 5, 9,
etc.
  [4] Sidonius, l. iii. Epist. 3, p. 65-68; Greg. Turon. l. ii. c. 24, in tom. ii.
p. 174; Jornandes, c. 45, p. 679. Perhaps Ecdicius was only the son-in-
law of Avitus, his wife's son by another husband.

His charity was equal to his courage: in a time of extreme scarcity four thousand poor were fed at his expense; and his private influence levied an army of Burgundians for the deliverance of Auvergne. From *his* virtues alone the faithful citizens of Gaul derived any hopes of safety or freedom; and even such virtues were insufficient to avert the impending ruin of their country, since they were anxious to learn, from his authority and example, whether they should prefer the alternative of exile or servitude.[1] The public confidence was lost; the resources of the state were exhausted; and the Gauls had too much reason to believe that Anthemius, who reigned in Italy, was incapable of protecting his distressed subjects beyond the Alps. The feeble emperor could only procure for their defence the service of twelve thousand British auxiliaries. Riothamus, one of the independent kings or chieftains of the island, was persuaded to transport his troops to the continent of Gaul: he sailed up the Loire, and established his quarters in Berry, where the people complained of these oppressive allies, till they were destroyed or dispersed by the arms of the Visigoths.[2]

One of the last acts of jurisdiction which the Roman senate exercised over their subjects of Gaul was the trial and condemnation of Arvandus, the Prætorian præfect. Sidonius, who rejoices that he lived under a reign in which he might pity and assist a state-criminal, has expressed, with tenderness and freedom, the faults of his indiscreet and unfortunate friend.[3] From the perils which he had escaped, Arvandus imbibed confidence rather than wisdom; and such was the various, though uniform, imprudence of his behaviour, that his prosperity must appear much more surprising than his downfall. The second præfecture, which he obtained within the term of five years, abolished the merit and popularity of his preceding administration. His easy temper was corrupted by flattery

---

[1] Si nullæ a republicâ vires, nulla præsidia, si nullæ, quantum rumor est, Anthemii principis opes, statuit, et auctore, nobilitas, seu patriam dimittere seu capillos (Sidon. l. ii. Epist. 1, p. 33). The last words (Sirmond, Not. p. 25) may likewise denote the clerical tonsure, which was indeed the choice of Sidonius himself.

[2] The history of these Britons may be traced in Jornandes (c. 45, p. 678), Sidonius (l. iii. Epistol. 9, p. 73, 74), and Gregory of Tours (l. ii. c. 18, in tom. ii. p. 170). Sidonius (who styles these mercenary troops argutos, armatos, tumultuosos, virtute, numero, contubernio, contumaces) addresses their general in a tone of friendship and familiarity.

[3] See Sidonius, l. i. Epist. 7, p. 15-20, with Sirmond's notes. This letter does honour to his heart as well as to his understanding. The prose of Sidonius, however vitiated by a false and affected taste, is much superior to his insipid verses.

and exasperated by opposition; he was forced to satisfy his importunate creditors with the spoils of the province; his capricious insolence offended the nobles of Gaul; and he sunk under the weight of the public hatred. The mandate of his disgrace summoned him to justify his conduct before the senate; and he passed the sea of Tuscany with a favourable wind, the presage, as he vainly imagined, of his future fortunes. A decent respect was still observed for the *Præfectorian* rank; and on his arrival at Rome Arvandus was committed to the hospitality, rather than to the custody, of Flavius Asellus, the count of the sacred largesses, who resided in the Capitol.[1] He was eagerly pursued by his accusers, the four deputies of Gaul, who were all distinguished by their birth, their dignities, or their eloquence. In the name of a great province, and according to the forms of Roman jurisprudence, they instituted a civil and criminal action, requiring such restitution as might compensate the losses of individuals, and such punishment as might satisfy the justice of the state. Their charges of corrupt oppression were numerous and weighty; but they placed their secret dependence on a letter which they had intercepted, and which they could prove, by the evidence of his secretary, to have been dictated by Arvandus himself. The author of this letter seemed to dissuade the king of the Goths from a peace with the *Greek* emperor: he suggested the attack of the Britons on the Loire; and he recommended a division of Gaul, according to the law of nations, between the Visigoths and the Burgundians.[2] These pernicious schemes, which a friend could only palliate by the reproaches of vanity and indiscretion, were susceptible of a treasonable interpretation; and the deputies had artfully resolved not to produce their most formidable weapons till the decisive moment of the contest. But their intentions were discovered by the zeal of Sidonius. He immediately apprised the unsuspecting criminal of his danger; and sincerely lamented, without any mixture of anger, the haughty presumption of Arvandus, who rejected, and even resented, the salutary advice of his friends. Ignorant of his real situation, Arvandus showed himself in the Capitol

---

[1] When the Capitol ceased to be a temple, it was appropriated to the use of the civil magistrate; and it is still the residence of the Roman senator. The jewellers, etc., might be allowed to expose their precious wares in the porticoes.

[2] Hæc ad regem Gothorum, charta videbatur emitti pacem cum Græco Imperatore dissuadens, Britannos super Ligerim sitos impugnari oportere demonstrans, cum Burgundionibus jure gentium Gallias dividi debere confirmans.

in the white robe of a candidate, accepted indiscriminate salutations and offers of service, examined the shops of the merchants, the silks and gems, sometimes with the indifference of a spectator and sometimes with the attention of a purchaser; and complained of the times, of the senate, of the prince, and of the delays of justice. His complaints were soon removed. An early day was fixed for his trial; and Arvandus appeared, with his accusers, before a numerous assembly of the Roman senate. The mournful garb which they affected excited the compassion of the judges, who were scandalised by the gay and splendid dress of their adversary: and when the præfect Arvandus, with the first of the Gallic deputies, were directed to take their places on the senatorial benches, the same contrast of pride and modesty was observed in their behaviour. In this memorable judgment, which presented a lively image of the old republic, the Gauls exposed, with force and freedom, the grievances of the province; and as soon as the minds of the audience were sufficiently inflamed, they recited the fatal epistle. The obstinacy of Arvandus was founded on the strange supposition that a subject could not be convicted of treason, unless he had actually conspired to assume the purple. As the paper was read, he repeatedly, and with a loud voice, acknowledged it for his genuine composition; and his astonishment was equal to his dismay when the unanimous voice of the senate declared him guilty of a capital offence. By their decree he was degraded from the rank of a præfect to the obscure condition of a plebeian, and ignominiously dragged by servile hands to the public prison. After a fortnight's adjournment the senate was again convened to pronounce the sentence of his death: but while he expected, in the island of Æsculapius, the expiration of the thirty days allowed by an ancient law to the vilest malefactors,[1] his friends interposed, the emperor Anthemius relented, and the præfect of Gaul obtained the milder punishment of exile and confiscation. The faults of Arvandus might deserve compassion; but the impunity of Seronatus accused the justice of the republic, till he was condemned and executed on the complaint of the people of Auvergne. That flagitious minister, the Catiline of his age and country, held a secret correspondence with the Visigoths to betray the province which he oppressed: his industry was continually exercised in the discovery of new taxes and obsolete

---

[1] *Senatusconsultum Tiberianum* (Sirmond, Not. p. 17); but that law allowed only ten days between the sentence and execution; the remaining twenty were added in the reign of Theodosius.

offences; and his extravagant vices would have inspired contempt if they had not excited fear and abhorrence.[1]

Such criminals were not beyond the reach of justice; but whatever might be the guilt of Ricimer, that powerful barbarian was able to contend or to negotiate with the prince whose alliance he had condescended to accept. The peaceful and prosperous reign which Anthemius had promised to the West was soon clouded by misfortune and discord. Ricimer, apprehensive or impatient of a superior, retired from Rome and fixed his residence at Milan; an advantageous situation, either to invite or to repel the warlike tribes that were seated between the Alps and the Danube.[2] Italy was gradually divided into two independent and hostile kingdoms; and the nobles of Liguria, who trembled at the near approach of a civil war, fell prostrate at the feet of the patrician, and conjured him to spare their unhappy country. "For my own part," replied Ricimer, in a tone of insolent moderation, "I am still inclined to embrace the friendship of the Galatian;[3] but who will undertake to appease his anger, or to mitigate the pride which always rises in proportion to our submission?" They informed him that Epiphanius, bishop of Pavia,[4] united the wisdom of the serpent with the innocence of the dove; and appeared confident that the eloquence of such an ambassador must prevail against the strongest opposition, either of interest or passion. Their recommendation was approved; and Epiphanius, assuming the benevolent office of mediation, proceeded without delay to Rome, where he was received with the honours due to his merit and reputation. The oration of a bishop in favour of peace may be easily supposed: he argued that, in all possible circumstances, the forgiveness of injuries must be an act of mercy, or magnanimity, or prudence; and he

---

[1] Catilina seculi nostri. Sidonius, l. ii. Epist. 1, p. 33; l. v. Epist. 13, p. 143; l. vii. Epist. 7, p. 185. He execrates the crimes and applauds the punishment of Seronatus, perhaps with the indignation of a virtuous citizen, perhaps with the resentment of a personal enemy.

[2] Ricimer, under the reign of Anthemius, defeated and slew in battle Beorgor, king of the Alani (Jornandes, c. 45, p. 678). His sister had married the king of the Burgundians, and he maintained an intimate connection with the Suevic colony established in Pannonia and Noricum.

[3] Galatam concitatum. Sirmond (in his notes to Ennodius [tom. i. p. 659]) applies this appellation to Anthemius himself. The emperor was probably born in the province of Galatia, whose inhabitants, the Gallo-Grecians, were supposed to unite the vices of a savage and a corrupted people.

[4] Epiphanius was thirty years bishop of Pavia (A.D. 467-497; see Tillemont, Mém. Ecclés. tom. xvi. p. 788). His name and actions would have been unknown to posterity if Ennodius, one of his successors, had not written his Life (Sirmond, Opera, tom. i. p. 1647-1692); in which he represents him as one of the greatest characters of the age.

seriously admonished the emperor to avoid a contest with a fierce barbarian, which might be fatal to himself, and must be ruinous to his dominions. Anthemius acknowledged the truth of his maxims; but he deeply felt, with grief and indignation, the behaviour of Ricimer; and his passion gave eloquence and energy to his discourse. " What favours," he warmly exclaimed, " have we refused to this ungrateful man? What provocations have we not endured? Regardless of the majesty of the purple, I gave my daughter to a Goth; I sacrificed my own blood to the safety of the republic. The liberality which ought to have secured the eternal attachment of Ricimer has exasperated him against his benefactor. What wars has he not excited against the empire? How often has he instigated and assisted the fury of hostile nations? Shall I now accept his perfidious friendship? Can I hope that *he* will respect the engagements of a treaty, who has already violated the duties of a son? " But the anger of Anthemius evaporated in these passionate exclamations: he insensibly yielded to the proposals of Epiphanius; and the bishop returned to his diocese with the satisfaction of restoring the peace of Italy by a reconciliation,[1] of which the sincerity and continuance might be reasonably suspected. The clemency of the emperor was extorted from his weakness; and Ricimer suspended his ambitious designs till he had secretly prepared the engines with which he resolved to subvert the throne of Anthemius. The mask of peace and moderation was then thrown aside. The army of Ricimer was fortified by a numerous reinforcement of Burgundians and Oriental Suevi: he disclaimed all allegiance to the Greek emperor, marched from Milan to the gates of Rome, and, fixing his camp on the banks of the Anio, impatiently expected the arrival of Olybrius, his Imperial candidate.

The senator Olybrius, of the Anician family, might esteem himself the lawful heir of the Western empire. He had married Placidia, the younger daughter of Valentinian, after she was restored by Genseric, who still detained her sister Eudoxia, as the wife, or rather as the captive, of his son. The king of the Vandals supported, by threats and solicitations, the fair pretensions of his Roman ally; and assigned, as one of the motives of the war, the refusal of the senate and people to acknowledge their lawful prince, and the unworthy preference which they

---

[1] Ennodius (p. 1659-1664) has related this embassy of Epiphanius; and his narrative, verbose and turgid as it must appear, illustrates some curious passages in the fall of the Western empire.

had given to a stranger.[1] The friendship of the public enemy
might render Olybrius still more unpopular to the Italians;
but when Ricimer meditated the ruin of the emperor Anthemius,
he tempted, with the offer of a diadem, the candidate who could
justify his rebellion by an illustrious name and a royal alliance.
The husband of Placidia, who, like most of his ancestors, had
been invested with the consular dignity, might have continued
to enjoy a secure and splendid fortune in the peaceful residence
of Constantinople; nor does he appear to have been tormented
by such a genius as cannot be amused or occupied unless by the
administration of an empire. Yet Olybrius yielded to the
importunities of his friends, perhaps of his wife; rashly plunged
into the dangers and calamities of a civil war; and, with the secret
connivance of the emperor Leo, accepted the Italian purple, which
was bestowed, and resumed, at the capricious will of a barbarian.
He landed without obstacle (for Genseric was master of the sea)
either at Ravenna or the port of Ostia, and immediately proceeded to the camp of Ricimer, where he was received as the
sovereign of the Western world.[2]

The patrician, who had extended his posts from the Anio to
the Milvian bridge, already possessed two quarters of Rome,
the Vatican and the Janiculum, which are separated by the
Tiber from the rest of the city;[3] and it may be conjectured that
an assembly of seceding senators imitated, in the choice of
Olybrius, the forms of a legal election. But the body of the
senate and people firmly adhered to the cause of Anthemius;
and the more effectual support of a Gothic army enabled him
to prolong his reign, and the public distress, by a resistance of
three months, which produced the concomitant evils of famine
and pestilence. At length Ricimer made a furious assault on
the bridge of Hadrian, or St. Angelo; and the narrow pass was

---

[1] Priscus Excerpt. Legation. p. 74 [p. 219. ed. Bonn]. Procopius de
Bell. Vandal. l. i. c. 6. p. 191 [tom. i. p. 336. ed. Bonn]. Eudoxia and her
daughter were restored after the death of Majorian. Perhaps the consulship of Olybrius (A.D. 464) was bestowed as a nuptial present.

[2] The hostile appearance of Olybrius is fixed (notwithstanding the
opinion of Pagi) by the duration of his reign. The secret connivance of
Leo is acknowledged by Theophanes and the Paschal Chronicle. We are
ignorant of his motives; but in this obscure period our ignorance extends
to the most public and important facts.

[3] Of the fourteen regions, or quarters, into which Rome was divided by
Augustus, only *one*, the Janiculum, lay on the Tuscan side of the Tiber.
But, in the fifth century, the Vatican suburb formed a considerable city;
and in the ecclesiastical distribution, which had been recently made by
Simplicius, the reigning pope, *two* of the *seven* regions or parishes of Rome
depended on the church of St. Peter. See Nardini Roma Antica, p. 67. It
would require a tedious dissertation to mark the circumstances in which I
am inclined to depart from the topography of that learned Roman.

defended with equal valour by the Goths till the death of Gilimer, their leader. The victorious troops, breaking down every barrier, rushed with irresistible violence into the heart of the city, and Rome (if we may use the language of a contemporary pope) was subverted by the civil fury of Anthemius and Ricimer.[1] The unfortunate Anthemius was dragged from his concealment and inhumanly massacred by the command of his son-in-law, who thus added a third, or perhaps a fourth, emperor to the number of his victims. The soldiers, who united the rage of factious citizens with the savage manners of barbarians, were indulged without control in the licence of rapine and murder: the crowd of slaves and plebeians, who were unconcerned in the event, could only gain by the indiscriminate pillage; and the face of the city exhibited the strange contrast of stern cruelty and dissolute intemperance.[2] Forty days after this calamitous event, the subject, not of glory, but of guilt, Italy was delivered, by a painful disease, from the tyrant Ricimer, who bequeathed the command of his army to his nephew Gundobald, one of the princes of the Burgundians. In the same year all the principal actors in this great revolution were removed from the stage; and the whole reign of Olybrius, whose death does not betray any symptoms of violence, is included within the term of seven months. He left one daughter, the offspring of his marriage with Placidia; and the family of the great Theodosius, transplanted from Spain to Constantinople, was propagated in the female line as far as the eighth generation.[3]

Whilst the vacant throne of Italy was abandoned to lawless barbarians,[4] the election of a new colleague was seriously agitated

---

[1] Nuper Anthemii et Ricimeris civili furore subversa est. Gelasius (in Epist. ad Andromach. apud Baron. A.D. 496, No. 42), Sigonius (tom. i. l. xiv. de Occidentali Imperio, p. 542, 543), and Muratori (Annali d'Italia tom. iv. p. 308, 309), with the aid of a less imperfect MS. of the Historia Miscella, have illustrated this dark and bloody transaction.

[2] Such had been the sæva ac deformis urbe totâ facies, when Rome was assaulted and stormed by the troops of Vespasian (see Tacit. Hist. iii. 82, 83); and every cause of mischief had since acquired much additional energy. The revolution of ages may bring round the same calamities; but ages may revolve without producing a Tacitus to describe them.

[3] See Ducange, Familiæ Byzantin. p. 74, 75. Areobindus, who appears to have married the niece of the emperor Justinian, was the eighth descendant of the elder Theodosius.

[4] The last revolutions of the Western empire are faintly marked in Theophanes (p. 102 [tom. i. p. 184, ed. Bonn]), Jornandes (c. 45, p. 679), the Chronicle of Marcellinus, and the Fragments of an anonymous writer, published by Valesius at the end of Ammianus (p. 716, 717 [tom. ii. p. 303 sq., ed. Bipon.]). If Photius had not been so wretchedly concise, we should derive much information from the contemporary histories of Malchus and Candidus. See his Extracts, p. 172-179 [p. 54-56, ed. Bekk].

in the council of Leo. The empress Verina, studious to promote the greatness of her own family, had married one of her nieces to Julius Nepos, who succeeded his uncle Marcellinus in the sovereignty of Dalmatia, a more solid possession than the title which he was persuaded to accept of Emperor of the West. But the measures of the Byzantine court were so languid and irresolute, that many months elapsed after the death of Anthemius, and even of Olybrius, before their destined successor could show himself, with a respectable force, to his Italian subjects. During that interval, Glycerius, an obscure soldier, was invested with the purple by his patron Gundobald; but the Burgundian prince was unable or unwilling to support his nomination by a civil war: the pursuits of domestic ambition recalled him beyond the Alps,[1] and his client was permitted to exchange the Roman sceptre for the bishopric of Salona. After extinguishing such a competitor, the emperor Nepos was acknowledged by the senate, by the Italians, and by the provincials of Gaul; his moral virtues and military talents were loudly celebrated; and those who derived any private benefit from his government announced in prophetic strains the restoration of the public felicity.[2] Their hopes (if such hopes had been entertained) were confounded within the term of a single year; and the treaty of peace, which ceded Auvergne to the Visigoths, is the only event of his short and inglorious reign. The most faithful subjects of Gaul were sacrificed by the Italian emperor to the hope of domestic security;[3] but his repose was soon invaded by a furious sedition of the barbarian confederates, who, under the command of Orestes, their general, were in full march from Rome to Ravenna. Nepos trembled at their approach; and, instead of placing a just confidence in the strength of Ravenna, he hastily escaped to his ships, and retired to his Dalmatian principality, on the opposite coast of the Hadriatic. By this shameful abdication he protracted his life

[1] See Greg. Turon. l. ii. c. 28, in tom. ii. p. 175. Dubos, Hist. Critique, tom. i. p. 613. By the murder or death of his two brothers, Gundobald acquired the sole possession of the kingdom of Burgundy, whose ruin was hastened by their discord.

[2] Julius Nepos armis pariter summus Augustus ac moribus. Sidonius, l. v. Ep. 16, p. 146. Nepos had given to Ecdicius the title of Patrician, which Anthemius had promised, decessoris Anthemii fidem absolvit. See l. viii. Ep. 7, p. 224 [l. v. Ep. 16, p. 146].

[3] Epiphanius was sent ambassador from Nepos to the Visigoths for the purpose of ascertaining the *fines Imperii Italici* (Ennodius in Sirmond, tom. i. p. 1665-1669). His pathetic discourse concealed the disgraceful secret which soon excited the just and bitter complaints of the bishop of Clermont.

about five years, in a very ambiguous state between an emperor and an exile, till he was assassinated at Salona by the ungrateful Glycerius, who was translated, perhaps as the reward of his crime, to the archbishopric of Milan.[1]

The nations who had asserted their independence after the death of Attila were established, by the right of possession or conquest, in the boundless countries to the north of the Danube; or in the Roman provinces between the river and the Alps. But the bravest of their youth enlisted in the army of *confederates*, who formed the defence and the terror of Italy;[2] and in this promiscuous multitude, the names of the Heruli, the Sciri, the Alani, the Turcilingi, and the Rugians, appear to have predominated. The example of these warriors was imitated by Orestes,[3] the son of Tatullus, and the father of the last Roman emperor of the West. Orestes, who has been already mentioned in this history, had never deserted his country. His birth and fortunes rendered him one of the most illustrious subjects of Pannonia. When that province was ceded to the Huns, he entered into the service of Attila, his lawful sovereign, obtained the office of his secretary, and was repeatedly sent ambassador to Constantinople, to represent the person and signify the commands of the imperious monarch. The death of that conqueror restored him to his freedom; and Orestes might honourably refuse either to follow the sons of Attila into the Scythian desert, or to obey the Ostrogoths, who had usurped the dominion of Pannonia. He preferred the service of the Italian princes, the successors of Valentinian; and, as he possessed the qualifications

[1] Malchus, apud Phot. p. 172 [p. 54 b, ed. Bekk.]. Ennod. Epigram. lxxxii. in Sirmond Oper. tom. i. p. 1879. Some doubt may however be raised on the identity of the emperor and the archbishop.
[2] Our knowledge of these mercenaries who subverted the Western empire is derived from Procopius (de Bell. Gothico. l. i. c. i. p. 308 [tom. ii. p. 6, ed. Bonn]). The popular opinion and the recent historians represent Odoacer in the false light of a *stranger* and a *king*, who invaded Italy with an army of foreigners, his native subjects.
[Of these peoples who formed at once the defence and the terror of Italy, nearly all originally came from the neighbourhood of the Baltic. The Heruli appear again later on. The Turcilingi are probably the same tribe which are described by Ptolemy (ii. 11, 14) under the corrupt form, Ρουτικλειοι, and are stated to be dwelling on the Vistula. The Sciri or Scirri are also placed by Pliny on the eastern side of the Vistula. The Rugii are first mentioned by Tacitus in the Germania (Germ. c. 43), who places them on the Baltic, and are perhaps the people of the gulf of Riga. Cf. Zeuss, *Die Deutschen und die Nachbarstämme*.—O. S.]
[3] Orestes, qui eo tempore quando Attila ad Italiam venit, se illi junxit, et ejus notarius factus fuerat. Anonym. Vales. p. 716 [Amm. Marc. tom. ii. p. 303, ed. Bipon.] He is mistaken in the date; but we may credit his assertion that the secretary of Attila was the father of Augustulus.

of courage, industry, and experience, he advanced with rapid steps in the military profession, till he was elevated, by the favour of Nepos himself, to the dignities of patrician and master-general of the troops. These troops had been long accustomed to reverence the character and authority of Orestes, who affected their manners, conversed with them in their own language, and was intimately connected with their national chieftains by long habits of familiarity and friendship. At his solicitation they rose in arms against the obscure Greek who presumed to claim their obedience; and when Orestes, from some secret motive, declined the purple, they consented, with the same facility, to acknowledge his son Augustulus as the emperor of the West. By the abdication of Nepos, Orestes had now attained the summit of his ambitious hopes; but he soon discovered, before the end of the first year, that the lessons of perjury and ingratitude which a rebel must inculcate will be retorted against himself, and that the precarious sovereign of Italy was only permitted to choose whether he would be the slave or the victim of his barbarian mercenaries. The dangerous alliance of these strangers had oppressed and insulted the last remains of Roman freedom and dignity. At each revolution their pay and privileges were augmented; but their insolence increased in a still more extravagant degree; they envied the fortune of their brethren in Gaul, Spain, and Africa, whose victorious arms had acquired an independent and perpetual inheritance; and they insisted on their peremptory demand that a *third* part of the lands of Italy should be immediately divided among them. Orestes, with a spirit which, in another situation, might be entitled to our esteem, chose rather to encounter the rage of an armed multitude than to subscribe the ruin of an innocent people. He rejected the audacious demand; and his refusal was favourable to the ambition of Odoacer, a bold barbarian, who assured his fellow-soldiers that, if they dared to associate under his command, they might soon extort the justice which had been denied to their dutiful petitions. From all the camps and garrisons of Italy the confederates, actuated by the same resentment and the same hopes, impatiently flocked to the standard of this popular leader; and the unfortunate patrician, overwhelmed by the torrent, hastily retreated to the strong city of Pavia, the episcopal seat of the holy Epiphanites. Pavia was immediately besieged, the fortifications were stormed, the town was pillaged; and although the bishop might labour, with much zeal and some success, to save the property of the church and the chastity of female captives, the tumult could only be appeased by the execution of Orestes.[1] His brother Paul was slain in an action near Ravenna; and the helpless Augustulus, who could no longer command the respect, was reduced to implore the clemency, of Odoacer.

That successful barbarian was the son of Edecon; who, in some remarkable transactions, particularly described in a preceding chapter, had been the colleague of Orestes himself. The honour of an ambassador should be exempt from suspicion; and Edecon had listened to a conspiracy against the life of his sovereign. But this apparent guilt was expiated by his merit or repentance: his rank was eminent and conspicuous; he enjoyed the favour of Attila; and the troops under his command, who guarded in their turn the royal village, consisted of a tribe of Sciri, his immediate and hereditary subjects. In the revolt of the nations they still adhered to the Huns; and, more than twelve years afterwards, the name of Edecon is honourably mentioned in their unequal contest with the Ostrogoths; which was terminated, after two bloody battles, by the defeat and dispersion of the Sciri.[2] Their gallant leader, who did not survive this national calamity, left two sons, Onulf and Odoacer, to struggle with adversity, and to maintain as they might, by rapine or service, the faithful followers of their exile. Onulf directed his steps towards Constantinople, where he sullied, by the assassination of a generous benefactor, the fame which he had acquired in arms. His brother Odoacer led a wandering life among the barbarians of Noricum, with a mind and a fortune suited to the most desperate adventures; and when he had fixed his choice, he piously visited the cell of Severinus, the popular saint of the country, to solicit his approbation and blessing. The lowness of the door would not admit the lofty stature of Odoacer: he was obliged to stoop; but in that humble attitude the saint could discern the symptoms of his future greatness; and addressing him in a prophetic tone, " Pursue (said he) your design; proceed to Italy, you will soon cast away this coarse garment of skins; and your wealth will be adequate to the

---

[1] See Ennodius (in Vit. Epiphan. Sirmond, tom. i. p. 1669. 1670). He adds weight to the narrative of Procopius, though we may doubt whether the devil actually contrived the siege of Pavia to distress the bishop and his flock.

[2] Jornandes, c. 53, 54, p. 692-695. M. de Buat (Hist. des Peuples de l'Europe, tom. viii. p. 221-228) has clearly explained the origin and adventures of Odoacer. I am almost inclined to believe that he was the same who pillaged Angers, and commanded a fleet of Saxon pirates on the ocean. Greg. Turon. l. ii. c. 18, in tom. ii. p. 170.

liberality of your mind." [1] The barbarian, whose daring spirit accepted and ratified the prediction, was admitted into the service of the Western empire, and soon obtained an honourable rank in the guards. His manners were gradually polished, his military skill was improved, and the confederates of Italy would not have elected him for their general unless the exploits of Odoacer had established a high opinion of his courage and capacity.[2] Their military acclamations saluted him with the title of king; but he abstained during his whole reign from the use of the purple and diadem,[3] lest he should offend those princes whose subjects, by their accidental mixture, had formed the victorious army which time and policy might insensibly unite into a great nation.

Royalty was familiar to the barbarians, and the submissive people of Italy was prepared to obey, without a murmur, the authority which he should condescend to exercise as the vice-gerent of the emperor of the West. But Odoacer had resolved to abolish that useless and expensive office; and such is the weight of antique prejudice, that it required some boldness and penetration to discover the extreme facility of the enterprise. The unfortunate Augustulus was made the instrument of his own disgrace; he signified his resignation to the senate; and that assembly, in their last act of obedience to a Roman prince, still affected the spirit of freedom and the forms of the constitution. An epistle was addressed, by their unanimous decree, to the emperor Zeno, the son-in-law and successor of Leo, who had lately been restored, after a short rebellion, to the Byzantine throne. They solemnly " disclaim the necessity, or even the wish, of continuing any longer the Imperial succession in Italy; since, in their opinion, the majesty of a sole monarch is sufficient to pervade and protect, at the same time, both the East and the West. In their own name, and in the name of the people,

---

[1] Vade ad Italiam, vade vilissimis nunc pellibus coopertus: sed multis cito plurima largiturus. Anonym. Vales. p. 717 [Amm. Marc. ii. p. 305, ed. Bipon.]. He quotes the Life of St. Severinus, which is extant, and contains much unknown and valuable history; it was composed by his disciple Eugippius (A.D. 511), thirty years after his death. See Tillemont, Mém. Ecclés. tom. xvi. p. 168-181.

[2] Theophanes, who calls him a Goth, affirms that he was educated, nursed (τράφεντος), in Italy (p. 102 [tom. i. p. 184, ed. Bonn]); and as this strong expression will not bear a literal interpretation, it must be explained by long service in the Imperial guards.

[3] Nomen regis Odoacer assumpsit, cum tamen neque purpurâ nec regalibus uteretur insignibus. Cassiodor. in Chron. A.D. 476. He seems to have assumed the abstract title of a king without applying it to any particular nation or country.

they consent that the seat of universal empire shall be transferred from Rome to Constantinople; and they basely renounce the right of choosing their master, the only vestige that yet remained of the authority which had given laws to the world. The republic (they repeat that name without a blush) might safely confide in the civil and military virtues of Odoacer; and they humbly request that the emperor would invest him with the title of Patrician, and the administration of the *diocese* of Italy." The deputies of the senate were received at Constantinople with some marks of displeasure and indignation: and when they were admitted to the audience of Zeno, he sternly reproached them with their treatment of the two emperors, Anthemius and Nepos, whom the East had successively granted to the prayers of Italy. " The first (continued he) you have murdered; the second you have expelled: but the second is still alive, and whilst he lives he is your lawful sovereign." But the prudent Zeno soon deserted the hopeless cause of his abdicated colleague. His vanity was gratified by the title of sole emperor, and by the statues erected to his honour in the several quarters of Rome; he entertained a friendly, though ambiguous, correspondence with the *patrician* Odoacer; and he gratefully accepted the Imperial ensigns, the sacred ornaments of the throne and palace, which the barbarian was not unwilling to remove from the sight of the people.[1]

In the space of twenty years since the death of Valentinian, nine emperors had successively disappeared; and the son of Orestes, a youth recommended only by his beauty, would be the least entitled to the notice of posterity, if his reign, which was marked by the extinction of the Roman empire in the West, did not leave a memorable era in the history of mankind.[2] The patrician Orestes had married the daughter of Count *Romulus*, of Petovio in Noricum: the name of *Augustus*, notwithstanding the jealousy of power, was known at Aquileia as a familiar surname; and the appellations of the two great founders, of the city and of the monarchy, were thus strangely united in the last

---

[1] Malchus, whose loss excites our regret, has preserved (in Excerpt. Legat. p. 93 [ed. Par.; p. 235, ed. Bonn]) this extraordinary embassy from the senate to Zeno. The anonymous fragment (p. 717) and the extract from Candidus (apud Phot. p. 176 [p. 55, ed. Bekk.]) are likewise of some use.

[2] The precise year in which the Western empire was extinguished is not positively ascertained. The vulgar era of A.D. 476 *appears* to have the sanction of authentic chronicles. But the two dates assigned by Jornandes (c. 46, p. 680) would delay that great event to the year 479; and though M. de Buat has overlooked *his* evidence, he produces (tom. viii. p. 261-288) many collateral circumstances in support of the same opinion.

of their successors.[1] The son of Orestes assumed and disgraced
the names of Romulus Augustus; but the first was corrupted
into Momyllus by the Greeks, and the second has been changed
by the Latins into the contemptible diminutive Augustulus.
The life of this inoffensive youth was spared by the generous
clemency of Odoacer; who dismissed him, with his whole family,
from the Imperial palace, fixed his annual allowance at six
thousand pieces of gold, and assigned the castle of Lucullus, in
Campania, for the place of his exile or retirement.[2] As soon
as the Romans breathed from the toils of the Punic war, they
were attracted by the beauties and the pleasures of Campania;
and the country-house of the elder Scipio at Liternum exhibited
a lasting model of their rustic simplicity.[3] The delicious shores
of the bay of Naples were crowded with villas; and Sylla
applauded the masterly skill of his rival, who had seated himself on the lofty promontory of Misenum, that commands, on
every side, the sea and land, as far as the boundaries of the
horizon.[4] The villa of Marius was purchased, within a few
years, by Lucullus, and the price had increased from two
thousand five hundred, to more than fourscore thousand,
pounds sterling.[5] It was adorned by the new proprietor with
Grecian arts and Asiatic treasures; and the houses and gardens
of Lucullus obtained a distinguished rank in the list of Imperial

[1] See his medals in Ducange (Fam. Byzantin. p. 81), Priscus (Excerpt.
Legat. p. 57 [p. 185, ed. Bonn]).   Maffei (Osservazioni Letterarie, tom. ii.
p. 314).   We may allege a famous and similar case.   The meanest subjects
of the Roman empire assumed the *illustrious* name of *Patricius*, which, by
the conversion of Ireland, has been communicated to a whole nation.

[2] Ingrediens autem Ravennam deposuit Augustulum de regno, cujus in-
fantiam misertus concessit ei sanguinem; et quia pulcher erat, tamen
donavit ei reditum sex millia solidos, et misit eum intra Campaniam cum
parentibus suis libere vivere.   Anonym. Vales. p. 716 [Amm. Marc. tom.
ii. p. 303, ed. Bipon.].   Jornandes says (c. 46, p. 680), in Lucullano Cam-
paniæ castello exsilii pœna damnavit.

[3] See the eloquent Declamation of Seneca (Epist. lxxxvi.).   The philosopher might have recollected that all luxury is relative; and that the
elder Scipio, whose manners were polished by study and conversation, was
himself accused of that vice by his ruder contemporaries (Livy, xxix. 19).

[4] Sylla, in the language of a soldier, praised his *peritia castrametandi*
(Plin. Hist. Natur. xviii. 7).   Phædrus, who makes its shady walks (*læta
viridia*) the scene of an insipid fable (ii. 5), has thus described the situation:—

> Cæsar Tiberius quum petens Neapolim,
> In Misenensem villam venisset suam;
> Quæ monte summo posita Luculli manu
> Prospectat Siculum et despicit Tuscum mare.

[5] From seven myriads and a half to two hundred and fifty myriads of
drachmæ.   Yet even in the possession of Marius it was a luxurious retirement.   The Romans derided his indolence; they soon bewailed his
activity.   See Plutarch in Mario [c. 34], tom. ii. p. 524.

palaces.[1] When the Vandals became formidable to the sea-coast, the Lucullan villa, on the promontory of Misenum, gradually assumed the strength and appellation of a strong castle, the obscure retreat of the last emperor of the West. About twenty years after that great revolution it was converted into a church and monastery, to receive the bones of St. Severinus. They securely reposed, amidst the broken trophies of Cimbric and Armenian victories, till the beginning of the tenth century; when the fortifications, which might afford a dangerous shelter to the Saracens, were demolished by the people of Naples.[2]

Odoacer was the first barbarian who reigned in Italy, over a people who had once asserted their just superiority above the rest of mankind. The disgrace of the Romans still excites our respectful compassion, and we fondly sympathise with the imaginary grief and indignation of their degenerate posterity. But the calamities of Italy had gradually subdued the proud consciousness of freedom and glory. In the age of Roman virtue the provinces were subject to the arms, and the citizens to the laws, of the republic, till those laws were subverted by civil discord, and both the city and the provinces became the servile property of a tyrant. The forms of the constitution, which alleviated or disguised their abject slavery, were abolished by time and violence; the Italians alternately lamented the presence or the absence of the sovereigns whom they detested or despised; and the succession of five centuries inflicted the various evils of military licence, capricious despotism, and elaborate oppression. During the same period, the barbarians had emerged from obscurity and contempt, and the warriors of Germany and Scythia were introduced into the provinces, as the servants, the allies, and at length the masters, of the Romans, whom they insulted or protected. The hatred of the people was suppressed by fear; they respected the spirit and splendour of the martial chiefs who were invested with the honours of the empire; and the fate of Rome had long depended on the sword

---

[1] Lucullus had other villas of equal, though various, magnificence at Baiæ, Naples, Tusculum, etc. He boasted that he changed his climate with the storks and cranes. Plutarch, in Lucull. [c. 39] tom. iii. p. 193.

[2] Severinus died in Noricum, A.D. 482. Six years afterwards his body, which scattered miracles as it passed, was transported by his disciples into Italy. The devotion of a Neapolitan lady invited the saint to the Lucullan villa, in the place of Augustulus, who was probably no more. See Baronius (Annal. Eccles. A.D. 496, No. 50, 51) and Tillemont (Mém. Ecclés. tom. xvi. p. 178-181), from the original Life by Eugippius. The narrative of the last migration of Severinus to Naples is likewise an authentic piece.

of those formidable strangers.   The stern Ricimer, who trampled
on the ruins of Italy, had exercised the power, without assuming
the title, of a king; and the patient Romans were insensibly
prepared to acknowledge the royalty of Odoacer and his barbaric
successors.

The king of Italy was not unworthy of the high station to
which his valour and fortune had exalted him: his savage
manners were polished by the habits of conversation; and he
respected, though a conqueror and a barbarian, the institutions,
and even the prejudices, of his subjects.   After an interval of
seven years, Odoacer restored the consulship of the West.   For
himself, he modestly, or proudly, declined an honour which was
still accepted by the emperors of the East; but the curule chair
was successively filled by eleven of the most illustrious senators;[1]
and the list is adorned by the respectable name of Basilius, whose
virtues claimed the friendship and grateful applause of Sidonius,
his client.[2]   The laws of the emperors were strictly enforced;
and the civil administration of Italy was still exercised by
the Prætorian præfect and his subordinate officers.   Odoacer
devolved on the Roman magistrates the odious and oppressive
task of collecting the public revenue; but he reserved for himself the merit of seasonable and popular indulgence.[3]   Like the
rest of the barbarians, he had been instructed in the Arian
heresy; but he revered the monastic and episcopal characters;
and the silence of the catholics attests the toleration which they
enjoyed.   The peace of the city required the interposition of
his præfect Basilius in the choice of a Roman pontiff: the decree
which restrained the clergy from alienating their lands was
ultimately designed for the benefit of the people, whose devotion
would have been taxed to repair the dilapidations of the church.[4]
Italy was protected by the arms of its conqueror; and its frontiers

[1] The consular Fasti may be found in Pagi or Muratori.   The consuls
named by Odoacer, or perhaps by the Roman senate, appear to have been
acknowledged in the Eastern empire.

[2] Sidonius Apollinaris (l. i. Epist. 9, p. 22, edit. Sirmond) has compared
the two leading senators of his time (A.D. 468), Gennadius Avienus and
Cæcina Basilius.   To the former he assigns the specious, to the latter the
solid, virtues of public and private life.   A Basilius junior, possibly his
son, was consul in the year 480.

[3] Epiphanius interceded for the people of Pavia; and the king first
granted an indulgence of five years, and afterwards relieved them from
the oppression of Pelagius, the Prætorian præfect (Ennodius, in Vit. St.
Epiphan. in Sirmond. Oper. tom. i. p. 1670-1672).

[4] See Baronius, Annal. Eccles. A.D. 483, No. 10-15.   Sixteen years afterwards the irregular proceedings of Basilius were condemned by pope Symmachus in a Roman synod.

were respected by the barbarians of Gaul and Germany, who had so long insulted the feeble race of Theodosius. Odoacer passed the Hadriatic, to chastise the assassins of the emperor Nepos, and to acquire the maritime province of Dalmatia. He passed the Alps, to rescue the remains of Noricum from Fava, or Feletheus, king of the Rugians, who held his residence beyond the Danube. The king was vanquished in battle, and led away prisoner; a numerous colony of captives and subjects was transplanted into Italy; and Rome, after a long period of defeat and disgrace, might claim the triumph of her barbarian master.[1]

Notwithstanding the prudence and success of Odoacer, his kingdom exhibited the sad prospect of misery and desolation. Since the age of Tiberius, the decay of agriculture had been felt in Italy; and it was a just subject of complaint that the life of the Roman people depended on the accidents of the winds and waves.[2] In the division and the decline of the empire, the tributary harvests of Egypt and Africa were withdrawn; the numbers of the inhabitants continually diminished with the means of subsistence; and the country was exhausted by the irretrievable losses of war, famine,[3] and pestilence. St. Ambrose has deplored the ruin of a populous district, which had been once adorned with the flourishing cities of Bologna, Modena, Rhegium, and Placentia.[4] Pope Gelasius was a subject of Odoacer; and he affirms, with strong exaggeration, that in Æmilia, Tuscany, and the adjacent provinces, the human species was almost extirpated.[5] The plebeians of Rome, who were fed by the hand of their master, perished or disappeared as soon as his liberality was suppressed; the decline of the arts reduced the

[1] The wars of Odoacer are concisely mentioned by Paul the Deacon (de Gest. Langobard. l. i. c. 19, p. 757, edit Grot.) and in the two Chronicles of Cassiodorus and Cuspinian. The Life of St. Severinus, by Eugippius, which the Count de Buat (Hist. des Peuples, etc., tom. viii. c. 1, 4, 8, 9) has diligently studied, illustrates the ruin of Noricum and the Bavarian antiquities.

[2] Tacit. Annal. iii. 53 [54]. The Recherches sur l'Administration des Terres chez les Romains (p. 351-361) clearly state the progress of internal decay.

[3] A famine, which afflicted Italy at the time of the irruption of Odoacer, king of the Heruli, is eloquently described in prose and verse by a French poet (Les Mois, tom. ii. p. 174, 206, edit. in 12mo.). I am ignorant from whence he derives his information; but I am well assured that he relates some facts incompatible with the truth of history.

[4] See the xxxixth epistle of St. Ambrose [tom. ii. p. 944, ed. Bened.] as it is quoted by Muratori, sopra le Antichità Italiane, tom. i. Dissert. xxi. p. 354.

[5] Æmilia, Tuscia, ceteræque provinciæ in quibus hominum prope nullus exsistit. Gelasius, Epist. ad Andromachum, ap. Baronium, Annal. Eccles. A.D. 496, No. 36.

industrious mechanic to idleness and want; and the senators, who might support with patience the ruin of their country, bewailed their private loss of wealth and luxury. One third of those ample estates, to which the ruin of Italy is originally imputed,[1] was extorted for the use of the conquerors. Injuries were aggravated by insults; the sense of actual sufferings was embittered by the fear of more dreadful evils; and as new lands were allotted to new swarms of barbarians, each senator was apprehensive lest the arbitrary surveyors should approach his favourite villa, or his most profitable farm. The least unfortunate were those who submitted without a murmur to the power which it was impossible to resist. Since they desired to live, they owed some gratitude to the tyrant who had spared their lives; and since he was the absolute master of their fortunes, the portion which he left must be accepted as his pure and voluntary gift.[2] The distress of Italy was mitigated by the prudence and humanity of Odoacer, who had bound himself, as the price of his elevation, to satisfy the demands of a licentious and turbulent multitude. The kings of the barbarians were frequently resisted, deposed, or murdered, by their *native* subjects; and the various bands of Italian mercenaries, who associated under the standard of an elective general, claimed a larger privilege of freedom and rapine. A monarchy destitute of national union and hereditary right hastened to its dissolution. After a reign of fourteen years Odoacer was oppressed by the superior genius of Theodoric, king of the Ostrogoths; a hero alike excellent in the arts of war and of government, who restored an age of peace and prosperity, and whose name still excites and deserves the attention of mankind.

[1] Verumque confitentibus, latifundia perdidere Italiam. Plin. Hist. Natur. xviii. 7 [§ 3].

[2] Such are the topics of consolation, or rather of patience, which Cicero ad Familiares, lib. ix. Epist. 17) suggests to his friend Papirius Pætus, under the military despotism of Cæsar. The argument, however, of "vivere pulcherrimum duxi," is more forcibly addressed to a Roman philosopher, who possessed the free alternative of life or death.

EVERYMAN'S LIBRARY
A LIST OF THE 990 VOLUMES
ARRANGED UNDER AUTHORS

Anonymous works are given under titles
Anthologies, Composite Volumes, Dictionaries, etc., are
arranged at the end of the list

November 1950. *The Publishers regret that some of the volumes are out of print.*
A Selected List is available showing volumes in stock.

LONDON: J. M. DENT & SONS LTD.

NEW YORK: E. P. DUTTON & CO. INC.